Yale Language Series, 5

EDITORS

Bernard Bloch

William S. Cornyn

Isidore Dyen

BEGINNING

JAPANESE

PART I

by Eleanor Harz Jorden

with the assistance of Hamako Ito Chaplin

New Haven and London, Yale University Press

Set in IBM Documentary type and
printed in the United States of America.

Library of Congress catalog card number: 62-16235
ISBN: 0-300-00135-5 (paper)

40   39

For
W. J. J.

Acknowledgments

I am indebted to many people — in Japan and the United States — for their assistance in the preparation of this book:

to Hajime Aikawa, Shiro Sugata, Hiroshi Sakamoto, Mayako Matsuda, Kazuhiko Mitsumoto, and Akira Kobayashi, who participated in the preparation of a short course, the expansion and revision of which was the basis for this text. I deeply appreciate their tireless efforts.

to Sayoko Kawamoto, Hiroshi Takano, Masayuki Minami, Yasukazu Tsukagoshi, and Reiko Hummel — and to Gabriel Cordova, supervisor of recording — for assistance in the preparation of the tape recordings that accompany the text. Mrs. Kawamoto was particularly helpful in performing many of the tiresome chores that preceded and followed actual recording, as well as in assisting in the final revision of the text.

to Mrs. Tomoko Tanaka Campen for her excellent illustrations, drawn with such meticulous care.

to the Language Development Section of the Department of Health, Education, and Welfare, for a grant which expedited the completion of the book and made possible the preparation of the accompanying tapes.

to the Center for Applied Linguistics of the Modern Language Association, for a grant which expedited the publishing of the book.

to Samuel E. Martin, of Yale University, for discussions which suggested several useful revisions.

to Kyoko Edayoshi, for her careful typing of the manuscript and for several valuable suggestions pertaining to the text.

To my teacher, Bernard Bloch of Yale University, who directed my formal study of linguistics and introduced me to the Japanese language, I continue to owe an immeasurable debt.

To Hamako Ito Chaplin, of Yale University, who has been directly involved in the preparation of this text — and previous versions of it — during the past six years, I wish to express my deepest appreciation for her capable assistance and enthusiastic cooperation. Mrs. Chaplin has willingly and cheerfully performed innumerable tasks of writing, rewriting, checking, editing, and recording, always giving evidence of her outstanding ability and uncompromising standards of excellence. It is impossible to express adequately my gratitude to her.

To my husband, William J. Jorden, I wish to express my thanks for his encouragement, his advice, and his patience.

E. H. J.

Washington, D.C.
January 1962

Contents

Contents

Introduction

Beginning Japanese (Parts I and II) contains thirty-five lessons, all of which have the same basic pattern and involve the same procedures. Each lesson requires many hours of class work supplemented by outside study and, if possible, laboratory work.

The method underlying this text is guided imitation; the aim is automaticity. Ideally, there are two teachers: under the supervision of a scientific linguist, who talks ABOUT Japanese, the student learns to speak the language in direct imitation of a tutor who is a native speaker of Japanese. The tutor drills on the Japanese in the text, providing an authentic model for the student to imitate. Statements on how the language is manipulated are included in the explanatory notes in the text, which may be supplemented, if necessary, by further discussions on the part of the linguist.

Language learning is overlearning. Through memorization of whole utterances, and substitution within and manipulation of these utterances, a student achieves the fluency and automaticity that are necessary for control of a language. Language learning involves acquiring a new set of habits, and habits must be automatic. Just as the experienced driver performs the mechanics of driving—turning on the engine, shifting gears, applying the brakes, etc.— unconsciously, and concentrates on where he is going, so the fluent speaker of a language is concerned with what he is saying rather than the mechanics of how he is saying it.

This textbook is concerned only with spoken Japanese. Reading and writing involve a different set of habits and are best begun after acquiring some basic control of the spoken language. It is suggested that students interested in studying written Japanese begin using an introductory reading text only after completing at least ten or fifteen lessons of this volume.[1]

The student should note the following general suggestions and warnings:

ALWAYS USE NORMAL SPEED. Do not permit yourself to speak more slowly than your tutor, and do not ask him to speak more slowly than is natural for him. The ability to understand slow, deliberate speech never heard outside of a classroom is of little practical value. The aim of the student should be to learn Japanese as it is spoken by the Japanese—not an artificial classroom dialect.

DRILL HOURS WITH A NATIVE TUTOR SHOULD BE CONDUCTED ENTIRELY IN JAPANESE FROM THE FIRST DAY. A class which fluctuates between Japanese and English, where valuable repetition and drill aimed at developing fluency are constantly interrupted by English questions and comments, never achieves the desired results. It is recommended that a specific time be designated as discussion period and that interruption of drill at

---

[1] For students who have completed Parts I and II, the forthcoming publication A Manual of Japanese Writing, by Chaplin and Martin, is suggested.

other times be avoided. A tutor who has not had technical linguistic training should not attempt technical explanations <u>about</u> Japanese. These are provided by the explanatory notes in the book and/or the scientific linguist.

REVIEW CONSTANTLY. DO NOT GO AHEAD TOO RAPIDLY. Remember that e a c h new lesson presupposes thorough mastery of what has gone before.

Do not assume that the patterns of Japanese will resemble those of English, or that distinctions made in English will be present in Japanese. EXPECT DIFFERENCES AND BE SURPRISED AT SIMILARITIES.

Remember that USAGE—NOT LOGIC—DETERMINES WHAT IS ACCEPTED IN A LANGUAGE. A native speaker is the final judge of whether or not an utterance is acceptable in his dialect. Differences of dialect, of course, cause frequent disagreement among native speakers. Not all dialect differences are geographical; many are social and educational.

PROCEDURES

1.   Basic Dialogues

Each of the thirty-five lessons begins with a group of <u>Basic Dialogues</u> which form the core of the lesson. A student controls a lesson to the extent to which he has learned the dialogues by heart. Thorough memorization of the dialogues means thorough mastery of the text. Memorization is achieved by direct imitation of the native tutor in class, and by repeated use of tapes in the laboratory or at home.

Basic Dialogues are presented with their English equivalents. Numbered utterances in the dialogues are <u>Basic Sentences</u>. New words or phrases occurring in a Basic Sentence for the first time are listed separately, immediately before the s e n t e n c e, as <u>breakdowns</u>. They a r e indented and not numbered.

Some lessons contain <u>Additional Vocabulary</u>, at the end of the Basic Dialogues. The words in these sections are always to be drilled within an appropriate pattern sentence, never in isolation.

Following the Basic Dialogues are <u>Notes on the Basic Dialogues</u>, containing assorted information on specific sentences. The numbering of the notes corresponds to that of the sentences.

2.   Grammatical Notes

Discussions of new patterns introduced in the Basic Dialogues are found in the <u>Grammatical Notes</u>. These are to be read outside of class after the Basic Dialogues have been introduced, but before proceeding to the drills.

In the Grammatical Notes, the procedure has been to introduce only material which will be of immediate practical use to a beginning student. No attempt is made to present the full scientific analysis of Japanese on which the text is based; rather, explanations are provided which will be useful within the framework of the Japanese material being studied.

3.   Drills

There are five basic kinds of drill in <u>Beginning Japanese</u>, each having a

special purpose.   However, the aim of all drills is the over-all aim of the
course: to develop fluency and automaticity.   Drills are to be performed in
class with a tutor, and in the laboratory or at home with tapes.   TEXTBOOKS
SHOULD BE CLOSED DURING DRILL PRACTICE IN CLASS.

a. Substitution Drills

The tutor gives a pattern sentence which the student repeats.   Immediately the tutor gives a word or phrase (called a cue) which the student substitutes appropriately in the original sentence.   The tutor follows immediately
with a new cue.

Example (English substitution drill):

Tutor:	Where did you put my book?
Student:	Where did you put my book?
Tutor:	pen
Student:	Where did you put my pen?
Tutor:	dictionary
Student:	Where did you put my dictionary?
	etc.

In more complicated substitution drills, there may be several substitution
items (a compound cue) for each new sentence; or the successive cues may
have to be substituted in different parts of the sentence; or the cue may require changes in the pattern sentence; or the cue may be given in its citation
form (i.e. the basic form that regularly occurs in a dictionary) and have to be
changed in order to occur within the pattern sentence.

Substitution drills whose cues occur in the same form in the pattern sentence are printed in two columns, with English equivalents on the left and drill
sentences with cues underlined on the right.   A drill that looks like this—

1.	Please give me a cig-arette.	Ta⌐bako o kudasa˥i.
2.	Please give me a match.	Ma˥tti o kudasai.
3.	Please give me a book. etc.	Ho˥ñ o kudasai.

is to be drilled:

Tutor:	Ta⌐bako o kudasa˥i.
Student:	Ta⌐bako o kudasa˥i.
Tutor:	ma˥tti
Student:	Ma˥tti o kudasai.
Tutor:	ho˥ñ
Student:	Ho˥ñ o kudasai.
	etc.

When cues occur in their citation forms and must be changed by the student,
they are given between virgules (//) immediately after the English equivalents
on the left.   A drill that looks like this—

1.	Please wait here.	Ko⌐ko de ma˥tte kudasai.
2.	Please study here. /beñkyoo-suru/	Ko⌐ko de beñkyoo-site kudasa˥i.

3. Please read here.   Ko⌐ko de yo⌐ñde kudasai.
    /yo⌐mu/
    etc.

is to be drilled:

Tutor: Ko⌐ko de ma⌐tte kudasai.
Student: Ko⌐ko de ma⌐tte kudasai.
Tutor: beñkyoo-suru
Student: Ko⌐ko de beñkyoo-site kudasa⌐i.
Tutor: yo⌐mu
Student: Ko⌐ko de yo⌐ñde kudasai.

b. Grammar Drills

Here, on the basis of a model provided at the beginning of the drill, the student is required to perform parallel manipulation on a series of utterances by the tutor. For example, he may be required to change each of the tutor's utterances to the corresponding negative, or the past tense, etc.

Grammar Drills are printed in two columns, with the tutor's utterances on the left and the student's responses on the right.

c. Response Drill

On the basis of the model or directions occurring at the beginning of the drill, the student provides a parallel response to a series of questions or remarks by the tutor.

Like Grammar Drills, Response Drills are printed in two columns, with the tutor's utterances on the left and the student's responses on the right. In cases requiring a response clue from the tutor, this is given between virgules immediately following the tutor's utterance.

Example (English response drill):

Tutor	Student
What did you buy? /a book/	I bought a book.
What did you borrow? /a pencil/ etc.	I borrowed a pencil.

d. Level Drill

Here, the student is asked to change the tutor's utterances to a different level of speech—to a more formal level, to the informal level, etc.

Again, this kind of drill is printed in two columns, with the tutor's utterance on the left and the student's equivalent on the right.

e. Expansion Drills

The usual kind of expansion drill in this text is a repetition drill which involves the buildup from short to long sentences. The tutor begins with a short sentence and gradually adds words and phrases to form a long, complex sentence. At each stage, the student repeats what the tutor has just said. These drills are printed in two columns, with the successively longer Japanese sentences on the right and English equivalents on the left.

In another kind of expansion drill, the student expands a pattern sentence with the cue provided by the tutor. A model is provided at the beginning of the drill. For such drills, the tutor's pattern sentence and cue (marked off with virgules) are in the left column, and the student's responses in the right column.

Drills are not meant to be grammatical puzzles for tricking the student; they are intended to develop fluency. The pace of all drills should be rapid. A student has mastered a drill only when he can provide the required oral responses promptly, fluently, and without reference to his textbook.

4. Supplementary Material

The supplementary material following the drills occurs in various forms: conversations of varying length (with English equivalents), narrative passages, and question drills.

When read aloud by the tutor, this material is a good test of comprehension—but it must be read at normal speed, and the students' books must be closed. It also provides a stimulus to conversation. The class can ask and answer questions pertaining to the material and make up similar material; and with conversations for which English equivalents are given, they may reconstruct the original conversations by referring only to the English.

5. Exercises

The final section of each lesson contains suggestions for additional practice appropriate to each lesson. These exercises should be performed orally. Only the student who is able to do them fluently and accurately is ready to proceed to the next lesson.

TAPES

The tape series which accompanies Beginning Japanese includes all Basic Dialogues, Drills, and Supplementary Material.

1. Basic Dialogues

Each dialogue is recorded four times:

(a) For listening

The dialogue (in its most contracted form) is spoken at normal speed just as you might overhear it.

LISTEN WITH YOUR BOOK CLOSED.

(b) For memorization

This phase includes breakdowns and Basic Sentences, followed by pauses[1] for students' repetition. Breakdowns are said once and Basic Sentences twice. When a contracted alternant occurs, it is said once, following the second repetition of the uncontracted equivalent.

REPEAT EVERYTHING ALOUD AND FOLLOW IN YOUR BOOK.

(c) For fluency

Each complete Basic Sentence is said once, with pause for repetition. For sentences which have a contracted equivalent, only the uncontract-alternant is included in this phase.

REPEAT ALOUD WITH YOUR BOOK CLOSED.

(d) For comprehension

This is a repetition of (a) above (the Dialogue for listening), but this time the student is expected to understand everything he hears.

LISTEN WITH YOUR BOOK CLOSED.

2. Drills

Students are expected to participate in the drills when working with tapes exactly as they do in the classroom, except that they may follow in their books as necessary.

For drills which require repetition — that is, most expansion drills — there are pauses on the tapes following each utterance to be repeated. For drills which require answering by the student — substitution, grammar, response, level, and some expansion drills — there is a pause on the tape permitting him to give his answer orally. This pause is <u>followed</u> by the correct response, which serves to reinforce — or correct — the student's response.

REPEAT OR ANSWER. FOLLOW IN YOUR BOOK AS NECESSARY.

3. Supplementary Material

During question drills, turn off the tape recorder after each question and take whatever time is necessary to answer. All other supplementary material is presented for comprehension practice.

LISTEN WITH YOUR BOOK CLOSED.

---

[1] All pauses on the tapes are timed to require the student to speak at a normal rate of speed. The student who cannot repeat within the allotted time is talking too slowly and needs more practice.

PRONUNCIATION

The so-called 'standard' dialect of Japanese (spoken by educated natives of Tokyo) can be described in terms of 113 distinct syllables, of the following kinds:

     5   single vowel
   67   consonant + vowel
   36   consonant + y + vowel
     5   single consonant

The student's first task is to learn (1) how the sounds of Japanese are pronounced and (2) how the Japanese sounds—which are different from the sounds of English—are represented in this text with the letters of our own alphabet. For (1), the student needs as a model a native speaker of Japanese and/or a recording made by a native speaker. For (2), he must study the chart and notes below, always bearing in mind that the letters are no more than arbitrary symbols which are meant to remind him of the actually occurring Japanese sounds. Although the symbols may seem unnecessarily arbitrary at the beginning, while the structure of Japanese is still unknown, the student becomes accustomed to them very quickly as he becomes familiar with the language.

Syllables of Japanese

1	2	3	4	5	6	7	8	9	10	11	12	13	14	15	16	17
a	ka	ga	ḡa	sa	za	ta	da	na	ha	pa	ba	ma	ya	ra	wa	k
i	ki	gi	ḡi	si	zi	ti	--	ni	hi	pi	bi	mi	--	ri	--	s
u	ku	gu	ḡu	su	zu	tu	--	nu	hu	pu	bu	mu	yu	ru	--	t
e	ke	ge	ḡe	se	ze	te	de	ne	he	pe	be	me	--	re	--	p
o	ko	go	ḡo	so	zo	to	do	no	ho	po	bo	mo	yo	ro	--	n̄
	kya	gya	ḡya	sya	zya	tya	--	nya	hya	pya	bya	mya	--	rya	--	
	kyu	gyu	ḡyu	syu	zyu	tyu	--	nyu	hyu	pyu	byu	myu	--	ryu	--	
	kyo	gyo	ḡyo	syo	zyo	tyo	--	nyo	hyo	pyo	byo	myo	--	ryo	--	

(In the following discussion, row numbers correspond to the numbers of the vertical rows in the chart above. IN THIS SECTION ONLY, syllables within a word are separated by hyphens to show syllable division, and capital letters represent a pitch level higher than that represented by lower-case letters.)

Row 1	The symbol:	stands for a sound approximately like:	but the Japanese sound:
	a	'a' in 'father'	is short and clipped
	i	'i' in 'machine'	is short and clipped
	u	'u' in 'put'	is short, clipped, and without lip-rounding
	e	'e' in 'bet'	is short and clipped
	o	'o' in 'horse'	is short and clipped

When two or more Japanese vowels follow each other directly, each one retains its original quality and length, but the sequence is regularly pronounced as a continuum. The occurrence of the same vowel symbol twice indicates a long vowel: e.g. aa represents a + a pronounced without a break.

A word in Japanese has at least as many syllables as it has vowels.

Practice 1[1]

a 'oh!'	A-o 'blue'	u-E 'top'	e 'picture'
A-a 'oh!'	I-i 'is good'	o-I 'nephew'	E-e 'yes'
A-i 'love'	i-E 'house'	o-O-i 'are many'	o-U 'owe'
A-u 'meet'	i-I-E 'no'	a-O-i 'is blue'	o-O-u 'conceal'

Row 2	The symbol:	stands for a sound approximately like:	but the Japanese sound:
	k before a, u, e, o	'c' in 'coot'	has less aspiration[2]
	ky, and k before i	'c' in 'cute'	has less aspiration[2]

The values of the vowel symbols remain the same as in Row 1 above.

Practice 2

ka-U 'buy'	a-KA-I 'is red'	ka-I-KE-E 'account'
ka-O 'face'	o-O-KI-i 'is big'	KYA-a 'eek!'
i-KE 'pond'	KE-e-ko 'practice'	KYO-o 'today'
ko-KO 'here'	ku-U-KO-O 'airport'	KYU-u 'grade'

---

[1] All the practice drills that follow are for pronunciation practice only.

[2] The corresponding English sound is followed by a strong puff of breath.

Row 3	The symbol:	stands for a sound approximately like:	but the Japanese sound:
g before a, u, e, o	'g' in 'begone'	in initial position is more fully voiced than the corresponding English initial [1]
gy, and g before i	'g' in 'regular'	in initial position is more fully voiced than the corresponding English initial [1]

Practice 3

GA-i 'injury'   gi-KO-O 'art'   GU-ke-e 'my elder
                                            brother'

GE-e 'craft'   GI-ka-i 'the Diet'   GYA-ku-i 'traitor-
                                            ous mind'

GO-i 'vocabulary'   go-KA-I 'misunderstand- gyo-O-KO-O 'good
                       ing'   fortune'

gi-KE-E 'brother-   gu-U-I 'a moral'   GYU-u 'beef'
  in-law'

Row 4

The symbol $\bar{g}$ represents a sound like the 'ng' of 'singer' [2] — that is, it is a sound made with the tongue in position for a g but with the air escaping through the nasal passages. In Japanese, this sound never occurs at the beginning of an utterance.

Like gy and g before i, $\bar{g}$y and $\bar{g}$ before i are pronounced with the tongue raised in a 'y' position, somewhat like the 'ngy' of 'bring you.'

The occurrence of $\bar{g}$ is a matter of dialect. While it is usually considered a feature of Tokyo Japanese, there are many Tokyo speakers who

---

[1] A voiced sound is one accompanied by vibration of the vocal cords. In English, a voiced consonant at the beginning of a word begins without voice (vibration); in Japanese, an initial voiced consonant is voiced throughout its articulation.

[2] This is a valid comparison only for those speakers of English who distinguish between the medial sounds of 'singer' and 'finger,' with the latter containing the medial sound of 'singer' + 'g.'

regularly use g instead, and there are still others who alternate freely be-
between the two. The situation, as far as this text is concerned, is
as follows:

  Where g is written, ḡ is NOT to be substituted.
  Where g̿ is written, g can ALWAYS be substituted.

Example:

  GA-i: G occurs in the speech of all speakers of Tokyo Japanese.

  KA-ḡu: Some speakers say KA-ḡu (with the nasal ḡ) consistently,
          others say KA-gu consistently, and still others alternate
          freely between the two pronunciations.

Whichever pronunciation a student uses, he must be able to understand both. [1] However, it should be pointed out that the dialect which
includes ḡ is considered the "prestige" dialect of Tokyo.

Practice 4

E-e-ḡa	KA-ḡe	ka-I-ḠI
'movie'	'shade'	'conference'
i-KA-ḡa	GO-ḡo	ka-I-ḠYA-KU [2]
'how?'	'afternoon'	'a jest'
KA-ḡu	ko-O-ḠO	ka-I-ḠYU-U
'furniture'	'spoken language'	'sea-cow'
a-O-ḡu	ku-ḠI	KO-o-ḡyo-o
'look up'	'nail'	'industry'

Row 5	The symbol:	stands for a sound approximately like:	but the Japanese sound:
	s before a, u, e, o	's' in 'see'	is pronounced further forward in the mouth
	sy, and s be-fore i	'sh' in 'she'	

---

[1] Accordingly, examples of g substitution for ḡ have been included on the
tapes that accompany this text.

[2] See the section on Whispered Syllables below.

Practice 5

A-sa 'morning'	o-SA-KE 'rice wine'	SYA-ka-i 'society'
a-SU 'tomorrow'	SU-ḡu 'right away'	HA-i-sya 'dentist'
A-se 'perspiration'	ko-O-SU-I 'perfume'	KYU-u-syu-u 'Kyushu'
a-SI 'leg'	o-I-SI-I 'is delicious'	sya-SYO-O 'conductor'
a-SO-KO 'there'	o-KA-SI-i 'is funny'	syu-U-SYO-O 'grief'

Row 6	The symbol:	stands for a sound approximately like:	but the Japanese sound:
	z before a, u,[1] e, o	'z' in 'bazaar'	is pronounced further forward in the mouth and is regularly fully voiced [2]
	zy, and z before i	'j' in 'reject'	

Practice 6

za-I-KA 'inventory'	GO-zi 'five o'clock'	ZYU-u 'ten'
KA-zu 'number'	KA-zi 'a fire'	KA-zyu 'fruit tree'
ki-ZU 'a cut'	zi-E-E 'self-defense'	zyo-O 'feeling'
ZE-e 'a tax'	ZYA-a 'well then'	zyo-SE-E 'womanhood'
ZO-o 'elephant'	zya-KO-O 'musk'	ko-O-ZYO-o 'factory'

Row 7	The symbol:	stands for a sound approximately like:	but the Japanese sound:
	t before a, e, o	't' in 'tip'	is pronounced with the tongue touching the teeth and with little aspiration
	ty, and t before i	'ch' in 'cheap'	is pronounced further forward in the mouth
	t before u	'ts' in 'tsetse fly'	is pronounced further forward in the mouth

[1] An alternate pronunciation of z before u is 'dz.'

[2] See footnote 1 on page xxiii.

Practice 7

ka-TA 'person'   TI-zu 'map'   o-SI-ḠO-TO-TYU-U
                                                        'in the middle of work'
ta-KA-i 'is high'   ti-I-SA-i 'is small'   ko-O-TYO-O 'director'
ki-I-TE 'listening'   o-TYA 'tea'   TYO-o-me-e 'long life'
to-O-KA 'ten days'   ko-O-TYA 'black tea'   TU-i-te 'concerning'
si-ḠO-TO 'work'   TYU-u-i 'warning'   tu-ZU-KI 'continuation'

Row 8	The symbol:	stands for a sound approximately like:	but the Japanese sound:
	d̲	'd' in 'redeem'	is pronounced with the tongue touching the teeth and is regularly fully voiced [1]

Practice 8

e-DA 'branch'   DE-te 'leaving'   KA-do 'street corner'
o-KA-DA (family name)   i-SO-i-de 'hurrying'   DO-ko 'where?'
ku-DA-SA-i 'give me'   de-KI-ḠO-to 'oc-   do-O-ḠU 'tool'
                                 currence'

Row 9	The symbol:	stands for a sound approximately like:	but the Japanese sound:
	n̲ before a̲, u̲, e̲, o̲	'n' in 'deny'	is pronounced with the tongue touching the teeth and is regularly fully voiced [1]
	ny̲, and n̲ before i̲	'n' in 'menu,' 'ave-nue,'[2] etc.	

---

[1] See footnote 1 on page xxiii.

[2] Applicable only for those speakers who use a ' —nyu' pronunciation.

Practice 9

NA-ka 'inside'	o-KA-NE 'money'	NYA-o 'meow'
KI-nu 'silk'	so-NO 'that'	gyu-U-NYU-U 'milk'
te-NU-ḠU-I 'towel'	NA-ni 'what?'	nyu-U-ZYO-O 'entrance'
NE-ko 'cat'	ni-KA-I 'second floor'	NYO-o-ḡo 'court lady'

Row 10	The symbol:	stands for a sound approximately like:	but the Japanese sound:
	h before a, e, o	'h' in 'hot'	has more friction
	hy, and h before i	'h' in 'humid'	
	H before u is made by bringing the upper and lower lips together and then puffing air out between them. Unlike English 'f,' which is the closest English sound, Japanese h before u does not involve the lower teeth in its production.		

Practice 10

HA-i 'yes'	hi-ḠE 'beard'	HYO-o 'hail'
HA-ha 'mother'	ko-O-HI-i 'coffee'	HU-u 'manner'
he-E 'wall'	HYU-u-zu 'fuse'	HU-ne 'boat'
HO-o 'direction'	hya-KU-DO '100 times'	HU-zi 'Fuji'

Row 11	The symbol:	stands for a sound approximately like:	but the Japanese sound:
	p before a, u, e, o	'p' in 'poor'	has less aspiration
	py, and p before i	'p' in 'pure'	

Practice 11

PA-a-zi 'purge'	PU-u-pu-u (noise of a horn)	PO-o-zu 'a pause'
a-PA-a-to 'apartment'	pe-E-ZI 'page'	PYU-u-pyu-u (noise of a whistle)
de-PA-a-to 'department store'	PO-ka-po-ka 'repeatedly'	pi-A-NO 'piano'

Row 12	The symbol:	stands for a sound approximately like:	but the Japanese sound:
	<u>b</u> before <u>a</u>, <u>u</u>, <u>e</u>, <u>o</u>	'b' in 'rebel'	is regularly fully voiced [1]
	<u>by</u>, and <u>b</u> before <u>i</u>	'b' in 'rebuke'	

Practice 12

BA-ta   ka-BE   sa-BI-SI-i
 'butter'   'wall'   'is lonely'
ta-BA-KO   bo-O   BYA-ku-e
 'cigarette'   'stick'   'white robe'
a-SO-BU   o-BO-e-te   BYU-u-byu-u
 'play'   'remembering'   (noise of a whistle)
a-BU-NA-I   e-BI   byo-O-BU
 'is dangerous'   'shrimp'   'screen'

Row 13	The symbol:	stands for a sound approximately like:	but the Japanese sound:
	<u>m</u> before <u>a</u>, <u>u</u>, <u>e</u>, <u>o</u>	'm' in 'remind'	is regularly fully voiced [1]
	<u>my</u>, and <u>m</u> before <u>i</u>	'm' in 'amuse'	

Practice 13

MA-e 'front'   mu-SU-ME 'daughter'   kyo-O-MI 'interest'
ma-TA 'again'   ME-e-zi 'Meiji'   mya-KU-DO-O 'pulse'
NO-mu 'drink'   I-tu mo 'always'   MYU-u-zu 'muse'
mu-KO-O 'over   MI-se-te 'showing'   ko-O-MYO-O 'great
 there'   deed'

---

[1] See footnote 1 on page xxiii.

Row 14	The symbol:	stands for a sound approximately like:	but the Japanese sound:
	y	'y' in 'year'	is regularly fully voiced [1]

Practice 14

ya-O-YA	o-YU	yo-SI-DA
'vegetable store'	'hot water'	(family name)
NA-g̃o-ya	yu-KI-yo	sa-YO-O
'Nagoya'	'snowy night'	'that way'
o-YA-SU-MI-NA-SA-i	yu-U-ME-E	o-HA-YO-O
'good night'	'famous'	'good morning'

Row 15

The Japanese r is a flap-r, made by flicking the tip of the tongue against the alveolar ridge (area behind the upper teeth). This sound closely resembles the 'r' in the British English pronunciation of 'very.' To speakers of American English, it often sounds like a d, but there are two main differences: (1) the Japanese r is shorter than d; and (2) in the production of r, the tip of the tongue makes contact with the alveolar ridge, whereas in the production of d, it is the area of the tongue immediately behind the tip that makes contact against the upper teeth. When r is immediately followed by i or y, the r articulation just described is accompanied by palatalization — that is, the back part of the tongue is in position to make a y sound, while the tip makes the flap-r.

Practice 15

ra-KU	o-HU-ro	rya-KU-ZI
'comfortable'	'bath'	'simplified character'
sa-YO-NA-RA	o-MO-SI-RO-i	ka-I-RYU-U
'goodbye'	'is interesting'	'ocean current'
BI-ru	ri-KO-O	ryu-U-KO-O
'building'	'clever'	'fashion'
RU-u-ru	ko-O-RI	RYO-o-zi
'rule'	'ice'	'consul'
KI-re-e	a-RI-g̃a-to-o	ryo-O-RI-ya
'pretty'	'thank you'	'restaurant'

---

[1] See footnote 1 on page xxiii.

Row 16	The symbol: <u> </u>	stands for a sound approximately like:	but the Japanese sound:
	<u>w</u>	'w' in 'want'	is regularly fully voiced [1]

Practice 16

wa-KA-i	wa-KA-ru	wa-RE-WA-RE
'is young'	'understand'	'we'
he-E-WA	yu-BI-WA	wa-SU-RE-RU
'peace'	'ring'	'forget'

Row 17

<u>K</u> occurs as a syllable by itself immediately preceding a syllable having initial <u>k</u> (i.e. a syllable of Row 2). The back of the tongue is raised as in the production of a single (that is, short) <u>k</u> and is held in that position for a full syllable beat before being released (compare the somewhat similar long 'k' in English 'bookkeeper'). The following syllable, which has initial <u>k</u>, is pronounced without aspiration—that is, without a puff of breath after the <u>k</u>.

<u>S</u> occurs as a syllable by itself immediately preceding a syllable having initial <u>s</u> (i.e. a syllable of Row 5). Its articulation lasts for a full syllable beat and has the same quality as the <u>s</u> that follows (compare the somewhat similar long 's' in English 'less sleep' and the long 'sh' in 'horse-show').

<u>T</u> occurs as a syllable by itself immediately preceding a syllable having initial <u>t</u> (i.e. a syllable of Row 7). The front of the tongue is pushed against the back of the upper teeth as in the production of a single (that is, short) <u>t</u> and is held in that position for a full syllable beat before being released (compare the somewhat similar long 't' in English 'hot tip'). The following syllable, which has initial <u>t</u>, is pronounced without aspiration.

<u>P</u> occurs as a syllable by itself immediately preceding a syllable having initial <u>p</u> (i.e. a syllable of Row 11). The lips are brought together as in the production of a single (that is, short) <u>p</u> and are held in that position for a full syllable beat before being released (compare the somewhat similar long 'p' in English 'top part'). The following syllable, which has initial <u>p</u>, is pronounced without aspiration.

---

[1] See footnote 1 on page xxiii.

All double (that is, long) consonants in Japanese are characterized by tenseness.

Practice 17 a

mi-K-KA 'three days'	a-S-SA-ri 'briefly'
yu-K-KU-ri 'slowly'	ma-S-SU-ḡu 'straight'
NI-k-ko-o 'Nikko'	i-S-SO-O 'more'
ha-K-KI-ri 'clearly'	za-S-SI 'magazine'
se-K-KYO-o 'sermon'	ma-S-SI-RO 'all white'
ha-K-KYU-U 'small salary'	i-S-SYU-U 'one round'
ka-T-TA 'bought'	i-P-PA-I 'full'
i-T-TE 'going'	i-P-PU-U 'odd'
TYO-t-to 'a bit'	ri-P-PO-O 'legislation'
ma-T-TI-ba-ko 'matchbox'	ha-P-PI 'workman's coat'
ko-MA-t-tya-t-ta '[I]'m upset'	ha-P-PYA-KU-ME '800 momme'
yo-T-TU-ME 'fourth thing'	ha-P-PYO-O 'announcement'

Row 17 (continued)

N̄ represents a syllabic nasal: it is a sound which always has a full syllable beat of its own—that is, it constitutes a syllable—and is always pronounced with the nasal passage open; but its pronunciation varies depending on the sound that immediately follows in the same word or a following word.

1. Before a syllable beginning with p, b, or m (that is, a syllable of Row 11, 12, or 13), n̄ represents a syllabic m. [1]

2. Before a syllable beginning with z, t, d, n, or r (that is, a syllable of Row 6, 7, 8, 9, or 15), n̄ represents a syllabic n. [1]

3. Before a syllable beginning with k, g, or ḡ (that is, a syllable of Row 2, 3, or 4), n̄ represents a syllabic ḡ. [1]

4. Elsewhere—that is, before a vowel (i.e. a syllable of Row 1) or a syllable beginning with s, h, y, or w (i.e. a syllable of Row 5, 10, 14, or 16) or at the end of an utterance— n̄ represents syllabic nasalization, articulated by raising the tongue toward the roof of the mouth but not making contact anywhere, and at the same time releasing the flow of air through the nasal passage and vibrating the vocal cords. When n̄ is followed by o, the o is anticipated and the combination sounds like n̄ + w + o. Similarly, n̄ followed by e sounds like n̄ + y + e.

---

[1] It constitutes a full syllable and is longer than the related sound which occurs as the initial part of a syllable.

Practice 17 b

   (1) sa-N̄-PO   (2) be-N̄-ZYO   (3) be-N̄-KYO-O
        'a walk'   'toilet'   'study'
        SA-ñ-ba-i   ke-N̄-TO-o   ni-HO-N̄-GI-ñ-ko-o
        'three cupfuls'   'a guess'   'Bank of Japan'
        a-N̄-MA-RI   KO-ñ-do   ni-HO-N̄-GO
        'too much'   'this time'   'Japanese language'
                         da-N̄-NA-SA-ma
                         'master'
                         BE-ñ-ri
                         'convenient'

          (4) te-N̄-I-N̄ 'store clerk'
              ni-HO-ñ o 'Japan (as direct object)'
              ni-HO-ñ e 'to Japan'
              sa-N̄-SE-E 'approval'
              HA-ñ-ha-ñ 'half and half'
              HO-ñ-ya 'bookstore'
              de-N̄-WA 'telephone'
              a-RI-MA-SE-ñ 'there isn't any'

Whispered Syllables

The Tokyo dialect of Japanese is characterized by the frequent occurrence of whispered (that is, voiceless[1]) syllables. Whenever an i or u vowel[2] occurs between any two voiceless consonants (k, s, t, p, or h), the vowel automatically becomes voiceless or, in some cases, is lost. This happens whether the two consonants come in the same word or in consecutive words.

---

[1] A voiceless sound is one which is not accompanied by vibration of the vocal cords.

[2] Other vowels are only occasionally affected.

Practice 18

In the following practice drills, whispered (i.e. voiceless or lost) vowels are crossed by a virgule (/).

kí-SYA	sú-SU-MU	hí-SYO
'train'	'advance'	'secretary'
kí-TE	sú-TE-RU	hí-TO
'coming'	'throw away'	'person'
kí-T-TE	na-SÚ-t-te	hí-P-PA-ru
'stamp'	'doing'	'pull'
kú-SYA-mi	tí-KA-i	hú-KA-i
'sneeze'	'is close'	'is deep'
NA-kú-te	tí-T-TO-mo	hú-SI-ḠI
'not being any'	'[not] a bit'	'strange'
sí-TE	tú-KI-MA-sí-ta	hú-TO-i
'doing'	'[I] arrived'	'is big around'
sí-T-TE	tú-TO-me-te	hú-T-TO-BO-o-ru
'knowing'	'being employed'	'football'
sú-KI-i	hí-KI-MA-sí-ta	hí-HA-N̄
'skiing'	'[I] pulled'	'criticism'

In the phrases in the left-hand column below, the final vowel of the first word is preceded AND followed by a voiceless consonant and accordingly is itself voiceless. In the phrases in the right-hand column, the final vowel of the first word is preceded but not f o l l o w e d by a voiceless consonant and accordingly has its full, voiced value—that is, it is accompanied by vibration of the vocal cords.

Practice 19

DO-t-tí ka 'either one'   DO-t-ti ḡa 'which one (as subject)?'

DE-sú kara 'therefore'   DE-su ḡa 'however'

I-tú kara 'since when?'   I-tu ma-de 'until when?'

hí-KO-o-kí to 'airplane and'   hí-KO-o-ki no 'of an airplane'

When an i or u vowel preceded by a voiceless consonant comes at the end of an utterance, the vowel either has its full voiced value or is whispered. There is variation depending on the speaker, the occasion, and the word in question. Alternants like the following occur commonly:

Practice 20

hí-TO-tú   or   hí-TO-tu 'one unit'

SO-o de-sú   or   SO-o de-su 'that's right'

o-HA-YO-O GO-ZA-I-MA-sú   or   o-HA-YO-O GO-ZA-I-MA-su
'good morning'

Accent

The rhythm of Japanese, unlike that of English, is regular and even: each syllable is given moderate, approximately equal stress, and has approximately equal length. However, some syllables seem more prominent than others. This prominence—or accent—is primarily a matter of pitch in Japanese, and only secondarily a matter of stress.

Any continuous Japanese sequence of one or more words is said to be accented if it contains at least one example of a single high-pitched syllable, or an uninterrupted series of high-pitched syllables, followed by an abrupt drop to a low-pitched syllable; and the accent is said to occur on the last (or only) high-pitched syllable, which is slightly stressed. Thus, an utterance that sounds like this:

$$a^{merikaryoozi}{}_{kan} \text{ 'American Consulate'}$$

is an accented utterance, and the accent occurs on the syllable zi, which is slightly stressed (i.e. louder).

For the purposes of this text, we recognize four significant pitch levels: two accented levels (high and medium-high) and two unaccented levels (neutral and low). These are not absolute pitch levels but are relative to each other within a given utterance.

Some Japanese utterances are accented and some are unaccented. The first syllable of an unaccented sequence of more than one syllable is automatically pronounced with low pitch, and the following syllables all have neutral pitch. An unaccented sequence which follows pause (that is, which occurs at the beginning of a sentence, or within a sentence after a pause) appears in this text without any special accent marks.

koko is pronounced ko^{ko} 'here'

asoko is pronounced a^{soko} 'there'

ano sakana is pronounced a$^{no\ sakana}$ 'that fish'

soko e iku is pronounced so$^{ko\ e\ iku}$ 'I'll go there'

moo iti-do itte is pronounced mo$^{o\ iti\text{-}do\ itte}$ 'saying it again'

However, when an unaccented word or phrase having the above pitch contour occurs in the middle of a sequence, the superscript symbol ⌐ appears over the single syllable which has low pitch: ⌐ indicates a rise in pitch from low level to neutral level. Thus:

kore wa zắssi da   is pronounced   ko$^{re\ wa}{}_{za}{}^{ssi\ da}$

'this is a magazine'

An accented sequence contains one or more of the following superscript symbols:[1]

Symbol	Meaning
⌐	Rise from neutral to high pitch
¬	Drop from high to neutral or low pitch
⊦	Rise from neutral to medium-high pitch
⊣	Drop from medium-high to neutral or low pitch

Thus:

do¬ozo is pronounced ^{do}ozo 'please'

a⌐na¬ta is pronounced a^{na}ta 'you'

a⌐o¬i is pronounced a^{o}i 'is blue'

wa⌐karimase¬n̄ is pronounced wa^{karimase}n̄ 'it isn't clear'

da⌐izyo¬obu is pronounced da^{izyo}obu 'safe'

mo⌐o iti-do itte kudasa¬i is pronounced mo$^{o\ iti\text{-}do\ itte\ kudasa}{}_{i}$ 'please say it again'

ki¬ree na o⊦zyo⊣osañ is pronounced ^{ki}ree na o^{zyo}osañ 'a pretty girl'

na¬ḡaku ka⊦karima⊣su kara is pronounced ^{na}ḡaku ka^{karima}su kara 'because it takes long'

o⌐oki¬i i⊦e⊣ desu is pronounced o^{oki}i i^{e} desu 'it's a big house'

Note the following rules and conventions:

(1) Only a word which contains ¬ or ⊣ is said to be accented, and the accent is said to occur on the syllable at whose end ¬ or ⊣ occurs.[2]

(2) Any word containing ⌐ or ⊦, or the first word after a pause, or any word beginning with low plus neutral pitch, marks the start of a new accent phrase.

(3) Except in special circumstances, the first or only accented sequence of syllables of an utterance is said to be within the pitch

---

[1] A single accented word never has more than one high-pitched sequence and therefore cannot contain more than two of the accent superscripts—one rising and one falling.

[2] Actually the rise in pitch symbolized by ⌐ or ⊦ is automatic, given the

range designated as "high." Subsequent accented sequences in the same sentence which have the same[1] or higher pitch are also said to be within the high range; those which have significantly lower pitch (i.e. lower than high but higher than neutral) are said to be "medium-high."

Whispered syllables in Japanese cannot be distinguished by pitch. Their position within the pitch coutour is determined by other linguistic criteria.

Since accent in Japanese is a matter of high pitch relative to a following low pitch, it is impossible to hear accent without a following low syllable. The occurrence of ⌐ at the end of a single word in this text means that the word ordinarily has that accent when a following low syllable occurs. For example, hasi 'edge' and ha⌐si⌐ 'bridge' sound alike in isolation—in both, the first syllable is lower pitched than the second syllable—but when they are followed by a neutral or low syllable, they contrast with each other:

hasi wa (ha$^{si\ wa}$) 'as for the edge,' but

ha⌐si⌐ wa (ha^{si} wa) 'as for the bridge';

hasi da (ha$^{si\ da}$) 'it's the edge,' but

ha⌐si⌐ da (ha^{si} da) 'it's the bridge'; etc.

Similarly, ki 'spirit' and ki⌐ 'tree' are alike in isolation, but compare:

ki wa (ki ^{wa}) 'as for the spirit' and

ki⌐ wa (^{ki} wa) 'as for the tree.'

Accordingly we do speak of Japanese words that are accented on the final syllable, although we recognize that the accent can be heard in only some occurrences.

When a word is accented on its next-to-last syllable and the final syllable has a whispered alternant, the accent is regularly marked. For example, i⌐kima⌐su means either i$\underline{\quad kima\quad}$su̜[2] or i$\underline{\quad kima\quad}$su.

---

boundaries of the accent phrase. It always occurs on the second syllable of the accent phrase, unless the accent itself falls on the first syllable, in which case only the first syllable is high-pitched. Symbols for the rise are included here to simplify the reading of the transcription for the beginning student. It is possible to represent Japanese accent by using a traditional accent mark on the last high syllable (where this text has ⌐ or ⌐), with no symbol to indicate the automatic rise—provided the boundaries of the accent phrase are identified. Thus: ho⌐ñ might be written hón, a⌐na⌐ta as anáta, i⌐kima⌐sita as ikimásita, mo⌐o iti-do itte kudasa⌐i as moo iti-do itte kudasái, and so on.

[1] 'Same' here refers to linguistic sameness, i. e. variation is within the bounds permitted by the native speaker for identification as the same. Usually, each successive occurrence of a given pitch level within a pause group represents a slightly lower alternant of that pitch.

[2] This is the more common alternant in Tokyo speech.

In animated or emphatic speech, the interval between pitch levels increases. In some cases, the interval between low and neutral pitch within one emphatic unaccented phrase may be as great as or greater than that between neutral and high pitch in a following unemphatic accented phrase. The symbol | (appearing only in Part II) marks the end of such an emphatic phrase. Thus:

        oyoso kyo⌐omi na⌉i <u>is pronounced</u> o$^{yoso\ kyo}$ $^{omi\ na}$ $_{i}$

        'on the whole I have no interest'

but:

        oyoso | kyo⌐omi na⌉i <u>is pronounced</u> o^{yoso} kyo$^{omi\ na}$ na$_{i}$

        'ON THE WHOLE I have no interest'

Accent presents difficulty for a foreign student of Japanese largely because of accent variation.[1] This variation is of three kinds:

(1) Variation in basic word accent

Many words have alternate accents within the Tokyo dialect. Thus, the accepted pronunciation of the word for 'policeman' is <u>zyuñsa</u> or <u>zyu⌉ñsa</u>; for 'streetcar,' <u>deñsya</u> or <u>de⌉ñsya</u>; for 'I,' <u>boku</u> or <u>bo⌉ku</u>.

(2) Gain and loss of accent in particular environments

Many basically unaccented· words sometimes acquire an accent, and many accented words sometimes lose their accent. For example, accented <u>ku⌐dasa⌉i</u> loses its accent following an accented -<u>te</u> word:

        i⌐tte kudasa⌉i 'please say [it]'
        ha⌐na⌉site kudasai 'please talk'

An unaccented -<u>te</u> word acquires an accent before <u>mo</u> and <u>kara</u>:

        itte 'saying [it]'

but:

        i⌐tte⌉ mo 'even if [I] say [it]'

and:

        i⌐tte⌉ kara 'after saying [it]'

(3) Variation in phrase accent

Many pairs of utterances, otherwise identical, are distinguished only by a difference in their phrase accent. Compare:

---

[1] The accents and intonations marked in this text follow those of the tapes that were recorded to accompany it, for all the material that was recorded.

(a) Kyo⌐oto e i⌐kima⌐sita ka 'did you go to Kyoto (or did you go somewhere else)?'

(b) Kyo⌐oto e i⌐kima⌐sita ka 'did you (or didn't you) go to Kyoto?'

(a) are wa ⌐na⌐ñ desu ka 'what is that?'

(b) a⌐re wa na⌐ñ desu ka 'what is THAT (in comparison with the other things)?'

(a) zu⌐ibuñ ya⌐su⌐i desu ⌐ne⌐e 'it's very CHEAP, isn't it'

(b) zu⌐ibuñ ya⌐su⌐i desu ⌐ne⌐e 'it's VERY cheap, isn't it'

(a) mo⌐tto ǔsiro 'further BACK'

(b) mo⌐tto usiro 'FURTHER back'

In general, it can be said that the occurrence of ⌐ or ⌐ on a word is a sign of primary interest in that word. Conversely, ⌐ is never a sign of interest or emphasis.

Superimposed on these kinds of variation is dialectal variation. The accent of Tokyo Japanese is different from that of other parts of Japan. A student working with a tutor who is not a native of Tokyo will find that the pitch contours marked in this text often do not match those used by his tutor.

Doesn't this mean, then, that the student of Japanese might just as well ignore accent? Not at all! The fact that two different accents are sometimes acceptable does not mean that any accent at all is permitted. (Some native speakers of English say 'dry cléaning' and others say 'drý cleaning,' but no speaker says 'dry cleaníng.') Further indication of the importance of accent is the fact that many pairs of utterances with different meanings are distinguished only by their accent.

Intonation

The following intonation symbols are used in this text:

1. Period .

A period ending a sentence indicates that the final syllable and all immediately preceding unaccented syllables are pronounced with low pitch level, with the final syllable — if it is not whispered — lowest of all. In the event that the sentence, or its final accent phrase, contains no accent — that is, if the final or only pitch contour of the sentence is low + neutral — a final period indicates only the onset of silence.

Period intonation occurs most commonly at the end of statements, suggestions, rhetorical questions, and questions asked indirectly. At the end of direct questions, it often indicates abruptness, stiffness, aloofness, etc.

Examples:

Wa⌐karimase⌐n desita. 'I didn't understand.'   is pronounced

   wa^{karimase}
            n desi_{ta}

Asuko e iku. 'I'm going to go there.'   is pronounced

   _asuko e iku

2. Question mark ?

A question mark ending a sentence indicates a rise in pitch on the final syllable, [1] usually with lengthening of that syllable. Question-mark intonation regularly changes a statement into a question, and is typical of familiar style.

Examples:

Wa⌐ka⌐ru? 'Is it clear?'   is pronounced   wa^{ka}ru^u

Kore? 'This one?'   is pronounced   ko^{re}^e

3. Rising hook ⌐

A rising hook ending a sentence indicates a slight rise in pitch on the final syllable only, usually without lengthening of that syllable. The final syllable may start on a high or a low pitch. [2] This intonation occurs with certain sentence particles and implies friendliness and interest in the reaction of the person addressed. Wherever a rising hook occurs, it is possible to substitute a period as an alternate intonation without changing the meaning beyond m a k i n g the sentence more abrupt. Examples:

Wa⌐karima⌐sita ka⌐   'Did you understand?'   is pronounced

   wa^{karima}sita ka⌐   or   wa^{karima}sita ^{ka⌐}

I⌐i desu yo⌐   'It's all right!'   is pronounced

   ⁱi desu yo⌐   or   ⁱi desu ^{yo⌐}

---

[1] With this intonation, the final syllable is never whispered.

[2] A high-pitched start is more common in women's speech.

4. Low bar _

A low bar ending a sentence indicates that the final syllable has neutral pitch. It usually is lengthened and there is a gradual fading into silence. This intonation denotes incompleteness.

Examples:

Ka⌐mawana⌐kereba_ 'If it doesn't matter...'   is pronounced

ka^{mawana}kerebaa_

So⌐o desu ḡa_ 'That's so but....'   is pronounced

so^o desu ḡaa_

5. Exclamation point !

An exclamation point ending a sentence indicates that the final syllable starts high and has slightly falling pitch. Articulation ends abruptly and there is no significant lengthening of the final syllable.

Example:

Ano ne! 'Say there!'   is pronounced   a^{no} ^{ne}

6. Asterisk *

An asterisk at the beginning of a sequence indicates a special exclamatory intonation in which all pitch levels of the sequence become successively higher with each occurrence. Examples:

* Yo⌐ku wa⌐karima⌐su ⌐ne⌐e. 'How well you understand!'

is pronounced yo^oku wa^{karima}su^{ne} _e

* I⌐i o⌐te⌐ñki desu ⌐ne⌐e. 'What nice weather!'   is pronounced

i_i o^{te}ñki de^{su} ^{ne}_e

7. Comma , and Semicolon ;

A comma within a sentence indicates a break within the utterance: X, Y means that there is a slight slowing down of articulation, with or without accompanying pause, at the end of X; that neutral syllables at the end of X have a low alternant of neutral pitch; and that Y starts a new accent phrase. [1]

---

[1] This means that if the first two syllables of Y have unaccented pitch, the first is low and the second neutral.

A semicolon marks the same general kind of division as a comma, but in sentences containing more than one such division, the semicolon is used to indicate a division of major rank.

Examples:

Su⌈peiñḡo o yamema⌉sita ḡa, ni⌈hoñḡo wa ma⌉da be⌐ñkyoo-site ima⌐su.
'I gave up Spanish, but Japanese I'm still studying.'

<u>is pronounced</u>

    peiñḡo o yamema   hoñḡo wa ma

su   sita ḡa ⁿⁱ   da be^{ñkyoo-site ima} su.

Zi⌈kañ ḡa na⌉i kara, su⌈peiñḡo o yamema⌉sita ḡa; ni⌈hoñḡo wa ma⌉da be⌐ñkyoo-site ima⌐su.
'I gave up Spanish because I have no time, but Japanese I'm still studying.'   <u>is pronounced</u>

   kañ ḡa na   peiñḡo o yamema   hoñḡo wa ma

zi   i kara ^{su}   sita ḡa ⁿⁱ   da be^{ñkyoo-}

   site ima

      su.

8. Dash —

A dash occurs within inverted sentences (cf. Lesson 11, Grammatical Note 5), indicating that what follows is to be pronounced without pause as if it were part of the preceding phrase. An accented sequence following the dash is medium-high.

Examples:

I⌐i desu ⌈ne⌉e — sore wa.   'Isn't it nice — that.'   <u>is pronounced</u>

  _ii desu ^{ne}e sore wa

I⌈kima⌉sita yo⌡[1] — Kyo⌐oto e.   'I went — to Kyoto.'   <u>is pronounced</u>

  _ikima_{sita} ^{yo⌡} kyo_{oto e}

---

[1] An intonation symbol which ordinarily occurs at the end of a sentence may occur in the middle of an inverted sentence.

Supplementary Pronunciation Drills

1. Vowel Combinations

a⌐raima⌐su 'wash   hiatari 'exposure   huañ
   (formal)'   to the sun'   'uneasiness'
arau 'wash   iu (yuu) [1]   huite
   (informal)'   'say'   'wiping'
a⌐rae⌐   su⌐mi⌐e 'ink   suehiro
   'wash!'   drawing'   'folding fan'
a⌐rao⌐o   ki⌐kio⌐ku 'hear (and   huoñ
   'let's wash'   keep in mind)'   'unrest'

deasi 'start'   do⌐a 'door'
deiri 'going in and out'   hi⌐ro⌐i 'is wide'
neuti 'value'   o⌐mo⌐u 'think'
neoki 'lying down and getting   ko⌐e 'voice
   up'

2. Short and Long Vowels

obasañ 'aunt'   ha⌐ 'tooth'
o⌐ba⌐asañ 'grandmother'   ha⌐a 'yes'

ozisañ 'uncle'   ki⌐te⌐ 'coming'
o⌐zi⌐isañ 'grandfather'   kiite 'listening'

ku⌐roo 'trouble'   husetu 'construction'
ku⌐uro 'air route'   huusetu 'rumor'

ki⌐re⌐ 'cloth'   se⌐gyoo 'management'
ki⌐ree 'pretty'   se⌐egyo control'

to⌐tte 'taking'   mu⌐ko 'bridegroom'
to⌐otte 'going through'   mukoo 'beyond'

tori 'bird'   oki 'open sea'
to⌐ori⌐ 'avenue'   o⌐oki⌐i 'is big'

---

[1] I + u is regularly pronounced yuu.

3. Short and Long Consonants

maki 'firewood' ite 'being'
maꜝkki 'the last years' itte 'going'

Masao (proper name) koꜞnaꜝ 'flour'
maꜞssaꜝo 'deep blue' koñna 'this kind'

nisi 'west' kono boosi 'this hat'
niꜝssi 'Japan and China' koꜝñ no boosi 'navy blue hat'

maꜞtiꜝ 'town' Suꜞpeꜝiñ 'Spain'
maꜝtti 'match' suꜞppaꜝi 'is sour'

4. <u>su</u> ~ <u>tu</u> Contrast

masu 'increase' suꜝri 'pickpocket' suꜞkiꜝ 'liking'
maꜝtu 'wait' turi 'fishing' tuꜞkiꜝ 'moon'

suꜝmi 'corner' suꜞgiꜝ 'past' susumu 'advance'
tuꜝmi 'crime' tuꜞgiꜝ 'next' tuꜞtuꜝmu 'wrap'

5. <u>d</u> ~ <u>r</u> Contrast

doꜝo 'how?' hodo 'extent' muda 'useless'
roꜝo 'prison' hoꜝro 'hood' mura 'village'

dañboo 'heating' maꜝde 'until' sode 'sleeve'
rañboo 'rough' maꜞreꜝ 'rare' sore 'that thing'

6. <u>n</u> ~ <u>ḡ</u> ~ <u>ñ</u> ~ <u>ñḡ</u> Contrast

kani 'crab' kaneñ 'a combustible' saꜝ ni 'in what follows'
kaꜞḡiꜝ 'key' kaḡeñ 'moderation' saꜝḡi 'fraud'
kaꜝñi severe cold' kaꜝñeñ 'hepatitis' sañi 'approval'
kaꜝñḡi 'Korean kañḡeñ 'restoration' saꜝñḡi 'participation in
  singing girl'   government'

7 Even Rhythm Practice

a 'oh!'
are 'that one'
asoko 'there'
toꜞkidokiꜝ 'sometimes'
ano sakana 'that fish'
ano tomodati 'that friend'
ano tomodati da 'it's that friend'
asoko no tomodati 'a friend from that place'
Amerika no tomodati 'an American friend'
Amerika no tomodati da 'it's an American friend'

8. Accent Contrasts

I⌐ma desu. 'It's now.'
I⌐ma⌐ desu. 'It's a living room.'

Ma⌐initi desu. 'It's every day.'
Ma⌐initi de⌐su. 'It's the Mainichi (a newspaper).'

Yo⌐nde kudasai. 'Please read [it].'
Yo⌐nde kudasa⌐i. 'Please call [him].'

Tu⌐yu de⌐su. 'It's the rainy season.'
Tu⌐yu desu. 'It's broth.'

A⌐tuku simasu. 'I'll make it hot.'
A⌐tuku sima⌐su. 'I'll make it thick.'

So⌐re o ki⌐ru kara_ 'Since I'm going to cut it . . .'
So⌐re o kiru⌐ kara_ 'Since I'm going to wear it . . .'

Ha⌐si desu. 'They're chopsticks.'
Ha⌐si de⌐su. 'It's the edge.'
Ha⌐si⌐ desu. 'It's a bridge.'

9. Intonation Contrasts

De⌐ki⌐ru. 'It's possible.'
De⌐ki⌐ru? 'Is it possible?'

So⌐o desyoo. 'That's probably so.'
So⌐o desyoo? 'That's so, isn't it?'

Sore. 'That one.'
Sore? 'That one?'

I⌐sogasi⌐i. 'I'm busy.'
I⌐sogasi⌐i? 'Are you busy?'

So⌐o desu ka. 'Oh.'
So⌐o desu ka⌐ 'Oh?'

Ti⌐gaima⌐su yo. 'They're different.'
Ti⌐gaima⌐su yo⌐ 'They're different.' [1]

---

[1] Differences in the English equivalents are also differences of intonation.

O⌐warima¬sita yo.   'I've finished.'
O⌐warima¬sita yo⌐   'I've finished.'[1]

I⌐kima¬su ka⌐   'Are you going?'
I⌐kima¬su ḡa⌐   'I'm going but...'

O⌐nazi de¬su yo.   'They're the same.'
O⌐nazi de¬su ḡa⌐   'They're the same but...'

Zyo⌐ozu¬ ni na⌐rima¬sita ⌐ne¬e.   'How proficient you've become!'
* Zyo⌐ozu¬ ni na⌐rima¬sita ⌐ne¬e.   'How proficient you've become!'[1]

A⌐ñmari dekimase¬ñ ⌐ne¬e.   'He can't do very much, can he!'
* A⌐ñmari dekimase¬ñ ⌐ne¬e.   'He can't do very much, can he!'[1]

SPECIAL SYMBOLS AND CONVENTIONS

1. ( ), *[ ]*, [ ]

In a Japanese sequence, material enclosed in parentheses ( ) may be omitted. In every case, the shorter utterance is less formal and/or less polite. Thus, a(b) means that ab and a both occur with the same meaning except that a is less formal and/or less polite than ab.

Italicized brackets *[ ]*, on the other hand, enclose material that is optional without a difference of formality and/or politeness level: a*[b]* means that both ab and a occur in the given context without significant distinction.

Square brackets [ ] in the English equivalent of a Japanese sequence enclose material which is needed for natural English but does not correspond to anything in the Japanese sequence. Conversely, parentheses in the English equivalent enclose explanatory material or something literally translated from the Japanese which is not needed in the English. Compare:

I⌐kima¬sita ka⌐   'Did [you] go?'

E¬e, i⌐kima¬sita.   'Yes, [I] did (go).'

---

[1] Differences in the English equivalents are also differences of intonation.

'You' and 'I' are needed for natural English but do not correspond to anything in the Japanese. 'Go' in the second sentence corresponds to something in the Japanese that is usually omitted in the English equivalent.

Square brackets and parentheses are used more frequently in the earlier lessons, as an aid to the beginning student.

2. ↑, ↓, +

A raised arrow pointing upward ↑ following a Japanese word or phrase indicates that the word or phrase is polite-honorific—that is, it exalts the person to whom it refers. Such a word is used only in reference to persons other than the speaker.

A raised arrow pointing downward ↓ following a Japanese word or phrase indicates that the word or phrase is polite-humble—that is, it humbles the person to whom it refers in deference to the person addressed. Such a word is used only in reference to the speaker, members of his family, or persons closely connected with him.

A raised plus sign + following a Japanese word or phrase indicates that the word or phrase is polite-neutral—that is, it is polite but does not exalt or humble the person to whom it refers or the person to whom it is addressed. Such a word is a neutral indication of politeness.

3. Miscellaneous

A radical √ enclosing the citation form of an inflected word indicates the given word in any or all of its derived inflected forms. Thus, √go (in English) is an abbreviation for go, goes, went, gone, etc.

Lit. is used throughout the text as an abbreviation for 'literally.'

In the Japanese material, only the first word in a sentence and names of persons and places are capitalized.

ROMANIZATION

Various systems of romanization—representation of the Japanese language by letters of the Roman alphabet—are in use in Japan today. The system used in this book is an adaptation of the Shin-kunrei-shiki 'New Official System' and will be designated as BJ Romanization. [1] Other common romanizations are

---

[1] However, Japanese words appearing throughout the book as non-quoted parts of English sentences (as in this explanatory paragraph) are spelled in Hepburn romanization.

Hepburn (also called Hyōjun-shiki 'Standard System') and Nippon-shiki 'Japanese System.' The differences among them are slight and can be learned with little difficulty. For example, the word for 'romanization' is variously represented as follows:

BJ:	roomazi
Shin-kunrei-shiki:	rômazi [1]
Hepburn:	rōmaji [1]
Nippon-shiki:	rōmadi [1]

Hepburn romanization is the system most familiar to Westerners; but there are three cogent reasons for not using it in a Japanese language textbook.

1. BJ, Shin-kunrei-shiki, and Nippon-shiki bear a direct relation to Japanese structure, whereas Hepburn has no such connection. Thus, in describing Japanese inflection, many statements become unnecessarily complicated and parallelism is obscured if Hepburn romanization is used. For example, compare the following:

In a text using BJ, Shin-kunrei-shiki, or Nippon-shiki:

To form the stem of -u-class verbals, change final -u to -i.

Corresponding statement in a text using Hepburn romanization:

To form the stem of -u-class verbals, change final -u to -i, but change final -tsu to -chi and final -su to -shi.

The complexity of the latter statement results not from "special cases" in Japanese verbal structure, but only from the fact that Hepburn romanization is based on languages of the West (its vowels have values roughly as in the Romance languages, its consonants as in English) rather than on the Japanese language.

2. For the student who plans to learn the native Japanese writing system, the transition from Hepburn is more difficult than from the other systems.

3. The Japanese themselves do not adhere consistently to any single system; in fact, they sometimes use a mixture of several within the same word! It therefore becomes necessary for the foreign student to familiarize himself with the symbols used in all the systems. BJ, Shin-kunrei-shiki, and Nippon-shiki romanizations take a little longer for the English-speaking student to master (though only in the initial stages); but once he has learned any one of them, he can switch to Hepburn with no trouble. The student who has used only Hepburn, however, finds the conversion to other systems a difficult one.

The minor differences between BJ on the one hand and Shin-kunrei-shiki and Nippon-shiki on the other result from an attempt to avoid certain inconsistencies and ambiguity in the latter systems. For example, in BJ, ee and ei consistently represent different and distinct sequences of sounds of Tokyo Japanese. The spelling of these sequences in all the other romanizations (including Hepburn) is inconsistent, so that it is often impossible for a student to be certain which value a given occurrence of ei represents.

---

[1] The long mark over the o is sometimes omitted.

CONVERSION TABLE OF ROMANIZATION[1]

Symbol in another romanization	Corresponding symbol in BJ
ā [2]	aa
ū [2]	uu
ē [2]	ee
ei	ee (or ei)
ye	e
ō [2]	oo
wo	o
-g-	-g̃- (or -g-)
shi	si
sha	sya
shu	syu
sho	syo
ji	zi
ja	zya
ju	zyu
jo	zyo
di	zi
dz	z
chi	ti
cha	tya
chu	tyu
cho	tyo
tsu	tu
fu	hu
-n'-	-ñ-
-n (final)	-ñ
-n + consonant other than y-	-ñ-
-mp-	-ñp-
-mb-	-ñb-
-mm-	-ñm-

---

[1] The left-hand column includes symbols and combinations which either do not occur in BJ Romanization, or else they correspond to more than one BJ symbol so that their interpretation is ambiguous.

[2] A circumflex (^) over a vowel has the same meaning as a macron (ˉ).

Classroom Instructions

1. Please listen.

2. Please say [it].
3. Please say [it] again.
4. Please answer.
5. Please speak in Japanese.
6. Please don't use English.
7. Please open [your] book.
8. Please look at [your] book.
9. Please don't look at [your] book.
10. Please close [your] book.
11. Please say [it] in chorus.
12. Please say [it] one (person) at a time.
13. Please speak more quickly.
14. Please speak more clearly.
15. Please speak in a louder voice.
16. Please ask Mr. (or Mrs. or Miss) Tanaka.

Ki⌐ite kudasa⌐i. or
Ki⌐ite (i)te kudasa⌐i.[2]
I⌐tte kudasa⌐i.
Mo⌐o iti-do itte kudasa⌐i.
Ko⌐ta⌐ete kudasai.
Ni⌐hoñgo de hana⌐site kudasai.
Eego (wa) tu⌐kawana⌐i de kudasai.
Hoñ (o) a⌐kete kudasa⌐i.
Hoñ (o) ⌐mi⌐te kudasai.
Hoñ (wa) ⌐mi⌐nai de kudasai.

Hoñ (o) ⌐to⌐zite kudasai.
Mi⌐ñna⌐ de i⌐tte kudasa⌐i.
Hi⌐tori-zu⌐tu i⌐tte kudasa⌐i.

Mo⌐tto ⌐ha⌐yaku ha⌐na⌐site kudasai.
Mo⌐tto ha⌐kki⌐ri ha⌐na⌐site kudasai.
Mo⌐tto ⌐o⌐oki na ⌐ko⌐e de ha⌐na⌐site kudasai.
Ta⌐naka-sañ ni kiite kudasa⌐i.

[1] These sentences are primarily for use by a Japanese instructor in giving classroom directions. It is suggested that introductory drill on them be conducted for the purpose of aural recognition.

[2] Accent of contracted alternant: Ki⌐ite⌐ te kudasai.

1

Introductory Lesson: Greetings and Useful Phrases

1.	Oh, Mr. (or Mrs. or Miss) Tanaka!	A˺a, Tanaka-sañ.
2.	Good morning.	O⌐hayoo (gozaima˺su).
3.	Good afternoon.	Koñniti wa.
4.	Good evening.	Koñbañ wa.
5.	How are you? or Are you well? (Lit. Is it health?)	O⌐ge˺ñki desu ka⌐
6.	Yes.	Ha˺i. or E˺e.
7.	[I'm fine,] thank you. And you? (Lit. As for you?)	Okaḡesama de. A⌐na˺ta wa?
8.	Goodnight.	O⌐yasumi-nasa˺i.
9.	Goodbye.	Sayo(o)nara.[2]
10.	Excuse me (on leaving).	Si⌐tu˺ree(-simasu).
11.	Excuse me (for what I did).	Si⌐tu˺ree-(simasita).
12.	No. or Not at all.	Iie.
13.	Don't mention it. or You're welcome.	Do˺o itasimasite.
14.	I'm sorry. or Thank you for your trouble.	Su⌐(m)imase˺ñ.
15.	I'm sorry (for what I did). or Thank you (for the trouble you took).	Su⌐(m)imase˺ñ desita.
16.	[Thanks] very much.	Do˺o mo.
17.	Thank you.	A⌐ri˺ḡatoo (gozaimasu).
18.	Thank you very much.	Do˺o mo a⌐ri˺ḡatoo (gozaimasu).
19.	Thank you (for what you did).	A⌐ri˺ḡatoo (gozaimasita).
20.	Please (speaker requesting something).	O⌐neḡai-sima˺su.
21.	Please (speaker offering something).	Do˺ozo.

NOTES ON THE BASIC SENTENCES[3]

1. -Sañ is added to a family name (as in <u>Tanaka-sañ</u>), a given name (as in Ta˺roo-sañ), or a family name plus a given name (as in <u>Tanaka ⌐Ta˺roo-sañ</u>), but it is NOT added to one's own name or to that of members of one's

---

[1] Be sure to read the Introduction before beginning.

[2] Alternate accent: Sa⌐yo(o)na˺ra.

[3] Numbers in this section correspond to Basic Sentence numbers.

own family or household when speaking to outsiders. Thus, Mr. Yamamoto calls Mr. Tanaka <u>Tanaka-sañ</u>, but Mr. Tanaka identifies himself simply as <u>Tanaka.</u>

2. <u>Ohayoo</u> is used when addressing a friend or colleague or inferior informally. O⌐hayoo gozaima⌐su is a formal greeting used in addressing a superior, or in any situation requiring formality.

5. O⌐ge⌐ñki is the honorific (↑) equivalent of <u>ge⌐ñki</u>. Only the latter may be used in reference to oneself. In referring to others, <u>ge⌐ñki</u> is plain and o⌐ge⌐ñki is polite. (O)⌐ge⌐ñki desu ka⌐ may occur as the equivalent of 'How are you?' 'How, is he?' 'How is she?' or 'How are they?,' provided the context makes the meaning clear.

6. In general, <u>ha⌐i</u> is a rather stiff word, whereas e⌐e is conversational. However, <u>ha⌐i</u> is the regular response to a knock at the door or the calling of one's name.

7. <u>Okaḡesama de</u> indicates the speaker's appreciation for interest in his personal affairs ('thanks for asking') and/or appreciation for assistance ('thanks to you'). It always accompanies, or itself implies, favorable or pleasant information.

9. <u>Sayonara</u> is the contracted, less formal equivalent of <u>sayoonara.</u>

10. Si⌐tu⌐ree-simasu means literally 'I [am about to] commit a rudeness.' It is a polite way of excusing oneself from someone's presence, sometimes in the sense 'Excuse me for a moment' and sometimes as 'Excuse me—goodbye.' Other uses will be introduced later.

11. Si⌐tu⌐ree-simasita is the past equivalent of the preceding and means literally 'I committed a rudeness.' It is an apology for something that has already been done.

12. <u>Iie</u> is used in negative replies to questions, in contradictions and denials, and as an informal reply to apologies, expressions of thanks, and compliments.

13. <u>Do⌐o itasimasite</u> is used alone, or with <u>iie</u>, as a formal reply to apologies, expressions of thanks, and compliments.

14. <u>Su⌐imase⌐ñ</u> is the contracted, less formal equivalent of <u>su⌐mimase⌐ñ.</u>

15. <u>Su⌐(m)imase⌐ñ desita</u> is the past equivalent of <u>su⌐(m)imase⌐ñ</u> and refers to an action already completed. It is commonly used to apologize or say thank you, by someone who is on the point of leaving. However, the non-past form is used in expressing thanks immediately upon receiving something.

16. <u>Do⌐o mo</u>, used alone as an expression of thanks, is informal. It means literally 'in every way.'

17, 18, 19. The forms with <u>gozaimasu</u> (or <u>gozaimasita</u>) are formal, and those without are informal. Compare 2, above.

19. <u>A⌐ri⌐ḡatoo gozaimasita</u> is the past equivalent of a⌐ri⌐ḡatoo gozaimasu and refers to an action already completed. See 15, above.

20. Among the more common English equivalents of o⌐negai-sima⌐su are such expressions as: 'Would you please do it?'; 'Please take care of things';

'Please do'; 'May I have it?'; 'I'd like to have it'; etc. The equivalent differs depending upon the context, but the basic meaning is always the
same—'I make a request'—and the word is humble (↓).

21. Do⌐ozo, which occurs by itself as an expression of offering or invitation
     ('Please have some'; 'Go ahead'; 'Here you are'; etc.), also occurs within
     sentences of request, making the request softer and less abrupt. Thus,
     do⌐ozo o⌐negai-sima⌐su is a softer equivalent of o⌐negai-sima⌐su alone.

DRILLS

A.   Response Drill

1.	Tanaka-sañ⌐	Ha⌐i.
2.	Ohayoo.	Ohayoo.
3.	O⌐hayoo gozaima⌐su.	O⌐hayoo gozaima⌐su.
4.	O⌐hayoo gozaima⌐su.	Ohayoo.
5.	Koñniti wa.	Koñniti wa.
6.	Koñbañ wa.	Koñbañ wa.
7.	O⌐ge⌐ñki desu ka⌐	Okaḡesama de.
8.	O⌐ge⌐ñki desu ka⌐	E⌐e, okaḡesama de. A⌐na⌐ta wa?
9.	O⌐ge⌐ñki desu ka⌐	E⌐e, a⌐ri⌐ḡatoo gozaimasu.
10.	O⌐yasumi-nasa⌐i.	O⌐yasumi-nasa⌐i.
11.	O⌐yasumi-nasa⌐i.	Sayonara.
12.	Sa⌐yoona⌐ra.	Sayoonara.
13.	Sayonara.	Sayonara.
14.	Sa⌐yoona⌐ra.	Sayonara.
15.	Sayonara.	O⌐yasumi-nasa⌐i.
16.	Si⌐tu⌐ree.	Do⌐ozo.
17.	Si⌐tu⌐ree-simasu.	Do⌐ozo.
18.	Si⌐tu⌐ree.	Sayonara.
19.	Si⌐tu⌐ree-simasu.	Sayoonara.
20.	Si⌐tu⌐ree.	Iie.
21.	Si⌐tu⌐ree-simasita.	Do⌐o itasimasite.
22.	Si⌐tu⌐ree-simasita.	Iie, do⌐o itasimasite.
23.	Su⌐mimase⌐ñ.	Iie.
24.	Su⌐mimase⌐ñ.	Iie, do⌐o itasimasite.
25.	Su⌐mimase⌐ñ desita.	Iie.
26.	Su⌐mimase⌐ñ desita.	Do⌐o itasimasite.
27.	A⌐ri⌐ḡatoo.	Iie.
28.	A⌐ri⌐ḡatoo gozaimasu.	Do⌐o itasimasite.
29.	A⌐ri⌐ḡatoo gozaimasita.	Iie, do⌐o itasimasite.
30.	Do⌐o mo a⌐ri⌐ḡatoo gozaimasita.	Iie, do⌐o itasimasite.
31.	Do⌐o mo.	Iie.
32.	Do⌐ozo.	Su⌐mimase⌐ñ.
33.	Do⌐ozo.	A⌐ri⌐ḡatoo gozaimasu.
34.	Do⌐ozo.	Do⌐o mo.
35.	O⌐negai-sima⌐su.	Do⌐ozo.
36.	O⌐negai-sima⌐su.	Ha⌐i ⌐do⌐ozo.
37.	Do⌐ozo o⌐negai-sima⌐su.	Do⌐ozo.

B. Level Drill[1]

1. Ohayoo.   O⌐hayoo ⌐gozaima⌐su.
2. Sayonara.   Sa⌐yoona⌐ra.
3. Si⌐tu⌐ree.   Si⌐tu⌐ree-simasu.   <u>or</u>
                               Si⌐tu⌐ree-simasita.
4. Ge⌐ñki desu ka┘   O⌐ge⌐ñki desu ka┘
5. Su⌐imase⌐ñ.   Su⌐mimase⌐ñ.
6. Su⌐imase⌐ñ desita.   Su⌐mimase⌐ñ desita.
7. A⌐ri⌐gatoo.   A⌐ri⌐gatoo gozaimasu.   <u>or</u>
                               A⌐ri⌐gatoo gozaimasita.
8. Do⌐o mo.   Do⌐o mo a⌐ri⌐gatoo gozaimasu.   <u>or</u>
                               Do⌐o mo a⌐ri⌐gatoo gozaimasita.
9. Do⌐o mo a⌐ri⌐gatoo.   Do⌐o mo a⌐ri⌐gatoo gozaimasu.   <u>or</u>
                               Do⌐o mo a⌐ri⌐gatoo gozaimasita.

EXERCISES

1. What would you say to Mr. Tanaka under the following circumstances?

    a. You have just met him in the morning.
    b. You have just met him in the afternoon.
    c. You have just met him in the evening.
    d. You offer him a cigarette.
    e. He has just given you something.
    f. He has just thanked you for something.
    g. You have just bumped into him.
    h. You are leaving.

2. Give Mr. Tanaka's reply to the preceding, wherever possible.

_____

[1] The utterances in the right-hand column are more formal or polite equivalents of the utterances in the left-hand column.

Lesson 1. Getting Around

BASIC DIALOGUES: FOR MEMORIZATION

(a)

Smith

a bit <u>or</u> a little	tyoꞌtto
please wait	maꞌtte kudasai
1. Just a minute!	Tyoꞌtto Ꞌmaꞌtte kudasai.
2. I don't understand.	Waꞁkarimaseꞁñ.

Tanaka

3. You don't understand?	Waꞁkarimaseꞁñ ka˩

Smith

one time	iti-do
one time more	moo iti-do
please say	iꞁtte kudasaꞁi
4. No (i.e. that's right). Please say [it] once more.	Eꞁe. Moꞁo iti-do itte kudasaꞁi.

(b)

Smith

5. Do you understand?	Waꞁkarimaꞁsu ka˩

Yamamoto

6. Yes, I do (understand).	Eꞁe, waꞁkarimaꞁsu.

Smith

7. How about Mr. Tanaka? (Lit. As for Mr. Tanaka?)	Tanaka-sañ wa?

Yamamoto

8. Mr. Tanaka doesn't understand.	Taꞁnaka-sañ wa wakarimaseꞁñ.

(c)

Tanaka

9. Did you understand?	Waꞁkarimaꞁsita ka˩

Smith

10. Yes, I did (understand).	Eꞁe waꞁkarimaꞁsita.

Tanaka

well <u>or</u> a good deal <u>or</u> often	yoꞁku

11. You understand [very] well,   Yo⌐ku wakarimasu ⌐ne⌐e.
     don't you.

Smith

12. Oh, no!   Do⌐o itasimasite.

(d)

Smith

13. Did you do [it]?   Si⌐ma⌐sita ka⌐

Tanaka

     all or the whole thing   ze⌐ñbu
14. Yes, I did [it] all.   E⌐e, ze⌐ñbu si⌐ma⌐sita.

Smith

15. Thanks for your trouble.   Go⌐ku⌐roosama (desita).

Tanaka

16. Don't mention it.   Do⌐o itasimasite.

(e)

Smith

17. Did you go?   I⌐kima⌐sita ka⌐

Tanaka

18. No, I didn't (go).   Iie, i⌐kimase⌐ñ desita.

Smith (to Yamamoto)

19. How about you?   A⌐na⌐ta wa?

Yamamoto

     yesterday   ki⌐no⌐o
20. I went yesterday.   Ki⌐noo ikima⌐sita.

(f)

Smith

     tomorrow   a⌐sita⌐
21. Are you going to go to-   A⌐sita ikima⌐su ka⌐
     morrow?

Yamamoto

     today   kyo⌐o
22. No, I'm going to go today.   Iie, kyo⌐o ikimasu.

Smith

23. How about Mr. Tanaka?   Tanaka-sañ wa?

Yamamoto

24. He isn't going to go.   I⌐kimase⌐ñ.

NOTES ON THE BASIC DIALOGUES[1]

7. When addressing Mr. Tanaka, <u>Tanaka-sañ wa?</u> is equivalent to 'How about you, Mr. Tanaka?' It is less direct and more polite in Japanese to refer to the person by his name than by a⌐na⌐ta 'you.'

12. <u>Do⌐o itasimasite</u>, in addition to its use as a reply to expressions of thanks and apology, occurs as a polite reply to compliments.

15. <u>Go⌐ku⌐roosama desita</u> — lit. 'it has been toil on your part' — is used especially commonly in addressing a subordinate. The alternant without <u>desita</u> is informal.

GRAMMATICAL NOTES

1. V e r b a l s

wa⌐karima⌐su[2]	'understanding takes place' <u>or</u> 'understanding will take place'
wa⌐karima⌐sita	'understanding took place' <u>or</u> 'understanding has taken place'
wa⌐karimase⌐ñ	'understanding does not take place' <u>or</u> 'understanding will not take place' <u>or</u> 'understanding has not taken place'
wa⌐karimase⌐ñ desita	'understanding did not take place'

In Japanese there are words which are constant (i.e. have only one form) and those which are inflected (i.e. take particular sets of endings; compare English 'listen, listened, listening, listens'). Among the inflected words is a large group having forms similar to the four listed above (in addition to other forms). All such words are hereafter called VERBALS. [3]

The four forms listed above are named as follows:

(a) Form ending in -<u>ma⌐su</u>: Formal non-past affirmative
     Meaning: 'something happens (or exists)'   <u>or</u>
                'something is going to or will happen (or exist)'

---

[1] Numbers in this section correspond to those of the sentences in the Basic Dialogues.

[2] For the accent, see Introduction, page xxxvi.

[3] Note that the term 'verbal' is being defined with particular respect to Japanese. It names the word-class to which all words inflected like wa⌐karima⌐su belong—namely, words having other forms ending in -<u>ma⌐sita</u>, -<u>mase⌐ñ</u>, etc.

(b) Form ending in -ma⌐sita: Formal past affirmative
   Meaning: 'something has happened (or existed)' or
            'something happened (or existed)'

(c) Form ending in -mase⌐n̄: Formal non-past negative
   Meaning: 'something does not happen (or exist)' or
            'something is not going to or will not happen (or exist)' or
            'something has not happened (or existed) up to the present
            time'

(d) Form ending in -mase⌐n̄ desita: Formal past negative
   Meaning: 'something did not happen (or exist)'

The particular meaning of a given form is determined by context.

Verbals are impersonal and can occur by themselves as complete standard
sentences. They can indicate the occurrence of an action or the existence of a
state without grammatical reference to a subject. Contrast English 'I understand,' 'he understands,' 'they understand,' etc., with Japanese wa⌐karima⌐su
'understanding takes place,' 'there is understanding.' Most commonly, a verbal occurring alone refers to the speaker in a statement and to the person addressed in a question. For example:

    I⌐kima⌐sita ka↲ 'Did you go?' (Lit. 'Did going take place?')
    E⌐e i⌐kima⌐sita. 'Yes, I went.' (Lit. 'Yes, going took place.')

Different topics are indicated sometimes by the context, sometimes by the specific mention of a topic (which in some circumstances is followed by the particle wa 'as for,' about which more will be said later). For example, continuing
the immediately preceding conversation:

    Tanaka-sañ wa? 'How about Mr. Tanaka?' (Lit. 'As for Mr. Tana-
    ka?')
    I⌐kimase⌐n̄ desita. 'He didn't go.' (Lit. 'Going didn't take place.')
    or
    Tanaka-sañ wa i⌐kimase⌐n̄ desita. 'Mr. Tanaka didn't go.' (Lit. 'As
    for Mr. Tanaka, going didn't take place.')

In the lessons that follow, new verbals will be introduced first alone in their
-ma⌐su form, with the dictionary form of the closest English equivalent, and
then in a sentence (in the -ma⌐su form or another form) with an appropriate
contextual equivalent. For example:

    write   ka⌐kima⌐su
  Are you going to write?   Ka⌐kima⌐su ka↲

WARNING: Note that the -ma⌐su form of a verbal regularly refers to repeated action or future action, but not present action. Thus si⌐ma⌐su means '[I] do'
or '[I] will do,' but never '[I] am doing.'

2. Question Particle ka

  A Japanese sentence ending with the question particle[1] ka is a question. Any

---

[1] More will be said about particles in general later on.

statement can be made into a question by adding <u>ka,</u> provided the meaning makes sense. Compare:

  (a) Wa⌐karimase⌐n. '[I] don't understand.' (Lit. 'There isn't understanding.')
  (b) Wa⌐karimase⌐n ka. '[You] don't understand?' <u>or</u> 'Don't [you] understand?' (Lit. 'There isn't understanding?')

Questions with <u>ka</u> end in rising intonation (represented in this text by the symbol ⌐) or in low intonation (represented by a period).

All sentences ending with the question particle <u>ka</u> are questions; but not all questions end with <u>ka.</u> For example, the phrase a⌐na⌐ta wa 'as for you' becomes a question when pronounced with question intonation (represented by a question mark).

3.   Answers to Yes-or-No Questions

Ha⌐i[1] usually means 'what you just said is right.' In answer to affirmative questions, it corresponds to English 'yes,' but in answer to negative questions that anticipate a negative answer, it usually confirms the negative and corresponds to English 'no.' <u>Iie</u>, the opposite of ha⌐i, means 'what you just said is wrong' and behaves in a parallel way: in answer to affirmative questions it corresponds to English 'no,' but in answer to negative questions that anticipate a negative answer, it usually contradicts the negative and corresponds to English 'yes.'

	Literal English Equivalent	Normal English Equivalent
I⌐kima⌐sita ka.	'Going took place?'	'Did you go?'
Ha⌐i. [I⌐kima⌐sita.] [2]	'That's right. [Going took place.]'	'Yes. [I did (go).]'
Iie. [I⌐kimase⌐n desita.]	'That's wrong. [Going didn't take place.]'	'No. [I didn't (go).]'
I⌐kimase⌐n desita ka.	'Going didn't take place?'	'Didn't you go?'
Ha⌐i. [I⌐kimase⌐n desita.]	'That's right. [Going didn't take place.]'	'No. [I didn't (go).]'
Iie. [I⌐kima⌐sita.]	'That's wrong. [Going took place.]'	'Yes. [I did (go).]'

WARNING: English usage is as unexpected for a Japanese studying English as Japanese usage is for an American studying Japanese. Be wary of single-word answers given by a Japanese who is not yet fluent in English. In answer to 'Don't you have any bananas?' a 'Yes' from many Japanese means 'Yes. We have no bananas.'

---

[1] Throughout this note, whatever is said about <u>ha⌐i</u> applies equally to e⌐e.

[2] Diagonal brackets ([---]) enclose optional portions of the **answer.**

To sum up: The meaning of ha⁷i and iie occurring in answer to a yes-or-no question usually depends on the inflected form of the preceding question: Ha⁷i means that the affirmative or negative of the question applies and iie means that it does not apply.

4. ne⁷e

Ne⁷e 'isn't it true!' at the end of a sentence indicates an exclamation. It sometimes indicates reflection or consideration, and it often implies agreement—actual or assumed—between speaker and person addressed, but it is not a question-word in its occurrences with statement intonation. Compare:

Tanaka-sañ wa ⌈yo⌉ku wakarimasu.   'Mr. Tanaka understands [very] well.'

Tanaka-sañ wa ⌈yo⌉ku wa⌐karima⌐su   'Does Mr. Tanaka understand well?'
ka⌣

Tanaka-sañ wa ⌈yo⌉ku wakarimasu   'Doesn't Mr. Tanaka understand well!'
⌈ne⌉e.   'How well Mr. Tanaka understands!'
                                        'Mr. Tanaka understands [very] well,
                                        doesn't he!' 'Come to think of it, Mr.
                                        Tanaka does understand well!' etc.

As always, unless the subject is explicitly stated, it is inferred from context. Thus, Wa⌈karimase⌉ñ ⌈ne⌉e. may mean 'You don't understand, do you!' or 'He doesn't understand, does he!' or 'They don't understand, do they!' or 'Come to think of it, I don't understand!' etc.

DRILLS

A. Substitution Drill

1. I did [it] all.   Ze⌉ñbu si⌐ma⌐sita.
2. I did a little.   Tyo⌉tto si⌐ma⌐sita.
3. I did [it] once.   I⌐ti-do sima⌉sita.
4. I did [it] yesterday.   Ki⌐noo sima⌉sita.
5. I did [it] today.   Kyo⌉o si⌐ma⌐sita.
6. I did [it] once more.   Mo⌐o iti-do sima⌉sita.

B. Substitution Drill

1. I went yesterday.   Ki⌐noo ikima⌉sita.
2. I went today.   Kyo⌉o i⌐kima⌐sita.
3. I did [it] today.   Kyo⌉o si⌐ma⌐sita.
4. I did [it] all.   Ze⌉ñbu si⌐ma⌐sita.
5. I understood [it] all.   Ze⌐ñbu wa⌐karima⌐sita.
6. I understood a little.   Tyo⌉tto wa⌐karima⌐sita.
7. I'll do a little.   Tyo⌉tto simasu.
8. I'll do [it] tomorrow.   A⌈sita sima⌉su.

C. Grammar Drill (based on Grammatical Note 1)

      Tutor: I⌐kima⌐su. (non-past verbal)
      Student: I⌐kima⌐sita. (past verbal)

1. Yo⌐ku wakarimasu.   Yo⌐ku wa⌐karima⌐sita.
2. A⌐ri⌐gatoo gozaimasu.   A⌐ri⌐gatoo gozaimasita.
3. Ze⌐ñbu simasu.   Ze⌐ñbu si⌐ma⌐sita.
4. Wa⌐karimase⌐ñ ka⌐   Wa⌐karimase⌐ñ desita ka⌐
5. Kyo⌐o ikimasu.   Kyo⌐o i⌐kima⌐sita.
6. Su⌐mimase⌐ñ.   Su⌐mimase⌐ñ desita.
7. Kyo⌐o si⌐ma⌐su ka⌐   Kyo⌐o si⌐ma⌐sita ka⌐
8. I⌐kima⌐su ka⌐   I⌐kima⌐sita ka⌐
9. Yo⌐ku wa⌐karimase⌐ñ.   Yo⌐ku wa⌐karimase⌐ñ desita.
10. Tanaka-sañ wa i⌐ki-   Tanaka-sañ wa i⌐kimase⌐ñ desita.
    mase⌐ñ.

D. Response Drill (based on Grammatical Note 3)

(What does the Ha⌐i. or Iie. answer to each of the following questions
mean?)

1. I⌐kima⌐su ka⌐ /Ha⌐i./   Ha⌐i, i⌐kima⌐su.
2. Si⌐mase⌐ñ ka⌐ /Iie./   Iie, si⌐ma⌐su.
3. Wa⌐karima⌐sita ka⌐   Ha⌐i, wa⌐karima⌐sita.
   /Ha⌐i./
4. I⌐kima⌐sita ka⌐ /Iie./   Iie, i⌐kimase⌐ñ desita.
5. Si⌐ma⌐sita ka⌐ /Ha⌐i./   Ha⌐i, si⌐ma⌐sita.
6. Wa⌐karima⌐su ka⌐ /Iie./   Iie, wa⌐karimase⌐ñ.
7. I⌐kimase⌐ñ ka⌐ /Ha⌐i./   Ha⌐i, i⌐kimase⌐ñ.
8. Si⌐ma⌐su ka⌐ /Iie./   Iie, si⌐mase⌐ñ.
9. Wa⌐karimase⌐ñ ka⌐   Ha⌐i, wa⌐karimase⌐ñ.
   /Ha⌐i./
10. I⌐kimase⌐ñ desita ka⌐   Iie, i⌐kima⌐sita.
    /Iie./
11. Si⌐mase⌐ñ desita ka⌐   Ha⌐i, si⌐mase⌐ñ desita.
    /Ha⌐i./
12. Wa⌐karimase⌐ñ desita   Iie, wa⌐karima⌐sita.
    ka⌐ /Iie./

E. Expansion Drill

1. Please say [it].   I⌐tte kudasa⌐i.
   Please say [it] all.   Ze⌐ñbu i⌐tte kudasa⌐i.
   Please say [it] all once.   Iti-do ⌐ze⌐ñbu i⌐tte kudasa⌐i.
   Please say [it] all once   Moo iti-do ⌐ze⌐ñbu i⌐tte kudasa⌐i.
   more.
2. [He] understands. [1]   Wa⌐karima⌐su.

_____

[1] Remember that the English equivalents given are not the only equivalents.
Depending on context, there are various possibilities.

	[He] understands, doesn't he!	Wa⌐karima⌐su ⌐ne⌐e.
	How well [he] understands!	Yo⌐ku wakarimasu ⌐ne⌐e.
	How well Mr. Tanaka understands!	Tanaka-san wa ⌐yo⌐ku wakarimasu ⌐ne⌐e.
3.	[He]'s going to go.	I⌐kima⌐su.
	Is [he] going to go?	I⌐kima⌐su ka˩
	Is [he] going to go tomorrow?	A⌐sita ikima⌐su ka˩
	Is Mr. Tanaka going to go tomorrow?	Tanaka-san wa a⌐sita ikima⌐su ka˩
4.	[He]'s not going to do [it].	Si⌐mase⌐n.
	[He] didn't do [it].	Si⌐mase⌐n desita.
	Didn't [he] do [it]?	Si⌐mase⌐n desita ka˩
	Didn't Mr. Tanaka do [it]?	Tanaka-san wa si⌐mase⌐n desita ka˩

EXERCISES

1. Tell Tanaka-san:

   a. to wait a minute.
   b. to repeat.
   c. that you didn't understand.
   d. that you are going tomorrow.
   e. that you'll do the whole thing.
   f. that you appreciate his trouble.

2. Ask Tanaka-san:

   a. if he understood.
   b. if he is going today.
   c. if he did [it] yesterday.
   d. if he understood the whole thing.
   e. if he is well.

3. Exclaim (using ne⌐e) to Tanaka-san:

   a. how well Yamamoto-san understands.
   b. how well Yamamoto-san understood.
   c. how well Yamamoto-san is.
   d. that Yamamoto-san doesn't understand.

Lesson 2. Getting Around (cont.)

BASIC DIALOGUES: FOR MEMORIZATION

(a)

Tanaka (looking at a new kind of ball-point pen)

that thing	sore
as for that thing	sore wa
what?	naˀn̄ or
	naˀni
what is it?	naˀn̄ desu ka

1. What is that? (Lit. As for that   Sore wa ⌈naˀn̄ desu ka⌟
    thing, what is it?)

Smith

which thing (of 3 or more)	doˀre

2. Which one is it? or Which   Doˀre desu ka⌟
    one do you mean?

Tanaka (pointing)

3. It's that one. or I mean   So⌈re deˀsu.
    that one.

Smith

oh	aˀa
pen	peˀn̄

4. Oh, that's a pen.   Aˀa, sore wa ⌈peˀn̄ desu.

Tanaka

pencil	en̄pitu
[it] isn't a pencil	e⌈n̄pitu zya arimaseˀn̄

5. Isn't it a pencil?   E⌈n̄pitu zya arimaseˀn̄ ka⌟

Smith

is new	a⌈tarasiˀi
new pen	a⌈tarasiˀi ⌈peˀn̄

6. No (i.e. that's right). It's a   Eˀe. A⌈tarasiˀi ⌈peˀn̄ desu yo⌟
    new pen.

Tanaka

that way _or_ thus _or_ so	soˀo

7. Oh, is that so? or Oh, really?   Aˀa, soˀo desu ka.
  or Oh?

(b)

Smith

that thing over there	are
as for that thing over there	are wa
dictionary	zi⌐biki¬ or
	zi¬syo

8. Is that (over there) a dictionary?   Are wa zi⌐biki¬ desu ka⌐

Tanaka

9. Yes, that's right (lit. it's that   E¬e, so¬o desu.
    way).

Smith

is small	ti⌐isa¬i

10. Isn't it small!   Ti⌐isa¬i desu ⌐ne⌐e.

Tanaka

11. It is, isn't it!   So¬o desu ⌐ne¬e.

Smith

is good or fine or all right	i¬i
good dictionary	i¬i zibiki

12. Is it a good dictionary?   I¬i zi⌐biki⌐ desu ka⌐

Tanaka

isn't good	yo¬ku a⌐rimase⌐ñ

13. No, it isn't (good)!   Iie, yo¬ku a⌐rimase⌐ñ yo⌐

Smith

14. Oh, really?   A¬a, so¬o desu ka.

(c)

Smith (looking for something to read)

this thing	kore
as for this thing	kore wa
is interesting or unusual or fun	o⌐mosiro¬i
book	ho¬ñ
interesting book	o⌐mosiro¬i ⌐ho⌐ñ

15. Is this an interesting book?   Kore wa o⌐mosiro¬i ⌐ho⌐ñ desu ka⌐

Tanaka

16. No, it isn't (interesting).   Iie, o⌐mosi¬roku a⌐rimase⌐ñ.

Smith

then or well then or in that case	zya¬a

17. Well then, [how about] that?   Zya¬a, sore wa?

Tanaka

	magazine	zassi
18.	Do you mean the magazine?	Za⌐ssi de˥su ka⌐
19.	That's [very] good!	So⌐re wa i˥i desu yo⌐
20.	Here!	Do˥ozo.

(d)

Smith (looking at some Japanese paperbacks)

| 21. | Is that a magazine? | Sore wa za⌐ssi de˥su ka⌐ |

Tanaka

| 22. | No, it isn't. | Iie, so˥o zya a⌐rimase˥n̄. |
| 23. | It's a book. | Ho˥n̄ desu yo⌐ |

Smith

| 24. | How about this one? | Kore wa? |

Tanaka

	be different <u>or</u> be wrong	ti⌐ḡaima˥su
25.	Oh, that's different.	A˥a, so⌐re wa tiḡaima˥su.
26.	That's a magazine.	So⌐re wa zassi de˥su.

(e)

Tanaka (to Smith, who is about to buy a newspaper)

	newspaper	sin̄bun̄
	good newspaper	i˥i sin̄bun̄
27.	That's not a [very] good news-paper, you know.	Sore wa ⌐i˥i sin̄bun̄ zya a⌐rimase˥n̄ yo⌐

Smith

28.	Oh?	So˥o desu ka.
	how?	do˥o
29.	How is this one?	Ko⌐re wa do˥o desu ka⌐

Tanaka

	same	onazi
30.	It's the same.	O⌐nazi de˥su.
	no good	da⌐me˥
31.	It's no good!	Da⌐me˥ desu yo.

ADDITIONAL VOCABULARY: OPPOSITES

A⌐tarasi˥i desu. 'It's new <u>or</u> fresh.'

O⌐mosiro˥i desu. 'It's interesting or fun <u>or</u> unusual.'

Hu⌐ru˥i desu. 'It's old (i.e. not new) or stale.'

Tu⌐mara˥nai desu. 'It's dull <u>or</u> bor-ing <u>or</u> trifling.'

Ti⌐isa⌐i desu. 'It's small.'   O⌐oki⌐i desu. 'It's big.'
I⌐i desu. 'It's good.'   {Wa⌐ru⌐i desu. 'It's bad.'
                                      {Da⌐me⌐ desu. 'It's no good.'

NOTES ON THE BASIC DIALOGUES

1. Na⌐n̄ occurs before d-, both na⌐n̄ and na⌐ni before t- and n-, and na⌐ni else-
    where.

7, 9, 11, 14. So⌐o desu. 'That's right.' occurs in answer to questions. So⌐o
    desu ⌐ne⌐e. 'That's right, isn't it.' follows statements (especially excla-
    mations ending in ne⌐e.) containing known or recognized information, and
    indicates agreement. So⌐o desu ka. 'Is that so?' follows statements con-
    taining information previously unknown or unrecognized, and indicates
    attention and interest. Thus:

    O⌐mosiro⌐i ⌐ho⌐n̄ desu ka⌐ 'Is it an interesting book?'
    So⌐o desu. 'That's right.'

    O⌐mosiro⌐i ⌐ho⌐n̄ desu ⌐ne⌐e. 'It's an interesting book, isn't it.'
    So⌐o desu ⌐ne⌐e. 'It is, isn't it.' (i.e. I knew that, and I agree.)

    O⌐mosiro⌐i ⌐ho⌐n̄ desu. 'It's an interesting book.'
    So⌐o desu ka. 'Is that so?' (i.e. I didn't know until you told me.)

12. Note these additional equivalents of i⌐i desu: 'it's fine,' 'it's nice,' 'it's
    all set,' 'it's all right,' 'it's all right as it is,' 'never mind,' 'don't both-
    er.'

20. In this context, do⌐ozo means 'take it,' or 'read it,' or 'look at it,' etc. —
    i.e. Tanaka is offering it to Smith.

25. Ti⌐gaima⌐su is a verbal (cf. Lesson 1, Grammatical Note 1). However, the
    non-past negative ti⌐gaimase⌐n̄ is comparatively rare and should be avoided
    by the beginning student.

31. Da⌐me⌐ desu may also refer to something that is broken or out of order or
    spoiled.

GRAMMATICAL NOTES

1. Adjectivals

    o⌐mosiro⌐i desu 'it's interesting'
    o⌐mosi⌐roku a⌐rimase⌐n̄ 'it isn't interesting'

    The words o⌐mosiro⌐i 'it's interesting,' tu⌐mara⌐nai 'it's dull,' a⌐tarasi⌐i
'it's new,' hu⌐ru⌐i 'it's old,' ti⌐isa⌐i 'it's small,' o⌐oki⌐i 'it's big,' i⌐i 'it's good,'
and wa⌐ru⌐i 'it's bad' are all members of a class of inflected Japanese words
having the following characteristics: they have a form ending in -ai, -oi, -ui,
or -ii, and a form ending in -ku (in addition to others). All such words will
hereafter be called ADJECTIVALS. The form ending in -i will be called the
INFORMAL NON-PAST (it refers to present or future time) or the CITATION

FORM; it is the form under which an adjectival is regularly listed in a dictionary and the form by which it is cited. The form ending in -ku will be called the
ADVERBIAL.   The adverbial is regularly made from the -i form (i.e. the informal non-past) by dropping the -i and adding -ku.[1] Thus:

Informal Non-Past (Citation Form)	Adverbial
o⌐mosiro¬i	o⌐mosi¬roku
tu⌐mara¬nai	tu⌐mara¬naku
a⌐tarasi¬i	a⌐tara¬siku
hu⌐ru¬i	hu¬ruku
ti⌐isa¬i	ti¬isaku
o⌐oki¬i	o¬okiku
wa⌐ru¬i	wa¬ruku

The only exception is i¬i : yo¬ku. I¬i is a newer form of yo¬i (which still occurs in present-day Japanese, alternating with i¬i), but the -ku form of the
word is always based on the older root.

Adjectivals, like verbals, are impersonal and may refer to any subject.
Context or a stated topic (sometimes followed by particle wa 'as for') makes
clear what is described.

An adjectival may o c c u r in its -i form alone as a sentence in informal
speech; with a following desu,[2] it becomes formal. In other words, the only
difference between an -i form alone and an -i form plus desu is degree of formality.   Thus:

	Informal	Formal
'It's interesting.'	O⌐mosiro¬i.	O⌐mosiro¬i desu.
'It's dull.'	Tu⌐mara¬nai.	Tu⌐mara¬nai desu.
'It's new.'	A⌐tarasi¬i.	A⌐tarasi¬i desu.
'It's old.'	Hu⌐ru¬i.	Hu⌐ru¬i desu.
'It's small.'	Ti⌐isa¬i.	Ti⌐isa¬i desu.
'It's big.'	O⌐oki¬i.	O⌐oki¬i desu.
'It's good.'	I¬i.	I¬i desu.
'It's bad.'	Wa⌐ru¬i.	Wa⌐ru¬i desu.

An adjectival which describes a verbal or any other inflected expression
occurs in its adverbial (-ku) form (cf. Yo¬ku wakarimasu ⌐ne⌐e. 'You understand [very] well, don't you! ').   When adjectivals occur before the negative
a⌐rimase¬n 'there isn't any,' we find:

---

[1] If the dictionary form is accented, the -ku form is also accented, but the
high-pitched sequence usually ends on an earlier syllable in the -ku form. However, many -ku forms occur with alternate accents.

[2] In this position, the adjectival is always accented, and the high-pitched
sequence normally ends on the next-to-last syllable. De¬su after an accented
word loses its accent.

Oˈmosiˈroku aˈrimaseˈñ.	'It isn't interesting.'
Tuˈmaraˈnaku aˈrimaseˈñ.	'It isn't dull.'
Aˈtaraˈsiku aˈrimaseˈñ.	'It isn't new.'
Huˈruku aˈrimaseˈñ.	'It isn't old.'
Tiˈisaku aˈrimaseˈñ.	'It isn't small.'
Oˈokiku aˈrimaseˈñ.	'It isn't big.'
Yoˈku aˈrimaseˈñ.	'It isn't good.'
Waˈruku aˈrimaseˈñ.	'It isn't bad.'

Since -maseˈñ forms are formal, non-past, and negative, the above combinations are also formal, non-past, and negative. They are further identified as the negative equivalents of adjectivals in their -i form plus desu. The formal adjectival pattern is outlined as follows:

Formal Non-Past Adjectival

Affirmative	Negative
-ai -oi -ui -ii } + desu.	-aku -oku -uku -iku } + aˈrimaseˈñ.

Note that in the negative combination, it is the aˈrimaseˈñ that is negative—not the -ku form. Tiˈisaku aˈrimaseˈñ, for example, means literally something like 'being small, there isn't.'

WARNING: All adjectivals end in -ai, -oi, -ui, or -ii (in their informal non-past form); but not every word ending in one of these combinations is an adjectival. The word must also have a -ku form in order to be classified as an adjectival.

Hereafter, all new adjectivals will be introduced first in their citation form followed immediately by /-ku/ and defined without a subject, and then in a sentence with an appropriate contextual equivalent. For example:

is hot	aˈtuˈi /-ku/
Isn't it hot?	Aˈtuku aˈrimaseˈñ ka⌐

2.   Nominals

The major word class of Japanese is a class of constants (i.e. uninflected words; those having only one form) which will hereafter be called NOMINALS. Any constant which in some of its uses occurs with deˈsu (meaning 'it is ——' or 'it will be ——') as a complete utterance is classed as a nominal.[1] The negative equivalent of nominal + deˈsu is nominal + zya + aˈrimaseˈñ 'it's not ——' or 'it won't be ——.' For example, soˈo is a constant which may occur with desu as a complete utterance: Soˈo desu. 'It's that way' or 'That's right.'

---

[1] Not all words classed as nominals occur in this pattern. Other identifying characteristics of nominals will be introduced later.

So⌐o is therefore classed as a nominal.   The negative of So⌐o desu. is So⌐o zya
a⌐rimase⌐n. 'It's not that way' or 'That's not right.'   Other examples are:

   ho⌐n 'book': Ho⌐n desu. 'It's a book.'
               Ho⌐n zya a⌐rimase⌐n. 'It's not a book.'

   Tanaka-san 'Mr. Tanaka': Ta⌐naka-san de⌐su. 'It's Mr. Tanaka.'
                         Ta⌐naka-san zya arimase⌐n. 'It's not Mr. Tana-
                         ka.'
   a⌐na⌐ta 'you': A⌐na⌐ta desu. 'It's you.'
               A⌐na⌐ta zya a⌐rimase⌐n. 'It's not you.'

   kore 'this thing': Ko⌐re de⌐su. 'It's this (thing).'
                  Ko⌐re zya arimase⌐n. 'It's not this (thing).'

The class of nominals includes—but is by no means limited to—all Japanese
words which stand for tangible objects: chair, man, milk, book, etc.

De⌐su regularly loses its accent when it follows an accented nominal.   Compare:

      Pe⌐n desu. 'It's a pen.'
      E⌐npitu de⌐su. 'It's a pencil.'

For the accent of zya + a⌐rimase⌐n following accented and unaccented nominals,
note the examples above.

Nominals do not distinguish between singular and plural number.   For example, ho⌐n may refer to one book or more than one; kore to this thing or these
things; etc.

Nominal + de⌐su sequences, like verbals and adjectivals, are impersonal and
may refer to any topic, stated explicitly or indicated only by the context. Thus,
depending on context, Ta⌐naka de⌐su may be equivalent to 'I'm Tanaka,' 'he's
Tanaka,' 'it's Tanaka,' etc.   Kore wa ⌐ho⌐n desu, with the topic indicated by
kore wa, means either 'this is a book' or 'these are books,' since nominals do
not distinguish between singular and plural.

An adjectival in its c i t a t i o n form may precede a nominal directly as a
descriptive word:

      o⌐mosiro⌐i ⌐ho⌐n 'an interesting book'
      o⌐oki⌐i zibiki 'a big dictionary'

This form may also precede an adjectival + nominal sequence:

      ti⌐isa⌐i o⌐mosiro⌐i ⌐ho⌐n 'a small interesting book'
      a⌐tarasi⌐i o⌐oki⌐i zibiki 'a new big dictionary'

Compare now these three constantly recurring, basic patterns of Japanese:

F o r m a l   N o n - P a s t

	Affirmative	Negative
Verbal Pattern	Verbal ending in -ma⌐su (wa⌐karima⌐su)	Verbal ending in -mase⌐n (wa⌐karimase⌐n)
Adjectival Pattern	Adjectival ending in -i + desu (o⌐oki⌐i desu)	Adjectival ending in -ku + a⌐rimase⌐n (o⌐okiku a⌐rimase⌐n)
Nominal Pattern	Nominal + de⌐su (ho⌐n desu)	Nominal + zya + a⌐rimase⌐n (ho⌐n zya a⌐rimase⌐n)

So⌐o desu 'that's right' and so⌐o zya a⌐rimase⌐n̄ 'that's not right' are frequently used in answer to a question that ends with a nominal + de⌐su ka, but
less commonly in answer to verbal or adjectival questions.   Thus:

I⌐kima⌐su ka⌐   E⌐e, i⌐kima⌐su.
                          Iie, i⌐kimase⌐n̄.

O⌐oki⌐i desu ka⌐   E⌐e, o⌐oki⌐i desu.
                          Iie, o⌐okiku a⌐rimase⌐n̄.

Pe⌐n̄ desu ka⌐   E⌐e, pe⌐n̄ desu. or E⌐e, so⌐o desu.
                          Iie, pe⌐n̄ zya a⌐rimase⌐n̄. or Iie, so⌐o
                          zya a⌐rimase⌐n̄.

In changing a sentence that ends with an adjectival + desu to its precise negative equivalent, the adjectival pattern is used; but a sentence that ends with a
nominal + de⌐su follows the nominal pattern in forming its exactly corresponding negative.   Compare:

Ho⌐n̄ wa o⌐mosiro⌐i desu.   Ho⌐n̄ wa o⌐mosi⌐roku a⌐rimase⌐n̄.
'The book is interesting.'   'The book isn't interesting.'

O⌐mosiro⌐i ⌐ho⌐n̄ desu.   O⌐mosiro⌐i ⌐ho⌐n̄ zya a⌐rimase⌐n̄.
'It's an interesting book.'   'It's not an interesting book.'

In conversation, however, a reply to a question does not always follow the
question pattern exactly.   Thus, in answer to:

Sore wa a⌐tarasi⌐i ⌐pe⌐n̄ desu ka⌐ 'Is that a new pen?'   (nominal pattern)

a common reply would be:

Iie, a⌐tara⌐siku a⌐rimase⌐n̄. 'No, it isn't new.' (adjectival pattern)

However, the exact negative equivalent would be:

Sore wa a⌐tarasi⌐i ⌐pe⌐n̄ zya a⌐rimase⌐n̄. 'That is not a new pen.'

Most new nominals can be recognized in the lessons that follow by a process
of elimination: if a word is not a verbal (identified by a -ma⌐su ending) or an
adjectival (identified by /-ku/) and is first introduced singly rather than in a
phrase, it is a nominal.   Other nominals, more difficult to recognize, can be
identified on the basis of other criteria to be introduced later.

3.   k o r e ,   s o r e ,   a r e ,   do⌐r e

These four words are all nominals.

Kore refers to a thing or things[1] close to the speaker—i.e. 'near me.'

Sore refers to a thing or things (a) removed from the speaker but close to
the person addressed—i.e. 'near you'; (b) within sight but slightly removed —

---

[1] These words are also used in reference to certain people; those who are
inferiors, members of one's own family, etc.

i.e. neither 'here' nor 'over yonder'—from both speaker and person addressed; or (c) already identified in what has gone before—i.e. 'that thing (or those things) already under discussion.' In meaning (c), the English equivalent is often 'it.'

Are refers to a thing or things 'over there' or 'over yonder,' removed from both speaker and person addressed, either within sight or out of sight. Like sore, it too may refer to something already identified in what has gone before, but it always refers to something removed and usually indicates some particular concrete object(s) being pointed out and defined in terms of a particular location. For example, 'medicine being manufactured today' would, after its first mention, usually be referred to as sore, whereas Mount Fuji would most often be referred to as are.

In a sequence containing both sore and are, are usually implies greater distance. But when sore—with meaning (b)—and are occur singly, it is impossible to define the distance from the speaker at which sore ceases to be used and are begins; the most that can be said is that sore means 'that-rather-near' and are means 'that-over-there.'

Do⌐re is an interrogative nominal meaning 'which one (of a specified group, usually containing at least three things)?'

4.   Particle yo

Like question particle ka, yo occurs at the end of sentences. It is a particle of emphasis: it means that the sentence is being stated with assurance. It is often used in warnings, in contradictions, and in informative exclamations. Sometimes it corresponds to conversational English 'you know,' 'I tell you,' 'say!' 'I'm sure,' etc.; but many times it corresponds to English exclamatory intonation and therefore is difficult to indicate in a written equivalent. Like sentences ending in ka, those ending in yo occur with rising or low intonation.

Compare:

> Da⌐me⌐ desu. 'It's no good.'
> Da⌐me⌐ desu ka⌐ 'Isn't it any good?'
> Da⌐me⌐ desu ⌐ne⌐e. 'It's no good, is it!' or 'Isn't it awful!' (i.e. I assume you know)
> Da⌐me⌐ desu yo. 'It's no good!' or 'It's no good, you know!' or 'Contrary to what you think, it's no good' or 'I'm telling you it's no good,' etc.

DRILLS

A. Substitution Drill

1.	What is that?	Sore wa ⌐na⌐n̄ desu ka⌐
2.	Is that a book?	Sore wa ⌐ho⌐n̄ desu ka⌐
3.	Is that a magazine?	Sore wa za⌐ssi de⌐su ka⌐
4.	Is that a newspaper?	Sore wa si⌐n̄buñ de⌐su ka⌐
5.	Is that a dictionary?	Sore wa ⌐zi⌐syo desu ka⌐

6. Is that the same?   Sore wa oˈnazi deˈsu kaↄ
7. Is that out of order?   Sore wa daˈmeˈ desu kaↄ
8. Is that today?   Sore wa ˈkyoˈo desu kaↄ
9. Is that tomorrow?   Sore wa aˈsitaˈ desu kaↄ
10. How is that?   Sore wa ˈdoˈo desu kaↄ

B. Substitution Drill

1. This is an interesting
   book, isn't it.   Kore wa oˈmosiroˈi ˈhoˈñ desu ˈneˈe.
2. That is an interesting
   book, isn't it.   Sore wa oˈmosiroˈi ˈhoˈñ desu ˈneˈe.
3. That is a good book,
   isn't it.   Sore wa ˈiˈi ˈhoˈñ desu ˈneˈe.
4. That is a good diction-
   ary, isn't it.   Sore wa ˈiˈi ziˈbikiˈ desu ˈneˈe.
5. That (over there) is a
   good dictionary, isn't it.   Are wa ˈiˈi ziˈbikiˈ desu ˈneˈe.
6. That (over there) is a
   big dictionary, isn't it.   Are wa oˈokiˈi ziˈbikiˈ desu ˈneˈe.
7. That (over there) is a
   big magazine, isn't it.   Are wa oˈokiˈi zaˈssi deˈsu ˈneˈe.
8. That (over there) is a
   dull magazine, isn't it.   Are wa tuˈmaraˈnai zaˈssi deˈsu
                                ˈneˈe.
9. That (over there) is a
   dull newspaper, isn t it.   Are wa tuˈmaraˈnai siˈñbuñ deˈsu
                                ˈneˈe.

C. Response Drill (based on Grammatical Note 2)

(What does the Eˈe. or Iie. answer to each of the following questions
mean?)

1. Peˈñ desu kaↄ /Eˈe./   Eˈe, peˈñ desu.
2. Eˈñpitu deˈsu kaↄ /Iie./   Iie, eˈñpitu zya arimaseˈñ.
3. Soˈo desu kaↄ /Eˈe./   Eˈe, soˈo desu.
4. Kyoˈo desu kaↄ /Iie./   Iie, kyoˈo zya aˈrimaseˈñ.
5. Siˈñbuñ deˈsu kaↄ /Eˈe./   Eˈe, siˈñbuñ deˈsu.
6. Oˈnazi deˈsu kaↄ /Iie./   Iie, oˈnazi zya arimaseˈñ.
7. Zaˈssi deˈsu kaↄ /Eˈe./   Eˈe, zaˈssi deˈsu.
8. Aˈsitaˈ desu kaↄ /Iie./   Iie, aˈsitaˈ zya aˈrimaseˈñ.
9. Daˈmeˈ desu kaↄ /Eˈe./   Eˈe, daˈmeˈ desu.
10. Taˈnaka-sañ deˈsu kaↄ   Iie, Taˈnaka-sañ zya arimaseˈñ.
    /Iie./

D. Response Drill (based on Grammatical Note 1)

(What does the Eˈe. or Iie. answer to each of the following questions
mean?)

1. Oˈokiˈi desu kaↄ /Eˈe./   Eˈe, oˈokiˈi desu.
2. Aˈtarasiˈi desu kaↄ /Iie./ Iie, aˈtaraˈsiku aˈrimaseˈñ.
3. Huˈruˈi desu kaↄ /Eˈe./   Eˈe, huˈruˈi desu.
4. Iˈi desu kaↄ /Iie./   Iie, yoˈku aˈrimaseˈñ.

5. Oˊmosiroˈi desu ka﬩ /Eˈe./   Eˈe, oˊmosiroˈi desu.
6. Tiˈisaˈi desu ka﬩ /Iie./   Iie, tiˈisaku aˈrimaseˈñ.
7. Waˈruˈi desu ka﬩ /Eˈe./   Eˈe, waˈruˈi desu.
8. Tuˈmaraˈnai desu ka﬩ /Iie./   Iie, tuˈmaraˈnaku aˈrimaseˈñ.
9. Iˈi desu ka﬩ /Eˈe./   Eˈe, iˈi desu.
10. Oˈokiˈi desu ka﬩ /Iie./   Iie, oˈokiku aˈrimaseˈñ.

E. Response Drill

(What does the <u>Iie.</u> answer to each of the following questions mean?)

1. Iˈkimaˈsu ka﬩ /Iie./   Iie, iˈkimaseˈñ.
2. Huˈruˈi desu ka﬩ /Iie./   Iie, huˈruku aˈrimaseˈñ.
3. Oˈnazi deˈsu ka﬩ /Iie./   Iie, oˈnazi zya arimaseˈñ.
4. Waˈkarimaseˈñ desita ka﬩   Iie, waˈkarimaˈsita.
    /Iie./
5. Siˈñbuñ zya arimaseˈñ ka﬩   Iie, siˈñbuñ deˈsu.
    /Iie./
6. Oˈmosiˈroku aˈrimaseˈñ   Iie, oˈmosiroˈi desu.
    ka﬩ /Iie./
7. Siˈmaˈsu ka﬩ /Iie./   Iie, siˈmaseˈñ.
8. Ziˈsyo zya aˈrimaseˈñ ka﬩   Iie, ziˈsyo desu.
    /Iie./
9. Aˈtarasiˈi desu ka﬩ /Iie./   Iie, aˈtaraˈsiku aˈrimaseˈñ.
10. Koˈre deˈsu ka﬩ /Iie./   Iie, koˈre zya arimaseˈñ.

F. Response Drill

Answer with <u>soˈo desu</u>, <u>soˈo desu ˈneˈe</u>, or <u>soˈo desu ka</u>, whichever is appropriate. Assume that each statement not ending with ˈneˈe contains new
information.

1. Waˈkarimaseˈñ desita.   Soˈo desu ka.
2. Oˈmosiroˈi desu ˈneˈe.   Soˈo desu ˈneˈe.
3. Zeˈñbu waˈkarimaˈsita.   Soˈo desu ka.
4. Peˈñ desu ka﬩   Soˈo desu.
5. Daˈmeˈ desu yo﬩   Soˈo desu ka.
6. Ziˈsyo desu ka﬩   Soˈo desu.
7. Iˈi desu ˈneˈe.   Soˈo desu ˈneˈe.
8. Tiˈḡaimaˈsu yo﬩   Soˈo desu ka.

G. Expansion Drill

1. [It] isn't a pen.   Peˈñ zya aˈrimaseˈñ.
    [It] isn't a new pen.   Aˈtarasiˈi ˈpeˈñ zya aˈrimaseˈñ.
    That isn't a new pen.   Sore wa aˈtarasiˈi ˈpeˈñ zya aˈri-
                                    maseˈñ.

    Isn't that a new pen?   Sore wa aˈtarasiˈi ˈpeˈñ zya aˈri-
                                    maseˈñ ka﬩

2. [It]'s a book.   Hoˈñ desu.
    [It]'s an interesting book.   Oˈmosiroˈi ˈhoˈñ desu.
    This is an interesting book.   Kore wa oˈmosiroˈi ˈhoˈñ desu.
    Isn't this an interesting   Kore wa oˈmosiroˈi ˈhoˈñ desu ˈneˈe.
      book!

3. [It]'s dull.   Tu⌐mara⌐nai desu.
    That's dull.   Sore wa tu⌐mara⌐nai desu.
    You know, that's dull.   Sore wa tu⌐mara⌐nai desu yo◡
    You know, Mr. Tanaka, that's   Tanaka-san, sore wa tu⌐mara⌐nai
      dull.   desu yo◡
4. [It] isn't [any] good.   Yo⌐ku a⌐rimase⌐ñ.
    The dictionary isn't [any]   Zi⌐biki⌐ wa ⌐yo⌐ku a⌐rimase⌐ñ.
      good.
    The small dictionary isn't   Ti⌐isa⌐i zi⌐biki⌐ wa ⌐yo⌐ku a⌐rimase⌐ñ.
      [any] good.
    The small dictionary isn't   Ti⌐isa⌐i zi⌐biki⌐ wa ⌐yo⌐ku a⌐rimase⌐ñ
      [any] good, is it!   ⌐ne⌐e.

EXERCISES

1. Tanaka-san asks you what it is. You answer that:

    a. it's a book.
    b. it's a newspaper.
    c. it's a pencil.
    d. it's an old magazine.
    e. it's a new pen.

2. Tanaka-san asks: Your answer:

    a. if it's interesting.   Yes, it is (interesting).
    b. if it's small.   No, it's big.
    c. if it's new.   No, it isn't (new).
    d. if it's the same.   No, it's different.
    e. if it's an interesting book.   No, it isn't interesting.
    f. if it's a new magazine.   No, it's old.
    g. what it is.   Which one do you mean?

3. Following the Basic Dialogues of this lesson, make up new conversations by
    replacing the nominals and adjectivals with other words of the same word-
    class, wherever possible. Practice the new conversations using appropriate
    props. For example, using a newspaper and a magazine, you might prac-
    tice Basic Dialogue (c) as follows:

    Smith: Kore wa a⌐tarasi⌐i za⌐ssi de⌐su ka◡
    Tanaka: Iie, a⌐tara⌐siku a⌐rimase⌐ñ.
    Smith: Zya⌐a, sore wa?
    Tanaka: Si⌐ñbuñ de⌐su ka◡
            So⌐re wa atarasi⌐i desu yo◡ Do⌐ozo.

Lesson 3. Shopping

NUMERALS

1 i⌐ti¬	10 zyu¬u	20 ni¬zyuu	30 sa¬ñzyuu
2 ni¬	11 zyu⌐uiti¬	21 ni¬zyuu iti	31 sa¬ñzyuu iti
3 sañ	12 zyu⌐uni¬	22 ni¬zyuu ni	32 sa¬ñzyuu ni
4 si¬ or yo¬ñ	13 zyu⌐usañ	23 ni¬zyuu sañ	33 sa¬ñzyuu sañ
5 go¬	14 zyu⌐usi¬	24 ni¬zyuu si	34 sa¬ñzyuu si
6 ro⌐ku¬	15 zyu⌐ugo	25 ni¬zyuu go	35 sa¬ñzyuu go
7 si⌐ti¬ or na¬na	16 zyu⌐uroku¬	26 ni¬zyuu roku	36 sa¬ñzyuu roku
8 ha⌐ti¬	17 zyu⌐usiti¬	27 ni¬zyuu siti	37 sa¬ñzyuu siti
9 ku¬ or kyu¬u	18 zyu⌐uhati¬	28 ni¬zyuu hati	38 sa¬ñzyuu hati
	19 zyu⌐uku	29 ni¬zyuu ku	39 sa¬ñzyuu ku

40 yo¬ñzyuu	50 go⌐zyu¬u	60 ro⌐kuzyu¬u	70 na⌐na¬zyuu
41 yo¬ñzyuu iti	51 go⌐zyuu iti¬	61 ro⌐kuzyuu iti¬	71 na⌐na¬zyuu iti
42 yo¬ñzyuu ni	52 go⌐zyuu ni¬	62 ro⌐kuzyuu ni¬	72 na⌐na¬zyuu ni
43 yo¬ñzyuu sañ	53 gozyuu sañ	63 rokuzyuu sañ	73 na⌐na¬zyuu sañ
44 yo¬ñzyuu si	54 go⌐zyuu si¬	64 ro⌐kuzyuu si¬	74 na⌐na¬zyuu si
45 yo¬ñzyuu go	55 go⌐zyuu go¬	65 ro⌐kuzyuu go¬	75 na⌐na¬zyuu go
46 yo¬ñzyuu roku	56 go⌐zyuu roku¬	66 ro⌐kuzyuu roku¬	76 na⌐na¬zyuu roku
47 yo¬ñzyuu siti	57 go⌐zyuu siti¬	67 ro⌐kuzyuu siti¬	77 na⌐na¬zyuu siti
48 yo¬ñzyuu hati	58 go⌐zyuu hati¬	68 ro⌐kuzyuu hati¬	78 na⌐na¬zyuu hati
49 yo¬ñzyuu ku	59 go⌐zyuu ku¬	69 ro⌐kuzyuu ku¬	79 na⌐na¬zyuu ku

80 ha⌐tizyu¬u	90 kyu¬uzyuu
81 ha⌐tizyuu iti¬	91 kyu¬uzyuu iti
82 ha⌐tizyuu ni¬	92 kyu¬uzyuu ni
83 hatizyuu sañ	93 kyu¬uzyuu sañ
84 ha⌐tizyuu si¬	94 kyu¬uzyuu si
85 ha⌐tizyuu go¬	95 kyu¬uzyuu go
86 ha⌐tizyuu roku¬	96 kyu¬uzyuu roku
87 ha⌐tizyuu siti¬	97 kyu¬uzyuu siti
88 ha⌐tizyuu hati¬	98 kyu¬uzyuu hati
89 ha⌐tizyuu ku¬	99 kyu¬uzyuu kyuu

100 hya⌐ku¬	1000 se¬ñ or i⌐sse¬ñ	10,000 i⌐tima¬ñ
200 ni⌐hyaku¬	2000 ni⌐se¬ñ	20,000 ni⌐ma¬ñ
300 sa⌐ñbyaku	3000 sa⌐ñze¬ñ	30,000 sa⌐ñma¬ñ
400 yo⌐ñhyaku	4000 yo⌐ñse¬ñ	40,000 yo⌐ñma¬ñ
500 go⌐hyaku¬	5000 go⌐se¬ñ	50,000 go⌐ma¬ñ
600 ro⌐ppyaku¬	6000 ro⌐kuse¬ñ	60,000 ro⌐kuma¬ñ
700 na⌐na¬hyaku	7000 na⌐nase¬ñ	70,000 na⌐nama¬ñ
800 ha⌐ppyaku¬	8000 ha⌐sse¬ñ	80,000 ha⌐tima¬ñ
900 kyu⌐uhyaku	9000 kyu⌐use¬ñ	90,000 kyu⌐uma¬ñ

BASIC DIALOGUES: FOR MEMORIZATION

(a)

Smith

cigarette(s) or tobacco	tabako
that cigarette or those cigarettes	sono tabako
how much?	i⌐kura or oikura[+]

1. How much are those cigarettes?   Sono tabako wa ⌐i⌐kura desu ka⌐

Clerk

which cigarette(s)?	do⌐no tabako

2. Which cigarettes are they? or   Do⌐no tabako desu ka⌐
    Which cigarettes do you mean?

Smith (picking up cigarettes)

this cigarette or these cigarettes	kono tabako

3. They're these cigarettes. or   Ko⌐no tabako de⌐su.
    I mean these cigarettes.

Clerk

1 yen	iti-eñ
2 yen	ni-eñ
3 yen	sañ-eñ
4 yen	yo⌐-eñ

4. They're ¥ 40.   Yo⌐ñzyu⌐u-eñ desu.

Smith

match(es)	ma⌐tti
this match or these matches	ko⌐no ma⌐tti

5. How about these matches?   Ko⌐no ma⌐tti wa?

Clerk

6. They're ¥ 2.   Ni-⌐eñ de⌐su.

Smith

here you are	ha⌐i

7. Here you are. ¥ 42.   Ha⌐i. Yo⌐ñzyuu ⌐ni⌐-eñ.

Clerk

8. Thank you.   A⌐ri⌐g̃atoo gozaimasu.

(b)

Tanaka (examining Smith's purchases on the counter)

ashtray(s)	ha⌐iza⌐ra
that little ashtray	sono ti⌐isa⌐i ha⌐iza⌐ra
pretty or clean	ki⌐ree

9. Isn't that little ashtray pretty!   Sono ti⌐isa⌐i ha⌐iza⌐ra wa ⌐ki⌐ree desu
                                          ⌐ne⌐e.

10. Was it ¥400?   Yo⌐ñhyaku⌐-eñ desita ka⌐

                          Smith

11. No, it wasn't (that way).   Iie. So⌐o zya a⌐rimase⌐ñ desita.

12. It was ¥200.   Ni⌐hyaku⌐-eñ desita yo⌐

                          Tanaka

13. (It was) ¥200?   Ni⌐hyaku⌐-eñ desita ka⌐

        is cheap or inexpensive   ya⌐su⌐i /-ku/
14. How cheap! (Lit. It's cheap,   Ya⌐su⌐i desu ⌐ne⌐e.
     isn't it.)

                          (c)

                          Smith

        that big dictionary over   ano o⌐oki⌐i zibiki
           there
15. How much was that big diction-   Ano o⌐oki⌐i zi⌐biki⌐ wa ⌐i⌐kura desita
     ary over there?   ka⌐

                          Tanaka

16. It was ¥1200.   Se⌐ñ nihyaku⌐-eñ desita.

                          Smith

        truth or true   hoñtoo
17. Is that true? or Really?   Ho⌐ñtoo de⌐su ka⌐
     or Do you really mean it?

        extremely or to a con-   zu⌐ibuñ
           siderable degree
18. How (very) cheap! (Lit. It's   Zu⌐ibuñ ya⌐su⌐i desu ⌐ne⌐e.
     very cheap, isn't it.)

                          (d)

                          Smith

19. How much was that?   Sore wa ⌐i⌐kura desita ka⌐

                          Tanaka

        this book   ko⌐no ho⌐ñ
20. Is it this book? or Do you   Ko⌐no ho⌐ñ desu ka⌐
     mean this book?

21. It was ¥250.   Ni⌐hyaku gozyu⌐u-eñ desita.

                          Smith

        not very much or not so   añmari + negative
           much or not too much
        is expensive   ta⌐ka⌐i /-ku/
22. It wasn't very expensive, was   A⌐ñmari ta⌐kaku a⌐rimase⌐ñ desita
     it.   ⌐ne⌐e.

NOTES ON THE BASIC DIALOGUES

1. When 'cigarette' is being distinguished from other things to smoke—cigars, pipes, etc.—ma⌐kita⌐bako is used.

   Oikura, the polite (+) equivalent of i⌐kura, is used more commonly—but not exclusively—by women.

7. Ha⌐i is frequently used when handing something over to someone.

17. Ho⌐ntoo de⌐su ka⌐ 'Is that true?' indicates livelier interest and greater surprise than So⌐o desu ka⌐ 'Is that so?' or 'Oh?'

GRAMMATICAL NOTES

1.   Numerals of Series I and Counter -eñ

The numerals listed on page 26 are Japanese numerals of Chinese origin; they will hereafter be designated as SERIES I NUMERALS. A second series, of native Japanese origin, will be introduced later.

Three numerals have alternate forms: '4' is yo⌐ñ or si⌐;[1] '7' is na⌐na or si⌐ti⌐; '9' is kyu⌐u or ku⌐. Depending on what follows, either the alternants are used interchangeably, or one alternant occurs much more commonly, or only one alternant occurs. Unfortunately, no general rules apply which will assist the student in choosing the correct alternant(s); he must learn each combination as it occurs.

Si⌐zyu⌐u occurs as a less common alternant of yo⌐ñzyuu, and si⌐tizyu⌐u as a less common alternant of na⌐na⌐zyuu.

Numerals from 1 to 100 are listed at the beginning of this lesson. Three-digit numerals are read in terms of the number of hundreds, the number of tens, and the single units. If a zero occurs within a written number, it is usually omitted in the spoken number. Thus:

   236: ni⌐hyaku sa⌐ñzyuu ro⌐ku⌐ (lit. '2 hundreds, 3 tens, 6')
   632: ro⌐ppyaku sa⌐ñzyuu ⌐ni⌐ (lit. '6 hundreds, 3 tens, 2')
   801: ha⌐ppyaku iti⌐ (lit. '8 hundreds, 1')

Four-digit numerals are read in terms of the number of thousands, the number of hundreds, the number of tens, and the single units. Thus:

   4578: yo⌐ñse⌐ñ gohyaku na⌐na⌐zyuu ha⌐ti⌐ (lit. '4 thousands, 5 hundreds, 7 tens, 8')
   8754: ha⌐sse⌐ñ na⌐na⌐hyaku go⌐zyuu si⌐ (lit. '8 thousands, 7 hundreds, 5 tens, 4')
   9023: kyu⌐use⌐ñ ⌐ni⌐zyuu sañ (lit. '9 thousands, 2 tens, 3')

---

[1] A third, less common alternant which occurs only in certain compounds is yo-.

Higher numerals often cause difficulties for English speakers and therefore require special attention. In reading numerals containing from five to eight digits,[1] the numeral is read in terms of how many ten-thousands (up to thousands of ten-thousands), how many thousands, how many hundreds, how many tens, and how many single units it contains. This can be simplified in the case of a written number by inserting a comma between the fourth and fifth digit counting from the right,[2] and reading what precedes the comma as an independent numeral + -ma⌐ñ 'ten-thousands.' Study the following examples:

12,345 (rewritten 1,2345) is read: i⌜tima⌝ñ ni⌐se⌝ñ ⌜sa⌝ñbyaku ⌜yo⌝ñzyuu ⌜go⌝ (lit. '1 ten-thousand, 2 thousands, 3 hundreds, 4 tens, 5')

123,456 (rewritten 12,3456) is read: zyu⌜unima⌝ñ sa⌐ñze⌝ñ ⌜yo⌝ñhyaku go- ⌜zyuu roku⌝ (lit. '12 ten-thousands, 3 thousands, 4 hundreds, 5 tens, 6')

1,234,567 (rewritten 123,4567) is read: hya⌜ku ni⌝zyuu sa⌐ñma⌝ñ yo⌜ñse⌝ñ gohyaku ro⌜kuzyuu siti⌝ (lit. '123 ten-thousands, 4 thousands, 5 hundreds, 6 tens, 7')

12,345,678 (rewritten 1234,5678) is read: se⌝ñ nihyaku ⌜sa⌝ñzyuu yo⌐ñma⌝ñ go⌜se⌝ñ roppyaku na⌜na⌝zyuu hati (lit. '1234 ten-thousands, 5 thousands, 6 hundreds, 7 tens, 8')

Note that the Japanese equivalent of a million is hya⌜kuma⌝ñ (lit. '100 ten-thousands,' i. e. 100,0000).

The occurrence of -ma⌝ñ in a numeral is always a signal of four digits to come. The digits may be zero. Thus:

go⌜ma⌝ñ	'50,000'
go⌜ma⌝ñ i⌜sse⌝ñ	'51,000'
go⌜ma⌝ñ hya⌜ku⌝	'50,100'
go⌜ma⌝ñ ⌜zyu⌝u	'50,010'
go⌜ma⌝ñ i⌜ti⌝	'50,001'

The numerals of Series I regularly occur independently in mathematics, in counting cadence, and in serial counting.

The monetary unit of Japan is the yen. To count yen, -eñ is added to the numerals of Series I.   Note, however, that before -eñ, '4' is yo⌝- instead of the more usual yo⌝ñ or si⌝. The forms from 1 to 10[3] are:

iti-eñ	'1 yen'	roku-eñ	'6 yen'
ni-eñ	'2 yen'	na⌜na⌝-eñ or siti-eñ	'7 yen'
sañ-eñ	'3 yen'	hati-eñ	'8 yen'
yo⌝-eñ	'4 yen'	kyu⌝u-eñ	'9 yen'
go⌝-eñ	'5 yen'	zyuu-eñ	'10 yen'

The corresponding question word is na⌝ñ-eñ 'how many yen?'

---

[1] Numerals larger than this are not treated in this text.

[2] In English, numerals are divided into groups of threes; in Japanese, into groups of fours.

[3] In all such lists in this text, only commonly occurring alternants are included.

Forms like -eñ, which do not occur as independent words but are joined with numerals in compounds, will hereafter be called COUNTERS; and compounds that consist of numeral + counter will be called NUMBERS. All numerals and numbers are nominals.

2. Demonstratives: kono, sono, ano, do'no

Kono 'this —,' sono 'that —,' ano 'that — over there,' and do'no 'which — [of three or more]?' belong to a small class of Japanese constants (words having only one form) which occur only as a modifier of a following nominal.[1] Words of this class will be called DEMONSTRATIVES. Examples:

ko'no pe'ñ 'this pen' (or, of course, 'these pens')
sono eñpitu 'that pencil'
a'no ho'ñ 'that book over there'
kono o'mosiro'i 'ho'ñ 'this interesting book'
do'no tabako 'which cigarettes?'
do'no Tanaka-sañ 'which Mr. Tanaka?'

These four words must not be confused with kore, sore, are, and do're, which are nominals. Compare:

Ko're de'su. 'It's this.'
Kore wa 'ho'ñ desu. 'This is a book.'
Ko'no ho'ñ desu. 'It's this book.'
So're zya arimase'ñ. 'It's not that.'
Sore wa 'pe'ñ zya a'rimase'ñ. 'That is not a pen.'
So'no pe'ñ zya a'rimase'ñ. 'It's not that pen.'

The spatial and referential relationships of kore, sore, and are described above (pages 21–22) apply equally to the corresponding demonstratives kono, sono, and ano.

3. Copula

De'su is a member of a certain set of inflected forms[2] which is neither a verbal (there are no forms ending in -ma'su, -ma'sita, etc.) nor an adjectival (there are no forms ending in -i or -ku). Actually, it is a unique set of forms; there are no other Japanese words with the same shapes or usage. Hereafter, de'su and its derived forms — symbolized as √de'su —[3] will be called the COPULA. The de'su form itself is the formal non-past of the copula, corresponding to the -ma'su form of a verbal.

---

[1] The nominal may have other modifiers as well. Note the fourth example.

[2] I.e. is one shape of a word having several shapes.

[3] The symbol √ indicates the enclosed word and its other forms. Thus √wa-'karima'su is a short-cut way of writing wa'karima'su, wa'karima'sita, etc.

It has already been pointed out that:

(a) de⌐su may follow an adjectival in its citation (-i) form, making the expression formal. The -i form alone is non-past informal; the -i form + de⌐su is non-past formal.

   o⌐oki⌐i desu 'it's big' (negative: o⌐okiku a⌐rimase⌐ñ 'it's not big')

(b) de⌐su may follow a nominal, meaning 'it is ——' or 'it will be ——' (non-past formal).

   ho⌐ñtoo de⌐su 'it's true' (negative: ho⌐ñtoo zya arimase⌐ñ 'it's not true')

In this lesson, the following new information is introduced:

(c) The past of de⌐su is de⌐sita[1] (also formal). It regularly occurs after a nominal, meaning 'it was ——.'

   kyo⌐o desu 'it's today'; kyo⌐o desita 'it was today.'

It sometimes follows an adjectival in its -i form, as the past equivalent of adjectival + de⌐su. However, this is only one of several formal past adjectival patterns,[2] and is not the most common pattern. An -i + desita pattern should not be used by a student without first checking with a native speaker of Japanese. If he hears it, however, he will have no trouble understanding it.

   (ya⌐su⌐i desu 'it's cheap'; ya⌐su⌐i desita 'it was cheap')

(d) Desita added to a formal non-past negative (ending in -mase⌐ñ) produces a formal past negative.

Formal Negatives

	Non-Past	Past
Verbal Pattern	wa⌐kariMASE⌐Ñ 'it isn't clear'	wa⌐kariMASE⌐Ñ DESITA 'it wasn't clear'
Adjectival Pattern	o⌐okiKU A⌐RIMASE⌐Ñ 'it isn't big'	o⌐okiKU A⌐RIMASE⌐Ñ DESITA 'it wasn't big'
Nominal Pattern	ho⌐ñtoo ZYA ARIMASE⌐Ñ 'it isn't true'	ho⌐ñtoo ZYA ARIMASE⌐Ñ DESITA 'it wasn't true'

---

[1] De⌐sita regularly loses its accent after an accented word.

[2] The others will be introduced later.

DRILLS

A. Substitution Drill

1.	Do you mean this dictionary?	Ko⌐no zibiki⌉ desu ka⌟
2.	Do you mean those cigarettes?	So⌐no tabako de⌉su ka⌟
3.	Do you mean those matches over there?	A⌐no ma⌉tti desu ka⌟
4.	Which book do you mean?	Do⌉no ʰho⁴n̄ desu ka⌟
5.	Do you mean this magazine?	Ko⌐no zassi de⌉su ka⌟
6.	Do you mean that newspaper?	So⌐no sin̄bun̄ de⌉su ka⌟
7.	Do you mean that ashtray over there?	A⌐no haiza⌉ra desu ka⌟
8.	Which Mr. Tanaka do you mean?	Do⌉no Taʰnaka-san̄ de⁴su ka⌟

B. Substitution Drill

1.	How much were those cigarettes?	Sono tabako wa ⌐i⌉kura desita ka⌟
2.	How much was that ashtray?	So⌐no haiza⌉ra wa ⌐i⌉kura desita ka⌟
3.	How much were those matches?	So⌐no ma⌉tti wa ⌐i⌉kura desita ka⌟
4.	How much was that newspaper?	Sono sin̄bun̄ wa ⌐i⌉kura desita ka⌟
5.	How much was that magazine?	Sono zassi wa ⌐i⌉kura desita ka⌟
6.	How much was that book?	So⌐no ho⌉n̄ wa ⌐i⌉kura desita ka⌟
7.	How much was that dictionary?	So⌐no zibiki⌉ wa ⌐i⌉kura desita ka⌟
8.	How much was that pencil?	Sono en̄pitu wa ⌐i⌉kura desita ka⌟
9.	How much was that pen?	So⌐no pe⌉n̄ wa ⌐i⌉kura desita ka⌟

C. Substitution Drill

1.	That big dictionary wasn't very expensive, was it!	Sono o⌐oki⌉i ziʰbiki⁴ wa a⌐n̄mari ta⌉kaku aʰrimase⁴n̄ desita ⌐ne⌉e.
2.	That new dictionary wasn't very expensive, was it!	Sono a⌐tarasi⌉i ziʰbiki⁴ wa a⌐n̄mari ta⌉kaku aʰrimase⁴n̄ desita ⌐ne⌉e.
3.	That new dictionary wasn't very big, was it!	Sono a⌐tarasi⌉i ziʰbiki⁴ wa a⌐n̄mari o⌉okiku aʰrimase⁴n̄ desita ⌐ne⌉e.
4.	That expensive dictionary wasn't very big, was it!	Sono ta⌐ka⌉i ziʰbiki⁴ wa a⌐n̄mari o⌉okiku aʰrimase⁴n̄ desita ⌐ne⌉e.
5.	That expensive dictionary wasn't very good, was it!	Sono ta⌐ka⌉i ziʰbiki⁴ wa a⌐n̄mari yo⌉ku aʰrimase⁴n̄ desita ⌐ne⌉e.
6.	That small dictionary wasn't very good, was it!	Sono ti⌐isa⌉i ziʰbiki⁴ wa a⌐n̄mari yo⌉ku aʰrimase⁴n̄ desita ⌐ne⌉e.
7.	That small dictionary wasn't too bad, was it!	Sono ti⌐isa⌉i ziʰbiki⁴ wa a⌐n̄mari wa⌉ruku aʰrimase⁴n̄ desita ⌐ne⌉e.
8.	That cheap dictionary wasn't too bad, was it!	Sono ya⌐su⌉i ziʰbiki⁴ wa a⌐n̄mari wa⌉ruku aʰrimase⁴n̄ desita ⌐ne⌉e.

D. Response Drill (based on Grammatical Note 3)

(Give the <u>iie</u> answer for each of the following.)

1. Aꜛno tabako deꜗsita ka⌐   Iie, aꜛno tabako zya arimaseꜗñ desita.
2. Ziꜗsyo desita ka⌐   Iie, ziꜗsyo zya aꜜrimaseꜜñ desita.
3. Kiꜗree desita ka⌐   Iie, kiꜗree zya aꜜrimaseꜜñ desita.
4. Hoꜛñtoo deꜗsita ka⌐   Iie, hoꜛñtoo zya arimaseꜗñ desita.
5. Taꜛnaka-sañ deꜗsita ka⌐   Iie, Taꜛnaka-sañ zya arimaseꜗñ de-
                                      sita.
6. Hyaꜛku-eñ deꜗsita ka⌐   Iie, hyaꜛku-eñ zya arimaseꜗñ desita.
7. Kiꜛnoꜗo desita ka⌐   Iie, kiꜛnoꜗo zya aꜜrimaseꜜñ desita.
8. Oꜛnazi deꜗsita ka⌐   Iie, oꜛnazi zya arimaseꜗñ desita.

E. Response Drill (based on Grammatical Note 3)

(Give the <u>iie</u> answer for each of the following, using the adjectival pattern.)

1. Oꜛmosiroꜗi zaꜜssi deꜜsita   Iie, oꜛmosiꜗroku aꜜrimaseꜜñ desita.
    ka⌐
2. Yaꜛsuꜗi haꜜizaꜜra desita ka⌐   Iie, yaꜛsuku aꜜrimaseꜜñ desita.
3. Oꜛokiꜗi ziꜜbikiꜜ desita ka⌐   Iie, oꜛokiku aꜜrimaseꜜñ desita.
4. Iꜗi ꜜhoꜜñ desita ka⌐   Iie, yoꜛku aꜜrimaseꜜñ desita.
5. Tuꜛmaraꜗnai zaꜜssi deꜜsita   Iie, tuꜛmaraꜗnaku aꜜrimaseꜜñ desita.
    ka⌐
6. Taꜛkaꜗi taꜜbako deꜜsita ka⌐   Iie, taꜗkaku aꜜrimaseꜜñ desita.
7. Aꜛtarasiꜗi siꜜñbuñ deꜜsita ka⌐ Iie, aꜛtaraꜗsiku aꜜrimaseꜜñ desita.
8. Tiꜛisaꜗi ziꜜbikiꜜ desita ka⌐   Iie, tiꜛisaku aꜜrimaseꜜñ desita.
9. Waꜛruꜗi ꜜhoꜜñ desita ka⌐   Iie, waꜗruku aꜜrimaseꜜñ desita.
10. Huꜛruꜗi siꜜñbuñ deꜜsita ka⌐   Iie, huꜛruku aꜜrimaseꜜñ desita.

F. Grammar Drill (based on Grammatical Note 2)

Tutor: Koꜛno hoꜗñ wa taꜛkaꜗi desu ꜛneꜗe. 'Isn't this book expensive!'
Student: Kore wa taꜛkaꜗi desu ꜛneꜗe. 'Isn't this expensive!'

1. Koꜛno peꜗñ wa yaꜛsuꜗi desu   Kore wa yaꜛsuꜗi desu ꜛneꜗe.
    ꜛneꜗe.
2. Soꜛno zibikiꜗ wa taꜛkaꜗi desu   Sore wa taꜛkaꜗi desu yo⌐
    yo⌐
3. Aꜛno haizaꜗra wa ꜛiꜗkura   Are wa ꜛiꜗkura desita ka⌐
    desita ka⌐
4. Doꜗno zaꜜssi deꜜsu ka⌐   Doꜗre desu ka⌐
5. Sono eñpitu wa daꜛmeꜗ desu   Sore wa daꜛmeꜗ desu ka⌐
    ka⌐
6. Ano siñbuñ wa huꜛruꜗi desu   Are wa huꜛruꜗi desu yo⌐
    yo⌐
7. Koꜛno hoꜗñ wa oꜛmosiroꜗi   Kore wa oꜛmosiroꜗi desu ꜛneꜗe.
    desu ꜛneꜗe.

G. Expansion Drill

1. It's pretty.   Kiꜗree desu.
    Isn't it pretty!   Kiꜗree desu ꜛneꜗe.
    Isn't the ashtray pretty!   Haꜛizaꜗra wa ꜛkiꜗree desu ꜛneꜗe.
    Isn't that ashtray pretty!   Soꜛno haizaꜗra wa ꜛkiꜗree desu ꜛneꜗe.

2. How much was it?   Iˈkura desita kaˍ
    How much was the dictionary?   Ziˈbikiˈ wa ˈiˈkura desita kaˍ
    How much was the big dic-   Oˈokiˈi ziˈbikiˈ wa ˈiˈkura desita kaˍ
    tionary?
    How much was this big dic-   Kono oˈokiˈi ziˈbikiˈ wa ˈiˈkura de-
    tionary?   sita kaˍ

3. It isn't expensive.   Taˈkaku aˈrimaseˈñ.
    It wasn't expensive.   Taˈkaku aˈrimaseˈñ desita.
    It wasn't very expensive.   Aˈñmari taˈkaku aˈrimaseˈñ desita.
    This book wasn't·very expen-   Koˈno hoˈñ wa aˈñmari taˈkaku aˈri-
    sive.   maseˈñ desita.

4. It isn't true.   Hoˈñtoo zya arimaseˈñ.
    It wasn't true.   Hoˈñtoo zya arimaseˈñ desita.
    That wasn't true.   Sore wa hoˈñtoo zya arimaseˈñ desita.
    You know, that wasn't true!   Sore wa hoˈñtoo zya arimaseˈñ desita
                                          yoˍ

SUPPLEMENTARY CONVERSATION

Smith: (Pointing) Oˈneḡai-simaˈsu.
Clerk: Koˈre deˈsu kaˍ
Smith: Eˈe.
Clerk: Doˈozo.
Smith: Iˈkura desu kaˍ
Clerk: Niˈseñ-eñ deˈsu.
Smith: Tyoˈtto taˈkaˈi desu ˈneˈe.
Clerk: (Showing another one) Koˈre wa yasuˈi desu. (Checking price tag) Seˈñ
        nihyakuˈ-eñ desu.
Smith: Aˈa, koˈre wa iˈi desu ˈneˈe. Oˈneḡai-simaˈsu. (Handing over money)
        Seˈñ nihyakuˈ-eñ. Haˈi.
Clerk: Aˈriˈḡatoo gozaimasu.

English Equivalent

Smith: May I see that, please? (Lit. I make a request.)
Clerk: (Do you mean) this one?
Smith: Yes.
Clerk: Here you are.
Smith: How much is it?
Clerk: (It's) ¥ 2000.
Smith: It's a little expensive, isn't it.
Clerk: This one is cheap. . . . It's ¥ 1200.
Smith: Oh, this one is fine! I'll take it. Here you are. ¥ 1200.
Clerk: Thank you.

EXERCISES

1. Read the following in Japanese:

        a.   27   c.   604
        b.   64   d.   358

e.	891	m.	3,456,789
f.	3,487	n.	7,250,000
g.	8,926	o.	10,500,000
h.	6,044	p.	¥360
i.	10,000	q.	¥1,800
j.	23,487	r.	¥36,000
k.	46,020	s.	¥650,000
l.	321,321	t.	¥1,000,000

2. The customer asks the price of the following objects and the clerk answers with the price indicated:

   a. those cigarettes.   (¥40)
   b. this ashtray.   (¥350)
   c. these matches.   (¥2)
   d. that pen over there.   (¥1000)
   e. that small dictionary.   (¥400)
   f. that big book.   (¥1800)

3. You ask: Tanaka-san answers:
   a. if this book is interest-   No, it isn't very interesting.
       ing.
   b. if that book was ¥350.   No, it was ¥450.
   c. if these cigarettes are   Which cigarettes do you mean?
       ¥40.
   d. if that thing over there   No, it's a pencil.
       is a pen.
   e. if these books are the   No, they're different.
       same.
   f. if this pen was ¥2500.   Yes, that's right.
   g. if that pencil is ¥10.   No, it's ¥15.
   h. if these pens are dif-   Yes, they are.
       ferent.
   i. if that is a good pen.   No, it's not very good.
   j. if it was an expensive   No, it wasn't very expensive.
       dictionary.

4. Practice the Basic Dialogues with variations and appropriate props.

Lesson 4. Shopping (cont.)

BASIC DIALOGUES: FOR MEMORIZATION

(a)

Clerk

1. Welcome!　　　　　　　　　　　　　I⌐rassya⌐i.　_or_
　　　　　　　　　　　　　　　　　　I⌐rassyaima⌐se.

Smith

furoshiki (cloth square for　　　　hurosiki
　wrapping)
furoshiki (as direct object)　　　hurosiki o
show _or_ let [someone] see　　　mi⌐sema⌐su
please show _or_ please let　　　　mi⌐sete kudasai
　[someone] see

2. Please show [me] that furoshiki　A⌐no hurosiki (o) mi⌐sete kudasai.
over there.

Clerk

is red　　　　　　　　　　　　　akai /-ku/[1]
red one(s)　　　　　　　　　　　a⌐ka⌐i no

3. Do you mean the red one? Here　A⌐ka⌐i no desu ka⌐」 Do⌐ozo.
you are.

Smith

is blue _or_ green　　　　　　　a⌐o⌐i /-ku/
blue one(s)　　　　　　　　　　a⌐o⌐i no
blue one(s) too　　　　　　　　a⌐o⌐i no mo

4. Please show me that blue one　Sono a⌐o⌐i no mo ⌐mi⌐sete kudasai.
too.

(. . . looking them over)

a little _or_ a few　　　　　　　su⌐ko⌐si
a little more _or_ a few more　　mo⌐o suko⌐si
big one(s)　　　　　　　　　　o⌐oki⌐i no
little bigger ones (as em-　　　mo⌐o suko⌐si o⌐oki⌐i no ḡa
　phatic subject)
be necessary _or_ need _or_ want　i⌐rima⌐su
[I] need but　　　　　　　　　　i⌐rima⌐su ḡa

5. I need a little bigger one but . . .　Mo⌐o suko⌐si o⌐oki⌐i no ḡa i⌐rima⌐su
　　　　　　　　　　　　　　　　　ḡa—

---

[1] This is the first example of an unaccented adjectival: akai, akaku, akai hurosiki, but a⌐ka⌐i desu, a⌐ka⌐i no.

37

Clerk (showing a third one)

is yellow	kiiroi /-ku/
yellow one(s)	ki⌐iro⌐i no
as for a yellow one	ki⌐iro⌐i no wa
how?	i⌐ka⌐ḡa⁺

6. How about this yellow one?   Kono ki⌐iro⌐i no(wa) i⌐ka⌐ḡa desu ka◡
   or How is this yellow one?

Smith

7. Let me see. . . .   or   So⌐o desu ⌐ne⌐e.
   Hmmm. . . .

it's pretty but	ki⌐ree desu ḡa

8. It's pretty but I'm afraid it   Ki⌐ree desu ḡa, tyo⌐tto▁
   won't do. . . (Lit. It's pretty
   but a bit. . .)

oh well or I guess	ma⌐a
this one (as direct object)	kore o
please give me	ku⌐dasa⌐i

9. Oh well, I'll take (lit. give me)   Ma⌐a, ko⌐re (o) kudasa⌐i.
   this one.

after that or and then or	sore kara
and	
red one(s) too	a⌐ka⌐i no mo

10. And give me this red one too.   Sore kara, kono a⌐ka⌐i no mo kudasai.

Clerk

in addition	hoka ni
something or anything	na⌐ni ka

11. Anything else?   Ho⌐ka ni na⌐ni ka?

Smith

just that	so⌐re dake⌐

12. That's all.   So⌐re dake⌐ desu.

13. Here you are — ¥1000.   Ha⌐i señ-eñ.

Clerk

a little	syo⌐osyoo⁺
please wait	o⌐mati-kudasa⌐i or
	o⌐mati-kudasaima⌐se

14. Just a moment, please.   Syo⌐osyoo o⌐mati-kudasa⌐i.   or
                                  Syo⌐osyoo o⌐mati-kudasaima⌐se.

(. . . returning with the wrapped package)

15. I'm sorry to have kept you   O⌐matase-itasima⌐sita. ⁺
    waiting.

every time	maido

16. Thank you (again and again).   Ma⌐ido ari⌐ḡatoo gozaimasu.

	again	mata
17.	Please [come] again.	Maˈta doˈozo.

Smith

18. Say there!   Tyoˈtto—

    ashtray (as emphatic   haˈizaˈra ḡa
      subject)
    be in a place (of inanimate   aˈrimaˈsu   or
      objects) or have   goˈzaimaˈsu +

19. Are there any ashtrays? or   Haˈizaˈra (ḡa) aˈrimaˈsu ka◡
    Do you have any ashtrays?

Clerk

    yes   haˈaˈ+
20. Yes, there are. or Yes, I   Haˈa, goˈzaimaˈsu. Doˈozo.
    have. Here you are.

Smith

    is black   kuˈroˈi /-ku/
    black one(s)   kuˈroˈi no
    black one(s) (as direct   kuˈroˈi no o
      object)
21. Please show me that black one. Sono kuˈroˈi no (o) ˈmiˈsete kudasai.

    is white   siˈroˈi /-ku/
    white one(s) too   siˈroˈi no mo
22. And please show me that white   Sore kara, sono siˈroˈi no mo
    one, too.   ˈmiˈsete kudasai.

. . .

23. I'll take this black one.   Kono kuˈroˈi no (o) kudasai.

Clerk

    as for the white one   siˈroˈi no wa
24. How about the white one?   Siˈroˈi no wa iˈkaˈḡa desu ka◡

Smith

    as for that one   sore wa
25. That one I don't want.   Soˈre wa irimaseˈn.

Clerk

26. Certainly. (I.e. I have under- Kaˈsikomarimaˈsita.ˈ
    stood your request and will do
    as you ask.)

Smith

    what (as direct object)?   naˈni o
    buy   kaˈimaˈsu

27. What did you buy?   Na꜒ni (o) ka˥ima꜒sita ka⌐

                           Tanaka

     book and magazine   ho꜒n̄ to zãssi
     book and magazine (as   ho꜒n̄ to zãssi o
       direct object)
28. I bought a book and a magazine.   Ho꜒n̄ to zaꜛssi (o) kaima꜒sita.

                           Smith

29. What about a newspaper?   Siñbuñ wa?

                           Tanaka

     oh!   a
     forget   waꜛsurema꜒su
30. Oh, I forgot. I'm sorry.   A. Waꜛsurema꜒sita. Suꜛmimase꜒n̄.

     as for a newspaper   siñbuñ wa
31. I didn't buy a newspaper.   Siñbuñ wa kaꜛimase꜒n̄ desita.

                           Smith

     later   a꜒to de
32. Well then, would you [get it]   Zya꜒a, a꜒to de oneg̃ai-simasu.
       later?

     match (as emphatic sub-   ma꜒tti g̃a
       ject)
33. Say, have you got a match?   Tyo꜒tto, ma꜒tti (g̃a) aꜛrima꜒su ka⌐

                           Tanaka

     as for a match   ma꜒tti wa
     there isn't but or I don't   aꜛrimase꜒n̄ g̃a
       have but
     lighter   ra꜒itaa
     lighter (as emphatic sub-   ra꜒itaa g̃a
       ject)
34. A match I don't have but I have   Ma꜒tti wa aꜛrimase꜒n̄ g̃a, ra꜒itaa g̃a
     a lighter. Here you are.   arimasu. Do꜒ozo.

                  NOTES ON THE BASIC DIALOGUES

1. Iꜛrassya꜒i and iꜛrassyaima꜒se, imperatives of the honorific verbal iꜛras-
    syaima꜒su 'come,' are regularly used for greeting a customer entering a
    store, restaurant, inn, etc., and also for welcoming a guest to one's home.
    The form with -ma꜒se, which is formal, is used by women and by male em-
    ployees of shops, restaurants, hotels, etc.

2. A furoshiki is a square of silk or cotton—or, more recently, plastic—used
    for wrapping packages which are to be hand-carried.

4. Aꜛo꜒i covers that portion of the spectrum which includes both the 'blue' and
    'green' of English. Additional Japanese color words of more limited mean-
    ing will be introduced later.

5. With the meaning 'a little' or 'a few,' su⌐ko'si and tyo'tto are interchange-
    able, except that tyo'tto is less formal; but only tyo'tto is used as a means
    of attracting attention (sentence 18) and as a polite refusal (sentence 8).

    The affirmative forms of i⌐rima'su more often mean 'need' and the nega-
    tive forms 'not want' (sentence 25).

6. I⌐ka'ḡa is a more polite equivalent of do'o which occurs in a more limited
    number of constructions.   Both are used in suggestions and in inquiring

    how something or someone is.   Thus, X (wa) $\left\{ \begin{array}{l} \text{⌐do'o} \\ \text{i⌐ka'ḡa} \end{array} \right\}$ desu ka 'how about

    X?' or 'how is X?'

7. Context, intonation, and/or rhythm make it possible to distinguish between
    so'o desu ⌐ne'e 'that's right, isn't it,' 'isn't that true!' and so'o desu ⌐ne'e
    'hmmm. . .'   The latter is often pronounced so'oo desu ⊦ne⌐ee.

8. Tyo'tto_ is an indirect, hesitant—and polite—refusal of a suggestion, re-
    quest, or invitation.

9. Ma'a indicates that what follows is said after some hesitation or with some
    reluctance.

14. Syo'osyoo is a more polite equivalent of su⌐ko'si which occurs commonly
    in this sentence.   O⌐mati-kudasa'i is a more polite equivalent of ma'tte
    kudasai.   The formal -ma'se alternant is used most often by women.
    (Compare the two alternants of sentence 1.)

15. O⌐matase-itasima'sita is a humble (⫯) word meaning literally 'I have caused
    you to wait.'

16. Ma⌐ido ari'ḡatoo gozaimasu is commonly used only by shopkeepers, clerks,
    restaurant employees, etc.

18. Tyo'tto is an informal word used to attract attention.

20. Ha'a is a polite equivalent of ha'i which occurs in the same kinds of pat-
    terns.

26. Ka⌐sikomarima'sita means 'certainly—I have understood what you want me
    to do' (never 'certainly—that's right').   It is addressed to a superior: for
    example, an employer or a customer.

GRAMMATICAL NOTES

1.   Particles: ḡa, o, wa, mo, to

    There is a class of uninflected (i.e. non-changing) Japanese words which
occur within or at the end of a sentence, but never at the beginning.   They are
never preceded by pause but rather they are regularly pronounced as though
they were part of the word before them.   Within sentences, they relate what
precedes to what follows.   At the end of sentences, they color the meaning of
the sentence as a whole, making it into a question, an exclamation, an emphatic
statement, etc.   All such words are PARTICLES.   Those that regularly occur
at the end of sentences—like question particle ka and emphatic particle yo—are
SENTENCE PARTICLES.

Japanese particles often correspond to English prepositions. Many times, however, they are reflected instead in a particular word order or stress-intonation pattern in English; and sometimes there is nothing that specifically corresponds to them in a natural English equivalent.

(a) ḡa

(1) When preceded by a non-past or past inflected word (i.e. verbal, or adjectival, or copula), ḡa marks a major division within a sentence: often it connects two sequences which are in contrast (corresponding to English 'but'); many times it separates a statement of fact from a related question or request (in which case, the most natural English equivalent is two independent sentences instead of two clauses with a connective).

Examples:

Ta⌐naka-san wa ikima⌐sita ḡa, Ya⌐mamoto-san wa ikimase⌐n desita. 'Mr. Tanaka went but Mr. Yamamoto didn't go.'
Ya⌐su⌐i desu ḡa, ki⌐ree desu. 'It's cheap but it's pretty.'
Ko⌐re wa ki⌐ree desu ḡa, so⌐re wa ki⌐ree zya a⌐rimase⌐n. 'This is pretty but that isn't (pretty).'
O⌐mosiro⌐i ⌐ho⌐n ḡa a⌐rima⌐su ḡa, i⌐ka⌐ḡa desu ka⌐ 'I have an interesting book. How about [reading] it?'

(2) Ḡa preceded by a nominal singles out the nominal as the subject[1] of a following inflected expression. Observe the location of the emphasis in the English equivalents.

Examples:

Ta⌐naka-san ḡa sima⌐sita. 'MR. TANAKA did [it].' (tells who did it)
Ko⌐re ḡa atarasi⌐i desu. 'THIS is new.' (tells which one is new)
So⌐re ḡa dame⌐ desu. 'THAT's out of order.' (tells which one is out of order)

(b) o

The particle o singles out the preceding nominal as the direct object[1] of a following inflected expression. Note the location of the emphasis in the English equivalents.

Examples:

So⌐re o kudasa⌐i. 'Give me THAT.' (tells which one I want)
Ra⌐itaa o ⌐mi⌐sete kudasai. 'Please show me some LIGHTERS.' (tells what I want to see)
Ta⌐bako o oneḡai-sima⌐su. 'I'd like a CIGARETTE.' (tells what I want to have)
Hu⌐rosiki o kaima⌐sita. 'I bought a FUROSHIKI.' (tells what I bought)

---

[1] The subject tells who or what does or is something, and the direct object tells who or what is directly acted upon. Thus, in 'Bill called John,' 'Bill' is the subject and 'John' the direct object; in 'John called Bill,' 'John' is the subject and 'Bill' the direct object.

(c) <u>wa</u>

The particle <u>wa</u> 'as for,' 'in reference to' following a nominal occurs in two kinds of constructions:

(1) It follows the general topic (often one already under discussion) about which something new or significant is about to be stated or asked:[1] <u>X wa</u> 'I am talking about X—listen to what I am about to say'; 'as for X, the following is significant.'

Examples:

> Tabako wa aˈrimaseˈñ. 'There AREN'T any cigarettes.' (in answer to the question 'Are there any cigarettes?'; i.e. 'I'm talking about cigarettes: what I want to say is that there AREN'T any.')
>
> Sore wa taˈkaˈi desu yo⌐ 'That one is EXPENSIVE, you know.' (i.e. 'I'm talking about that: what I want to say is that it's EXPENSIVE.')
>
> Kore wa ˈraˈitaa desu. 'This is a LIGHTER.' (i.e. 'I'm talking about this: what I want to say is that it's a LIGHTER.')

(2) <u>Wa</u> also occurs as the particle of comparison following a topic which is being compared:[2] <u>X wa</u> 'X in comparison with others' or 'insofar as we're talking about X.'

Examples:

> Taˈbako wa arimaseˈñ. 'Cigarettes I don't have.'
>
> Soˈre wa takaˈi desu yo⌐ 'That one (in comparison with others) is expensive, you know.'
>
> Koˈre wa raˈitaa desu. 'This (in comparison with others) is a lighter.'

Note: <u>Wa</u> NEVER follows an interrogative word (i.e. a word that asks a question: 'what?' 'who?' 'when?' 'where?' etc.) and it NEVER follows the word or phrase that answers an interrogative word in a preceding question.

Now compare the following pairs:

> Maˈtti ḡa aˈrimaseˈñ. 'There aren't any MATCHES.' (tells what is lacking)
>
> Maˈtti wa aˈrimaseˈñ. 'There AREN'T any matches.' (answers the question 'Are there any matches?')

> Koˈre ḡa akaˈi desu. 'THIS is red.' (tells which one is red)
>
> Kore wa aˈkaˈi desu. 'This is RED.' (tells what color this is)

---

[1] In this construction, the word after <u>wa</u> regularly begins a new accent phrase. (See Introduction, page xxxv.)

[2] In this construction, the word after <u>wa</u> often does not begin a new accent phrase. (See Introduction, page xxxv.)

Ta⌐bako o kaima⌐sita.   'I bought CIGARETTES.'   (tells what I bought)
Ta⌐bako wa kaima⌐sita.   'Cigarettes I bought.'   (tells what happened to
    cigarettes in comparison with other things)

Si⌐ñbuñ o wasurema⌐sita. 'I forgot the NEWSPAPER.' (tells what I for-
    got)
Si⌐ñbuñ wa wasurema⌐sita. 'The newspaper I forgot.' (tells what happened
    to the newspaper in comparison with other things)

A phrase ending with <u>wa</u> usually occurs at, or near, the beginning of the
sentence. A phrase ending with subject particle <u>ḡa</u> usually precedes one ending
with <u>o</u>. However, a departure from the usual order changes only the emphasis.

Now study and compare the following examples.

Tanaka-sañ wa ⌐ho⌐ñ o ka⌐ima⌐sita. 'Mr. Tanaka bought a BOOK.' (tells
    what Mr. Tanaka bought)
Tanaka-sañ ḡa ⌐ho⌐ñ o ka⌐ima⌐sita.   'MR. TANAKA bought a BOOK.'
    (tells who bought what)
Ho⌐ñ wa Ta⌐naka-sañ ḡa kaima⌐sita.   'MR. TANAKA bought the book.'
    (tells who bought the book being talked about)

There are some verbals which may occur with both a <u>wa</u> and a <u>ḡa</u> phrase but
never with an <u>o</u> phrase.   Three such verbals have already been introduced:
wa⌐karima⌐su 'understand' or 'be clear'; a⌐rima⌐su 'be in a place' or 'have';
i⌐rima⌐su 'need' or 'be necessary.' With all such verbals, both the person who
understands (has, needs, etc.) and the thing or person affected are followed by
<u>wa</u> or <u>ḡa</u>, depending on emphasis.   Note the following examples of some of the
possible combinations:

Ta⌐naka-sañ ḡa irima⌐su. 'MR. TANAKA needs [it].'
Pe⌐ñ ḡa irimasu. 'I need a PEN.'
Tanaka-sañ wa ⌐pe⌐ñ ḡa irimasu. 'Mr. Tanaka needs a PEN.'
Pe⌐ñ wa Ta⌐naka-sañ ḡa irima⌐su. 'The pen, MR. TANAKA needs.'
Ko⌐re ḡa wakarimase⌐ñ. 'I don't understand THIS.'
Ko⌐re wa Tanaka-sañ wa wakarima⌐su. 'This (in comparison with others)
    Mr. Tanaka (in comparison with others) UNDERSTANDS.'
Tanaka-sañ wa zi⌐biki⌐ ḡa a⌐rimase⌐ñ. 'Mr. Tanaka doesn't have a DIC-
    TIONARY.'

Ḡa, <u>wa</u>, and <u>o</u> are frequently omitted, [1] particularly in short
sentences; the result is a slightly less formal alternant. (Watch the parentheses
in the Basic Dialogues and note where these particles are optional.)

(d) <u>mo</u>

The particle <u>mo</u> following a nominal means 'also,' 'too,' or—with a negative—'/not/ either.' A phrase ending in <u>mo</u> occurs as the subject or object or
topic of a following inflected expression, without particles <u>ga</u>, <u>o</u>, <u>wa</u>.

---

[1] But the <u>wa</u> of comparison is rarely omitted.

Examples:

Ta⌐naka-sañ mo ikima⌐sita. 'Mr. Tanaka went too.'
Ta⌐naka-sañ mo wasurema⌐sita. 'Mr. Tanaka forgot too.' or 'I forgot
  Mr. Tanaka, too.'
Ko⌐re mo i⌐i desu. 'This is good, too.'
So⌐re mo so⌐o desu. 'That's right, too.'
Ko⌐re mo wakarimase⌐ñ. 'I don't understand this either.'

(e) <u>to</u>

The particle <u>to</u> 'and' joins nominals (which may be preceded by descriptive
phrases. It does not regularly join verbals or adjectivals.

Examples:

ta⌐bako to ma⌐tti 'cigarettes and matches'
kore to sore 'this and that'
aⁿa⌐ta to Tānaka-sañ 'you and Mr. Tanaka'
ho⌐ñ to zāssi to siñbuñ 'a book and a magazine and a newspaper'
o⌐oki⌐i zi˥biki˥ to ti⌐isa⌐i ˥ho˥ñ 'a big dictionary and a small book'

A series of two or more nominals joined by <u>to</u> occurs in the same kinds of
constructions as a nominal alone. Thus:

Ta⌐bako to ma⌐tti o ku˥dasa˥i. 'Please give me a cigarette and match.'
Tanaka-sañ to Ya⌐mamoto-sañ de⌐su. 'It's Mr. Tanaka and Mr. Yamamoto.'
Ho⌐ñ to zāssi to siñbuñ ḡa arima⌐su. 'There's a book and a magazine
  and a newspaper.'

2.   a⌐rima⌐su ～ go⌐zaima⌐su

A⌐rima⌐su and go⌐zaima⌐su, meaning 'some THING is located in a place' or
'have,' are verbals of identical lexical meaning, but a⌐rima⌐su is plain and
go⌐zaima⌐su is polite-neutral.[1]

An utterance containing √a⌐rima⌐su may be made more polite by substituting
√go⌐zaima⌐su in its corresponding form. The reverse, however, is not always
true: some utterances containing √go⌐zaima⌐su do not occur with a corresponding form of √a⌐rima⌐su (for example, o⌐hayoo gozaima⌐su).

In general, persons of equal status in the Japanese social structure use the
same politeness and formality level in conversing. Which level they use is determined by the formality of the situation and of the individuals involved as
well as by the closeness of their friendship. In conversations between persons
occupying different positions in the social scale (for example, employer and
employee, customer and salesgirl, etc.), the person of lower position usually

---

[1] Both are formal because of their -ma⌐su endings.

uses a more polite and/or formal level of speech.[1] In general, women use polite speech more commonly than men; √goˊzaimaˊsu, for example, is much more typical of women's speech than of men's.

It is important to distinguish carefully between the use of nominal + √aˊrimaˊsu and nominal + √deˊsu. Note the following contrasts:

Affirmative	Negative
Ziˈbikiˈ (ḡa) arimasu.	Ziˈbikiˈ (ḡa) aˊrimaseˊñ.
'There's a DICTIONARY.'	'There isn't a DICTIONARY.'
or 'I have a DICTIONARY.'	or 'I don't have a DICTIONARY.'
Ziˈbikiˈ wa arimasu.	Ziˈbikiˈ wa aˊrimaseˊñ.
'There is a dictionary (in	'There isn't a dictionary (in com-
comparison with other things).'	parison with other things).' or
or 'A dictionary I have.'	'A dictionary I don't have.'
Ziˈbikiˈ desu.	Ziˈbikiˈ zya aˊrimaseˊñ.
'It's a dictionary.'	'It isn't a dictionary.'

In each column the first two examples express existence or location in a place, or possession; the last example expresses equivalence or definition.

3. kuˈdasaˈi and Verbal Gerunds

Kuˈdasaˈi is the imperative of the verbal kuˈdasaimaˊsuˈ '[someone] gives me.' Since it is a polite word, the imperative is often translated as 'please give me' and the -maˊsu form as '[someone] is kind enough to give me.'

In addition to the four inflected forms described in Lesson 1, verbals have a form ending in -te (or -de). This form will be called the GERUND or, more simply, the -TE FORM.

	Formal Non-Past	Gerund
'be (inanimate)' or 'have'	aˊrimaˊsu	aˊtte
'say'	iˈimaˊsu	itte
'go'	iˈkimaˊsu	itte
'need'	iˈrimaˊsu	itte
'buy'	kaˈimaˊsu	katte
'wait'	maˈtimaˊsu	maˊtte
'show'	miˈsemaˊsu	miˈsete
'do'	siˈmaˊsu	site
'be different'	tiḡaimaˊsu	tiḡatte
'understand'	waˈkarimaˊsu	waˈkaˈtte
'forget'	waˈsuremaˊsu	wasurete

---

[1] This, of course, is not necessarily reflected in every part of the conversation but refers to the over-all level.

A verbal in its gerund form + ku⌐dasa¬i is a polite imperative expression. Ku⌐dasa¬i regularly loses its accent when the preceding word or phrase is accented. Examples:

mi⌐sema¬su '[I] show'	mi¬sete kudasai 'please show'
	[lit. 'please give me showing']
ka⌐ima¬su '[I] buy'	ka⌐tte kudasa¬i 'please buy'
ma⌐tima¬su '[I] wait'	ma¬tte kudasai 'please wait'
i⌐ima¬su '[I] say'	i⌐tte kudasa¬i 'please say'
i⌐kima¬su '[I] go'	i⌐tte kudasa¬i 'please go'[1]
si⌐ma¬su '[I] do'	si⌐te kudasa¬i 'please do'

The -te form has other uses which will be introduced later.

Ku⌐dasa¬i may also be preceded by a nominal (+ o):[2] E⌐npitu (o) kudasa¬i. 'Please give me a pencil.'

O⌐mati-kudasa¬i, in Basic Sentence 14, is an example of another ku⌐dasa¬i pattern which will be discussed in a later lesson. It is equivalent to ma¬tte kudasai except that it is more polite. Ku⌐dasaima¬se is a formal equivalent of ku⌐dasa¬i and is used most commonly by women.

4. no 'one(s)'

The no introduced in this lesson[3] is a nominal meaning 'one' or 'ones.' Like its English equivalents, it is used to refer to something or someone whose specific identity is known from the context. Thus, Japanese ya⌐su¬i no (o) ka⌐i-ma⌐sita and its English equivalents 'I bought a cheap one' or 'I bought cheap ones' are used when the objects referred to are known.

Unlike the nominals which have occurred previously, no is always preceded by a modifier. An adjectival preceding no is always accented, as it is before √de¬su: an unaccented adjectival acquires an accent on its pre-final syllable (cf. akai, but a⌐ka¬i no and a⌐ka¬i desu).

5. Fragments

All Japanese sentences which consist of, or end with, a past or non-past or imperative[4] inflected form, with or without one or more sentence particles

---

[1] I⌐tte kudasa¬i 'please say' and i⌐tte kudasa¬i 'please go' are distinguished in the spoken language only by context.

[2] See Grammatical Note 1 above.

[3] See Basic Sentences 3, 4, 5, 6, 10, 21, 22, 23, 24.

[4] Or tentative (to be introduced later).

immediately following, are MAJOR SENTENCES.   All other sentences are MINOR SENTENCES or FRAGMENTS.   Some of the fragments that have appeared are: Koñbañ wa. Tyo⌐tto. Ha⌐i.

In conversational Japanese, a sentence may end in the middle of what would be a major sentence if a portion of the preceding context were repeated and the complete meaning is clear to the hearer; such utterances are also fragments. Examples:

Na⌐ni (o) ka⌐ima⌐sita ka⌐ 'What did you buy?'
   Siñbuñ (o). 'A newspaper.' (i. e. Si⌐ñbuñ (o) kaima⌐sita. 'I bought a newspaper.')

Ta⌐ka⌐i desu ⌐ne⌐e. 'It's expensive, isn't it.'
   E⌐e, zu⌐ibuñ. 'Yes, very.' (i. e. E⌐e, zu⌐ibuñ ta⌐ka⌐i desu. 'Yes, it's very expensive.')

Ta⌐naka-sañ wa wakarima⌐sita. A⌐na⌐ta wa? (i.e. A⌐na⌐ta wa wa⌐karima⌐sita ka⌐) 'Mr. Takana understood. How about you? (i.e. As for you, was there understanding?)'

Particularly common are fragments ending with ḡa 'but.' In some cases, the ḡa implies a specific contrast to be supplied by the listener, as:

Si⌐ñbuñ to zassi o kaima⌐sita ka⌐   'Did you buy a newspaper and a magazine?'
Si⌐ñbuñ wa kaima⌐sita ḡa_   'A newspaper I bought but [I didn't buy a magazine].'

Many times, however, X ḡa is simply a softer, more hesitant, less positive way of saying X—indicating for example 'so-and-so is the case but. . .is that all right? or should I do anything about it? or do you want to say something different? or why do you ask? etc. In contrast with sentence-final yo, which indicates finality and assurance on the part of the speaker, final ḡa is indirect and polite. Often, the closest English equivalent of this ḡa is an intonation expressing hesitation.

Examples:

Ma⌐tti o kudasai. 'Please give me a match.'
   A⌐rimase⌐ñ ḡa_ 'I haven't any but [do you want me to get some?]'

Ko⌐re wa irimase⌐ñ. So⌐re o kudasa⌐i. 'I don't want this one. Give me that one.'
   O⌐nazi de⌐su ḡa_ 'It's the same but [I'll give it to you if you want it].'

Ta⌐naka-sañ de⌐su ka⌐ 'Are you Mr. Tanaka?'
   E⌐e, Ta⌐naka de⌐su ḡa_ 'Yes, I'm Tanaka but [what would you like? or why do you ask?]'

DRILLS

A. Substitution Drill

1.	Do you have a furoshiki?	Hu⌐rosiki (g̃a) arima⌐su ka⌟
2.	Do you have a lighter?	Ra⌐itaa (g̃a) a⌐rima⌐su ka⌟
3.	Do you have a match?	Ma⌐tti (g̃a) a⌐rima⌐su ka⌟
4.	Do you have a cigarette?	Ta⌐bako (g̃a) arima⌐su ka⌟
5.	Do you have an ashtray?	Ha⌐iza⌐ra (g̃a) a⌐rima⌐su ka⌟
6.	Do you have a pencil?	E⌐ñpitu (g̃a) arima⌐su ka⌟
7.	Do you have a pen?	Pe⌐ñ (g̃a) a⌐rima⌐su ka⌟
8.	Do you have a dictionary?	Zi⌐syo (g̃a) a⌐rima⌐su ka⌟

B. Substitution Drill

1.	Please give me that furoshiki over there.	A⌐no hurosiki (o) kudasa⌐i.
2.	Please give me that lighter.	So⌐no ra⌐itaa (o) kudasai.
3.	Please give me those matches over there.	A⌐no ma⌐tti (o) kudasai.
4.	Please give me those cigarettes.	So⌐no tabako (o) kudasa⌐i.
5.	Please give me that ashtray over there.	A⌐no haiza⌐ra (o) kudasai.
6.	Please give me that pencil.	So⌐no eñpitu (o) kudasa⌐i.
7.	Please give me that pen over there.	A⌐no pe⌐ñ (o) kudasai.
8.	Please give me that dictionary.	So⌐no zi⌐syo (o) kudasai.
9.	Please give me that book over there.	A⌐no ho⌐ñ (o) kudasai.
10.	Please give me that newspaper.	So⌐no siñbuñ (o) kudasa⌐i.

C. Substitution Drill

1.	Please let me see that blue furoshiki.	Sono a⌐o⌐i hurosiki (o) ⌐mi⌐sete kudasai.
2.	Please let me see that small dictionary over there.	Ano ti⌐isa⌐i zi⌐biki⌐ (o) ⌐mi⌐sete kudasai.
3.	Please let me see that big book.	Sono o⌐oki⌐i ⌐ho⌐ñ (o) ⌐mi⌐sete kudasai.
4.	Please let me see that white ashtray over there.	Ano si⌐ro⌐i ha⌐iza⌐ra (o) ⌐mi⌐sete kudasai.
5.	Please let me see that new magazine.	Sono a⌐tarasi⌐i zassi (o) ⌐mi⌐sete kudasai.
6.	Please let me see that black pen over there.	Ano ku⌐ro⌐i ⌐pe⌐ñ (o) ⌐mi⌐sete kudasai.

7.	Please let me see that red pencil.	Sono a⌈kai eñpitu (o) mi⌉sete kudasai.
8.	Please let me see that old newspaper over there.	Ano hu⌈ru⌉i siñbuñ (o) ⊢mi⊣sete kudasai.

D. Substitution Drill

(Make whatever particle changes are necessary.)

1.	What did you buy?	Na⌉ni (o) ka⊢ima⊣sita ka⌟
2.	What did you do?	Na⌉ni (o) si⊢ma⊣sita ka⌟
3.	What did you forget?	Na⌉ni (o) wa⊢surema⊣sita ka⌟
4.	What do you need?	Na⌉ni (ḡa) i⊢rima⊣su ka⌟
5.	What do you have? or What is there?	Na⌉ni (ḡa) a⊢rima⊣su ka⌟
6.	What don't you understand?	Na⌉ni (ḡa) wa⊢karimase⊣ñ ka⌟
7.	Which one don't you understand?	Do⌉re (ḡa) wa⊢karimase⊣ñ ka⌟
~~8.~~	~~Which one is the same?~~	~~Do⌉re (ḡa) o⊢nazi de⊣su ka⌟~~
~~9.~~	~~Which one is no good?~~	~~Do⌉re (ḡa) da⊢me⊣ desu ka⌟~~
10.	Which one is a dictionary?	Do⌉re (ḡa) zi⊢biki⊣ desu ka⌟

E. Grammar Drill (based on Grammatical Notes 1 and 4)

Tutor: Sono a⌈kai ho⌉ñ (o) kudasai. / a⌈o⌉i/ 'Please give me that red book.'

Student: Sono a⌈o⌉i no mo kudasai. 'Please give me that blue one, too.'

1.	O⌈oki⌉i zi⊢biki⊣ (o) ka⊢ima⊣sita. /ti⌈isa⌉i/	Ti⌈isa⌉i no mo ka⊢ima⊣sita.
2.	A⌈kai eñpitu (o) oneḡai-sima⌉su. /ku⌈ro⌉i/	Ku⌈ro⌉i no mo oneḡai-simasu.
3.	Kono hu⌈ru⌉i ⊢ma⊣tti (wa) da⌈me⌉ desu. /a⌈tarasi⌉i/	Kono a⌈tarasi⌉i no mo da⊢me⊣ desu.
4.	Ya⌈su⌉i hurosiki (o) ka⊢ima⊣sita. /ta⌈ka⌉i/	Ta⌈ka⌉i no mo ka⊢ima⊣sita.
5.	Sono ku⌈ro⌉i ⊢ho⊣ñ (o) ⊢mi⊣sete kudasai. /akai/	Sono a⌈ka⌉i no mo ⊢mi⊣sete kudasai.
6.	Kono si⌈ro⌉i hurosiki (wa) ta⌈ka⌉i desu. /ku⌈ro⌉i/	Kono ku⌈ro⌉i no mo ta⊢ka⊣i desu.
7.	Sono ki⌈iroi haiza⌉ra (o) kudasai. /a⌈o⌉i/	Sono a⌈o⌉i no mo kudasai.
8.	Tu⌈mara⌉nai ⊢ho⊣ñ (o) ka⊢ima⊣sita. /o⌈mosiro⌉i/	O⌈mosiro⌉i no mo ka⊢ima⊣sita.

F. Response Drill (based on Grammatical Note 1)[1]

   1. Are wa ⌐na⌐n desu ka↲   [Are wa] hu⌐rosiki de⌐su.
      /hurosiki/
   2. Na⌐ni ḡa i⌐rima⌐su ka↲   E⌐ñpitu ḡa irima⌐su.
      /eñpitu/
   3. Na⌐ni o ka⌐ima⌐sita ka↲   Ha⌐iza⌐ra o ka⌐ima⌐sita.
      /ha⌐iza⌐ra/
   4. A⌐tarasi⌐i zassi wa ⌐do⌐re   [A⌐tarasi⌐i zassi wa] a⌐re de⌐su.
      desu ka↲   /are/
   5. Do⌐re ḡa da⌐me⌐ desu ka↲   Ko⌐re ḡa dame⌐ desu.
      /kore/
   6. Kore wa i⌐ka⌐ḡa desu ka↲   [Kore wa] da⌐me⌐ desu.
      /da⌐me⌐/
   7. Do⌐re o ka⌐ima⌐sita ka↲   A⌐o⌐i no o ka⌐ima⌐sita.
      /a⌐o⌐i no/
   8. Do⌐no ⌐pe⌐ñ ḡa da⌐me⌐   A⌐no pe⌐ñ ḡa da⌐me⌐ desu.
      desu ka↲   /a⌐no pe⌐ñ/
   9. A⌐no pe⌐ñ wa ⌐do⌐o desu ka↲   [A⌐no pe⌐ñ wa] da⌐me⌐ desu.
      /da⌐me⌐/
 10. Do⌐no zi⌐biki⌐ ḡa i⌐rima⌐su   So⌐no zibiki⌐ ḡa irimasu.
      ka↲   /so⌐no zibiki⌐/

G. Response Drill (based on Grammatical Notes 1 and 2)

   1. Zi⌐biki⌐ (ḡa) a⌐rima⌐su ka↲   E⌐e, [zi⌐biki⌐ (ḡa)] arimasu.
      /E⌐e./
   2. Zi⌐biki⌐ (ḡa) a⌐rima⌐su ka↲   Iie, [zi⌐biki⌐ (wa)] a⌐rimase⌐ñ.
      /Iie./
   3. Zi⌐biki⌐ desu ka↲   /Iie./   Iie, zi⌐biki⌐ zya a⌐rimase⌐ñ.
   4. Hu⌐rosiki (ḡa) gozaima⌐su   Ha⌐a, [hu⌐rosiki (ḡa)] gozaima⌐su.
      ka↲   /Ha⌐a./
   5. Hu⌐rosiki (ḡa) gozaima⌐su   Iie, [hu⌐rosiki (wa)] gozaimase⌐ñ.
      ka↲   /Iie./
   6. Hu⌐rosiki de⌐su ka↲   /Iie./   Iie, hu⌐rosiki zya arimase⌐ñ.
   7. Ha⌐iza⌐ra (ḡa) a⌐rima⌐su   E⌐e, [ha⌐iza⌐ra (ḡa)] arimasu.
      ka↲   /E⌐e./
   8. Ha⌐iza⌐ra (ḡa) a⌐rima⌐su   Iie, [ha⌐iza⌐ra (wa)] a⌐rimase⌐ñ.
      ka↲   /Iie./
   9. Ha⌐iza⌐ra desu ka↲   /Iie./   Iie, ha⌐iza⌐ra zya a⌐rimase⌐ñ.

---

[1] Particles ordinarily designated as optional are not so marked in this exercise because drill on the particles is the purpose of the exercise.

H. Expansion Drill

1. Please show [it to me].   Mi⌐sete kudasai.
    Please show [me] a furo-   Hu⌐rosiki (o) mi⌐sete kudasai.
    shiki.
    Please show [me] that furo-   A⌐no hurosiki (o) mi⌐sete kudasai.
    shiki.
    Say, please show [me] that   Tyo⌐tto, a⌐no hurosiki (o) mi⌐sete ku-
    furoshiki.   dasai.

2. I need [it].   I⌐rima⌐su.
    I need a small one.   Ti⌐isa⌐i no (ḡa) irimasu.
    I need a little smaller one.   Mo⌐o suko⌐si ti⌐isa⌐i no (ḡa) iri-
                                            masu.
    I need a little smaller one   Mo⌐o suko⌐si ti⌐isa⌐i no (ḡa) i⌐ri-
    but [do you have one?]   ma⌐su ḡa_

3. I'd like [it].   O⌐neḡai-sima⌐su.
    I'd like a red one too.   A⌐ka⌐i no mo oneḡai-simasu.
    I'd like this red one, too.   Kono a⌐ka⌐i no mo oneḡai-simasu.
    And I'd like this red one,   Sore kara, kono a⌐ka⌐i no mo oneḡai-
    too.   simasu.

4. [He] bought [it].   Ka⌐ima⌐sita.
    [He] bought a dictionary.   Zi⌐biki⌐ (o) ka⌐ima⌐sita.
    [He] bought a magazine and   Za⌐ssi to zibiki⌐ (o) ka⌐ima⌐sita.
    a dictionary.
    Mr. Tanaka bought a maga-   Tanaka-sañ (wa) za⌐ssi to zibiki⌐ (o)
    zine and a dictionary.   ka⌐ima⌐sita.

5. Aren't there any?   A⌐rimase⌐ñ ka_
    Aren't there any ashtrays?   Ha⌐iza⌐ra (wa) a⌐rimase⌐ñ ka_
    Aren't there any cheap ash-   Ya⌐su⌐i ha⌐iza⌐ra (wa) a⌐rimase⌐ñ
    trays?   ka_
    Aren't there any ashtrays   Mo⌐o suko⌐si ya⌐su⌐i ha⌐iza⌐ra (wa)
    that are a little cheaper?   a⌐rimase⌐ñ ka_

6. It's a dictionary.   Zi⌐biki⌐ desu.
    Is it a dictionary?   Zi⌐biki⌐ desu ka_
    Is it a new dictionary?   A⌐tarasi⌐i zi⌐biki⌐ desu ka_
    Which one is a new dic-   Do⌐re ḡa a⌐tarasi⌐i zi⌐biki⌐ desu ka_
    tionary?

SHORT DIALOGUE PRACTICE

1. Do you have a match?   Ma⌐tti (ḡa) a⌐rima⌐su ka_
      No, I haven't.   Iie, a⌐rimase⌐ñ.
    How about a lighter?   Ra⌐itaa wa?
      I don't have a lighter   Ra⌐itaa mo a⌐rimase⌐ñ.
      either.

2. Do you have magazines?   Za⌐ssi (ḡa) arima⌐su ka_
      No, we haven't.   Iie, a⌐rimase⌐ñ.

How about papers?   Siñbuñ wa?
Papers we have.   Si⌐ñbuñ wa arima⌐su.

3.   Do you have a pencil?   E⌐ñpitu (ḡa) gozaima⌐su ka⌐
     Yes, I have.   Ha⌐a, go⌐zaima⌐su.
     How about a pen?   Pe⌐ñ wa?
     I have a pen, too.   Pe⌐ñ mo gozaimasu.

4.   Do you have a cigarette?   Ta⌐bako (ḡa) arima⌐su ka⌐
     Yes, I have.   E⌐e, a⌐rima⌐su.
     How about a match?   Ma⌐tti wa?
     A match I don't have.   Ma⌐tti wa a⌐rimase⌐ñ.

5.   Did you buy a book?   Ho⌐ñ (o) ka⌐ima⌐sita ka⌐
     Yes, I did (buy).   E⌐e, ka⌐ima⌐sita.
     How about a magazine?   Zassi wa?
     I bought a magazine, too.   Za⌐ssi mo kaima⌐sita.

6.   Did you buy a pen?   Pe⌐ñ (o) ka⌐ima⌐sita ka⌐
     No, I didn't.   Iie, ka⌐imase⌐ñ desita.
     How about a pencil?   Eñpitu wa?
     I didn't buy a pencil either.   E⌐ñpitu mo kaimase⌐ñ desita.

7.   Did you buy a paper?   Si⌐ñbuñ (o) kaima⌐sita ka⌐
     Yes, I did.   E⌐e, ka⌐ima⌐sita.
     How about a magazine?   Zassi wa?
        A magazine I didn't buy.   Za⌐ssi wa kaimase⌐ñ desita.

8.   Did you buy a book?   Ho⌐ñ (o) ka⌐ima⌐sita ka⌐
     No, I didn't.   Iie, ka⌐imase⌐ñ desita.
     How about a dictionary?   Zi⌐biki⌐ wa?
     A dictionary I bought.   Zi⌐biki⌐ wa ka⌐ima⌐sita.

9.   Did you buy cigarettes and   Ta⌐bako to ma⌐tti (o) ka⌐ima⌐sita ka⌐
     matches?

        Cigarettes I bought but   Ta⌐bako wa kaima⌐sita ḡa, ma⌐tti wa
        matches I didn't buy.   ka⌐imase⌐ñ desita.

10. Did you buy a magazine?   Za⌐ssi (o) kaima⌐sita ka⌐
     A magazine I didn't buy but   Za⌐ssi wa kaimase⌐ñ desita ḡa, siñ-
     I bought a paper.   buñ (o) kaima⌐sita.

11. Do you need a pen and pen-   Pe⌐ñ to e⌐ñpitu (ḡa) irima⌐su ka⌐
     cil?

        A pen I need but a pencil   Pe⌐ñ wa i⌐rima⌐su ḡa, eñpitu wa
        I don't need.   irimase⌐ñ.

12. Do you need a pen?   Pe⌐ñ (ḡa) i⌐rima⌐su ka⌐
     A pen I don't need but I   Pe⌐ñ wa i⌐rimase⌐ñ ḡa, e⌐ñpitu (ḡa)
     need a pencil.   irima⌐su.

SUPPLEMENTARY CONVERSATIONS

1. Smith (calling a clerk): O⌐negai-sima⌐su. So⌐no pe⌐ñ o ⌐mi⌐sete kudasai.
   Clerk: I⌐rassya⌐i. Do⌐no ⌐pe⌐ñ desu ka⌡
   Smith: Sono ku⌐ro⌐i no desu.
   Clerk: Do⌐ozo.
   Smith: I⌐kura desu ka⌡
   Clerk: Ni⌐señ-eñ de⌐su.
   Smith: Tyo⌐tto ta⌐ka⌐i desu ⌐ne⌐e. Mo⌐o suko⌐si ya⌐su⌐i no wa a⌐rimase⌐ñ
          ka⌡
   Clerk: Kono a⌐ka⌐i no wa i⌐ka⌐ga desu ka. Se⌐ñ-eñ de⌐su ga⌐
   Smith: So⌐o desu ⌐ne⌐e. Sore mo ⌐tyo⌐tto⌐
   Clerk: A⌐a, ko⌐re wa ika⌐ga desu ka⌡ Se⌐ñ nihyaku⌐-eñ desu.
   Smith (trying it out): A⌐a, ko⌐re wa i⌐i ⌐pe⌐ñ desu ⌐ne⌐e. Ko⌐re o kudasa⌐i.
   Clerk: A⌐ri⌐gatoo gozaimasu. E⌐ñpitu mo ika⌐ga desu ka⌡
   Smith: E⌐ñpitu wa irimase⌐ñ. (Handing over money) Se⌐ñ gohyaku⌐- eñ.
          Ha⌐i.
   Clerk: Syo⌐osyoo o⌐mati-kudasa⌐i.

                          .   .   .

   Clerk (returning with package and change): O⌐matase-itasima⌐sita. Sa⌐ñ-
          byaku⌐-eñ desu. Ma⌐ido ari⌐gatoo gozaimasu. Ma⌐ta do⌐ozo.

2. Smith: Tyo⌐tto.
   Clerk: I⌐rassyaima⌐se.
   Smith: Are wa ⌐na⌐ñ desu ka⌡
   Clerk: A⌐re de⌐su ka⌡ Ha⌐iza⌐ra desu.
   Smith: So⌐o desu ka. Ki⌐ree desu ⌐ne⌐e. Tyo⌐tto ⌐mi⌐sete kudasai.
   Clerk: Ki⌐iro⌐i no desu ka⌡
   Smith: E⌐e.
   Clerk: Do⌐ozo.
   Smith: Ano a⌐ka⌐i no mo ⌐mi⌐sete kudasai.
   Clerk: Ka⌐sikomarima⌐sita.
   Smith: I⌐kura desu ka⌡
   Clerk: Ki⌐iro⌐i no wa sa⌐ñbyaku⌐-eñ desu. A⌐ka⌐i no wa ⌐sa⌐ñbyaku go⌐zyu⌐u-
          eñ desu.
   Smith: O⌐nazi zya arimase⌐ñ ⌐ne⌐e.
   Clerk: Ha⌐a. Ki⌐iro⌐i no wa ⌐tyo⌐tto ti⌐isa⌐i desu.
   Smith: A⌐a, so⌐o desu ka. A⌐ka⌐i no o ku⌐dasa⌐i.
   Clerk: A⌐ri⌐gatoo gozaimasu.
   Smith: Tyo⌐tto ⌐ma⌐tte kudasai. Ki⌐iro⌐i no mo onegai-simasu.
   Clerk: Ka⌐sikomarima⌐sita. Ho⌐ka ni na⌐ni ka?
   Smith: So⌐re dake⌐ desu.
   Clerk: Ro⌐ppyaku gozyu⌐u-eñ desu.
   Smith: Señ-eñ. Ha⌐i.
   Clerk: Syo⌐osyoo o⌐mati-kudasaima⌐se.

                          .   .   .

   Clerk: O⌐matase-itasima⌐sita. Sa⌐ñbyaku go⌐zyu⌐u - eñ d e s u . Do⌐o mo
          a⌐ri⌐gatoo gozaimasita.

English Equivalents

1. Smith: Would you wait on me? Please show me that pen.
   Clerk: (Welcome.) Which pen do you mean?
   Smith: (It's) that black one.
   Clerk: Here you are.
   Smith: How much is it?
   Clerk: It's ¥ 2000.
   Smith: It's a little expensive, isn't it. Don't you have a little cheaper
   one?
   Clerk: How about this red one? It's ¥ 1000. . . .
   Smith: Hmmm. I'm afraid that one won't do either.
   Clerk: Oh, how about this one? It's ¥ 1200.
   Smith: Oh, this is a good pen, isn't it. I'll take this one.
   Clerk: Thank you. How about a pencil, too?
   Smith: I don't need any pencils. Here you are. ¥ 1500.
   Clerk: Just a moment, please.

         .   .   .

   Clerk: I'm sorry to have kept you waiting. [Your change] is ¥ 300. Thank
   you. Please come again.

2. Smith: Say there!
   Clerk: (Welcome.)
   Smith: What are those things?
   Clerk: Those? They're ashtrays.
   Smith: Oh? Aren't they pretty. Let me have a look.
   Clerk: Do you mean a yellow one?
   Smith: Yes.
   Clerk: Here you are.
   Smith: Let me see that red one, too.
   Clerk: Certainly.
   Smith: How much are they?
   Clerk: The yellow one is ¥ 300. The red one is ¥ 350.
   Smith: They're not the same, are they.
   Clerk: No (i.e. that's right). The yellow one is a little small[er].
   Smith: Oh? I'll take the red one.
   Clerk: Thank you.
   Smith: Just a minute. I'd like the yellow one, too.
   Clerk: Certainly. Anything else?
   Smith: That's all.
   Clerk: (It's) ¥ 650.
   Smith: Here you are. ¥ 1000.
   Clerk: Just a moment, please.

         .   .   .

   Clerk: I'm sorry to have kept you waiting. [Your change] is ¥ 350. Thank
   you very much.

EXERCISES

1. Mr. Smith asks the clerk: The clerk replies:

    a. to show him that big   Which one do you mean?
        book.
    b. if he has any small dic-   I do, but they aren't very good.
        tionaries.
    c. for that.   Here you are.
    d. for cigarettes and   Anything else?
        matches.
    e. how much that red   It's ¥ 350.
        furoshiki is.
    f. if that blue ashtray is   No, it's ¥ 500.
        ¥ 400.

2. Mr. Smith has just entered a stationery store.

    a. The clerk greets Mr. Smith.
    b. Mr. Smith asks if they have any pens.
    c. The clerk answers that they do.
    d. Mr. Smith asks the clerk to show him a black pen.
    e. The clerk shows him one and says that it is a fine pen.
    f. Mr. Smith asks the price.
    g. The clerk answers that it is ¥ 2500.
    h. Mr. Smith remarks that it is very expensive. He asks if they have
        any that are a little cheaper.
    i. The clerk answers that they have, but they aren't black. He suggests
        a blue one. It costs ¥ 1500.
    j. Mr. Smith thinks the blue pen is pretty. He remarks that it isn't very
        expensive. He decides to buy it.
    k. The clerk thanks Mr. Smith and asks if he wants anything else.
    l. Mr. Smith says that that's all he wants, and gives the clerk ¥ 2000.
    m. The clerk asks him to wait a moment. When he returns, he apolo-
        gizes for having kept Mr. Smith waiting and gives him ¥ 500 change.
        He thanks Mr. Smith and invites him to come again.
    n. Mr. Smith says goodbye.

3. Practice the Basic Dialogues with variations and appropriate props.

Lesson 5. Shopping (cont.)

BASIC DIALOGUES: FOR MEMORIZATION

(a)

Smith

more | moˈtto
1. Do you have more of these? | Kore (wa) ˈmoˈtto aˈrimaˈsu ka⌐
(Lit. As for these, are there more?)

Clerk

much or many | taˈkusaˈn̄
2. Yes, we have lots of those. | Haˈa, sore wa taˈkusan̄ gozaimaˈsu.
(Lit. As for those, there are many.)

Smith

one unit	hiˈtoˈ-tu → hi·to-tzu
two units	huˈta-tuˈ hi,1A-+zu
three units	mi-ˈttuˈ
four units	yo-ˈttuˈ
five units	iˈtuˈ-tu → Hi tzu-+zu
six units	mu-ˈttuˈ
seven units	naˈnaˈ-tu
eight units	ya-ˈttuˈ
nine units	koˈkoˈno-tu
ten units	toˈo
eleven units	zyuˈuitiˈ → ぢゅ-iˈ 円升
twelve units	zyuˈuniˈ

3. I'd like five. | Iˈtuˈ-tu oneḡai-simasu.

4. And then give me three of those white ones, too. | Sore kara, sono siˈroˈi no mo mi-ˈttu kudasaˈi.

Clerk

I'm sorry but | suˈmimaseˈn̄ ḡa
5. I'm sorry but that is all we have of the white ones. | Suˈmimaseˈn̄ ḡa, siˈroˈi no wa soˈre dakeˈ desu.
(Lit. As for the white ones, it's just that.)

Smith

three units more | moˈo mi-ttuˈ
6. Then give me three more of these. | Zyaˈa, kore (o) moˈo mi-ttu kudasaˈi.

57

(b)

Smith

how many units?   i⌐kutu or
                                       oikutu +

7. How many of these do you   Kore (wa) ⌐i⌐kutu aʰrima⌐su ka⌐
    have? (Lit. As for these, how
    many are there?)

Clerk

8. We have five (but) . . .   I⌐tu⌐-tu goʰzaima⌐su ḡa⌐

Smith

    just three units   mi-⌐ttu dake⌐
9. I'd like just three.   Mi-⌐ttu dake oneḡai-sima⌐su.

    one long, cylindrical unit   i⌐p-poñ
    two long, cylindrical units   ni⌐-hoñ
    three long, cylindrical units   sa⌐ñ-boñ
10. And then give me three of those   Sore kara, sono eñpitu mo ⌐sa⌐ñ-boñ
    pencils, too.   kudasai.

Clerk

    color   i⌐ro⌐
    what (kind of) color?   do⌐ñna iro
    is good or fine   yorosii /-ku/
11. What color would you like?   Do⌐ñna i⌐ro⌐ ḡa yoʰrosi⌐i desu ka⌐
    (Lit. What kind of color is
    good?)

Smith

12. I'd like one red one and two   A⌐ka⌐i no (o) ʰi⌐p-poñ to, a⌐o⌐i no (o)
    blue ones.   ⌐ni⌐-hoñ oneḡai-simasu.

(c)

Smith

    paper   ka⌐mi⌐
    this kind of paper   ko⌐ñna kami⌐
    one thin, flat unit   i⌐ti⌐-mai
    two thin, flat units   ni⌐-mai
    three thin, flat units   sa⌐ñ-mai
13. How much is one sheet of this   Ko⌐ñna kami⌐ (wa) i⌐ti⌐ - mai ⌐i⌐kura
    kind of paper?   desu ka⌐

Clerk

14. It's ¥20.   Ni⌐zyuu-eñ desu.

Smith

15. Give me two sheets of the red   A⌐ka⌐i no (o) ʰni⌐-mai to, si⌐ro⌐i no
    and three sheets of the white.   (o) ⌐sa⌐ñ-mai kudasai.

one bound unit (as, a book,   i⌐s-satu⌐
    magazine, etc.)
two bound units   ni⌐-satu
three bound units   sa⌐ñ-satu

16. And then I'd like two of these   Sore kara, kono ti⌐isa⌐i zi⌐biki⌐ mo
small dictionaries, too.   ⌐ni⌐-satu onegai-simasu.

(d)

Tanaka

17. What are you going to buy?   Na⌐ni (o) ka⌐ima⌐su ka⌐

Smith

I or me   watakusi or
     bo⌐ku (man's word; has unac-
      cented alternant)

18. (Do you mean) me?   Wa⌐takusi de⌐su ka⌐ or
    Bo⌐ku desu ka⌐

map   ti⌐zu
19. I'm going to buy a map.   Ti⌐zu (o) kaimasu.

(to the clerk)

Tokyo   Tookyoo
map of Tokyo   To⌐okyoo no ti⌐zu
20. Say! Do you have maps of   Tyo⌐tto. To⌐okyoo no ti⌐zu (ga) a⌐ri-
Tokyo?   ma⌐su ka⌐

Clerk

both big ones and small   o⌐oki⌐i no mo ti⌐isa⌐i no mo
   ones
21. Yes. We have (both) big ones   Ha⌐a. O⌐oki⌐i no mo ti⌐isa⌐i no mo
and small ones (but) . . .   go⌐zaima⌐su ga—

Smith

just   tyo⌐tto
22. (Just) let me have a look.   Tyo⌐tto ⌐mi⌐sete kudasai.

. . .

23. Oh, this one is fine.   A⌐, ko⌐re ga i⌐i desu.

24. Give me two.   Ni⌐-mai kudasai.

(e)

Smith

today's newspaper   kyo⌐o no siñbuñ
25. Don't you have today's paper?   Kyo⌐o no siñbuñ (wa) a⌐rimase⌐ñ ka⌐

Clerk

yesterday's newspaper   kinoo no siñbuñ
26. No (i.e. that's right). This is   E⌐e, kore wa ki⌐noo no siñbuñ de⌐su.
yesterday's paper.

as for today's (one) <u>or</u>   kyo⌐o no wa
 today's (one), compara-
 tively speaking
soon <u>or</u> any minute <u>or</u>   su⌐ḡu
 right away
come   ki⌐ma⌐su

27. Today's (one) will come any   Kyo⌐o no wa ⌐su⌐ḡu ki⌐ma⌐su yo⌐
     minute.

ADDITIONAL PLACE NAMES

Japan	Ni⌐ho⌐n̄ <u>or</u>	England	Iḡirisu <u>or</u>
	Ni⌐ppo⌐n̄		Eekoku
Fukuoka	Hu⌐ku⌐oka	London	Ro⌐n̄don̄
Hokkaido	Ho⌐kka⌐idoo	France	Hurañsu
Honshu	Ho⌐n̄syuu	Paris	Pa⌐rii
Kobe	Ko⌐obe	Germany	Do⌐itu
Kyushu	Kyu⌐usyuu	Berlin	Beruriñ
Nara	Na⌐ra	U.S.S.R.	So⌐reñ <u>or</u>
Nikko	Ni⌐kkoo		So⌐bie⌐to
Osaka	Oosaka	Moscow	Mosukuwa
Sapporo	Sapporo	India	I⌐n̄do
Shikoku	Si⌐ko⌐ku	Korea	Tyo⌐ose⌐n̄
Yokohama	Yokohama	China	Tyu⌐uḡoku
		Formosa	Ta⌐iwa⌐n̄
U.S.A.	Amerika <u>or</u>	(Communist	Tyuukyoo)[1]
	Beekoku	China	
New York	Nyu⌐uyo⌐oku		
San Fran-	Sa⌐n̄hurañsi⌐suko		
cisco			
Washington	Wa⌐si⌐n̄ton̄		

NOTES ON THE BASIC DIALOGUES

8. 'We have five but—how many do you want? <u>or</u> is that enough? <u>or</u> did you
    want more than that? <u>or</u> I hope that is enough (etc.)'

11. <u>Yorosii</u> resembles <u>i⌐i</u> in meaning and general usage, but is a more polite
     word. It occurs in the negative only under special circumstances.

18. Bo⌐ku occurs in men's speech and is less polite than <u>watakusi</u>, which is
     used by both men and women. <u>Watakusi</u> is often contracted to <u>watasi</u> by
     men and women, and to <u>atasi</u> by women.

21. 'We have big ones and small ones but—which kind did you want?'

22. Tyo⌐tto 'just' is not interchangeable with <u>su⌐ko⌐si</u>.

27. The gerund of <u>ki⌐ma⌐su</u> is <u>ki⌐te⌐</u>.

---

[1] This name has become obsolete.

GRAMMATICAL NOTES

1. Numerals: Series II

The numerals of Series I (i⌐ti¬, ni¬, sań, etc.) were introduced in Lesson 3. The second numeral series, of native Japanese origin, is introduced in this lesson:

hi⌐to¬-	'1'	mu-	'6'
huta-	'2'	na⌐na¬-	'7'
mi-	'3'	ya-	'8'
yo-	'4'	ko⌐ko¬no-	'9'
i⌐tu¬-	'5'	to- or to¬o-	'10'

This second series goes only as far as 10; beyond 10, Series I (zyu⌐uiti¬, zyu⌐uni¬, etc.) is used.

The numerals of Series I occur both as independent words (for example, in mathematics) and in number compounds (for example, combined with -eń to count yen); but the numerals of Series II usually occur only in number compounds. Combined with -⌐t⌐/tu 'unit,'[1] the numerals of Series II are used to count unit objects which are inanimate (see the list preceding Basic Sentence 3 in this lesson; note that in to¬o '10 units,' the longer alternant for 10 occurs, without the -⌐t⌐/tu which occurs in the equivalents of '1 unit' through '9 units'). To count the number of units beyond 10, the numerals of Series I are used independently.

Thus, '1' in reply to the question 'What is 3 minus 2?' is i⌐ti¬, but '1' in reply to the question 'How many chairs do you need?' is hi⌐to¬-tu; '11' in reply to both of the questions 'What is 21 minus 10?' and 'How many chairs do you need?' is zyu⌐uiti¬.

The question word corresponding to the hi⌐to¬-tu, hu⌐ta-tu¬ series is i¬kutu (polite, oikutu) 'how many units?' Oikutu is used more commonly, but not exclusively, by women.

Single units of some objects are always counted with the hi⌐to¬-tu, hu⌐ta-tu¬ series; some things are never counted with it (i.e. they use a specialized counter); and units of some objects are counted either with the hi⌐to¬-tu, hu⌐ta-tu¬ series or with a specialized counter (with some variation among individual speakers).[2]

---

[1] They also enter into other combinations, some of which will be introduced later. Examples: hi⌐to¬-bań '1 night'; hi⌐to¬-kumi '1 set'; hi⌐to¬-asi '1 pace.'

[2] In the last case there may be a difference of meaning, depending on whether the hi⌐to¬-tu, hu⌐ta-tu¬ series or a specialized counter is used. For example, in reference to tabako, i¬p-poń, ni¬-hoń, etc. refer only to individual cigarettes, but hi⌐to¬-tu, hu⌐ta-tu¬ etc. may also be used to count packages of cigarettes.

2. C o u n t e r s :   -hoñ, -mai, -satu

Single units of objects which are thin and flat in shape—sheets, blankets, furoshiki, handkerchiefs, plates, boards, rugs, leaves, etc.—are counted with the counter -mai, which combines with numerals of Series I.   Numbers from 1 to 10 are:

i⌐ti¬-mai	'1 thin, flat unit'	ro⌐ku¬-mai	'6 thin, flat units'
ni¬-mai	'2 thin, flat units'	na⌐na¬-mai or	
sa¬ñ-mai	'3 thin, flat units'	si⌐ti¬-mai	'7 thin, flat units'
yo¬ñ-mai or		ha⌐ti¬-mai	'8 thin, flat units'
yo-mai	'4 thin, flat units'	kyu¬u-mai	'9 thin, flat units'
go-mai	'5 thin, flat units'	zyu¬u-mai	'10 thin, flat units'

Question word: na¬ñ-mai 'how many thin, flat units?'

Single units of objects which are long and cylindrical in shape—pens, pencils, cigarettes, bottles, arms, legs, trees, poles, cutflowers, etc.—are counted with the counter -hoñ, which combines with numerals of Series I.   Some combinations of numeral + counter in this series undergo assimilation: namely, '1,' '3,' '6,' '8,' '10.'   The numbers from one to ten are:

i¬p-poñ	'1 long, cylindrical unit'
ni¬-hoñ	'2 long, cylindrical units'
sa¬ñ-boñ	'3 long, cylindrical units'
yo¬ñ-hoñ or si¬-hoñ	'4 long, cylindrical units'
go-hoñ	'5 long, cylindrical units'
ro¬p-poñ	'6 long, cylindrical units'
na⌐na¬-hoñ or si⌐ti¬-hoñ	'7 long, cylindrical units'
ha¬p-poñ or ha⌐ti¬-hoñ	'8 long, cylindrical units'
kyu¬u-hoñ	'9 long, cylindrical units'
zi¬p-poñ or zyu¬p-poñ	'10 long, cylindrical units'

Question word: na¬ñ-boñ 'how many long, cylindrical units?'

Single units of bound objects—books, magazines, albums, etc.—are counted with the counter -satu, which combines with numerals of Series I.   Some combinations of numeral + counter in this series undergo assimilation: namely, '1,' '8,' '10.'   The numbers from one to ten are:

i⌐s-satu¬	'1 bound unit'	ro⌐ku-satu¬	'6 bound units'
ni¬-satu	'2 bound units'	na⌐na¬-satu or	
sa¬ñ-satu	'3 bound units'	si⌐ti-satu¬	'7 bound units'
yo¬ñ-satu	'4 bound units'	ha⌐s-satu¬	'8 bound units'
go-⌐satu¬	'5 bound units'	kyu¬u-satu	'9 bound units'
		zi⌐s-satu¬ or	
		zyu⌐s-satu¬	'10 bound units'

Question word: na¬ñ-satu 'how many bound units?'

Numbers are nominals and accordingly occur in the same kinds of patterns as nominals. They occur frequently in the nominal pattern described in the following note.

3.   Extent

A Japanese word or phrase which asks or answers the question 'how many?'
'how much?' 'how far?' or 'how long?' with reference to an inflected expression, regularly occurs without a following particle.[1] Compare:

Pe⌐ñ o kudasai. 'Please give me a pen.' (tells WHAT I want)
Su⌐ko⌐si kudasai. 'Please give me a little (or a few).' (tells HOW MUCH
   or HOW MANY I want)
Hu⌐rosiki g̃a arima⌐su. 'I have a furoshiki.' (tells WHAT I have)
I⌐ti⌐-mai arimasu. 'I have one (thin, flat object).' (tells HOW MANY I
   have)

Hurosiki (g̃a) i⌐ti⌐-mai arimasu. 'I have one furoshiki.' (lit. 'There are furoshiki to the extent of one thin, flat unit.') contains the information of the last
two sentences. In Japanese, the WHAT occurs as the subject or object or topic
followed by particle g̃a, o, or wa, and the HOW MANY or HOW MUCH occurs
as an extent expression, without a following particle.

When the WHAT is apparent from the context, it is regularly omitted. For
example, in Zyu⌐u-eñ kudasa⌐i. 'Please give me ¥ 10,' zyuu-eñ tells HOW
MUCH I want; the WHAT (i.e. money) is apparent from the counter and is not
explicitly stated.

Examples:

Kore (o) ⌐mo⌐tto oneg̃ai-simasu. 'I'd like more of this.' (Lit. 'I'd like
   this to a greater extent.')
Sore (o) ⌐ze⌐ñbu si⌐ma⌐sita. 'I did all of that.' (Lit. 'I did that to the extent of the whole thing.')
Ha⌐iza⌐ra (g̃a) ta⌐kusañ irima⌐su. 'I need lots of ashtrays.' (Lit. 'Ashtrays are needed to the extent of many.')
Eñpitu (g̃a) ⌐na⌐ñ-boñ a⌐rima⌐su ka˩   'How many pencils are there?'
   (Lit. 'There are pencils to the extent of how many long, cylindrical
   units?')
Ha⌐iza⌐ra (o) mi-⌐ttu kaima⌐sita. 'I bought three ashtrays.' (Lit. 'I bought
   ashtrays to the extent of three units.')

The hi⌐to⌐-tu, hu⌐ta-tu⌐ series is regularly used to count all the many inanimate unit objects for which there are no specialized counters. It is also frequently used alternatively with specialized counters for counting inanimate unit
objects which do have specialized counters. This series, then, is safer for the
beginning student to use until his stock of specialized counters is enlarged.
For example, if a student didn't know the counter -satu and said Ho⌐ñ o hu⌐ta-tu
kaima⌐sita 'I bought two books,' a Japanese would have no difficulty understanding him, whereas if he substituted the mathematical ni⌐ without a counter, most
Japanese listeners would be baffled.

---

[1] Irrespective of formality. This is different from the optional omission of
g̃a, wa, and o in conversation.

The order of the WHAT preceding the quantity expression in the above examples is the usual one. The reverse order also exists, however, with no difference in basic structure but only in emphasis. Thus: Ta˥kusa˥n̄ ha˥i-za˥ra ḡa irimasu. 'I need LOTS of ashtrays.'

The particle to 'and' may occur with extent patterns. A common pattern consists of—

nominal being counted or measured (+ particle wa, ḡa, or o)
+ extent expression
+ to,
+ nominal being counted or measured (+ particle wa, ḡa, or o)
+ extent expression

Thus:

Ka˥mi˥ (o) ˥ni˥- mai to, eñpitu (o) ˥sa˥n̄-bon̄ ka˥ima˥sita.   'I bought two sheets of paper and three pencils.'

See also Basic Sentences 12 and 15.

4.   Particle no

The particle no occurs between nominals with the meaning 'the preceding nominal describes the following nominal'—that is to say, A no B is an A kind of B. For example:

To˥okyoo no ti˥zu	'Tokyo map(s)' or 'map(s) of Tokyo'
Amerika no tabako	'American cigarettes' or ' cigarettes in America'
asita no siñbuñ	'tomorrow's newspaper(s)' or 'newspaper(s) tomorrow'
Tookyoo no siñbuñ	'Tokyo newspaper(s)' or 'Tokyo's newspaper(s)' or 'newspapers in Tokyo'
Tookyoo no Tanaka-sañ	'Mr. Tanaka from Tokyo' or 'Mr. Tanaka in Tokyo'
a˥na˥ta no zibiki	'your dictionary'
wa˥takusi no ho˥n̄	'my book'

There is no single word in English which is exactly equivalent to no. Sometimes (by no means always) it corresponds to English 'of.' A nominal + no sequence may indicate possession, location, origin, or other things; but in every instance, it is descriptive.

An adjectival or demonstrative describing a nominal has no connecting particle; but a nominal describing a nominal is regularly followed by no. Compare:

a˥tarasi˥i zassi 'new magazine'
kono zassi 'this magazine'
Nihon̄ no zassi 'Japanese magazine'

When a nominal has more than one describing word or phrase, a nominal + no sequence may be separated from the nominal it describes by another descriptive word or phrase.[1] Thus:

Tookyoo no o⌐oki¬i ⌐ti¬zu 'a big map of Tokyo'
  (ti¬zu described by Tookyoo and o⌐oki¬i)

Tanaka-sañ no so⌐no ho¬ñ 'that book of Mr. Tanaka's'
  (ho¬ñ described by Tanaka-sañ and sono)

Tanaka-sañ no To⌐okyoo no ti¬zu 'Mr. Tanaka's map of Tokyo'
  (ti¬zu described by Tanaka-sañ and Tookyoo)

It is also possible for the nominal of a nominal + no sequence to be described:[2]

a⌐tarasi¬i zassi no kami   'the paper in new magazines'
  (ka⌐mi¬ described by zassi, which is described by a⌐tarasi¬i)

so⌐no zibiki¬ no kami   'the paper in that dictionary'
  (ka⌐mi¬ described by zi⌐biki¬, which is described by sono)

Ni⌐hoñ no ho¬ñ no kami[3]   'the paper in Japanese books'
  (ka⌐mi¬ described by ho¬ñ, which is described by Ni⌐ho¬ñ)

In some special cases, a nominal describes another nominal directly without an intervening no (for example: mo⌐o suko¬si 'a little more'). Such combinations should be memorized as they occur.

When particle no immediately precedes the nominal no 'one(s),' the two no are contracted to a single no: that is, x no no is contracted to x no [4] (with no accented if x is unaccented). The contraction occurs in the same kinds of patterns as nominals. Compare:

---

[1] In such cases, the two descriptive words or phrases are usually not in the same accent phrase.

[2] In such cases, the descriptive words or phrases are usually in the same accent phrase.

[3] With different intonation, these three phrases could mean 'new paper in (or for) magazines,' 'that paper in (or for) dictionaries,' 'Japanese paper in (or for) books.' With these meanings, the final nominal in each case has two modifiers (cf. the examples in the preceding group above).

[4] x no (in which no = particle) and x no (the contraction of x no no) are distinguished by context: the former must be followed by a nominal which it describes.

Ta⌐naka-sañ de⌐su. 'It's Mr. Tanaka.'

Ta⌐naka-sañ no ho⌐ñ desu. 'It's Mr. Tanaka's book.'

Ta⌐naka-sañ no⌐ desu. 'It's Mr. Tanaka's (one).'

(Tanaka-sañ no 'Mr. Tanaka's' + no 'one' = Ta⌐naka-sañ no⌐   'one belonging to Mr. Tanaka')

Tookyoo wa o⌐oki⌐i desu. 'Tokyo is big.'

To⌐okyoo no ti⌐zu wa o⌐oki⌐i desu. 'The map of Tokyo is big.'

To⌐okyoo no⌐ wa o⌐oki⌐i desu. 'The one of Tokyo is big.'

(Tookyoo no 'of Tokyo' + no 'one' = To⌐okyoo no⌐ 'the one of Tokyo')

A⌐tarasi⌐i To⌐okyoo no ti⌐zu wa o⌐oki⌐i desu. 'The new map of Tokyo is big.'

A⌐tarasi⌐i To⌐okyoo no⌐ wa o⌐oki⌐i desu. 'The new one of Tokyo is big.' (No 'one' modified by a⌐tarasi⌐i and by Tookyoo no, with no + no contracted to a single no)

5. koñna, soñna, añna, do⌐ñna

Koñna 'this kind (of),' soñna and añna 'that kind (of),' and do⌐ñna 'what kind (of)?' modify nominals directly, without an intervening particle. The nominals may or may not be preceded by other descriptive words or phrases. The spatial and relational meanings of this series are parallel to those of the kore and kono series.

Examples:

> koñna eñpitu 'this kind of pencil'
> so⌐ñna ti⌐zu 'that kind of map'
> a⌐ñna waru⌐i ⌐ho⌐ñ 'a bad book like that'
> do⌐ñna a⌐tarasi⌐i ⌐pe⌐ñ 'what kind of new pen?'

The Japanese equivalent of 'what color?' is do⌐ñna iro (lit. 'what kind of color?') or the compound word naniiro.

6. moo ~ mo⌐tto

Mo⌐tto means 'more.' It occurs as an extent expression with verbals (mo⌐tto ka⌐ima⌐sita 'I bought more'), adjectivals (mo⌐tto ⌐i⌐i 'it's better'), and a nominal + √de⌐su (mo⌐tto ⌐ki⌐ree desu 'it's prettier').

Moo means 'more' IF FOLLOWED IMMEDIATELY WITHIN THE SAME ACCENT PHRASE BY A NUMBER OR INDEFINITE QUANTITY EXPRESSION.[1]

---

[1] Ta⌐kusa⌐ñ 'many' or 'much' does not occur in this pattern.

Examples:

> moo iti-do 'one time more'
> mo⌐o iti⌐-mai 'one thin, flat unit more'
> mo⌐o hyaku⌐-eñ '¥100 more'
> mo⌐o suko⌐si 'a little more'

7. dake

A nominal followed by dake 'just,' 'only,' 'no more than' may occur as an extent expression without a following particle.

Examples:

> Ta⌐naka-sañ dake ikima⌐sita. 'Just Mr. Tanaka went.'
> Su⌐ko⌐si dake onegai-simasu. 'I'd like just a little.'
> O⌐mosiro⌐i zassi wa ko⌐re dake⌐ desu.[1] 'This is the only interesting magazine.' (Lit. 'As for interesting magazines, it's just this.')

8. —— mo —— mo

x mo y mo, in which x and y are subject or object nominals (with or without preceding descriptive expressions), means 'both x and y' or 'x AND y.' With a negative, it means 'neither x nor y,' 'not x OR y.'

Examples:

> Pe⌐ñ mo e⌐ñpitu mo arima⌐su. 'There are pens AND pencils.'
> Ti⌐isa⌐i ⌐ti⌐zu mo o⌐oki⌐i ⌐ti⌐zu mo ku⌐dasa⌐i. 'Give me the small map AND the big map.'
> A⌐na⌐ta no mo Ta⌐naka-sañ no⌐ mo onegai-simasu. 'I'd like both yours (lit. your one) and Mr. Tanaka's (one).'
> Pe⌐ñ mo e⌐ñpitu mo arimase⌐ñ. 'I don't have a pen OR a pencil.'

DRILLS

A. Substitution Drill

1. I'd like one of those.	Sore (o) hi⌐to⌐-tu onegai-simasu.
2. I'd like two of those (thin, flat objects).	Sore (o) ⌐ni⌐-mai onegai-simasu.
3. I'd like three of those (bound objects).	Sore (o) ⌐sa⌐ñ-satu onegai-simasu.
4. I'd like four of those (long, cylindrical objects).	Sore (o) ⌐yo⌐ñ-hoñ onegai-simasu.

---

[1] Dake is regularly accented (da⌐ke⌐) in its occurrences before √desu.

  5. I'd like more of that.   Sore (o) ⌐motto⌐ oneḡai-simasu.
  6. I'd like a little more of that. Sore (o) mo⌐o sukōsi oneḡai-simasu.
  7. I'd like one more of those.   Sore (o) mo⌐o hito⌐-tu oneḡai-simasu.
  8. I'd like all of that.   Sore (o) ⌐ze⌐ñbu oneḡai-simasu.
  9. I'd like just a little of that. Sore (o) su⌐ko⌐si dake oneḡai-simasu.
 10. I'd like ten of those.   Sore (o) to⌐o oneḡai-sima⌐su.

B. Substitution Drill

  1. I bought lots of cigarettes.   Tabako (o) ta⌐kusañ kaima⌐sita.
  2. I bought one ashtray.   Ha⌐iza⌐ra (o) hi⌐to⌐-tu ka⌐ima⌐sita.
  3. I bought three maps.   Ti⌐zu (o) ⌐sa⌐n-mai ka⌐ima⌐sita.
  4. I bought a little paper.   Ka⌐mi⌐ (o) su⌐ko⌐si ka⌐ima⌐sita.
  5. I bought ten pencils.   Eñpitu (o) ⌐zyu⌐p-poñ ka⌐ima⌐sita.
  6. I bought two dictionaries.   Zi⌐biki⌐ (o) ⌐ni⌐-satu ka⌐ima⌐sita.
  7. I bought three furoshiki.   Hurosiki (o) ⌐sa⌐ñ-mai ka⌐ima⌐sita.
  8. I bought one pen.   Pe⌐ñ (o) ⌐i⌐p-poñ ka⌐ima⌐sita.
  9. I bought one book.   Ho⌐ñ (o) i⌐s-satu kaima⌐sita.
 10. I bought five sheets of paper. Ka⌐mi⌐ (o) go-⌐mai kaima⌐sita.

C. Substitution Drill

  1. I have both a newspaper and   Si⌐ñbuñ mo zassi mo arima⌐su.
     a magazine. [1]
  2. I have neither a newspaper   Si⌐ñbuñ mo zassi mo arimase⌐ñ.
     nor a magazine.
  3. I bought both a newspaper   Si⌐ñbuñ mo zassi mo kaima⌐sita.
     and a magazine.
  4. I forgot both the newspaper   Si⌐ñbuñ mo zassi mo wasurema⌐sita.
     and the magazine.
  5. I have both a newspaper and   Si⌐ñbuñ mo zassi mo gozaima⌐su.
     a magazine.
  6. I have neither a newspaper   Si⌐ñbuñ mo zassi mo gozaimase⌐ñ.
     nor a magazine.
  7. I'd like both a newspaper   Si⌐ñbuñ mo zassi mo oneḡai-sima⌐su.
     and a magazine.
  8. Please give me both a news-   Si⌐ñbuñ mo zassi mo kudasa⌐i.
     paper and a magazine.
  9. Please show me both the   Si⌐ñbuñ mo zassi mo mi⌐sete kudasai.
     newspaper and the magazine.

D. Substitution Drill

  1. That's all there are of ash-   Ha⌐iza⌐ra wa so⌐re dake⌐ desu.
     trays.

----

[1] In any given situation, the use of 'a' or 'the' in the English equivalents
would be determined by the context in which the Japanese sentence occurred.

2. That's all there are of dictionaries.   Zi⌐biki⌐ wa so⌐re dake⌐ desu.

3. That's all there are of this kind (of one).   Ko⌐ñna no⌐ wa so⌐re dake⌐ desu.

4. That's all there are of new ones.   A⌐tarasi⌐i no wa so⌐re dake⌐ desu.

5. That's all there are of good ones.   I⌐i no wa so⌐re dake⌐ desu.

6. That's all there are of red ones.   A⌐ka⌐i no wa so⌐re dake⌐ desu.

7. That's all there are of maps of America.   A⌐merika no ti⌐zu wa so⌐re dake⌐ desu.

8. That's all there are of today's papers.   Kyo⌐o no siñbuñ wa so⌐re dake⌐ desu.

9. That's all there are of yesterday's (ones).   Ki⌐no⌐o no wa so⌐re dake⌐ desu.

10. That's all there are of English ones.   I⌐ḡirisu no⌐ wa so⌐re dake⌐ desu.

E. Substitution Drill

1. What (kind of) color would you like? (Lit. What kind of color is good?)   Do⌐ñna i⌐ro⌐ ḡa yo⌐rosi⌐i desu ka⌐

2. Which one would you like?   Do⌐re ḡa yo⌐rosi⌐i desu ka⌐

3. What would you like?   Na⌐ni ḡa yo⌐rosi⌐i desu ka⌐

4. Which map would you like?   Do⌐no ⌐ti⌐zu ḡa yo⌐rosi⌐i desu ka⌐

5. What kind of map would you like?   Do⌐ñna ⌐ti⌐zu ḡa yo⌐rosi⌐i desu ka⌐

6. Would you like this kind of paper?   Ko⌐ñna kami⌐ ḡa yo⌐rosi⌐i desu ka⌐

7. Would you like that kind of magazine?   So⌐ñna zassi ḡa yorosi⌐i desu ka⌐

8. Would you like that map?   A⌐no ti⌐zu ḡa yo⌐rosi⌐i desu ka⌐

F. Substitution Drill (based on Grammatical Note 4)

(Insert the substitution item in the model sentence as a modifier of pe⌐ñ with or without a following particle as required.)

1. Please show me that pen.   So⌐no pe⌐ñ (o) ⌐mi⌐sete kudasai.

2. Please show me your pen.   A⌐na⌐ta no ⌐pe⌐ñ (o) ⌐mi⌐sete kudasai.

3. Please show me a good pen.   I⌐i ⌐pe⌐ñ (o) ⌐mi⌐sete kudasai.

4. Please show me this kind of pen.   Ko⌐ñna pe⌐ñ (o) ⌐mi⌐sete kudasai.

5. Please show me a black pen.   Ku⌐ro⌐i ⌐pe⌐ñ (o) ⌐mi⌐sete kudasai.

6. Please show me an American pen.   A⌐merika no pe⌐ñ (o) ⌐mi⌐sete kudasai.

7. Please show me Mr. Tanaka's pen.   Ta⌐naka-sañ no pe⌐ñ (o) ⌐mi⌐sete kudasai.

8. Please show me that pen over there.   A⌐no pe⌐ñ (o) ⌐mi⌐sete kudasai.

9. Please show me a blue pen.   A⌐o⌐i ⌐pe⌐ñ (o) ⌐mi⌐sete kudasai.
10. Please show me a Japanese   Ni⌐hoñ no pe⌐ñ (o) ⌐mi⌐sete kudasai.
    pen.

G. Grammar Drill (based on Grammatical Note 4)

       Tutor: To⌐okyoo no ti⌐zu desu. 'It's a map of Tokyo.'
       Student: To⌐okyoo no⌐ desu. 'It's one of Tokyo.'

1. Si⌐ñbuñ no kami⌐ desu ka⌐   Si⌐ñbuñ no⌐ desu ka⌐
2. O⌐oki⌐i ⌐ti⌐zu (o) ka⌐ima⌐si-   O⌐oki⌐i no (o) ka⌐ima⌐sita.
    ta.
3. Ta⌐naka-sañ no ra⌐itaa desu   Ta⌐naka-sañ no⌐ desu ka⌐
    ka⌐
4. A⌐na⌐ta no ⌐ho⌐ñ desu ka⌐   A⌐na⌐ta no desu ka⌐
5. Kyo⌐o no siñbuñ (wa) ⌐su⌐ḡu   Kyo⌐o no (wa) ⌐su⌐ḡu kimasu.
    kimasu.
6. A⌐merika no pe⌐ñ (o) ⌐mi⌐-   A⌐merika no⌐ (o) ⌐mi⌐sete kudasai.
    sete kudasai.
7. Wa⌐takusi no siñbuñ de⌐su   Wa⌐takusi no⌐ desu yo⌐
    yo⌐
8. A⌐kai eñpitu (o) oneḡai-   A⌐ka⌐i no (o) oneḡai-simasu.
    sima⌐su.

H. Expansion Drill

1. I'd like [it].   O⌐neḡai-sima⌐su.
    I'd like three.   Mi-⌐ttu oneḡai-sima⌐su.
    I'd like three white ones,   Si⌐ro⌐i no mo mi-⌐ttu oneḡai-sima⌐su.
       too.
    I'd like three of those white   Sono si⌐ro⌐i no mo mi-⌐ttu oneḡai-si-
       ones, too.   ma⌐su.

2. I bought [it].   Ka⌐ima⌐sita.
    I bought two (long cylin-   Ni⌐-hoñ ka⌐ima⌐sita.
       drical units).
    I bought two pencils.   Eñpitu (o) ⌐ni⌐-hoñ ka⌐ima⌐sita.
    I bought one pen and two   Pe⌐ñ (o) ⌐i⌐p-poñ to, eñpitu (o) ⌐ni⌐-
       pencils.   hoñ ka⌐ima⌐sita.

3. How much is [it]?   I⌐kura desu ka⌐
    How much is one (thin, flat   I⌐ti⌐-mai ⌐i⌐kura desu ka⌐
       unit)?
    How much is one sheet of   Ka⌐mi⌐ (wa) i⌐ti⌐-mai ⌐i⌐kura desu ka⌐
       paper?
    How much is one sheet of   Ko⌐ñna kami⌐ (wa) i⌐ti⌐-mai   ⌐i⌐kura
       this kind of paper?   desu ka⌐

4. Do you have [any]?   Go⌐zaima⌐su ka⌐
    Do you have maps too?   Ti⌐zu mo go⌐zaima⌐su ka⌐

	Do you have maps of America too?	A⌈merika no ti⌉zu mo go⊢zaima⊣su ka⌟
	Do you have maps of England AND maps of America?	I⌈ḡirisu no ti⌉zu mo A⌈merika no ti⌉zu mo go⊢zaima⊣su ka⌟
5.	It's a dictionary.	Zi⌈biki⌉ desu.
	It's a new dictionary.	A⌈tarasi⌉i zi⊢biki⊣ desu.
	It's my new dictionary.	Bo⌉ku no a⌈tarasi⌉i zi⊢biki⊣ desu.
	This is my new dictionary.	Kore wa ⌈bo⌉ku no a⌈tarasi⌉i zi⊢biki⊣ desu.
6.	I don't want [it]!	I⌈rimase⌉n̄ yo⌟
	I don't want any books!	Ho⌉n̄ wa i⌈rimase⌉n̄ yo⌟
	I don't want any dull books!	Tu⌈mara⌉nai ⊢ho⊣n̄ wa i⌈rimase⌉n̄ yo⌟
	I don't want any dull books like that!	So⌈n̄na tumara⌉nai ⊢ho⊣n̄ wa i⌈rimase⌉n̄ yo⌟

SUPPLEMENTARY CONVERSATIONS

1. Smith: Sore o to⌈o kudasa⌉i.
 Clerk: To⌉o desu ka⌟ Ha⌉i.
 Smith: A⌉a, tyo⌉tto ⊢ma⊣tte kudasai. Zyu⌈uni oneḡai-sima⌉su.
 Clerk: Mo⌈o huta-tu⌉ desu ka⌟
 Smith: E⌉e, so⌉o desu.
 Clerk: Ka⌈sikomarima⌉sita. A⌈ri⌉ḡatoo gozaimasu.

2. Smith: Sono a⌈o⌉i ha⊢iza⊣ra o mu-⌈ttu kudasa⌉i.
 Clerk: Su⌈mimase⌉n̄ ḡa, kore wa i⌈tu⌉-tu da⌈ke⌉ desu ḡa_
 Smith: So⌉o desu ka_ Ano ki⌈iro⌉i no wa?
 Clerk: A⌈re mo itu⌉-tu da⊢ke⊣ desu. Do⌉o mo su⊢mimase⊣n̄.

English Equivalents

1. Smith: Give me ten of those.
 Clerk: Ten? All right.
 Smith: Oh, wait a minute. I'd like twelve.
 Clerk: Two more?
 Smith: Yes, that's right.
 Clerk: Certainly. Thank you.

2. Smith: Give me six of those blue ashtrays.
 Clerk: I'm sorry but there are only five of these (lit. as for these, it's just five). . .
 Smith: Oh? How about those yellow ones?
 Clerk: There are (lit. It is) just five of those, too. I'm very sorry.

EXERCISES

1. Ask for each of the following:

    a. one cigarette
    b. two of those dictionaries
    c. three red pencils
    d. ten sheets of this kind of white paper
    e. five of those small ashtrays
    f . one of those magazines
    g. two of these blue furoshiki
    h. a few of these
    i. all of that
    j. more of those
    k. a little more of that
    l. one more of those (i.e. ashtrays)
    m. one more of those (i.e. pens)
    n. one more of those (i.e. furoshiki)
    o. one more of those (i.e. books)
    p. one sheet of white paper and two sheets of blue paper
    q. two red pencils and three black ones

2. Practice the Basic Dialogues with variations and appropriate props.

Lesson 6. Locating People and Things

(a)

Tanaka

that place <u>or</u> there	soko
embassy	taⁿisiⁿkañ
American Embassy	Aⁿmerika-taisiⁿkañ
1. Is that (place) the American Embassy?	Soko (wa) Aⁿmerika-taisiⁿkañ desu ka˩

Smith

consulate	ryoⁿoziⁿkañ
2. No, it's the consulate.	Iie, ryoⁿoziⁿkañ desu yo˩

Tanaka

what place? <u>or</u> where?	doⁿko
3. Where's the embassy?	Taⁿisiⁿkañ wa ⁿdoⁿko desu ka˩

Smith

in Tokyo	Tookyoo ni
4. It's in Tokyo.	Toⁿokyoo ni arimaⁿsu.
this place <u>or</u> here	koko
as for in this place <u>or</u> in this place, comparatively speaking	koⁿko niⁿ wa
5. There isn't [one] here.	Koⁿko niⁿ wa aⁿrimaseⁿñ.

(b)

Smith (pointing)

station	eⁿki
Tokyo Station	Toⁿokyoⁿo-eki
this one (of two) <u>or</u> this way <u>or</u> hereabouts <u>or</u> here	kotira
side <u>or</u> direction <u>or</u> alternative	hoⁿo
this side <u>or</u> this direction	koⁿtira no hoⁿo
6. Is Tokyo Station this way? <u>or</u> Is Tokyo Station in this direction <u>or</u> on this side?	Toⁿokyoⁿo-eki (wa) koⁿtira deⁿsu ka˩ Toⁿokyoⁿo-eki (wa) koⁿtira no hoⁿo desu ka˩

Stranger

building (Western style)	bi˥ru
beyond <u>or</u> over there <u>or</u> the far side	mukoo
beyond the building	bi˥ru no mŭkoo

7. Yes. It's beyond that big build-ing.   E˥e. Ano o˻oki˥i ˺bi˥ru no mu˻koo de˥su.

Smith

8. I see. Thank you.   Wa˻karima˥sita. A˻ri g̃atoo gozaima-sita.

(c)

Smith

that place over there <u>or</u> over there	asoko <u>or</u> asuko
hotel (Western style)	ho˥teru
it's probably a hotel	ho˥teru desyoo

9. Do you suppose that (place) is a hotel?   Asuko (wa) ˻ho˥teru desyoo ka.

Yamamoto

hmm   sa˥a

10. I wonder. . . .   Sa˥a. Do˥o desyoo ka ˺ne˥e.

Tanaka

11. Oh, that IS a hotel.   A˥a, ho˥teru desu yo⌐

Smith

12. It's probably expensive, isn't it. <u>or</u> It must be expensive!   Ta˻ka˥i desyoo ˻ne˥e.

Yamamoto

13. It must be (that way)!   So˥o desyoo ˻ne˥e.

(d)

Smith

be in a place (of animate beings)	i˻ma˥su <u>or</u> o˻rima˥su ⌐ <u>or</u> i˻rassyaima˥su ⌐

14. Is Mr. Tanaka [in]?   Tanaka-sañ (wa) i˻ma˥su ka⌐   <u>or</u> Tanaka-sañ (wa) i˻rassyaima˥su ka⌐

Yamamoto

15. No, he isn't.   Iie, i˻mase˥ñ. <u>or</u> Iie, o˻rimase˥ñ. <u>or</u> Iie, i˻rassyaimase˥ñ.

Smith

which one (of two)?   or   do⌐tira
   which way?   or
   whereabouts? or where?
   in what place? or where?   do⌐ko ni   or
                                    do⌐tira ni

16. Where is he?   Do⌐ko ni i⌐ma⌐su ka↲   or
                                    Do⌐tira ni i⌐rassyaima⌐su ka↲

Yamamoto

   in Kyoto   Kyo⌐oto ni
17. He's in Kyoto.   Kyo⌐oto ni imasu.   or
                                    Kyo⌐oto ni orimasu.   or
                                    Kyo⌐oto ni irassyaimasu.

(e)

Smith

   in this area or around   kono heñ ni
      here
   telephone   deñwa   or
                                    o⌐de⌐ñwa +

18. Is(n't) there a telephone   Kono heñ ni deñwa (wa) arimase⌐ñ
     around here?   ka↲

Tanaka

   front   ma⌐e
   front of the station   e⌐ki no ⌐ma⌐e
   side   yoko
   both in front and at the   ma⌐e ni mo yo⌐ko ni⌐ mo
      side
19. There is (indeed). There's   A⌐rima⌐su yo↲ E⌐ki no ⌐ma⌐e ni mo
     [one] in front of the station yo⌐ko ni⌐ mo arimasu.
     AND at the side.

   department store   de⌐pa⌐ato
   in the department store too   de⌐pa⌐ato ni mo
20. And then there's [one] in that Sore kara, sono de⌐pa⌐ato ni mo ari-
     department store, too.   masu.

Smith

   building   ta⌐temo⌐no
21. Which building is the depart- De⌐pa⌐ato (wa) ⌐do⌐no ta⌐temo⌐no desu
     ment store?   ka↲   or
                                    Do⌐no ta⌐temo⌐no ḡa de⌐pa⌐ato desu
                                    ka↲

Tanaka

   next door or adjoining   tonari
   next door to the station   e⌐ki no tōnari
22. It's next door to the station. E⌐ki no to⌐nari de⌐su.

(f)

Smith

	post office	yu┌ubi┐ñkyoku
	the post office here <u>or</u> the post office in this place	ko┌ko no yuubi┐ñkyoku
23.	Where's the post office in this place?	Ko┌ko no yuubi┐ñkyoku (wa) ┌do┐ko ni a├rima┤su ka⌣

Tanaka

	vicinity	so┐ba
	immediate vicinity	su┐ḡu ├so┤ba
	right near the station	e┐ki no ┌su┐ḡu ├so┤ba
24.	The post office? It's right near the station.	Yu┌ubi┐ñkyoku desu ka⌣ E┐ki no ┌su┐ḡu ├so┤ba ni arimasu.
	bank	giñkoo
	next door to the bank	giñkoo no to┐nari
	the building next door to the bank	giñkoo no to┌nari no bi┐ru
25.	It's [the building] next door to the big bank.	O┌oki┐i giñkoo no to┌nari [no bi┐ru] desu.[1]

(g)

Smith

	inquire	u┌kaḡaima┐su ↓
	I'm just going to ask [you something] (but)	tyo┐tto u├kaḡaima┤su ḡa
	Imperial Hotel	Te┌ekoku-ho┐teru
26.	Excuse me but where is the Imperial Hotel?	Tyo┐tto u├kaḡaima┤su ḡa, Te┌ekoku-ho┐teru (wa) ┌do┐ko desyoo ka.

Stranger

	ahead	saki
	a little further ahead	mo┌o suko┐si saki
27.	The Imperial Hotel? It's a little further ahead.	Te┌ekoku-ho┐teru desu ka⌣ Mo┌o suko┐si saki desu.

Smith

	left	hidari
	the left side <u>or</u> toward the left	hi┌dari no ho┐o
28.	Is it [on] the left side?	Hi┌dari no ho┐o desu ka⌣

---

[1] Accent of short alternant: <u>de┐su.</u>

Stranger

right	mi⎴gi
the right side <u>or</u> toward the right	mi⌐gi no ho⌐o

29. No, it's [on] the right side.   Iie, mi⎴gi no ho⌐o desu.

Smith

Nikkatsu Building	Ni⌐kkatu⌐-biru[1]
beyond the Nikkatsu Building	Ni⌐kkatu⌐-biru no mŭkoo

30. Is it beyond the Nikkatsu Build-   Ni⌐kkatu⌐-biru no mu⌐koo de⌐su ka˩
ing?

Stranger

this side	temae

31. No, it's this side [of it].   Iie, te⌐mae de⌐su.

ADDITIONAL VOCABULARY[2]

bookstore	ho⌐ñya
cigar store	tabakoya
drugstore	kusuriya
fish market	sakanaya
flower shop	ha⌐na⌐ya
inn (Japanese style)	ryokañ
meat market	ni⌐ku⌐ya
park	kooeñ
school	gakkoo
store <u>or</u> shop (small)	mi⌐se⌐
theater	gekizyoo
toilet	be⌐ñzyo⌐ [3] <u>or</u> te⌐a⌐rai <u>or</u> o⌐tea⌐rai + [4] <u>or</u> to⌐iretto
vegetable store	yaoya

NOTES ON THE BASIC DIALOGUES

1. Words like A⌐merika-taisi⌐kañ, To⌐okyo⌐o-eki (sentence 6), Te⌐ekoku-ho⌐te-ru (sentence 26), and Nikkatu-biru (sentence 30) are single, compound

---

[1] Has unaccented alternant.

[2] Practice these words as substitutes for deñwa in Basic Sentence 18 (cf. Drill G, page 86.

[3] Man's word.

[4] Woman's word.

nominals, w h i c h name specific buildings o r organizations. Compare Tŏokyoᷱo-eki 'Tokyo Station' and Tŏokyoo no eᷱki 'station(s) in Tokyo' — i.e. any one(s) at all.

7.   Remember that an A no B combination (in which A and B are nominals) refers to a kind of B.   Thus, biᷱru no mukoo is a kind of mukoo, i.e. 'the far side described by the building' or 'beyond the building.' Muᷢkoo no biᷱru, on the other hand, is a kind of biᷱru, i.e. 'the building described by the far side' or 'the building over there.'

8.   Waᷢkarimaᷱsita often means 'I have understood what you just said (i.e. the information you just gave me, or what you just told me to do).'

18.   The negative here occurs as a less direct — and slightly more polite — alternative. It does not mean that the speaker expects a negative reply.

21.   Taᷢtemoᷱno is the general word for 'building,' but biᷱru is commonly used only in reference to large, Western-style buildings. The f i r s t alterna- tive of sentence 21 means literally ' As for the department store, which building is it? '

23.   Koko here refers to 'this place' meaning 'this town' or 'this village' or 'this particular section.' Koᷢko no yuubiᷱñkyoku is another example of the particle no between nominals the first of which describes the second.

24.   Suᷱg̃u ᷣsoᷣba is an example of one nominal describing another without the intervening particle no. Only certain nominals occur in this pattern.

26.   √Uᷢkag̃aimaᷱsu (gerund ukag̃atte) is a humble polite verbal. Tyoᷱtto uᷣka- g̃aimaᷣsu g̃a and suᷢmimaseᷱñ g̃a are both common Japanese equivalents of English 'excuse me but': the former is used when the speaker is about to request information, and the latter is an apology for interrupting, bothering, etc. Thus, in stopping a stranger on the street to ask for di- rections, either one may be used; in asking someone to do something, however, the former does not occur.

27.   Saki usually means ' ahead — on the same street or route,' whereas mukoo 'beyond,' 'over there' is a word of more general meaning.

GRAMMATICAL NOTES

1.   C o p u l a :   T e n t a t i v e

   Deᷢsyoᷱo is the less positive, less direct equivalent of deᷱsu. It will here- after be called the TENTATIVE of deᷱsu. Compare:

> Hoᷱñ desu. 'It's a book.'
> Hoᷱñ desyoo. 'It's probably a book,' 'I think it's a book,' 'It must be a book,' etc.

Both deᷱsu and deᷢsyoᷱo are formal.

   Like deᷱsu, deᷢsyoᷱo may refer to present or future time, and it follows nominals and adjectivals. (Other uses will be introduced later.) It is unaccented when the preceding word or phrase is accented.

Examples:

> Ta⌐naka-sañ desyo⌐o. 'It probably is (or will be) Mr. Tanaka.'
> I⌐i desyoo. 'I guess it's all right.'
> So⌐o desyoo. 'I guess that's right.'
> O⌐mosiro⌐i desyoo. 'It's probably interesting.'

In questions, the less direct de⌐syo⌐o is slightly more polite than de⌐su. Compare:

> Do⌐ko desu ka↗ 'Where is it?'
> Do⌐ko desyoo ka. 'Where would it be?' 'Where do you suppose it is?' etc. — or simply 'Where is it?'

The indicated difference in intonation is common.

Both de⌐syo⌐o statements and de⌐syo⌐o ka questions are often followed by exclamatory ne⌐e (Lesson 1, Grammatical Note 4). Thus:

> Da⌐me⌐ desyoo ⌐ne⌐e. 'It must be out of order!' 'I guess it is out of order, isn't it.'
> Ya⌐su⌐i desyoo ⌐ne⌐e. 'It must be cheap!' 'I guess it is cheap, isn't it.'
> Na⌐ñ desyoo ka ⌐ne⌐e. 'What DO you suppose it is!' 'I'm wondering what it is,' 'What is it indeed!'
> Do⌐o desyoo ka ⌐ne⌐e. 'I wonder [about what you said],' 'I wonder how [what you said] would be,' 'How WOULD it be!'

WARNING: Be sure to distinguish between the pronunciation of de⌐syo⌐o (de-⌐syo⌐-o) and de⌐su yo (de⌐-su-yo). The former indicates doubt, probability, indefiniteness, indirectness, etc., whereas the latter indicates certainty, assurance, emphasis, etc.

2. do⌐ko desu ka ~ do⌐ko ni a⌐rima⌐su ka

X de⌐su (in which X is a nominal) has two basic meanings: '[it] is X' or '[it] is described by X.' Accordingly, depending on context, To⌐okyoo de⌐su means either '[it] is Tokyo' or '[it] is described by—i.e. has something to do with—Tokyo.' Compare:

> Koko wa To⌐okyoo de⌐su. 'This (place) is Tokyo.'

and:

> Ta⌐isi⌐kañ wa To⌐okyoo de⌐su. 'The embassy is described by Tokyo' —i.e. 'The embassy is in Tokyo.'

In other words, if √de⌐su is preceded by a place word (or phrase), the combination may signify equivalence or it may describe the location of something or someone. Accordingly, do⌐ko desu ka, depending on context, means either 'what place is it?' or 'what place describes it?'—i.e. 'where is it?'

Examples:

> Koko wa ⌐do⌐ko desu ka↗ 'What place is this (place)?'
> Tanaka-sañ wa ⌐do⌐ko desu ka↗ 'Mr. Tanaka is described by what place?'—i.e. 'Where is Mr. Tanaka?'

Koko wa O⌐osaka de⌐su. 'This (place) is Osaka.'
A⌐no ho⌐teru wa O⌐osaka de⌐su. 'That hotel is described by Osaka'—
i.e. 'That hotel is in Osaka.'

There is a second construction, used only in describing location:

$$\text{Place expression} + \underline{\text{ni}} + \begin{cases} \sqrt{a^{\ulcorner}\text{rima}^{\urcorner}\text{su}} \\ \sqrt{i^{\ulcorner}\text{ma}^{\urcorner}\text{su}} \end{cases}$$

A⌐rima⌐su in its location meaning refers to inanimate objects and i⌐ma⌐su refers to the location of animate beings. The particle ni follows the place expression which tells where something or someone is.

Examples:

Ta⌐isi⌐kañ wa To⌐okyoo ni arima⌐su.   'The embassy is located in
   Tokyo.'
Tanaka-sañ wa ⌐do⌐ko ni i⌐ma⌐su ka⌐ 'Where (i.e. in what place) is
   Mr. Tanaka located?'
A⌐no ho⌐teru wa O⌐osaka ni arima⌐su.   'That hotel is located in
   Osaka.'

To sum up: Place expression + de⌐su means either '[it] is the place' or
'[it] is described by the place.' In the latter meaning, it is used more or less
interchangeably with a pattern consisting of place expression + ni + a⌐rima⌐su
∼ i⌐ma⌐su. '[something or somebody] is located in the place.' Thus, the
equivalent of 'it is the front' is ma⌐e desu; the equivalent of 'it is in front' is
ma⌐e desu or ma⌐e ni arimasu.

3.   i⌐ma⌐su ∼ o⌐rima⌐su ∼ i⌐rassyaima⌐su

These three verbals all occur with the same lexical meaning: 'an animate
object is located in a place.' They differ only in politeness.

I⌐ma⌐su belongs to the plain level—the level of a⌐rima⌐su, wa⌐karima⌐su,
ka⌐ima⌐su, etc.

Like go⌐zaima⌐su, o⌐rima⌐su and i⌐rassyaima⌐su are polite words, but
go⌐zaima⌐su is neutrally polite (+), whereas o⌐rima⌐su is humble (↓) and i⌐ras-
syaima⌐su is honorific (↑).

O⌐rima⌐su is used most commonly in reference to oneself, members of one's
own family, and one's own close friends, or in any situation where the speaker
wishes to talk politely without exalting the position of the subject to which the
verbal refers. I⌐rassyaima⌐su, on the other hand, exalts the position of its
subject and, accordingly, is NEVER USED IN REFERENCE TO ONESELF.
Compare:

Employee: Ta⌐naka-sañ irassyaima⌐su ka⌐ 'Is Mr. Tanaka (i.e. the boss)
   in?'
Tanaka's Secretary: Ha⌐a, i⌐rassyaima⌐su. 'Yes, he is.'

Visitor: Ta⌐naka-sañ irassyaima⌐su ka⌐ 'Is Mr. Tanaka in?'
Tanaka's co-worker: Ha⌐a, o⌐rima⌐su. 'Yes, he is.'

Oᴵrimaᴵsu and iᴵrassyaimaᴵsu, like many other polite words introduced previously, are used more commonly—though by no means exclusively—by women.

4. Particle ni of Location

The particle ni 'in,' 'on,' 'at' follows a nominal of place which indicates the location of something animate or inanimate, and is followed by √aᴵrimaᴵsu or √iᴵmaᴵsu or a more polite equivalent (cf. Note 2 above).

Examples:

> Aᴵsoko ni arimaᴵsu. 'It's over there (lit. in that place).'
> Asoko ni koᴵoeñ ḡa arimaᴵsu. 'Over there there's a park.'
> Gaᴵkkoo no maᴵe ni imasu. '[He] is in front of the school.'
> Teᴵekoku-hoᴵteru ni orimasu. 'I'm at the Imperial Hotel.'

Note that particle ni is not ordinarily used in desu sentences. Compare:

> Tonari wa giᴵñkoo deᴵsu. 'Next door is a bank.'

but:

> Tonari ni giᴵñkoo ḡa arimaᴵsu. '(In the place) next door there's a bank.'

5. Multiple Particles

In Japanese there are many occurrences of multiple particles—sequences of more than one consecutive particle. That is to say, a particle may follow a sequence that ends with a particle. Study the following examples:

> waᴵtakusi no hoᴵñ ni 'in my book'
> waᴵtakusi no hoᴵñ ni mo 'in my book too,' as in—
> Taᴵnaka-sañ no hoᴵñ ni arimasu. . . . Waᴵtakusi no hoᴵñ ni mo arimasu. 'It's in Mr. Tanaka's book. . . . It's in my book, too.'
> koko ni 'in this place'
> koᴵko niᴵ wa[1] 'in this place, comparatively speaking,' as in—
> Doᴵko ni aᴵrimaᴵsu ka⌋ . . . Toᴵokyoo ni arimaᴵsu. Koᴵko niᴵ wa aᴵrimaseᴵñ. 'Where is it? . . . It's in Tokyo. It isn't here.'

Particles wa and mo may follow ni and various other particles which will be introduced later; but they replace, rather than follow, ḡa and o. Compare the following groups:

> { Koᴵko ni arimaᴵsu. 'It's here.'
> { Soᴵko niᴵ wa aᴵrimaseᴵñ. 'It isn't there.'
> { Aᴵsoko niᴵ mo aᴵrimaᴵñ. 'It isn't over there either.'

---

[1] Particle ni acquires an accent when it follows an unaccented word and is followed by an unaccented particle.

$\begin{cases}$ Ta⌐bako g̃a arima⌐su. 'There are cigarettes.'
Ma⌐tti mo arimasu. 'There are matches, too.'
Ra⌐itaa wa a⌐rimase⌐ñ. 'There isn't a lighter.' $\end{cases}$

$\begin{cases}$ Ho⌐ñ o ka⌐ima⌐sita. 'I bought a book.'
Za⌐ssi mo kaima⌐sita. 'I bought a magazine, too.'
Siñbuñ wa ka⌐imase⌐ñ desita. 'A paper I didn't buy.' $\end{cases}$

6.   Place - Word Series

koko	kotira	ko⌐tti⌐
soko	sotira	so⌐tti⌐
asoko	atira	a⌐tti⌐
do⌐ko	do⌐tira	do⌐tti

The above words—all nominals—bear an obvious resemblance to the kore, kono, and koñna series.

The first group (koko, soko, etc.) refer specifically to place:

koko 'this place' or 'here'
soko 'that place' or 'there'
asoko[1] 'that place over there' or 'over there'
do⌐ko 'what place?' or 'where?'

The words of the second group (kotira, sotira, etc.) have several meanings:

(1) they refer to one alternative out of two possibilities.[2]

Compare: Do⌐re desu ka⌣ . . . Ko⌐re de⌐su.   'Which one (of three or more) is it? . . . It's this one.'

and: Do⌐tira desu ka⌣ . . . Ko⌐tira de⌐su. 'Which one (of two) is it? . . . It's this one.'

(2) they have a directional meaning. In a different context—for example, pointing to a fork in the road—the last example above would have a different meaning:

Do⌐tira desu ka⌣ . . . Ko⌐tira de⌐su. 'Which way is it? . . . It's this way.'

(3) they have an indefinite locational meaning: 'hereabouts,' 'thereabouts,' 'whereabouts.' The indirect and vague, as mentioned before, is more polite in Japanese than the direct and specific; accordingly, the kotira series with meaning (3) often occurs as a polite equivalent of the koko

---

[1] Asuko is an alternant of asoko. It is particularly common in rapid speech.

[2] The kore series more commonly refers to inanimate objects, but the kotira series in meaning (1) refers equally to animate beings and to objects.

series.   Thus, in asking a stranger for the location of something,
do⌐tira desyoo ka [lit.] 'whereabouts would it be?' is simply a more indirect — and therefore m o r e polite — way of s a y i n g 'where is it?'
Similarly, with polite √go⌐zaima⌐su a n d √i⌐rassyaima⌐su, the kotira
series is more common than the koko series. Do⌐tira ni i⌐rassyaima⌐su
ka is a more polite way of saying do⌐ko ni i⌐ma⌐su ka 'where is he?'

One further use of the kotira series will be introduced later.

Summary: kotira 'this one (of two),' 'this way,' 'hereabouts,' 'here'

   sotira and atira[1] 'that way (of two),' 'that way,' 'thereabouts,'
   'there'

   do⌐tira 'which one (of two)?' 'which way?' 'whereabouts?'
   'where?'

The ko⌐tti⌐ series in an informal, contracted equivalent of the kotira series.
Its members have the same meanings but they are used in less formal speech.

7.   -ya

Product name + -ya means 'place where the product is sold' or 'dealer in
the product.' Thus:

tabako 'cigarette' or 'tobacco'   tabakoya 'cigar store' or 'tobacco dealer'
ho⌐ñ 'book'   ho⌐ñya 'bookstore' or 'book dealer'
ha⌐na⌐ 'flower'   ha⌐na⌐ya 'flower shop' or 'florist'
kusuri 'medicine'   kusuriya 'drugstore' or 'druggist'
ni⌐ku⌐ 'meat'   ni⌐ku⌐ya 'meat market' or 'butcher'
sakana 'fish'   sakanaya 'fish market' or 'fish man'

The dealer is often addressed with the appropriate -ya word + -sañ. For
example:

   Ku⌐suriyasañ de⌐su ka⌐   'Are you the druggist?'

DRILLS

A.   Substitution Drill

   1.   Where is that?   Sore (wa) ⌐do⌐ko desu ka⌐
   2.   Which one (of three or   Sore (wa) ⌐do⌐re desu ka⌐
        more) is that?
   3.   How is that? or   Sore (wa) ⌐do⌐o desu ka⌐
        How about that?

---

[1] The differences between the two words are parallel to the differences between sore and are (cf. Lesson 2, Grammatical Note 3).

    4. What is that?   Sore (wa) ⌈na⌉n̄ desu ka⌒

    5. Which way (<u>or</u> which of
        two, <u>or</u> whereabouts) is
        that?   Sore (wa) ⌈do⌉tira desu ka⌒

    6. Which building is that?   Sore (wa) ⌈do⌉no ˥bi˥ru desu ka⌒

    7. How is that? <u>or</u>   Sore (wa) i⌈ka⌉ḡa desu ka⌒
        How about that?

    8. How much is that?   Sore (wa) ⌈i⌉kura desu ka⌒

    9. How many yen is that?   Sore (wa) ⌈na⌉n̄-en̄ desu ka⌒

  10. Which way (<u>or</u> which of
        two, <u>or</u> whereabouts) is
        that?   Sore (wa) ⌈do⌉tti desu ka⌒

B. Substitution Drill

    1. It's beyond the embassy.   Ta⌈isi⌉kan̄ no mu⌈koo de⌉su.

    2. It's in front of the embassy. Ta⌈isi⌉kan̄ no ⌈ma⌉e desu.

    3. It's at the side of the em-
        bassy.   Ta⌈isi⌉kan̄ no yo⌈ko de⌉su.

    4. It's next door to the em-
        bassy.   Ta⌈isi⌉kan̄ no to⌈nari de⌉su.

    5. It's near the embassy.   Ta⌈isi⌉kan̄ no ⌈so⌉ba desu.

    6. It's right near the embassy. Ta⌈isi⌉kan̄ no ⌈su⌉ḡu ˥so˥ba desu.

    7. It's up ahead, past the em-
        bassy.   Ta⌈isi⌉kan̄ no sa⌈ki de⌉su.

    8. It's this side of the em-
        bassy.   Ta⌈isi⌉kan̄ no te⌈mae de⌉su.

    9. It's to the right of the em-
        bassy.   Ta⌈isi⌉kan̄ no mi⌈ḡi de⌉su.

  10. It's to the left of the em-
        bassy.   Ta⌈isi⌉kan̄ no hi⌈dari de⌉su.

C. Substitution Drill

    1. It's the store over there.   Mu⌈koo no mise⌉ desu.

    2. It's the store in front.   Ma⌉e no mi˥se˥ desu.

    3. It's the store at the side.   Yo⌈ko no mise⌉ desu.

    4. It's the store next door.   To⌈nari no mise⌉ desu.

    5. It's the store right near.   Su⌉ḡu ˥so˥ba no mi˥se˥ desu.

    5. It's the store up ahead.   Sa⌈ki no mise⌉ desu.

    7. It's the store on the right. Mi⌈ḡi no mise⌉ desu.

    8. It's the store on the left.   Hi⌈dari no mise⌉ desu.

    9. It's a store in Tokyo.   To⌈okyoo no mise⌉ desu.

  10. It's a store in America.   A⌈merika no mise⌉ desu.

D. Substitution Drill

    (The Japanese sentences with the intonations as marked correspond to Eng-
lish sentences having the emphasis on the final word or words.)

    1. It's the school next door   Ko⌈oen̄ no tonari no gakkoo de⌉su.
        to the park.

2. It's the park next (door) to the school.

Ga⌐kkoo no tonari no kooeñ de¬su.

3. It's the vegetable store next door to the florist.

Ha⌐na¬ya no to⌐nari no yaoya de¬su.

4. It's the florist next door to the vegetable store.

Ya⌐oya no tonari no hana¬ya desu.

5. It's the cigar store next door to the bookstore.

Ho¬ñya no to⌐nari no tabakoya de¬su.

6. It's the bookstore next door to the cigar store.

Ta⌐bakoya no tonari no ho¬ñya desu.

7. It's the drugstore next door to the meat market.

Ni⌐ku¬ya no to⌐nari no kusuriya de¬su.

8. It's the meat market next door to the drugstore.

Ku⌐suriya no tonari no niku¬ya desu.

9. It's the post office next door to the bank.

Giñkoo no tonari no yuubi¬ñkyoku desu.

10. It's the bank next door to the post office.

Yu⌐ubi¬ñkyoku no to⌐nari no giñkoo de¬su.

E. Substitution Drill

1. The park is next (door) to the school. [1]

Kooeñ wa ga⌐kkoo no tonari de¬su.

2. The school is next door to the park.

Gakkoo wa ko⌐oeñ no tonari de¬su.

3. The florist is next door to the vegetable store.

Ha⌐na¬ya wa ya⌐oya no tonari de¬su.

4. The vegetable store is next door to the florist.

Yaoya wa ha⌐na¬ya no to⌐nari de¬su.

5. The bookstore is next door to the cigar store.

Ho¬ñya wa ta⌐bakoya no tonari de¬su.

6. The cigar store is next door to the bookstore.

Tabakoya wa ⌐ho¬ñya no to⌐nari de¬su.

7. The meat market is next door to the drugstore.

Ni⌐ku¬ya wa ku⌐suriya no tonari de¬su.

8. The drugstore is next door to the meat market.

Kusuriya wa ni⌐ku¬ya no to⌐nari de¬su.

9. The bank is next door to the post office.

Giñkoo wa yu⌐ubi¬ñkyoku no to⌐nari de¬su.

10. The post office is next door to the bank.

Yu⌐ubi¬ñkyoku wa gi⌐ñkoo no tonari de¬su.

---

[1] In order to correspond to the Japanese sentences, the emphasis of the English sentences in this drill must fall on the second half of the sentence. After mastering the drill in its present form, go through it again replacing every <u>wa</u> with ḡa; now the emphasis in the English shifts to the first half of the sentence.

F. Substitution Drill

1. Next (door) to the school
    is a park.[1]

    Gakkoo no tonari wa koʳoeñ deˈsu.

2. Next door to the park is a
    school.

    Kooeñ no tonari wa gaˈkkoo deˈsu.

3. Next door to the vegetable
    store is a florist.

    Yaoya no tonari wa haˈnaˈya desu.

4. Next door to the florist is
    a vegetable store.

    Haˈnaˈya no tonari wa yaʳoya deˈsu.

5. Next door to the cigar store
    is a bookstore.

    Tabakoya no tonari wa ʳhoˈñya desu.

6. Next door to the bookstore
    is a cigar store.

    Hoˈñya no tonari wa taˈbakoya deˈsu.

7. Next door to the drugstore
    is a meat market.

    Kusuriya no tonari wa niˈkuˈya desu.

8. Next door to the meat mar-
    ket is a drugstore.

    Niˈkuˈya no tonari wa kuˈsuriya deˈsu.

9. Next door to the post office
    is a bank.

    Yuˈubiˈñkyoku no tonari wa giˈñkoo
    deˈsu.

10. Next door to the bank is a
    post office.

    Giñkoo no tonari wa yuˈubiˈñkyoku
    desu.

G. Substitution Drill

1. Is(n't) there a telephone
    around here?

    Kono heñ ni deˈñwa (wa) arimaseˈñ
    ka⏌

2. Is(n't) there a station around
    here?

    Kono heñ ni ʳeˈki (wa) aʳrimaseˈñ ka⏌

3. Is(n't) there a hotel around
    here?

    Kono heñ ni ʳhoˈteru (wa) aʳrimaseˈñ
    ka⏌

4. Is(n't) there a department
    store around here?

    Kono heñ ni deʳpaˈato (wa) aʳrimaseˈñ
    ka⏌

5. Is(n't) there a bank around
    here?

    Kono heñ ni giˈñkoo (wa) arimaseˈñ ka⏌

6. Is(n't) there a consulate
    around here?

    Kono heñ ni ryoʳoziˈkañ (wa) aʳrima-
    seˈñ ka⏌

7. Is(n't) there an embassy
    around here?

    Kono heñ ni taˈisiˈkañ (wa) aʳrimaseˈñ
    ka⏌

8. Is(n't) there a post office
    around here?

    Kono heñ ni yuˈubiˈñkyoku (wa) aʳrima-
    seˈñ ka⏌

---

[1] In order to correspond to the Japanese sentences, the emphasis of the
English sentences in this drill must fall on the second half of the sentence. After mastering the drill in its present form, go through it again replacing every
wa with ḡa; now the emphasis in the English shifts to the first half of the sentence.

H. Substitution Drill

1. Excuse me, but where is   Tyo⌐tto u⌐kaḡaima⌐su ḡa, A⌐merika-
    the American Embassy?   taisi⌐kañ (wa) ⌐do⌐ko desyoo ka.
2. Excuse me, but where is   Tyo⌐tto u⌐kaḡaima⌐su ḡa, To⌐okyo⌐o-
    Tokyo Station?   eki (wa) ⌐do⌐ko desyoo ka.
3. Excuse me, but where is   Tyo⌐tto u⌐kaḡaima⌐su ḡa, Te⌐ekoku-
    the Imperial Hotel?   ho⌐teru (wa) ⌐do⌐ko desyoo ka.
4. Excuse me, but where is   Tyo⌐tto u⌐kaḡaima⌐su ḡa, Nikkatu-
    the Nikkatsu Building?   biru (wa) ⌐do⌐ko desyoo ka.
5. Excuse me, but where is   Tyo⌐tto u⌐kaḡaima⌐su ḡa, Ni⌐hoñ-
    the Bank of Japan?   gi⌐ñkoo (wa) ⌐do⌐ko desyoo ka.
6. Excuse me, but where is   Tyo⌐tto u⌐kaḡaima⌐su ḡa, E⌐ekoku-
    the British Embassy?   taisi⌐kañ (wa) ⌐do⌐ko desyoo ka.
7. Excuse me, but where is   Tyo⌐tto u⌐kaḡaima⌐su ḡa, To⌐okyoo-
    the Tokyo Hotel?   ho⌐teru (wa) ⌐do⌐ko desyoo ka.
8. Excuse me, but where is   Tyo⌐tto u⌐kaḡaima⌐su ḡa, A⌐merika-
    the Bank of America?   gi⌐ñkoo (wa) ⌐do⌐ko desyoo ka.

I. Grammar Drill (based on Grammatical Note 5)

   Tutor: Ko⌐ko ni arima⌐su. /soko/ 'It's here.' /'there'/
   Student: So⌐ko ni⌐ mo arimasu. 'It's there, too.'

1. E⌐ki no ⌐ma⌐e ni arimasu.   E⌐ki no yo⌐ko ni⌐ mo arimasu.
    /yoko/
2. Tanaka-sañ (wa) To⌐okyoo   Ya⌐mamoto-sañ mo Tookyoo ni ima⌐su.
    ni ima⌐su. /Yamamoto-
    sañ/
3. Tookyoo ni ryo⌐ozi⌐kañ (ḡa)   Ko⌐obe ni mo ryo⌐ozi⌐kañ (ḡa) arima-
    arimasu. /Ko⌐obe/   su.
4. Koko (wa) o⌐tea⌐rai desu.   A⌐suko mo otea⌐rai desu.
    /asuko/
5. Koko ni o⌐tea⌐rai (ḡa)   A⌐suko ni⌐ mo o⌐tea⌐rai (ḡa) arima-
    arimasu. /asuko/   su.
6. Zi⌐syo (o) ka⌐ima⌐sita.   Si⌐ñbuñ mo kaima⌐sita.
    /siñbuñ/
7. Ta⌐bako (o) oneḡai-sima⌐su.   Ra⌐itaa mo oneḡai-sima⌐su.
    /ra⌐itaa/
8. Kono heñ ni ni⌐ku⌐ya (wa)   Kono heñ ni sa⌐kanaya mo arimase⌐ñ.
    a⌐rimase⌐ñ. /sakanaya/

J. Grammar Drill (based on Grammatical Note 1)

   Tutor   Pe⌐ñ desu. 'It's a pen.'
   Student: Pe⌐ñ desyoo. 'It's probably a pen.'

1. Hu⌐ru⌐i desu.   Hu⌐ru⌐i desyoo.
2. Ga⌐kkoo de⌐su.   Ga⌐kkoo desyo⌐o.
3. So⌐o desu.   So⌐o desyoo.
4. Na⌐ñ desu ka⌐   Na⌐ñ desyoo ka.
5. Ta⌐naka-sañ no⌐ desu.   Ta⌐naka-sañ no⌐ desyoo.
6. So⌐o desu ⌐ne⌐e.   So⌐o desyoo ⌐ne⌐e.

    7. Ta⌐ka⌐i desu ⌐ne⌐e.   Ta⌐ka⌐i desyoo ⌐ne⌐e.

    8. Do⌐ko desu ka⌐   Do⌐ko desyoo ka.

K.   Response Drill (based on Grammatical Note 2)

    (Give the answer in the same basic form as the question.)

    1. Koko (wa) ⌐do⌐ko desu ka⌐   Ko⌐obe desu.
       /Ko⌐obe/

    2. A⌐merika-taisi⌐kañ (wa)   To⌐okyoo ni arima⌐su.
       ⌐do⌐ko ni arimasu ka⌐
       /Tookyoo/

    3. Asoko ni ⌐na⌐ni (ḡa) arimasu   Ko⌐oeñ (ḡa) arima⌐su.
       ka⌐ /kooeñ/

    4. Kooeñ (wa) ⌐do⌐ko ni arima-   A⌐soko ni arima⌐su.
       su ka⌐ /asoko/

    5. Kooeñ (wa) ⌐do⌐ko desu ka⌐   A⌐soko de⌐su.
       /asoko/

    6. Tanaka-sañ (wa) ⌐do⌐ko ni   A⌐soko ni ima⌐su.
       imasu ka⌐   /asoko/

    7. Te⌐ekoku-ho⌐teru no ⌐ma⌐e   Ko⌐oeñ de⌐su.
       (wa) ⌐na⌐ñ desu ka⌐
       /kooeñ/

    8. Te⌐ekoku-ho⌐teru no ⌐ma⌐e   Ko⌐oeñ (ḡa) arima⌐su.
       ni ⌐na⌐ni (ḡa) arimasu
       ka⌐ /kooeñ/

    9. Kooeñ (wa) ⌐do⌐ko desu ka⌐   Te⌐ekoku-ho⌐teru no ⌐ma⌐e desu.
       /Te⌐ekoku-ho⌐teru no
       ⌐ma⌐e/

   10. Kooeñ (wa) ⌐do⌐ko ni ari-   Te⌐ekoku-ho⌐teru no ⌐ma⌐e ni ari-
      masu ka⌐   /Te⌐ekoku-   masu.
      ho⌐teru no ⌐ma⌐e/

L.   Level Drill[1]

    1. Ta⌐naka-sañ ima⌐su ka⌐   Ta⌐naka-sañ irassyaima⌐su ka⌐
    2. Ta⌐bako arima⌐su ka⌐   Ta⌐bako gozaima⌐su ka⌐
    3. Tyo⌐tto ⌐ma⌐tte kudasai.   Syo⌐osyoo o⌐mati-kudasa⌐i.
    4. Tanaka-sañ (wa) ⌐do⌐ko ni   Tanaka-sañ (wa) ⌐do⌐tira ni i⌐rassyai-
      i⌐ma⌐su ka⌐   ma⌐su ka⌐
    5. I⌐kura desu ka⌐   O⌐ikura de⌐su ka⌐
    6. I⌐kutu a⌐rima⌐sita ka⌐   O⌐ikutu gozaima⌐sita ka⌐
    7. Ge⌐ñki desu ka⌐   O⌐ge⌐ñki desu ka⌐

---

[1] The sentences on the right are more polite equivalents of the sentences on
the left.

8. Ta⌐naka ima⌐su ka⌐ ¹   Ta⌐naka orima⌐su ka⌐
9. Kono heñ ni yu⌐ubi⌐ñkyoku   Kono heñ ni yu⌐ubi⌐ñkyoku (wa) go⌐za-
   (wa) a⌐rimase⌐ñ ka⌐   imase⌐ñ ka⌐
10. Tanaka-sañ (wa) i⌐mase⌐ñ   Tanaka-sañ (wa) i⌐rassyaimase⌐ñ de-
    desita ka⌐   sita ka⌐

M. Expansion Drill

1. [It]'s beyond.   Mu⌐koo de⌐su.
   [It]'s beyond the post office. Yu⌐ubi⌐ñkyoku no mu⌐koo de⌐su.
   [It]'s beyond the big post of- O⌐oki⌐i yu⌐ubi⌐ñkyoku no mu⌐koo
   fice.   de⌐su.
   [It]'s beyond that big post   Ano o⌐oki⌐i yu⌐ubi⌐ñkyoku no mu⌐koo
   office.   de⌐su.
   Tokyo Station is beyond that   To⌐okyo⌐o - eki (wa) ano o⌐oki⌐i yu⌐u-
   big post office.   bi⌐ñkyoku no mu⌐koo de⌐su.

2. [It]'s probably expensive.   Ta⌐ka⌐i desyoo.
   [It] must be expensive!   Ta⌐ka⌐i desyoo ⌐ne⌐e.
   The inn must be expensive!   Ryokañ (wa) ta⌐ka⌐i desyoo ⌐ne⌐e.
   The new inn must be expen-   A⌐tarasi⌐i ryokañ (wa) ta⌐ka⌐i desyoo
   sive!   ⌐ne⌐e.
   A new inn like that must be   So⌐ñna atarasi⌐i ryokañ (wa) ta⌐ka⌐i
   expensive!   desyoo ⌐ne⌐e.

3. There is.   A⌐rima⌐su.
   There's a toilet.   To⌐iretto (ḡa) arimasu.
   There's a toilet over there,   A⌐soko ni⌐ mo ⌐to⌐iretto (ḡa) arima-
   too.   su.
   There's a toilet here AND   Ko⌐ko ni⌐ mo a⌐soko ni⌐ mo ⌐to⌐iret-
   over there.   to (ḡa) arimasu.

4. There is.   A⌐rima⌐su.
   Where is [it]?   Do⌐ko ni a⌐rima⌐su ka⌐
   Where is the hotel?   Ho⌐teru (wa) ⌐do⌐ko ni a⌐rima⌐su ka⌐
   Where is the new hotel?   A⌐tarasi⌐i ⌐ho⌐teru (wa) ⌐do⌐ko ni a⌐ri-
                                     ma⌐su ka⌐
   Where is the new hotel in   Oosaka no a⌐tarasi⌐i ⌐ho⌐teru (wa)
   Osaka?   ⌐do⌐ko ni a⌐rima⌐su ka⌐

5. There isn't [any].   A⌐rimase⌐ñ.
   Isn't there [any]?   A⌐rimase⌐ñ ka⌐
   Is(n't) there an inn?   Ryo⌐kañ (wa) arimase⌐ñ ka⌐
   Is(n't) there a good inn?   I⌐i ryo⌐kañ (wa) arimase⌐ñ ka⌐
   Is(n't) there a good inn   Kono heñ ni ⌐i⌐i ryo⌐kañ (wa) arima-
   around here?   se⌐ñ ka⌐

---

¹ Spoken for example by a relative of Mr. Tanaka's.

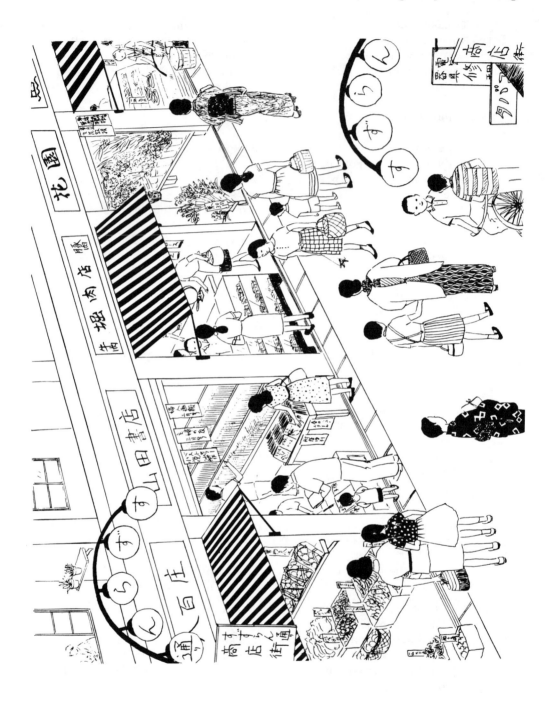

6. What is [it]?

   What is the big building?

   What is the big building on
   the right?

   What is the big building to
   the right of the station?

   Naˈñ desyoo ka.

   Oˈokiˈi ˈbiˈru (wa) ˈnaˈñ desyoo ka.

   Miḡi no oˈokiˈi ˈbiˈru (wa) ˈnaˈñ desyoo ka.

   Eˈki no miḡi no oˈokiˈi ˈbiˈru (wa)
   ˈnaˈñ desyoo ka.

7. [It]'s a florist.

   Is [it] a florist?

   Is [it] a new florist?

   Is [it] that new florist?

   Which shop is that new
   florist?

   Haˈnaˈya desu.

   Haˈnaˈya desu ka⌐

   Aˈtarasiˈi haˈnaˈya desu ka⌐

   Sono aˈtarasiˈi haˈnaˈya desu ka⌐

   Doˈno miˈseˈ ḡa sono aˈtarasiˈi
   haˈnaˈya desu ka⌐

8. There's a drugstore.

   There's a big drugstore.

   [Up] ahead there's a big
   drugstore.

   A little ahead there's a big
   drugstore.

   A little further ahead there's
   a big drugstore.

   Kuˈsuriya (ḡa) arimaˈsu.

   Oˈokiˈi kuˈsuriya (ḡa) arimaˈsu.

   Saki ni oˈokiˈi kuˈsuriya (ḡa) arimaˈ-
   su.

   Suˈkoˈsi saki ni oˈokiˈi kuˈsuriya (ḡa)
   arimaˈsu.

   Moˈo sukoˈsi saki ni oˈokiˈi kuˈsuriya (ḡa) arimaˈsu.

SHORT SUPPLEMENTARY DIALOGUES

1. A: Waˈtakusi no ziˈsyo ˈdoˈko desu ka⌐
   B: Koˈko deˈsu yo⌐

2. A: Kyoˈo no siñbuñ koˈko deˈsu yo⌐
   B: Waˈkarimaˈsita.   Doˈo mo.

3. A: Taˈnaka-sañ to Yamamoto-sañ imaˈsu ka⌐
   B: Taˈnaka-sañ wa imaˈsu ḡa, Yaˈmamoto-sañ wa imaseˈñ.

4. Visitor: Taˈnaka-sañ irassyaimaˈsu ka⌐
   Secretary: Haˈa, iˈrassyaimaˈsu. Syoˈosyoo oˈmati-kudasaˈi.

5. Mrs. Tanaka (calling her husband's office): Taˈnaka orimaˈsu ka⌐
   Secretary: Haˈa, iˈrassyaimaˈsu. Syoˈosyoo oˈmati-kudasaimaˈse.

6. A: Beˈñzyoˈ koˈttiˈ desu ka⌐
   B: Iie, soˈttiˈ desu yo.

7. A: Soˈñna hoˈñ (wa) taˈkaˈi desyoo ˈneˈe.
   B: Soˈo desyoo ˈneˈe.

8. A: Sore wa ˈnaˈñ desyoo ka.
   B: Naˈñ desyoo ka ˈneˈe.

9. A: Soko wa gaˈkkoo desyoˈo ka.
   B: Saˈa. Doˈo desyoo ka ˈneˈe.

10. A: Iˈi desu ka⌐
    B: Maˈa ˈiˈi desyoo.

English Equivalents

1. A: Where's my dictionary?
    B: Here it is!

2. A: Today's paper is [over] here!
    B: I see.   Thanks.

3. A: Are Mr. Tanaka and Mr. Yamamoto in?
    B: Mr. Tanaka is (in) but Mr. Yamamoto isn't (in).

4. Visitor: Is Mr. Tanaka in?
    Secretary: Yes, he is (in).   Just a moment, please.

5. Mrs. Tanaka: Is [Mr.] Tanaka in?
    Secretary: Yes, he is (in).   Just a moment, please.

6. A: Is the toilet this way?
    B: No, it's that way.

7. A: A book like that must be expensive!
    B: It must be!

8. A: What do you suppose that is?
    B: What DO you suppose it is! (or   What is it, indeed!)

9. A: Would that (place) be a school?
    B: I wonder . . .

10. A: Is it all right?
     B (reluctantly): I guess it probably is (all right).

—oOo—

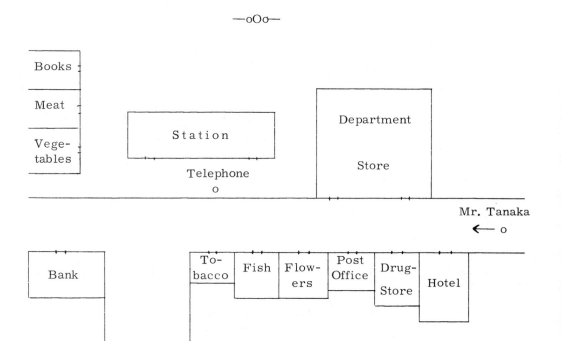

EXERCISES

1. Answer the following on the basis of the diagram on page 92.

    a. True – False

        (1) E⌐ki no ˥ma˥e ni de⌐nwa ḡa arima˥su.
        (2) E⌐ki no tonari wa de⌐pa˥ato desu.
        (3) Ga⌐kkoo wa arima˥su ḡa, gi⌐nkoo wa arimase˥n.
        (4) Yu⌐ubi˥nkyoku no tonari ni sa⌐kanaya ḡa arima˥su.
        (5) E⌐ki no yoko ni mi⌐se˥ ḡa arimasu.

    b. Answer the following questions for Mr. Tanaka, who is facing in the di-
        rection of the arrow.

        (1) Ginkoo wa sa⌐ki de˥su ka⌐
        (2) E⌐ki wa ⌐do˥tira desyoo ka⌐
        (3) Kono hen ni ⌐ho˥nya wa a˥rimase˥n ka⌐
        (4) Do˥nna mi˥se˥ ḡa ˥e˥ki no yo˥ko ni arima˥su ka⌐
        (5) Yaoya wa ⌐e˥ki no te⌐mae de˥su ka⌐

2. Using the diagram on page 92, other similar diagrams, photographs, or
    models, take turns asking and answering questions about the identity and
    location of the buildings. Always use 'left' and 'right' relative to a posi-
    tion facing the front of a building.

3. You ask a stranger: The stranger replies:

    a. where the American Em-   It's that way.
        bassy is.
    b. where the Imperial Hotel   It's near the Nikkatsu Building.
        is.
    c. where Tokyo Station is.   It's beyond that big building.
    d. where the British Consulate   It's this side of that white building.
        is.
    e. if there is(n't) a telephone   There's [one] in front of the station.
        around here.
    f. if that is the Nikkatsu Ho-   No, it's the Imperial Hotel.
        tel.
    g. if Tokyo is in this direction.   No, it's that way.
    h. if there is(n't) a post office   There is. It's next to that big bank.
        around here.
    i. if the Imperial Theater is on   No, it's on the right.
        the left.

4. Practice the Basic Dialogues with variations and appropriate props.

Lesson 7. Around Town

BASIC DIALOGUES: FOR MEMORIZATION

(a)

Smith

now	i⌐ma
to what place?	do⌐ko e or
	do⌐ko ni or
	do⌐tira e or
	do⌐tira ni
go	i⌐kima⌐su or
	ma⌐irima⌐su ↓ or
	i⌐rassyaima⌐su ↑

1. Where are you going to go now?

   I⌐ma ⌐do⌐ko |e/ni| i⌐kima⌐su ka⌐   or

   I⌐ma ⌐do⌐tira |e/ni| i⌐rassyaima⌐su ka⌐

Tanaka

movie theater	e⌐eḡa⌐kañ
to a movie theater	e⌐eḡa⌐kañ e or
	e⌐eḡa⌐kañ ni

2. I'm going to go to a movie (theater).

   E⌐eḡa⌐kañ |e/ni| ikimasu.   or

   E⌐eḡa⌐kañ |e/ni| mairimasu.

3. Won't you go too?   or Wouldn't you [like to] go too?

   A⌐na⌐ta mo i⌐kimase⌐ñ ka⌐   or
   A⌐na⌐ta mo i⌐rassyaimase⌐ñ ka⌐

Smith

4. Thank you but I'm afraid I can't [just] now.

   A⌐ri⌐ḡatoo gozaimasu ḡa, i⌐ma wa
   ⌐tyo⌐tto⌐

(b)

Smith

Marunouchi Building (in Tokyo)	Maru-biru
to the Maru-biru	Maru-biru e or
	Maru-biru ni
want to go or would like to go	ikitai /-ku/
street or road or way	miti

5. I want to go to the Maru-biru but I don't know the way (lit. the road isn't clear).

Ma⌐ru‑biru | e / ni | ikita⌐i ñ desu ḡa, mi⌐ti ḡa wakarimase⌐ñ.

    write or draw
    would you write (or draw) for me

ka⌐kima⌐su
ka⌐ite ku⌐dasaimase⌐ñ ka

6. Would you (just) draw a map for me?

Tyo⌐tto, ti⌐zu (o) ⌐ka⌐ite ku⌐dasaimase⌐ñ ka⌐

Tanaka

    avenue or wide street

to⌐ori⌐

7. A map? The Maru-biru is a little further along this street (but)...

Ti⌐zu desu ka⌐ Maru-biru (wa) ko⌐no toori⌐ no mo⌐o suko⌐si sa⌐ki de⌐su ḡa⌐

Smith

8. Then I don't need a map, do I.

Zya⌐a, ti⌐zu wa i⌐rimase⌐ñ ⌐ne⌐e.

(c)

Smith

    (a section between Tokyo and Yokohama)
    to Kawasaki

Kawasaki

Kawasaki e or
Kawasaki ni

    teach or inform
    would you teach (or inform) me?

o⌐siema⌐su
o⌐siete kudasaimase⌐ñ ka

9. I want to go to Kawasaki. Would you show me the way?

Ka⌐wasaki | e / ni | ikita⌐i ñ desu ḡa, mi⌐ti (o) osiete kudasaimase⌐ñ ka⌐

Tanaka

    space between
    between Tokyo and Yokohama

aida
Tookyoo to Yokohama no aida

10. Kawasaki? Why, it's between Tokyo and Yokohama.

Ka⌐wasaki de⌐su ka⌐ To⌐okyoo to Yokohama no aida de⌐su yo⌐

Smith

11. Oh? Then, it's that road, isn't it.

So⌐o desu ka. Zya⌐a, so⌐no miti de⌐su ⌐ne⌐e.

Tanaka

12. That's right.

So⌐o desu yo⌐

(d)

Smith

    policeman

zyuñsa[1]

---

[1] Alternate accent: zyu⌐ñsa.

13. Is(n't) there a policeman around   Kono heñ ni zyuˢñsa (wa) imaseˈñ kaˌ
    here?

Tanaka

    police box   koobañ
14. There's a police box over there.   Asoko ni koˢobañ ḡa arimaˈsu yoˌ

Smith (to policeman)

    hospital   byooiñ
    St. Luke's Hospital   Seˢeroka-byoˈoiñ
15. Say! Where (or which way) is   Tyoˈtto. Seˢeroka-byoˈoiñ (wa) ˢdoˈ-
    St. Luke's Hospital?   tira desu kaˌ

Policeman

    up ahead from here   kono saki
16. St. Luke's Hospital? Why, it's   Seˢeroka-byoˈoiñ desu kaˌ Kono saki
    the big building on the left side   no hiˢdari no hoˈo no oˢokiˈi taˢte-
    up ahead (from here).   moˈno desu yoˌ

Smith

17. I see. Thank you very much.   Waˢkarimaˈsita.   Doˈo mo aˢriˈḡa-
                                          too gozaimasita.

(e)

Tanaka

    by means of what?   naˈñ de
    let's go   iˢkimasyoˈo   or
                                          maˢirimasyoˈo ↓

    shall we go?   iˢkimasyoˈo ka   or
                                          maˢirimasyoˈo ka
18. How shall we go?   Naˈñ de iˢkimasyoˈo ka.   or
                                          Naˈñ de maˢirimasyoˈo ka.

Smith

    taxi   taˈkusii
    by taxi   taˈkusii de
19. Let's go by taxi.   Taˈkusii de iˢkimasyoˈo.   or
                                          Taˈkusii de maˢirimasyoˈo.

. . .

Driver

20. Where to?   Doˈtira |e / ni| ?

Tanaka

    as far as Tokyo Station   Toˢokyoˈo-eki made
    please go   iˢtte kudasaˈi
21. (Go as far as) Tokyo Station,   Toˢokyoˈo - eki made (iˢtte kudasaˈi).
    please.

. . .

Smith

be in a hurry	i ⌐so͟gima⌐su
please don't hurry	i ⌐so͟ga⌐nai de kudasai
22. Please don't go so fast.	Aṉmari i⌐so͟ga⌐nai de kudasai.

. . .

Driver

23. [This] is Tokyo Station   To⌐okyo⌐o-eki desu ͟ga‒
     (but) . . .

Tanaka

automobile	zi⌐do⌐osya
car or cart	kuruma
back or rear	usiro
at the back	usiro de
bring to a halt	to⌐mema⌐su
please bring to a halt	to⌐mete kudasa⌐i
24. Please stop in back of that	Ano ku⌐ro⌐i kuruma no u⌐siro de to-
black car.	mete kudasa⌐i.

(f)

Passenger

(section of Tokyo)	Giṉza
1-chome	i⌐t-tyoome⌐
2-chome	ni- ⌐tyoome⌐
as far as 4-chome	yo⌐ṉ-tyoome⌐ made
25. (Go as far as) Ginza 4-chome,	Gi⌐ṉza yoṉ-tyoome⌐ made (i⌐tte ku-
please. . . .	dasa⌐i). . . .

| is dangerous | abunai /-ku/ |
| 26. Oh! Look out! | A. Abunai. |

Driver

| safe or all right | da⌐izyo⌐obu |
| 27. It's all right! . . . | Da⌐izyo⌐obu desu yo. . . . |

28. [This] is 4-chome (but) . . .   Yo⌐ṉ-tyoome⌐ desu ͟ga‒

Passenger

next	tu⌐͟gi⌐
street corner	ka⌐do
next corner	tu⌐͟gi⌐ no ⌐ka⌐do
make a turn	ma⌐͟garima⌐su
turn a corner	ka⌐do o ma⌐͟garima⌐su
turn to the right	mi⌐͟gi e ma͟garima⌐su or
	mi⌐͟gi ni ma͟garima⌐su
please turn	ma⌐͟gatte kudasa⌐i
29. Please turn right at the next	Tu⌐͟gi⌐ no ⌐ka⌐do (o) mi⌐͟gi |e| ma-
corner. (Lit. Please turn	͟gatte kudasa⌐i. . . . |ni|
the next corner to the right.) . . .	

straight	maˢssuˡg̅u
going straight along this street	kono miti o maˢssuˡg̅u itte
end of a street or corridor	tukiatari
turn at the end of the street	tuˢkiatari o mag̅arimaˡsu

30. Please go straight along this street, and turn (to the) left at the end. . . .

Kono miti (o) maˢssuˡg̅u itte, tuki-atari (o) hiˢdari $\begin{vmatrix} e \\ ni \end{vmatrix}$ mag̅atte kuda-saˡi. . . .

at that place over there	asoko de

31. Please stop over there. . . .   Aˢsoko de tomete kudasaˡi. . . .

go back	moˊdorimaˡsu
please go back	moˢdoˡtte kudasai

32. Please back up a little. . . .   Tyoˡtto moˢdoˡtte kudasai. . . .

33. Here we are! Thanks (for your trouble).

Koˢko deˡsu yo⌐ Goˢkuˡroosama.

NOTES ON THE BASIC DIALOGUES

1. Iˡma 'now' is a nominal (iˡma desu 'it's now'; iˡma zya aᶦrimaseᶧn̄ 'it isn't now'). Iˡma with a non-past verbal refers to immediate future, and with a past verbal to immediate past: Iˡma simasu 'I'll do [it] now'; iˡma siᶜmaᶧsita 'I just did [it].'

5. Remember that √waˢkarimaˡsu is never preceded by particle o. Both the person who understands and the thing which is clear are followed by g̅a or wa, depending upon emphasis.

7. 'It's a little further along this street but—if you want a map, I'll draw one.' Toˢoriˡ usually refers to a broad avenue, whereas miti is any street or road. As the second part of a compound, toˢoriˡ becomes -doori: thus, Yaˢesu-doˡori 'Yaesu Avenue,' Naˢmiki-doˡori 'Namiki Avenue.'

9. Miˢsemaˡsu means 'show—i.e. let someone see'; oˢsiemaˡsu means 'show —i.e. explain.' Note particle g̅a connecting a statement of fact with a related question or request.

14. Koobañ 'police boxes' are booths located at frequent intervals throughout Japanese cities where one or more policemen are on duty at all times.

16. Taˢtemoˡno has three modifiers in this sentence: kono saki, hiˢdari no hoˡo, and oˢokiˡi. The first two are nominal modifiers, each followed by particle no. Oˢokiˡi, an adjectival modifier, takes no connecting particle.

21. Itte here is the gerund of iˢkimaˡsu 'go.' This itte is not to be confused with the itte of moˢo iti-do itte kudasaˡi 'please say it once more,' the gerund of iˢimaˡsu ' say.' The two gerunds sound alike; they are distinguished only by context in the spoken language.

22. The gerund of iˢsog̅imaˡsu is iˢsoˡide. This is the first example of a

gerund ending in -de instead of the more common -te.

23. 'This is Tokyo Station but—where shall I go from here? or where do you want to get out?'

24. 'Stop' here means 'stop the taxi,' 'bring the taxi to a halt.'

26. Note the use of the informal adjectival. The formal equivalent would be aˈbunaˈi desu.

27. Daˈizyoˈobu, a nominal, has many English equivalents: 'safe,' 'all right,' 'O.K.,' 'don't worry,' 'I can manage,' etc. The underlying meaning is one of safety or security or lack of concern.

28. See 23 above.

GRAMMATICAL NOTES

1. Adjectivals Ending in -tai 'want to —'

Take a verbal in its -maˈsu form: replace -maˈsu with -tai, and the result is an ADJECTIVAL meaning 'want to (or would like to) do so-and-so.'[1] For example:

kaˈkimaˈsu '[I] write'	kaˈkitaˈi '[I] want to write'
iˈkimaˈsu '[I] go'	ikitai '[I] want to go'
kaˈimaˈsu '[I] buy'	kaitai '[I] want to buy'
siˈmaˈsu '[I] do'	sitai '[I] want to do'

Like all other adjectivals, a -tai form alone is informal. The formal equivalent is the informal + deˈsu—in this case, yielding -taˈi desu—and the formal negative is the derived -ku form + aˈrimaseˈñ. Compare:

  tiˈisaˈi desu '[it] is small' : tiˈisaku aˈrimaseˈñ '[it] is not small'
  iˈkitaˈi desu '[I] want to go' : iˈkitaku arimaseˈñ '[I] don't want to go'

A common formal pattern, frequently followed by ḡa 'but,' is -taˈi ñ desu— an example of the pattern adjectival + nominal + deˈsu (cf. tiˈisaˈi ˈhoˈñ desu 'it is a small book'). Ñ[2] is a nominal meaning something like ˈmatter,' 'fact,' 'case,' and iˈkitaˈi ñ desu means literally 'it is a wanting-to-go matter.'

The adjectival + ñ desu pattern is not limited to -tai adjectivals; any other adjectival may occur in the same construction. Thus:

---

[1] Whether or not a -tai word is accented depends on the verbal root from which it is derived. But all adjectivals—and therefore all -tai words—are accented in their occurrences before √deˈsu.

[2] Ñ is the contraction of a nominal no, which occurs in more formal, precise speech.

a⌈buna⌉i ñ desu 'it is dangerous' (lit. 'it is a matter of being dangerous')

i⌉i ñ desu 'it's fine' (lit. 'it is a matter of being fine')

The alternative with n̄ is considered softer and less abrupt than the alternative
without n̄. More will be said about this pattern later.

The particle ḡa 'but' frequently follows a -tai pattern. In final position it
serves to qualify and/or soften the preceding: 'I'd like to do so-and-so but—
do you mind?' or 'is it all right?' or 'I don't know how to proceed' or 'I can't,'
etc. (Cf. Lesson 4, Grammatical Note 5.)

In statements, -tai patterns usually refer to the speaker, and in questions,
to the person addressed.

-Tai words have one special characteristic: the direct object (followed by
particle o) of a verbal often becomes the subject (followed by particle ḡa) of
the adjectival -tai derivative. Thus:

Si⌈ñbuñ o kaima⌉su. 'I am going to buy a newspaper.'

but:

Si⌈ñbuñ ḡa kaita⌉i ñ desu ḡa_ 'I want to buy a newspaper but . . .'

Siñbuñ o kaitai also occurs and has the same meaning. With many -tai words
the ḡa alternant is more common, but with some o is more usual. Observe individual examples as they occur.

WARNING: A -tai question means 'do you WANT to do so-and-so?' 'is so-
and-so what you want to do?' in a literal sense. It does not carry the same
connotation as English questions beginning 'would you like to do so-and-so?';
these are invitations, and the usual Japanese equivalent is a negative question.
Example:

A⌈sita kimase⌉n̄ ka_ 'Won't you come tomorrow?' 'Would(n't) y o u
like to come tomorrow?' etc.

Compare also Basic Sentence 3 in this lesson.

2.   Verbal Tentative

The tentative of a formal verbal is made by changing the -ma⌉su ending to
-masyo⌉o (compare de⌉su and de⌈syo⌉o). One English equivalent is 'let's do
so-and-so' or, in a question, 'shall we do so-and-so?'; another will be introduced in a later lesson.

Examples:

So⌈o simasyo⌉o. 'Let's do that.' or 'Let's do [it] that way.'
I⌈soḡimasyo⌉o. 'Let's hurry.'
I⌈kimasyo⌉o ka. 'Shall we go?'

In polite speech, the humble form—not the honorific—is used:

Ma⌈irimasyo⌉o ka. 'Shall we go?'
Ma⌈irimasyo⌉o. 'Let's go.'

Note: The use of the assertive sentence particle yo following the formal tentative—for example, i⌐kimasyo⌐o yo 'let's go!'—is typical of women's speech.

3.   Particles e 'to,' ni 'to,' ma⌐de 'as far as,' de 'at,' de 'by means of,' o 'through'

    a. e and ni

      A nominal of place followed by particle e 'to' modifies an inflected expression directly or is followed by another particle; it indicates a goal. When a phrase ending in e modifies a nominal, it is regularly followed by no. Examples:

> Do⌐ko e i⌐kimasyo⌐o ka.   'Where (lit. to what place) shall we go?'
> Tanaka-sañ wa To⌐okyoo e kima⌐su ka⌐   'Is Mr. Tanaka coming to Tokyo?'
> Ko⌐oeñ e⌐ mo i⌐kima⌐sita. 'I went to the park, too.'
> Kyo⌐oto e wa i⌐kimase⌐ñ desita. 'I didn't go to Kyoto (in comparison with other places).'
> To⌐okyoo e no miti de⌐su ka⌐ 'Is it the road to Tokyo?'

In this pattern, ni 'to' may usually be used instead of e. For example, the first two sentences cited just above could be changed to Do⌐ko ni i⌐kimasyo⌐o ka. and Tanaka-sañ wa To⌐okyoo ni kima⌐su ka⌐ with no significant difference in meaning. This ni must not be confused with ni meaning 'in'; the two particles are distinguished by the immediate context, particularly the accompanying verbal. Compare:

> Kyo⌐oto ni arimasu. 'It's in Kyoto.'
> Kyo⌐oto ni ikimasu. 'I'm going to Kyoto.'
> Ga⌐kkoo ni imase⌐ñ desita. '[He] wasn't in school.'
> Ga⌐kkoo ni kimase⌐ñ desita. '[He] didn't come to school.'

Sometimes a larger context is required. For example, i⌐rassyaima⌐su has been introduced as the honorific equivalent of both i⌐ma⌐su and i⌐kima⌐su. Therefore, depending on context, ga⌐kkoo ni irassyaima⌐su might mean 'he is in school' or 'he is going to go to school.'

    b. ma⌐de

      A nominal of place followed by ma⌐de 'as far as,' 'up to and including but not beyond' occurs as a modifier of inflected expressions directly or followed by another particle, and indicates how far something proceeds. When a phrase ending in ma⌐de modifies a nominal, it is regularly followed by no. Ma⌐de normally loses its accent when it follows an accented word.

    Examples:

> Do⌐ko made i⌐kima⌐sita ka⌐ 'How far (lit. as far as what place) did you go?'
> Ko⌐ko ma⌐de si⌐ma⌐sita. 'I did [it] as far as this point' (indicating a place in the lesson, for example).

A⌐merika·e⌐ wa[1] i⌐kima⌐sita ḡa, Nyu⌐uyo⌐oku made wa[1] i⌐kimase⌐ñ
desita.   'I did go to America, but I didn't go as far as New York.'
To⌐okyoo ma⌐de no mi⌐ti de⌐su ka⌐   'Is it the road [that goes] as
far as Tokyo?'

c.   de 'at,' 'in'

A nominal of place followed by particle de occurs as a modifier of inflected expressions directly or followed by another particle, and indicates the
place where something happens. This is in contrast with the pattern consisting
of a place word + ni + √ a⌐rima⌐su or √ i⌐ma⌐su meaning 'something or someone
is statically located in a place.'   Examples:

A⌐soko de tomete kudasa⌐i. 'Please stop [the car] over there.'
De⌐pa⌐ato de ka⌐ima⌐sita. 'I bought [it] at a department store.'
Ho⌐ñya de wa[1] ka⌐imase⌐ñ desita. 'I didn't buy [it] at a bookstore.'
Ga⌐kkoo de kakima⌐sita. 'I wrote [it] at school.'
Do⌐ko de si⌐masyo⌐o ka. 'Where shall we do [it]?'

d.   de 'by means of'

A nominal + de 'by means of' occurs as a modifier of an inflected expression directly or followed by another particle and indicates the means by
which an action is accomplished.   Examples:

Ta⌐kusii de ki⌐ma⌐sita. 'I came by taxi.'
E⌐ñpitu de kakima⌐sita. 'I wrote with a pencil.'
Pe⌐ñ de wa[1] ka⌐kimase⌐ñ desita. 'I didn't write with a pen.'
Ma⌐tti de si⌐ma⌐sita. 'I did [it] with a match.'

e.   o 'through,' 'along'

A nominal of place + o followed by a word of motion indicates the place
through which the motion takes place.   Examples:

A⌐no miti o ikimasyo⌐o. 'Let's go along that street.'
Tu⌐gi⌐ no ⌐ka⌐do o ma⌐gatte kudasa⌐i. 'Please turn the next corner.'
(Lit. 'Please make a turn through the next corner.')

Like particle o which follows a direct object (for example, ho⌐ñ o ka⌐ima⌐sita
'I bought a book'), this o is often omitted in conversation.

4.   Verbal Gerund + ku⌐dasaimase⌐ñ ka

Reread Grammatical Note 3 of Lesson 4.

The gerund (i. e. the -te or -de form) of a verbal + ku⌐dasaimase⌐ñ ka—lit.
'won't you [be kind enough to] give me?'—is a very polite request, softer and

---

[1] Wa = the wa of comparison.

less direct than one consisting of a gerund + the imperative ku⌐dasa⌐i.   Examples:

> Ma⌐tte ku⌐dasaimase⌐n̄ ka⌐ 'Would you be kind enough to wait for
> me?' (Lit. 'Won't you [be kind enough to] give me waiting?')
> Mi⌐sete ku⌐dasaimase⌐n̄ ka⌐ 'Would you be kind enough to show me?'
> (Lit. 'Won't you [be kind enough to] give me showing?')
> O⌐siete kudasaimase⌐n̄ ka⌐ 'Would you be kind enough to instruct
> me?' (Lit. 'Won't you [be kind enough to] give me instructing?')

5. . . . ma⌐ssu⌐ḡu itte . . . ma⌐ḡatte kudasa⌐i

Observe the following four pairs of independent sentences:

1. (a) Kono miti (o) ma⌐ssu⌐ḡu i⌐tte kudasa⌐i. 'Please go straight along
    this street.'
    (b) Tukiatari (o) hi⌐dari e maḡatte kudasa⌐i. 'Please turn left at the
    end.'

2. (a) Kono miti (o) ma⌐ssu⌐ḡu ikimasu. '[I] go (or will go) straight along
    this street.'
    (b) Tukiatari (o) hi⌐dari e maḡarima⌐su. '[I] turn (or will turn) left at
    the end.'

3. (a) Kono miti (o) ma⌐ssu⌐ḡu i⌐kima⌐sita. '[I] went straight along this
    street.'
    (b) Tukiatari (o) hi⌐dari e maḡarima⌐sita. '[I] turned left at the end.'

4. (a) Kono miti (o) ma⌐ssu⌐ḡu i⌐kimasyo⌐o. 'Let's go straight along this
    street.'
    (b) Tukiatari (o) hi⌐dari e maḡarimasyo⌐o. 'Let's turn left at the end.'

Each pair can be combined into a single, complex sentence, meaning 'A and
[then] B,' simply by replacing the inflected word or phrase at the end of the
first sentence with its corresponding gerund.[1] The gerund regularly ends with
comma intonation, and the next word begins a new accent phrase. Thus:

1. Kono miti (o) ma⌐ssu⌐ḡu itte, tukiatari (o) hi⌐dari e maḡatte kudasa⌐i.
    'Please go straight along this street, and turn left at the end.'

2. Kono miti (o) ma⌐ssu⌐ḡu itte, tukiatari (o) hi⌐dari e maḡarima⌐su. '[I]
    go (or will go) straight along this street, and turn left at the end.'

3. Kono miti (o) ma⌐ssu⌐ḡu itte, tukiatari (o) hi⌐dari e maḡarima⌐sita. '[I]
    went straight along this street and turned left at the end.'

4. Kono miti (o) ma⌐ssu⌐ḡu itte, tukiatari (o) hi⌐dari e maḡarimasyo⌐o.
    'Let's go straight along this street, and turn left at the end.'

---

[1] When three or more sentences are combined in this way, the inflected
word or phrase at the end of every sentence except the last is replaced by the
corresponding gerund.

Note that regardless of whether the sentence final is past, non-past, tentative, imperative, etc., the gerund is used in the middle. In other words, the
time and mode of complex sentences like these are determined only by the time
and mode of the inflected forms at the end of the sentence and by context—unless, of course, a time word like 'today,' 'tomorrow,' etc. furnishes additional
time evidence.

6. i⌐kima⌐su ~ ma⌐irima⌐su ~ i⌐rassyaima⌐su

I⌐kima⌐su 'go' is a plain formal verbal, and ma⌐irima⌐su and i⌐rassyaima⌐su
are polite formal verbals with the same meaning.   Ma⌐irima⌐su, a humble
verbal, is used in polite speech in reference to oneself or members of one's
own family, while i⌐rassyaima⌐su, an honorific, is used in reference to persons
other than the speaker, in an exalting sense.

The following is a chart of the verbals introduced thus far that have polite
equivalents:

Meaning	Plain Formal	P o l i t e F o r m a l		
		Neutral +	Humble ‖	Honorific ‖
'be located (inanimate) or have'	a⌐rima⌐su	go⌐zaima⌐su		
'be located (animate)'	i⌐ma⌐su		o⌐rima⌐su	i⌐rassyaima⌐su
'go'	i⌐kima⌐su		ma⌐irima⌐su	i⌐rassyaima⌐su

7. kono saki

Kono saki means 'up ahead, from here,' and sono saki means 'up ahead,
from there,' 'further (along the road) than that.' Words of the kono series plus
other nominals of place have parallel meanings.   For example:

> ko⌐no ma⌐e 'in front of this'
> sono usiro 'in back of that'
> ano mukoo 'beyond that'
> kono tonari 'next door to this [place]'
> so⌐no so⌐ba 'near that'

8. -tyoome 'chome'

With the exception of the names of a few main arteries, street names are
rarely used in Japan. Addresses are usually given in terms of location within

particular sections, and directions are regularly given in terms of landmarks —hence the common use of maps and diagrams and the frequent stops at police boxes for instructions.

One of the divisions into which some sections of a city are divided is the -tyoome. While it is one of the smallest divisions, its size is not fixed, and there may be considerable variation among the -tyoome of a given section. The numerals of Series I (i⌐ti¬, ni¬, sañ, etc.) combine with -tyoome to name (not count!) the -tyoome. Study the following list, noting particularly the forms for '1,' '8,' and '10':

i⌐t-tyoome¬	'1-chome' [1]	ro⌐ku-tyoome¬	'6-chome'
ni-⌐tyoome¬	'2-chome'	na⌐na-tyoome¬	'7-chome'
sa⌐ñ-tyoome¬	'3-chome'	ha⌐t-tyoome¬	'8-chome'
yo⌐ñ-tyoome¬	'4-chome'	kyu⌐u-tyoome¬	'9-chome'
go-⌐tyoome¬	'5-chome'	zi⌐t-tyoome¬ or	
		zyu⌐t-tyoome¬	'10-chome'

na⌐ñ-tyoome¬ 'what number chome?'

The lower numbers occur more frequently.

DRILLS

A. Substitution Drill

(Insert no whenever appropriate.)

1.	Please turn the next corner.	Tu⌐gi¬ no ⌐ka¬do (o) ma⌐gatte kudasa¬i.
2.	Please turn that corner.	A⌐no ka¬do (o) ma⌐gatte kudasa¬i.
3.	Please turn the corner where the school is.	Ga⌐kkoo no ka¬do (o) ma⌐gatte kudasa¬i.
4.	Please turn the corner where the department store is.	De⌐pa¬ato no ⌐ka¬do (o) ma⌐gatte kudasa¬i.
5.	Please turn the corner where the police box is.	Ko⌐obañ no ka¬do (o) ma⌐gatte kudasa¬i.
6.	Please turn the corner where the hospital is.	Byo⌐oiñ no ka¬do (o) ma⌐gatte kudasa¬i.
7.	Please turn the corner where the drugstore is.	Ku⌐suriya no ka¬do (o) ma⌐gatte kudasa¬i.
8.	Please turn the corner where the cigar store is.	Ta⌐bakoya no ka¬do (o) ma⌐gatte kudasa¬i.

---

[1] This is the usual English equivalent, although 'chome 1' or '1st chome' would be more accurate.

B. Substitution Drill

1. It's between Tokyo and Yo-
    kohama.
    Tookyoo to Yoᒥkohama no aida deᒣsu.

2. It's between Japan and
    America.
    Niᒥhoᒣñ to Aᒥmerika no aida deᒣsu.

3. It's between a bank and
    a department store.
    Giñkoo to deᒥpaᒣato no aᒥida deᒣsu.

4. It's between a bookstore
    and a flower shop.
    Hoᒣñya to haᒥnaᒣya no aᒥida deᒣsu.

5. It's between the embassy
    and the consulate.
    Taᒥisiᒣkañ to ryoᒥoziᒣkañ no aᒥida
    deᒣsu.

6. It's between the books and
    the magazines.
    Hoᒣñ to zaᒥssi no aida deᒣsu.

7. It's between Mr. Tanaka
    and Mr. Yamamoto.
    Tanaka-sañ to Yaᒥmamoto-sañ no ai-
    da deᒣsu.

8. It's between the car and
    the taxi.
    Kuruma to ᒥtaᒣkusii no aᒥida deᒣsu.

C. Substitution Drill

1. MR. TANAKA went.
    Taᒥnaka-sañ ḡa ikimaᒣsita.

2. Mr. Tanaka (compared with
    the others) went.
    Taᒥnaka-sañ wa ikimaᒣsita.

3. Mr. Tanaka went, too.
    Taᒥnaka-sañ mo ikimaᒣsita.

4. He went by cab.
    Taᒣkusii de iᒥkimaᒣsita.

5. He went along that street.
    Soᒥno miti (o) ikimaᒣsita.

6. He went to the bank.
    Giᒥñkoo e ikimaᒣsita.

7. He went to the bank.
    Giᒥñkoo ni ikimaᒣsita.

8. He went as far as the bank.
    Giᒥñkoo maᒣde iᒥkimaᒣsita.

D. Substitution Drill

1. Please stop here.
    Koᒥko de tomete kudasaᒣi.

2. Please wait here.
    Koᒥko de maᒣtte kudasai.

3. Please write here.
    Koᒥko de kaᒣite kudasai.

4. Please do [it] here.
    Koᒥko de site kudasaᒣi.

5. Please buy [it] here.
    Koᒥko de katte kudasaᒣi.

6. Please say [it] here.
    Koᒥko de itte kudasaᒣi.

E. Grammar Drill (based on Grammatical Note 2)

Tutor: Aᒥsoko e ikimaᒣsu. 'I'm going to go there.'
Student: Aᒥsoko e ikimasyoᒣo. 'Let's go there.'

1. Eᒥeḡaᒣkañ e maᒥirimaᒣsu.
    Eᒥeḡaᒣkañ e maᒥirimasyoᒣo.

2. Tiᒣzu (o) kaᒥkimaᒣsu.
    Tiᒣzu (o) kaᒥkimasyoᒣo.

3. Iᒥsoḡimaᒣsu.
    Iᒥsoḡimasyoᒣo.

4. Gaᒥkkoo no maᒣe de toᒥme-
    maᒣsu.
    Gaᒥkkoo no maᒣe de toᒥmemasyoᒣo.

5. Tuᒥḡiᒣ no ᒥkaᒣdo (o) maᒥḡa-
    rimaᒣsu.
    Tuᒥḡiᒣ no ᒥkaᒣdo (o) maᒥḡarimasyoᒣo.

6. Ka⌐do made mo˥dorima˧su.   Ka⌐do made mo˥dorimasyo˧o.
7. Kyo⌐o no si˥ñbuñ (o) kai-   Kyo⌐o no si˥ñbuñ (o) kaimasyo˧o.
   ma˧su.
8. So˹o sima⌐su.   So˹o simasyo˹o.

F. Grammar Drill (based on Grammatical Note 1)

       Tutor: Ma˹ru-biru e ikima⌐su. 'I'm going to go to the Maru-biru.'
       Student: Maru-biru e i˹kita⌐i ñ desu ḡa_ 'I'd like to go to the Maru-
                biru (but) . . .'

   1. A˹sita⌐ mo i˥kima⌐su.   A˹sita⌐ mo i˹kita⌐i ñ desu ḡa_
   2. Eñpitu de kakima⌐su.   Eñpitu de ka˹kita⌐i ñ desu ḡa_
   3. E˹eḡa˹kañ no ˥ka˧do (o)   E˹eḡa˹kañ no ˥ka˧do (o) ma˹garita⌐i
      ma˥ḡarima˧su.   ñ desu ḡa_
   4. Ze⌐ñbu si˥ma⌐su.   Ze⌐ñbu si˹ta⌐i ñ desu ḡa_
   5. Yu˹ubi⌐ñkyoku e i˥kima⌐su.   Yu˹ubi⌐ñkyoku e i˹kita⌐i ñ desu ḡa_
   6. A˹tarasi⌐i ku˥ruma (o) kai-   A˹tarasi⌐i kuruma (o) ka˹ita⌐i ñ desu
      ma˧su.   ḡa_
   7. Tyo⌐tto u˥kaḡaima˧su ḡa_   Tyo⌐tto u˹kaḡaita⌐i ñ desu ḡa_
   8. A˹soko de tomema⌐su.   A˹soko de to˹meta⌐i ñ desu ḡa_

G. Grammar Drill (based on Grammatical Note 4)

       Tutor: A˹na⌐ta no siñbuñ (o) ˹mi˹sete kudasai. 'Please show me your
                paper.'
       Student: A˹na⌐ta no siñbuñ (o) ˹mi˹sete ku˹dasaimase˧ñ ka˩ 'Would
                you be kind enough to show me your paper?'

   1. Pe⌐ñ de ˥ka˧ite kudasai.   Pe⌐ñ de ˥ka˧ite ku˥dasaimase˧ñ ka˩
   2. Ko˹ko de tomete kudasa⌐i.   Ko˹ko de tomete kudasaimase⌐ñ ka˩
   3. Ka⌐do made mo˹do⌐tte kuda-   Ka⌐do made mo˹do⌐tte ku˥dasaima-
      sai.   se˧ñ ka˩
   4. A˹sita⌐ mo i˹tte kudasa⌐i.   A˹sita⌐ mo i˹tte kudasaimase⌐ñ ka˩
   5. Mi˹ti (o) osiete kudasa⌐i.   Mi˹ti (o) osiete kudasaimase⌐ñ ka˩
   6. Mo˹o iti-do itte kudasa⌐i.   Mo˹o iti-do itte kudasaimase⌐ñ ka˩
   7. Tu˹ḡi⌐ no ˥ka˧do (o) ma-   Tu˹ḡi⌐ no ˥ka˧do (o) ma˹ḡatte kudasa-
      ˹ḡatte kudasa⌐i.   imase⌐ñ ka˩
   8. Koko de ˹ma⌐tte kudasai.   Koko de ˹ma⌐tte ku˥dasaimase˧ñ ka˩

H. Grammar Drill (based on Grammatical Note 5)

       Tutor: Ko˹no miti (o) itte kudasa⌐i. Tu˹ḡi⌐ no ˥ka˧do (o) ma˹ḡatte
                kudasa⌐i. 'Please go along this street. Please turn at the
                next corner.' (2 sentences)
       Student: Kono miti (o) itte, tu˹ḡi⌐ no ˥ka˧do (o) ma˹ḡatte kudasa⌐i.
                'Please go along this street and turn at the next corner.'
                (1 complex sentence)

   1. Ka⌐do made mo˥dorima˧sita.   Ka⌐do made mo˥do⌐tte, so˹ko de to-
      So˹ko de tomema⌐sita.   mema⌐sita.
   2. To˹okyo⌐o-eki no ˥ma˧e de   To˹okyo⌐o-eki no ˥ma˧e de tŏmete,
      to˹mete kudasa⌐i.   soko de ˹ma⌐tte kudasai.
      Soko de ˹ma⌐tte kudasai.

3. Tu⌐g̃i˥ no ⌐ka˥do (o) mi⌐g̃i
   e mag̃arima˥su.
   Ano miti (o) tu⌐kiatari ma˥de
   ikimasu.

   Tu⌐g̃i˥ no ⌐ka˥do (o) mĩg̃i e ma-
   g̃atte, ano miti (o) tu⌐kiatari ma˥de
   ikimasu.

4. Ho˥ñya e i⌐kimasyo˥o.
   A⌐tarasi˥i zi⌐biki˥ (o) ka⌐i-
   masyo˥o.

   Ho˥ñya e itte, a⌐tarasi˥i zi⌐biki˥ (o)
   ka⌐imasyo˥o.

I. Grammar Drill

Tutor: Wa⌐karima˥su.   'It's clear.' (affirmative)
Student: Wa⌐karimase˥ñ.   'It isn't clear.' (negative)

1. A⌐buna˥i desu.
2. Gi⌐ñkoo no ma˥e desu.
3. Ma⌐g̃arima˥sita.
4. Ma⌐ssu˥g̃u desu.
5. I⌐kita˥i desu.
6. To⌐mema˥su.
7. E⌐eg̃a˥kañ desita.
8. A⌐o˥i desu.

A⌐bunaku arimase˥ñ.
Gi⌐ñkoo no ma˥e zya a⌐rimase˥ñ.
Ma⌐g̃arimase˥ñ desita.
Ma⌐ssu˥g̃u zya a⌐rimase˥ñ.
I⌐kitaku arimase˥ñ.
To⌐memase˥ñ.
E⌐eg̃a˥kañ zya a⌐rimase˥ñ desita.
A˥oku a⌐rimase˥ñ.

J. Level Drill[1]

1. Ta⌐bako (g̃a) arima˥su ka⤵
2. I˥ma i⌐kimasyo˥o.
3. Ta⌐naka ima˥su ka⤵
4. Tanaka-sañ (wa) ⌐do˥ko ni
   i⌐kima˥su ka⤵
5. Tanaka-sañ (wa) ⌐do˥ko ni
   i⌐ma˥su ka⤵
6. Tyo˥tto ⌐ma˥tte kudasai.
7. I˥kutu a⌐rima˥sita ka⤵
8. Watakusi (wa) i⌐kimase˥ñ
   desita.

Ta⌐bako (g̃a) gozaima˥su ka⤵
I˥ma ma⌐irimasyo˥o.
Ta⌐naka orima˥su ka⤵
Tanaka-sañ (wa) ⌐do˥tira ni i⌐rassya-
   ima˥su ka⤵
Tanaka-sañ (wa) ⌐do˥tira ni i⌐rassya-
   ima˥su ka⤵
Syo˥osyoo o⌐mati-kudasa˥i.
O⌐ikutu gozaima˥sita ka⤵
Watakusi (wa) ma⌐irimase˥ñ desita.

K. Expansion Drill

1. I'm not going to go.
   Wouldn't you [like to] go?
   Wouldn't you [like to] go
     to a movie (theater)?
   Wouldn't you [like to] go
     to a movie (theater), too?

I⌐kimase˥ñ.
I⌐kimase˥ñ ka⤵
E⌐eg̃a˥kañ e i⌐kimase˥ñ ka⤵

A⌐na˥ta mo e⌐eg̃a˥kañ e i⌐kimase˥ñ
   ka⤵

---

[1] In each case, the sentence on the right is the polite equivalent of the sentence on the left.

2. I don't understand.
    I don't know the way.
    I want to go, but I don't
    know the way.
    I want to go to Yokohama,
    but I don't know the way.

Wa⌐karimase⌐ñ.
Mi⌐ti ḡa wakarimase⌐ñ.
I⌐kita⌐i ñ desu ḡa, mi⌐ti ḡa wakari-
    mase⌐ñ.
Yo⌐kohama e ikita⌐i ñ desu ḡa, mi⌐ti
    ḡa wakarimase⌐ñ.

3. Would(n't) you give [it] to
    me?
    Would you be kind enough
    to teach me?
    Would you be kind enough
    to show me the way?
    I'd like to go. Would you
    be kind enough to show
    me the way?
    I'd like to go to the Imperi-
    al Theater. Would you
    be kind enough to show
    me the way?

Ku⌐dasaimase⌐ñ ka⌐

O⌐siete kudasaimase⌐ñ ka⌐

Mi⌐ti (o) osiete kudasaimase⌐ñ ka⌐

I⌐kita⌐i ñ desu ḡa, mi⌐ti (o) osiete
    kudasaimase⌐ñ ka⌐

Te⌐ekoku-ḡe⌐kizyoo e i⌐kita⌐i ñ desu
    ḡa, mi⌐ti (o) osiete kudasaimase⌐ñ
    ka⌐

4. It's a building.
    It's a big building.
    It's a big building on the
    right.
    It's a big building on the
    right up ahead.
    It's a big building on the
    right up ahead of that
    hospital.

Ta⌐temo⌐no desu.
O⌐oki⌐i ta⌐temo⌐no desu.
Mi⌐ḡi no ho⌐o no o⌐oki⌐i ta⌐temo⌐no
    desu.
Saki no mi⌐ḡi no ho⌐o no o⌐oki⌐i ta-
    ⌐temo⌐no desu.
Sono byooiñ no saki no mi⌐ḡi no ho⌐o
    no o⌐oki⌐i ta⌐temo⌐no desu.

5. Let's go.
    Shall we go?
    Shall we go by cab?
    Shall we go to the station
    by cab?

I⌐kimasyo⌐o.
I⌐kimasyo⌐o ka.
Ta⌐kusii de i⌐kimasyo⌐o ka.
E⌐ki e ⌐ta⌐kusii de i⌐kimasyo⌐o ka.

6. I brought [it] to a halt.
    I brought the car to a halt.
    I stopped the car in front.
    I stopped the car in front of
    the school.

To⌐mema⌐sita.
Ku⌐ruma (o) tomema⌐sita.
Ma⌐e de ku⌐ruma (o) tomema⌐sita.
Ga⌐kkoo no ma⌐e de ku⌐ruma (o) to-
    mema⌐sita.

7. Please make a turn.
    Please make a turn to the
    right.
    Please go as far as the end
    of the street and turn to
    the right.
    Please go along this street
    as far as the end, and
    turn to the right.

Ma⌐ḡatte kudasa⌐i.
Mi⌐ḡi e maḡatte kudasa⌐i.

Tu⌐kiatari ma⌐de itte, mi⌐ḡi e ma-
    ḡatte kudasa⌐i.

Kono miti (o) tu⌐kiatari ma⌐de itte,
    mi⌐ḡi e maḡatte kudasa⌐i.

8. Please stop. [1]   To⌐mete kudasa⌐i.
    Please stop there.   So⌐ko de tomete kudasa⌐i.
    Please back up and stop   Mo⌐do⌐tte, so⌐ko de tomete kudasa⌐i.
       there.
    Please back up as far as   Ka⌐do made mo⌐do⌐tte, so⌐ko de to-
       the corner and stop   mete kudasa⌐i.
       there.

SUPPLEMENTARY CONVERSATIONS

1. Cab driver: Do⌐tira made?
   Smith: Go⌐tañda⌐[2]-eki made.
   Cab driver: Ha⌐i wa⌐karima⌐sita.
   Smith: Añmari i⌐soğa⌐nai de kudasai◡
   Cab driver: Da⌐izyo⌐obu desu yo. . . .   Ko⌐ko ğa Gotañda⌐-eki desu ğa‿
   Smith: Ko⌐no e⌐ki no ⌐so⌐ba no byo⌐oiñ e ikita⌐i ñ desu ğa, kono heñ
                ni ko⌐obañ wa arimase⌐ñ ka◡   Byo⌐oiñ wa koobañ no usiro
                de⌐su ğa‿
   Cab driver: A⌐soko ni koobañ ğa arima⌐su yo◡   Ho⌐ñya no mi⌐ği no ho⌐o
                desu.
   Smith: A⌐a, so⌐o desu ⌐ne⌐e.   So⌐no koobañ no ka⌐do o hi⌐dari e ma-
                ğatte kudasa⌐i.
   Cab driver: Ha⌐i.
   Smith: Mo⌐o suko⌐si sa⌐ki ma⌐de i⌐tte kudasa⌐i. A.   Ko⌐ko de⌐su yo◡
                Go⌐ku⌐roosama. I⌐kura desu ka◡
   Cab driver: Ni⌐hyaku⌐-eñ desu. A⌐ri⌐ğatoo gozaimasu.

2. Smith: Tyo⌐tto u⌐kağaima⌐su ğa, To⌐okyoo-gi⌐ñkoo ko⌐no heñ   de⌐su
                ka◡
   Stranger: To⌐okyoo-gi⌐ñkoo desu ka◡   Ni⌐hoñ-gi⌐ñkoo zya a⌐rimase⌐ñ
                ka◡   Ni⌐hoñ-gi⌐ñkoo wa so⌐no depa⌐ato no to⌐nari de⌐su ğa‿
   Smith: To⌐okyoo-gi⌐ñkoo desu ğa‿
   Stranger: So⌐o desu ka. Ko⌐no heñ ni⌐ wa a⌐rimase⌐ñ yo◡

English Equivalents

1. Cab driver: Where to? (lit. How far?)
   Smith: (As far as) Gotanda Station.
   Cab driver: All right.
   Smith: Don't go so fast.
   Cab driver: Don't worry! . . . Here's Gotanda Station (but) . . .
   Smith: I want to go to a hospital near this station. Is(n't) there a po-

---

[1] Lit. 'bring something to a halt.'
[2] Section of Tokyo.

lice box around here? The hospital is behind the police box (but)...[1]

Cab driver: There's a police box over there! It's to the right of the bookstore.

Smith: Oh, that's right. Turn left at the corner where that police box is.

Cab driver: All right.

Smith: Go a little further ahead. Oh, this is the place! Thanks (for your trouble). How much is it?

Cab driver: (It's) ¥ 200. Thank you.

2. Smith: Excuse me but is the Bank of Tokyo around here?

Stranger: The Bank of Tokyo? Don't you mean the Bank of Japan? The Bank of Japan is next door to that department store (but)...

Smith: It's the Bank of Tokyo [I'm looking for] (but)...[2]

Stranger: Oh? It's not around here.

EXERCISES

1. Give the following instructions to the taxi driver:

    a. Imperial Hotel, please.
    b. American Embassy, please.
    c. St. Luke's Hospital, please.
    d. Please hurry.
    e. Please don't go so fast.
    f. Turn right.
    g. Turn left.
    h. Go straight.
    i. Turn right at the next corner.
    j. Turn left at the corner where the bank is.
    k. Stop here.
    l. Stop in front of the department store.
    m. Stop in back of that taxi.
    n. Back up a little.
    o. Back up to the corner.
    p. Look out!

2. Using a detailed street map of any area—real or imaginary—practice conversations between a taxi driver and his customer by choosing particular destinations and giving explicit directions.

―――――――――――

[1] 'but—where is the police box?'

[2] 'but—maybe it isn't around here.'

3. Practice conversations between Mr. Smith and a Japanese stranger, asking how to reach particular destinations.

4. Practice the Basic Dialogues with appropriate variations and props.

Lesson 8. Time

BASIC DIALOGUES: FOR MEMORIZATION

(a)

Tanaka

what time?	na⌐n-zi
1. What time is it (now)?	I⌐ma ⌐na⌐n-zi desu ka⌐ or
	I⌐ma ⌐na⌐n-zi?

Yamamoto

one o'clock	i⌐ti⌐-zi
2. It's one o'clock.	I⌐ti⌐-zi (desu).

Tanaka

exactly	tyoodo
3. Is it exactly one o'clock?	Tyo⌐odo iti⌐-zi desu ka⌐ or
	Tyo⌐odo iti⌐-zi?

Yamamoto

two minutes or minute two[1]	ni⌐-huñ
minute two past or after	ni-⌐hu⌐ñ-suḡi
4. No. It's 1:02. or No. It's two minutes after one.	Iie. I⌐ti⌐-zi ⌐ni⌐-huñ (desu). or
	Iie. I⌐ti⌐-zi ni-⌐hu⌐ñ-suḡi (desu).

Tanaka

clock or watch	tokee
5. This watch is out of order.	Kono tokee (wa) da⌐me⌐ (desu).
ten minutes or minute ten	zi⌐p-puñ or
	zyu⌐p-puñ
minute ten before the hour	zi⌐p-pu⌐ñ-mae
6. It says (lit. is) ten minutes before.	Zi⌐p-pu⌐ñ-mae (desu).

(b)

Tanaka

first day of the month	tu⌐itati⌐
7. Is today the first?	Kyo⌐o (wa) tu⌐itati⌐ desu ka⌐

---

[1] I.e. 'minute two of a sixty-minute hour.'

113

Smith

second day of the month	hutu-ka
or two days	
8. Why no, it's the second.	Iie. Hu⌐tu-ka de⌐su yo⌐

Tanaka

Monday	getuyoo[1] or
	ge⌐tuyo⌐obi
9. It isn't Monday?	Ge⌐tuyoo zyà arimase⌐n ka⌐

Smith

Tuesday	ka⌐yo⌐o (bi)[2]
Wednesday	su⌐iyo⌐o (bi)[2]
Thursday	mo⌐kuyo⌐o (bi)[2]
Friday	ki⌐nyo⌐o (bi)[2]
Saturday	do⌐yo⌐o (bi)[2]
Sunday	nitiyoo or
	ni⌐tiyo⌐obi
10. No (i.e. that's right). It's Tuesday.	E⌐e, ka⌐yo⌐o desu yo⌐

Tanaka

11. Oh, that's right!	A⌐a, so⌐o desu ⌐ne⌐e.

(c)

Tanaka

when	i⌐tu
come	ki⌐ma⌐su or
	ma⌐irima⌐su ⌐ or
	i⌐rassyaima⌐su ⌐
12. When did you come here?	I⌐tu ko⌐ko e kima⌐sita ka⌐ or
	I⌐tu ko⌐tira e irassyaima⌐sita ka⌐

Smith

three years or the year three	san-nen
three years before or ago	sa⌐n-nen ma⌐e
at a time three years ago	sa⌐n-nen ma⌐e ni
13. I came three years ago.	Sa⌐n-nen ma⌐e ni ki⌐ma⌐sita. or
	Sa⌐n-nen ma⌐e ni ma⌐irima⌐sita.
Meiji Era (1868–1912)	me⌐ezi
Taisho Era (1912–1926)	taisyoo
Showa Era (1926–1989)	syoowa

---

[1] Alternate accented form: ge⌐tuyo⌐o.

[2] Short form has unaccented alternant.

Heisei Era (1989–)	heesee
14. That was Heisei 3.	Sore wa heesee sa⌐n-neñ de⌐sita.

Tanaka

airplane	hi⌐ko⌐oki
15. Did you come by plane?	Hi⌐ko⌐oki de ki⌐ma⌐sita ka⌐ or
	Hi⌐ko⌐oki de i⌐rassyaima⌐sita ka⌐

Smith

ship	hu⌐ne
16. No. I came by ship.	Iie, hu⌐ne de ki⌐ma⌐sita. or
	Iie, hu⌐ne de ma⌐irima⌐sita.

Tanaka

about how long?	dono-ḡurai
be required or take	ka⌐karima⌐su
17. About how long did it take?	Do⌐no-ḡurai kakarima⌐sita ka⌐

Smith

two weeks	ni-⌐syu⌐ukañ
about two weeks	ni-⌐syuukañ-ḡu⌐rai
18. It took about two weeks.	Ni-⌐syuukañ-ḡu⌐rai ka⌐karima⌐sita.

(d)

Tanaka

day before yesterday	o⌐toto⌐i
19. Say, I went to Nikko the day before yesterday.	Ototoi ⌐Ni⌐kkoo e i⌐kima⌐sita yo⌐

Smith

20. Oh? How was it?	So⌐o desu ka. Do⌐o desita ka⌐

Tanaka

exceedingly or very	totemo or
	tottemo
21. It was very pretty. Wouldn't you [like to] go too?	To⌐ttemo ki⌐ree desita. A⌐na⌐ta mo i⌐kimase⌐ñ ka⌐

Smith

from here	koko kara
22. I'd like to go some (lit. one) time. About how long does it take from here to Nikko?	Iti-do i⌐kita⌐i ñ desu ḡa, ko⌐ko kara Ni⌐kkoo made do⌐no-ḡurai kakarima⌐su ka⌐

Tanaka

electric train or street car	de⌐ñsya[1]

---

[1] Has unaccented alternant.

(steam) train	ki⌐sya⌐
bus	ba⌐su
three hours	sa⌐ñ-zi⌐kañ
three hours and a half	sa⌐ñ-zikañ-ha⌐ñ
about three hours and a half	sa⌐ñ-zikañ-hañ-ḡu⌐rai

23. I went by electric train. It took about three hours and a half.

Watakusi wa ⌐de⌐ñsya de i⌐kima⌐sita ḡa, sa⌐ñ- zikañ- hañ- ḡu⌐rai ka⌐kari-ma⌐sita.

(e)

Smith

vacation or holiday or time off	ya⌐sumi⌐ or oyasumi †

24. When is your vacation?

Oyasumi (wa) ⌐i⌐tu desu ka⌐

Tanaka

this year	kotosi
August	ha⌐ti-ḡatu⌐
about August	ha⌐ti-ḡatu-go⌐ro

25. This year it will be about August (but) . . .

Kotosi wa ha⌐ti-ḡatu-ḡo⌐ro desu ḡa_

Smith

one month	i⌐k-ka⌐ḡetu

26. Will it be a month?

I⌐k-ka⌐ḡetu desu ka⌐

Tanaka

27. Heavens no!

To⌐ñde mo arimase⌐ñ.

ten days or tenth of the month	too-ka

28. It will be ten days.

To⌐o-ka de⌐su yo_

NOTES ON THE BASIC DIALOGUES

1. The Japanese equivalent WITH i⌐ma and the English equivalent WITHOUT 'now' are more usual.

5. Tokee is the general term for 'timepiece,' covering all kinds of clocks and watches. There are more specific terms which can be used when it is necessary to distinguish among different kinds of timepieces.

9, 10. The shorter forms of the days of the week, without -bi, are less formal, and common in conversation.

12. Particle e may be replaced here by particle ni (cf. Lesson 7, Grammatical Note 3 a).

14. The Japanese regularly count years according to eras, which in recent times have coincided with the reigns of their emperors. Each era, or reign, has its own name. When a new emperor takes the throne, a new

era begins; the remainder of the current calendar year is the year 1 (ga⌐nneñ) of that era, the next calendar year is the year 2, and so on. Thus 1926—the end of the Taisho Era—began as Taisho 15 (the 15th year of Taisho) but, with the accession of a new emperor, became Showa 1; 1927 was Showa 2.   To distinguish the Western system, seereki is used to designate the Christian Era: syoowa 35, for example, corresponds to seereki 1960.

17. Ka⌐karima⌐su (gerund ka⌐ka⌐tte) means 'take' or 'require,' as in 'take time,' 'take money.'   Like wa⌐karima⌐su, i⌐rima⌐su, and a⌐rima⌐su, ka⌐karima⌐su may occur with particles ḡa and/or wa, but never with particle o.   Ka⌐karima⌐su frequently occurs with extent constructions, as in the present instance, with no particle.

19. See Note 12 above.

21. Tottemo is the more emphatic alternant of totemo.   Intensifying words like totemo and zu⌐ibuñ have a complicated distribution, and students can learn where they occur only by observing how native speakers use them. For example, before ta⌐ka⌐i, both totemo and zu⌐ibuñ occur frequently, but before i⌐i, only totemo is common.   Distinguishing among the meanings of these intensifying words is something like trying to distinguish among degrees of intensity of English 'it is very difficult,' 'it is extremely difficult,' 'it is terribly difficult,' 'it is exceedingly difficult,' 'it is awfully difficult,' etc.
Note the use of negative + ka as an invitation.

22. Note the use of particle ḡa connecting a statement with a related question.

23. Here the particle ḡa connects a qualification with the direct answer to a question.   The answer to the question 'how long does it take?' is 'it took about three hours and a half,' but this answer is subject to the immediately preceding qualification—'I went by electric train.'

25. 'but—why do you ask?'

27. To⌐nde mo arimase⌐ñ is an emphatic rejection of what has been said and, accordingly, must be used with caution.   Common English equivalents are 'Ridiculous!' 'Far from it!' 'Nothing of the kind!' 'Don't be silly!' 'Never happen!'

28. The same sentence in a different context could mean 'It is (or will be) the tenth (of the month).'

GRAMMATICAL NOTES

1. **Time Counters:** -huñ, -zi, -zikañ, -ka/-niti, -syuukañ, -ḡatu, -kaḡetu, -neñ

The above counters can be divided into three groups:

A. those that combine with numerals to NAME:
   (1) -zi—to name the o'clocks
   (2) -ḡatu—to name the calendar months

B.   those that combine with numerals to COUNT:
   (1) -zikañ—to count the number of hours
   (2) -syuukañ—to count the number of weeks
   (3) -kaḡetu—to count the number of months

C.   those that combine with numerals to NAME AND COUNT:
   (1) -huñ—to name the minute of a sixty-minute hour and count the number of minutes
   (2) -ka/-niti—to name the days of the month[1] and count the number of days
   (3) -neñ—to name the years[2] and count the number of years

With the exception of -ka/-niti, all the above counters combine with numerals of Series I (i⌐ti⌐, ni⌐, sañ, etc.). -Ka/-niti combines with some numerals of Series I and some of Series II (the hi⌐to⌐, huta, mi series), and there are some irregular forms.

Study the following lists, noting particularly the assimilated forms (for example, ro⌐ku⌐ + -huñ = ro⌐p-puñ) and the irregular forms (for example, hutu-ka, nano-ka, etc.).

-huñ		-zi		-zikañ	
i⌐p-puñ	'1 minute' or 'minute 1'	i⌐ti⌐-zi	'1 o'clock'	i⌐ti-zi⌐kañ	'1 hour'
ni⌐-huñ	'2 minutes' or 'minute 2'	ni⌐-zi	'2 o'clock'	ni-⌐zi⌐kañ	'2 hours'
sa⌐ñ-puñ	'3 minutes' or 'minute 3'	sa⌐ñ-zi	'3 o'clock'	sa⌐ñ-zi⌐kañ	'3 hours'
yo⌐ñ-puñ	'4 minutes' or 'minute 4'	yo⌐-zi	'4 o'clock'	yo-⌐zi⌐kañ	'4 hours'
go⌐-huñ	'5 minutes' or 'minute 5'	go⌐-zi	'5 o'clock'	go-⌐zi⌐kañ	'5 hours'
ro⌐p-puñ	'6 minutes' or 'minute 6'	ro⌐ku⌐-zi	'6 o'clock'	ro⌐ku-zi⌐kañ	'6 hours'
na⌐na⌐-huñ or si⌐ti⌐-huñ	'7 minutes' or 'minute 7'	si⌐ti⌐-zi	'7 o'clock'	na⌐na-zi⌐kañ or si⌐ti-zi⌐kañ	'7 hours'
ha⌐ti⌐-huñ or ha⌐p-puñ	'8 minutes' or 'minute 8'	ha⌐ti⌐-zi	'8 o'clock'	ha⌐ti-zi⌐kañ	'8 hours'
kyu⌐u-huñ	'9 minutes' or 'minute 9'	ku⌐-zi	'9 o'clock'	ku-⌐zi⌐kañ	'9 hours'
zi⌐p-puñ or zyu⌐p-puñ	'10 minutes' or 'minute 10'	zyu⌐u-zi	'10 o'clock'	zyu⌐u-zi⌐kañ	'10 hours'
na⌐ñ-puñ	'how many minutes?' or 'what minute?'	na⌐ñ-zi	'what time?'	na⌐ñ-zi⌐kañ	'how many hours?'

---

[1] Except the first day of the month, for which there is the special word tu⌐itati⌐.

[2] Except the year 1. See the note on sentence 14 above. There are also counters -neñkañ and -kaneñkañ, which combine with numerals to count (but not name) years and hence belong in Group B above.

-ka/-niti

(tu⌐itati¬	'the first day of the month')		
i⌐ti-niti¬	'one day'		
hutu-ka	'the second'	or	'2 days'
mi-kka	'the third'	or	'3 days'
yo-kka	'the fourth'	or	'4 days'
itu-ka	'the fifth'	or	'5 days'
mu-ika	'the sixth'	or	'6 days'
nano-ka	'the seventh'	or	'7 days'
yoo-ka	'the eighth'	or	'8 days'
ko⌐kono-ka¬	'the ninth'	or	'9 days'
too-ka	'the tenth'	or	'10 days'
zyu⌐uiti-niti¬	'the eleventh'	or	'11 days'
zyu⌐uni-niti¬	'the twelfth'	or	'12 days'
zyu¬usañ-niti	'the thirteenth'	or	'13 days'
zyu¬uyo-kka	'the fourteenth'	or	'14 days'
zyu¬ugo-niti	'the fifteenth'	or	'15 days'
zyu⌐uroku-niti¬	'the sixteenth'	or	'16 days'
zyu⌐usiti-niti¬	'the seventeenth'	or	'17 days'
zyu⌐uhati-niti¬	'the eighteenth'	or	'18 days'
zyu¬uku-niti	'the nineteenth'	or	'19 days'
hatu-ka	'the twentieth'	or	'20 days'
ni¬zyuu i⌐ti-niti¬	'the twenty-first'	or	'21 days'
ni¬zyuu ni-¬niti¬	'the twenty-second'	or	'22 days'
ni¬zyuu ⌐sa¬ñ-niti	'the twenty-third'	or	'23 days'
ni¬zyuu yo-kka	'the twenty-fourth'	or	'24 days'
ni¬zyuu ⌐go¬-niti	'the twenty-fifth'	or	'25 days'
ni¬zyuu ro⌐ku-niti¬	'the twenty-sixth'	or	'26 days'
ni¬zyuu si⌐ti-niti¬	'the twenty-seventh'	or	'27 days'
ni¬zyuu ha⌐ti-niti¬	'the twenty-eighth'	or	'28 days'
ni¬zyuu ⌐ku¬-niti	'the twenty-ninth'	or	'29 days'
sa⌐ñzyu¬u-niti	'the thirtieth'	or	'30 days'
sa¬ñzyuu i⌐ti-niti¬	'the thirty-first'	or	'31 days'
na¬ñ-niti	'what date?'	or	'how many days?'

-syuukañ

i⌐s-syu¬ukañ	'1 week'
ni-⌐syu¬ukañ	'2 weeks'
sa⌐ñ-syu¬ukañ	'3 weeks'
yo⌐ñ-syu¬ukañ	'4 weeks'
go-⌐syu¬ukañ	'5 weeks'
ro⌐ku-syu¬ukañ	'6 weeks'
na⌐na-syu¬ukañ or	
si⌐ti-syu¬ukañ	'7 weeks'
ha⌐s-syu¬ukañ	'8 weeks'
kyu⌐u-syu¬ukañ	'9 weeks'
zi⌐s-syu¬ukañ or	
zyu⌐s-syu¬ukañ	'10 weeks'
na⌐ñ-syu¬ukañ	'how many weeks?'

-ḡatu		-kaḡetu	
i⌐ti-ḡatu¬	'January'	i⌐k-ka¬ḡetu	'1 month'
ni-⌐ḡatu¬	'February'	ni-⌐ka¬ḡetu	'2 months'
sa⌐n̄-ḡatu	'March'	sa⌐n̄-ka¬ḡetu	'3 months'
si-⌐ḡatu¬	'April'	yo⌐n̄-ka¬ḡetu	'4 months'
go¬-ḡatu	'May'	go-⌐ka¬ḡetu	'5 months'
ro⌐ku-ḡatu¬	'June'	ro⌐k-ka¬ḡetu	'6 months'
si⌐ti-ḡatu¬	'July'	si⌐ti-ka¬ḡetu or	
ha⌐ti-ḡatu¬	'August'	na⌐na-ka¬ḡetu	'7 months'
ku¬-ḡatu	'September'	ha⌐ti-ka¬ḡetu or	
zyu⌐u-ḡatu¬	'October'	ha⌐k-ka¬ḡetu	'8 months'
zyu⌐uiti-ḡatu¬	'November'	ku-⌐ka¬ḡetu or	
zyu⌐uni-ḡatu¬	'December'	kyu⌐u-ka¬ḡetu	'9 months'
		zi⌐k-ka¬ḡetu or	
na⌐n̄-ḡatu	'what month?'	zyu⌐k-ka¬ḡetu	'10 months'
		na⌐n̄-ka¬ḡetu	'how many months?'

-nen̄	
i⌐ti¬-nen̄	'1 year'
(ga¬n̄nen̄	'the year 1')
ni¬-nen̄	'2 years' or 'the year 2'
sañ-nen̄	'3 years' or 'the year 3'
yo-nen̄	'4 years' or 'the year 4'
go-nen̄	'5 years' or 'the year 5'
ro⌐ku¬-nen̄	'6 years' or 'the year 6'
si⌐ti¬-nen̄ or	
na⌐na¬-nen̄	'7 years' or 'the year 7'
ha⌐ti¬-nen̄	'8 years' or 'the year 8'
ku-nen̄ or	
kyu¬u-nen̄	'9 years' or 'the year 9'
zyu¬u-nen̄	'10 years' or 'the year 10'
na¬n̄-nen̄	'how many years?' or 'what year?'

The regular order of Japanese dates is year–month–day, with the smaller unit always following the larger. The units are usually joined without intervening particles. [1] Examples:

---

[1] But they can be joined by particle no. Ni-ḡatu kŏkono-ka might be compared to 'February 9th,' and ni-⌐ḡatu no kokono-ka¬ to 'the 9th of February [rather than of another month].'

⌈syoowa⌋ ⌜zyu⌉uku-neñ ⌜sa⌉ñ-ḡatu mĭ-kka 'March 3, 19 ⌈Showa⌋
    (= A. D. 1944)'
⌈seereki⌋ ⌜se⌉ñ ⌐kyu⌐uhyaku go⌜zyu⌉u-neñ hăti-ḡatu mŭ-ika
    'August 6, 1950 ⌈Christian era⌋ '

-Ha⌉ñ added to a number means 'a half added to the preceding':

    i⌜ti-zi-ha⌉ñ '1:30'
    i⌜ti-zikañ-ha⌉ñ 'one hour and a half'
    ni-⌜neñ-ha⌉ñ 'two years and a half'

But hañ- + counter means 'a half of one counter unit' (not all counters occur in this combination):

    ha⌜ñ-zi⌉kañ 'a half hour'
    ha⌜ñ-niti⌉ 'a half day'

2.   Telling   Time

    For telling time in terms of the hour only, a numeral + counter -zi is used.
Thus:

    Yo⌉-zi desu. 'It's 4 o'clock.'

To indicate time before the hour, ma⌉e is added, and to indicate time after the hour, su⌜ḡi⌉ is added. Thus:

    Si⌜ti-zi ma⌉e desu. 'It's before 7.'
    Ku-⌜zi suḡi⌉ desu. 'It's after 9.'

    To tell time in terms of hours and minutes, two patterns are used. The simpler pattern consists of the o'clock + the minute. This corresponds to the English pattern of '2:10,' '8:15,' '10:45,' etc. Thus:

    Ni⌐-zi ⌜zyu⌉p-puñ desu. 'It's 2:10.' (Lit. 'It's 2 o'clock minute 10.')
    Ha⌜ti⌉-zi ⌜zyu⌉ugo-huñ desu. 'It's 8:15.'
    Zyu⌉u-zi ⌜yo⌉ñzyuu ⌐go⌐-huñ desu. 'It's 10:45.'

The alternate pattern consists of (a) the o'clock + the minute before + -mae 'before' (when the minute hand is in the left half of the clock; compare English '5 of 2,' '20 minutes to 3,' 'a quarter of 8,' etc.); and (b) the o'clock + the minute after + -suḡi 'beyond' (when the minute hand is in the right half of the clock; compare English ' 10 after 2,' 'a quarter past 3,' etc.). The accent of the minute expression shifts to the first syllable of the counter. Thus:

    Ni⌉-zi go-⌜hu⌉ñ-mae desu. 'It's 5 of 2.' (Lit. 'It's 2 o'clock minute 5 before.')
    Ha⌜ti⌉-zi zyu⌜ugo-hu⌉ñ-mae desu.   'It's a quarter of 8.'
    Ni⌉-zi zi⌜p-pu⌉ñ-suḡi desu. 'It's 10 after 2.'
    Sa⌉ñ-zi zyu⌜ugo-hu⌉ñ-suḡi desu. 'It's a quarter after 3.'

    In all the above examples, -huñ occurs as a naming counter (cf. Group C of the preceding grammatical note), telling WHICH minute of the hour. -Huñ also occurs as an enumerating counter, telling HOW MANY minutes, before ma⌉e 'ago,' 'before' and also in various other expressions. Compare the following:

Zi⌐p-pu⌐n̄-mae desita.   'It was 10 of.'   (i. e. it was 10 minutes before
the hour)
Zi⌐p-puñ ⌐ma⌐e desita.
      or   } 'It was 10 minutes ago.'
Zi⌐p-puñ ma⌐e desita.

Sentences like those in the groups above are differentiated by accent.   Elsewhere, context determines whether -huñ is naming or counting.

3.   Informal Speech

The subject of speech levels has already been introduced in connection with
the occurrence of parallel pairs such as a⌐rima⌐su and go⌐zaima⌐su, i⌐kima⌐su
and i⌐rassyaima⌐su, ge⌐ñki and o⌐ge⌐ñki, i⌐kura and oikura.   In general, we
can speak of two major levels: the POLITE and the PLAIN.   The polite includes NEUTRAL POLITE (like go⌐zaima⌐su+), HUMBLE (like ma⌐irima⌐su+),
and HONORIFIC (like i⌐rassyaima⌐su+).   In addition to politeness levels, there
are formality levels—the FORMAL and the INFORMAL.   A given verbal may
be formal polite, informal polite, formal plain, or informal plain.   Verbals
ending in -ma⌐su and all of its derived forms (-ma⌐sita, -mase⌐ñ, -mase⌐ñ desita, and -masyo⌐o) and copula forms de⌐su, de⌐sita, and de⌐syo⌐o are all
formal forms.   Thus, a⌐rima⌐su is formal plain style, whereas go⌐zaima⌐su
is formal polite; i⌐kima⌐su is formal plain, but ma⌐irima⌐su and i⌐rassyaima⌐su
are formal polite. [1]

In general, a sentence is assigned to the level of its final (or only) inflected
word—provided, of course, that it has an inflected word.   Other features of the
sentence may make it a more or less formal and/or polite degree of that major
level.   A speech sequence is said to belong to the level which characterizes
most of its sentences.

The ability to choose the appropriate level for any given situation requires
a thorough knowledge of Japanese social structure.   In general, the informal
style of speech is used most commonly in addressing friends and in speaking to
social inferiors in informal situations; formal speech is used in addressing
strangers, casual acquaintances, and superiors, and in speaking to social inferiors in formal situations; polite words are usually used in reference to persons of equal or superior social standing; the plain level is usually used in
reference to persons of equal or inferior social standing; women use polite and
formal speech more commonly than men.   This is at best an oversimplification;
one of the most complicated phases of the problem for a foreigner is to determine the bases for social inferiority and superiority in the Japanese system,
and to know when a formal, comparatively stiff style of speech is appropriate
and when it is fitting to be informal.

---

[1] Informal equivalents will be introduced later.

The following are two patterns typical of the informal style of speech:[1]

a. Adjectivals and nominals occur at the end of statements without the de⌐su which follows them in formal speech.

Examples:

Formal	Informal
O⌐oki⌐i desu. 'It's big.'	O⌐oki⌐i. 'It's big.'
Pe⌐n̄ desu. 'It's a pen.'	Pe⌐n̄. 'A pen.'

Note that the only difference between an adjectival + desu and an adjectival alone is in the formality; an adjectival in its -i form has tense and is a complete, major—but informal—sentence when it occurs alone. A nominal, on the other hand, has no tense and occurs as a sentence by itself only in fragments (cf. Lesson 4, Grammatical Note 5) similar to English sentences like these: 'A book.' 'Some bread.' 'That ashtray.' etc.

b. Adjectivals and nominals occur with question-mark intonation in questions, without the de⌐su + ka which occurs in formal speech.

Examples:

Formal	Informal
O⌐oki⌐i desu ka↲ 'Is it big?'	O⌐oki⌐i? 'Is it big?'
Pe⌐n̄ desu ka↲ 'Is it a pen?'	Pe⌐n̄? 'A pen?'

But note the following:

Formal	Informal[2]
So⌐o desu ka↲ 'Is that right?'	So⌐o? 'Really?'
So⌐o desu ka. 'Is that right.'	A⌐a ⌐so⌐o. 'Oh.' or 'Oh?'
So⌐o desu ⌐ne⌐e. 'That's right, isn't it.'	So⌐o. 'Right.'
So⌐o desu. 'That's right.'	So⌐o. 'Right.'

The first form in each column is more animated than the second and shows livelier interest. The difference between So⌐o. occurring as the informal equivalent of So⌐o desu. and of So⌐o desu ⌐ne⌐e. is determined by context.

Additional informal patterns and forms will be introduced later.

---

[1] But these are by no means the only informal equivalents of the given formal patterns.

[2] Again, each informal expression mentioned here is only one of several possibilities; others will be described later.

4.   P a r t i c l e s :   <u>kara</u> 'f r o m ,' <u>ni</u> (t i m e   w h e n)

a. <u>kara</u> 'from'

The particle <u>kara</u> following a nominal means 'from.' A phrase ending
with <u>kara</u> may modify an inflected expression directly, or it may be followed by another particle.   When a <u>kara</u> phrase describes a nominal it
is followed by <u>no</u>.   Examples:

Kyo⌐oto kara ki┌ma┐sita. 'I came from Kyoto.'
Asita ⌐ku┐-zi kara ko⌐ko ni ima┐su.   'I'll be here from 9 o'clock [on]
tomorrow.'
Ta⌐naka-sañ kara wa kimase┐ñ desita. 'It didn't come from Tanaka
[but where it did come from I don't know].'
Are wa ⌐Ni┐kkoo kara no ┌ba┐su desu ka⌐」 'Is that the bus from Nik-
ko?'

Compare also <u>sore kara</u> 'from that' (i.e. 'after that' or 'next').

b. <u>ni</u> 'in,' 'on,' 'at'

Time expressions modifying an inflected expression, and indicating the
time at which something happens, a r e divided into two main groups:
those which occur without a following particle, and those which are followed by <u>ni</u>.   (Compare the English use of 'on' with days of the week,
'in' with months and years, 'at' with hours of the day, and no preposi-
tion with 'today,' 'tomorrow,' 'yesterday,' etc.)   In general, time words
whose meaning is relative to the time of usage—for example, i┌ma 'now,'
kyo┐o 'today,' a⌐sita┐ 'tomorrow,' and ki⌐no┐o 'yesterday'—occur without a following particle, while other time expressions are more apt to
take <u>ni</u>, but the rule is not hard and fast.

Some time expressions —for example, those ending with -ğo┐ro (cf. the
following note)—occur both with or without <u>ni</u> in this kind of construction.

Examples:

I┐tu i┌kima┐su ka⌐」 'When are you going to go?'
A⌐sita sima┐su. 'I'll do [it] tomorrow.'
I┐ma ka┌kima┐sita. 'I just wrote [it].'
Ku┐-zi ⌐xyu┐ugohuñ ni ki┌ma┐sita. 'I came at 9:15.'
Si⌐ti-ğatu┐ ni i┌kimasyo┐o. 'Let's go in July.'
To⌐o-ka ni kaima┐sita. 'I bought [it] on the tenth.'

Such time expressions, both those with <u>ni</u> and those without <u>ni</u>, may be
followed by particles <u>wa</u> or <u>mo</u>:

Kyo┐o wa i┌kima┐su ğa⌐ 'Today (in comparison with other times) I'll
go but . . .'
Si⌐ti-ğatu┐ ni wa i┌kima┐su ğa⌐   'In July (in comparison with other
times) I'll go but . . .'
A⌐sita┐ mo kimasu. 'I'll come tomorrow, too.'
To⌐o-ka ni┐ mo kimasu. 'I'll come on the tenth, too.'

All the preceding applies only when the time expression tells when

something occurs. Time expressions also occur in other nominal constructions. Compare the following pairs of examples:

1. (a) Sore (wa) ⌐na⌐n̄ desu ka⌐ 'What is that?'
    (b) Kyo⌐o (wa) na⌐ñyo⌐obi desu ka⌐ 'What day is today?'

2. (a) Na⌐ni ḡa ⌐i⌐i desyoo ka. 'What would be good?'
    (b) Na⌐ñyo⌐obi ḡa ⌐i⌐i desyoo ka. 'What day would be good?'

3. (a) A⌐merika no zido⌐osya desu. 'It's an American car.'
    (b) Ro⌐kuzyu⌐u-neñ no zi⌐do⌐osya desu. 'It's a '60 car.'

5. -ḡo⌐ro ~ -ḡu⌐rai 'about'

-Ḡo⌐ro is added to time expressions which ask or answer the question
'when?'; it means 'approximate point of time.'

-Ḡu⌐rai 'approximate quantity' is added to quantity expressions which ask
or answer the questions 'how much?' 'how many?' 'how far?' or 'how long?'
and to kono, sono, ano, and do⌐no.

An expression ending with -ḡo⌐ro is always a nominal time expression but
one ending with -ḡu⌐rai may be any kind of nominal quantity expression.

Speaking in terms of the time counter groups introduced in Grammatical
Note 1 above, those in Group A (-zi and -ḡatu) may be followed by -ḡo⌐ro; those
in Group B (-zikañ, -syuukañ, and -kaḡetu) may be followed by -ḡu⌐rai; and
those in Group C (-huñ, -ka/-niti, and -neñ) may be followed by -ḡo⌐ro when
naming a time and by -ḡu⌐rai when counting time.

Before -ḡo⌐ro and -ḡu⌐rai, an accented word regularly loses its accent; and
in some combinations, -ḡo⌐ro and -ḡu⌐rai also lose their accents (note examples
below).

Examples:

        itu-ḡoro 'about when?'
        sa⌐ñ-zi-ḡo⌐ro 'about 3 o'clock'
        sa⌐ñ-zi zi⌐p-puñ-ḡo⌐ro 'about 3:10'
        go-⌐huñ-mae-ḡo⌐ro 'about five minutes of [the hour]'
        go-⌐huñ-suḡi-ḡo⌐ro 'about 5 minutes after [the hour]'
        do⌐yoobi-ḡo⌐ro 'about Saturday'
        to⌐o-ka-ḡo⌐ro 'about the 10th of the month'
        se⌐ñ ⌐kyu⌐uhyaku go⌐zyuu-neñ-ḡo⌐ro 'about 1950'
        dono-ḡurai 'about how much?'
        kono-ḡurai 'about this much'
        zi⌐p-puñ-ḡu⌐rai 'about 10 minutes'
        sa⌐ñ-zikañ-ḡu⌐rai 'about 3 hours'
        to⌐o-ka-ḡu⌐rai 'about 10 days'
        yo⌐ñ-kaḡetu-ḡu⌐rai 'about 4 months'
        zyu⌐u-neñ-ḡu⌐rai 'about 10 years'
        to⌐o-ḡu⌐rai 'about 10 (units)'
        hya⌐ku-eñ-ḡu⌐rai 'about ¥ 100'

When a phrase ending in -ḡo⌐ro tells the approximate time at which something happens, it may occur with particle <u>ni</u>, but more commonly occurs with-out it (cf. Grammatical Note 4b above). Compare English 'I'm going [at] about 4 o'clock.'

Examples:

Sa⌈ñ-zi-g̅o⌉ro [ni] i⌐kimasyo⌐o. 'Let's go [at] about 3 o'clock.'
Sa⌈ñ-g̅atu-g̅o⌉ro [ni] ki⌐ma⌐sita. 'He came [in] about March.'
So⌐no ho⌐ñ wa syŏowa zyu⌐u-neñ-g̅o⌉ro [ni] ka⌐kima⌐sita.   'That book he wrote [in] about Showa 10.'

6.   ki⌈ma⌉su ~ ma⌈irima⌉su ~ i⌈rassyaima⌉su

Ki⌈ma⌉su 'come' is a plain formal verbal; ma⌈irima⌉su and i⌈rassyaima⌉su are polite formal verbals with the same meaning. Ma⌈irima⌉su, a humble verbal, refers to the actions of the speaker (or members of his own family), in polite speech. I⌈rassyaima⌉su, an honorific verbal, refers to the actions of persons other than the speaker, whose position is being elevated or exalted, in polite speech.

Three meanings for i⌈rassyaima⌉su and two for ma⌈irima⌉su have now been introduced. Study the following chart:

	Plain Formal	Polite Formal	
		Humble ↓	Honorific ↑
'be located (animate)'	i⌈ma⌉su	o⌈rima⌉su	i⌈rassyaima⌉su
'go'	i⌈kima⌉su	ma⌈irima⌉su	i⌈rassyaima⌉su
'come'	ki⌈ma⌉su	ma⌈irima⌉su	i⌈rassyaima⌉su

Ki⌈ma⌉su regularly means motion toward—and i⌈kima⌉su motion away from—the speaker's position. Thus, the Japanese equivalent of 'I'm not com-ing to school tomorrow' said, for example, during a telephone conversation from outside, with someone at the school, would be A⌈sita⌉ wa ga⌐kkoo e iki-mase⌐ñ lit. 'I'm not going to school tomorrow.' A⌈sita⌉ wa ga⌐kkoo e kimase⌐ñ would be said only by someone actually at the school.

DRILLS

A.   Substitution Drill

1. It took 2 hours.   Ni-⌈zi⌉kañ ka⌐karima⌐sita.
2. It took 2 minutes.   Ni⌉-huñ ka⌐karima⌐sita.
3. It took 2 days.   Hu⌈tu-ka kakarima⌉sita.
4. It took 2 years.   Ni⌉-neñ ka⌐karima⌐sita.
5. It took 2 months.   Ni-⌈ka⌉g̅etu ka⌐karima⌐sita.
6. It took 2 weeks.   Ni-⌈syu⌉ukañ ka⌐karima⌐sita.
7. It took 2½ years.   Ni-⌈neñ-ha⌉ñ ka⌐karima⌐sita.

8. It took 2½ hours.   Ni-⌐zikañ-ha⌐ñ ka⌐karima⌐sita.
9. It took a half day.   Ha⌐ñ-niti kakarima⌐sita.
10. It took a half hour.   Ha⌐ñ-zi⌐kañ ka⌐karima⌐sita.

B. Substitution Drill

1. I did [it] at 2 o'clock.   Ni⌐-zi ni si⌐ma⌐sita.
2. I did [it] 2 days ago.   Hu⌐tu-ka ma⌐e ni si⌐ma⌐sita.
3. I did [it] in Showa 2.   Syoowa ⌐ni⌐-neñ ni si⌐ma⌐sita.
4. I did [it] in February.   Ni-⌐gatu⌐ ni si⌐ma⌐sita.
5. I did [it] at 2:30.   Ni-⌐zi-ha⌐ñ ni si⌐ma⌐sita.
6. I did [it] on Tuesday.   Ka⌐yo⌐obi ni si⌐ma⌐sita.
7. I did [it] 2 hours ago.   Ni-⌐zikañ ma⌐e ni si⌐ma⌐sita.
8. I did [it] on the second.   Hu⌐tu-ka ni sima⌐sita.

C. Substitution Drill

1. I went to the station by   Kyo⌐o ⌐e⌐ki e ⌐ba⌐su de i⌐kima⌐sita.
    bus today.
2. I went to the station by   Kinoo ⌐e⌐ki e ⌐ba⌐su de i⌐kima⌐sita.
    bus yesterday.
3. I went to the hospital by   Kinoo byǒoiñ e ⌐ba⌐su de i⌐kima⌐sita.
    bus yesterday.
4. I went to the hospital by   Kinoo byǒoiñ e ⌐ta⌐kusii de i⌐kima⌐si-
    taxi yesterday.   ta.
5. I came to the hospital by   Kinoo byǒoin e ⌐ta⌐kusii de ki⌐ma⌐sita.
    taxi yesterday.
6. I came to the hospital by   Ototoi byǒoiñ e ⌐ta⌐kusii de ki⌐ma⌐si-
    taxi the day before yes-   ta.
    terday.
7. I came to school by taxi   Ototoi gǎkkoo e ⌐ta⌐kusii de ki⌐ma⌐si-
    the day before yesterday.   ta.
8. I came to school by elec-   Ototoi gǎkkoo e ⌐de⌐ñsya de ki⌐ma⌐si-
    tric train the day before   ta.
    yesterday.
9. I came here by electric   Ototoi kǒko e ⌐de⌐ñsya de ki⌐ma⌐sita.
    train the day before yes-
    terday.
10. I came here by plane the   Ototoi kǒko e hi⌐ko⌐oki de ki⌐ma⌐si-
    day before yesterday.   ta.
11. I came here by plane this   Kotosi kǒko e hi⌐ko⌐oki de ki⌐ma⌐si-
    year.   ta.
12. I came here by ship this   Kotosi kǒko e ⌐hu⌐ne de ki⌐ma⌐sita.
    year.

D. Substitution Drill

1. I came 10 years ago.   Zyu⌐u-neñ ma⌐e ni ki⌐ma⌐sita.
2. I came 5 minutes ago.   Go-⌐huñ ma⌐e ni ki⌐ma⌐sita.
3. I came 1 hour ago.   I⌐ti-zikañ ma⌐e ni ki⌐ma⌐sita.
4. I came 10 days ago.   To⌐o-ka ma⌐e ni ki⌐ma⌐sita.

5. I came 6 months ago.   Ro⌐k-kaḡetu ma⌐e ni ki⌐ma⌐sita.
6. I came 3 weeks ago.   Sañ-syuukañ ma⌐e ni ki⌐ma⌐sita.
7. I came a little (while) ago.   Su⌐ko⌐si ⌐ma⌐e ni ki⌐ma⌐sita.
8. I came a little (while) ago.   Tyo⌐tto ⌐ma⌐e ni ki⌐ma⌐sita.

E. Substitution Drill

1. When is that?   Sore (wa) ⌐i⌐tu desu ka⌐
2. What is that?   Sore (wa) ⌐na⌐ñ desu ka⌐
3. Which one is that?   Sore (wa) ⌐do⌐re desu ka⌐
4. Where is that?   Sore (wa) ⌐do⌐ko desu ka⌐
5. How is that?   Sore (wa) ⌐do⌐o desu ka⌐
6. What month is that?   Sore (wa) ⌐na⌐ñ-ḡatu desu ka⌐
7. What time is that?   Sore (wa) ⌐na⌐ñ-zi desu ka⌐
8. What day is that?   Sore (wa) na⌐ñyo⌐obi desu ka⌐
9. How much is that?   Sore (wa) ⌐i⌐kura desu ka⌐
10. How many yen is that?   Sore (wa) ⌐na⌐ñ-eñ desu ka⌐

F. Substitution Drill

1. I went from the hotel.   Ho⌐teru kara i⌐kima⌐sita.
2. I went by train.   Ki⌐sya⌐ de i⌐kima⌐sita.
3. I went as far as the station. E⌐ki made i⌐kima⌐sita.
4. I went on the third.   Mi-⌐kka ni ikima⌐sita.
5. I went along that road.   So⌐no miti (o) ikima⌐sita.
6. I went.   Wa⌐takusi⌐ ḡa ikima⌐sita.
7. I (in comparison with oth-   Wa⌐takusi wa ikima⌐sita.
    ers) went.
8. I went the day before yes-   O⌐totoi ikima⌐sita.
    terday.
9. I went about 9 o'clock.   Ku-⌐zi-ḡo⌐ro i⌐kima⌐sita.
10. I went to the consulate.   Ryo⌐ozi⌐kañ e i⌐kima⌐sita.

G. Grammar Drill (based on Grammatical Note 5)

         Tutor: Yo⌐-zi desu. 'It's 4 o'clock.'
         Student: Yo-⌐zi-ḡo⌐ro desu. 'It's about 4 o'clock.'

1. To⌐o-ka ima⌐sita.   To⌐o-ka-ḡu⌐rai i⌐ma⌐sita.
2. To⌐o-ka ni ima⌐sita.   To⌐o-ka-ḡo⌐ro i⌐ma⌐sita.
3. Ku⌐-ḡatu desu.   Ku-⌐ḡatu-ḡo⌐ro desu.
4. Mo⌐kuyo⌐o ni i⌐kimasyo⌐o.   Mo⌐kuyoo-ḡo⌐ro i⌐kimasyo⌐o.
5. Go-⌐neñ ima⌐sita.   Go-⌐neñ-ḡu⌐rai i⌐ma⌐sita.
6. Go-⌐neñ ni ima⌐sita.   Go-⌐neñ-ḡo⌐ro i⌐ma⌐sita.
7. Zyu⌐s-syu⌐ukañ desita.   Zyu⌐s-syuukañ-ḡu⌐rai desita.
8. Zi⌐p-puñ ka⌐karima⌐sita.   Zi⌐p-puñ-ḡu⌐rai ka⌐karima⌐sita.

H. Level Drill (The sentences on the right are the plain equivalents of the po-
    lite sentences on the left.)

    1. I⌐tu ko⌐tira e irassyaima⌐si-   I⌐tu ko⌐ko e kima⌐sita ka⌐
        ta ka⌐

2. Ya⌐mamoto orima⌐su ka⌐   Ya⌐mamoto ima⌐su ka⌐
3. I⌐ma ma⌐irimasyo⌐o ka.   I⌐ma i⌐kimasyo⌐o ka.

4. Ta⌐naka-san irassyaima⌐su | ima⌐su |
   ka⌐   Ta⌐naka-san | kima⌐su | ka⌐
                                                | ikima⌐su|

5. Ra⌐itaa go⌐zaima⌐su ka⌐   Ra⌐itaa a⌐rima⌐su ka⌐
6. Ni⌐-nen ⌐ma⌐e ni ko⌐tira   Ni⌐-nen ⌐ma⌐e ni ko⌐ko e kima⌐sita.
   e mairima⌐sita.
7. Do⌐tira e i⌐rassyaima⌐su   Do⌐ko e i⌐kima⌐su ka⌐
   ka⌐
8. To⌐nde mo gozaimase⌐n.   To⌐nde mo arimase⌐n.

I. Level Drill (The sentences on the right are informal equivalents of the sentences on the left.)

   1. Kyo⌐o tu⌐itati⌐ desu ka⌐   Kyo⌐o tu̅itati?
   2. Tyo⌐odo yo⌐-zi desu.   Tyo⌐odo yo⌐-zi.
   3. A⌐a, so⌐o desu ka.   A⌐a, so⌐o.
   4. To⌐ttemo i⌐i desu.   To⌐ttemo i⌐i.
   5. Yo⌐rosi⌐i desu ka⌐   Yorosii?
   6. Sore ⌐na⌐n desu ka⌐   Sore ⌐na⌐ni?

J. Expansion Drill

   1. [He] went.   I⌐kima⌐sita.
      [He] went to France.   Hu⌐ransu e ikima⌐sita.
      [He] went to France six   Ro⌐k-kagetu ma⌐e ni Hu⌐ransu e iki-
      months ago.   ma⌐sita.
      Mr. Tanaka went to France   Tanaka-san (wa) ro⌐k-kagetu ma⌐e ni
      six months ago.   Hu⌐ransu e ikima⌐sita.

   2. I came.   Ki⌐ma⌐sita.
      I came on the 24th.   Ni⌐zyuu yo-⌐kka ni kima⌐sita.
      I came on August 24th.   Hati-gatu ⌐ni⌐zyuu yo-⌐kka ni kima⌐si-
                                    ta.
      I came on August 24, 35 (i.e. Sa⌐nzyuu go-nen hāti-gatu ⌐ni⌐zyuu yo-
      of the Showa Era).   ⌐kka ni kima⌐sita.

   3. About how many days does it   Na⌐n-niti-gu⌐rai ka⌐karima⌐su ka⌐
      take?
      About how many days does it   Hu⌐ne de na⌐n-niti-gu⌐rai ka⌐karima⌐-
      take by ship?   su ka⌐
      About how many days does it   A⌐merika ma⌐de ⌐hu⌐ne de na⌐n-niti-gu⌐-
      take by ship, as far as   rai ka⌐karima⌐su ka⌐
      America?
      About how many days does it   Ni⌐ho⌐n kara A⌐merika ma⌐de ⌐hu⌐ne de
      take from Japan as far as   na⌐n-niti-gu⌐rai ka⌐karima⌐su ka⌐
      America by ship?

4. I'd like to go . . .   I⌐kita⌐i ñ desu ḡa_
    I'd like to go by car . . .   Zi⌐do⌐osya de i⌐kita⌐i ñ desu ḡa_
    I'd like to go to Nikko by   Ni⌐kkoo e zi⌐do⌐osya de i⌐kita⌐i ñ desu
    car . . .   ḡa_
    I'd like to go to Nikko by   Iti-do ⌐Ni⌐kkoo e zi⌐do⌐osya de i⌐kita⌐i
    car some (lit. one) time . . .   ñ desu ḡa_

5. It will probably be about   Si⌐ti-ḡatu-ḡo⌐ro desyoo.
    July.
    [His] vacation will probably   Oyasumi (wa) si⌐ti-ḡatu-ḡo⌐ro desyoo.
    be about July.
    [His] vacation this year will   Kotosi no oyasumi (wa) si⌐ti-ḡatu-ḡo⌐-
    probably be about July.   ro desyoo.
    Mr. Tanaka's vacation this   Tanaka-sañ no kōtosi no oyasumi (wa)
    year will probably be   si⌐ti-ḡatu-ḡo⌐ro desyoo.
    about July.

6. [They]'re good!   I⌐i desu yo_
    [They]'re very good!   To⌐ttemo i⌐i desu yo_
    The new hotels are very   A⌐tarasi⌐i ⌐ho⌐teru (wa) to⌐ttemo i⌐i
    good!   desu yo_
    The new hotels in Tokyo   Tookyoo no a⌐tarasi⌐i ⌐ho⌐teru (wa)
    are very good!   to⌐ttemo i⌐i desu yo_

QUESTION SUPPLEMENT

Answer the following questions, using a calendar when necessary:

1. I⌐ti-zi⌐kañ wa ⌐na⌐ñ-puñ desu ka_
2. I⌐ti-niti⌐ wa na⌐ñ-zi⌐kañ desu ka_
3. I⌐s-syu⌐ukañ wa ⌐na⌐ñ-niti desu ka_
4. I⌐k-ka⌐ḡetu wa na⌐ñ-niti-ḡu⌐rai desu ka_
5. I⌐k-ka⌐ḡetu wa na⌐ñ-syuukañ-ḡu⌐rai desu ka_
6. I⌐ti⌐-neñ wa ⌐na⌐ñ-niti desu ka_
7. I⌐ti⌐-neñ wa na⌐ñ-syu⌐ukañ desu ka_
8. I⌐ti⌐-neñ wa na⌐ñ-ka⌐ḡetu desu ka_
9. Kyo⌐o wa na⌐ñyo⌐obi desu ka_
10. A⌐sita⌐ wa ⌐na⌐ñ-niti desu ka_
11. Ki⌐no⌐o wa ⌐na⌐ñ-niti na⌐ñyo⌐obi desita ka_
12. O⌐toto⌐i wa ni⌐tiyoo de⌐sita ka_
13. Kotosi no iti-ḡatu hātu-ka wa na⌐ñyo⌐obi desu ka_
14. Kotosi no ⌐go⌐-ḡatu mī-kka wa na⌐ñyo⌐obi desu ka_
15. Kotosi no sīti-ḡatu ⌐ni⌐zyuu si⌐ti-niti⌐ wa na⌐ñyo⌐obi desu ka_
16. Kotosi no hāti-ḡatu hūtu-ka wa na⌐ñyo⌐obi desu ka_
17. Ko⌐tosi no Kurisu⌐masu ['Christmas'] wa na⌐ñyo⌐obi desu ka_
18. Watakusi wa ha⌐ñ-zikañ ma⌐e ni ki⌐ma⌐sita. Na⌐ñ-zi ni ki⌐ma⌐sita
    ka_
19. Watakusi wa tyōodo sa⌐ñ-kaḡetu ma⌐e ni ⌐Ni⌐kkoo e i⌐kima⌐sita. Na⌐ñ-
    ḡatu ⌐na⌐ñ-niti ni i⌐kima⌐sita ka_

20. Watakusi wa tyóodo i⌐s-syuukañ ma⌐e ni ko⌐no kuruma o kaima⌐sita.
    Na⌐ñ-niti ni ka⌐ima⌐sita ka⌐

21. Syoowa ⌐zyu⌐u-neñ wa seereki ⌐na⌐ñ-neñ desita ka⌐

22. Me⌐ezi ⌐ga⌐ñneñ wa seereki ⌐na⌐ñ-neñ desita ka⌐

23. Kotosi wa ⌐na⌐ñ-neñ desu ka⌐

EXERCISES

1. Mr. Tanaka has asked what time it is. Give the following answers:

    a. It's 4 o'clock.
    b. It's just 7:30.
    c. It's 10 after 6.
    d. It's 10:45.
    e. It's 5:15.
    f. It's about 7 o'clock.
    g. It's about a quarter to eight.
    h. It's 2:28.
    i. It's one minute after 1.
    j. It's 10 to 12.
    k. It's 20 to 11.
    l. It's probably about 9.

2. Mr. Tanaka has just asked you when you came here. Tell him that you came:

    a. In 1955.
    b. In January.
    c. In March, 1953.
    d. On April 14th.
    e. In Showa 29.
    f. About six months ago.
    g. About two years ago.
    h. About ten weeks ago.

3. Using a calendar, practice asking and answering questions pertaining to dates and days of the week.

4. Practice asking and answering questions on how long it takes from one given geographical point to another by a given mode of transportation. The geographical points may include everything f r o m countries to buildings within a c i t y. Timetables are useful as the basis for some questions.

5. Practice the Basic Dialogues with appropriate variations.

Lesson 9. Time (cont.)

BASIC DIALOGUES: FOR MEMORIZATION

(a)

Tanaka

every day	ma⌐initi
return home	ka⌐erima⌐su or
	o⌐kaeri ni narima⌐su ⌐

1. What time do you go home every day?

Ma⌐initi ⌐na⌐ñ-zi ni ka⌐erima⌐su ka⌐
or
Ma⌐initi ⌐na⌐ñ-zi ni o⌐kaeri ni narima⌐su ka⌐

Smith

usually	taitee
sometimes	to⌐kidoki⌐

2. I usually go home at 5:30, but sometimes I go home about 6.

Taitee go-⌐zi-ha⌐ñ ni ka⌐erima⌐su ga, tokidoki ro⌐ku-zi-go⌐ro kaerimasu.

Tanaka

morning	a⌐sa
home	uti or
	otaku ⌐
go out or leave	de⌐ma⌐su or
	o⌐de ni narima⌐su ⌐

3. What time do you leave home in the morning?

A⌐sa ⌐na⌐ñ-zi ni u⌐ti (o) dema⌐su ka⌐
or
A⌐sa ⌐na⌐ñ-zi ni o⌐taku (o) ode ni narima⌐su ka⌐

Smith

always	i⌐tu mo
a little after 8	ha⌐ti⌐-zi tyo⌐tto sugi⌐

4. I always leave at a little after 8.

I⌐tu mo ha⌐ti⌐-zi tyo⌐tto sugi⌐ ni demasu.

going out or leaving	de⌐te
business office	zi⌐mu⌐syo
arrive	tu⌐kima⌐su

5. I leave the house about 8, and arrive at the office about 9.

Ha⌐ti-zi-go⌐ro u⌐ti (o) de⌐te, ku-⌐zi-go⌐ro zi⌐mu⌐syo ni tukimasu.

(b)

Tanaka

6. (About) when are you going back to America? | I⌈tu-ḡoro Amerika ni kaerima⌉su ka⌣ *or* I⌈tu-ḡoro Amerika ni okaeri ni narima⌉su ka⌣

Smith

by October | zyu⌈u-ḡatu⌉ made ni

7. I'd LIKE to go back by October (but) . . . | Zyu⌈u-ḡatu⌉ made ni ka⌈erita⌉i ñ desu ḡa—

Tanaka

be possible *or* can do | de⌈kima⌉su *or* o⌈deki ni narima⌉su†

8. Can't you? | De⌈kimase⌉ñ ka⌣ *or* O⌈deki ni narimase⌉ñ ka⌣

Smith

9. Hmm. I wonder. | Sa⌉a. Do⌉o desyoo ka ⌐ne⌐e.

(c)

At a government office

Employee

tomorrow morning | a⌈sita no a⌉sa

please come | ki⌈te⌉ kudasai *or* i⌈rassya⌉tte† kudasai *or* i⌈ra⌉site † kudasai

10. Please come again tomorrow morning. | A⌈sita no a⌉sa ma⌈ta kite⌉ kudasai. *or* A⌈sita no a⌉sa ma⌈ta irassya⌉tte kudasai. *or* A⌈sita no a⌉sa ma⌈ta ira⌉site kudasai.

Tanaka

I guess I'll come | ki⌈masyo⌉o *or* ma⌈irimasyo⌉o ↓

shall I come? | ki⌈masyo⌉o ka *or* ma⌈irimasyo⌉o ka ↓

11. What time shall I come? | Na⌉ñ-zi ni ki⌐masyo⌐o ka. *or* Na⌉ñ-zi ni ma⌐irimasyo⌐o ka.

Employee

by 9 o'clock | ku⌉-zi made ni

12. Please come by 9 o'clock.   Ku⌐-zi made ni ki⌐te⌐ kudasai.
                                            or
                                    Ku⌐-zi made ni i⌐rassya⌐tte kudasai.
                                          or
                                    Ku⌐-zi made ni i⌐ra⌐site kudasai.

Tanaka

    is fast or early   ha⌐ya⌐i /-ku/
13. That's early!   Ha⌐ya⌐i desu ⌐ne⌐e.

    be(come) distressing or   ko⌐marima⌐su
    troublesome or annoy-
    ing or inconvenient or
    perplexing
14. I'm afraid that will be a bit   Tyo⌐tto ko⌐marima⌐su ḡa_
    inconvenient...

Employee

15. Well then, how about 10   Zya⌐a, zyu⌐u-zi wa ⌐do⌐o desu ka.
    o'clock?   or
                                        Zya⌐a, zyu⌐u-zi wa i⌐ka⌐ḡa desu
                                        ka.

Tanaka

    fine   ke⌐kkoo+
    by 10 o'clock   zyu⌐u-zi made ni
16. That's fine. I'll come by   I⌐i desu yo_ Zyu⌐u-zi made ni kima-
    10.   su.
                                        or
                                      Ke⌐kkoo desu. Zyu⌐u-zi made ni ma-
                                      irimasu.

(d)

Secretary

    until what time?   na⌐ñ-zi made
    how long? (i.e. from   na⌐ñ-zi kara ⌐na⌐ñ-zi made
    what time until
    what time?)
    I guess I'll be or stay   i⌐masyo⌐o or
                                       o⌐rimasyo⌐o⌐
    shall I be or stay?   i⌐masyo⌐o ka or
                                      o⌐rimasyo⌐o ka⌐
17. How long shall I stay here   Asita ⌐na⌐ñ-zi kara ⌐na⌐ñ-zi made ko-
    tomorrow?   ⌐ko ni orimasyo⌐o ka_

Smith

    afternoon or p.m.   go⌐ḡo
    until 3 o'clock   sa⌐ñ-zi made
    please be or stay   i⌐te kudasa⌐i or
                                       i⌐rassya⌐tte⌐ kudasai or
                                       i⌐ra⌐site⌐ kudasai

18. Please be [here] from 9 in the morning until 3 in the afternoon.

A˥sa ⌈ku˩-zi kara ⌈go˥go ⌈sa˥ñ-zi made i˩te kudasa˥i.

Secretary

19. Certainly. I'll be here (lit. come) by 9.

Ka⌈sikomarima˥sita. Ku˥-zi made ni mairimasu.

(e)

Smith

this morning

ke˥sa

20. Did you go to the bank this morning?

Ke˥sa gi⌈ñkoo e ikima˥sita ka⌣

Tanaka

make no difference or be all right

ka⌈maimase˥ñ

21. No, I'm going later. Is that all right?

Iie, a˥to de i˩kima˥su ga, ka⌈maima-se˥ñ ka⌣

Smith

until 3 o'clock

sa˥ñ-zi made

22. The bank closes at (lit. is until) 3, you know.

Giñkoo (wa) ⌈sa˥ñ-zi made desu yo⌣

Tanaka

well then or then
I guess I'll go

zya
i⌈kimasyo˥o or
ma⌈irimasyo˥o↑

23. Oh, of course! Then I guess I'll go now.

A. ⌈So˥o ˩so˩o. Zya, i˥ma i˩kima-syo˩o.

NOTES ON THE BASIC DIALOGUES

1. Ma˥initi: compare also ma˥iasa 'every morning,' maisyuu 'every week,' maituki or mai̇getu 'every month,' and maitosi or maineñ 'every year.' All are time nominals and all occur without particle ni indicating time when something happens.

   Ka⌈erima˥su means 'return to a place where one habitually spends time— one's own home, office, native land, etc.' The gerund (-te form) of ka⌈e-rima˥su is ka⌈ette.

2. Remember that after -ġo˥ro, time particle ni is optional but more often omitted. Ni does not occur after taitee and to⌈kidoki˥.

3. A˥sa is another time word which indicates time when something happens, without a following particle.

   Note these expressions: Place word + o + de⌈ma˥su 'leave a place'; place word + kara + de⌈ma˥su 'leave from a place.'

5. De⌐te is the gerund (-te form) of de⌐ma⌐su. The gerund of tu⌐kima⌐su is
   tu⌐ite. Zi⌐mu⌐syo ni tukimasu may be replaced by zi⌐mu⌐syo e tukimasu
   without significant difference in meaning.

6. Amerika e or Amerika ni. Compare the preceding note.

7. 'I'd like to, but—I don't know whether I can or not.'

8. Like √wa⌐karima⌐su, √a⌐rima⌐su, √i⌐rima⌐su, and √ka⌐karima⌐su, √de⌐ki-
   ma⌐su does not occur with particle o. Both the person who can and the
   thing which is possible are followed by particles wa or g̃a, depending on
   emphasis. The gerund (-te form) of de⌐kima⌐su is de⌐kite.

10. Note the difference between a⌐sita no a⌐sa ki⌐te⌐ kudasai (in which a⌐sita⌐
    describes a⌐sa) 'please come tomorrow morning' and asita ⌐a⌐sa ki⌐te⌐
    kudasai (in which both a⌐sita⌐ and a⌐sa tell 'time when' and modify ki⌐te⌐
    kudasai) 'please come tomorrow, in the morning.'

    Ki⌐te⌐ is the gerund (-te form) of ki⌐ma⌐su. I⌐rassya⌐tte and i⌐ra⌐site are
    alternate gerunds of the honorific i⌐rassyaima⌐su 'come,' 'go,' or 'be,'
    with i⌐ra⌐site the less stiff and more conversational of the two.

13. Like all adjectivals, ha⌐ya⌐i occurs in its adverbial (-ku) form when it
    modifies an inflected expression. Thus: ha⌐yaku a⌐rimase⌐ñ 'it isn't fast
    or early,' ha⌐yaku si⌐te kudasa⌐i 'do [it] quickly or early,' ha⌐yaku ki-
    ⌐ma⌐sita 'I came early or quickly,' etc. Compare: Ha⌐ya⌐i ⌐ta⌐kusii de
    ki⌐ma⌐sita 'I came in a fast taxi' and ha⌐yaku ⌐ta⌐kusii de ki⌐ma⌐sita 'I
    came quickly by taxi.'

14. Ko⌐marima⌐su and ko⌐marima⌐sita have many varied English equivalents:
    'Oh, dear!' 'What am I going to do?' 'What a mess I'm in!' 'This is a
    bad situation'; etc. The -ma⌐su form usually refers to a general or future
    situation, while the -ma⌐sita form indicates either that the difficult situa-
    tion has taken place (i.e. I'm affected now) or did take place. Both what
    is troublesome and the person affected are followed by particles wa or g̃a
    depending on emphasis. The gerund of ko⌐marima⌐su is ko⌐ma⌐tte.

    The final g̃a qualifies the statement politely: 'It will be a bit inconvenient
    but—I don't like to insist on your making a change' or 'I don't like to men-
    tion it,' etc. Basic Sentence 14 is a close equivalent of English 'I'm afraid
    it will be a bit inconvenient. . .'

16. The nominal ke⌐kkoo is a polite word which usually occurs in affirmative
    statements. Like adjectivals i⌐i and yorosii, it refers to situations which
    are 'fine,' 'good,' 'all right,' and also to those which are 'fine as they
    are—nothing more needed.' Accordingly, in some contexts the closest
    English equivalent is 'never mind.'

18. Go⌐g̃o is used both as a conversational term for 'afternoon' and as a tech-
    nical term corresponding to English p.m. In the latter meaning, its op-
    posite is go⌐zeñ 'a.m.,' while the conversational word for morning is a⌐sa.
    Go⌐g̃o occurs both with and without following particle ni in indicating time
    when something happens.

    Ite is the gerund (-te form) of i⌐ma⌐su.

20. Ke⌐sa occurs without a following particle in indicating time when something
    happens.

21. Ka⌐maimase⌐ñ, a verbal negative whose corresponding affirmative is comparatively rare, has many English equivalents: 'It makes no difference'; 'It doesn't matter'; 'I don't care'; 'I don't mind'; 'It doesn't bother me'; 'It's all right'; etc. Ko⌐marima⌐su usually occurs as its opposite. Thus: Ko⌐marima⌐su ka␣ 'Will it be inconvenient?' . . . 'Iie, ka⌐maimase⌐ñ. 'No, it doesn't matter.'

23. Repeated so⌐o is emphatic. So⌐o here is the informal equivalent of so⌐o desu ⌐ne⌐e. Zya is a more clipped, terse alternant of zya⌐a.

GRAMMATICAL NOTES

1. Verbals: More About the Tentative

In Lesson 7, Grammatical Note 2, the tentative of verbals was introduced, meaning 'let's do so-and-so' in statements, and 'shall we do so-and-so?' in questions. Thus:

> I⌐kimasyo⌐o ka. 'Shall we go?'
> E⌐e, i⌐kimasyo⌐o. 'Yes, let's go.'

The verbal tentative has a second use, distinguished from the first only by context. It may indicate a suggestion by the speaker directed to himself alone: 'I guess I'll do so-and-so'; and in its more common use—in questions—this second kind of tentative is an offer: 'Shall I do so-and-so?' In such cases, the affirmative reply is an appropriate imperative, or o⌐negai-sima⌐su, or another request expression. Possible negative replies include i⌐i desu and the more polite ke⌐kkoo desu meaning 'never mind.'

Examples:

> Ti⌐zu (o) ka⌐kimasyo⌐o ka. 'Shall I draw a map?'
> E⌐e, ka⌐ite kudasai. 'Yes, please (draw).' or
> E⌐e, o⌐negai-sima⌐su. 'Yes, please do.'
>
> Ta⌐bako (o) kaimasyo⌐o ka. 'Shall I buy some cigarettes?'
> Iie, i⌐i desu yo. or ⎫ 'No, never mind.'
> Iie, ke⌐kkoo desu. ⎭

2. Verbals: Honorific Equivalents Ending in √na⌐rima⌐su

The polite verbals previously introduced (√go⌐zaima⌐su, √i⌐rassyaima⌐su, etc.) were words which had to be memorized along with their plain equivalents because structurally they were unrelated. Such polite verbals are limited in number. Far more common are those having the same root as their plain equivalents.

One of the most common types of honorific (†) consists of the polite o- prefixed to the stem of a plain verbal (the stem is the -ma⌐su form minus -ma⌐su) + particle ni + √na⌐rima⌐su. (√Na⌐rima⌐su as an independent verbal means 'become,' 'come to be'; it will occur in later lessons.) The form of √na⌐rima⌐su shows whether the combination is non-past or past, affirmative or negative, etc. The accent of the combination occurs on √na⌐rima⌐su. The combination is the honorific equivalent of the corresponding plain verbal.

Examples:

Plain	(Stem)	Honorific (↑) Equivalent
ka⌐eri maˈsu	(kaˈeri)	o⌐kaeri ni narimaˈsu '[he] returns (or will return) home'
de⌐maˈsita	(deˈ)	o⌐de ni narimaˈsita '[he] went out'
tu⌐kimaseˈñ	(tuˈki)	o⌐tuki ni narimaseˈñ '[he] doesn't (or won't) arrive or hasn't arrived'
de⌐kimaseˈñ desita	(deˈki)	o⌐deki ni narimaseˈñ desita '[he] couldn't do it'

The gerund of the honorific is o- + verbal stem + ni + naˈtte.

The corresponding form for √iˈmaˈsu, √iˈkimaˈsu, and √kiˈmaˈsu is irregular: o⌐ide ni √narimaˈsu.   Like √iˈrassyaimaˈsu, it occurs as the honorific equivalent of all three plain verbals.

Like all honorifics, these are used only in reference to persons other than the speaker, in polite speech. The plain equivalent is used as a corresponding non-honorific form. Thus:

> A: Tanaka-sañ (wa) o⌐wakari ni narimaˈsu ka⌐
>   'Does Mr. Tanaka understand?'
>
> B: Haˈa, o⌐wakari ni narimaˈsu.
>   'Yes, he understands.'
>
> A: A⌐naˈta mo o⌐wakari ni narima⁴su ka⌐
>   'Do you understand too?'
>
> B: Haˈa, wa⌐takusi mo wakarimaˈsu.
>   'Yes, I understand too.'

WARNING: Don't try to make up o-⌐(stem) ni √narimaˈsu honorific equivalents for all plain verbals. As always, let the usage of native speakers be your guide.

3.   Particles: maˈde 'until,' maˈde ni 'by'

a. maˈde 'until'

Reread Lesson 7, Grammatical Note 3b.

The particle maˈde after a time expression means 'until' — i.e. 'up to and including part or all of.'

Examples:

> a⌐sitaˈ made 'until tomorrow'
> iˈtu made 'until when?'

iˈti- g̃atu maˈdeᴵ 'until January'
iˈma maˈdeᴵ 'until now'

b. <u>maˈde ni</u> 'by'

The particle sequence <u>maˈde ni</u> preceded by a time expression means 'at a point in the time until,' i.e. 'by' the given time. It regularly occurs with an inflected expression which indicates action.

Examples:

Aˈsitaˈ made ni kimasu. 'He'll come by tomorrow.'
Iˈti-g̃atu maˈde ni tukimasu. 'He'll arrive by January.'
Iˈma maˈde ni deˈmaᴴsita. 'It has left by now.'
Kuᴴ-zi maˈde niᴴ wa kaerimasu. 'By 9 (comparatively speaking) I'll be home (lit. return home).'

4. √deˈsu Following a Particle

Besides occurring after adjectivals and nominals, √deˈsu also occurs immediately after phrases which end in some particles—for example, it may follow <u>kara</u> and <u>maˈde</u> but it rarely follows <u>wa</u>, <u>g̃a</u>, or <u>o</u> directly. √Deˈsu is accented if the preceding phrase is unaccented.

Examples:

Saˈñ-zi made desu. 'It is until 3'—i.e. 'it lasts until 3' or 'it ends at 3' or 'it closes at 3' or 'it is open until 3.'

Saˈñ-zi kara desu. 'It is from 3'—i.e. 'it begins at 3' or 'it opens at 3.'

The negative equivalent of a sequence ending in particle + √deˈsu ends in particle + <u>zya aˈrimaseˈñ</u>:

Saˈñ-zi kara zya aᴴrimaseᴴñ. 'It isn't from 3 o'clock'—i.e. 'it doesn't begin at 3' or 'it doesn't open at 3.'

DRILLS

A. Substitution Drill

1.	I usually come by bus.	Taitee ˈbaˈsu de kimasu.
2.	I sometimes come by bus.	Tokidoki ˈbaˈsu de kimasu.
3.	I always come by bus.	Iˈtu mo ˈbaˈsu de kimasu.
4.	I come by bus a good deal.	Yoˈku ˈbaˈsu de kimasu.
5.	I come by bus every day.	Maˈiniti ˈbaˈsu de kimasu.

---

[1] Note the irregular accent of this phrase.

6. I come by bus in the afternoon.

Go⌐go ⌐ba⌐su de kimasu.

7. I come by bus in the morning.

A⌐sa ⌐ba⌐su de kimasu.

8. I come by bus every morning.

Ma⌐iasa ⌐ba⌐su de kimasu.

B. Substitution Drill

1. Mr. Tanaka HAS LEFT.
2. MR. TANAKA left.
3. He left the office.
4. He left from the office.
5. He left today.
6. He left in the afternoon.
7. He left at 8 o'clock.
8. He left by 8 o'clock.
9. I left, too.

Tanaka-sañ (wa) de⌐ma⌐sita.
Ta⌐naka-sañ ḡa dema⌐sita.
Zi⌐mu⌐syo (o) de⌐ma⌐sita.
Zi⌐mu⌐syo kara de⌐ma⌐sita.
Kyo⌐o de⌐ma⌐sita.
Go⌐go [ni] de⌐ma⌐sita.
Ha⌐ti⌐-zi ni de⌐ma⌐sita.
Ha⌐ti⌐-zi made ni de⌐ma⌐sita.
Wa⌐takusi mo dema⌐sita.

C. Substitution Drill

1. Please come again to-
   morrow.
2. Please come again in the
   afternoon.
3. Please come again on
   Monday.
4. Please come again in
   April.
5. Please come again about
   4.
6. Please come again at 7:30.
7. Please come again tomorrow morning.
8. Please come again tomorrow about 10.

Asita ma⌐ta kite⌐ kudasai.

Go⌐go ma⌐ta kite⌐ kudasai.

Ge⌐tuyo⌐obi ni ma⌐ta kite⌐ kudasai.

Si-⌐ḡatu⌐ ni ma⌐ta kite⌐ kudasai.

Yo-⌐zi-ḡo⌐ro ma⌐ta kite⌐ kudasai.

Si⌐ti-zi-ha⌐ñ ni ma⌐ta kite⌐ kudasai.
A⌐sita no a⌐sa ma⌐ta kite⌐ kudasai.

Asita zyu⌐u-zi-ḡo⌐ro ma⌐ta kite⌐ kudasai.

D. Substitution Drill

1. I'm going later. Is that
   all right?
2. I'm not coming tomorrow.
   Is that all right?
3. I'd like to go home early.
   Is that all right?
4. I'm going to leave from the
   office. Is that all right?
5. I'll arrive about 10. Is
   that all right?
6. I'll be [here] until afternoon. Is that all right?

A⌐to de i⌐kima⌐su ḡa, ka⌐maimase⌐ñ
ka⌐

A⌐sita kimase⌐ñ ḡa, ka⌐maimase⌐ñ ka⌐

Ha⌐yaku ka⌐erita⌐i ñ desu ḡa, ka⌐ma-
imase⌐ñ ka⌐

Zi⌐mu⌐syo kara de⌐ma⌐su ḡa, ka⌐mai-
mase⌐ñ ka⌐

Zyu⌐u-zi-ḡo⌐ro tu⌐kima⌐su ḡa, ka⌐ma-
imase⌐ñ ka⌐

Go⌐go made i⌐ma⌐su ḡa, ka⌐maimase⌐ñ
ka⌐

7. I bought a cheap furoshiki.
Is that all right?

Ya⌐su⌉i hu⌐rosiki (o) kaima⌐sita ḡa,
ka⌐maimase⌉ñ ka⌐

8. There aren't any cigarettes.
Is that all right?

Ta⌐bako (wa) arimase⌉ñ ḡa, ka⌐mai-
mase⌉ñ ka⌐

9. This one is a little different.
Is that all right?

Kore (wa) su⌐ko⌉si ti⌐ḡaima⌉su ḡa,
ka⌐maimase⌉ñ ka⌐

10. It's a little expensive. Is
that all right?

Su⌐ko⌉si ta⌐ka⌉i desu ḡa, ka⌐maima-
se⌉ñ ka⌐

E. Substitution Drill

1. I was here from morning
until afternoon.

A⌉sa kara ⌐go⌉ḡo made ko⌐ko ni ima⌉-
sita.

2. I was in the office from 9
until 5.

Ku⌉-zi kara ⌐go⌉-zi made zi⌐mu⌉syo ni
i⌐ma⌐sita.

3. I was at home from Friday
until Sunday.

Ki⌐ñyo⌉o kara ni⌐tiyoo ma⌐de u⌐ti ni ima⌉-
sita.

4. I was at the hospital from
April until August.

Si-⌐ḡatu⌉ kara ha⌐ti-ḡatu⌉ made byo⌐oiñ
ni ima⌐sita.

5. I was in school from the
year 30 until this year.

Sa⌐ñzyu⌉u-neñ kara ko⌐tosi ma⌐de ga⌐k-
koo ni ima⌐sita.

6. I was in the park from
about 10 until about 11:30.

Zyu⌐u-zi-ḡo⌉ro kara zyu⌐uiti-zi-hañ-
ḡo⌉ro made ko⌐oeñ ni ima⌐sita.

7. I was at that hotel from the
first until the tenth.

Tu⌐itati⌉ kara to⌐o-ka ma⌐de a⌐no ho⌉-
teru ni i⌐ma⌐sita.

8. I was at an inn in Kyoto
from the day before yes-
terday until yesterday.

O⌐toto⌉i kara ki⌐no⌉o made ⌐Kyo⌉oto no
ryo⌐kañ ni ima⌐sita.

9. I was in the post office
from 10 to 10 until 5 af-
ter.

Zyu⌐u-zi zyu⌐p-pu⌉ñ-mae kara go-⌐hu⌉ñ-
suḡi made yu⌐ubi⌉ñkyoku ni i⌐ma⌐si-
ta.

10. I was at Mr. Tanaka's
house from yesterday
morning until this morn-
ing.

Ki⌐noo no a⌉sa kara ⌐ke⌉sa made Ta⌐na-
ka-sañ no otaku ni ima⌐sita.

F. Substitution Drill

1. I am always at home about
8.

I⌉tu mo ha⌐ti-zi-ḡo⌉ro u⌐ti ni ima⌐su.

2. I usually am at home about
8.

Taitee ha⌐ti-zi-ḡo⌉ro u⌐ti ni ima⌐su.

3. I usually am at home at
exactly 9.

Taitee tyo⌐odo ku⌉-zi ni u⌐ti ni ima⌐su.

4. I usually am in the office
at exactly 9.

Taitee tyo⌐odo ku⌉-zi ni zi⌐mu⌉syo ni
imasu.

5. I usually arrive at the office at exactly 9.

Taitee tyo⌐odo ku⌉-zi ni zi⌐mu⌉syo ni
tukimasu.

6. Every day I arrive at the
office at exactly 9.

Ma⌉initi tyo⌐odo ku⌉-zi ni zi⌐mu⌉syo ni
tukimasu.

7. Every day I arrive at the office at a little before 9. — Ma꜆initi ⌜ku꜆-zi ⌜tyo꜆tto ⊢ma⊣e ni zi⌜mu꜆syo ni tukimasu.
8. Every day I arrive at school at a little before 9. — Ma꜆initi ⌜ku꜆-zi ⌜tyo꜆tto ⊢ma⊣e ni ga⌜kkoo ni tukima꜆su.
9. Every day I go to school at a little before 9. — Ma꜆initi ⌜ku꜆-zi ⌜tyo꜆tto ⊢ma⊣e ni ga⌜kkoo ni ikima꜆su.

G. Grammar Drill

Tutor: I꜆ma desu ka ‿ 'Is it now?' (affirmative)
Student: I꜆ma zya a⊢rimase⊣ñ ka ‿ 'Isn't it now?' (negative)

1. Ma꜆initi desu ka ‿ — Ma꜆initi zya a⊢rimase⊣ñ ka ‿
2. O⌜wakari ni narima꜆su ka ‿ — O⌜wakari ni narimase꜆ñ ka ‿
3. Ke꜆sa desita yo ‿ — Ke꜆sa zya a⊢rimase⊣ñ desita yo ‿
4. Sa꜆ñ-zi kara desu ka ‿ — Sa꜆ñ-zi kara zya a⊢rimase⊣ñ ka ‿
5. Kinoo o⌜kaeri ni narima꜆sita ka ‿ — Kinoo o⌜kaeri ni narimase꜆ñ desita ka ‿
6. Ha⌜ya꜆i desu ka ‿ — Ha꜆yaku a⊢rimase⊣ñ ka ‿
7. Yo꜆-zi made desu ka ‿ — Yo꜆-zi made zya a⊢rimase⊣ñ ka ‿
8. De⌜kima꜆sita ka ‿ — De⌜kimase꜆ñ desita ka ‿
9. A⌜na꜆ta mo o⊢de ni narima⊣su ka ‿ — A⌜na꜆ta mo o⊢de ni narimase⊣ñ ka ‿
10. Ta⌜naka-sañ no꜆ desu yo ‿ — Ta⌜naka-sañ no꜆ zya a⊢rimase⊣ñ yo ‿

H. Response Drill[1]

Tutor: I⌜kimasyo꜆o ka. 'Shall I go?' (an offer)
Student: E꜆e, i⌜tte kudasa꜆i. 'Yes, please (go).' (affirmative answer)

1. Ti꜆zu (o) ka⊢kimasyo⊣o ka. — E꜆e, ka꜆ite kudasai.
2. Ma⌜timasyo꜆o ka. — E꜆e, ma꜆tte kudasai.
3. Wa⌜takusi mo mairimasyo꜆o ka. — Ha꜆a, i⌜ra꜆site kudasai.
4. A⌜sita꜆ mo ki⊢masyo⊣o ka. — E꜆e, ki⌜te꜆ kudasai.
5. Ko⌜re (o) simasyo꜆o ka. — E꜆e, si⌜te kudasa꜆i.
6. Mo⌜o iti-do iimasyo꜆o ka. — E꜆e, i⌜tte kudasa꜆i.
7. Ro⌜ku꜆-zi made i⊢masyo⊣o ka. — E꜆e, i⌜te kudasa꜆i.
8. Si⌜ñbuñ mo kaimasyo꜆o ka. — E꜆e, ka⌜tte kudasa꜆i.

---

[1] Based on Grammatical Note 1. After practicing the drill in its given form, practice it with o⌜negai-sima꜆su as an alternate affirmative reply, and with i꜆i desu and ke꜆kkoo desu as negative replies.

I. Level Drill[1]

1. I⌐tu-ḡoro kaerima⌐su ka⌐   I⌐tu-ḡoro okaeri ni narima⌐su ka⌐
2. Wa⌐surema⌐sita ka⌐   O⌐wasure ni narima⌐sita ka⌐
3. To⌐kee (ḡa) arima⌐su ka⌐   To⌐kee (ḡa) gozaima⌐su ka⌐
4. Na⌐ñ-zi ni u⌐ti (o) dema⌐su   Na⌐ñ-zi ni o⌐taku (o) ode ni narima⌐su
   ka⌐   ka⌐

5. Go⌐ḡo made i⌐ma⌐su ka⌐

   Go⌐ḡo made | i⌐rassyaima⌐su / o⌐ide ni narima⌐su | ka⌐

6. I⌐tu ko⌐ko ni kima⌐sita ka⌐

   I⌐tu ko⌐tira ni | irassyaima⌐sita / oide ni narima⌐sita | ka⌐

7. Wa⌐karima⌐sita ka⌐   O⌐wakari ni narima⌐sita ka⌐
8. Na⌐ñ-niti-ḡo⌐ro tu⌐kima⌐su   Na⌐ñ-niti-ḡo⌐ro o⌐tuki ni narima⌐su ka⌐
   ka⌐

J. Expansion Drill

1. I guess I'll come.   Ki⌐masyo⌐o.
   Shall I come?   Ki⌐masyo⌐o ka.
   Shall I come again?   Ma⌐ta kimasyo⌐o ka.
   Shall I come again tomor-   A⌐sita mata kimasyo⌐o ka.
      row?

2. I go back.   Ka⌐erima⌐su.
   I go back to Kyoto.   Kyo⌐oto ni kaerimasu.
   I go back to Kyoto in June.   Ro⌐ku-ḡatu⌐ ni ⌐Kyo⌐oto ni kaerimasu.
   I usually go back to Kyoto   Taitee ro⌐ku-ḡatu⌐ ni ⌐Kyo⌐oto ni kae-
      in June.   rimasu.

3. I'm [here].   I⌐ma⌐su.
   I'm in the office.   Zi⌐mu⌐syo ni imasu.
   I'm in the office until 5:30.   Go-⌐zi-ha⌐ñ made zi⌐mu⌐syo ni imasu.
   I'm in the office from 9   Ku⌐-zi kara go-⌐zi-ha⌐ñ made zi⌐mu⌐-
      until 5:30.   syo ni imasu.
   I'm in the office every day   Ma⌐initi ⌐ku⌐-zi kara go-⌐zi-ha⌐ñ made
      from 9 to 5:30.   zi⌐mu⌐syo ni imasu.

4. [He] arrived.   Tu⌐kima⌐sita.
   [He] arrived in America.   A⌐merika ni tukima⌐sita.
   [He] arrived in America   Ni-⌐syuukañ-ḡu⌐rai ⌐ma⌐e ni A⌐meri-
      about 2 weeks ago.   ka ni tukima⌐sita.
   Mr. Tanaka arrived in   Tanaka-sañ (wa) ni-⌐syuukañ-ḡu⌐rai
      America about 2 weeks   ⌐ma⌐e ni A⌐merika ni tukima⌐sita.
      ago.

---

[1] In each case the sentence on the right is the polite equivalent of the sentence on the left.

5. Is it all right?   Ka⌐maimase⌐ñ ka⌐
   I'd like to leave. Is it   De⌐ta⌐i ñ desu ḡa, ka⌐maimase⌐ñ ka⌐
   all right?
   I'd like to leave here. Is   Ko⌐ko (o) deta⌐i ñ desu ḡa, ka⌐maima-
   it all right?   se⌐ñ ka⌐
   I'd like to leave here by 3   Sa⌐ñ-zi made ni ko⌐ko (o) deta⌐i ñ de-
   o'clock. Is it all right?   su ḡa, ka⌐maimase⌐ñ ka⌐

6. I arrived.   Tu⌐kima⌐sita.
   I arrived in Japan.   Ni⌐ho⌐ñ ni tu⌐kima⌐sita.
   I arrived in Japan on the   Zyu⌐ugo-niti ni Ni⌐ho⌐ñ ni tu⌐kima⌐si-
   15th.   ta.
   I left America on the 1st   Tu⌐itati⌐ ni A⌐merika (o) de⌐te, zyu⌐u-
   and arrived in Japan on   go-niti ni Ni⌐ho⌐ñ ni tu⌐kima⌐sita.
   the 15th.

7. I can't do [it].   De⌐kimase⌐ñ.
   I can't do [it] (I tell you).   De⌐kimase⌐ñ yo⌐
   All of it, I can't do (I tell   Ze⌐ñbu wa de⌐kimase⌐ñ yo⌐
   you).
   I can do a little but I can't   Su⌐ko⌐si wa de⌐kima⌐su ḡa, ze⌐ñbu wa
   do all of it (I tell you).   de⌐kimase⌐ñ yo.

8. It's troublesome.   Ko⌐marima⌐su.
   It's troublesome (I tell you).   Ko⌐marima⌐su yo⌐
   It's a little troublesome (I   Tyo⌐tto ko⌐marima⌐su yo⌐
   tell you).
   This is a little troublesome   Kore wa ⌐tyo⌐tto ko⌐marima⌐su yo⌐
   (I tell you).
   That doesn't matter, but   So⌐re wa kamaimase⌐ñ ḡa, kore wa
   this is a little troublesome   ⌐tyo⌐tto ko⌐marima⌐su yo⌐
   (I tell you).

SUPPLEMENTARY CONVERSATIONS

(with questions)

1. Yamamoto (a visitor): Ta⌐naka-sañ irassyaima⌐su ka⌐
   Secretary: Ta⌐naka-sañ de⌐su ka⌐ Yo⌐kohama e irassyaima⌐sita ḡa_
   Yamamoto: So⌐o desu ka. Na⌐ñ-zi-ḡo⌐ro o⌐kaeri ni narima⌐su ka⌐
   Secretary: Yo⌐ku wa⌐karimase⌐ñ ḡa, ni-⌐zi-ḡo⌐ro desyoo.
   Yamamoto: So⌐o desu ka. Zya⌐a, ma⌐ta a⌐to de ma⌐irimasyo⌐o. Do⌐o mo
              a⌐ri⌐ḡatoo gozaimasita.
   Secretary: Do⌐o itasimasite.

Questions (Answer in Japanese on the basis of the above conversation.)

       1. Tanaka-sañ wa i⌐ma⌐su ka⌐
       2. Tanaka-sañ wa ⌐do⌐ko ni i⌐ma⌐su ka⌐
       3. Tanaka-sañ wa ⌐i⌐tu ka⌐erima⌐su ka⌐

    4. Yamamoto-sañ wa ⌐do⌐o si⌐ma⌐su ka⌐[1]

2. Mr. Smith: A⌐sita⌐ kara[2] Ka⌐makura⌐[3] e ikima⌐su ḡa, a⌐na⌐ta mo īti-do i⌐ki-
                  mase⌐ñ ka⌐

        Tanaka: A⌐ri⌐ḡatoo gozaimasu ḡa_

        Smith: Tu⌐ḡi⌐ no ni⌐tiyo⌐obi wa ⌐do⌐o desu ka.

        Tanaka: A⌐ri⌐ḡatoo gozaimasu. Tu⌐ḡi⌐ no ni⌐tiyo⌐obi ⌐na⌐ñ-niti desyoo
                  ka.

        Smith: Ha⌐tu-ka de⌐su ḡa_ Do⌐o desu ka. I⌐kimase⌐ñ ka⌐

        Tanaka: A⌐ri⌐ḡatoo gozaimasu. Ka⌐maimase⌐ñ ka⌐

        Smith: E⌐e, do⌐ozo ⌐do⌐ozo. Na⌐ñ de i⌐kima⌐su ka⌐

        Tanaka: So⌐o desu ⌐ne⌐e. De⌐ñsya de i⌐kima⌐su ḡa_

        Smith: Na⌐ñ-zi-ḡo⌐ro tu⌐kima⌐su ka⌐ Tookyoo kara tyóodo i⌐ti-zi⌐kañ
                  ka⌐karima⌐su ḡa_

        Tanaka: Zya⌐a, zyu⌐u-zi-ḡo⌐ro Ka⌐makura-eki e tu⌐kimasyo⌐o ka.

        Smith: I⌐i desu yo_ Bo⌐ku wa ⌐zyu⌐u-zi made ni ⌐e⌐ki e itte, e⌐ki no
                  ⌐ma⌐e ni imasu.

        Tanaka: A⌐ri⌐ḡatoo gozaimasu. Do⌐ozo o⌐negai-sima⌐su.

        Smith: Zya⌐a mata.

        Tanaka: Sayonara.

        Smith: Sayonara.

Questions:

    1. Su⌐misu-sañ wa a⌐sita⌐ kara ⌐do⌐ko e i⌐kima⌐su ka⌐

    2. Ta⌐naka-sañ mo asita ikima⌐su ka⌐

    3. Tanaka-sañ wa na⌐ñyo⌐obi ni i⌐kima⌐su ka⌐

    4. Tanaka-sañ wa ⌐na⌐ñ-niti ni i⌐kima⌐su ka⌐

    5. Tanaka-sañ wa ⌐na⌐ñ de i⌐kima⌐su ka⌐

    6. Tanaka-sañ wa ⌐na⌐ñ-zi ni Ka⌐makura e tukima⌐su ka⌐

    7. To⌐okyoo kara Kamakura ma⌐de ⌐de⌐ñsya de do⌐no-ḡurai kakarima⌐su
        ka⌐

    8. Su⌐misu-sañ wa tu⌐ḡi⌐ no ni⌐tiyo⌐obi no ⌐na⌐ñ-zi ni Ka⌐makura-e⌐ki
        e i⌐kima⌐su ka⌐

    9. Kamakura wa ⌐do⌐ko desu ka.

---

[1] 'What (lit. how) will Mr. Yamamoto do?'

[2] Lit. 'I go from tomorrow' —i.e. 'I go tomorrow and stay on.'

[3] A resort city near Yokohama.

English Equivalents of Conversations

1. Yamamoto: Is Mr. Tanaka in?
    Secretary: Mr. Tanaka? He went to Yokohama but [is there anything I can do for you?]
    Yamamoto: Oh. (About) what time will he be back?
    Secretary: I'm not sure but it will probably be about 2 o'clock.
    Yamamoto: Oh. Then I guess I'll come again later. Thank you very much.
    Secretary: Not at all.

2. Mr. Smith: I'm going to Kamakura tomorrow to stay for a while. Won't you come (lit. go[1]) too some (lit. one) time?
    Tanaka: Thank you but . . .
    Smith: How about next Sunday?
    Tanaka: Thank you. What date is next Sunday?
    Smith: It's the 20th. . . . How about it? Won't you come?
    Tanaka: Thank you. (Hesitantly) Will it be all right?
    Smith: Yes. Please [come]! How will you come?
    Tanaka: Let's see. I'll come by electric train but [will that be convenient?]
    Smith: About what time will you arrive? It takes just an hour from Tokyo . . .
    Tanaka: Well then, shall I arrive at Kamakura Station about 10?
    Smith: That will be fine. I'll go to the station by 10, and I'll be in front (of the station).
    Tanaka: Thank you. Would you do that [i.e. meet me]?
    Smith: Well then, [I'll see you] again.
    Tanaka: Goodbye.
    Smith: Goodbye.

EXERCISES

1. You ask Mr. Tanaka: Mr. Tanaka replies:

    a. to come again tomorrow   Certainly.
        afternoon.
    b. if you should come again   Please do.
        tomorrow afternoon.
    c. how long (i.e. until what   Until 5:30.
        time) he will be here.
    d. what time he goes home.   Usually at 5:00.
    e. if he always goes home at   No. Sometimes I go home at
        about 5:00.   about 6:00.

---

[1] Reread Lesson 8, Grammatical Note 6, last paragraph.

    f. what time you should   By 10:30.
       come on Saturday.

    g. what time he is coming   At 10:30.
       on Saturday.

    h. how late the post office   I think it's until about 5:30.
       is open.

    i. to wait until 4:30.   I'm sorry but I can't.

    j. to stay here from 12:00   All right.
       to 1:00.

    k. if Mr. Yamamoto has gone   Yes, he went home at 5:00.
       home.

    l. when he is returning to   I'd like to go back tomorrow.
       Tokyo.

    m. to come here by 6:30.   I'm afraid that's a bit inconven-
                                            ient.

    n. if you should draw a map.   No, never mind.

    o. if he is coming here again   Yes, at 8:45.
       tomorrow morning.

    p. if he is coming here again   No, on the 20th.
       on the 19th.

    q. if he will be here until   No, I'm going home at 5:00.
       6:00.

    r. if he will be in Tokyo until   No, I'm returning to Osaka in
       March.   February.

    s. if you should turn this cor- No, to the right.
       ner to the left.

    t. if you should back up a   It doesn't matter.
       little.

    u. what time he leaves home   Usually, at 7:45.
       in the morning.

    v. when he arrived in Kyoto.   I came here in March of this
                                            year.

2. Using a timetable, real or made up, practice asking and answering questions like the following:

    (Time) ni (place) o de⌐ma¬sita. ⌐Na¬ñ-zi ni (another place) ni tu⌐kima¬sita
    ka?

    (Time) ni (place) ni tu⌐kima¬sita. Na¬ñ-zi ni (another place) o de⌐ma¬sita
    ka?

3. Practice asking and answering questions like the following:

    Ge⌐tuyo¬o kara ki⌐ñyo¬o made ⌐na¬ñ-niti a⌐rima¬su ka⌐
    Sa¬ñ-zi kara ku-⌐zi-ha¬ñ made na⌐ñ-zi¬kañ a⌐rima¬su ka⌐
    Si-g̃atu tu⌐itati¬ kara, ⌐go¬-g̃atu ⌐sa¬ñzyuu i⌐ti-niti¬ made, na⌐ñ-ka¬g̃etu a⌐ri-
    ma¬su ka⌐

4. Practice the Basic Dialogues with appropriate variations.

Lesson 10. Meeting People

BASIC DIALOGUES: FOR MEMORIZATION

(a)

Smith

female	o⌐ñna⌐
person	hi⌐to⌐ or
	ka⌐ta⌐ ↑
woman	o⌐ña no hito⌐ or
	o⌐ña no kata⌐ ↑
who?	da⌐re or
	do⌐nata ↑

1. Who is that woman? Ano o⌐ña no hito⌐ (wa) ⌐da⌐re desu ka⌐

or

Ano o⌐ña no kata⌐ (wa) ⌐do⌐nata desu ka⌐

or

Ano o⌐ña no kata⌐ (wa) ⌐do⌐nata de (i)rassyaimasu ka⌐

Tanaka

an American	a⌐merika⌐ziñ

2. Do you mean the American? A⌐merika⌐ziñ desu ka⌐

Smith

a Japanese	ni⌐hoñzi⌐ñ

3. No, I mean the Japanese. Iie, ni⌐hoñzi⌐ñ desu.

Tanaka

4. Oh, that (person) is Miss (or Mrs.) Yamada. A⌐a, a⌐no⌐ hito wa Ya⌐mada-sañ de⌐su.

or

A⌐a, a⌐no kata⌐ wa Ya⌐mada-sañ de⌐su.

or

A⌐a, a⌐no kata⌐ wa Ya⌐mada-sañ de (i)rassyaima⌐su.

Smith

friend	tomodati or
	otomodati ↑

5. Is she a friend? To⌐modati de⌐su ka⌐

or

O⌐tomodati de⌐su ka⌐

or

O⌐tomodati de (i)rassyaima⌐su ka⌐

148

Tanaka

name	namae <u>or</u> onamae ꜜ‾
know	si⸢tte (i)ma⸣su <u>or</u> si⸢tte orima⸣su ꜜ‾ <u>or</u> si⸢tte (i)rassyaima‾⸣su ꜜ

6. No, she isn't a friend, but I know her name.

Iie, to⸢modati zya arimase⸣ñ g̃a, na⸢mae wa sitte (i)ma⸣su.

<u>or</u>

Iie, to⸢modati de⸣ wa go⸢ꜜzaimase⸣ñ g̃a, o⸢namae wa sitte orima⸣su.

(b)

Smith

rudeness <u>or</u> rude it is rude [of me] but	si⸢tu⸣ree si⸢tu⸣ree desu g̃a <u>or</u> si⸢tu⸣ree de gozaimasu g̃a

7. Excuse me [for asking] but [what is] your name?

Si⸢tu⸣ree desu g̃a, onamae wa?

<u>or</u>

Si⸢tu⸣ree de gozaimasu g̃a,   onamae wa?

Sato

8. I'm Yukio Sato.

Sa⸣too Yu⸢kio de⸣su.

<u>or</u>

Sa⸣too Yu⸢kio de gozaima⸣su.

Smith

work	sig̃oto <u>or</u> o⸢si⸣g̃oto ꜜ‾

9. What do you do? (Lit. As for your work?)

O⸢si⸣g̃oto wa?

Sato

for the American Embassy	A⸢merika-taisi⸣kañ ni
become employed be employed	tu⸢tomema⸣su tu⸢to⸣mete (i)masu <u>or</u> tu⸢to⸣mete orimasu ꜜ‾ <u>or</u> tu⸢to⸣mete (i)rassyaimasu ꜜ

10. I'm working for the American Embassy.

A⸢merika-taisi⸣kañ ni tu⸢to⸣mete (i)masu.

<u>or</u>

A⸢merika-taisi⸣kañ ni tu⸢to⸣mete orimasu.

(c)

Smith

marry	ke⸢kkoñ-sima⸣su

be married   ke˥kkoñ-site (i)ma˥su   <u>or</u>
                                                      ke˥kkoñ-site orima˥su ⸸   <u>or</u>
                                                      ke˥kkoñ-site (i)rassyaima˥su ⸸

11. Excuse me [for asking] but   Si˥tu˥ree desu ğa, ke˥kkoñ-site (i)ma˥-
      are you married?   su ka⌟
                                                          <u>or</u>
                                                      Si˥tu˥ree de gozaimasu ğa, ke˥kkoñ-
                                                      site (i)rassyaima˥su ka⌟

                                Tanaka

single   hi˥to˥ri   <u>or</u>
                                                      ohitori ⸸

12. No, I'm single.   How about   Iie, hi˥to˥ri desu.   A˥na˥ta wa?
      you?   <u>or</u>
                                                      Iie, hi˥to˥ri de gozaimasu. A˥na˥ta wa?

                                Smith

13. I'm married.   Ke˥kkoñ-site (i)ma˥su.
                                                              <u>or</u>
                                                      Ke˥kkoñ-site orima˥su.

                                Tanaka

child   kodomo   <u>or</u>
                                                      okosañ ⸸

14. (a) Do you have any   Ko˥domo (ğa) arima˥su ka⌟
            children?   <u>or</u>
                                                      O˥kosañ (ğa) gozaima˥su ka⌟
      <u>or</u>
      (b) Are there any children   Ko˥domo (ğa) ima˥su ka⌟
            [in your family]?   <u>or</u>
                                                      O˥kosañ (ğa) irassyaima˥su ka⌟

                                Smith

1 person   hi˥to˥-ri
2 people   hu˥ta-ri˥
3 people   sa˥ñ-ni˥ñ
15. (a) Yes, I have two.   E˥e, hu˥tari arima˥su.
                                                              <u>or</u>
      <u>or</u>   E˥e, hu˥tari gozaima˥su.

      (b) Yes, there are two.   E˥e, hu˥tari ima˥su.
                                                              <u>or</u>
                                                      E˥e, hu˥tari orima˥su.

                                Tanaka

how old?   i˥kutu   <u>or</u>
                                                      oikutu ⸸

16. How old are they?   I˥kutu desu ka⌟
                                                              <u>or</u>
                                                      O˥ikutu de˥su ka⌟
                                                              <u>or</u>
                                                      O˥ikutu de (i)rassyaima˥su ka⌟

Smith

1 year old	hiˈtoˈ-tu
2 years old	huˈta-tuˈ
being 12 years old	zyuˈuniˈ de
this month	koñ̄getu
become	naˈrimaˈsu
become 8 years old	ya-ˈttuˈ ni narimasu

17. One is 12 and the other (lit. one more person) will be 8 this month.

Hiˈtoˈ-ri wa zyuˈuniˈ de, moˈo hitoˈ-ri wa koñ̄getu ya-ˈttuˈ ni narimasu.

Tanaka

both	doˈtira mo[1]
male	oˈtokoˈ
boy	oˈtokoˈ no ko or oˈtokoˈ no okosañ †

18. Are both boys?

Dotira mo oˈtokoˈ no ko desu ka⌟

or

Dotira mo oˈtokoˈ no oˈkosañ de (i)ra-ssyaimaˈsu ka⌟

Smith

over or top or top-most or oldest	ue
under or below or bottom or youngest	sita
being a boy	oˈtokoˈ no ko de
girl	oˈñnaˈ no ko or oˈñnaˈ no okosañ †

19. No. The older is a boy and the younger is a girl.

Iie. Uˈe wa otokoˈ no ko de, sita wa oˈñnaˈ no ko desu.

or

Iie. Uˈe wa otokoˈ no ko de, sita wa oˈñnaˈ no ko de gozaimasu.

(d)

Smith

that child	aˈnoˈ ko or ano okosañ †
child of what place (i.e. what household)?	doˈko no ko or doˈtira no okosañ †

---

[1] Has unaccented alternant (cf. sentence following).

20. Whose child is that? (Lit.   A⌐no⌐ ko (wa) ⌐do⌐ko no ko ⌐de⌐su ka⌐
    That child is the child of   or
    what place?)   Ano okosañ (wa) ⌐do⌐tira no o⌐kosañ
                                            de gozaima⌐su ka⌐

                        Tanaka

    belonging or pertaining   uti no or
    to one's household   otaku no ⌐
21. Why, that's our Taro.   Uti no ⌐Ta⌐roo desu yo⌐
                                               or
                                            Uti no ⌐Ta⌐roo de gozaimasu yo⌐

                        Smith

    Master Taro   Ta⌐roo-tyañ
22. (Is he) your Taro?   Otaku no ⌐Ta⌐roo-tyañ desu ka.
                                               or
                                            Otaku no ⌐Ta⌐roo-tyañ de (i)rassyai-
                                            masu ka.

    become big   o⌐okiku narimasu or
                                            o⌐okiku o⌐nari ni narima⌐su⌐
23. Hasn't he grown!   * O⌐okiku na⌐rima⌐sita ⌐ne⌐e.
                                               or
                                            * O⌐okiku o⌐nari ni narima⌐sita ⌐ne⌐e.

                        ADDITIONAL NATIONALITIES

                (All the following words refer to people only.[1])

    Japanese   ni⌐hoñzi⌐ñ or
                                            ni⌐ppoñzi⌐ñ

    American   a⌐merika⌐ziñ or
                                            be⌐ekoku⌐ziñ

    Korean   tyo⌐oseñzi⌐ñ
                                            (or ka⌐ñkoku⌐ziñ[2])

    Chinese   tyu⌐uḡoku⌐ziñ
                                            (or si⌐na⌐ziñ[3])

    Englishman   i⌐ḡirisu⌐ziñ or
                                            e⌐ekoku⌐ziñ

---

[1] Compare:
   Ni⌐hoñzi⌐ñ desu. 'He's Japanese.'
   Ni⌐hoñ no⌐ desu. 'It's Japanese.'

[2] Refers to South Koreans only. Preferred by them to preceding older
term, which refers to all Koreans.

[3] Formerly a commonly used word, now considered insulting by many
Chinese.

Frenchman	hu⌐rañsu⌐zin
German	do⌐itu⌐ziñ
Russian	ro⌐sia⌐ziñ
Indian (from India)	i⌐ñdo⌐ziñ
what nationality?	na⌐ni⌐ziñ

NOTES ON THE BASIC DIALOGUES

Sentences for which alternate forms are given are in the order of increasing politeness. Polite alternants are used more commonly, but not exclusively, by women.

5. The polite otomodati usually refers to someone else's friend(s), but some women use it in reference to their own friends as well—i.e. as a polite neutral (+) word.

6. Si⌐tte ima⌐su 'know' implies knowledge, whereas wa⌐karima⌐su 'understand,' 'can tell,' 'be clear' implies understanding or recognition by the senses. For example, I know (si⌐tte ima⌐su) Mr. Tanaka—perhaps because I have been introduced to him—but I can tell (wa⌐karima⌐su) who Mr. Tanaka is— perhaps because he is the only Japanese in the room.

   The wa following namae is the wa of comparison: i.e. 'even if I don't know her well, her name I know.'

7. The nominal si⌐tu⌐ree + desu (or de go⌐zaima⌐su) ḡa is common before questions of a personal nature. It is also used to introduce an interruption.

8. Remember that -sañ is not used with one's own name.

   The family name precedes the given name in Japanese. When -sañ is used with the full name, it comes last, after the given name (for example, Sa⌐too Yŭkio - sañ). -Sañ may also be used with the given name alone.

Additional examples of family names:

Aoyama	Ikeda	Ueda
Gotoo	Kimura	Watanabe
Hasimoto	Oota	Yamada
Hatoyama	Ta⌐mura	Yosida

Additional examples of given names:

Men's		Women's	
Haruo	Siḡeru	Ha⌐nako	Ma⌐sako
Hi⌐rosi	Syo⌐ozi	Ha⌐ru	Mi⌐dori
Masao	Ta⌐roo	Harue	Si⌐ḡe
Masaru	Yosio	Ha⌐ruko	Yo⌐siko
Sa⌐buro⌐o	Zi⌐roo	Haruyo	Yu⌐kiko

11. Ke⌐kkoñ-sima⌐su is one of a vast number of verbals consisting of a nominal compounded with the verbal √si⌐ma⌐su 'make' or 'do.' Kekkoñ is a
nominal meaning 'marriage.'

14. √A⌐rima⌐su occurs with both animate and inanimate subjects (corresponding to objects in English) when it means 'have'; thus, ko⌐domo ḡa √arima⌐su
(polite √go⌐zaima⌐su) 'have children.' In the given context, 14 (a) and (b)
and 15 (a) and (b) are used almost interchangeably, except for differences
of politeness.

18. Do⌐tira mo is used in reference to inanimate objects as well as living beings.

19. Compare: u⌐e no ho⌐ñ 'top book' and ho⌐ñ no ue 'top of the book'; si⌐ta no
ho⌐ñ 'bottom book' and ho⌐ñ no sita 'under the book.'

22. -Tyañ is added to boys' and girls' given names. It is polite, but less
formal than -sañ. While it is used in talking TO one's own children, it is
not ordinarily used in talking ABOUT them to those outside the family or
circle of very close friends.

GRAMMATICAL NOTES

1. √de⌐su: Polite Equivalents

√de⌐su ~ √de go⌐zaima⌐su ~ √de (i)⌐rassyaima⌐su

The polite neutral (+) equivalent of de⌐su following a nominal or a particle
is de go⌐zaima⌐su (de = the gerund of de⌐su). The past is de go⌐zaima⌐sita, and
the tentative de go⌐zaimasyo⌐o.

Examples:

	Plain	Polite +
'It's a book.'	Ho⌐ñ desu.	Ho⌐ñ de gozaimasu.
'It's that one.'	So⌐re de⌐su.	So⌐re de gozaima⌐su.
'It was pretty.'	Ki⌐ree desita.	Ki⌐ree de gozaimasita.
'It's probably the same.'	O⌐nazi desyo⌐o.	O⌐nazi de gozaimasyo⌐o.
'It's until tomorrow.'	A⌐sita⌐ made desu.	A⌐sita⌐ made de gozaimasu.

WARNING: Do not confuse the above with:

'There's a book.' or		
'I have a book.'	Ho⌐ñ (ḡa) arimasu.	Ho⌐ñ (ḡa) gozaimasu.

The negative equivalent of de go⌐zaima⌐su following a nominal or a particle
is de[1] wa go⌐zaimase⌐ñ (past, de⌐ wa go⌐zaimase⌐ñ desita).

---

[1] De is accented before wa, unless an accented word or phrase precedes.

Examples:

	Plain	Polite +
'It isn't a book.'	Ho⌐n zya a⌐rimase⌐ñ.	Ho⌐ñ de wa go⌐zaimase⌐ñ.
'It isn't that.'	So⌐re zya arimase⌐ñ.	So⌐re de⌐ wa go⌐zaimase⌐ñ.
'It wasn't a taxi.'	Ta⌐kusii zya a⌐rimase⌐ñ desita.	Ta⌐kusii de wa go⌐zaimase⌐ñ desita.
'It doesn't start at 3 o'clock.'	Sa⌐ñ-zi kara zya a⌐rimase⌐ñ.	Sa⌐ñ-zi kara de wa go⌐zaimase⌐ñ.

Actually, zya is the contracted equivalent of de⌐ wa, and the two can be used interchangeably anywhere, with only a difference of formality.

If a nominal (with or without following particle) + de⌐su refers to a PERSON other than the speaker, it has a second polite equivalent which is honorific (†) —namely, nominal + de (i)⌐rassyaima⌐su[1] (past, de (i)⌐rassyaima⌐sita; tentative, de (i)⌐rassyaimasyo⌐o; negative, de⌐ wa i⌐rassyaimase⌐ñ; past negative, de⌐ wa i⌐rassyaimase⌐ñ desita).

Thus:

	Plain	Polite
'He is Mr. Sato.'	Sa⌐too-sañ desu.	(Neutral) Sa⌐too-sañ de go-zaimasu. or (Honorific) Sa⌐too-sañ de (i)rassyaimasu.

But:

	Plain	Polite
'I am Mr. Sato.'	Sa⌐too desu.	Sa⌐too de gozaimasu.

The de go⌐zaima⌐su alternative represents simply a polite style of speech, whereas the de (i)⌐rassyaima⌐su alternative exalts the person under discussion besides being a polite style of speech. Of the two, the latter is more common— unless, of course, the speaker is talking politely about himself, a member of his own family, or someone of inferior social status.

WARNING: De⌐su following an adjectival (for example, ta⌐ka⌐i) is NOT replaced by de go⌐zaima⌐su or de (i)⌐rassyaima⌐su in the polite style.

---

[1] The form without i- is a contracted form, very common in conversation. Compare the end of Note 2 following.

2. Verbal Gerund + √i⌐ma⌐su

The non-past of a verbal usually refers to repeated or future punctual[1] occurrence.

A present or future durative[1] action or state is regularly indicated by a
verbal gerund + i⌐ma⌐su. This pattern means either (a) 'an action is now or
will be taking place over a period of time' or (b) 'the state resulting from an
action now exists, or will exist, over a period of time.' Meaning (b) is more
common among verbals which never take a direct object—particularly among
verbals indicating motion from one place to another and among those which
basically mean 'become so-and-so.' Depending on the individual verbal, the
subject may be animate or inanimate.
Examples:

Non-Past	Gerund + i⌐ma⌐su
Meaning (a)	
si⌐ma⌐su '[someone] does' or '[someone] will do'	si⌐te ima⌐su '[someone] is doing' or '[someone] will be doing'
ka⌐kima⌐su '[someone] writes' or '[someone] will write'	ka⌐ite imasu '[someone] is writing' or '[someone] will be writing'
ka⌐ima⌐su '[someone] buys' or '[someone] will buy'	ka⌐tte ima⌐su '[someone] is buying' or '[someone] will be buying'
Meaning (b)	
ke⌐kkoñ-sima⌐su '[someone] gets married' or '[someone] will get married'	ke⌐kkoñ-site ima⌐su '[someone] is married' or '[someone] will be married (i.e. in a married state)'
tu⌐tomema⌐su '[someone] becomes employed' or '[someone] will become employed'	tu⌐to⌐mete imasu '[someone] is em-ployed' or '[someone] will be employed (i.e. in an employed state)'
i⌐kima⌐su '[someone] goes' or '[someone] will go'	i⌐tte ima⌐su[2] '[someone] is gone' or '[someone] will be gone'

---

[1] PUNCTUAL indicates simple occurrence without any reference to duration
of time, whereas DURATIVE indicates occurrence over a period of time, during which something else may happen. Compare: 'I wrote a letter' (punctual)
and 'I was writing a letter' (durative).

[2] Also occurs with meaning (a): '[Someone] is going (i.e. repeatedly, over a
period of time)' as in 'He is going to that school.'

Gerund + i⌐ma⌐su may also indicate an action or state which began in the past and is still continuing. A time expression + particle <u>kara</u> tells when the action or state began and a time expression without following particle tells how long the action or state has been continuing. Thus:

Kyo⌐neñ kara ⌐ma⌐tte imasu. 'I have been waiting since last year.' (Lit. 'I am waiting from last year.')

Ni⌐-neñ ⌐ma⌐e kara tu⌐to⌐mete imasu. 'I have been employed for the last two years.' (Lit. 'I am employed from two years ago.')

Sa⌐ñ-neñ-g̃u⌐rai o⌐siete ima⌐su. 'I have been teaching for about three years.'

Si⌐tte ima⌐su, meaning literally '[someone] is in a state of having come to know'—i.e. '[someone] knows'—is another example of the gerund + i⌐ma⌐su pattern. The opposite is si⌐rimase⌐ñ '[someone] doesn't know' (lit. '[someone] has not come to know').¹

Following a gerund, √i⌐ma⌐su and its more polite equivalents √o⌐rima⌐su and √i⌐rassyaima⌐su may occur in the affirmative or negative, non-past or past, etc., with corresponding equivalents. Thus:

> ma⌐tte orimasu 'I'm waiting'
> ke⌐kkoñ-site irassyaimase⌐ñ '[he] is not married'
> ka⌐ite i⌐ma⌐sita '[I] was writing'
> ka⌐ette i⌐mase⌐ñ desita '[I] wasn't back (home)'

In rapid speech, the initial <u>i-</u> of √i⌐ma⌐su and √i⌐rassyaima⌐su is regularly dropped after a gerund. Thus:

> ke⌐kkoñ-site rassyaimase⌐ñ
> ka⌐ite masita
> ka⌐ette ma⌐se⌐ñ desita

3. √de⌐su: Gerund

The gerund of √de⌐su is <u>de</u>. Preceded by a nominal or particle, it occurs in the middle of sentences, coordinate with what follows (cf. Lesson 7, Grammatical Note 5). Thus:

2 sentences: A⌐merika⌐ziñ desu. 'I'm an American.'
              A⌐merika-taisi⌐kañ ni tu⌐to⌐mete imasu. 'I work for the American Embassy.'

1 sentence: A⌐merika⌐ziñ de, A⌐merika-taisi⌐kañ ni tu⌐to⌐mete imasu. 'I'm an American and I work for the American Embassy.'

---

¹ WARNING: Do not attempt to use the corresponding negative of si⌐tte ima⌐su (i.e. ~ i⌐mase⌐ñ) or the corresponding -ma⌐su affirmative of si⌐rimase⌐ñ.

Additional examples:

> Ue wa zyu⌐uni⌐ de, sita wa ya-⌐ttu⌐ desu.   'The older one is 12 and the
> younger one is 8.'
>
> Dotira mo ōnazi de, dotira mo da⌐me⌐ desu.   'They're both the same
> and they're both no good.'
>
> Sono kuruma wa I⌐girisu no⌐ de, to⌐ttemo taka⌐i desu yo.   'That car is
> a British one and it's very expensive.'

4.   Adjectival + √na⌐rima⌐su ~ Nominal + ni + √na⌐rima⌐su

An adjectival modifying an inflected expression is regularly in its adverbial
(-ku) form:

> Yo⌐ku na⌐rima⌐sita.   '[It] has become good.' or '[It] has improved.'
> Ta⌐kaku narimasu.   '[It] gets (or is going to get) expensive.'
> O⌐okiku na⌐rimase⌐ñ.   '[It] doesn't (or won't) get big.' or '[It] hasn't
> grown big.'
> Ya⌐suku na⌐rimase⌐ñ desita.   '[It] didn't get cheap.'
> I⌐kitaku narima⌐sita.   'I've reached the point where I want to go.'(Lit.
> 'I've become wanting to go.')

When the goal of √na⌐rima⌐su is a nominal, the nominal is followed by the
goal particle ni: X ni √na⌐rima⌐su 'become X,' 'get to be X.'

> De⌐pa⌐ato ni na⌐rima⌐sita.   '[It] has become a department store.'
> Da⌐me⌐ ni narimasu.   '[It] gets (or will get) bad.'
> To⌐modati ni⌐ wa[1] na⌐rita⌐ku a⌐rimase⌐ñ.   'I don't want to become a
> friend.'
> O⌐nazi ni⌐ wa[1] na⌐rimase⌐ñ desita.   '[It] didn't become the same.'

Note the regular difference in usage between:

> I⌐kura desu ka⌐   'How much is it?'   (i.e. one item)

and:

> I⌐kura ni na⌐rima⌐su ka⌐   'How much does it (or will it) come to?'
> (i.e. several items purchased)

Na⌐rima⌐su frequently corresponds to an English future, provided a change
in situation is involved. Compare:

> 'It will be cheap tomorrow' (i.e. it isn't today): A⌐sita⌐ wa ⌐ya⌐suku
> narimasu.
> 'It will be cheap tomorrow, too' (i.e. as it is today; no change): A⌐si-
> ta⌐ mo ya⌐su⌐i desu.

---

[1] The wa of comparison.

5. Counting People and Their Ages

The counter for people has two shapes, -ri for '1' and '2' and -niñ for higher numerals. -Ri combines with the numerals of Series II and -niñ with the numerals of Series I. Thus:

hi⌐to⌐-ri '1 person'	ro⌐ku⌐-niñ '6 people'
hu⌐ta-ri⌐ '2 people'	si⌐ti⌐-niñ '7 people'
sa⌐ñ-ni⌐ñ '3 people'	ha⌐ti⌐-niñ '8 people'
yo-⌐ni⌐ñ '4 people'	ku-⌐ni⌐ñ '9 people'
go-⌐ni⌐ñ '5 people'	zyu⌐u-niñ '10 people'

na⌐ñ-niñ 'how many people?'

The numbers used in counting people's ages are identical with those used in counting unit objects (hi⌐to⌐-tu, hu⌐ta-tu⌐, mi-⌐ttu⌐, etc.; see Lesson 5, Grammatical Note 1), except for the special word ha⌐tati '20 years old.' '20 units' is ni⌐zyuu.

Compare the following examples:

Hi⌐to⌐ri no kodomo wa o⌐ñna⌐ no ko desu. 'One child is a girl.'
Hi⌐to⌐tu no kodomo wa o⌐ñna⌐ no ko desu. 'The one-year-old child is a girl.'

DRILLS

A. Substitution Drill

1. Who is your friend? — Otomodati (wa) ⌐do⌐nata desu ka⌐
2. Where is your friend? — Otomodati (wa) ⌐do⌐ko desu ka⌐
3. How is your friend? — Otomodati (wa) i⌐ka⌐ḡa desu ka⌐
4. How old is your friend? — Otomodati (wa) o⌐ikutu de⌐su ka⌐
5. Is your friend English? — Otomodati (wa) i⌐ḡirisu⌐ziñ desu ka⌐
6. Is your friend single? — Otomodati (wa) o⌐hitori de⌐su ka⌐
7. Which one (lit. person) is your friend? — Otomodati (wa) ⌐do⌐no ka⌐ta⌐ desu ka⌐
8. What kind of person is your friend? — Otomodati (wa) ⌐do⌐ñna ka⌐ta⌐ desu ka⌐

B. Substitution Drill

1. A woman has come. — O⌐ñna no hito⌐ (ḡa) ki⌐ma⌐sita.
2. A man has come. — O⌐toko no hito⌐ (ḡa) ki⌐ma⌐sita.
3. A little girl has come. — O⌐ñna⌐ no ko (ḡa) ki⌐ma⌐sita.
4. A little boy has come. — O⌐toko⌐ no ko (ḡa) ki⌐ma⌐sita.
5. A friend (i.e. a lady) has come. — O⌐ñna no tomodati (ḡa) kima⌐sita.
6. A friend (i.e. a man) has come. — O⌐toko no tomodati (ḡa) kima⌐sita.

C.   Substitution Drill

1.	I'm working for the American Embassy.	Aꟲmerika-taisiꟲkañ ni tuꟲtoꟲmete (i)-masu.
2.	I'm working for the British Consulate.	Eꟲekoku-ryooziꟲkañ ni tuꟲtoꟲmete (i)-masu.
3.	I'm working for the Bank of Japan.	Niꟲhoñ-giꟲñkoo ni tuꟲtoꟲmete (i)masu.
4.	I'm working for the Yokohama Post Office.	Yoꟲkohama-yuubiꟲñkyoku ni tuꟲtoꟲmete (i)masu.
5.	I'm working for a Tokyo department store.	Toꟲokyoo no depaꟲato ni tuꟲtoꟲmete (i)masu.
6.	I'm working for a Kyoto hotel.	Kyoꟲoto no ꟲhoꟲteru ni tuꟲtoꟲmete (i)-masu.
7.	I'm working for St. Luke's Hospital.	Seꟲeroka-byoꟲoiñ ni tuꟲtoꟲmete (i)masu.
8.	I'm working for an American school.	Aꟲmerika no gakkoo ni tutoꟲmete (i)-masu.

D.   Substitution Drill

1.	Who did [it]?	Daꟲre ḡa siꟲmaꟲsita ka⌐
2.	Who doesn't understand?	Daꟲre ḡa waꟲkarimaseꟲñ ka⌐
3.	Who wants to go?	Daꟲre ḡa iꟲkitaꟲi ñ desu ka⌐
4.	Who is here?	Daꟲre ḡa iꟲmaꟲsu ka⌐
5.	Who wrote [it]?	Daꟲre ḡa kaꟲkimaꟲsita ka⌐
6.	Who bought [it]?	Daꟲre ḡa kaꟲimaꟲsita ka⌐
7.	Who needs [it]?	Daꟲre ḡa iꟲrimaꟲsu ka⌐
8.	Who is waiting?	Daꟲre ḡa ꟲmaꟲtte (i)masu ka⌐
9.	Who isn't here?	Daꟲre ḡa iꟲmaseꟲñ ka⌐
10.	Who didn't come?	Daꟲre ḡa kiꟲmaseꟲñ desita ka⌐

E.   Substitution Drill

1.	One (person) is 12 and the other is 10.	Hiꟲtoꟲ-ri wa zyuꟲuniꟲ de, moꟲo hitoꟲ-ri wa ꟲtoꟲo desu.
2.	One (person) is 8 and the other is 4.	Hiꟲtoꟲ-ri wa ya-ꟲttuꟲ de, moꟲo hitoꟲ-ri wa yo-ꟲttuꟲ desu.
3.	One (person) is 20 and the other is 21.	Hiꟲtoꟲ-ri wa ꟲhaꟲtati de, moꟲo hitoꟲ-ri wa ꟲniꟲzyuu iꟲtiꟲ desu.
4.	One (person) is French and the other is German.	Hiꟲtoꟲri wa huꟲrañsuꟲziñ de, moꟲo hitoꟲ-ri wa doꟲituꟲziñ desu.
5.	One (person) is a boy and the other is a girl.	Hiꟲtoꟲ-ri wa oꟲtokoꟲ no ko de, moꟲo hi-toꟲ-ri wa oꟲñnaꟲ no ko desu.
6.	One (person) is a man and the other is a woman.	Hiꟲtoꟲ-ri wa oꟲtoko no hitoꟲ de, moꟲo hitoꟲ-ri wa oꟲñna no hitoꟲ desu.
7.	One (person) is a policeman and the other is a druggist.	Hiꟲtoꟲ-ri wa zyuñsa de, moꟲo hitoꟲ-ri wa kuꟲsuriya deꟲsu.
8.	One (person) is a book dealer and the other is a florist.	Hiꟲtoꟲ-ri wa ꟲhoꟲñya de, moꟲo hitoꟲ-ri wa haꟲnaꟲya desu.

F. Substitution Drill

1. One woman came.   Oʳñna no hitoꜛ (ḡa) hiʳtoꜛ-ri kiᵗma�-si-
                                 ta.
2. Two friends came.   Tomodati (ḡa) huʳta-ri kimaꜛsita.
3. Three children came.   Kodomo (ḡa) saʳñ-niñ kimaꜛsita.
4. Four policemen came.   Zyuñsa (ḡa) yo-ʳniñ kimaꜛsita.
5. Five Koreans came.   Tyoʳoseñziꜛñ (ḡa) go-ʳniñ kimaꜛsita.
6. Six Russians came.   Roʳsiaꜛziñ (ḡa) roʳkuꜛ-niñ kiᵗmaᴸsita.
7. Seven Indians came.   Iꜛñdoꜛziñ (ḡa) siʳtiꜛ-niñ kiᵗmaᴸsita.
8. Eight Chinese came.   Tyuʳuḡokuꜛziñ (ḡa) haʳtiꜛ-niñ kiᵗmaᴸ-
                                 sita.

G. Substitution Drill

1. I'm doing [it] now.   Iꜛma siᵗte (i)maᴸsu.
2. I've been doing [it] for the Ziꜛp-puñ ᵗmaᴸe kara siᵗte (i)maᴸsu.
    last 10 minutes.
3. I've been waiting for the   Ziꜛp-puñ ᵗmaᴸe kara ᵗmaᴸtte (i)ma-
    last 10 minutes.   su.
4. I've been waiting since last Kyoꜛneñ[1] kara ᵗmaᴸtte (i)masu.
    year.
5. I've been teaching since last Kyoꜛneñ kara oᵗsiete (i)maᴸsu.
    year.
6. I've been teaching for about Zyuʳu-neñ-ḡuꜛrai oᵗsiete (i)maᴸsu.
    10 years.
7. I've been employed for about Zyuʳu-neñ-ḡuꜛrai tuᵗtoᴸmete (i)masu.
    10 years.
8. I'm employed now.   Iꜛma tuᵗtoᴸmete (i)masu.

H. Grammar Drill (based on Grammatical Note 4)

        Tutor: Oʳokiꜛi desu. '[It] is big.'
        Student: Oꜛokiku naᵗrimaᴸsita. '[It] has become big.'

1. Aʳkaꜛi desu.   Aʳkaku narimaꜛsita.
2. Geꜛñki desu.   Geꜛñki ni naᵗrimaᴸsita.
3. Tuʳmaraꜛnại desu.   Tuʳmaraꜛnaku naᵗrimaᴸsita.
4. Iꜛi desu.   Yoꜛku naᵗrimaᴸsita.
5. Haꜛtati desu.   Haꜛtati ni naᵗrimaᴸsita.
6. Oʳmosiroꜛi desu.   Oʳmosiroꜛku naᵗrimaᴸsita.
7. Toʳmodati deꜛsu.   Toʳmodati ni narimaꜛsita.
8. Waʳruꜛi desu.   Waʳruku naᵗrimaᴸsita.
9. Daʳmeꜛ desu.   Daʳmeꜛ ni naᵗrimaᴸsita.
10. Aʳbunaꜛi desu.   Aʳbunaku narimaꜛsita.

I. Grammar Drill (based on Grammatical Note 3)

        Tutor: Ue wa oʳtokoꜛ no ko desu. Sita wa oʳñnaꜛ no ko desu. 'The
                 oldest is a boy. The youngest is a girl.' (2 sentences)
        Student: Ue wa oʳtokoꜛ no ko de, sita wa oʳñnaꜛ no ko desu. 'The old-
                 est is a boy and the youngest is a girl.' (1 sentence)

---

[1] Kyoꜛneñ 'last year'

1. Tomodati wa ni⌐hoñzi⌐ñ desu. A⌐merika-gi⌐ñkoo ni tu⌐to⌐mete (i)masu.

   Tomodati wa ni⌐hoñzi⌐ñ de, A⌐merika-gi⌐ñkoo ni tu⌐to⌐mete (i)masu.

2. Ta⌐roo-tyañ wa ko⌐ko⌐no-tu desu. Ha⌐ruko-tyañ wa na⌐na⌐-tu desu.

   Ta⌐roo-tyañ wa ko⌐ko⌐no-tu de, Ha⌐ruko-tyañ wa na⌐na⌐-tu desu.

3. Ni⌐ho⌐ñ de ke⌐kkoñ-sima⌐sita. A⌐merika e kaerima⌐sita.

   Ni⌐ho⌐ñ de kekkoñ-site, A⌐merika e kaerima⌐sita.

4. Kore wa wa⌐takusi no⌐ desu. Sore wa ⌐tomodai no⌐ desu.

   Kore wa wa⌐takusi no⌐ de, sore wa to-⌐modati no⌐ desu.

5. A⌐no ka⌐do ni mo⌐do⌐tte kudasai. Mi⌐ḡi e maḡatte kudasa⌐i.

   A⌐no ka⌐do ni mo⌐do⌐tte, mi⌐ḡi e ma-ḡatte kudasa⌐i.

6. Kono hurosiki wa ni⌐hyaku⌐-eñ desu. Sore wa sa⌐ñbyaku⌐-eñ desu.

   Kono hurosiki wa ni⌐hyaku⌐-eñ de, so-re wa sa⌐ñbyaku⌐-eñ desu.

7. Tu⌐itati⌐ wa ge⌐tuyo⌐o desu. Nano-ka wa ni⌐tiyoo de⌐su.

   Tu⌐itati⌐ wa ge⌐tuyo⌐o de, nano-ka wa ni⌐tiyoo de⌐su.

8. Ha⌐ti⌐-zi ni u⌐ti (o) dema⌐sita. Ro⌐ku-zi-ḡo⌐ro ka⌐erima⌐sita.

   Ha⌐ti⌐-zi ni u⌐ti (o) de⌐te, ro⌐ku-zi-ḡo⌐ro ka⌐erima⌐sita.

J. Response Drill

(Give the corresponding negative reply—same politeness level—to each question.)

1. To⌐modati de⌐su ka⌐   To⌐modati zya arimase⌐ñ.
2. Si⌐ma⌐su ka⌐   Si⌐mase⌐ñ.
3. Si⌐te (i)ma⌐su ka⌐   Si⌐te (i)mase⌐ñ.
4. Ga⌐kkoo de gozaima⌐su ka⌐   Ga⌐kkoo de⌐ wa go⌐zaimase⌐ñ.
5. O⌐toto⌐i de go⌐zaima⌐sita ka⌐   O⌐toto⌐i de wa go⌐zaimase⌐ñ desita.
6. So⌐no kata⌐ (wa) a⌐merika⌐ziñ de (i)rassyaimasu ka⌐   So⌐no kata⌐ (wa) a⌐merika⌐ziñ de wa i⌐rassyaimase⌐ñ.
7. Tanaka-sañ (wa) tu⌐to⌐mete (i)rassyaimasu ka⌐   Tanaka-sañ (wa) tu⌐to⌐mete (i)⌐rassyaimase⌐ñ.
8. Si⌐tu⌐ree desu ka⌐   Si⌐tu⌐ree zya a⌐rimase⌐ñ.
9. Si⌐tte (i)ma⌐su ka⌐   Si⌐rimase⌐ñ.
10. A⌐buna⌐i desu ka⌐   A⌐bunaku arimase⌐ñ.

K. Level Drill (The sentences on the right are the polite equivalents of those on the left.)

1. Do⌐ko desu ka⌐   Do⌐tira de gozaimasu ka⌐
2. I⌐tu desu ka⌐   I⌐tu de gozaimasu ka⌐
3. A⌐sita⌐ desu.   A⌐sita⌐ de gozaimasu.

4. Ko⌐re de⌐su.   Ko⌐re de gozaima⌐su.
5. U⌐siro de⌐su.   U⌐siro de gozaima⌐su.
6. Ya⌐sumi⌐ desu ka⌐   O⌐yasumi de gozaima⌐su ka⌐
7. Ra⌐itaa desu.   Ra⌐itaa de gozaimasu.
8. Ga⌐kkoo de⌐su.   Ga⌐kkoo de gozaima⌐su.

L. Level Drill (The sentences on the right are the polite equivalents of those
    on the left.)

1. Na⌐ñ desu ka⌐   Na⌐ñ de gozaimasu ka⌐
2. A⌐na⌐ta (wa) Ta⌐naka-sañ   A⌐na⌐ta (wa) Ta⌐naka-sañ de (i)ras-
    de⌐su ka⌐   syaima⌐su ka⌐
3. Wa⌐surema⌐sita ka⌐   O⌐wasure ni narima⌐sita ka⌐
4. Ko⌐domo (ḡa) ima⌐su ka⌐   O⌐kosañ (ḡa) │irassyaima⌐su   │ka⌐
                                                          │oide ni narima⌐su │
5. Na⌐ñ-zi ni ki⌐ma⌐sita   Na⌐ñ-zi ni │i⌐rassyaima⌐sita   │ka⌐
    ka⌐   │o⌐ide ni narima⌐sita│
6. O⌐tomodati de⌐su ka⌐   O⌐tomodati de (i)rassyaima⌐su ka⌐
7. Ko⌐domo (ḡa) arima⌐su   O⌐kosañ (ḡa) gozaima⌐su ka⌐
    ka⌐
8. Do⌐ko ni tu⌐to⌐mete (i)ma-   Do⌐tira ni tu⌐to⌐mete (i)rassyaimasu
    su ka⌐   ka⌐
9. Na⌐ni (ḡa) i⌐rima⌐su ka⌐   Na⌐ni (ḡa) o⌐iri ni narima⌐su ka⌐
10. Watakusi wa ke⌐kkoñ-site   Watakusi wa ke⌐kkoñ-site orimase⌐ñ.
    imase⌐ñ.

M. Expansion Drill

1. I don't know.   Si⌐rimase⌐ñ.
    The name I don't know.   Na⌐mae wa sirimase⌐ñ.
    He's employed but I don't   Tu⌐to⌐mete (i)masu ḡa, na⌐mae wa si-
    know his name.   rimase⌐ñ.
    He's employed here (lit. for   Ko⌐ko ni tuto⌐mete (i)masu ḡa, na⌐mae
    this place) but I don't know   wa sirimase⌐ñ.
    his name.

2. Are you working (lit. doing   Si⌐ḡoto (o) site (i)ma⌐su ka⌐
    work)?
    What kind of work are you   Do⌐ñna si⌐ḡoto (o) site (i)ma⌐su ka⌐
    doing?
    What kind of work are you   I⌐ma ⌐do⌐ñna si⌐ḡoto (o) site (i)ma⌐su
    doing now?   ka⌐
    Excuse me [for asking],   Si⌐tu⌐ree desu ḡa, i⌐ma ⌐do⌐ñna si⌐ḡo-
    but what kind of work are   to (o) site (i)ma⌐su ka⌐
    you doing now?

3. [They]'re in America.   A⌐merika ni ima⌐su.
    Both are in America.   Do⌐tira mo A⌐merika ni ima⌐su.
    I have two (people) but both   Hu⌐ta-ri arima⌐su ḡa, do⌐tira mo A⌐me-
    are in America.   rika ni ima⌐su.
    I have two children but both   Kodomo ḡa hu⌐ta-ri arima⌐su ḡa, do⌐ti-
    are in America.   ra mo A⌐merika ni ima⌐su.

4. It's become expensive.   Ta⌐kaku na┌rima┐sita.
    It's become awfully expen-   Zu⌐ibuñ ⌐ta⌐kaku na┌rima┐sita.
    sive.
    It's become awfully expen-   Kotosi ⌐zu⌐ibuñ ⌐ta⌐kaku na┌rima┐sita.
    sive this year.
    Meat has become awfully   Ni⌐ku⌐ wa kŏtosi ⌐zu⌐ibuñ ⌐ta⌐kaku na-
    expensive this year.   ┌rima┐sita.
    Meat has become awfully   Ni⌐ku⌐ wa kŏtosi ⌐zu⌐ibuñ ⌐ta⌐kaku na-
    expensive this year,   ┌rima┐sita ⌐ne⌐e.
    hasn't it!

5. Would you be kind enough   Ka⌐ite ku┌dasaimase┐ñ ka ⌐
    to write [it]?
    Would you be kind enough   Pe⌐ñ de ┌ka┐ite ku┌dasaimase┐ñ ka ⌐
    to write [it] with a pen?
    Would you be kind enough   Onamae o ⌐pe⌐ñ de ┌ka┐ite ku┌dasa-
    to write your name with   imase┐ñ ka ⌐
    a pen?
    I'm sorry but would you   Su⌐mimase⌐ñ g̃a, onamae o ⌐pe⌐ñ de
    be kind enough to write   ┌ka┐ite ku┌dasaimase┐ñ ka ⌐
    your name with a pen?

6. How old is [he]?   O⌐ikutu de (i)rassyaima┐su ka ⌐
    How old is Taro?   Ta┐roo-tyañ (wa) o⌐ikutu de (i)rassya-
                                           ima┐su ka ⌐
    How old is your Taro?   O⌐taku no Ta┐roo-tyañ (wa) o⌐ikutu de
                                           (i)rassyaima┐su ka ⌐
    Excuse me [for asking],   Si⌐tu⌐ree desu g̃a, o⌐taku no Ta┐roo-
    but how old is your   tyañ (wa) o⌐ikutu de (i)rassyaima┐-
    Taro?   su ka ⌐

SUPPLEMENTARY SELECTIONS

(with questions)

(Give precise answers for each group of questions according to the information contained in the statements that precede them.)

1. Ko⌐domo g̃a sañ-niñ ima┐su. Ha┐ruko g̃a ŭe no ko de, ⌐to⌐o desu. Tu⌐g̃i⌐ wa
    ⌐Ta┐roo de, na⌐na┐-tu desu. Zi┐roo g̃a sĭta no ko de, si-g̃atu⌐ ni yo-⌐ttu⌐ ni
    narimasu.

        Kodomo g̃a ⌐na┐ñ-niñ i┌ma┐su ka ⌐
        Ue no ko no namae wa ⌐na┐ñ desu ka ⌐
        Ue wa o⌐toko┐ no ko desu ka ⌐
        Da┐re g̃a ┌to┐o desu ka ⌐
        Ta┐roo-tyañ wa ⌐i⌐kutu desu ka ⌐
        Sita wa o⌐ñna┐ no ko desu ka ⌐
        Zi┐roo-tyañ wa ⌐i┐ma ⌐i⌐kutu desu ka ⌐
        Ue no ko g̃a si-g̃atu⌐ ni yo-⌐ttu⌐ ni na┌rima┐su ka ⌐

2. Ke⌐sa a⌐merika⌐ziñ to i⌐girisu⌐ziñ ḡa wa⌐takusi no zimu⌐syo e ki⌐ma⌐sita.
    A⌐merika⌐ziñ wa o⌐toko no hito⌐ de, A⌐merika-gi⌐ñkoo ni tu⌐to⌐mete imasu.
    I⌐girisu⌐ziñ wa o⌐ñna no hito⌐ de, E⌐ekoku-taisi⌐kañ ni tu⌐to⌐mete imasu.
    A⌐merika⌐ziñ no namae wa ⌐Su⌐misu de, i⌐girisu⌐ziñ no namae wa ⌐Zyo⌐oñzu
    desu.

        Na⌐ñ-niñ wa⌐takusi no zimu⌐syo e ki⌐ma⌐sita ka﹄
        Do⌐tira mo a⌐merika⌐ziñ desu ka﹄
        Do⌐tira ḡa o⌐ñna no hito⌐ desu ka﹄
        Do⌐tira ḡa ta⌐isi⌐kañ ni tu⌐to⌐mete imasu ka﹄
        Do⌐tira ḡa ⌐Su⌐misu-sañ desu ka﹄

3. Yamamoto-sañ wa go-⌐neñ ma⌐e ni ke⌐kkoñ-sima⌐sita.   Tanaka-sañ wa
    kōtosi zyu⌐uni-ḡatu⌐ ni ke⌐kkoñ-sima⌐su.

        Do⌐tira ḡa ⌐i⌐ma ke⌐kkoñ-site ima⌐su ka﹄
        So⌐no⌐ hito wa ⌐na⌐ñ-neñ ni ke⌐kkoñ-sima⌐sita ka﹄
        So⌐no⌐ hito wa ⌐na⌐ñ-neñ kara ke⌐kkoñ-site ima⌐su ka﹄
        So⌐no⌐ hito wa ⌐na⌐ñ-neñ ⌐ma⌐e kara ke⌐kkoñ-site ima⌐su ka﹄
        So⌐no⌐ hito wa ⌐na⌐ñ-neñ ke⌐kkoñ-site ima⌐su ka﹄
        Do⌐tira ḡa ko⌐tosi kekkoñ-sima⌐su ka﹄

EXERCISES

1. Using pictures of familiar people, practice asking and answering questions
    about their names, nationalities, marital status, and age.

2. You ask Mr. Tanaka: Mr. Tanaka replies:

    a. what his name is.   I'm Taro Tanaka.
    b. to write his name.   I'm sorry but I don't have a pencil.
    c. how old he is.   I'm 52.
    d. what kind of work he does. I work for the Bank of Japan.
    e. if he is married.   Yes, I am.
    f. if he has any children.   Yes, I have three.
    g. who that is.   That's Yukio Sato.
    h. who that Japanese is.   He's a friend.
    i. who that woman is.   I don't know her name but she works
                                       for the embassy.
    j. if Mr. Jones is American.   No, he's English.

3. Practice the Basic Dialogues with appropriate variations.

Lesson 11. Meeting People (cont.)

BASIC DIALOGUES: FOR MEMORIZATION

(a)

(Mr. and Mrs. Tanaka meet Mr. Smith)

Mr. Tanaka

    a while (long or short)   si⌐ba⌐raku
1. Mr. Smith! It's been a long   Su⌐misu-sañ. Si⌐ba⌐raku desita.
    time [since I last saw you].

Mr. Smith

2. Oh, Mr. Tanaka! It <u>has</u> been   A⌐a, Tanaka-sañ. Si⌐ba⌐raku desita
    a long time.   ⌐ne⌐e.

Mr. Tanaka

    everyone <u>or</u> everything   miñna
    everyone   mi⌐na⌐sañ ⌐
3. Is everyone well?   Mi⌐na⌐sañ o⌐ge⌐ñki desu ka⌐

Mr. Smith

4. Yes, thank you. Is everyone   E⌐e, okaḡesama de. O⌐taku no mi-
    at your house [well], too?   na⌐sañ mo?

Mr. Tanaka

5. Yes, thank you.   E⌐e, a⌐ri⌐ḡatoo gozaimasu.

    wife   ka⌐nai <u>or</u>
        o⌐kusañ ⌐
6. Mr. Smith, this is my wife.   Su⌐misu-sañ. Kore (wa) ⌐ka⌐nai de-
        su.

(addressing his wife)

    this person   kotira
7. This is Mr. Smith from the   Kotira (wa) A⌐merika-taisi⌐kañ no
    American Embassy.   ⌐Su⌐misu-sañ desu.

Mr. Smith

    the first time   ha⌐zi⌐mete
    meet <u>or</u> see (a person)   o⌐me ni kakarima⌐su ⌐
    how <u>do you</u> do   ha⌐zimema⌐site <u>or</u>
    how do you do (lit. I meet   ha⌐zi⌐mete ome ni kakarimasu ⌐
    you for the first time)
8. Are you Mrs. [Tanaka]? I'm   O⌐kusañ desu ka⌐ Su⌐misu desu. Ha-
    [Mr.] Smith. How do you do.   ⌐zimema⌐site.

Mrs. Tanaka

9. I'm [Mrs.] Tanaka. How do   Ta⌐naka⌐ de gozaima⌐su. Ha⌐zi⌐mete
    you do. I'm glad to meet   ome ni kakarimasu. Do⌐ozo yŏrosi-
    you.   ku.

         Japanese language   nihoñḡo   or
                                        nippoñḡo
10. You can [speak] Japanese very   Nihoñḡo (ḡa) ⌐yo⌐ku o⌐deki ni nari-
    well, can't you!   ma⌐su ⌐ne⌐e.

                             Mr. Smith

         study   be⌐ñkyoo-sima⌐su
         be studying   beñkyoo-site (i)ru (informal)   or
                                        be⌐ñkyoo-site (i)ma⌐su

         because [I] am studying   be⌐ñkyoo-site (i)ru⌐ kara   or
         or [I] am studying, so   be⌐ñkyoo-site (i)ma⌐su kara
11. Oh, no! I am studying so I can   Do⌐o itasimasite. Be⌐ñkyoo-site (i)ru⌐
    [speak it] a little but . . .   kara, su⌐ko⌐si wa de⌐kima⌐su ḡa_
                                                or
                                        Do⌐o itasimasite. Be⌐ñkyoo-site (i)-
                                        ma⌐su kara, su⌐ko⌐si wa de⌐kima⌐su
                                        ḡa_

         considerably or more   nakanaka
            than expected
         is difficult   muzukasii /-ku/
12. It's quite difficult, isn't it—   Na⌐kanaka muzukasi⌐i desu ⌐ne⌐e—ni-
    Japanese.   hoñḡo wa.

                            Mrs. Tanaka

         foreign language   gaikokuḡo
         is easy   yasasii /-ku/
13. Foreign languages aren't easy,   Ga⌐ikokuḡo wa yasasiku gozaimase⌐ñ
    are they!   ⌐ne⌐e.

                                (b)
                              Smith

14. Whose is this?   Kore (wa) ⌐da⌐re no desu ka_

                              Tanaka

15. It's Mr. Kobayashi's, isn't   Ko⌐bayasi-sañ no⌐ desyoo?
    it?

                              Smith

16. It isn't yours?   A⌐na⌐ta no zya a⌐rimase⌐ñ ka_

                              Tanaka

17. No (i.e. that's right). It's   E⌐e, a⌐no⌐ hito no desu.
    his.

                              Smith

18. What about yours?   A⌐na⌐ta no wa?

Tanaka

19. Hmm. I wonder where it is. It was here but . . .	Sa⌉a. Do⌉ko desyoo ka ⊢ne⊣e. Ko⌈ko ni arima⌉sita ḡa_

(c)

Smith

is late or slow	osoi /-ku/
become late	o⌈soku na⌉ru (informal) or o⌈soku narima⌉su
because it becomes late or it becomes late so	o⌈soku na⌉ru kara or o⌈soku narima⌉su kara
20. Well, it's getting late so if you'll excuse me . . .	Zya⌉a, o⌈soku na⌉ru kara, si⌈tu⌉ree. or Zya⌉a, o⌈soku narima⌉su kara, si⌈tu⌉-ree-simasu.

Tanaka

meet or see a person	a⌈ima⌉su
21. Well, I'll see you again. Goodbye.	Zya⌉a, ma⌈ta (aimasyo⌉o). Sayonara_

Smith

to everyone	mi⌈na⌉sañ ni †
22. Give my regards to everyone. Goodbye.	Mi⌈na⌉sañ ni yo͞rosiku. Sayonara_

(d)

Smith

why?	na⌉ze
why? or how?	do⌉o site
23. Why aren't you going to go?	Na⌉ze i⊢kimase⊣ñ ka⌣ or Do⌉o site i⊢kimase⊣ñ ka⌣

Tanaka

father	ti⌈ti⌉ or o⌈to⌉osañ †
sickness or sick	byooki or gobyooki †
is sick	byooki da (informal) or byo⌈oki de⌉su
because [he] is sick or [he] is sick so	byo⌈oki da⌉ kara or byo⌈oki de⌉su kara
24. Because my father is sick.	Ti⌈ti⌉ ḡa byo⌈oki da⌉ kara. or Ti⌈ti⌉ ḡa byo⌈oki de⌉su kara.

Smith

25. He's sick?	Go⌈byooki de⌉su ka.
26. That's too bad.	I⌈kemase⌉ñ ⌈ne⌉e.
27. Take care.	Odaizi ni.

Tanaka

28. Thank you.	A⌈ri⌉ḡatoo gozaimasu.

(e)

Smith

last night	yu⌐ube⌐
Foreign Office	ga⌐imu⌐syoo
meet <u>or</u> see Mr. Yamada	Ya⌐mada-sañ ni aima⌐su

29. You know, I saw Mr. Yamada   Yuube ga⌐imu⌐syoo no Ya⌐mada-sañ ni
    from the Foreign Office last   aima⌐sita yo⌐
    night.

Tanaka

30. You did? Was it the first   So⌐o desu ka. Ha⌐zi⌐mete desita ka⌐
    time?

Smith

31. Yes, that's right.   E⌐e, so⌐o desu.

Tanaka

32. He's a fine man, isn't he?   I⌐i ka⌐ta⌐ desyoo?

Smith

33. Yes, very.   E⌐e, tottemo.

FAMILY TERMS [1]

	Plain or Humble[†] Word	Polite Honorific[†] Word
family	ka⌐zoku	go⌐ka⌐zoku
grandfather	so⌐hu	o⌐zi⌐isañ [2]
grandmother	so⌐bo	o⌐ba⌐asañ [3]
parent	o⌐ya⌐	oyaḡosañ
both parents	ryo⌐osiñ	go⌐ryo⌐osiñ
father	ti⌐ti⌐	o⌐to⌐osañ
mother	ha⌐ha	o⌐ka⌐asañ
son	musuko	musukosañ <u>or</u> bo⌐ttyañ
daughter	mu⌐sume⌐	musumesañ <u>or</u> o⌐zyo⌐osañ
husband	syu⌐ziñ	go⌐syu⌐ziñ
wife	ka⌐nai	o⌐kusañ

---

[1] Practice these words according to the pattern of Drill I, page 185.

[2] Also means 'old man.'

[3] Also means 'old woman.'

	Plain or Humble [†] Word	Polite Honorific [†] Word
uncle	ozi	ozisañ [1]
aunt	oba	obasañ [2]
brothers and/or sisters [3]	kyo˺odai	go˹kyo˺odai
older brother	a˺ni	ni˹isañ or o˹ni˹isañ
older sister	ane	ne˹esañ or o˹ne˹esañ
younger brother	o˹tooto˺	otootosañ
younger sister	i˹mooto˺	imootosañ or oimotosañ
cousin	i˹to˺ko	oitokosañ
nephew	oi	oiḡosañ
niece	me˹e	meeḡosañ
grandchild	ma˹ḡo˺	omaḡosañ

ADDITIONAL LANGUAGE NAMES [4]

(All the following words refer to languages only)

English	eeḡo
French	hurañsuḡo
German	doituḡo
Russian	rosiaḡo
Korean	tyooseñḡo
Chinese	tyuuḡokuḡo (or sinaḡo [5])
Spanish	supeiñḡo

NOTES ON THE BASIC DIALOGUES

3. For Americans from the South, mi˹na˺sañ is the most common equivalent of 'you-all.'

---

[1] Also an informal word for 'man' used especially commonly by children and in talking to children; often used in reference to a close friend of the family.

[2] Also means 'woman'; its usage parallels that of ozisañ.

[3] I.e. 'siblings.'

[4] Practice these words as substitutes for nihoñḡo in Basic Sentence 10 (cf. Drill A, page 181.

[5] Formerly a commonly used word, now considered insulting by many Chinese.

7. The kotira series is frequently used in reference to people. In this usage, it is polite (+). Kotira, depending on context, means either 'this person — close to me' or 'this person — i.e. myself.' Similarly, sotira means 'that person — not far away' or 'the person I'm addressing — i.e. you.'

8, 9. In Japanese, it is customary to repeat one's own name according to the patterns of Basic Sentences 8 and 9, immediately upon being introduced.

Ha⌐zi⌐mete is a nominal: ha⌐zi⌐mete desu 'it's the first time'; ha⌐zi⌐mete zya a⌐rimase⌐ñ 'it's not the first time.' Its formal equivalent ha⌐zime-ma⌐site is used only in introductions as a shorter equivalent of humble-polite ha⌐zi⌐mete ome ni kakarimasu.

Yorosiku is the adverbial (-ku form) of the adjectival yorosii. Do⌐ozo yorosiku means 'please [treat our acquaintance] favorably.' A person who is being introduced regularly says ha⌐zimema⌐site OR ha⌐zi⌐mete ome ni kakarimasu AND/OR do⌐ozo yorosiku.

Note the use of polite speech by Mrs. Tanaka in addressing Mr. Smith— typical in the given situation. Mr. Smith may use plain or polite speech, depending on circumstances of position, age, etc.

10. In reference to a language, √de⌐kima⌐su 'be possible' or 'can do' means 'know' or 'can speak.' Remember that both the thing that is possible and the person to whom it is possible are followed by particles g̃a and/or wa.

11. √Be⌐ñkyoo-sima⌐su is a compound verbal (like √ke⌐kkoñ-sima⌐su) made up of the nominal beñkyoo 'study (noun)' + √si⌐ma⌐su 'do.'

The wa here is the wa of comparison: 'A little I can speak it but—not very well.'

13. Gaikoku means 'foreign country' and gaikokug̃o is the language of a foreign country. Gaikokuziñ means 'foreigner'; this word frequently occurs in the abbreviated form gaiziñ, which now usually refers to Westerners.

Ya⌐sasiku gozaimase⌐ñ is the polite (+) equivalent of ya⌐sasiku arimase⌐ñ. Remember that √a⌐rima⌐su can regularly be replaced by the appropriate form of √go⌐zaima⌐su to form a polite equivalent.

14–18. Note the contraction of particle no + nominal no into a single no.

19. 'It was here but—I don't know where it is now.'

20. O⌐soku narima⌐sita 'it has become late' is often used as an apology for being late.

21. A⌐ima⌐su is a formal plain verbal, and o⌐me ni kakarima⌐su (sentence 9 above) is its humble (↓) equivalent. The honorific (↑) equivalent is o⌐ai ni narima⌐su. These verbals usually mean 'meet' or 'see' in the sense 'meet up with and talk to,' not 'catch sight of' or 'look at.' The person seen or met is followed by particle ni (sentence 29 below).

Ma⌐ta aimasyo⌐o means '(I guess) I'll see you again' or 'let's meet again.'

23. As an equivalent of 'why?' do⌐o site (literally 'doing how?') is softer and less direct than na⌐ze.

26. I⌐kemase⌐ñ is a verbal negative which has taken on a specialized meaning

(compare su⌐mimase¬ñ). It is used to prohibit ('it won't do,' 'you mustn't do that'), and with ne¬e, it occurs as an   expression of sympathy in regard to a matter of not too serious a nature.

27. Odaizi ni is an admonition to 'treat yourself — or someone close to you — carefully.' Daizi (polite odaizi') is a nominal meaning 'important,' 'valuable.'

Family terms:

The plain words in the list of family terms, besides being used as general terms without reference to any particular individuals, are used in talking about members of one's own family, whereas the polite words are used in polite reference to members of the families of others. O⌐zi¬isañ, o⌐ba¬asañ, o⌐to¬osañ, o⌐ka⌐asañ, ozisañ, obasañ, ni¬isañ, and ne¬esañ are also used in addressing one's own relatives.   Thus:

> ti⌐ti¬ 'my father,' 'a father'
> o⌐to¬osañ 'your father,' 'his father,' etc., and 'Father!'

In reference to someone else's young son and daughter, bo¬ttyañ and o⌐zyo¬osañ are more polite than musukosañ and musumesañ; but the latter terms are regularly used in reference to someone else's adult son and daughter. Bo¬ttyañ may also be used in addressing boys and o⌐zyo¬osañ in addressing girls and young ladies, not related to the speaker.

O¬kusañ is the regular polite way to address married women — including strangers.   It is the Japanese equivalent of 'madam' and 'Mrs. ——.'

To distinguish among different members of a given family, kinship terms are regularly used preceded by the family name + no. Thus:

> Ta⌐naka-sañ no gosyu¬zZiñ 'Mr. Tanaka'
> Ta⌐naka-sañ no o¬kusañ 'Mrs. Tanaka'
> Ta⌐naka-sañ no ozyo¬osañ 'Miss Tanaka'
> Ta⌐naka-sañ no bo¬ttyañ 'Master Tanaka'

GRAMMATICAL NOTES

1.   V e r b a l s :   I n f o r m a l   N o n - p a s t ,   S t e m ,   a n d   G e r u n d

A verbal ending in -ma¬su is formal, non-past, and affirmative. Its informal equivalent — i. e. informal, non-past, affirmative — introduced in this lesson for the first time, is the form regularly listed in dictionaries and will hereafter be referred to as the CITATION FORM. A verbal stem (the -ma¬su form minus -ma¬su) and gerund (the -te form) are related to the citation form according to regular patterning.

Toward the end of this note is a chart listing the informal non-past affirmative (i. e. the citation form; other informal forms will be introduced later), stem, gerund, and English equivalent of verbals introduced thus far. Study the chart carefully while noting the following points:

(1) Informal Non-past Affirmative (Citation Form)

Henceforth, all new verbals will be cited in this form when they first occur.

THIS FORM IS IDENTICAL IN MEANING WITH THE -MA⌐SU FORM
EXCEPT THAT IT IS LESS FORMAL. Don't make the very common
mistake of equating it with the English infinitive and then translating it
'to do so-and-so.' Just as Wa⌐karima⌐su. may occur as a complete sentence meaning 'It's clear.' 'I understand.' so Wa⌐ka⌐ru. occurs with the
same meanings, as its informal equivalent.

Verbals may be divided into 4 groups:

(a) The -RU GROUP includes verbals which have -ru in the informal (ci-
    tation form) corresponding to -ma⌐su in the formal. In all such verbals,
    the vowel preceding -ru is e or i.

    Example: de⌐ru/de⌐ma⌐su 'go out'

(b) The -U GROUP includes verbals which have -u in the informal (citation
    form) corresponding to -ima⌐su in the formal. In all such verbals, the
    -u is preceded by one of 8 consonants—t, r, s, k, ḡ, b, m, or n—or by a
    vowel other than e.

    Example: ka⌐eru/ka⌐erima⌐su 'return (home)'

(c) The -ARU GROUP includes verbals which have -aru in the informal
    (citation form) corresponding to -aima⌐su in the formal. This group
    includes only 5 verbals, all of which are polite.

    Example: ku⌐dasa⌐ru/ku⌐dasaima⌐su 'give me'

(d) The IRREGULAR GROUP includes only 2 verbals:

    suru/si⌐ma⌐su 'do'
    ku⌐ru/ki⌐ma⌐su 'come'

In subsequent lessons, a new verbal will be identified at its first appearance according to its group. For example:

    ka⌐ke⌐ru /-ru/

(2) Stem

The stem is the -ma⌐su form minus -ma⌐su. [1] It is the form to which the

---

[1] The stem is accented if the citation form is accented. The accent of the
citation form must be learned for each verbal. A -ma⌐su form is regularly
accented on the ma syllable except in environments where the accent is lost.

adjectival -tai ending, meaning 'want to do so-and-so,' is added (for example, KAItai 'want to buy,' IKItai 'want to go,' etc.).[1] The polite nominals
which are derived from verbals and which occur in polite patterns consist
of the polite prefix o- plus the stem[2] (for example, o⌐DEKI ni narima⌐su
ka 'can you do it?'; o⌐KAERI ni narima⌐su ka 'are you going to go home?').
Other uses of the stem will be introduced later.

To determine the stem, given the citation form:

(a) for verbals of the -ru group, drop the -ru ending.

Example: wasureru 'forget,' stem wasure

(b) for verbals of the -u group, change final -u to -i.

Example: kau 'buy,' stem kai

(c) for verbals of the -aru group, change final -aru to -ai.

Example: go⌐za⌐ru 'be,' 'have,' stem go⌐za⌐i

(d) irregular:

suru 'do,' stem si
ku⌐ru 'come,' stem ki⌐

(3) Gerund (the -te form)

The gerund has been introduced in the following patterns:

O⌐namae o KA⌐ITE kudasai. 'Please write your name.'
O⌐namae o KA⌐ITE ku└dasaimase⌐ñ ka↲ 'Would you be kind enough to
   write your name?'
So⌐re o KA⌐ITE, ka⌐erima⌐sita. 'I wrote it and went home.'
Na⌐mae o KA⌐ITE (i)masu. 'I'm writing my name.'

Other uses will be introduced later.

To determine the gerund, given the citation form:

(a) for -ru verbals, change the final -ru to -te.

Example: wasureru 'forget' : wasurete

---

[1] When -tai is added to an accented stem, the combination is accented on
syllable ta; when it is added to an unaccented stem, the combination is also unaccented.

[2] The combination is an unaccented word.

(b) for -u verbals: change final—

-tu to -tte	Example: ma⌐tu 'wait' : ma⌐tte
-ru to -tte	ka⌐eru 'return' : ka⌐ette
vowel + -u to vowel + -tte	kau 'buy' : katte
-su to -site	ha⌐na⌐su 'speak' : ha⌐na⌐site
-ku to -ite	ka⌐ku 'write' : ka⌐ite
-g̃u to -ide	i⌐so⌐g̃u 'hurry' : i⌐so⌐ide
-bu to -ñde	yobu[1] 'call' : yoñde
-mu to -ñde	yo⌐mu[1] 'read' : yo⌐ñde
-nu to -ñde	sinu[1] 'die' : siñde (unique example)

(c) for -aru verbals, change the final -aru to -atte, but note also the alternate forms in the chart below.

      Example: i⌐rassya⌐ru 'go,' 'come,' 'be': i⌐rassya⌐tte
                                   (and i⌐ra⌐site)

(d) irregular:

    suru 'do' : site
    ku⌐ru 'come' : ki⌐te⌐

A stem and gerund are accented only if the informal non-past (citation) form from which they are derived is accented. In the -ru group, the accent of the stem and gerund occurs one syllable nearer the beginning of the word than the accent of the citation form, unless that accent is on the first syllable (example: non-past mi⌐se⌐ru, stem mi⌐se, gerund mi⌐sete); elsewhere, the accent of the stem and gerund regularly occurs on the same syllable as the accent of the citation form (example: non-past ka⌐ku, stem ka⌐ki, gerund ka⌐ite). [2]

Once you have learned the five -aru and two irregular verbals, any other verbal not ending in -eru or -iru must belong to the -u group. A verbal ending in -eru or -iru may belong to the -ru group or the -u group; this cannot be determined unless other inflected forms of the word are known or unless the word is specifically identified as to group. Compare:

    iru (-ru) 'be in a place (animate)':

        stem i
        formal i⌐ma⌐su
        gerund ite

    iru (-u) 'be needed':

        stem iri
        formal i⌐rima⌐su
        gerund itte

---

[1] These verbals and others ending in -bu and -mu will occur in later lessons. They are mentioned here only for the sake of completeness.

[2] The accent of ki⌐te⌐, gerund of ku⌐ru, is irregular.

VERBALS

	Informal Non-past (Citation Form)	Stem	Gerund	English Equivalent
-RU Group:	de˹ki˺ru	de˹ki	de˹kite	'be possible'
	de˹ru	de˹	de˹te	'go out'
	iru[1]	i	ite	'be in a place (animate)'
	mi˹se˺ru	mi˹se	mi˹sete	'show'
	osieru	osie	osiete	'teach,' 'inform'
	tomeru	tome	tomete	'bring to a halt'
	tu˹tome˺ru	tu˹to˺me	tu˹to˺mete	'become employed'
	wasureru	wasure	wasurete	'forget'

	Informal Non-past (Citation Form)	Stem	Gerund	English Equivalent
-U Group:				
-tu	ma˹tu	ma˹ti	ma˹tte	'wait'
-ru	a˹ru	a˹ri	a˹tte	'be in a place (inanimate),' 'have'
	iru	iri	itte	'be needed'
	ka˹eru	ka˹eri	ka˹ette	'return home'
	ka˹ka˺ru	ka˹ka˺ri	ka˹ka˺tte	'be required' (ome ni ~ ↓ 'meet')
	ko˹ma˹ru	ko˹ma˹ri	ko˹ma˹tte	'be upsetting'
	maḡaru	maḡari	maḡatte	'make a turn'
	ma˹iru ↓	ma˹iri	ma˹itte	'come,' 'go'
	mo˹do˹ru	mo˹do˹ri	mo˹do˹tte	'go back,' 'back up'
	na˹ru	na˹ri	na˹tte	'become' (o- + stem ni ~ = honorific)
	o˹ru ↓	o˹ri	o˹tte	'be in a place (animate)'
	siru	siri	sitte	'come to know'
	wa˹ka˹ru	wa˹ka˹ri	wa˹ka˹tte	'be comprehensible'
-Vowel + u	a˹u	a˹i	a˹tte	'meet,' 'see (a person)'

---

[1] (i)ru, (i), (i)te following a gerund.

	iu[1]	ii	itte	'say'
	kau	kai	katte	'buy'
	tiḡau	tiḡai	tiḡatte	'be different'
	ukaḡau ꜛ	ukaḡai	ukaḡatte	'inquire'
-su	ha⌐na¬su	ha⌐na¬si	ha⌐na¬site	'talk'
-ku	ka¬ku	ka¬ki	ka¬ite	'write,' 'draw'
	tu¬ku	tu¬ki	tu¬ite	'arrive'
	iku	iki	itte[2]	'go'
-ḡu	i⌐so¬ḡu	i⌐so¬ḡi	i⌐so¬ide	'be in a hurry'

-ARU Group:	go⌐za¬ru+ [3]	go⌐za¬i	———	'be in a place (inanimate),' 'have'
	i⌐rassya¬ru ꜛ	i⌐rassya¬i	i⌐rassya¬tte or i⌐ra¬site	'go,' 'come,' 'be in a place (animate)'
	ku⌐dasa¬ru ꜛ	ku⌐dasa¬i	ku⌐dasa¬tte or ku⌐dasu¬tte	'give to me'
Irregular Group:	ku¬ru	ki¬	ki⌐te¬	'come'
	suru	si	site	'make,' 'do' (beñkyoo-～ 'study,' kekkoñ-～ 'marry,' etc.)

In informal speech, used most commonly in addressing close friends, relatives, or inferiors, the majority of inflected forms that occur are informal. They occur at the end of sentences as well as within longer sentences, in the informal speech of both men and women—but with specific differences. Remember that it is possible to be polite and informal at the same time, for example with forms like i⌐rassya¬ru ꜛ. Informal speech will be discussed in greater detail in later lessons.

Even in formal speech, informal inflected forms frequently occur as nonfinal inflected forms, in some patterns. (There is no difference here between the speech of men and women except that men use informal forms more frequently.) For one such pattern, see Note 3 below.

---

[1] The combination i + u is regularly pronounced yuu. The spelling iu is preferred here because it helps the student determine the other inflected forms.

[2] Itte, the gerund of iku, is an irregular form, but since it is the only irregular form, iku is not listed among the irregular verbs.

[3] This form is rare in conversational Japanese.

2. Copula: Informal Non-past da

The informal equivalent of de⌐su is da, which will hereafter be designated as the citation form of the copula. It occurs after nominals and particles.

Examples:

> so⌐o da 'that's right'
> sa⌐ñ-zi made da 'it's until 3 o'clock'

De, the gerund of the copula, has already been introduced. The copula has no form corresponding to a verbal stem.

WARNING: Remember that the informal equivalent of an adjectival + de⌐su is the adjectival alone. Thus: ta⌐ka⌐i desu 'it's expensive' (formal); ta⌐ka⌐i 'it's expensive' (informal).

Study the following chart:

Affirmative Non-past Inflectional Patterns

	Formal	Informal
Verbal Pattern	Verbal ending in -ma⌐su (wa⌐karima⌐su)	Verbal ending in -[r]u (wa⌐ka⌐ru)
Adjectival Pattern	Adjectival ending in -i + de⌐su (o⌐oki⌐i desu)	Adjectival ending in -i (o⌐oki⌐i)
Nominal[1] Pattern	Nominal[1] + de⌐su (ho⌐ñ desu)	Nominal[1] + da (ho⌐ñ da)

3. Particle kara 'so'

The particle kara following a nominal and meaning 'from' was described in Lesson 8, Grammatical Note 4.

Following an inflected expression (verbal, adjectival, or copula) in the non-past or past or tentative, affirmative or negative, kara means 'so,' 'therefore,' or 'because,' with the following differences in word order: x kara y 'x so y,' 'x therefore y,' or 'because x y.' In this pattern, kara usually ends with comma intonation.

Examples:

> A⌐sita ikima⌐su kara, kyo⌐o wa i⌐kimase⌐ñ.
> 'I'm going tomorrow, so today I'm not going to go.'

---

[1] With or without following particle.

Wa⌐karimase⌐ñ desita kara, mo⌐o iti-do itte kudasa⌐i.
'I didn't understand so please say it again.'
Ta⌐ka⌐i desyoo kara, ka⌐imase⌐ñ.
'It's probably expensive so I'm not going to buy it.'
Ta⌐kaku a⌐rimase⌐ñ kara, mo⌐o hito⌐-tu ka⌐imasyo⌐o.
'They're not expensive so let's buy one more.'
Tanaka-sañ wa byo⌐oki de⌐su kara, ki⌐mase⌐ñ.
'Mr. Tanaka isn't going to come because he's sick.'

An informal inflected expression before <u>kara</u> has the same meaning (except for formality) as its formal equivalent in the same position. Before <u>kara</u>, a normally unaccented verbal or nominal-plus-da expression acquires an accent on its final syllable, and a non-past adjectival on its next-to-last syllable.

A⌐sita iku⌐ kara, kyo⌐o wa i⌐kimase⌐ñ. [1]
Ta⌐ka⌐i kara, ka⌐imase⌐ñ. 'It's expensive so I'm not going to buy it.'
Tanaka-sañ wa byo⌐oki da⌐ kara, ki⌐mase⌐ñ. [1]

A major sentence as a whole is assigned to the level of its final inflected form. That form is as formal as, or more formal than, inflected forms occurring earlier in the sentence. [2]

Compare:

    (a) Be⌐ñkyoo-site (i)ru⌐ kara, su⌐ko⌐si wa⌐ka⌐ru.
    (b) Be⌐ñkyoo-site (i)ru⌐ kara, su⌐ko⌐si wakarimasu.
    (c) Be⌐ñkyoo-site (i)ma⌐su kara, su⌐ko⌐si wakarimasu.

All three sentences mean 'I am studying so I understand a little.' Sentence (a) is said to be informal because final <u>wa⌐ka⌐ru</u> is informal, and sentences (b) and (c) are both said to be formal because of final <u>wa⌐karima⌐su</u>, which is formal. Within the formal style, sentence (c) is more formal than (b) because its non-final inflected form <u>(i)⌐ma⌐su</u> is also formal.

A sentence (i.e. a fragment) may consist of a sequence ending with <u>kara</u> if the over-all meaning is clear from the context. For example:

    (To a taxi driver) I⌐sogima⌐su kara_ 'I'm in a hurry so [please go fast].'
    Ta⌐kusii de i⌐kima⌐su ka_ . . . Iie. Ku⌐ruma ga arima⌐su kara_ 'Are you going by taxi? . . . No. I have a car so [I don't need a cab].'

---

[1] The English equivalent is the same as for the corresponding sentence just above.

[2] Ḡa 'but' is one of the few particles which is usually preceded only by an inflected form of the same level as the final one in the sentence. An informal inflected form before ḡa occurs only in men's informal speech.

Do⌐o site i⌐kimase⌐ñ ka⌐ . . . Ki⌐noo ikima⌐sita kara. 'Why aren't you going to go? . . . Because I went yesterday [I'm not going to go].'

Na⌐ze ka⌐imase⌐ñ ka⌐ . . . Ta⌐ka⌐i kara. 'Why aren't you going to buy it? . . . Because it's expensive [I'm not going to buy it].'

A minor sentence like the last, ending with an informal form + kara, may occur in both informal and formal speech (determined by the formality of final inflected forms in surrounding sentences), but one ending with a formal form + kara occurs only in formal speech.

4. d e s y o o ?

Sentence-final desyoo with question-mark intonation indicates a question which anticipates agreement from the person addressed. Thus:

Koñna tokee wa ta⌐ka⌐i desyoo? 'Watches like these a r e expensive, aren't they?'

Kore to are wa ōnazi desyoo? 'This one and that one are the same, aren't they?'

Koko no giñkoo wa ⌐sa⌐ñ-zi made desyoo? 'The banks here are [open] until 3, aren't they?'

Desyoo? in sentence-final position is always unaccented. It often occurs with shortening of the final vowel (desyo?).

5.   I n v e r t e d S e n t e n c e s

Na⌐kanaka muzukasi⌐i desu ⌐ne⌐e —nihoñḡo wa

The above is an example of a Japanese INVERTED SENTENCE. If the order of the first part (na⌐kanaka muzukasi⌐i desu ⌐ne⌐e) and the second part (nihoñḡo wa) is reversed, the result is a standard Japanese sentence of identical meaning except that it is more formal. Inverted sentences are common in conversation.

Examples:

Standard	Inverted
Sore wa ⌐na⌐ñ desu ka.	Na⌐ñ desu ka—sore wa. [1]
'What is that?'	'What is [it]—that thing?'
So⌐ko e ikima⌐sita yo.	I⌐kima⌐sita yo—soko e.
'You know, I went there.'	'You know, I went—to that place.'

---

[1] For the dash, see Introduction, page xli.

<table>
<tr><th>Standard</th><th>Inverted</th></tr>
</table>

Standard	Inverted
Siˉn̄buñ o kaimaˀsita ꜛneꜜe. 'You bought the news- paper, didn't you.' Soꜛre wa iˀi desu yo↲ 'Why, that's fine.'	Kaꜛimasita ꜛneꜜe — siñbuñ o. 'You bought [it], didn't you — the newspaper.' Ĩ꜀i desu yo↲ — sore wa. 'It's fine — that.'

What normally occurs as a kind of sentence-final intonation occurs within an inverted sentence at the end of the first part, with the initial word of the second part pronounced as if it were part of the same accent phrase. An intonation other than period intonation is indicated by its regular symbol, preceding the dash (cf. the last example above).

DRILLS

A. Substitution Drill

1. You can [speak] Japanese very well, can't you!
   Nihoñḡo (ḡa) ꜛyoꜜku deꜛkimaꜜsu ꜛneꜜe.

2. You can [speak] English very well, can't you!
   Eeḡo (ḡa) ꜛyoꜜku deꜛkimaꜜsu ꜛneꜜe.

3. You can [speak] French very well, can't you!
   Hurañsuḡo (ḡa) ꜛyoꜜku deꜛkimaꜜsu ꜛneꜜe.

4. You can [speak] Chinese very well, can't you!
   Tyuuḡokuḡo (ḡa) ꜛyoꜜku deꜛkimaꜜsu ꜛneꜜe.

5. You can [speak] Spanish very well, can't you!
   Supeiñḡo (ḡa) ꜛyoꜜku deꜛkimaꜜsu ꜛneꜜe.

6. You can [speak] German very well, can't you!
   Doituḡo (ḡa) ꜛyoꜜku deꜛkimaꜜsu ꜛneꜜe.

7. You can [speak] Russian very well, can't you!
   Rosiaḡo (ḡa) ꜛyoꜜku deꜛkimaꜜsu ꜛneꜜe.

8. You can [speak] foreign languages very well, can't you!
   Gaikokuḡo (ḡa) ꜛyoꜜku deꜛkimaꜜsu ꜛneꜜe.

B. Substitution Drill

1. You know, I met Mr. Yamada from the Foreign Office last night.
   Yuube gaꜛimuꜜsyoo no Yaꜛmada-sañ ni aimaꜜsita yo↲

2. You know, I met Mr. Yamada from the Foreign Office for the first time.
   Haꜛziꜜmete gaꜛimuꜜsyoo no Yaꜛmada-sañ ni aimaꜜsita yo↲

3. You know, I met Mr. Yamada from the Bank of Japan for the first time.
   Haꜛziꜜmete Niꜛhoñ-giꜜñkoo no Yaꜛmada-sañ ni aimaꜜsita yo↲

4. You know, I met your (older) brother from the Bank of Japan for the first time.
   Haꜛziꜜmete Niꜛhoñ-giꜜñkoo no oꜛniꜜisañ ni aꜛimaꜜsita yo↲

5. You know, I met your (older) brother from the Bank
of Japan for the first time.

Ha⌐zi⌐mete Ni⌐hoñ-gi⌐ñkoo no o⌐ni⌐isañ
ni o⌐me ni kakarima⌐sita yo⌐

6. You know, I met your (older) brother from the Bank
of Japan the day before
yesterday.

Ototoi Ni⌐hoñ-gi⌐ñkoo no o⌐ni⌐isañ ni
o⌐me ni kakarima⌐sita yo⌐

C. Grammar Drill (based on Grammatical Note 4)

Tutor: Ta⌐ka⌐i desu. 'It's expensive.'
Student: Ta⌐ka⌐i desyoo? 'It's expensive, isn't it?'

1. Mi⌐ñna onazi de⌐su.
2. Koñna sigoto (wa) mu⌐zu-
kasi⌐i desu.
3. Gakkoo (wa) ⌐ku⌐-zi kara
desu.
4. Gekizyoo no tonari (wa)
ku⌐suriya de⌐su.
5. A⌐no ba⌐su (wa) Yo⌐koha-
ma ma⌐de desu.
6. Ko⌐ñna huru⌐i kuruma (wa)
o⌐so⌐i desu.
7. A⌐no zibiki⌐ (wa) Tānaka-
sañ no ⌐bo⌐ttyañ no desu.
8. Yokohama (wa) a⌐no toori⌐
desu.

Miñna onazi desyoo?
Koñna sigoto (wa) mu⌐zukasi⌐i desyoo?

Gakkoo (wa) ⌐ku⌐-zi kara desyoo?

Gekizyoo no tonari (wa) kūsuriya desyoo?
A⌐no ba⌐su (wa) Yo⌐kohama ma⌐de desyoo?
Ko⌐ñna huru⌐i kuruma (wa) o⌐so⌐i desyoo?
A⌐no zibiki⌐ (wa) Tānaka-sañ no ⌐bo⌐t-
tyañ no desyoo?
Yokohama (wa) a⌐no toori⌐ desyoo?

D. Grammar Drill (based on Grammatical Note 5)

Tutor: I⌐i desu ⌐ne⌐e— sore wa. 'Isn't it nice— that!' (inverted order)
Student: Sore wa ⌐i⌐i desu ⌐ne⌐e. 'That's nice, isn't it!' (standard order)

1. Yo⌐ku wa⌐karima⌐su ⌐ne⌐e—
nihoñgo ḡa.
2. Mu⌐zukasi⌐i desu yo⌐ — koñna sigoto wa.
3. Ya⌐sasi⌐i desu ⌐ne⌐e— kore
wa.
4. Ka⌐ima⌐sita yo⌐ — a⌐tara-
si⌐i kuruma o.
5. Yu⌐ube ikima⌐sita ⌐ne⌐e—
Te⌐ekoku-ge⌐kizyoo ni.
6. O⌐kaeri ni narima⌐su ka⌐
— i⌐ma.
7. O⌐okiku na⌐rima⌐sita ⌐ne⌐e
— bo⌐ttyañ wa.
8. A⌐rimase⌐ñ yo⌐ — tabako
ḡa.

Nihoñgo ḡa ⌐yo⌐ku wa⌐karima⌐su ⌐ne⌐e.

Koñna sigoto wa mu⌐zukasi⌐i desu yo⌐

Kore wa ya⌐sasi⌐i desu ⌐ne⌐e.

A⌐tarasi⌐i kuruma o ka⌐ima⌐sita yo⌐

Te⌐ekoku-ge⌐kizyoo ni yu⌐ube ikima⌐si-
ta ⌐ne⌐e.
I⌐ma o⌐kaeri ni narima⌐su ka⌐

Bo⌐ttyañ wa ⌐o⌐okiku na⌐rima⌐sita
⌐ne⌐e.
Tabako ḡa a⌐rimase⌐ñ yo⌐

E. Grammar Drill (based on Grammatical Note 3)

      (Retain the formal level before <u>kara</u>)

      Tutor: Be⌐ñkyoo-site (i)ma⌐su. Wa⌐karima⌐su. 'I'm studying. I understand.'

      Student: Be⌐ñkyoo-site (i)ma⌐su kara, wa⌐karima⌐su. 'I'm studying so I understand.'

1. I⌐ma be⌐ñkyoo-site (i)mase⌐ñ. Mi⌐ñna wasurema⌐sita.	I⌐ma be⌐ñkyoo-site (i)mase⌐ñ k a r a, mi⌐ñna wasurema⌐sita.
2. Tyo⌐oseñḡo (ḡa) dekimase⌐ñ. Wa⌐karimase⌐ñ desita.	Tyo⌐oseñḡo (ḡa) dekimase⌐ñ kara, wa⌐karimase⌐ñ desita.
3. Sa⌐ñ-zi suḡi⌐ desu. U⌐ti e kaerimasyo⌐o.	Sa⌐ñ-zi suḡi⌐ desu kara, u⌐ti e kaerimasyo⌐o.
4. Ha⌐zi⌐mete desu. A⌐ñmari wakarimase⌐ñ.	Ha⌐zi⌐mete desu kara, a⌐ñmari wakarimase⌐ñ.
5. Ta⌐kusii wa ta⌐ka⌐i desu. De⌐ñsya de i⌐kimasyo⌐o.	Ta⌐kusii wa ta⌐ka⌐i desu kara, de⌐ñsya de i⌐kimasyo⌐o.
6. I⌐soḡima⌐su. Ha⌐yaku site kudasai.	I⌐soḡima⌐su kara, ha⌐yaku site kudasai.
7. A⌐ñmari ki⌐ree zya a⌐rimase⌐ñ desita. Ka⌐imase⌐ñ desita.	A⌐ñmari ki⌐ree zya a⌐rimase⌐ñ desita kara, ka⌐imase⌐ñ desita.
8. Hu⌐ne wa o⌐so⌐i desu. Hi⌐ko⌐oki de i⌐kima⌐sita.	Hu⌐ne ,wa o⌐so⌐i desu kara, hi⌐ko⌐oki de i⌐kima⌐sita.
9. Hu⌐ruku na⌐rima⌐sita. A⌐tarasi⌐i no (ḡa) ka⌐ita⌐i ñ desu ḡa_	Hu⌐ruku na⌐rima⌐sita kara, a⌐tarasi⌐i no (ḡa) ka⌐ita⌐i ñ desu ḡa_
10. Byo⌐oki ni narima⌐sita. Kyo⌐o wa de⌐kimase⌐ñ.	Byo⌐oki ni narima⌐sita kara, kyo⌐o wa de⌐kimase⌐ñ.

F. Level Drill[1]

      Tutor: A⌐sita ikima⌐su kara. (formal verbal) } 'Because I'm going
      Student: A⌐sita iku⌐ kara. (informal verbal)   to go tomorrow.'

1. Tanaka-sañ (ḡa) ⌐yo⌐ku de⌐kima⌐su kara.	Tanaka-sañ (ḡa) ⌐yo⌐ku de⌐ki⌐ru kara.
2. Sa⌐ñ-ḡatu ni Tōokyoo de ke⌐kkoñ-sima⌐su kara.	Sa⌐ñ-ḡatu ni Tōokyoo de ke⌐kkoñ-suru⌐ kara.

---

[1] This drill is based on Grammatical Notes 1 and 3. After practicing it in its given form, reverse the procedure, with the tutor giving the sentence on the right and the student the sentence on the left

3. I⌐tu mo tu⌐itati⌐ ni ko⌐ko
ni tukima⌐su kara.

4. Ka⌐mi⌐ ḡa ta⌐kusañ iri-
ma⌐su kara.

5. Zyu⌐u-neñ ⌐ma⌐e kara
tu⌐to⌐mete (i)⌐ma⌐su
kara.

6. A⌐sa ha⌐ti⌐-zi wa ⌐tyo⌐tto
ko⌐marima⌐su kara.

7. Tu⌐ḡi⌐ no ⌐ka⌐do (o)
ma⌐ḡarima⌐su kara.

8. Ma⌐initi ro⌐ku-zi-ḡo⌐ro
zi⌐mu⌐syo (o) de⌐ma⌐su
kara.

9. Koñḡetu A⌐merika e okaeri ni narima⌐su kara.

10. Tookyoo (o) ⌐yo⌐ku si⌐tte
(i)ma⌐su kara.

11. Koko kara yo-⌐zikañ-ḡu⌐-
rai ka⌐karima⌐su kara.

12. Tanaka-sañ mo ⌐Ni⌐kkoo
e i⌐rassyaima⌐su kara.

I⌐tu mo tu⌐itati⌐ ni ko⌐ko ni tu⌐ku kara.

Ka⌐mi⌐ ḡa ta⌐kusañ iru⌐ kara.

Zyu⌐u-neñ ⌐ma⌐e kara tu⌐to⌐mete
(i)⌐ru⌐ kara.

A⌐sa ha⌐ti⌐-zi wa ⌐tyo⌐tto ko⌐ma⌐ru kara.

Tu⌐ḡi⌐ no ⌐ka⌐do (o) ma⌐ḡaru⌐ kara.

Ma⌐initi ro⌐ku-zi-ḡo⌐ro zi⌐mu⌐syo (o)
⌐de⌐ru kara.

Koñḡetu A⌐merika e okaeri ni na⌐ru
kara.

Tookyoo (o) ⌐yo⌐ku si⌐tte (i)ru⌐ kara.

Koko kara yo-⌐zikañ-ḡu⌐rai ka⌐ka⌐ru
kara.

Tanaka-sañ mo ⌐Ni⌐kkoo e i⌐rassya⌐-
ru kara.

G. Level Drill[1]

Tutor: Byo⌐oki de⌐su kara. (formal inflected word) ⎱ 'Because I'm
Student: Byo⌐oki da⌐ kara. (informal inflected word) ⎰   sick.'

1. Dotira mo da⌐me⌐ desu kara.
2. A⌐tarasi⌐i kuruma (wa) ta-
⌐ka⌐i desu kara.
3. Koñna miti (wa) a⌐buna⌐i
desu kara.
4. A⌐no⌐ hito (wa) zyu⌐ñsa
de⌐su kara.
5. A⌐no mise⌐ (wa) ha⌐na⌐ya
desu kara.
6. Ko⌐ñna ho⌐ñ (wa) o⌐mosi-
ro⌐i desu kara.
7. Kyo⌐o go-⌐zi ma⌐e ni
ka⌐erita⌐i desu kara.
8. Tanaka-sañ (wa) ⌐i⌐i to-
⌐modati de⌐su kara.

Dotira mo da⌐me⌐ da kara.

A⌐tarasi⌐i kuruma (wa) ta⌐ka⌐i kara.

Koñna miti (wa) a⌐buna⌐i kara.

A⌐no⌐ hito (wa) zyu⌐ñsa da⌐ kara.

A⌐no mise⌐ (wa) ha⌐na⌐ya da kara.

Ko⌐ñna ho⌐ñ (wa) o⌐mosiro⌐i kara.

Kyo⌐o go-⌐zi ma⌐e ni ka⌐erita⌐i kara.

Tanaka-sañ (wa) ⌐i⌐i to⌐modati da⌐
kara.

---

[1] This drill is based on Grammatical Note 2.   Again, practice it both in its given form and in reverse.

H. Level Drill[1]

1. Na⌐ñ-zi-ḡo⌐ro ka⌐erima⌐su   Na⌐ñ-zi-ḡo⌐ro o⌐kaeri ni narima⌐su
    ka↵   ka↵
2. O⌐kusañ desu ka↵   O⌐kusañ de (i)⌐rassyaima⌐su ka↵

3. A⌐sita⌐ mo ki⌐te⌐ kudasai.   A⌐sita⌐ mo | i⌐rassya⌐tte | kudasai.
                                                 | o⌐ide ni na⌐tte |

4. Mi⌐na⌐sañ o⌐ge⌐ñki desu   Mi⌐na⌐sañ o⌐ge⌐ñki de (i)⌐rassyaima⌐su
    ka↵   ka↵
5. Ha⌐zi⌐mete desyoo?   Ha⌐zi⌐mete de gozaimasyoo?
6. Si⌐ba⌐raku desita.   Si⌐ba⌐raku de gozaimasita.
7. Kore (wa) ⌐da⌐re no desu   Kore (wa) ⌐do⌐nata no de go⌐zaima⌐su
    ka↵   ka↵
8. Ni⌐hoñḡo (o) beñkyoo-site   Ni⌐hoñḡo (o) beñkyoo-site (i)rassyai-
    (i)ma⌐su ka↵   ma⌐su ka↵

I. Response Drill

        Tutor: O⌐kusañ desu ka↵ 'Is it your wife?'
        Student: E⌐e, ka⌐nai desu. 'Yes, it's my wife.'

1. Ni⌐isañ desu ka↵   E⌐e, a⌐ni desu.
2. O⌐zyo⌐osañ desu ka↵   E⌐e, mu⌐sume⌐ desu.
3. O⌐ka⌐asañ desu ka↵   E⌐e, ha⌐ha desu.
4. Bo⌐ttyañ desu ka↵   E⌐e, mu⌐suko de⌐su.
5. Ne⌐esañ desu ka↵   E⌐e, a⌐ne de⌐su.
6. O⌐to⌐osañ desu ka↵   E⌐e, ti⌐ti⌐ desu.
7. O⌐iḡosañ de⌐su ka↵   E⌐e, o⌐i de⌐su.
8. Go⌐syu⌐ziñ desu ka↵   E⌐e, syu⌐ziñ desu.

J. Expansion Drill

1. [He] can do it, can't he!   O⌐deki ni narima⌐su ⌐ne⌐e.
    [He] can do it very well,   Yo⌐ku o⌐deki ni narima⌐su ⌐ne⌐e.
      can't he!
    [He] can [speak] English   Eeḡo (ḡa) ⌐yo⌐ku o⌐deki ni narima⌐su
      very well, can't he!   ⌐ne⌐e.
    Mr. Tanaka can [speak]   Tanaka-sañ (wa) ëeḡo (ḡa) ⌐yo⌐ku o-
      English very well, can't   ⌐deki ni narima⌐su ⌐ne⌐e.
      he!
    Mr. Tanaka at the Foreign   Ga⌐imu⌐syoo no Tänaka-sañ (wa) ëeḡo
      Office can [speak] Eng-   (ḡa) ⌐yo⌐ku o⌐deki ni narima⌐su ⌐ne⌐e.
      lish very well, can't he!

---

[1] In each case, the sentence on the right is a more polite equivalent of the
sentence on the left.

2. [They]'re good, aren't they!
   [They]'re quite good, aren't
     they!
   They're quite good, aren't
     they—American pens!
   They're quite good, aren't
     they—American pens like
     this!

    I⌐i desu ˥ne˦e.
    Na⌐kanaka i⌐i desu ˥ne˦e.

    Na⌐kanaka i⌐i desu ˥ne˦e—A˥merika
    no pe˦ñ wa.
    Na⌐kanaka i⌐i desu ˥ne˦e—ko⌐ñna Ame-
    rika no pe˦ñ wa.

3. It's interesting, isn't it?
   It's quite interesting, isn't
     it?
   The work is quite interest-
     ing, isn't it?
   This kind of work is quite
     interesting, isn't it?

    O⌐mosiro⌐i desyoo?
    Na⌐kanaka omosiro⌐i desyoo?

    Siḡoto (wa) na⌐kanaka omosiro⌐i de-
    syoo?
    Koñna siḡoto (wa) na⌐kanaka omosiro⌐i
    desyoo?

4. I'm not going to go.
   Today I'm not going to go.
   [She]'s sick so today I'm
     not going to go.
   My wife is sick too, so
     today I'm not going to go.
   My mother AND my wife
     are sick so today I'm not
     going to go.

    I⌐kimase⌐ñ.
    Kyo⌐o wa i⌐kimase⌐ñ.
    Byo⌐oki da⌐ kara, kyo⌐o wa i⌐kimase⌐ñ.

    Ka⌐nai mo byo⌐oki da⌐ kara, kyo⌐o wa
    i⌐kimase⌐ñ.
    Ha⌐ha mo ⌐ka⌐nai mo byo⌐oki da⌐ kara,
    kyo⌐o wa i⌐kimase⌐ñ.

5. Please study.
   Please study some more.
   It will get interesting so
     please study some more.
   From this point [on] it will
     get interesting so please
     study some more.
   Japanese will get interest-
     ing from this point [on] so
     please study some more.

    Be⌐ñkyoo-site kudasa⌐i.
    Mo⌐tto be˥ñkyoo-site kudasa˦i.
    O⌐mosi⌐roku ˥na˦ru kara, mo⌐tto be-
    ˥ñkyoo-site kudasa˦i.
    Kore kara o⌐mosi⌐roku ˥na˦ru kara,
    mo⌐tto be˥ñkyoo-site kudasa˦i.

    Nihoñḡo wa ko̅re kara o⌐mosi⌐roku
    ˥na˦ru kara, mo⌐tto be˥ñkyoo-site
    kudasa˦i.

6. You know, I met [her].
   You know, I met [his]
     wife.
   You know, I met Mrs. Ko-
     bayashi.
   You know, I met Mrs. Ko-
     bayashi for the first
     time.
   You know, I met Mrs. Ko-
     bayashi for the first
     time, at the Imperial
     Theater.
   You know, I met Mrs. Ko-

    A⌐ima⌐sita yo↲
    O⌐kusañ ni a⌐ima˦sita yo↲

    Ko⌐bayasi-sañ no o⌐kusañ ni a⌐ima˦-
    sita yo↲
    Ha⌐zi⌐mete Ko⌐bayasi-sañ no o⌐kusañ
    ni a⌐ima˦sita yo↲

    Te⌐ekoku-ge⌐kizyoo de ha⌐zi⌐mete Ko-
    ⌐bayasi-sañ no o⌐kusañ ni a⌐ima˦si-
    ta yo↲

    Yuube Te⌐ekoku-ge⌐kizyoo de ha⌐zi⌐-

bayashi for the first   mete Ko⌐bayasi-sañ no o⌐kusañ ni
time, at the Imperial   a⌐ima⌐sita yo⌐
Theater last night.

SHORT SUPPLEMENTARY DIALOGUES

(The following are commonly occurring exchanges at meeting or parting.)

1. Guest: De⌐ wa, si⌐tu⌐ree-simasu.
   Host[ess]: Sayoonara. Ma⌐ta do⌐ozo. O⌐kusañ ni yōrosiku.
   Guest: A⌐ri⌐gatoo gozaimasu. Sayoonara.

2. Tanaka: O⌐soku na⌐ru kara, si⌐tu⌐ree.
   Yamamoto: Zya⌐a, mata.
   Tanaka: Sayonara.

3. Watanabe: Kore wa ti⌐ti⌐ desu.   Ko⌐no kata⌐ wa A⌐merika - ryoozi⌐kañ no
               ⌐Su⌐misu-sañ desu.
   Father: Wa⌐tanabe de⌐su. Do⌐ozo yōrosiku.
   Smith: Su⌐misu desu. Ha⌐zimema⌐site.

4. Tanaka: Kore wa ⌐ha⌐ha de gozaimasu.   Kotira wa Nyu⌐uyo⌐oku no
               ⌐Zyo⌐oñzu-sañ de irassyaimasu.
   Mother: Ta⌐naka de gozaima⌐su. Ha⌐zi⌐mete ome ni kakarimasu.
   Jones: Zyo⌐oñzu de gozaimasu. Ha⌐zimema⌐site. Do⌐ozo yōrosiku.

5. Tanaka: A⌐a, Kobayasi-sañ. Si⌐ba⌐raku.
   Kobayashi: Si⌐ba⌐raku. Mi⌐na⌐sañ o⌐ge⌐ñki?
   Tanaka: E⌐e, okagesama de. Otaku mo?
   Kobayashi: E⌐e. A⌐ri⌐gatoo.

6. Employee: Zya⌐a, si⌐tu⌐ree-simasu.
   Employer: Go⌐ku⌐roosama. Sayonara.

7. Yamamoto: Ka⌐nai ga byo⌐oki de⌐su kara, kyo⌐o wa ⌐ha⌐yaku ka⌐erita⌐i ñ
               desu ga⌐
   Watanabe: Go⌐byooki de⌐su ka⌐ I⌐kemase⌐ñ ⌐ne⌐e. Odaizi ni.
   Yamamoto: A⌐ri⌐gatoo gozaimasu.

8. Visitor: Ta⌐naka-sañ irassyaima⌐su ka⌐
   Secretary: Ha⌐a irassyaimasu. Syo⌐osyoo o⌐mati-kudasa⌐i.

English Equivalents

1. Guest: Well, I must be leaving.
   Host[ess]: Goodbye. Please come again. Regards to your wife.
   Guest: Thank you. Goodbye.

2. Tanaka: It's getting late so if you'll excuse me . . .
   Yamamoto: Well, [I'll see you] again.
   Tanaka: Goodbye.

3.   Watanabe: This is my father.   This is Mr./Mrs./Miss Smith from the
                    American Consulate.
     Father: (I'm Watanabe.) I'm glad to meet you.
     Smith: (I'm Smith.) How do you do.

4.   Tanaka: This is my mother.   This is Mr./Mrs./Miss Jones from New
                    York.
     Mother: (I'm Tanaka.) How do you do?
     Jones: (I'm Jones.) How do you do? I'm glad to meet you.

5.   Tanaka: Oh, Mr./Mrs./Miss Kobayashi!   I haven't seen you for
                    ages.
     Kobayashi: It has been a long time. Is everyone well?
     Tanaka: Yes, thank you. [Everyone at] your house too?
     Kobayashi: Yes, thanks.

6.   Employee: Well, I'll be leaving.
     Employer: (Thanks for your trouble.) Goodbye.

7.   Yamamoto: My wife is sick so today I'd like to go home early . . .
     Watanabe: She's sick? That's too bad. Take care.
     Yamamoto: Thank you.

8.   Visitor: Is Mr. Tanaka in?
     Secretary: Yes, he is. Just a moment, please.

EXERCISES

1.   On the basis of the following family tree, answer the questions below.

          (M = Male; F = Female; Number = Age)

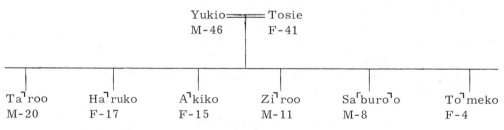

     a.   Fill in the blanks:

          1.   Yu⌐kio-san no o⌐kusan no namae wa _____ de⌐su.
          2.   Yu⌐kio-san to Tosie-san no ozyo⌐osan no namae wa _____ to _____
               to _____ desu.
          3.   Yukio-san wa ⌐Ta⌐roo-san no _____ desu.
          4.   Ta⌐roo-san no o⌐ka⌐asan no namae wa _____ de⌐su.
          5.   Yukio-san wa To⌐sie-san no _____ desu.
          6.   Yu⌐kio-san to Tosie-san no _____ wa ⌐Ta⌐roo-san to ⌐Zi⌐roo-san to
               Sa⌐buro⌐o-san desu.

7. _____ to _____ to _____ wa o⌐toko¬ de, _____ to _____ to _____ wa o⌐ñna¬ ⌐desu.

8. _____ wa ⌐ha¬tati desu.

b. Answer the following questions:

1. Yukio-sañ to Tosie-sañ wa o̅kosañ g̅a ⌐na¬ñ-niñ imasu ka⌟

2. Bo⌐ttyañ g̅a ⌐na¬ñ-niñ imasu ka⌟

3. Ta⌐roo-sañ to ⌐Zi¬roo-sañ to Sa⌐buro¬o-sañ wa o⌐ikutu de¬su ka⌟

4. Tosie-sañ wa o⌐toko¬ desu ka⌟

5. To⌐meko-sañ wa ya-⌐ttu¬ desu ka⌟

6. Yu⌐kio-sañ no o⌐kusañ wa o⌐ikutu de¬su ka⌟

7. Ko⌐no ka¬zoku wa ⌐na¬ñ-niñ desu ka⌟

c. Determine whether the following statements are true or false:

1. A⌐kiko-sañ wa ⌐Ha¬ruko-sañ no mu⊦sumesañ de⌐su.

2. Yukio-sañ wa ⌐To¬meko-sañ no o⊦to⌐osañ desu.

3. Ta⌐roo-sañ wa hu⌐ta-tu¬ desu.

4. To⌐meko-sañ wa Yu̅kio-sañ to Tosie-sañ no u⌐e no ozyo¬osañ desu.

5. Ha⌐ruko-sañ wa zyu⌐usiti¬ de, A⌐kiko-sañ wa ⌐zyu¬ugo de, do⌐tira mo otoko¬ no ko desu.

6. Yukio-sañ to Tosie-sañ wa o⌐zyo¬osañ g̅a go-⌐niñ arima¬su.

2. Within the framework of the vocabulary and sentence patterns you have learned, practice asking and answering questions concerning families, and on the basis of the information acquired, draw family trees similar to the above.

3. Practice introductions. Take turns performing introductions and being introduced.

4. (a) Give the single Japanese word which is the equivalent of each of the following:

(Example: kodomo no kodomo   Answer: ma⌐g̅o¬)

1. ti⌐ti¬ to ⌐ha¬ha

2. o⌐ya no ha¬ha

3. oya no o⌐toko no kyo¬odai

4. oñna no kodomo

5. kyo⌐odai no o⌐ñna¬ no ko

(b) For each of the following words, give a defining phrase:

(Example: musuko   Answer: otoko no kodomo)

1. so⌐hu

2. oba

3. ha⌐ha

4. oi

5. i⌐to¬ko

5. Practice the Basic Dialogues with appropriate variations.

Lesson 12. Telephoning

BASIC DIALOGUES: FOR MEMORIZATION

(a)

Smith

to Mr. Hashimoto	Hasimoto-sañ ni
telephone (verb)	de⌐ñwa o kake⌐ru /-ru/
number	ba⌐ñḡo⌐o
telephone number	de⌐ñwaba⌐ñḡoo
what number?	na⌐ñ-bañ

1. I'd like to telephone Mr. Hashimoto. What (number) is
his telephone number?

Ha⌐simoto-sañ ni deñwa (o) kaketa⌐i
ñ desu ḡa, de⌐ñwaba⌐ñḡoo (wa) ⌐na⌐ñ-
bañ desyoo ka.

Tanaka

business company or	kaisya
company office	

2. Do you mean his home('s), or
his office('s)?

O⌐taku no⌐ desu ka, ka⌐isya no⌐ desu
ka⌐

Smith

3. I mean his office('s).

Ka⌐isya no⌐ desu.

Tanaka

4. I don't know either. . . .

Wa⌐takusi mo sirimase⌐ñ ḡa—

Smith

telephone book	deñwatyoo
see or look at	mi⌐ru /-ru/

5. Then would you look it up in
(lit. look at) the phone book?

Zya⌐a, de⌐ñwatyoo (o) mi⌐te ku⌐da-
saimase⌐ñ ka—

Yamamoto

6. Are you talking about Mr.
Hashimoto's telephone [num-
ber]?

Ha⌐simoto-sañ no deñwa de⌐su ka—

number 21	ni⌐zyuu i⌐ti⌐-bañ or
	hu⌐ta⌐zyuu i⌐ti⌐-bañ

7. It's 481-7921.

Yo⌐ñhyaku ha⌐ti⌐zyuu i⌐ti⌐ no, na-
⌐na⌐señ ⌐kyu⌐uhyaku hu⌐ta⌐zyuu i⌐ti⌐-
bañ desu.

Smith

extension	naiseñ

8. How about the extension?

Naiseñ wa?

190

Yamamoto

9. The extension I don't know. . . .   Na⌐iseñ wa sirimase⌐ñ ḡa_

Smith

telephone operator (i.e.   ko⌐oka⌐ñsyu
  central or switchboard)
ask a question or listen   kiku /-u/
  or hear
ask the operator   ko⌐oka⌐ñsyu ni kiku
10. Then would you ask the oper- ʹ   Zya⌐a, ko⌐oka⌐ñsyu ni ki⌐ite kudasa-
  ator?   imase⌐ñ ka⌐

(b)

(On the telephone)

Smith

11. Hello (on the telephone) or   Mo⌐simosi.
  Say there!

Operator

12. Hello. (This is the) Bank   Mo⌐simosi. Ni⌐hoñ-gi⌐ñkoo de go-
  of Japan.   zaimasu.

Smith

number 10   zyu⌐u-bañ or
                                      to⌐o-bañ

13. Extension 210, please.   Naiseñ ni⌐hyaku ⌐to⌐o-bañ |e / ni| onee̅ai-
                                      simasu.
                                          or
                                      Naiseñ ni⌐hyaku ⌐to⌐o-bañ (o) onee̅ai-
                                      simasu.

14. Hello. Is Yoshio Hashi-   Mo⌐simosi. Ha⌐simoto Yosio - sañ
  moto there?   ima⌐su ka⌐

Secretary

the person addressed   sotira
who?   do⌐tirasama ꜛ
15. Who is calling, please?   Sotira (wa) ⌐do⌐tirasama de (i)⌐ras-
  (Lit. Who are you?)   syaima⌐su ka⌐

Smith

16. This is [Mr.] Smith of the   A⌐merika-taisi⌐kañ no ⌐Su⌐misu desu
  American Embassy. . . .   ḡa_

Secretary

seat or assigned place   se⌐ki or
                                      o⌐se⌐ki ꜛ
be at one's place   se⌐ki ni iru
17. Mr. Hashimoto isn't at his   Hasimoto - sañ (wa) ⌐i⌐ma o⌐se⌐ki ni
  desk (lit. place) [just] now. . . . i⌐rassyaimase⌐ñ ḡa_

Smith

later	notihodo
make a telephone call	deñwa-suru or
	o⌐de¬ñwa-suru⁺

18. Well then, I'll call again later   Zya¬a, ma⌐ta notihodo ode¬ñwa - si-
     (so). . .   masu kara⌐

Secretary

19. Thank you very much.   Do¬o mo su⌐mimase¬ñ.

(c)

(On the telephone)

Smith

the Yoshida residence	Yosida-sañ no otaku ↑

20. Is this the Yoshida resi-   Sotira (wa) Yo⌐sida-sañ no otaku de
     dence?   (i)rassyaima¬su ka⌐

Maid

that way or thus or so	sayoo

21. Yes, that's right.   Ha¬a, sa⌐yoo de gozaima¬su.

Smith

master	da⌐ñnasa¬ma ↑
mistress	o¬kusañ ↑ or
	o¬kusama ↑

22. Is Mr. Yoshida (lit. the mas-   Da⌐ñnasa¬ma i⌐rassyaima⌐su ka⌐
     ter) in?

Maid

away from home	ru¬su or
	o⌐ru¬su ↑

23. He's out [just] now. . . .   I¬ma o⌐ru¬su de gozaimasu ḡa⌐

Smith

24. About what time will he be   Na⌐ñ-zi-ḡo¬ro o⌐kaeri ni narima⌐su
     back?   ka⌐

Maid

he probably returns (or	ka¬eru desyoo or
will return) home	o⌐kaeri ni na¬ru desyoo ↑

25. He will probably be back by   Ro⌐ku-zi-ḡo¬ro ma⌐de ni⌐ wa o⌐ka-
     about 6 o'clock. . . .   eri ni na⌐ru desyoo ḡa⌐

Smith

excuse me (i.e. for break-	go⌐meñ-kudasa¬i or
ing away or interrupting)	go⌐meñ-kudasaima¬se

26. I see. Goodbye.   Wa⌐karima¬sita. Go⌐meñ-kudasa¬i.

Maid

27. Goodbye.   Go⌐meñ-kudasaima¬se.

(d)

(On the telephone)

Yamamoto

zero   re⌐e <u>or</u>
                                              ze⌐ro
number 4   yo⌐ñ-bañ
28. Hello. Is this 080-0704?   Mo⌐simosi. Sotira (wa) ⌐re⌐e ha⌐ti-
                                              zyu⌐u no, re⌐e na⌐na⌐hyaku ⌐yo⌐ñ-bañ
                                              desu ka⌐

Secretary

29. Yes, that's right. . . .   Ha⌐a, sa⌐yoo de gozaima⌐su ḡa⌐

Yamamoto

30. Is Mr. Yamada in?   Ya⌐mada-sañ ima⌐su ka⌐

Secretary

in the middle of work   siḡoto-tyuu <u>or</u>
                                              osiḡoto-tyuu ↑
31. He's busy [just] now. . . .   I⌐ma o⌐siḡoto-tyuu de (i)rassyaima⌐su
                                              ḡa⌐

Yamamoto

the person speaking   kotira
Japan Travel Bureau   ko⌐otuuko⌐osya
free time <u>or</u> leisure   hima <u>or</u>
                                              ohima ↑
time <u>or</u> occasion   to⌐ki⌐
at a free time   hi⌐ma na toki⌐ [ni]
32. This is [Mr.] Yamamoto of   Kotira (wa) ko⌐otuuko⌐osya no Ya-
     the Japan Travel Bureau.   ⌐mamoto de⌐su ḡa, o⌐hima na toki⌐
     Please give me a call when   [ni] o⌐de⌐ñwa (o) kudasai.
     he is free.

Secretary

33. Certainly.   Ka⌐sikomarima⌐sita.

Yamamoto

34. Goodbye.   Sayonara.

Secretary

35. Goodbye.   Go⌐meñ-kudasaima⌐se.

NOTES ON THE BASIC DIALOGUES

1. The <u>ni</u> following <u>Hasimoto-sañ</u> is the <u>ni</u> of goal: 'I want to make a tele-
    phone call TO Mr. Hashimoto.' Compare <u>Yo⌐kohama ni ikima⌐sita</u> 'I went
    to Yokohama.' Following a place expression, both goal particles —<u>ni</u> and

e — occur, but following a person, only <u>ni</u> is used.

Ba⌐n̄go⌐o means 'number' in the sense of 'assigned number' or 'serial number' — not 'mathematical numeral.' Similarly, na¹n̄-ban̄ means 'what assigned number?' or 'what serial number?'

2. <u>Kaisya</u> 'private company' is also commonly used in reference to the office of such a company. While zi⌐mu¹syo 'business office' has a broader meaning (it includes a private individual's office, an embassy, etc.), it is used less commonly than <u>kaisya</u> in situations where <u>kaisya</u> applies. As the second part of a compound, <u>kaisya</u> often becomes -g̃aisya (for example, ga⌐sug̃a¹isya 'gas company').

4. 'I don't know either but—is there any way I can help you?'

5. <u>Mi¹ru</u> more commonly refers to seeing or looking at things. When used with a personal object, it means 'look at': for example, it is used in reference to a doctor's looking at a patient. When 'see a person' corresponds to 'meet and talk to,' the Japanese equivalent is a¹u.

9. 'The extension I don't know but—is there any way I can help you?'

10. Note the following particles which occur with <u>kiku</u>: the person who asks, listens, or hears is followed by particle g̃a (or <u>wa</u>); the thing asked, listened to, or heard is followed by particle <u>o</u> (or <u>wa</u>); the person asked or listened to is followed by particle <u>ni</u>; the person from whom something is heard is followed by particle <u>kara</u> or <u>ni</u>.

11. Mo¹simosi is the most common way of saying hello on the telephone. It is also a polite way of attracting attention (in this usage it is similar to, but more polite than, tyo¹tto)—particularly when addressing strangers.

When making a telephone call in Japan, it is the person who places the call who usually says <u>mo¹simosi</u> first; he speaks when he hears a click at the other end of the line.

13. The first alternant means 'I'd like [to be connected] to extension 210.' The second alternant means 'I'd like extension 210.'

15. Do¹tirasama and <u>do¹natasama</u> are honorific words, more polite than <u>do¹</u>-nata alone. Do¹tirasama is especially common in telephone conversations.

16. 'This is Mr. Smith but—may I speak to Mr. Hashimoto?'

17. 'Mr. Hashimoto isn't at his desk but—is there anything I can do?'

18. 'I'll call later so—you won't have to do anything.'

<u>Notihodo</u> is a formal equivalent of a¹to de.

21. Sa⌐yoo de gozaima¹su is the polite equivalent of <u>so¹o desu</u>.

22. Da⌐n̄nasa¹ma is used commonly by s e r v a n t s and i n conversations with servants. It is also sometimes used as a synonym for go⌐syu¹zin̄.

O¹kusama is a more polite equivalent of <u>o¹kusan̄</u>. Compare also the very p o l i t e words o⌐to¹osama 'father,' o⌐ka¹asama 'mother,' go⌐syu¹zin̄sama 'husband,' o⌐zyo¹osama 'daughter,' etc.; the comparable form for bo¹ttyan̄ 'son' is o͡bo⌐ttyama.   Note also that -sama is added to proper names as a more polite equivalent of -sañ (for example, Tanaka-sama).

25.   'He'll probably be back . . . but—I can't be sure.'

The wa is the wa of comparison.

26.   Go⌐meñ-kudasa⌐i is also used when entering a house or a shop, to attract attention.   Compare English 'Hello there!' and 'Is anybody home?'

Go⌐meñ-kudasaima⌐se is the formal equivalent of gomeñ-kudasai, used most commonly by women, and by men who are employees of shops, restaurants, hotels, etc.

29.   'That's right but—what can I do for you?'

32.   Koosya (as in ko⌐otuuko⌐osya) refers to a public corporation, whereas kai-sya is a private company.

GRAMMATICAL NOTES

A Japanese telephone number consisting of two numerical parts—for example, 481-5021—is regularly read in one of the following ways:

1) The first number (i.e. the exchange number) is read in terms of individual digits and is followed by particle no; the second number is also read as individual digits.   In this system '4' is regularly yo⌐ñ (not si⌐), '7' is na⌐na (not si⌐ti⌐), '9' is kyu⌐u (not ku⌐); '2' has a special alternant ni⌐i, and '5' go͡o; '0' is ze⌐ro or re⌐e and is regularly included in reading.   Thus:

    yo⌐ñ hati i⌐ti⌐ no, go͡o ⌐ze⌐ro ⌐ni⌐i iti
    '(lit.) five zero two one of four eight one'

            or

2) The exchange number is read as an independent number (in terms of hundreds, tens, and units, if it consists of three digits) and is followed by particle no; the following four-digit number is read in terms of thousands, hundreds, tens, and digits, plus counter -bañ 'number.'   An initial zero in the exchange number is read re⌐e or ze⌐ro; otherwise it is often omitted in this style of reading.   Thus:

    yo⌐ñhyaku ha⌐tizyu⌐u i⌐ti⌐ no, go⌐se⌐ñ [⌐re⌐e] ni⌐zyuu i⌐ti⌐-bañ
    '(lit.) number five thousand twenty-one of four hundred eighty-one'

In this system, '4', '7', and '9' have the same alternants as above; '2' is ni⌐ or hu⌐ta⌐, and '10' is zyu⌐u or to⌐o.

Formerly, the second type of reading described above (i.e. the style used in Dialogue A of this lesson) was more common, but recently the first type has become more prevalent.

The numerals of Series I (with alternants for '2' and '10' from Series II) combine with the counter -baṇ to name telephone numbers, seat numbers, license numbers, etc.   The numbers from 1 to 10 are:

iˡtiˡ-baṇ	'number 1'	roˡkuˡ-baṇ	'number 6'
niˡ-baṇ or		naˡnaˡ-baṇ	'number 7'
huˡtaˡ-baṇ	'number 2'	haˡtiˡ-baṇ	'number 8'
saṇ-baṇ	'number 3'	kyuˡu-baṇ	'number 9'
yoˡṇ-baṇ	'number 4'	zyuˡu-baṇ or	
go-baṇ	'number 5'	toˡo-baṇ	'number 10'
	naˡṇ-baṇ	'what number?'	

2.   desyoo Following a Non-past Verbal

Desyoo, the formal tentative of da indicating probability or uncertainty, has been introduced previously as occurring after an adjectival ending in -i, a nominal, or a phrase ending with a particle:

> Taˡkaˡi desyoo.   'It's probably expensive.'
> Daˡmeˡ desyoo.   'It's probably no good.'
> Tanaka-saṇ kara desyoo?   'It's from Mr. Tanaka, isn't it?'

Desyoo also occurs after non-past[1] verbals, informal or formal.   Since desyoo is formal, the combination is always classified as formal; but a formal verbal + desyoo is more formal than an informal verbal + desyoo.

When it follows an accented verbal, desyoo is unaccented:

> Kuˡru desyoo.

A normally unaccented verbal + desyoo is accented according to one of two possible patterns, depending upon the speaker; either the verbal acquires an accent on its final syllable, or desyoo is accented on its next-to-last syllable:

> Iˡkuˡ desyoo.
>   or
> Iˡku desyoˡo.

Desyoo following a verbal indicates probability or uncertainty or indirectness, just as it does after words of other classes:

> Iˡku desyoˡo.   'He probably goes (or probably will go).'
> Beˡṇkyoo-site (i)ru desyoˡo.   'He's probably studying (or probably will be studying).'
> Waˡkarimaˡsu desyoo?   'It's clear, isn't it?'
> Aˡni ni ˡaˡu desyoo ka.   'Do you suppose you'll see my older brother?'

---

[1] Desyoo occurs after past forms also.   These patterns, as well as all informal negatives, will be taken up later.

Ta┐roo-tyañ wa ┌na┐ni o si┗te (i)ru desyo┙o ka.   'What do you suppose
Taro is doing?'
Si┗tte (i)ru desyo┐o ka ┗ne┙e. 'I wonder if he does know!'
Ka┌maimase┐ñ desyoo? 'It doesn't matter, does it?'

Do not confuse a verbal + <u>desyoo</u> with a tentative verbal, which indicates a
suggestion:[1]

Ka┌u desyo┐o. '[Someone] probably buys (<u>or</u> will probably buy) [it].'
Ka┌imasyo┐o. 'Let's buy [it].' <u>or</u> 'I guess I'll buy [it].'

3.   Alternate Questions

Two questions occurring within a sentence with the pattern <u>A ka B ka</u> are
alternate questions—'is it A, or is it B?'

Examples:

Ko┌marima┐su ka, ka┌maimase┐ñ ka.   'Is it inconvenient, or doesn't it
matter?'
O┌mosiro┐i desu ka, tu┌mara┐nai desu ka. 'Is it interesting, or is it
dull?'
O┌nazi de┐su ka, ti┌gaima┐su ka.   'Is it the same or is it different?'
Ma┐e desu ka, u┌siro de┐su ka.   'Is it in front, or is it in back?'

4.   <u>na</u>

Prior to this lesson, words or phrases used as descriptions of nominals
have been of four kinds:

1.   An adjectival (or a sequence ending with an adjectival)

Examples: ta┌ka┐i zi┗do┙osya 'expensive car'
to┌temo i┐i hito 'a very nice person'

2.   A demonstrative

Example: kono tokee 'this watch'

3.   A nominal + <u>no</u> or a nominal phrase (consisting of a nominal preceded
by descriptive words and/or followed by particles) + <u>no</u>

Examples: a┌na┐ta no ┗ho┙ñ 'your book'
o┌mosiro┐i ┗ho┙ñ no namae 'the name of an interesting
book'
A┌merika kara no hu┐ne 'a ship from America'

---

[1] In the standard spoken language, a verbal + <u>desyoo</u> may refer to first,
second, or third person, but a tentative verbal regularly refers to the first
person.

4.   A nominal alone (in special combinations only)

   Examples: su⌐ḡu ┌so┙ba 'immediate vicinity'
              tyo┐tto ┌ma┙e 'a little before'

Within the class of nominals, there is a subclass having the following special characteristic: when they describe another nominal, they are followed by
na.

   Examples:

      hi⌐ma na toki┐ 'time of leisure'
      ki┐ree na uti 'a pretty house'
      si⌐tu┐ree na hito 'a rude person'

All na-nominals describe qualities; but since not all quality nominals take
na, they must be memorized as they occur. Ge┐ñki 'healthy,' 'peppy,' for
example, is a na-nominal, but byooki 'sick' is not:

      ge┐ñki na kodomo 'a healthy child'
      byooki no kodomo 'a sick child'

Among the nominals introduced up to this point, the following are na-
nominals:

      (o)┌ge┐ñki 'healthy,' 'peppy'
      da┌me┐ 'no good'
      ki┐ree 'pretty,' 'clean'
      da┌izyo┐obu 'safe'
      ke┐kkoo 'fine'
      si⌐tu┐ree 'rude'
      (o)hima 'free (of time)'
      da┐izi 'important,' 'valuable'

In the lessons that follow, all na-nominals will be so designated when they
are first introduced.

Besides being followed by na when describing another nominal, na-nominals
regularly occur before various forms of √da, and before particle ni (as in
da⌐me┐ ni na┌rima┙sita 'it went bad' [lit. 'it became no good']).

DRILLS

A. Substitution Drill

   1. When you are free, please   O⌐hima na toki┐ ni o⌐de┐ñwa (o) kuda-
       give me a call.   sai.
   2. When you are free, please   O⌐hima na toki┐ ni ma⌐ta kite┐ kuda-
       come again.   sai.
   3. When you are free, please   O⌐hima na toki┐ ni ko⌐re (o) mi┐te ku-
       look at this.   dasai.
   4. When you are free, please   O⌐hima na toki┐ ni a⌐re (o) mi┐sete
       let me see that.   kudasai.
   5. When you are free, please   O⌐hima na toki┐ ni mi⌐ti (o) osiete
       show me the way.   kudasa┐i.

6. When you are free, please draw a map.

O⌐hima na toki⌐ ni ⌐ti⌐zu (o) ⌐ka⌐ite kudasai.

7. When you are free, please come to see me (lit. come to my house).

O⌐hima na toki⌐ ni u⌐ti e ira⌐site kudasai.

8. When you are free, please telephone Mr. Tanaka.

O⌐hima na toki⌐ ni Ta⌐naka-sañ ni deñwa (o) ka⌐kete kudasai.

B. Substitution Drill

1. I saw [it] at that school.
A⌐no gakkoo de mima⌐sita.

2. I asked at that school.
A⌐no gakkoo de kikima⌐sita.

3. I telephoned at that school.
A⌐no gakkoo de deñwa-sima⌐sita.

4. I saw [him] at that school.
A⌐no gakkoo de aima⌐sita.

5. I studied at that school.
A⌐no gakkoo de beñkyoo-sima⌐sita.

6. I wrote [it] at that school.
A⌐no gakkoo de kakima⌐sita.

7. I bought [it] at that school.
A⌐no gakkoo de kaima⌐sita.

8. I did [it] at that school.
A⌐no gakkoo de sima⌐sita.

C. Substitution Drill

1. I asked (or heard [it] or listened).
Wa⌐takusi ḡa kikima⌐sita.

2. I (comparatively speaking) asked (or heard [it] or listened).
Wa⌐takusi wa kikima⌐sita.

3. I too asked (or heard [it] or listened).
Wa⌐takusi mo kikima⌐sita.

4. I asked (or heard [it] from) a friend.
To⌐modati ni kikima⌐sita.

5. I heard [it] from a friend.
To⌐modati kara kikima⌐sita.

6. I asked (or heard or listened to) that.
So⌐re o kikima⌐sita.

7. That I asked (or heard or listened to).
So⌐re wa kikima⌐sita.

8. I asked (or heard or listened to) that, too.
So⌐re mo kikima⌐sita.

9. I asked (or heard [it] or listened) at the Japan Travel Bureau.
Ko⌐otuuko⌐osya de ki⌐kima⌐sita.

10. I asked (or heard [it] or listened) at 3 o'clock.
Sa⌐ñ-zi ni ki⌐kima⌐sita.

D. Substitution Drill

1. I'd like to telephone a friend. . . .
To⌐modati ni deñwa (o) kaketa⌐i ñ desu ḡa_

2. I'd like to telephone my home. . . .

U⌐ti | ni / e | deñwa (o) kaketa⌐i ñ desu ḡa_

3. I'd like to telephone a cous-   O⌐osaka no ito⌐ko ni de⌐ñwa (o) ka-
   in in Osaka. . . .   keta⁻i ñ desu ḡa‿

4. I'd like to telephone my un-   Kyo⌐oto no o⌐zi ni deñwa (o) kake-
   cle in Kyoto. . . .   ta⁻i ñ desu ḡa‿

5. I'd like to telephone Mrs.   Ha⌐simoto-sañ no o⌐kusañ ni de⌐ñwa
   Hashimoto. . . .   (o) kaketa⁻i ñ desu ḡa‿

6. I'd like to telephone Miss   Ko⌐bayasi-sañ no ozyo⌐osañ ni de⌐ñ-
   Kobayashi. . . .   wa (o) kaketa⁻i ñ desu ḡa‿

7. I'd like to telephone my   Ko⌐domo no gakkoo │ ni │ deñwa (o)
   child's school. . . .   │ e │
      kaketa⁻i ñ desu ḡa‿

8. I'd like to telephone the   Ko⌐otuuko⌐osya │ ni │ de⌐ñwa (o) ka-
   Japan Travel Bureau. . . .   │ e │
      keta⁻i ñ desu ḡa‿

9. I'd like to telephone (our)   U⌐ti no Zi⌐roo ni de⌐ñwa (o) kake-
   Jiro. . . .   ta⁻i ñ desu ḡa‿

10. I'd like to telephone Mr.   Ga⌐imu⌐syoo no Ta⌐naka-sañ ni deñ-
    Tanaka at the Foreign   wa (o) kaketa⁻i ñ desu ḡa‿
    Office. . . .

E. Substitution Drill

1. He'll probably return home   Ro⌐ku-zi-ḡo⌐ro made ni wa o⌐kaeri
   by about 6 o'clock.   ni na⁻ru desyoo.

2. He'll probably return home   A⌐sita ma⌐de ni wa o⌐kaeri ni na⁻ru
   by tomorrow.   desyoo.

3. He'll probably come (or go)   A⌐sita ma⌐de ni wa i⌐rassya⁻ru de-
   by tomorrow.   syoo.

4. He'll probably come (or go)   Su⌐iyo⌐o made ni wa i⌐rassya⁻ru de-
   by Wednesday.   syoo.

5. He'll probably arrive by   Su⌐iyo⌐o made ni wa o⌐tuki ni na⁻ru
   Wednesday.   desyoo.

6. He'll probably arrive by   Si-⌐ḡatu⌐ made ni wa o⌐tuki ni na⁻ru
   April.   desyoo.

7. He'll probably be able to   Si-⌐ḡatu⌐ made ni wa o⌐deki ni na⁻ru
   do [it] by April.   desyoo.

8. He'll probably be able to   Tu⌐itati⌐ made ni wa o⌐deki ni na⁻ru
   do [it] by the first.   desyoo.

9. He'll probably leave by the   Tu⌐itati⌐ made ni wa o⌐de ni na⁻ru
   first.   desyoo.

10. He'll probably leave by a   Zyu⌐ugo-hu⌐ñ-suḡi made ni wa o⌐de
    quarter after.   ni na⁻ru desyoo.

F. Grammar Drill (based on Grammatical Note 2)

    (Use the informal verbal before desyoo.)

    Tutor: Asita ⌐Ni⌐kkoo ni ikimasu. '[He] is going to go to Nikkoo to-
              morrow.'

    Student: Asita ⌐Ni⌐kkoo ni i⌐ku desyo⁻o. '[He] is probably going to
              go to Nikkoo tomorrow.'

1. Ma⌈ta asita aima⌉su.   Ma⌈ta asita a⌉u desyoo.
2. So⌈re wa komarima⌉su.   So⌈re wa koma⌉ru desyoo.
3. U⌈ti no usiro de tomema⌉su.   U⌈ti no usiro de tomeru desyo⌉o.
4. Ko⌈ñna siḡoto wa dekima⌉su.   Ko⌈ñna siḡoto wa deki⌉ru desyoo.
5. Ni⌈hoñḡo to eeḡo wa wakari-   Ni⌈hoñḡo to eeḡo wa waka⌉ru desyoo.
   ma⌉su.
6. Ko⌈re to sore wa tiḡaima⌉-   Ko⌈re to sore wa tiḡau desyo⌉o.
   su.
7. Hi⌈ma na toki⌉ ni mi⌐ma⌐su.   Hi⌈ma na toki⌉ ni ⌐mi⌐ru desyoo.
8. Asoko ni tabako (ḡa) ⌈mo⌉t-   Asoko ni tabako (ḡa) ⌈mo⌉tto ⌐a⌐ru
   to arimasu.   desyoo.
9. Go⌉ḡo made u⌐ti ni ima⌐su.   Go⌉ḡo made u⌐ti ni iru desyo⌐o.
10. A⌈sita Yokohama ni tuki-   A⌈sita Yokohama ni tu⌉ku desyoo.
    ma⌉su.

G. Grammar Drill (based on Grammatical Note 3)

   Tutor: I⌈kima⌉su. I⌈kimase⌉ñ. 'I'll go. I won't go.' (2 statements)
   Student: I⌈kima⌉su ka, i⌈kimase⌉ñ ka˩ 'Are you going, or aren't you
            going?' (alternate questions)

1. Ryo⌈kañ de⌉su. Ho⌉teru   Ryo⌈kañ de⌉su ka, ho⌉teru desu ka˩
   desu.
2. Si⌈tte (i)ma⌉su. Si⌈rima-   Si⌈tte (i)ma⌉su ka, si⌈rimase⌉ñ ka˩
   se⌉ñ.
3. Mu⌈zukasi⌉i desu. Ya⌈sa-   Mu⌈zukasi⌉i desu ka, ya⌈sasi⌉i desu
   si⌉i desu.   ka˩
4. Bo⌉ttyañ no desu. O⌈zyo⌉o-   Bo⌉ttyañ no desu ka, o⌈zyo⌉osañ no
   sañ no desu.   desu ka˩
5. Ki⌈no⌉o desita. O⌈toto⌉i   Ki⌈no⌉o desita ka, o⌈toto⌉i desita ka˩
   desita.
6. Ke⌈kkoñ-site ima⌉su. O⌈hi-   Ke⌈kkoñ-site (i)ma⌉su ka, o⌈hitori
   tori de⌉su.   de⌉su ka˩
7. De⌈kima⌉sita. De⌈kimase⌉ñ   De⌈kima⌉sita ka, de⌈kimase⌉ñ desita
   desita.   ka˩
8. Sa⌉ñ-zi made desu. Yo⌉-zi   Sa⌉ñ-zi made desu ka, yo⌉-zi made
   made desu.   desu ka˩

H. Grammar Drill (based on Grammatical Note 4)

   Tutor: Ko⌈no ho⌉ñ (wa) ta⌈ka⌉i desu ⌈ne⌉e. 'This book is expensive,
            isn't it.'
   Student: Kore (wa) ta⌈ka⌉i ⌐ho⌐ñ desu ⌈ne⌉e. 'This is an expensive
            book, isn't it.'

1. Ano kodomo (wa) ⌈ge⌉ñki   Are (wa) ⌈ge⌉ñki na ko⌐domo de⌐su
   desu ⌈ne⌉e.   ⌈ne⌉e.
2. Ko⌈no ba⌉su (wa) o⌈so⌉i desu   Kore (wa) o⌈soi ba⌉su desu ⌈ne⌉e.
   ⌈ne⌉e.
3. So⌈no mise⌉ (wa) sáki de-   Sore (wa) sa⌈ki no mise⌉ desyoo?
   syoo?

4. Kono siḡoto (wa) ⌈ma⌉initi
   desyoo?

   Kore (wa) ⌈ma⌉initi no siḡoto desyoo?

5. O⌈zyo⌉osañ (wa) ⌈ki⌉ree desu
   ⌈ne⌉e.

   Ki⌈ree na o┗zyo┛osañ desu ⌈ne⌉e.

6. So⌈no ka⌉do (wa) tu⌈ḡi⌉ desyoo?

   Sore (wa) tu⌈ḡi⌉ no ┗ka┛do desyoo?

7. A⌈no zido⌉osya (wa) hu⌈ru⌉i
   desu ⌈ne⌉e.

   Are (wa) hu⌈ru⌉i zi┗do┛osya desu
   ⌈ne⌉e.

8. Ano zyuñsa (wa) si⌈tu⌉ree
   desita ⌈ne⌉e.

   Are (wa) si⌈tu⌉ree na zyu┗ñsa de┛si-
   ta ⌈ne⌉e.

9. Kono miti (wa) a⌈buna⌉i
   desu ⌈ne⌉e.

   Kore (wa) a⌈bunai miti de⌉su ┗ne┛e.

I.   Expansion Drill

1. [He] didn't know.   Si⌈rimase⌉ñ desita.
   I asked, but [he] didn't   Ki⌈kima⌉sita ḡa, si⌈rimase⌉ñ desita.
   know.
   I asked the telephone num-   De⌈ñwaba⌉ñḡoo (o) ki┗kima┛sita ḡa,
   ber, but [he] didn't know.   si⌈rimase⌉ñ desita.
   I asked the telephone num-   Ga⌈imu⌉syoo no de┗ñwaba┛ñḡoo (o)
   ber of the Foreign Office,   ki┗kima┛sita ḡa, si⌈rimase⌉ñ de-
   but [he] didn't know.   sita.
   I asked my friend the tele-   Tomodati ni ga⌈imu⌉syoo no de┗ñwa-
   phone number of the For-   ba┛ñḡoo (o) ki┗kima┛sita ga, si⌈ri-
   eign Office, but [he]   mase⌉ñ desita.
   didn't know.

2. I'll probably see [him].   A⌉u desyoo.
   I'll probably see your   O⌈tomodati ni a⌉u desyoo.
   friend.
   I'm going to go, so I'll   I⌈kima⌉su kara,   o⌈tomodati ni a⌉u
   probably see your   desyoo.
   friend.
   I'm going to go to the Ja-   Ko⌈otuuko⌉osya e i┗kima┛su kara,
   pan Travel Bureau, so   o⌈tomodati ni a⌉u desyoo.
   I'll probably see your
   friend.
   I'm going to go to the Ja-   I⌉ma ko⌈otuuko⌉osya e i┗kima┛su ka-
   pan Travel Bureau now,   ra, o⌈tomodati ni a⌉u desyoo.
   so I'll probably see your
   friend.

3. You know, I saw [it].   Mi⌈ma⌉sita yo⌿
   You know, I saw [it] for the   Ha⌈zi⌉mete mi┗ma┛sita yo⌿
   first time.
   You know, I saw the house   Uti (o) ha⌈zi⌉mete mi┗ma┛sita yo⌿
   for the first time.
   You know, I saw a pretty   Ki⌉ree na uti (o) ha⌈zi⌉mete mi┗ma┛-
   house for the first   sita yo⌿
   time.

You know, I saw your son's
pretty house for the first
time.

Musukosañ no ⌐ki⌐ree na uti (o) ha-
⌐zi⌐mete mi⌐ma⌐sita yo⌐

You know, I saw your son's
pretty house for the first
time last night.

Yuube musukosañ no ⌐ki⌐ree na uti
(o) ha⌐zi⌐mete mi⌐ma⌐sita yo⌐

4. Did you ask?

Ki⌐kima⌐sita ka⌐

Did you ask the operator?

Ko⌐oka⌐ñsyu ni ki⌐kima⌐sita ka⌐

Did you see [it] or did you
ask the operator?

Mi⌐ma⌐sita ka, ko⌐oka⌐ñsyu ni ki⌐ki-
ma⌐sita ka⌐

Did you look at the phone
book or did you ask the
operator?

De⌐ñwatyoo (o) mima⌐sita ka, ko⌐o-
ka⌐ñsyu ni ki⌐kima⌐sita ka⌐

5. Is it number 2?

Hu⌐ta⌐-bañ desu ka⌐

Is it number 22?

Hu⌐ta⌐zyuu hu⌐ta⌐-bañ desu ka⌐

Is it number 422?

Yo⌐ñhyaku hu⌐ta⌐zyuu hu⌐ta⌐-bañ desu
ka⌐

Is it number 0422?

Re⌐e ⌐yo⌐ñhyaku hu⌐ta⌐zyuu hu⌐ta⌐-bañ
desu ka⌐

Is it (number) 081-0422?

Re⌐e ha⌐tizyu⌐u i⌐ti⌐ no, re⌐e ⌐yo⌐ñ-
hyaku hu⌐ta⌐zyuu hu⌐ta⌐-bañ desu
ka⌐

Is this (i.e. the person I'm
addressing) (number)
081-0422?

Sotira (wa) ⌐re⌐e ha⌐tizyu⌐u i⌐ti⌐ no,
re⌐e ⌐yo⌐ñhyaku hu⌐ta⌐zyuu hu⌐ta⌐-
bañ desu ka⌐

SUPPLEMENTARY CONVERSATIONS

1. Smith: Ki⌐mura-sañ no deñwaba⌐ñḡoo o si⌐tte ma⌐su ka⌐

   Tanaka: Tyo⌐tto ⌐ma⌐tte kudasai⌐ . . . Go⌐hyaku nana⌐zyuu i⌐ti⌐ no,
             sa⌐ñze⌐ñ ⌐yo⌐ñzyuu i⌐ti⌐-bañ desu yo⌐

   Smith: Ma⌐e wa so⌐no bañḡo⌐o desita ḡa, i⌐ma wa ⌐so⌐o zya a⌐rima-
             se⌐ñ yo.

   Tanaka: A⌐a, so⌐o desu ka⌐ Zya⌐a, kinoo Ha⌐simoto-sañ ḡa Kimura-
             sañ ni deñwa-sima⌐sita kara, Ha⌐simoto-sañ wa sitte ru⌐ de-
             syoo.

   Smith: Zya⌐a, Ha⌐simoto-sañ ni kikimasyo⌐o. Do⌐o mo su⌐mimase⌐ñ.

   Tanaka: Iie.

2. Mr. Tanaka: Mo⌐simosi⌐

   Maid: Mo⌐simosi⌐

   Mr. Tanaka: Ya⌐mada-sañ no otaku de⌐su ka⌐

   Maid: Ha⌐a, sa⌐yoo de gozaima⌐su.

   Mr. Tanaka: Yu⌐kio-sañ ima⌐su ka⌐

   Maid: Bo⌐ttyañ wa ⌐i⌐ma ga⌐kkoo de gozaima⌐su ḡa, do⌐tira-sama de
                i⌐rassyaima⌐su ka⌐

Mr. Tanaka: Azabu¹ no Ta⌐naka de⌐su ḡa, na⌐ñ-zi-ḡo⌐ro ka⌐erima⌐su ka⌐

Maid: Kyo⌐o wa do⌐yo⌐o desu kara i⌐ti-zi-ḡo⌐ro o⌐kaeri ni narima⌐su
            ḡa, notihodo ko⌐tira kara ode⌐ñwa si⌐masyo⌐o ka.

Mr. Tanaka: Iie. Ma⌐ta a⌐to de ⌐bo⌐ku ḡa de⌐ñwa suru⌐ kara.

Maid: Sa⌐yoo de gozaima⌐su ka⌐

Mr. Tanaka: Zya⌐a, sayonara.

Maid: Go⌐meñ-kudasaima⌐se.

3. Smith: Tyo⌐tto de⌐ñwa (o) kaketa⌐i ñ desu ḡa⌐

    Tanaka: Ko⌐no deñwa do⌐ozo.

    Smith: A⌐ri⌐ḡatoo. De⌐ñwaba⌐ñḡoo si⌐rimase⌐ñ ḡa⌐

    Tanaka: De⌐ñwatyoo arima⌐su yo⌐ Do⌐nata ni ka⌐keta⌐i ñ desu ka⌐

    Smith: Ki⌐mura Yosio de⌐su.

    Tanaka: Ki⌐mura Yosio de⌐su ka⌐ Tyo⌐tto ⌐ma⌐tte kudasai⌐ A⌐a, A⌐o⌐-
             yama¹ ro⌐ku-tyoome⌐ no Ki⌐mura-sañ de⌐su ka⌐

    Smith: E⌐e, so⌐o desu.

    Tanaka: Yo⌐ñhyaku ha⌐tizyu⌐u i⌐ti⌐ no, yo⌐ñse⌐ñ happyaku ⌐to⌐o-bañ de-
             su yo.

    Smith: Tyo⌐tto ⌐ma⌐tte kudasai—ka⌐kima⌐su kara.

    Tanaka: Do⌐ozo. E⌐ñpitu arima⌐su ka⌐

    Smith: E⌐e, a⌐rima⌐su. Su⌐mimase⌐ñ ḡa, mo⌐o iti-do itte kudasaima-
             se⌐ñ ka⌐

    Tanaka: Yo⌐ñhyaku ha⌐tizyu⌐u i⌐ti⌐ no, yo⌐ñse⌐ñ happyaku ⌐to⌐o-bañ de-
             su yo.

    Smith: Do⌐o mo su⌐mimase⌐ñ desita.

    Tanaka: Do⌐o itasimasite.

English Equivalents

1. Smith: Do you know Mr. Kimura's telephone number?
    Tanaka: Just a minute. It's 571-3041.
    Smith: It was that number before, but it isn't that now.
    Tanaka: Oh? Well then, Mr. Hashimoto telephoned Mr. Kimura yes-
              terday so Mr. Hashimoto probably knows.
    Smith: Well then, I'll ask Mr. Hashimoto. Thanks very much.
    Tanaka: Not at all.

2. Mr. Tanaka: Hello.
    Maid: Hello.
    Mr. Tanaka: Is this the Yamada residence?
    Maid: Yes, it is.
    Mr. Tanaka: Is Yukio there?

---

¹
  A section of Tokyo.

Maid: He (lit. the young master) is [at] school now.   Who is calling, please?

Mr. Tanaka: This is Mr. Tanaka in Azabu.   About what t i m e will he be home?

Maid: Today is Saturday so he'll be home about 1.   Do you want him to call you later? (Lit. Shall we call later from this side?)

Mr. Tanaka: No. (Because) I'll call again later.

Maid: Oh.

Mr. Tanaka: Well, goodbye.

Maid: Goodbye.

3. Smith: I'd (just) like to make a telephone call. . . .

Tanaka: Here, [use] this telephone.

Smith: Thanks.   I don't know the telephone number. . . .

Tanaka: I have a telephone book.   Who is it you want to call?

Smith: It's Yoshio Kimura.

Tanaka: Yoshio Kimura?   Just a minute. . . .   Oh, is it Mr. Kimura in Aoyama 6-chome?

Smith: Yes, that's right.

Tanaka: It's 481-4810.

Smith: Just a minute—because I'm going to write it [down].

Tanaka: Certainly.   Do you have a pencil?

Smith: Yes, I have.   I'm sorry but would you say it again?

Tanaka: It's 481-4810.

Smith: Thanks very much.

Tanaka: You're welcome.

EXERCISES

1. Read the following telephone numbers aloud in Japanese:

    a. 371-3923   f. 251-0360
    b. 481-1333   g. 622-2011
    c. 047-3092   h. 996-0520
    d. 891-1510   i. 291-5272, extension 607
    e. 611-6161   j. 631-0044, extension 941

2. Mr. Tanaka has just telephoned and asked for Mr. Yamamoto.   Give the following answers, practicing different levels, if appropriate:

    a. Just a moment, please.
    b. Mr. Yamamoto isn't at his desk just now. . . .
    c. Mr. Yamamoto is busy just now.   Would you like him to call later? (Lit. Shall we call later from this side?)
    d. Mr. Yamamoto is in Osaka.   He'll be back tomorrow.
    e. Who is calling, please?
    f. Mr. Yamamoto is in Mr. Sato's office just now.   It's extension 243.
    g. Mr. Yamamoto is away from home just now.   He'll be back on the first of the month. (Mrs. Yamamoto speaking)

     h. Mr. Yamamoto is at the office. He'll be back at about 6:00. (Mrs. Yamamoto speaking)

     i. Mr. Yamamoto will be away from home until Saturday. (Maid speaking)

     j. Do you mean Yosio Yamamoto, or Yukio Yamamoto?

3. Practice the Basic Dialogues with appropriate variations.

Lesson 13. Telephoning (cont.)

BASIC DIALOGUES: FOR MEMORIZATION

(a)

Sakamoto

1. Hello. Is Mr. Smith there?

    Mo⌐simosi ⌐ Su⌐misu - sañ i⌐ras-
    syaima⌐su ka⌐

Secretary

   set out or go out
2. No. He stepped out for a
    minute. . . .

   dekakeru /-ru/
   Iie, tyo⌐tto de⌐kakema⌐sita ḡa⌐

Sakamoto

   message or the giving
      of a message
   make or do
   request

   kotozuke   or
      okotozuke +
   itasu⌐ /-u/
   ne⌐ḡa⌐u ⌐/-u/   or
      o⌐neḡai-itasima⌐su ⌐

3. Well then, I'd like to leave a
    message for Mr. Smith.

    Zya⌐a, Su⌐misu - sañ ni o⌐kotozuke
    (o) oneḡai-itasima⌐su.

Secretary

4. Certainly.

    Do⌐ozo.

Sakamoto

   university
   Tokyo University

   daiḡaku
   To⌐okyoo-da⌐iḡaku   or
      Toodai

5. This is [Mr.] Sakamoto at
    Tokyo University. . . .

    Kotira (wa) To͞odai no Sa⌐kamoto de
    gozaima⌐su ḡa⌐

Secretary

6. Yes.

    Ha⌐a.

Sakamoto

   this evening or tonight
   say
   say that or say [it] that
      way

   ko⌐ñbañ
   o⌐ssya⌐ru⌐ /-aru/
   so⌐o ossya⌐ru

7. Please tell him that I will be
    waiting in front of the Maru-
    biru at 7 o'clock this evening.
    (Lit. I'll be waiting in front of
    the Maru-biru at 7 o'clock this
    evening so please say [it] that
    way.)

    Ko⌐ñbañ si⌐ti⌐ - zi ni Ma⌐ru-biru no
    ma⌐e de ⌐ma⌐tte orimasu kara, so⌐o
    ossya⌐tte kudasai.

207

Secretary

report <u>or</u> communicate
or convey a message

tutaeru /-ru/   <u>or</u>
o⌐tutae-itasima⌐su ↓

8. I understand. I'll give him your
message.

Wa⌐karima⌐sita. O⌐tutae-itasima⌐-
su.

(b)

Tanaka

9. Hello.

Mo⌐simosi.

Yamamoto

10. Hello. . . . Hello.

Mo⌐simosi_ . . . Mo⌐simosi.

Tanaka (in a louder voice)

is far

tooi /-ku/

have trouble hearing (on
the phone)

deñwa ḡa tooi

voice

ko⌐e

with a loud voice

o⌐oki⌐i ⌐ko⌐e de <u>or</u>
o⌐oki na ⌐ko⌐e de

speak <u>or</u> talk

ha⌐na⌐su /-u/

11. Hello. Say, I can't hear so
please talk in a little louder
voice.

Mo⌐simosi_ Tyo⌐tto, deñwa ḡa to-
⌐oi⌐ desu kara ne? Mo⌐o suko⌐si ⌐o⌐o-
ki na ⌐ko⌐e de ha⌐na⌐site kudasai.

Yamamoto (still louder)

be audible <u>or</u> can hear

kikoeru /-ru/

12. Hello. Hello. Can you hear
[me]?

Mo⌐simosi_ Mo⌐simosi_ Ki⌐koe-
ma⌐su ka_

Tanaka (shouting)

cut <u>or</u> cut off <u>or</u> hang
up (the telephone)

ki⌐ru /-u/

13. It's no good so I'll hang up now
and call again later.

Da⌐me⌐ desu kara ne? I⌐ma ⌐ki⌐tte
ne? Ma⌐ta a⌐to de de⌐ñwa-sima⌐su
yo.

(c)

Smith

know

go⌐zo⌐ñzi desu ↓

14. Do you know Mr. Ito's telephone [number]?

Itoo-sañ no deñwa (o) go⌐zo⌐ñzi desu
ka_

Tanaka

don't know

zo⌐ñzimase⌐ñ ↓

15. No, I don't know [it]. . . .

Iie, zo⌐ñzimase⌐ñ ḡa_

Yoshida

know

zo⌐ñzite orimasu ↓

name card <u>or</u> calling   meesi
    card
16. I know—because I have Mr.   Wa⌐takusi wa zo⌐ṅzite o r i m a s u _
    Ito's card.   I⌐too-sañ no meesi ḡa gozaima⌐su
                               kara.

Smith

read   yo⌐mu /-u/
17. Would you read it for me?   Yo⌐ṅde ku⌐dasaimase⌐ṅ ka↴

slowly   yu⌐kku⌐ri
18. I'm going to write it [down]   Ka⌐kima⌐su kara yu⌐kku⌐ri onegai-
    so [read it] slowly, please.   simasu.

(d)

Secretary

make <u>or</u> do   na⌐sa⌐ru ↑ /-aru/
make a telephone call   o⌐de⌐ṅwa-nasaru↑
19. Did you telephone the school?   Gakkoo |ni / e| o⌐de⌐ṅwa-nasaimasita

                            ka↴

Smith

talking <u>or</u> a talk <u>or</u>   hanasi   or
  a story   ohanasi↑
in the middle of talking   hanasi-tyuu   <u>or</u>
                     ohanasi-tyuu↑

nobody   dare mo /+ negative/
answer (the telephone)   de⌐ru /-ru/
20. Five minutes ago the line was   Go-⌐huṅ ma⌐e ni wa ha⌐nasi-tyuu
    busy but now no one answers. . . .   de⌐sita ḡa, i⌐ma wa da⌐re mo dema-
                            se⌐ṅ ḡa_

Secretary

strange   he⌐ṅ /na/
21. Isn't that strange!   He⌐ṅ desu ⌐ne⌐e.

(e)

Tanaka

22. Hello. Is this Tokyo Uni-   Mo⌐simosi_ To⌐odai de⌐su ka↴
    versity?
Stranger

23. Wrong number.   Ti⌐gaima⌐su.

Tanaka

24. Oh, I'm sorry. (Lit. I   A. Si⌐tu⌐ree-simasita.
    committed a rudeness.)

(f)

Husband

out of order   kosyoo
25. This telephone is out of or-   Kono deñwa kŏsyoo da yo↲
der.

Wife (testing phone)

do what? or act how?   do⌐o suru
26. It is, isn't it. What are you   Hoñtoo ⌐ne⌐e. Do⌐o suru?
going to do?

Husband

borrow or rent   kariru /-ru/
say to the operator or   ko⌐oka⌐ñsyu ni iu
tell the operator
27. I'm going to borrow the tele-   Tonari no deñwa karite, ko⌐oka⌐ñsyu
phone next door and tell the   ni i⌐u⌐ yo.
operator.

(On the telephone)

say! or hey there!   ano ne
fix or repair   na⌐o⌐su /-u/
28. Say! 401-5602 is out of order   Ano ne? Yo⌐ñhyaku i⌐ti⌐ no ne? Go-
so please fix it.   ⌐se⌐ñ rŏppyaku ⌐ni⌐-bañ wa ne? Ko-
⌐syoo da⌐ kara ne? Na⌐o⌐site kuda-
sai.

(g)

Mr. Tanaka

(Mr.) Sato   Sa⌐too-kuñ
is busy   i⌐soḡasi⌐i /-ku/ or
o⌐isoḡasi⌐i↑ /-ku/
29. Sato, are you busy?   Sa⌐too-kuñ, i⌐soḡasi⌐i?

Mr. Sato

30. No, not especially.   Iie, betu ni↲ [1]

Mr. Tanaka

call or summon   yobu /-u/

---

[1] Regularly followed by the negative in longer sentences.

31. Call Okada—because he has   Okada-kuñ yoñde—deᵗñwa daᵗkara.
    (lit. it is) a phone call.

Mr. Sato

32. Where is Okada now?   Okada-kuñ ꞌima ꞌdoꞌko?

Mr. Tanaka

room   heᵗyaᵗ or
                                     oheya †
33. He's in the next room.   Toᵗnari no heyaᵗ ni iru yo⌐

NOTES ON THE BASIC DIALOGUES

Dialogue (a): Sakamoto uses polite speech in talking to Smith's secretary
as a sign of respect for Smith.

2. 'He stepped out but—is there anything I can do?'

Dekakeru means 'go out' or 'set out' or 'start out,' whereas deᵗru means
'go out' or 'leave' or 'emerge.'

3. Itasu is the polite humble (†) equivalent of suru, both as an independent
word and as part of compounds like beñkyoo - suru (humble, beñkyoo-
itasu).

7. Oᵗssyaᵗru is the polite honorific equivalent of iu, used as an exalting
form in reference to people other than the speaker, in polite speech. It
belongs to the same subclass of verbals as iᵗrassyaᵗru, kuᵗdasaᵗru, and
goᵗzaᵗru: its stem is oᵗssyaᵗi and its -maᵗsu form oᵗssyaimaᵗsu.

11. The opposite of oᵗokiᵗi (or oᵗoki na) ᵗkoᵗe is tiᵗisaᵗi (or tiᵗisa na) ᵗkoᵗe
'low voice.'

Remember that verbals ending in -su in their citation form have gerunds
ending in -site.

12. Kikoeru is another verbal which does not occur with particle o. Both the
thing which is audible and the person who can hear are followed by particle
wa or g̃a.

13. Kiᵗru, like iru 'be necessary,' is a verbal ending in -iru but belonging to
the -u class of verbals: stem, kiᵗri; -maᵗsu form, kiᵗrimaᵗsu; gerund,
kiᵗtte.

14, 15, 16. The verbal zoᵗñziᵗru † (-ru) 'come to know' is not included in the
lists of this book.   It will occur only in the following forms:

zoᵗñzite (i)masu and zoᵗñzite orimasu 'I know (humble equivalents of
siᵗtte (i)maᵗsu and siᵗtte orimaᵗsu)

zoᵗñzimaseᵗñ 'I don't know' (humble equivalent of siᵗrimaseᵗñ)

goᵗzoᵗñzi desu (desita, desyoo, etc.) '[you] know (knew, probably know,
etc.)' (honorific equivalent of siᵗtte [i]maᵗsu [(i)maᵗsita, etc.])

15. 'No, I don't know it but—is there anything I can do?'

16. <u>Meesi</u> are used in Japan in professional circles to a much greater extent than calling cards are used in America. They are regularly exchanged by new acquaintances. They usually include name, title, business affiliation, address, and telephone number.

17. Verbals ending in -<u>mu</u> in their citation form have gerunds ending in -ñde.

18. Yu⌐kku┐ri means 'slowly,' 'without hurrying,' 'in a relaxed way.' Unlike the adjectival <u>osoi</u>, it has no connotation of lateness.

19. Na⌐sa┐ru is the polite honorific equivalent of <u>suru</u>, both as an independent word and as part of compounds like <u>beñkyoo-suru</u> (honorific, be⌐ñkyoo-na-sa┐ru). Compare:

'Did you study?'   'Yes, I studied.'

Plain: Be⌐ñkyoo-sima┐sita ka⌣   E┐e, be⌐ñkyoo-sima┐sita.
Polite: Be⌐ñkyoo-nasaima┐sita ka⌣   Ha┐a, be⌐ñkyoo-itasima┐sita.

Na⌐sa┐ru, like o⌐ssya┐ru above (sentence 7), belongs to the same subclass of verbals as i⌐rassya┐ru, ku⌐dasa┐ru, and go⌐za┐ru: its stem is na⌐sa┐i and its gerund na⌐sa┐tte (alternant: na⌐su┐tte). These five verbals are the only members of the -<u>aru</u> subclass.

20. 'Now no one answers but—I wonder why.' The two <u>wa</u>'s in this sentence are <u>wa</u> of comparison.

25. Note also: <u>kosyoo-suru</u> 'break down.'

28. <u>Ano ne</u> is a less polite equivalent of <u>tyo┐tto</u> 'say there!' It does not ordinarily occur in polite c o n v e r s a t i o n, but is used most commonly in addressing close friends and inferiors. It is usually wise to avoid it when speaking to strangers whose position is not known.

29. -<u>Kuñ</u>, like -<u>sañ</u>, is added to the family or given names of persons other than the speaker. However, it is a man's word, and is usually used by men in reference to men. It is an informal word and implies familiarity. It may be compared to the English use of a last name without 'Mr.' as a term of address.

30. When <u>betu ni</u> occurs alone, it implies an appropriate negative. Here, it means <u>betu ni i⌐soḡa┐siku a⌐rimase┐ñ</u> 'I'm not especially busy.'

31. Verbals ending in -<u>bu</u> in their citation form have gerunds ending in -ñde. Note the difference in accent between <u>yo┐ñde</u> 'reading' and <u>yoñde</u> 'calling.'

GRAMMATICAL NOTES

1.   <u>ne?</u> and the E x p l i c i t   S t y l e

Ne? occurs at the end of sentences and means 'are you following me?' or 'do you understand me?' or 'do you agree with me?' It must not be confused with confirming or exclamatory <u>ne┐e</u>.   <u>Ne?</u> is an actual question, inviting agreement or acknowledgment. Compare:

Ta⌜ka⌝i desu ⌜ne⌝e. 'Isn't it expensive!' 'It's expensive, isn't it.'
Ta⌜ka⌝i desu ne? 'It's expensive, don't you think so?'

The latter is similar to: Ta⌜ka⌝i desyoo?

When speaking explicitly, or when speaking in a situation where there is some question of the comprehension of the listener (for example, when talking on the telephone, or when giving complicated instructions or explanations, or when talking to an inferior, etc.), it is common to break up a long sentence into a series of shorter sentences ending in ne? The shorter the sentences, the more explicit they are. The listener usually replies to each of these sentences with ha⌝i, e⌝e, ha⌝a, so⌝o, etc.— or with a nod—indicating that he is following the conversation.

However, the frequent occurrence of ne in ordinary, non-explicit conversation is usually a sign of informality and familiarity; to use it appropriately and naturally is very difficult for a foreigner. Beginning students of Japanese should use it sparingly except in the situations described above.

Compare:

Ordinary style:

Asita tyo⌜odo ku⌝-zi ni ko⌜ko e kite⌝ kudasai.
'Please come here tomorrow at 9 sharp.'

Explicit style:

Asita ne? 'Tomorrow—understand?'
Ha⌝i. 'Yes.'
Tyo⌜odo ku⌝-zi ni ne? 'At 9 sharp—understand?'
Ha⌝i. 'Yes.'
Ko⌜ko e kite⌝ kudasai. 'Come here.'
Ha⌝i. Ka⌜sikomarima⌝sita. 'Yes. Certainly.'

Compare also sentences 11, 13, and 28 in the Basic Dialogues.

2.   More About Informal Speech

In informal speech, informal inflected forms occur in sentence-final position and before sentence particles as well as within longer sentences. The following are a few of the common patterns:

(a) Informal verbals and adjectivals occur in sentence-final position in statements and questions, in the speech of men and women. [1]

---

[1] But informal honorific verbals in this position are typical of women's speech. Example: I⌜rassya⌝ru? 'Are you going (or coming)?' or 'Will you be here?'

	Formal	Informal
'It's clear.'	Wa⌐karima⌐su.	Wa⌐ka⌐ru.
'Is it clear?'	Wa⌐karima⌐su ka⌐	Wa⌐ka⌐ru?
'It's expensive.'	Ta⌐ka⌐i desu.	Ta⌐ka⌐i.
'Is it expensive?'	Ta⌐ka⌐i desu ka⌐	Ta⌐ka⌐i?

(b) Both men and women use nominals in sentence-final position in statements and questions as the informal equivalents of nominal + de⌐su or de⌐su ka (cf. Lesson 8, Grammatical Note 3); but the occurrence of a nominal + informal da in statement-final position is typical only of men's speech.

	Formal	Informal	
		Men	Women
'It's true.'	Ho⌐ntoo de⌐su.	Hoñtoo.	Hoñtoo.
		or	
		Hoñtoo da.	
'Is it true?'	Ho⌐ntoo de⌐su ka⌐	Hoñtoo?	Hoñtoo?

(c) Informal verbals and adjectivals occur before sentence particle yo and before ne⌐[e] predominantly in informal men's speech.

	Formal	Informal— Men
'It is clear (I tell you).'	Wa⌐karima⌐su yo⌐	Wa⌐ka⌐ru yo⌐
'It is expensive (I tell you).'	Ta⌐ka⌐i desu yo⌐	Ta⌐ka⌐i yo⌐
'It's clear, isn't it?'	Wa⌐karima⌐su ne?	Wa⌐ka⌐ru ne?
'It's expensive, isn't it!'	Ta⌐ka⌐i desu ⌐ne⌐e.	Ta⌐ka⌐i ⌐ne⌐e.

(d) As the informal equivalent of a nominal + de⌐su + yo or ne⌐[e], men regularly use nominal + da + yo or ne⌐[e], while women use nominal + yo or ne⌐[e].

	Formal	Informal	
		Men	Women
'It is true (I tell you).'	Ho⌐ntoo de⌐su yo⌐	Hoñtoo da yo⌐	Hoñtoo yo⌐
'It's true, isn't it!'	Ho⌐ntoo de⌐su ⌐ne⌐e.	Hoñtoo da ⌐ne⌐e.	Hoñtoo ⌐ne⌐e.

Basic Dialogues (f) and (g) in this lesson are informal. Sentences 25, 27, and 33 are typical of men's informal speech, and Hoñtoo ⌐ne⌐e. in 26 is typical of women's informal speech. The remaining sentences of these two dialogues occur in the speech of both men and women, except that -kuñ of sentences 29, 31, and 32 would ordinarily be replaced by -sañ in women's speech.

3.   Gerunds As Informal Requests

The gerund of a verbal may occur in sentence-final position, or pre-final before a particle, as an informal request. It is normally used in addressing an equal who is well known to the speaker, or an inferior.

Examples:

> So⌐re o mi⌐sete. 'Show me that.'
> Tyo⌐tto ⌐ma⌐tte yo. 'Wait a minute!'
> Yu⌐kku⌐ri ha⌐na⌐site ne? 'Speak slowly, would you?'

The gerund of an honorific is also often used in this way by women, in informal but polite requests.

Examples:

> Ko⌐tti⌐ e i⌐ra⌐site. 'Come here.'
> Tyo⌐tto o⌐mati ni na⌐tte. 'Wait a minute.'
> Yu⌐kku⌐ri o⌐hanasi ni na⌐tte ne? 'Speak slowly, would you?'

4.   Verbals: Humble Equivalents in √-suru and √-itasu

A compound verbal consisting of the polite prefix o- + a verbal stem + √suru (or its humble equivalent √itasu) is a humble equivalent of the verbal, used in reference to oneself, members of one's own family, etc. The form with √itasu is more humble than the corresponding form with √suru. Study the following chart:

Plain (Citation Form)	Polite (Citation Form)	
	Humble ↓	Honorific ↑
yobu 'call'	oyobi-suru or oyobi-itasu	o⌐yobi ni na⌐ru
ha⌐na⌐su 'speak'	ohanasi-suru or ohanasi-itasu	o⌐hanasi ni na⌐ru
tutaeru 'report'	otutae-suru or otutae-itasu	o⌐tutae ni na⌐ru

A corresponding humble form does NOT exist for all verbals. Some verbals have only special humble equivalents with unrelated roots (for example, iku and ku⌐ru have the humble equivalent ma⌐iru; iru has o⌐ru; etc.), and some have no commonly occurring humble equivalents.

In general, honorific (↑) verbals are more common than humble (↓) verbals.

Humbling oneself represents a greater degree of politeness in Japanese than exalting others. Accordingly, it is not unusual to use a plain verbal in reply to an honorific question (cf. Lesson 9, Grammatical Note 2):

> Oᒥyobiˀ ni narimaˀsita kaⵥ 'Did you call?'
> Eˀe, yoᒥbimaˀsita. 'Yes, I did (call).'

The use of oᒥyobi-simaˀsita (or oᒥyobi-itasimaˀsita) in the above reply would be an indication of considerable deference.

However, some humble polite verbals are extremely common. Oᒥneḡai-simaˀsu and oᒥneḡai-itasimaˀsu are humble polite equivalents of neᒥḡaimaˀsu (informal, neᒥḡaˀu[1]). In this case, the humble polite forms probably occur more commonly than the plain form.

Another commonly occurring example of a polite humble verbal is oᒥmatase-itasimaˀsita, based on the plain verbal maᒥtaseˀru /-ru/ 'make [someone] wait.'

5. oᒥokiˀi ∼ oˀoki na

A few adjectivals—for example, oᒥokiˀi and tiᒥisaˀi—have a derived nominal which is a na-nominal (see Lesson 12, Grammatical Note 4). It is formed by dropping the final -i of the adjectival and moving the accent toward the beginning of the word (oᒥokiˀi ∼ oˀoki, tiᒥisaˀi ∼ tiˀisa). These nominals are used in combination with na to describe a following nominal: oˀoki na ᒥhoˀn̄ 'big book,' tiˀisa na zibiki 'small dictionary,' etc.

Thus, oᒥokiˀi MODIFYING A FOLLOWING NOMINAL is interchangeable with oˀoki na, and tiᒥisaˀi with tiˀisa na.

DRILLS

A. Substitution Drill

1.	Who is reading [it]?	Daˀre ḡa ᒥyoˀn̄de (i)masu kaⵥ
2.	Who is calling?	Daˀre ḡa yoᒥn̄de (i)maˀsu kaⵥ
3.	Who is fixing [it]?	Daˀre ḡa naᒥoˀsite (i)masu kaⵥ
4.	Who is speaking?	Daˀre ḡa haᒥnaˀsite (i)masu kaⵥ
5.	Who is saying [it]?	Daˀre ḡa iˀtte (i)maˀsu kaⵥ
6.	Who is renting (or borrowing) [it]?	Daˀre ḡa kaᒥrite (i)maˀsu kaⵥ
7.	Who is listening (or asking)?	Daˀre ḡa kiᒥite (i)maˀsu kaⵥ

---

[1] This verbal, in all its forms, is usually used only in reference to the speaker.

8. Who is cutting [it]?   Da⌉re ḡa ⌐ki⌐tte (i)masu ka⌟
9. Who is looking at [it]?   Da⌉re ḡa ⌐mi⌐te (i)masu ka⌟
10. Who is waiting?   Da⌉re ḡa ⌐ma⌐tte (i)masu ka⌟

B. Substitution Drill

1. Whom are you calling?   Da⌉re o yo⌐ñde (i)ma⌐su ka⌟
2. Whom are you waiting for?   Da⌉re o ⌐ma⌐tte (i)masu ka⌟ [1]
3. Whom are you looking at?   Da⌉re o ⌐mi⌐te (i)masu ka⌟
4. What are you looking at?   Na⌉ni o ⌐mi⌐te (i)masu ka⌟
5. What are you reading?   Na⌉ni o ⌐yo⌐ñde (i)masu ka⌟
6. What are you fixing?   Na⌉ni o na⌐o⌐site (i)masu ka⌟
7. What are you saying?   Na⌉ni o i⌐tte (i)ma⌐su ka⌟
8. What are you listening to?   Na⌉ni o ki⌐ite (i)ma⌐su ka⌟
9. What are you cutting?   Na⌉ni o ⌐ki⌐tte (i)masu ka⌟
10. What are you writing?   Na⌉ni o ⌐ka⌐ite (i)masu ka⌟

C. Substitution Drill

1. I'm going to read this   Ke⌉sa ko⌐no siñbuñ (o) yomima⌉su.
   paper this morning.
2. I'm reading this paper   Ke⌉sa ko⌐no siñbuñ (o) yo⌐ñde (i)ma-
   this morning.   su.
3. I was reading this paper   Ke⌉sa ko⌐no siñbuñ (o) yo⌐ñde (i)ma-
   this morning.   sita.
4. I read this paper this   Ke⌉sa ko⌐no siñbuñ (o) yomima⌉sita.
   morning.
5. Let's read this paper   Ke⌉sa ko⌐no siñbuñ (o) yomimasyo⌉o.
   this morning.
6. He's probably going to   Ke⌉sa ko⌐no siñbuñ (o) yo⌉mu desyoo.
   read this paper this
   morning.
7. He's probably reading   Ke⌉sa ko⌐no siñbuñ (o) yo⌐ñde (i)⌐ru
   this paper this morn-   desyo⌐o.
   ing.
8. Do you suppose he's   Ke⌉sa ko⌐no siñbuñ (o) yo⌐ñde (i)⌐ru
   reading this paper this   desyo⌐o ka.
   morning?
9. Shall we (or I) read this   Ke⌉sa ko⌐no siñbuñ (o) yomimasyo⌉o
   paper this morning?   ka.
10. Please read this paper   Ke⌉sa ko⌐no siñbuñ (o) yo⌐ñde kuda-
   this morning.   sai.

---

[1] Note: X o ⌐ma⌐tu 'wait for X,' 'await X.'

D.   Substitution Drill

1.   I'm not especially busy.   Betu ni i⌈soḡa⌉siku a⌐rimase⌐n̄.
2.   I don't especially want to   Betu ni i⌈kitaku arimase⌐n̄.
     go.
3.   It doesn't especially mat-   Betu ni ka⌈maimase⌐n̄.
     ter.
4.   I'm not in any special   Betu ni i⌈soḡimase⌐n̄.
     hurry.
5.   It isn't especially strange.   Betu ni ⌈he⌉n̄ zya a⌐rimase⌐n̄.
6.   It isn't especially far.   Betu ni to⌈oku arimase⌐n̄.
7.   It isn't especially difficult.   Betu ni mu⌈zukasiku arimase⌐n̄.
8.   It isn't especially rude.   Betu ni si⌈tu⌉ree zya a⌐rimase⌐n̄.

E.   Substitution Drill

1.   Nobody answers.   Da⌈re mo demase⌐n̄.
2.   Nobody knows. or I don't   Da⌈re mo sirimase⌐n̄.
     know anybody.
3.   Nobody understands.   Da⌈re mo wakarimase⌐n̄.
4.   Nobody can.   Da⌈re mo dekimase⌐n̄.
5.   Nobody is here.   Da⌈re mo imase⌐n̄.
6.   Nobody wants to do [it].   Da⌈re mo sitaku arimase⌐n̄.
7.   Nobody is busy.   Da⌈re mo isoḡa⌉siku a⌐rimase⌐n̄.
8.   Nobody is sick.   Da⌈re mo byooki zya arimase⌐n̄.
9.   Nobody is out (of the   Da⌈re mo ru⌉su zya a⌐rimase⌐n̄.
     house).
10. Nobody has free time.   Da⌈re mo hima ḡa arimase⌐n̄.

F.   Substitution Drill

1.   I know—because I have   Wa⌈takusi wa zo⌉n̄zite orimasu—
     Mr. Ito's card.   I⌐too-san no meesi (ḡa) gozaima⌐-
                                               su kara.

2.   I know—because I read the   Wa⌈takusi wa zo⌉n̄zite orimasu—si-
     paper.   ⌐n̄bun (o) yomima⌐sita kara.
3.   I know—because I looked at   Wa⌈takusi wa zo⌉n̄zite orimasu—de-
     the phone book.   ⌐n̄watyoo (o) mima⌐sita kara.
4.   I know—because I heard [it]   Wa⌈takusi wa zo⌉n̄zite orimasu—to-
     from a friend.   ⌐modati kara kikima⌐sita kara.
5.   I know—because I studied   Wa⌈takusi wa zo⌉n̄zite orimasu—
     hard.   ⌐yo⌐ku be⌐n̄kyoo-sima⌐sita kara.
6.   I know—because I asked a   Wa⌈takusi wa zo⌉n̄zite orimasu—
     policeman.   zyu⌐n̄sa ni kikima⌐sita kara.
7.   I know—because I go there   Wa⌈takusi wa zo⌉n̄zite orimasu—
     a good deal.   ⌐yo⌐ku a⌐soko e mairima⌐su ka-
                                              ra.
8.   I know—because I telephone   Wa⌈takusi wa zo⌉n̄zite orimasu—
     him every day.   a⌐no⌐ hito ni ⌐ma⌐initi de⌐n̄wa
                                              (o) kakema⌐su kara.

9. I know—because I come
   (or go) by car.

Waᵗtakusi wa zoˀñzite orimasu—ku-
ᵗruma de mairima⁴su kara.

10. I know—because I was able
    to hear well.

Waᵗtakusi wa zoˀñzite orimasu—
ᵗyo⁴ku kiᵗkoema⁴sita kara.

G. Substitution Drill

1. Call Mr. Okada—because
   he has a phone call.

Okada-kuñ (o) yoñde—deᵗñwa da⁴
kara.

2. Call Mr. Okada—because
   this won't do.

Okada-kuñ (o) yoñde—koᵗma⁴ru
kara.

3. Call Mr. Okada—because
   I want to see [him].

Okada-kuñ (o) yoñde—aᵗita⁴i kara.

4. Call Mr. Okada—because
   I'm in a hurry.

Okada-kuñ (o) yoñde—iᵗso⁴g̱u kara.

5. Call Mr. Okada—because
   I want to talk [to him].

Okada-kuñ (o) yoñde—haᵗnasita⁴i
kara.

6. Call Mr. Okada—because
   it's out of order.

Okada-kuñ (o) yoñde—koᵗsyoo da⁴
kara.

7. Call Mr. Okada—because
   I'm going out for a minute.

Okada-kuñ (o) yoñde— tyo⁴tto de-
ᵗkakeru⁴ kara.

8. Call Mr. Okada—because
   it's no good.

Okada-kuñ (o) yoñde—daᵗme⁴ da
kara.

H. Substitution Drill

1. Please tell him that I'll be
   waiting in front of the Maru-biru. [1]

Maᵗru-biru no maˀe de ᵗmaˀtte (i)ru
kara, soˀo itte kudasaˀi.

2. Please tell him that I want
   to talk [to him] at (lit.
   from) about 3:30.

Sañ-zi-hañ-ḡoro kara haᵗnasitaˀi kara, soˀo itte kudasaˀi.

3. Please tell him that I want
   to go home early today.

Kyoˀo ᵗhaˀyaku kaᵗeritaˀi kara, soˀo
itte kudasaˀi.

4. Please tell him that I'll telephone again later.

Maᵗta aˀto de deñwa-suruˀ kara,
soˀo itte kudasaˀi.

5. Please tell him that I'm going to the office by bus today.

Kyoˀo k̄aisya e ᵗbaˀsu de iᵗku⁴ kara,
soˀo itte kudasaˀi.

6. Please tell him that I'll be
   studying at home tonight.

Koˀñbañ uᵗti de beñkyoo-site (i)ruˀ kara, soˀo itte kudasaˀi.

7. Please tell him that our
   car is out of order.

Uti no kuruma (wa) koˀsyoo daˀ kara,
soˀo itte kudasaˀi.

---

[1] Lit. 'I'll be waiting in front of the Maru-biru so please say [it] that way.'

8. Please tell him that I'll
    be busy through tomorrow.

A⌐sita⌐ made i⌐soḡasi⌐i kara, so⌐o itte kudasa⌐i.

9. Please tell him that school
    lasts (lit. is) until 4.

Ga⌐kkoo (wa) yo⌐-zi made da kara,
so⌐o itte kudasa⌐i.

10. Please tell him that Mr. Ta-
    naka is on vacation this
    month.

Ta⌐naka-sañ (wa) koñḡetu yasumi⌐ da
kara, so⌐o itte kudasa⌐i.

I.   Response Drill

1. To⌐oi⌐ desu ka꜔   Iie, to⌐oku arimase⌐ñ.
2. He⌐ñ desu ka꜔   Iie, he⌐ñ zya a⌐rimase⌐ñ.
3. I⌐soḡasi⌐i desu ka꜔   Iie, i⌐soḡa⌐siku a⌐rimase⌐ñ.
4. A⌐na⌐ta (wa) ko̅re (o) go⌐zo⌐-
    ñzi desu ka꜔   Iie, zo⌐ñzimase⌐ñ.
5. A⌐no ka⌐ta (wa) ko̅re (o) go-
    ⌐zo⌐ñzi desu ka꜔   Iie, go⌐zo⌐ñzi zya a⌐rimase⌐ñ. [1]
6. Ko⌐syoo de⌐su ka꜔   Iie, ko⌐syoo zya arimase⌐ñ.

J.   Level Drill [2]

1. Yu⌐kku⌐ri neḡaimasu.   Yu⌐kku⌐ri oneḡai- { simasu.
                                               itasimasu.

2. Yo⌐bimasyo⌐o ka.   O⌐yobi- { simasyo⌐o
                                      itasimasyo⌐o } ka.

3. Si⌐rimase⌐ñ.   Zo⌐ñzimase⌐ñ.
4. Ke⌐sa da⌐iḡaku e ikima⌐sita.   Ke⌐sa da⌐iḡaku e mairima⌐sita.
5. Si⌐tu⌐ree-simasita.   Si⌐tu⌐ree-itasimasita.
6. Ta⌐naka-sañ ni aima⌐sita.   Ta⌐naka-sañ ni ome ni kakarima⌐si-
                               ta.
7. O⌐de⌐ñwa si⌐masyo⌐o ka. O⌐de⌐ñwa i⌐tasimasyo⌐o ka.
8. So⌐o tutaema⌐su.   So⌐o otutae- { sima⌐su.
                                          itasima⌐su.

K.   Level Drill [3]

1. Kosyoo da ne?   (M)   Ko⌐syoo de⌐su ne?

---

[1] Compare the preceding humble answer (referring to the speaker) with this
honorific answer (referring to someone else).

[2] In each case, sentences on the right are humble equivalents of the sentences on the left.

[3] Based on Grammatical Note 2. In each case, the sentence on the right is
a formal equivalent of the sentence on the left. Informal sentences marked (M)
occur predominantly in men's speech and those marked (W) predominantly in
women's speech.

2. I⌐so͞gasi⌐i?   I⌐so͞gasi⌐i desu ka↲

3. He⌐ñ ⌐ne⌐e.   (W)   He⌐ñ desu ⌐ne⌐e.

4. I⌐ma ⌐tyo⌐tto dekakeru   (M)   I⌐ma ⌐tyo⌐tto de⌐kakema⌐su yo↲
   yo↲

5. Kikoeru?   Ki⌐koema⌐su ka↲

6. Wa⌐ru⌐i yo↲   (M)   Wa⌐ru⌐i desu yo↲

7. Do⌐re (o) ⌐yo⌐mu?   Do⌐re (o) yo⌐mima⌐su ka↲

8. So⌐o yo↲   (W)   So⌐o desu yo↲

9. Na⌐ñ de ⌐ki⌐ru?   Na⌐ñ de ki⌐rima⌐su ka↲

10. Zu⌐ibuñ tooi yo↲   (M)   Zu⌐ibuñ to⌐oi⌐ desu yo↲

L. Expansion Drill

1. Telephone. [1]   Deñwa-site.
    YOU telephone.   A⌐na⌐ta ḡa deñwa-site.
    [I] am busy so YOU tele-   I⌐so͞gasi⌐i kara, a⌐na⌐ta ḡa deñwa-si-
    phone.   te.
    [I] am very busy so YOU   To⌐ttemo iso͞gasi⌐i kara, a⌐na⌐ta ḡa
    telephone.   deñwa-site.
    I am very busy so YOU   Bo⌐ku wa to⌐ttemo iso͞gasi⌐i kara,
    telephone.   a⌐na⌐ta ḡa deñwa site.

2. Would you speak?   Ha⌐na⌐site ku⌐dasaimase⌐ñ ka↲
    Would you speak in a loud   O⌐oki na ⌐ko⌐e de ha⌐na⌐site ku⌐da-
    voice?   saimase⌐ñ ka↲
    Would you speak in a louder   Mo⌐tto ⌐o⌐oki na ⌐ko⌐e de ha⌐na⌐site
    voice?   ku⌐dasaimase⌐ñ ka↲
    I can't hear so would you   Ki⌐koemase⌐ñ kara, mo⌐tto ⌐o⌐oki na
    speak in a louder voice?   ⌐ko⌐e de ha⌐na⌐site ku⌐dasaima-
                                                se⌐ñ ka↲
    I can't hear very well so   Yo⌐ku ki⌐koemase⌐ñ kara, mo⌐tto
    would you speak in a   ⌐o⌐oki na ⌐ko⌐e de ha⌐na⌐site ku⌐-
    louder voice?   ⌐dasaimase⌐ñ ka↲

3. It's all right (I tell you).   Da⌐izyo⌐obu desu yo↲
    Now it's all right (I tell   I⌐ma wa da⌐izyo⌐obu desu yo↲
    you).
    It was out of order but   Ko⌐syoo de⌐sita ḡa, i⌐ma wa da⌐i-
    now it's all right (I   zyo⌐obu desu yo↲
    tell you).
    Yesterday it was out of   Ki⌐no⌐o wa ko⌐syoo de⌐sita ḡa, i⌐ma
    order but now it's all   wa da⌐izyo⌐obu desu yo↲
    right (I tell you).

---

[1] This English sentence and its Japanese equivalent are equally abrupt.

4. It can't be heard, can
    it!

    [He] speaks in a low voice,
    so you can't hear [him]
    (isn't that so)!

    [He] always speaks in a low
    voice so you can't hear
    [him] (isn't that so)!

    He always speaks in a low
    voice so you can't hear
    [him] (isn't that so)!

Ki⌐koemase⌐n̄ ⌐ne⌐e.

Ti⌐isa na ⌐ko⌐e de ha⌐na⌐su kara,
ki⌐koemase⌐n̄ ⌐ne⌐e.

I⌐tu mo ⌐ti⌐isa na ⌐ko⌐e de ha⌐na⌐su
kara, ki⌐koemase⌐n̄ ⌐ne⌐e.

A⌐no⌐ hito (wa) ⌐i⌐tu mo ⌐ti⌐isa na
⌐ko⌐e de ha⌐na⌐su kara, ki⌐koe-
mase⌐n̄ ⌐ne⌐e.

5. I'll convey [the message].
    I'll convey [it] all.
    I'll convey all of that.
    I'll convey all of that by
    telephone.
    I'll convey all of that by
    telephone now.

O⌐tutae-sima⌐su.
Ze⌐n̄bu otutae-simasu.
Sore (o) ⌐ze⌐n̄bu otutae-simasu.
Den̄wa de so̐re (o) ⌐ze⌐n̄bu otutae-
simasu.
I⌐ma den̄wa de so̐re (o) ⌐ze⌐n̄bu otu-
tae-simasu.

6. Would you say [it]?
    Would you say [it] once
    more?
    I didn't understand so would
    you say [it] once more?

    I didn't understand your
    name so would you say
    [it] once more?
    I'm sorry but I didn't under-
    stand your name so would
    you say it once more?

O⌐ssya⌐tte ku⌐dasaimase⌐n̄ ka↵
Mo⌐o iti-do ossya⌐tte ku⌐dasaima-
se⌐n̄ ka↵
Wa⌐karimase⌐n̄ desita kara, mo⌐o
iti-do ossya⌐tte ku⌐dasaimase⌐n̄
ka↵
O⌐namae (ḡa) wakarimase⌐n̄ desita
kara, mo⌐o iti-do ossya⌐tte ku⌐da-
saimase⌐n̄ ka↵
Su⌐mimase⌐n̄ ḡa; o⌐namae (ḡa) waka-
rimase⌐n̄ desita kara, mo⌐o iti-do
ossya⌐tte ku⌐dasaimase⌐n̄ ka↵

SHORT INFORMAL DIALOGUES

(M = man; W = woman; X = either)

1. X(1): Iku?
    X(2): Iku.

2. X: I⌐i?
    M: Da⌐me⌐ da yo.

3. W: Ki⌐ree ⌐ne⌐e.
    M: So⌐o da ⌐ne⌐e.

4. X: Wa⌐ka⌐ru?
    M: Wa⌐ka⌐ru yo↵

5. X: Kosyoo?
    W: So⌐o yo↵

6. M: He˥ñ da ⌐ne⌐e.
   W: So˥o ⌐ne⌐e.

7. X: Sore ⌐do˥o?
   M: O⌐mosiro˥i yo⌟

8. M(1): Sore ⌐na˥ni?
   M(2): A⌐tarasi˥i deñwatyoo.
   M(1): Tyo˥tto ⌐mi⌐sete. . . . O⌐oki˥i ⌐ne˥e.
   M(2): So˥o da ⌐ne˥e.

9. M(1): Tyo˥tto, ta˥kusii yo⌐bu⌐ kara, koko de ⌐ma˥tte te.¹
   M(2): Bo⌐ku ḡa deñwa-suru˥ kara.
   M(1): I˥i yo. Boku ḡa suru yo.

10. X: Su˥misu-sañ si̅tte ru?
    M: E˥e, yo˥ku.
    X: A⌐no˥ hito ni̅hoñḡo de⌐ki˥ru?
    M: Na⌐kanaka yo˥ku de⌐ki⌐ru yo⌟ Yo-⌐neñ-ḡu⌐rai ⌐ma⌐e kara be⌐ñkyoo
        site ru⌐ kara.

SUPPLEMENTARY TELEPHONE CONVERSATIONS

1. Jones: Mo˥simosi⌟
   Secretary: Ni⌐hoñḡo-ga˥kkoo de gozaimasu.
   Jones: Ta⌐isi˥kañ no ⌐Zyo˥oñzu desu ḡa; kyo˥o wa ga⌐kkoo e iki-
               mase˥ñ² kara, Sa⌐too-sañ ni so˥o itte kudasa˥i.
   Secretary: Wa⌐karima˥sita. Do˥o mo a⌐ri˥ḡatoo gozaimasita.
   Jones: O⌐neḡai-sima˥su. Sayonara.

2. Mr. Matsumoto: Mo˥simosi⌟ Ta˥mura-sañ no o⌐taku de⌐su ka⌟
   Mrs. Tamura: Ha˥i. Sa⌐yoo de gozaima˥su.
   Mr. Matsumoto: Kotira wa Ma⌐tumoto de˥su ḡa; su⌐mimase˥ñ ḡa, otonari
                   no ⌐U˥eno ⌐Ha˥ruko - sañ o yo⌐ñde kudasaimase⌐ñ ka⌟
   Mrs. Tamura: Ha˥i. Syo˥osyoo o⌐mati-kudasaima⌐se.

                          . . . . .

   Miss Ueno: Mo˥simosi. O⌐matase-itasima˥sita.
   Mr. Matsumoto: Aa, Ha˥ruko-sañ? Bo˥ku desu. O⌐ge˥ñki?
   Miss Ueno: E˥e. A⌐na˥ta mo?

---

¹ Ma˥tte (i)te 'be waiting,' 'stay here and wait.'

² Compare Japanese gakkoo e IKIMASEN̄ (lit. 'I'm not going to school') and
English 'I'm not COMING to school (where you are).

Mr. Matsumoto:	Ko˺ñbañ o˺hima?
Miss Ueno:	E˺e. Hi˹ma de˺su ḡa_
Mr. Matsumoto:	Ni˹tiḡeki[1] e ikimase˺ñ ka⌐
Miss Ueno:	A˹ri˺ḡatoo. Na˺ñ-zi kara?
Mr. Matsumoto:	Go-˹zi-ha˺ñ kara. Go˺-zi ni o˹taku e ikima˹su yo.
Miss Ueno:	Zya˺a, ma˺tte masu kara, o˹neḡai-sima˺su.
Mr. Matsumoto:	Zya˺a, ma˺ta a˺to de.
Miss Ueno:	E˺e. Notihodo ne? Do˺o mo a˹ri˺ḡatoo.
Mr. Matsumoto:	Sayonara.
Miss Ueno:	Sayonara.

3.	Mr. Yamada:	Mo˺simosi_
	Maid:	Mo˺simosi_ Ya˹mada de gozaima˺su. [2]
	Mr. Yamada:	Yo˺si-sañ?
	Maid:	Ha˺a, sa˹yoo de gozaima˺su. Da˹ñnasa˺ma de irassyai-masu ka⌐
	Mr. Yamada:	E˺e, bo˺ku. O˺kusañ iru?
	Maid:	Iie, tyo˺tto o˹dekake ni narima˺sita ḡa_
	Mr. Yamada:	A˺a, so˺o. Ano ne? Ko˺ñbañ ne?
	Maid:	Ha˺a.
	Mr. Yamada:	A˹merika-taisi˺kañ no ˹Su˺misu-sañ no o˹taku e iku˹ ka ra ne?
	Maid:	Ha˺a.
	Mr. Yamada:	O˺kusañ ni so˹o itte˺ yo.
	Maid:	Ha˺a, o˹tutae-itasima˺su. Na˹ñ-zi-ḡo˺ro o˹kaeri ni narima˺su ka⌐
	Mr. Yamada:	Zyu˹uiti-zi suḡi˺ ni ˹na˹ru yo.
	Maid:	Ha˺a, wa˹karima˺sita.
	Mr. Yamada:	Zya˺a.
	Maid:	Go˹meñ-kudasaima˺se.

English Equivalents

1.	Jones:	Hello.
	Secretary:	This is the Japanese Language School.
	Jones:	This is [Mr.] Jones from the Embassy. Please tell Mr. Sato that I'm not coming to school today.
	Secretary:	Certainly. Thank you very much [for calling].
	Jones:	Please take care of this for me. Goodbye.

---

[1] Abbreviated name of Nihoñ-gekizyoo, a theater in Tokyo.

[2] A maid usually answers the telephone with the name of her employer.

2. Mr. Matsumoto: Hello. Is this the Tamura residence?
   Mrs. Tamura: Yes, it is.
   Mr. Matsumoto: This is [Mr.] Matsumoto. I'm sorry to bother you but would you call Miss Haruko Ueno (who lives) next door?
   Mrs. Tamura: Yes. Just a moment, please.

                          . . . . .

   Miss Ueno: Hello. (I'm sorry to have kept you waiting.)
   Mr. Matsumoto: Oh, Haruko? It's me. How are you?
   Miss Ueno: Fine. And you?
   Mr. Matsumoto: Are you free tonight?
   Miss Ueno: Yes, I'm free but [why do you ask?]
   Mr. Matsumoto: Would you like to go to the Nichigeki?
   Miss Ueno: Thanks. (From) what time?
   Mr. Matsumoto: (From) 5:30. I'll come to your house at 5.
   Miss Ueno: Well, I'll be waiting so do [come].
   Mr. Matsumoto: Well, [I'll talk to you] again later.
   Miss Ueno: Yes, later (right?). Thanks very much.
   Mr. Matsumoto: Goodbye.
   Miss Ueno: Goodbye.

3. Mr. Yamada: Hello.
   Maid: Hello. This is the Yamada residence.
   Mr. Yamada: Yoshi?
   Maid: Yes. Is this Mr. [Yamada]?
   Mr. Yamada: Yes, it's me. Is Mrs. [Yamada] in?
   Maid: No. She went out for a while but [is there anything I can do?]
   Mr. Yamada: Oh. Say! Tonight—
   Maid: Yes.
   Mr. Yamada: I'm going to the home of Mr. Smith from the American Embassy so—
   Maid: Yes.
   Mr. Yamada: Tell Mrs. [Yamada] (that).
   Maid: Yes. I'll give her the message. About what time will you be home?
   Mr. Yamada: It will be after 11.
   Maid: I understand.
   Mr. Yamada: Well then. . . .
   Maid: Goodbye.

EXERCISES

1. Make the following telephone calls:

   a. Call the Tanaka home and ask if Mrs. Tanaka is in.
   b. Call the American Embassy and leave a message for Mr. Smith that you are not coming today.
   c. Call your home and tell the maid that you are going to the Satos' house and will be home about 11:30.

      d. Call a friend and ask her to go to the Nichigeki with you. Tell her you'll come to her house at 2:30.

      e. Call Mr. Sato's house and ask Mr. Sato to call (i.e. summon) Mr. Yoshio Ito who lives next door. [1]

      f. Call Mr. Yamamoto's house and ask when Mr. Yamamoto is returning to Tokyo.

      g. Report that Extension 636 is out of order and request that it be fixed.

2.   Leave the following telephone messages for Mr. Yoshida:

      a. You'll be waiting in front of the Nichigeki at 6 this evening.

      b. You want to see him before 3 o'clock today.

      c. You are leaving the office early today because your wife is sick.

      d. You'll telephone him from Osaka tomorrow morning at about 10:30.

      e. You'll be at Tokyo University today until 5:30.

      f. Your new office telephone number is 481-7600.

      g. Mr. Smith arrived at Yokohama last night and is now at the Imperial Hotel.

3.   Practice the conversations preceding the Exercises, using other politeness and/or formality levels.

4.   Practice the Basic Dialogues with appropriate variations.

---

[1] This is normal procedure when someone does not have a telephone.

Lesson 14. Eating and Drinking

BASIC DIALOGUES: FOR MEMORIZATION

(a)

(Tanaka has taken Smith to a restaurant)

Waitress

already or yet or now
  already or soon now
place an order

mo⌐o /+ affirmative/

tyuumoñ-suru   or
  tyuumoñ-itasu⁺ or
  go⌐tyuumoñ-nasa⌐ru⁺

1. Have you ordered yet?

Mo⌐o go⌐tyuumoñ-nasaima⌐sita ka⌐

Tanaka

it is yet [to happen]
not yet

ma⌐da da
ma⌐da /+ negative/

2. No, not yet.

Iie, ma⌐da desu.

    or

No, I haven't (ordered yet).

Iie, ma⌐da tyu⌐umoñ-simase⌐ñ.

Waitress

into what?

na⌐ñ ni   or
na⌐ni ni

3. What would you like?
(Lit. Into what shall I make
[it]?)

Na⌐ñ ni i⌐tasimasyo⌐o ka.

Tanaka (to Smith)

thing
eat

mo⌐no⌐
ta⌐be⌐ru /-ru/   or
  itadaku⁺ /-u/ or
  mesiaḡaru⁺ /-u/

4. What (kind of things) shall
we eat?

Do⌐ñna mo⌐no⌐ (o) ta⌐bemasyo⌐o
ka.

Smith

5. What WOULD be good?

Na⌐ni ḡa yo⌐rosi⌐i desyoo ka ⌐ne⌐e.

Waitress

tempura (kind of Japa-
nese food)

teñpura

6. How about tempura?

Teñpura (wa) i⌐ka⌐ḡa de go⌐zaima-
syo⌐o ka.

227

Tanaka (to Smith)

into tempura   teñpura ni
make it tempura or   teñpura ni suru
    decide on tempura
7. Shall we decide on tempura?   Te⌐ñ⌐pura ni simasyo⌐o ka.

Smith

8. That will be fine!   Ke⌐kkoo desu ⌐ne⌐e.

Tanaka (to waitress)

9. Then let's make [it] that   Zya, so⌐o simasyo⌐o.
    (way).

        Japanese rice wine   sake   or
                                                         osake +

        bring (of things)   mo⌐tte ku⌐ru
10. And please bring some sake   Sore kara, sa⌐ke mo motte⌐ kite
    too.   kudasai.

(to Smith)

is cold (of weather)   sa⌐mu⌐i /-ku/
is hot   a⌐tu⌐i /-ku/
is delicious   oisii /-ku/
11. It's cold so hot sake will   Sa⌐mu⌐i kara, a⌐tu⌐i sake (wa) o⌐i-
    probably taste good, won't   si⌐i desyoo ne?
    it?

(b)

(Tanaka has invited Smith to have something to drink with him)

Tanaka

beer   bi⌐iru
drink   no⌐mu /-u/   or
                                                         itadaku˦/-u/   or
                                                         mesiaḡaru˦/-u/
12. Will you have some beer?   Bi⌐iru (o) me˧siaḡarima˦su ka⌐

Smith

13. Thank you. I will (drink).   A⌐ri⌐ḡatoo gozaimasu. I⌐tadakima⌐-
                                                   su.

Tanaka (to waitress)

14. Two bottles of beer, please.   Bi⌐iru (o) ⌐ni⌐-hoñ oneḡai-simasu.
    (Lit. I'd like beer to the ex-
    tent of two long, cylindrical
    units.)

. . .

Tanaka (when beer is brought)

15. Here you are.   Do⌐ozo.

Smith

16. (I'll have some.)   I⌐tadakima⌐su.

    is cold   tumetai /-ku/
17. Isn't it delicious—cold   O⌐isi⌐i desu ⌐ne⌐e—tu⌐metai bi⌐iru
    beer!   wa.

    . . .

Tanaka

    one glassful <u>or</u> cupful   i⌐p-pai
18. How about another glass?   Mo⌐o i⌐p-pai i⌐ka⌐ḡa desu ka⌐

Smith

    half   ha⌐ṅbu⌐ṅ
19. Well, just half, please.   Zya⌐a, ha⌐ṅbuṅ dake oneḡai-sima⌐su.

    . . .

Tanaka

20. Won't you have a little   Mo⌐o suko⌐si me⌐siaḡarimase⌐ṅ
    more?   ka⌐

Smith

21. No, thank you. (Lit. No,   Iie, mo⌐o ta⌐kusa⌐ṅ desu.
    already it's a lot <u>or</u> fine.)   <u>or</u>
                                                    Iie, mo⌐o ⌐ke⌐kkoo desu.

    a feast <u>or</u> delicious   gotisoo   <u>or</u>
    food and/or drink   gotisoosama +
22. It was delicious.   Go⌐tisoosama de⌐sita.

(c)

(Smith and Yamamoto meet on the street)

Yamamoto

    is pale   a⌐o⌐i /-ku/
    face <u>or</u> expression   kao
    be pale   a⌐o⌐i kao o suru
23. Mr. Smith. You're pale!   Su⌐misu-saṅ. A⌐o⌐i ka⌐o (o) site
                                                    (i)ma⌐su yo⌐

24. What happened?   Do⌐o simasita ka.

Smith

    shrimp <u>or</u> prawn   ebi
    shrimp tempura   ebi no teṅpura
    become spoiled   i⌐ta⌐mu /-u/
    became spoiled (informal)   i⌐ta⌐ṅda
    spoiled shrimp   i⌐ta⌐ṅda ebi
    it was shrimp (informal)   e⌐bi da⌐tta
25. Last night I ate shrimp tem-   Yuube Giṅza de e⌐bi no teṅpura (o)
    pura in the Ginza (but) I got   tabema⌐sıta ḡa; i⌐ta⌐ṅda e⌐bi da⌐tta
    sick because it was bad   kara, byo⌐oki ni narima⌐sita yo.
    shrimp.

Yamamoto

26. That's too bad.   I⌐kemase⌝n̄ ⌐ne⌝e.

Smith

medicine   kusuri
take (of medicine)   no⌝mu /-u/
get well <u>or</u> recover   na⌐o⌝ru /-u/

27. I took some medicine but   Ku⌐suri (o) nomima⌝sita ḡa, ma⌝da
     I'm not better (lit. I have-   na⌐orimase⌐n̄.
     n't recovered) yet.

Yamamoto

28. Take care of yourself.   Odaizi ni.

(d)

(Tanaka and Smith are in a tea shop)

Smith

make a request <u>or</u>   ta⌐no⌝mu /-u/
  place an order
requested <u>or</u> ordered   ta⌐no⌝n̄da
  (informal)
probably requested <u>or</u> or-   ta⌐no⌝n̄da desyoo
  dered

29. You ordered a long time ago,   Zu⌝ibun̄ ⌐ma⌐e ni ta⌐no⌐n̄da desyoo?
     didn't you?

Tanaka

30. Yes. I ordered about ten   E⌝e.   Mo⌝o zyu⌐p-pun̄-ḡu⌝rai ⌐ma⌐e
     minutes ago (already) but   ni ta⌐nomima⌐sita ḡa, ma⌝da mo⌐tte
     they haven't brought [it]   kimase⌐n̄ ⌐ne⌝e.
     yet, have they!

Smith

31. They'll probably bring it   Mo⌝o mo⌐tte ku⌐ru desyoo ḡa, o⌐so⌝i
     soon now but they are   desu ⌐ne⌝e.
     slow, aren't they!

(e)

(Two friends are talking)

Tanaka

ate (informal)   ta⌝beta
32. Did you eat that?   A⌐re ta⌝beta?

Yamamoto

too much <u>or</u> so much   an̄mari / + affirmative/
is spicy <u>or</u> salty   ka⌐ra⌝i /-ku/
was spicy <u>or</u> salty (in-   ka⌝rakatta
  formal)

33. No, because it was too spicy.   Iie, an̄mari ⌐ka⌝rakatta kara.

Tanaka

34. It was spicy?   Ka⌐rakatta?

Yamamoto

    yeah   ñ [1]
    is bad-tasting   ma⌐zu⌐i /-ku/
    was bad-tasting (in-   ma⌐zukatta
      formal)
35. Yeah. It tasted awful!   N̄. To⌐ttemo ma⌐zukatta yo.

(f)

Tanaka

36. How about a cigarette?   Ta⌐bako do⌐o desu ka↵

Smith

    smoke   no⌐mu /-u/ or
                          suu /-u/
37. No, I don't smoke.   Iie, no⌐mimase⌐ñ.

Tanaka

38. You don't smoke? Since   No⌐mimase⌐ñ ka↵ I⌐tu kara desu
    when?   ka↵

Smith

    last month   se⌐ñḡetu
    quit or give up   yameru /-ru/
39. Why, I quit last month.   Se⌐ñḡetu ya⌐mema⌐sita yo.

ADDITIONAL EATING AND DRINKING VOCABULARY [2]

1. Shall we eat at a Ginza   Gi⌐nza no teñpuraya de tabemasyo⌐o
    tempura shop?   ka.

    dining room   syokudoo
    noodle shop   so⌐ba⌐ya or osobaya [+]
    restaurant (Japanese style)   ryo⌐ori⌐ya
    restaurant (Western style)   re⌐sutorañ

---

[1] Man's word, informal.

[2] Drill on the new words by substituting them for the underlined word in the pattern sentence.

sushi shop	su⌐si⌐ya <u>or</u> osusiya +
tearoom	kissateñ [1]

2. I'd like a little more
    <u>shrimp</u>.

<u>Ebi</u> (o) mo⌐o suko⌐si oneḡai-simasu.

fish	sakana <u>or</u> osakana +
meat	ni⌐ku⌐ <u>or</u> o⌐ni⌐ku +
fowl <u>or</u> chicken	tori
egg	ta⌐ma⌐ḡo
vegetable	yasai <u>or</u> o⌐ya⌐sai +
fruit	ku⌐da⌐mono
cooked rice <u>or</u> food	go⌐hañ
uncooked rice	ko⌐me⌐ <u>or</u> okome +
bread and butter	pa⌐ñ to ⌐ba⌐ta
toast	to⌐osuto
cake <u>or</u> sweets	o⌐ka⌐si +
noodles	so⌐ba <u>or</u> o⌐so⌐ba +
sashimi (raw fish)	sa⌐simi⌐ <u>or</u> osasimi +
sushi (rice with fish, sea-weed, egg, etc.)	su⌐si <u>or</u> o⌐su⌐si +
sukiyaki (stew of vegetables with meat or chicken or fish)	sukiyaki
tempura (batter-fried fish and vegetables)	teñpura
sugar	sa⌐to⌐o <u>or</u> osatoo +
salt	si⌐o⌐ <u>or</u> o⌐si⌐o +
pepper	ko⌐syo⌐o
soy sauce	syooyu <u>or</u> osyooyu +

3. Please bring some <u>sake</u>.

<u>Sa⌐ke</u> (o) motte⌐ kite kudasai.

cold water	mizu <u>or</u> omizu +
hot water	oyu +
coffee	ko⌐ohi⌐i
tea	otya +
black tea	kootya
milk	mi⌐ruku <u>or</u> gyuunyuu
ice	koori

4. Don't you want a <u>knife</u>?

Na⌐ihu wa i⌐rimase⌐ñ ka⌐

fork	ho⌐oku
spoon	su⌐pu⌐ñ

---

[1] With <u>kissateñ</u>, substitute no⌐mimasyo⌐o for ta⌐bemasyo⌐o in the pattern sentence.   Alternate accent: ki⌐ssa⌐teñ.

chopsticks	ha⌐si or o⌐ha⌐si+
dish	sara or osara+
bowl	wañ or owañ+
napkin	na⌐pukiñ
tray	oboñ+
glass for drinking	koppu
cup or small bowl (Japa- nese style)	tyawañ or o⌐tya⌐wañ+
cup (with handles)	ko⌐ohiizya⌐wañ

5. It's so spicy that it does-   A⌐ñmari kara⌐i kara, o⌐isiku arima-
    n't taste good.   se⌐ñ.

is weak or thin (of liquids) or is light (of colors)	usui /-ku/
is strong or thick (of liquids) or is dark (of colors)	ko⌐i /-ku/
is sweet or sugary or insufficiently salted	amai /-ku/
is bitter	ni⌐ga⌐i /-ku/
is acid or sour	su⌐ppa⌐i /-ku/

NOTES ON THE BASIC DIALOGUES

1. Tyuumoñ (honorific, gotyuumoñ †) is a commonly occurring nominal.
    Example: Gotyuumoñ wa? 'Your order?'

4. Mo⌐no⌐ refers to things that are tangible.

    Ta⌐be⌐ru 'eat' has a second honorific equivalent, o⌐tabe ni na⌐ru, which is
    less common than—and not quite as polite as—mesiagaru. Both honorific
    equivalents are, of course, used only in polite speech, in reference to the
    action of someone other than the speaker. Conversely, the humble equiv-
    alent refers to the action of the speaker, in polite speech.

10. Mo⌐tte ku⌐ru means literally 'come holding' or 'come carrying.' Mo⌐tte
    is the gerund of the verbal mo⌐tu 'hold,' 'have,' 'own.' Note also motte
    iku 'take (something somewhere)' (lit. 'go holding'). The polite equiva-
    lents of these words are: humble (†), mo⌐tte ma⌐iru honorific (†), mo⌐tte
    irassya⌐ru and mo⌐tte oide ni na⌐ru.

12. No⌐mu 'drink' has a second honorific equivalent, o⌐nomi ni na⌐ru, which
    is not quite as polite as mesiagaru. See the note on Sentence 4 above.

16. A guest always says i⌐tadakima⌐su (or an equivalent) just before beginning
    to eat or drink.

17. Tumetai is the general term meaning 'is cold,' but it is rarely used in
    reference to weather or atmosphere. Sa⌐mu⌐i, on the other hand, refers
    only to weather and atmosphere. A⌐tu⌐i is the opposite of both
    words.

21. The second alternative is more polite. Both are refusals of second or later helpings. Ke˹kkoo desu (without mo˺o) is a commonly occurring polite refusal of a first offering. I˹i and yorosii are also used as refusals in the same kinds of patterns.

22. Go˹tisoosama (de˹sita) is regularly said, upon finishing eating or drinking, by a guest to his host, or by a person served to the person who prepared or served the food and/or drink. It is also said by a guest at the conclusion of a visit during which refreshments were served.

29. Ta˹no˺mu 'make a request' is a verbal of more general meaning than tyuumoñ-suru 'place an order for something.' The thing requested is followed by particle o (or wa); the person of whom the request is made is followed by particle ni (i.e. the request is made TO someone). Compare:

I asked Mr. Tanaka (= I asked him a question):
  Ta˹naka-sañ ni kikima˺sita.
and
I asked Mr. Tanaka (= I asked him to do something):
  Ta˹naka-sañ ni tanomima˺sita.

Ta˹no˺mu [yo] is used by men as a plain informal equivalent of o˹negai-sima˺su.

Eating and Drinking Vocabulary:

In general, where alternate forms are given, women almost invariably use the polite alternant, whereas men use either, depending on the level of politeness being used. In a few cases—for example, otya 'tea' (the drink) and oyu 'hot water'—the polite form is regularly used by both men and women.

GRAMMATICAL NOTES

1. Verbals: Informal Past

The informal past of a verbal is made by changing the final -e of the gerund to -a. Thus, the informal past always ends in -ta or -da. It is the exact equivalent of the -ma˺sita form except that it is informal. The informal past and the gerund regularly have the same accent. Examples:

Informal Non-past (Citation Form)	Gerund	Informal Past	Formal Past
(-ru): ta˹be˺ru 'eat'	ta˹bete	ta˹beta	ta˹bema˺sita
mi˹ru 'see'	mi˹te	mi˹ta	mi˹ma˺sita
(-u): ma˹tu 'wait'	ma˹tte	ma˹tta	ma˹tima˺sita
ka˹eru 'return'	ka˹ette	ka˹etta	ka˹erima˺sita
kau 'buy'	katte	katta	ka˹ima˺sita
ha˹na˺su 'talk'	ha˹na˺site	ha˹na˺sita	ha˹nasima˺sita
ka˹ku 'write'	ka˹ite	ka˹ita	ka˹kima˺sita
iku 'go'	itte (irreg.)	itta	i˹kima˺sita

i「so「gu 'be in a hurry'	i「so」ide	i「so」ida	i「sogima」sita
yobu 'call'	yonde	yonda	yo「bima」sita
yo」mu 'read'	yo」nde	yo」nda	yo「mima」sita
(-aru): o「ssya」ru ǂ 'say'	o「ssya」tte	o「ssya」tta	o「ssyaima」sita
(Ir-reg.): ku」ru 'come	ki「te」	ki」ta [1]	ki「ma」sita
suru 'do'	site	sita	si「ma」sita

2. Adjectivals: Informal and Formal Past

The informal past of an adjectival is made by dropping the final -i of the non-past and adding -katta. If the non-past is unaccented, the past is regularly accented on the syllable immediately preceding the -katta; if the non-past is accented, the past is also accented but usually on an earlier syllable. [2]

Examples:

Informal Non-past (Citation Form)	Informal Past
amai 'is sweet'	a「ma」katta 'was sweet'
a「tu」i 'is hot'	a」tukatta 'was hot'
hu「ru」i 'is old'	hu」rukatta 'was old'
muzukasii 'is difficult'	mu「zukasi」katta 'was difficult'
ti「isa」i 'is small'	ti」isakatta 'was small'
ikitai 'wants to go'	i「kita」katta 'wanted to go'

The comparatively rare formal past consisting of an adjectival in its -i form + formal desita (for example, ta「ka」i desita 'it was expensive') has already been mentioned in Lesson 3, Grammatical Note 3(c). Another formal past adjectival pattern consists of an informal past adjectival ending in -katta + formal desu.

Examples:

	Informal Past	Formal Past
'was sweet'	a「ma」katta	a「ma」katta desu
'was hot'	a」tukatta	a」tukatta desu
'was old'	hu」rukatta	hu」rukatta desu
'was difficult'	mu「zukasi」katta	mu「zukasi」katta desu

---

[1] Note the difference in accent between this form and the gerund.

[2] However, an accented -tai word is accented on the -ta- syllable in both the non-past and the past: ta「beta」i 'want to eat,' ta「beta」katta 'wanted to eat.'

3.   Copula: Informal Past

The past of <u>da</u> is <u>da˥tta</u>. It is the informal equivalent of <u>de˥sita</u>, but like <u>da</u>, it follows nominals and particles but does NOT occur immediately after verbals or adjectivals. It regularly loses its accent following an accented word or phrase.

Examples:

Informal Non-past	Informal Past	Formal Past

tomodati da
  'it's a friend'
	to˹modati da˥tta
	  'it was a friend'
		to˹modati de˥sita

tomodati kara da
  'it's from a friend'
	to˹modati kara da˥tta
	  'it was from a
	    friend'
		to˹modati kara de˥sita

Now study the following chart:

	Affirmative Past Inflectional Patterns	
	Formal	Informal
Verbal Pattern	Verbal ending in -<u>ma˥sita</u> (wa˹karima˥sita)	Verbal ending in -<u>ta</u> (wa˹ka˥tta)

Adjectival Pattern	Adjectival ending in:
	-<u>katta</u> + <u>desu</u>
	  (o˥okikatta desu)
	or
	-<u>i</u> + <u>desita</u>
	  (o˹oki˥i desita)
		Adjectival ending in:
		-<u>katta</u>
		  (o˥okikatta)

Nominal[1] Pattern	Nominal + <u>de˥sita</u> (ho˥ñ desita)	Nominal + <u>da˥tta</u> (ho˥ñ datta)

4.   Uses of the Informal Past

In informal speech, the uses of verbal and adjectival informal past forms parallel the uses of corresponding non-past forms, but there are some differences between the uses of non-past <u>da</u> and past <u>da˥tta</u>.

The following are past equivalents of the non-past examples in Lesson 13, Grammatical Note 2. Compare and study them carefully.

---

[1] With or without following particle.

	Formal	Informal— Men and Women
'It was clear.'	Wa⌐karima⌐sita.	Wa⌐ka⌐tta.
'Was it clear?'	Wa⌐karima⌐sita ka˩	Wa⌐ka⌐tta?
'It was expensive.'	Ta⌐kakatta desu.	Ta⌐kakatta.
	(or Ta⌐ka⌐i desita.)	
'Was it expensive?'	Ta⌐kakatta desu ka˩	Ta⌐kakatta?
	(or Ta⌐ka⌐i desita ka˩)	
'It was true.'	Ho⌐ntoo de⌐sita.	Ho⌐ntoo da⌐tta.
'Was it true?'	Ho⌐ntoo de⌐sita ka˩	Ho⌐ntoo da⌐tta?

Informal — Men

'It was clear (I tell you).'	Wa⌐karima⌐sita yo˩	Wa⌐ka⌐tta yo˩
'It was clear, wasn't it?'	Wa⌐karima⌐sita ne?	Wa⌐ka⌐tta ne?
'It was expensive (I tell you).'	Ta⌐kakatta desu yo˩	Ta⌐kakatta yo˩
	(or Ta⌐ka⌐i desita yo˩)	
'It was expensive, wasn't it!'	Ta⌐kakatta desu ⌐ne⌐e.	Ta⌐kakatta ⌐ne⌐e.
	(or Ta⌐ka⌐i desita ⌐ne⌐e.)	
'It was true (I tell you).'	Ho⌐ntoo de⌐sita yo˩	Ho⌐ntoo da⌐tta yo˩
'It was true, wasn't it!'	Ho⌐ntoo de⌐sita ⌐ne⌐e.	Ho⌐ntoo da⌐tta ⌐ne⌐e.

In formal speech, the use of verbal and adjectival informal past forms before de⌐syo⌐o, and of verbal, adjectival, and copula informal past forms before particle <u>kara</u> 'so' is parallel to that of corresponding non-past forms. The accentuation is also parallel. Thus:

Informal (or formal[1]) past + formal tentative <u>de⌐syo⌐o</u> = 'it probably happened <u>or</u> was true' or 'it probably has happened <u>or</u> has been true' (formal)

Examples:

I⌐tta desyo⌐o. 'He probably went.'
Yo⌐nde (i)ta desyoo. 'He was probably reading.'
Wa⌐karima⌐sita desyoo? 'You understood, didn't you?'
Ta⌐kakatta desyoo? 'It was expensive, wasn't it?'
Mi⌐ta⌐katta desyoo. 'He probably wanted to see [it].'
Wa⌐ka⌐tta desyoo ka. 'Do you suppose he understood?' or 'Did you understand?' (indirect)

---

[1] A formal verbal may also occur before formal de⌐syo⌐o. The combination is more formal than an informal verbal + <u>de⌐syo⌐o</u>. See the third example following.

Informal (or formal[1]) past + kara 'so' = 'so-and-so happened (o r w a s true) so' or 'so-and-so has happened (or has been true) so'

Examples:

Kinoo ⌐yo⌐ku be⌐ñkyoo-sita⌐ kara, kyo⌐o wa ⌐yo⌐ku wakarimasu. 'I studied hard yesterday so today I understand well.'

Ta⌐kakatta kara, ka⌐imase⌐ñ desita.   'It was expensive so I didn't buy [it].'

Ma⌐zu⌐i ku⌐da⌐mono datta kara, a⌐ñmari tabemase⌐ñ desita. 'It was awful fruit so I didn't eat very much.'

In addition, the informal past da⌐tta (or, less commonly, formal de⌐sita) following a nominal or particle may occur before the formal tentative de⌐syo⌐o with the meaning 'it probably was or has been so-and-so.'

Thus:

Formal Non-past Tentative	Formal Past Tentative
To⌐modati desyo⌐o. 'He's probably a friend.'	To⌐modati da⌐tta desyoo. 'He was probably a friend.'
To⌐modati kara desyo⌐o. 'It's probably from a friend.'	To⌐modati kara da⌐tta desyoo. 'It was probably from a friend.'
Ho⌐ñtoo desyo⌐o. 'It's probably true.'	Ho⌐ñtoo de⌐sita desyoo? 'It was true, wasn't it?'

5.   mo⌐o + Affirmative; ma⌐da + Negative

Mo⌐o plus an affirmative means 'already' or 'yet,' or 'now already,' 'now—after a change has taken place,' 'soon now.'

Ma⌐da plus a negative means 'not yet.' The non-past negative indicates that something has not happened up to the present moment (cf. Lesson 1, Grammatical Note 1).

Ma⌐da occurs in the iie answer to a mo⌐o question, and mo⌐o occurs in the iie answer to a ma⌐da question:

Tanaka-sañ wa ⌐mo⌐o ki⌐ma⌐sita ka↲ 'Has Mr. Tanaka come already?'
     Ha⌐i, mo⌐o ki⌐ma⌐sita. 'Yes, he's come already.'
     Iie, ⌐ma⌐da ki⌐mase⌐ñ. 'No, he hasn't come yet.'

Tanaka-sañ wa ⌐ma⌐da ki⌐mase⌐ñ ka↲ 'Hasn't Mr. Tanaka come yet?'
     Ha⌐i, ⌐ma⌐da ki⌐mase⌐ñ. 'That's right. He hasn't come yet.'
     Iie, ⌐mo⌐o ki⌐ma⌐sita. 'That's not right. He's already come.'

---

[1] A formal inflected form may also occur before kara in formal speech, as a more formal alternant. Many examples have already occurred.

Ma⌐da desu, meaning literally 'It is yet [to happen],' is the closest Japanese equivalent of English 'It hasn't happened yet'; 'Not yet.'

WARNING: Do not confuse the mo⌐o described above with moo (unaccented) occurring with immediately following numbers and indefinite quantity words, meaning 'more.' Compare the following examples:

> Mo⌐o su⌐ko⌐si ta⌐bema⌐sita.   'I've eaten a little, already.'

> Mo⌐o suko⌐si ta⌐bema⌐sita.   'I ate a little more.'

6.   Goal Patterns with √suru

A nominal X + particle ni of goal + √suru[1] means 'make [something] into X,' 'make it X,' 'decide on X.' Compare the following pairs:

> A⌐sita simasyo⌐o. 'Let's do [it] tomorrow.'
> (Tells when we should do something)
>
> A⌐sita⌐ ni si⌐masyo⌐o. 'Let's make [it] tomorrow.' or
>   'Let's decide on tomorrow.'
> (Tells what day we should decide on)

> So⌐o sima⌐sita. 'We did [it] that way.'
> So⌐re ni sima⌐sita. 'We decided on that one.'

> Hi⌐to⌐-tu si⌐masyo⌐o. 'Let's do one.'
>
> Hi⌐to⌐-tu ni si⌐masyo⌐o. 'Let's make [it] into one' (for example, several sentences into one lesson, or several small packages into one bundle, or all the dough into one cake, etc.)

Similarly, a waitress asks Na⌐n ni (i⌐ta)simasyo⌐o ka '(Into) what shall I make [your order]?'

Now reread Lesson 10, Grammatical Note 4.

If √na⌐ru, preceded by nominal + ni, or the -ku form of an adjectival, is replaced by the corresponding form of √suru, the English equivalent changes from 'become X' to 'make [it] X.' Study the following pairs:[2]

---

[1] Or, of course, a more polite alternative.

[2] The subjects and objects of the English equivalents will vary, as always, depending on the context.

⎰ O⌐nazi ni narima⌐sita. 'They have become the same.'
⎱ O⌐nazi ni sima⌐sita. 'I made them the same.'

⎰ Na⌐niiro ni narima⌐sita ka↲ 'What color did it become?'
⎱ Na⌐niiro ni sima⌐sita ka↲ 'What color did you make it?'

⎰ O⌐okiku na⌐rima⌐sita. 'It has become big.'
⎱ O⌐okiku si⌐ma⌐sita. 'I made it big.'

⎰ A⌐tuku narimasu. 'It will become hot.'
⎱ A⌐tuku simasu. 'I will make it hot.'

7.   Counter -<u>hai</u>

Glassfuls and cupfuls are counted with the counter -<u>hai</u>, which combines
with numerals of Series I. Numbers from one to ten are:

i⌐p-pai ' 1 glassful <u>or</u> cupful'
ni⌐-hai ' 2 glassfuls <u>or</u> cupfuls'
sa⌐ñ-bai ' 3 glassfuls <u>or</u> cupfuls'
yo⌐ñ-hai ' 4 glassfuls <u>or</u> cupfuls'
go-hai ' 5 glassfuls <u>or</u> cupfuls'
ro⌐p-pai ' 6 glassfuls <u>or</u> cupfuls'
na⌐na⌐-hai <u>or</u> si⌐ti⌐-hai ' 7 glassfuls <u>or</u> cupfuls'
ha⌐p-pai <u>or</u> ha⌐ti⌐-hai ' 8 glassfuls <u>or</u> cupfuls'
kyu⌐u-hai ' 9 glassfuls <u>or</u> cupfuls'
zi⌐p-pai <u>or</u> zyu⌐p-pai ' 10 glassfuls <u>or</u> cupfuls'

na⌐ñ-bai 'how many glassfuls <u>or</u> cupfuls?'

DRILLS

A. Substitution Drill

1. Shall we decide on tem-   Te⌐ñpura ni simasyo⌐o ka.
    pura? [1]
2. Shall we decide on suki-   Su⌐kiyaki ni simasyo⌐o ka.
    yaki?
3. Shall we decide on sushi?   O⌐su⌐si ni si⌐masyo⌐o ka.
4. Shall we decide on noodles?   O⌐so⌐ba ni si⌐masyo⌐o ka.
5. Shall we decide on rice   Sa⌐ke ni simasyo⌐o ka.
    wine?

----

[1] Or 'Shall we (<u>or</u> I) make it tempura?'

6. Shall we decide on sa-
    shimi?

Sa⌐simi˥ ni si├masyo˦o ka.

7. Shall we decide on beer?

Bi˥iru ni si├masyo˦o ka.

8. Shall we decide on coffee?

Ko⌐ohi˥i ni si├masyo˦o ka.

9. Shall we decide on chick-
    en?

To⌐ri ni simasyo˥o ka.

10. Shall we decide on fish?

Sa⌐kana ni simasyo˥o ka.

B. Substitution Drill

1. Shall I make [it] hot?

A˥tuku si├masyo˦o ka.

2. It got hot.

A˥tuku na├rima˦sita.

3. It got cold.

Tu⌐metaku narima˥sita.

4. I'll make [it] cold.

Tu⌐metaku sima˥su yo↲

5. I'm going to make [it] into
    a school.

Ga⌐kkoo ni sima˥su yo↲

6. It has become a school.

Ga⌐kkoo ni narima˥sita.

7. It has become a company.

Ka⌐isya ni narima˥sita.

8. He'll probably make [it]
    into a company.

Ka⌐isya ni suru desyo˥o.

9. He'll probably make [it]
    cheap.

Ya˥suku su├ru desyo˦o.

10. It will probably get cheap.

Ya˥suku ├na˦ru desyoo.

C. Substitution Drill

1. I've been eating here for
    about two years now (al-
    ready).

Mo˥o ni-⌐nen-ḡu˥rai kŏko de ⌐ta˥bete
(i)masu yo↲

2. I've been eating here for
    about six months now.

Mo˥o ro⌐k-kaḡetu-ḡu˥rai kŏko de
⌐ta˥bete (i)masu yo↲

3. I've been buying here for
    about six months now.

Mo˥o ro⌐k-kaḡetu-ḡu˥rai kŏko de
ka⌐tte (i)ma˥su yo↲

4. I've been buying here for
    about two weeks now.

Mo˥o ni-⌐syuukañ-ḡu˥rai kŏko de ka-
⌐tte (i)ma˥su yo↲

5. I've been studying here
    for about two weeks now.

Mo˥o ni-⌐syuukañ-ḡu˥rai kŏko de be-
⌐ñkyoo-site (i)ma˥su yo↲

6. I've been studying here for
    about four hours now.

Mo˥o yo-⌐zikañ-ḡu˥rai kŏko de be⌐ñ-
kyoo-site (i)ma˥su yo↲

7. I've been reading here for
    about four hours now.

Mo˥o yo-⌐zikañ-ḡu˥rai kŏko de ⌐yo˥-
ñde (i)masu yo↲

8. I've been reading here for
    about twenty minutes now.

Mo˥o ni⌐zip-puñ-ḡu˥rai kŏko de ⌐yo˥-
ñde (i)masu yo↲

9. I've been waiting here for
    about twenty minutes now.

Mo˥o ni⌐zip-puñ-ḡu˥rai kŏko de ⌐ma˥-
tte (i)masu yo↲

D. Substitution Drill

1. I (compared with others)
    ate [it].

Wa⌐takusi wa tabema˥sita.

2. The sashimi (compared with other things) [I] ate. — Sa⌐simi˥ wa ta˧bema˥sita.

3. [I] ate sashimi. — Sa⌐simi˥ o ta˧bema˥sita.
4. I ate [it]. — Wa˧takusi ḡa tabema˥sita.
5. I ate [it], too. — Wa˧takusi mo tabema˥sita.
6. [I] ate sashimi, too. — Sa⌐simi˥ mo ta˧bema˥sita.
7. [I] ate with chopsticks. — O⌐ha˥si de ta˧bema˥sita.
8. [I] ate at home. — U˥ti de tabema˥sita.
9. [I] ate at eight. — Ha⌐ti˥-zi ni ta˧bema˥sita.
10. [I] ate starting at eight. — Ha⌐ti˥-zi kara ta˧bema˥sita.

E. Substitution Drill

1. It's delicious, isn't it—this beer. — O⌐isi˥i desu ⌐ne˥e—ko˧no bi˥iru wa.
2. It's hot, isn't it—this tea. — A⌐tu˥i desu ⌐ne˥e—kono otya wa.
3. It's cold, isn't it—this room. — Sa⌐mu˥i desu ⌐ne˥e—ko˧no heya˥ wa.
4. It's cold, isn't it—this milk. — Tu⌐meta˥i desu ⌐ne˥e—ko˧no mi˥ruku wa.
5. It's awful(-tasting), isn't it—this fish. — Ma⌐zu˥i desu ⌐ne˥e—kono sakana wa.
6. It's sour, isn't it—this fruit. — Su⌐ppa˥i desu ⌐ne˥e—ko˧no kuda˥mono wa.
7. It's bitter, isn't it—this coffee. — Ni⌐ḡa˥i desu ⌐ne˥e—ko˧no koohi˥i wa.
8. It's spicy, isn't it—this sushi. — Ka⌐ra˥i desu ⌐ne˥e—ko˧no osu˥si wa.
9. It's sweet, isn't it—this cake. — A⌐ma˥i desu ⌐ne˥e—ko˧no oka˥si wa.
10. It's strong, isn't it—this (black) tea. — Ko˥i desu ⌐ne˥e—kono kootya wa.

F. Substitution Drill

1. Please bring two bottles of sake. — Sake (o) ⌐ni˥-hon̄ mo˧tte˥ kite kudasai.
2. Please bring two glasses of beer. — Bi˥iru (o) ⌐ni˥-hai mo˧tte˥ kite kudasai.
3. Please bring three knives. — Na⌐ihu (o) ⌐sa˥n̄-bon̄ mo˧tte˥ kite kudasai.
4. Please bring three pieces of toast. — To˥osuto (o) ⌐sa˥n̄-mai mo˧tte˥ kite kudasai.
5. Please bring three glasses of milk. — Mi˥ruku (o) ⌐sa˥n̄-bai mo˧tte˥ kite kudasai.
6. Please bring one fork. — Ho˥oku (o) ⌐i˥p-pon̄ mo˧tte˥ kite kudasai.
7. Please bring one glass of water. — Mizu (o) ⌐i˥p-pai mo˧tte˥ kite kudasai.
8. Please bring a little more rice. — Go˥han̄ (o) mo⌐o suko˥si mo˧tte˥ kite kudasai.

9. Please bring two cups. — Tyawañ (o) hu⌜tatu motte⌝kite kudasai.

10. Please bring two cups of tea. — Otya (o) ⌜ni⌝-hai mo⊢tte⊣ kite kudasai.

G. Response Drill

(Reply in the negative.)

1. Ya⌜sai de⌝su ka⌋ — Iie, ya⌜sai zya arimase⌝ñ.
2. A⌜ma⌝i desu ka⌋ — Iie, a⌜maku arimase⌝ñ.
3. Ya⌜mema⌝sita ka⌋ — Iie, ya⌜memase⌝ñ desita.
4. Syo⌜kudoo de⌝su ka⌋ — Iie, syo⌜kudoo zya arimase⌝ñ.
5. O⌜sobaya kara de⌝su ka⌋ — Iie, o⌜sobaya kara zya arimase⌝ñ.
6. Ku⌜suri de⌝sita ka⌋ — Iie, ku⌜suri zya arimase⌝ñ desita.
7. Su⌜ppa⌝i desu ka⌋ — Iie, su⌜ppa⌝ku a⊢rimase⊣ñ.
8. Ko⌝i desu ka⌋ — Iie, ko⌝ku a⊢rimase⊣ñ.

H. Response Drill (based on Grammatical Note 5)

1. Mo⌝o ta⌜bema⌝sita ka⌋ /iie/ — Iie, ma⌝da ta⌜bemase⌝ñ.
2. Ma⌝da na⌜orimase⌝ñ ka⌋ /iie/ — Iie, mo⌝o na⌜orima⌝sita.
3. Mo⌝o ku⌜suri (o) nomima⌝sita ka⌋ /e⌝e/ — E⌝e, mo⌝o ku⌜suri (o) nomima⌝sita.
4. Ma⌝da ta⌜nomimase⌝ñ ka⌋ /e⌝e/ — E⌝e, ma⌝da ta⌜nomimase⌝ñ.
5. Mo⌝o de⌜kima⌝sita ka⌋ /iie/ — Iie, ma⌝da de⌜kimase⌝ñ.
6. Ma⌝da ka⌜erimase⌝ñ ka⌋ /iie/ — Iie, mo⌝o ka⌜erima⌝sita.
7. Mo⌝o ku⌜ruma (o) naosima⌝sita ka⌋ /e⌝e/ — E⌝e, mo⌝o ku⌜ruma (o) naosima⌝sita.
8. Ma⌝da a⌜imase⌝ñ ka⌋ /e⌝e/ — E⌝e, ma⌝da a⌜imase⌝ñ.
9. Mo⌝o wa⌜karima⌝sita ka⌋ /iie/ — Iie, ma⌝da wa⌜karimase⌝ñ.
10. Ma⌝da de⌜ñwa-simase⌝ñ ka⌋ /iie/ — Iie, mo⌝o de⌜ñwa-sima⌝sita.

I. Level Drill (based on Grammatical Notes 1 and 4)

Tutor: Mo⌝o i⌜kima⌝sita kara. (formal verbal)
Student: Mo⌝o i⌜tta⌝ kara. (informal verbal)
'Because I already went.'

1. Sa⌜ke (o) yamema⌝sita kara. — Sa⌜ke (o) yameta⌝ kara.
2. Miti de to⌜modati ni aima⌝sita kara. — Miti de to⌜modati ni a⌝tta kara.
3. I⌜sogima⌝sita kara. — I⌜so⌝ida kara.
4. Mo⌝o i⌜ti-neñ-gu⌝rai ⊢ma⊣e ni yo⌜mima⌝sita kara. — Mo⌝o i⌜ti-neñ-gu⌝rai ⊢ma⊣e ni ⌜yo⌝ñda kara.

5. Ka⌐nai mo ko̅domo mo   Ka⌐nai mo ko̅domo mo byo⌐oki ni na⌐-
   byo⌐oki ni narima⌐sita   tta kara.
   kara.
6. Hu⌐ru⌐i sa⌐kana (o) tabe-   Hu⌐ru⌐i sa⌐kana (o) ta⌐beta kara.
   ma⌐sita kara.
7. Kinoo ⌐yo⌐ku be⌐ñkyoo-   Kinoo ⌐yo⌐ku be⌐ñkyoo-sita⌐ kara.
   sima⌐sita kara.
8. To⌐modati kara karima⌐-   To⌐modati kara karita⌐ kara.
   sita kara.
9. Ti⌐isa na ⌐ko⌐e de ha⌐na-   Ti⌐isa na ⌐ko⌐e de ha⌐na⌐sita kara.
   sima⌐sita kara.
10. Yuube ⌐bi⌐iru (o) ta⌐kusañ   Yuube ⌐bi⌐iru (o) ta⌐kusañ no⌐ñda
    nomima⌐sita kara.   kara.

J.   Grammar Drill (based on Grammatical Notes 1, 2, 3, and 4)

Tutor: I⌐ku desyo⌐o. 'He'll probably go.' (non-past)
Student: I⌐tta desyo⌐o. 'He probably went.' (past)

1. Kyo⌐o de⌐ñwa (o) nao⌐su   Kyo⌐o de⌐ñwa (o) nao⌐sita desyoo.
   desyoo.
2. Ze⌐ñbu tu⌐taeru desyo⌐o.   Ze⌐ñbu tu⌐taeta desyo⌐o.
3. Koñna sara (wa) ta⌐ka⌐i   Koñna sara (wa) ⌐ta⌐kakatta desyoo.
   desyoo.
4. Byo⌐oki desyo⌐o.   Byo⌐oki da⌐tta desyoo.
5. Kyo⌐o to⌐temo isog̅asi⌐i   Kyo⌐o to⌐temo isog̅a⌐sikatta desyoo.
   desyoo.
6. Ha⌐yaku na⌐o⌐ru desyoo.   Ha⌐yaku na⌐o⌐tta desyoo.
7. Sono sig̅oto (wa) tu⌐mara⌐-   Sono sig̅oto (wa) tu⌐mara⌐nakatta de-
   nai desyoo.   syoo.
8. Ko⌐no koohi⌐i (wa) ma⌐zu⌐i   Ko⌐no koohi⌐i (wa) ⌐ma⌐zukatta de-
   desyoo.   syoo.
9. Sono tori (wa) o⌐isi⌐i de-   Sono tori (wa) o⌐isi⌐katta desyoo.
   syoo.
10. Ha⌐nasi-tyuu desyo⌐o.   Ha⌐nasi-tyuu da⌐tta desyoo.

K.   Level Drill [1]

1. Ko⌐marima⌐sita ⌐ne⌐e.   Ko⌐ma⌐tta ⌐ne⌐e.   (M)
2. So⌐re (wa) yo⌐katta desu.   So⌐re (wa) yo⌐katta.
3. So⌐no⌐ hito no ⌐ko⌐e (wa)   So⌐no⌐ hito no ⌐ko⌐e (wa) ⌐he⌐ñ datta
   ⌐he⌐ñ desita yo↲   yo↲   (M)

---

[1] In each case, the sentence on the right is the informal equivalent of the
sentence on the left.   M = more typical of men's speech; W = more typical of
women's speech.

4. A⌐no kissa⌐teñ no o⌐ka⌐si   A⌐no kissa⌐teñ no o⌐ka⌐si (wa) o⌐isi⌐-
   (wa) o⌐isi⌐katta desu ⌐ne⌐e.   katta ⌐ne⌐e.   (M)

5. Mo⌐o o⌐kaeri ni narima⌐si-   Mo⌐o o⌐kaeri ni na⌐tta?   (W)
   ta ka⌐

6. Sono miti (wa) da⌐izyo⌐obu   Sono miti (wa) da⌐izyo⌐obu datta?
   desita ka⌐

7. So⌐no ho⌐ñ (wa) to⌐temo   So⌐no ho⌐ñ (wa) to⌐temo omosi⌐rokatta-
   omosi⌐rokatta desu.   ta.

8. Na⌐ni (o) go⌐tyuumoñ-   Na⌐ni (o) go⌐tyuumoñ-nasa⌐tta?   (W)
   nasaima⌐sita ka⌐

9. Sono sakana (wa) da⌐me⌐   Sono sakana (wa) da⌐me⌐ datta.
   desita.

10. Mo⌐o zi⌐p-puñ-ḡu⌐rai ⌐ma⌐e   Mo⌐o zi⌐p-puñ-ḡu⌐rai ⌐ma⌐e ni de̅ka-
    ni de⌐kakema⌐sita yo⌐   keta yo⌐   (M)

L. Expansion Drill

1. They haven't brought it.   Mo⌐tte kimase⌐ñ yo⌐
   They haven't brought it yet.   Ma⌐da mo⌐tte kimase⌐ñ yo⌐
   I ordered but they haven't   Tyu⌐umoñ-sima⌐sita ḡa, ma⌐da mo-
     brought it yet.   ⌐tte kimase⌐ñ yo⌐
   I ordered coffee but they   Ko⌐ohi⌐i (o) tyu⌐umoñ-sima⌐sita ḡa,
     haven't brought it yet.   ma⌐da mo⌐tte kimase⌐ñ yo⌐
   I ordered coffee about fif-   Zyu⌐ugo-huñ-ḡu⌐rai ⌐ma⌐e ni ko⌐o-
     teen minutes ago but they   hi⌐i (o) tyu⌐umoñ-sima⌐sita ḡa,
     haven't brought it yet.   ma⌐da mo⌐tte kimase⌐ñ yo⌐
   I ordered coffee about fif-   Mo⌐o zyu⌐ugo-huñ-ḡu⌐rai ⌐ma⌐e ni
     teen minutes ago (al-   ko⌐ohi⌐i (o) tyu⌐umoñ-sima⌐sita
     ready) but they haven't   ḡa, ma⌐da mo⌐tte kimase⌐ñ yo⌐
     brought it yet.

2. I got sick.   Byo⌐oki ni narima⌐sita yo.
   Because it was bad, I got   Da⌐me⌐ datta kara, byo⌐oki ni nari-
     sick.   ma⌐sita yo.
   Because that fish was bad,   Sono sakana wa da⌐me⌐ datta kara,
     I got sick.   byo⌐oki ni narima⌐sita yo.
   I ate fish. Because the fish   Sa⌐kana (o) tabema⌐sita ḡa; sono
     was bad, I got sick.   sakana wa da⌐me⌐ datta kara, byo-
                                       ⌐oki ni narima⌐sita yo.
   I ate fish at a cheap dining   Ya⌐su⌐i syokudoo de sa⌐kana (o) ta-
     room. Because the fish   bema⌐sita ḡa; sono sakana wa da-
     was bad, I got sick.   ⌐me⌐ datta kara, byo⌐oki ni nari-
                                       ma⌐sita yo.
   The day before yesterday   Ototoi ya⌐su⌐i syokudoo de sa⌐kana
     I ate fish at a cheap din-   (o) tabema⌐sita ḡa; sono s a k a n a
     ing room. Because the   wa da⌐me⌐ datta kara, byo⌐oki ni
     fish was bad, I got sick.   narima⌐sita yo.

3. [They] eat.   Ta⌐bema⌐su.
   [They] eat with chopsticks.   Ha⌐si de tabemasu.

Japanese eat with chop-
sticks.

Ni⌐hoñzi⌐ñ wa ⌐ha⌐si de tabemasu.

Americans eat with knives
and forks, but Japanese
eat with chopsticks.

A⌐merika⌐ziñ wa ⌐na⌐ihu to ⌐ho⌐oku
de ta╴bema╴su ḡa, ni⌐hoñzi⌐ñ wa
⌐ha⌐si de tabemasu.

4. He has probably arrived. . . .

Tu⌐ita desyoo ḡa_

He has probably arrived
home. . . .

O⌐taku ni tu⌐ita desyoo ḡa_

He has probably arrived
home already. . . .

Mo⌐o o⌐taku ni tu⌐ita desyoo ḡa_

He left about an hour ago
so he has probably ar-
rived home already. . . .

I⌐ti-zikañ-ḡu⌐rai ╴ma╴e ni ⌐de⌐ta kara, mo⌐o o⌐taku ni tu⌐ita desyoo
ḡa_

He left the office about an
hour ago so he has prob-
ably arrived home al-
ready. . . .

I⌐ti-zikañ-ḡu⌐rai ╴ma╴e ni zi⌐mu⌐syo
(o) ╴de╴ta kara, mo⌐o o⌐taku ni tu⌐-
ita desyoo ḡa_

5. Let's make it tomorrow.

A⌐sita⌐ ni si╴masyo╴o.

I'm busy so let's make it
tomorrow.

I⌐soḡasi⌐i kara, a⌐sita⌐ ni si╴ma-
syo╴o.

I'm very busy so let's
make it tomorrow.

To⌐ttemo isoḡasi⌐i kara, a⌐sita⌐ ni
si╴masyo╴o.

Today I'm very busy so
let's make it tomorrow.

Kyo⌐o wa to⌐ttemo isoḡasi⌐i k a r a,
a⌐sita⌐ ni si╴masyo╴o.

6. I telephoned.

De⌐ñwa-sima⌐sita.

I telephoned his home.

O⌐taku e deñwa-sima⌐sita.

I wanted to talk so I telephoned his home.

Ha⌐nasita⌐katta kara, o⌐taku e deñ-
wa-sima⌐sita.

I didn't see him but I
wanted to talk to him so
I telephoned his home.

A⌐imase⌐ñ desita ḡa; ha⌐nasita⌐katta
kara, o⌐taku e deñwa-sima⌐sita.

I didn't see him at the office but I wanted to talk
to him so I telephoned
his home.

Kaisya de a⌐imase⌐ñ desita ḡa; ha-
⌐nasita⌐katta kara, o⌐taku e deñwa-
sima⌐sita.

SUPPLEMENTARY CONVERSATION

(Two friends, Mr. Tanaka and Mr. Sato, sit down in a restaurant and are ap-
proached by a waitress)

Waitress: I⌐rassyaima⌐se. Na⌐ñ ni i╴tasimasyo╴o ka.
Tanaka: Mo⌐o hito⌐-ri ╴ku╴ru kara, tyo⌐tto ╴ma╴tte kudasai.
Waitress: Ha⌐a.
Tanaka: (to Sato)   Osoi ⌐ne⌐e—Yosida-kuñ wa.
Sato: So⌐o da ⌐ne⌐e.   Na⌐ñ ni suru?
Tanaka: Tori wa?

Sato: Yosida-kuñ wa tŏri wa dame.
Tanaka: So˥o ˥so˩o. Te⌐ñpura wa do˥o? Te⌐ñpura wa ta˥beta ne? — boku no
             uti de.
Sato: So˥o datta ˥ne˩e.

             (Mr. Yoshida arrives)

Yoshida: O⌐soku narima˥sita. Su⌐mimase˥ñ.
Tanaka ⎞
Sato   ⎠ :   Iie.
Tanaka: Na˥ñ ni suru?
Sato: Te⌐ñpura do˥o?
Yoshida: A˥a, i˥i ⌐ne˥e.
Sato: Zya˥a, te⌐ñpura tano˥mu yo. (To waitress) Tyo˥tto_
Waitress: Ha˥a. Na˥ñ ni i˥tasimasyo˩o ka.
Sato: Teñpura mi-⌐ttu oneḡai-sima˥su.
Waitress: Ha˥a, ka⌐sikomarima˥sita.
Tanaka: (to Yoshida and Sato) Bi˥iru mo ˥no˩mu?
Yoshida: No˥mu yo⌟ — tu˥meta˩i no o.
Sato: (to waitress) Zya˥a, bi˥iru mo. A⌐rima˥su ka⌟ — tu˥meta˩i no ḡa.
Waitress: Ha˥a gozaimasu. O⌐bi˥iru ¹ mo⌐tte mairimasyo˥o ka.
Sato: O⌐neḡai-sima˥su.

                    ·   ·   ·

Waitress: O⌐matase-itasima˥sita. Do˥ozo. Te⌐ñpura wa notihodo motte mai-
             rima˥su.
Tanaka: (to Yoshida and Sato) Tu⌐metai bi˥iru wa ŏisii ⌐ne˥e.

                    ·   ·   ·

Yoshida: O⌐isi˥katta ⌐ne˥e — ko˥no bi˩iru wa.
Sato: Mo˥tto ta˥no˩mu?
Yoshida: Mo˥o takusañ. Zu⌐ibuñ ˥no˩ñda yo⌟
Tanaka: (to Sato) Mo⌐o suko˥si ˥do˥o?
Sato: Boku mo ⌐mo˥o ⌐zu⌐ibuñ ˥no˩ñda kara_
Waitress: O⌐matase-itasima˥sita. Do˥ozo. Go˥hañ mo mo˥tte mairimasyo˩o
             ka.
Tanaka: O⌐neḡai-sima˥su.
Waitress: Ka⌐sikomarima˥sita.

                    ·   ·   ·

Yoshida: O⌐tya oneḡai-sima˥su.
Waitress: Ha˥a ˥ha˩a.
Tanaka: (to Yoshida and Sato) O⌐isi˥katta ˥ne˩e.

---

¹ The polite o⌐bi˥iru⁺ is regularly used by restaurant and hotel personnel.

Sato: Sa⌐kana g̃a atara⌐sikatta kara, o⌐isi⌐katta ˩ne˪e.
Yoshida: O⌐isii teñpura da⌐tta kara, ta⌐kusañ ta⌐beta yo˩
Tanaka: (to waitress) Tyo⌐tto_ I⌐kura?
Waitress: A⌐ri˜g̃atoo gozaimasu. Se⌐ñ happyaku ro⌐kuzyu⌐u-eñ de gozaimasu.
Yoshida: Kyo⌐o wa ⌐bo⌐ku g̃a_
Tanaka: Iie, boku g̃a_
Sato: Niseñ-eñ. Ha⌐i.

                              . . .

Waitress: Ma⌐ido ari˜g̃atoo gozaimasu. Hyaku yo⌐ñzyu⌐u-eñ. Do⌐ozo. Ma⌐ta
            do⌐ozo.

Tanaka ⎫
        ⎬: (to Sato) Do⌐o mo su˩mimase˪ñ. Gotisoosama.
Yoshida ⎭

Sato: Iie iie.

                    English Equivalent

Waitress: (Welcome.) What would you like?
Tanaka: One more is coming so just a minute.
Waitress: Certainly.
Tanaka: (to Sato) He's late, isn't he— Yoshida.
Sato: He is, isn't he. What are you going to have (lit. decide on)?
Tanaka: How about chicken?
Sato: Chicken is out for Yoshida.
Tanaka: That's right. How about tempura? Tempura he ate, didn't he— at
            my house?
Sato: He did, didn't he.
Yoshida: (joining his friends) I'm sorry I'm late.
Tanaka ⎫
        ⎬: Not at all.
Sato   ⎭
Tanaka: What are you going to have?
Sato: How about tempura?
Yoshida: Oh, fine!
Sato: Then I'll order tempura. (Calling waitress) Miss!
Waitress: Yes. What would you like?
Sato: We'd like three [orders of] tempura.
Waitress: Yes, certainly.
Tanaka: (to Yoshida and Sato) Are you going to have beer, too?
Yoshida: I'll have some— some that's cold.
Sato: (to waitress) Well then, beer too. Do you have some— some that's
            cold?
Waitress: Yes, we have. Shall I bring beer?
Sato: Yes, please.

                    . . .

Waitress: I'm sorry to have kept you waiting. Here you are. The tempura
            I'll bring later.
Tanaka: (to Yoshida and Sato) Isn't cold beer good!

Yoshida: Wasn't it good—this beer!
Sato: Do you want more?
Yoshida: No, thank you. I had an awful lot.
Tanaka: (to Sato) How about a little more?
Sato: I've had an awful lot already too so. . . .
Waitress: (bringing the tempura) I'm sorry to have kept you waiting. Here
             you are. Shall I bring some rice too?
Tanaka: Yes, please.
Waitress: Certainly.

                        . . .

Yoshida: We'd like some tea.
Waitress: Certainly.
Tanaka: (to Yoshida and Sato) Wasn't it good!
Sato: The fish was fresh so it WAS good, wasn't it!
Yoshida: It was delicious tempura so I ate a lot.
Tanaka: (to waitress) Miss! How much?
Waitress: (Thank you.) It's ¥1860.
Yoshida: Today I [will pay the check].
Tanaka: No, I [will pay].
Sato: (paying) Here. ¥2000.
Waitress: (Returning with change) Thank you. Here you are, ¥140. Please
             come again.
Tanaka
Yoshida }: (to Sato) Thank you very much. It was delicious.
Sato: Not at all.

EXERCISES

1. Tell the waitress:

      a. to bring 2 (portions of) sashimi.
      b. to bring some water.
      c. to bring more sake.
      d. that your tea is cold.
      e. that your coffee is weak.
      f. that the fish tastes bad.
      g. that you haven't ordered yet.
      h. that you want a little more rice.
      i. that you don't want any cake.
      j. that you enjoyed your meal.

2. Ask your guest: Your guest replies:

      a. what he will have   I'll have some sushi.
          to eat.
      b. if he will have some   Yes, thank you.
          sake.
      c. if he will have some   No, thank you.
          more beer.

      d. if he will have some   Just half, please.
           more coffee.
      e. if he would like sugar.   Just a little, please.

3.   Turn back to Level Drill I on pages 243–44. Make up questions for which the sentences of this drill would be appropriate answers. For example, using the model sentence <u>Moo i'tta kara.</u>, an appropriate question would be: <u>Doo site gʰiñkoo e ikimaseʰñ ka⌐</u> 'Why aren't you going to go to the bank?' Then drill on the questions together with their answers (informal alternants).

4.   Practice the Basic Dialogues using appropriate variations.

Lesson 15. Eating and Drinking (cont.)

BASIC DIALOGUES: FOR MEMORIZATION

(a)

At the office

Smith

together	issyo
dining or a meal	syokuzi or
	osyokuzi †
dine or eat a meal	syokuzi o suru
dine together	issyo ni syokuzi o suru
1. Shall we have lunch [1] together?	I⌐ssyo ni syokuzi (o) simasyo⌐o ka.

Tanaka

2. Haven't you eaten yet?	Ma⌐da ta˦bemase˦ñ ka↵
doesn't know (informal)	siranai
didn't know (informal)	si⌐rana⌐katta
with Mr. Saito	Saitoo-sañ to
together with Mr. Saito	Saitoo-sañ to issyo
eat together	i⌐ssyo ni tabe⌐ru
3. I didn't know so today I ate early (already) with Mr. Saito. . . .	Si⌐rana⌐katta kara, kyo⌐o wa ⌐mo⌐o Saitoo-sañ to issyo ni ⌐ha⌐yaku ta-˦bema˦sita g̃a↵

Smith

other or another	hoka
day	hi⌐
another day	ho⌐ka no hi⌐
4. Well then, let's make it another day.	Zya⌐a, ho⌐ka no hi⌐ ni si˦masyo˦o.

Tanaka

whatever day of the week it is or any day of the week at all	na⌐ñyo⌐o(bi) de mo
5. Yes. Any day at all will be fine.	E⌐e. Na⌐ñyo⌐o de mo ˦i˦i desu yo↵

---

[1] Or breakfast or dinner.

251

(b)

In a restaurant

Tanaka

which alternative

6. Which *[alternative]* would
   be better, noodles or sushi?

do˥tira no ˥ho˦o

So˥ba to ˹su˺si to, do˥tira *[no ˥ho˦o]*
ḡa ˥i˦i desyoo ka.

Smith

whichever of two it is
   or either one

7. Either one is fine, but let's
   make it sushi, shall we?

do˹tira de˺ mo

Do˹tira de mo i˥i desu ḡa, su˥si ni
si˥masyo˦o ne?

Tanaka (to waitress)

one portion

8. We'd like two portions of
   sushi.

iti-niñmae

Su˥si (o) ni-˹niñmae oneḡai-sima˥su.

. . .

bill or accounting or
   check

9. Check, please.

kaikee or
   okaikee⁺

Ka˹ikee (o) oneḡai-sima˥su.

10. How much does it come to?

I˹kura ni na˥rima˦su ka⌟

Waitress

11. It's ¥150 for one portion so
    it comes to ¥300.   Thank
    you.

Iti-niñmae hya˹ku gozyu˥u-eñ de go-
˥zaima˦su kara, sa˹ñbyaku˺-eñ ni
narimasu.   Ma˹ido ari˺ḡatoo gozaimasu.

(c)

Mrs. Smith (arriving home)

noon meal

stomach
become empty

12. I had lunch early so I'm
    hungry. (Lit. Lunch was
    early so my stomach has
    become empty.)

hi˹rugo˺hañ or
   o˹hirugo˺hañ⁺

onaka
suku /-u/

O˹hirugo˺hañ (ḡa) ˹ha˺yakatta kara,
o˹naka ḡa sukima˥sita yo⌟

a meal
come into being or
   be(come) completed

13. Is dinner ready?

go˥hañ
de˹ki˺ru /-ru/

Go˥hañ (ḡa) de˹kima˺sita ka⌟

Maid

soon now or any minute
   now

mo˹o su˥ḡu

14. It will be ready any minute now. . . .   Mo⌐o su⌐g̃u de⌐kima⌐su g̃a⌐

(d)

Mr. Tanaka

pleasing   su⌐ki⌐ /na/   or
              osuki⁺ /na/

15. Which [alternative] do you prefer— sukiyaki or sushi?   Sukiyaki to ⌐su⌐si to, do⌐tira [no ⌐ho⌐o] g̃a o⌐suki de⌐su ka⌐

Mr. Smith

the alternative of suki-yaki   su⌐kiyaki no ho⌐o

16. Me, I prefer sukiyaki.   Boku wa su⌐kiyaki [no ho⌐o] g̃a su-⌐ki⌐ desu yo. [1]

Mr. Tanaka

more than sukiyaki   su⌐kiyaki yo⌐ri
the alternative of sushi   su⌐si no ⌐ho⌐o

17. Oh? I like sushi more than sukiyaki.   So⌐o desu ka. Boku wa su⌐kiyaki yo⌐ri ⌐su⌐si [no ⌐ho⌐o] g̃a su⌐ki⌐ desu.

however or but   si⌐ka⌐si
to the highest degree   i⌐ti⌐bañ
the one that's most pleasing   i⌐tibañ suki⌐ na no

18. But what I like best is tempura.   Si⌐ka⌐si, i⌐tibañ suki⌐ na no wa te⌐ñ-pura de⌐su yo.

Mr. Smith

19. Oh, tempura?   A⌐a, te⌐ñpura de⌐su ka.

20. I like tempura best, too.   Bo⌐ku mo teñpura g̃a itibañ suki⌐ desu yo.

to the extent of tempura or as much as tem-pura   teñpura hodo

21. I like sukiyaki too, but not so much as tempura.   Su⌐kiyaki mo suki⌐ desu g̃a, te⌐ñpura hodo zya arimase⌐ñ yo.

(e)

Tanaka

for dining or for a meal   syokuzi ni

---

[1] Accent of short alternant: <u>suki⌐</u>.

being fish and meat and   sakana to ni⌐ku⌐ to tŏri de
   fowl
[being] among fish and   sakana to ni⌐ku⌐ to tŏri no uti
   meat and fowl   [de]

22. Mr. Smith is coming to our   Su⌐misu - sañ (ḡa) u⌐ti e syokuzi ni
     house for dinner. Which do   irassyaima⌐su ḡa; sakana to ni⌐ku⌐
     you suppose he would like   to tŏri │de   │, do⌐re ḡa i⌐ti-
     best, fish, meat, or fowl?   │no uti [de] │
                                            bañ osuki desyo⌐o ka.

Jones

isn't meat (informal)   ni⌐ku⌐ zya ⌐na⌐i
it probably isn't meat   ni⌐ku⌐ zya ⌐na⌐i desyoo
wouldn't it be meat?   ni⌐ku⌐ zya ⌐na⌐i desyoo ka

23. Hmm. I'm not sure but would-   Sa⌐a, yo⌐ku wa⌐karimase⌐ñ ḡa; ni-
     n't it be meat?   ⌐ku⌐ zya ⌐na⌐i desyoo ka.

Tanaka

24. I suppose so.   So⌐o desyoo ⌐ne⌐e.

Jones

whichever (of three or   do⌐re de mo
   more) it is or   any
   one at all
most Americans   ta⌐itee no Amerika⌐ziñ

25. I guess any one (of the three   Ma⌐a, do⌐re de mo ⌐i⌐i desyoo ḡa;
     alternatives) would be fine,   sa⌐simi⌐ wa ta⌐itee no Amerika⌐ziñ
     but sashimi most Americans   wa a⌐ñmari suki⌐ zya a⌐rimase⌐ñ ḡa_
     don't like very much. . . .

Tanaka

26. That's right, isn't it.   So⌐re wa so⌐o desu ⌐ne⌐e.

(f)

Mr. Tanaka

27. Which do you like better—   Bi⌐iru to săke to, do⌐tti [no ⌐ho⌐o]
     beer or sake?   ḡa suki?

Mr. Yamamoto

the alternative of beer   bi⌐iru no ⌐ho⌐o
by far   zutto
a drink or beverage   no⌐mi⌐mono
displeasing   kirai /na/

28. I like beer much more—   Bi⌐iru [no ⌐ho⌐o] ḡa zu⌐tto suki⌐ da
     since I hate hot drinks.   yo—a⌐tu⌐i no⌐mi⌐mono (wa) ki⌐rai
                                            da⌐ kara.

Mr. Tanaka

29. Tea too?   Otya mo?

Mr. Yamamoto

of course <u>or</u> to be sure	mo⌐ti⌐roñ
very pleasing	da⌐isuki /na/

30. Oh, tea is different. Of course
I like it a lot! | A⌐a, otya wa tiḡau. Mo⌐ti⌐roñ ⌐da⌐i-
suki da yo.

(g)

Mr. Tanaka

throat	no⌐do
become dry	ka⌐wa⌐ku /-u/

31. I'm thirsty. (Lit. My throat
has become dry.) | No⌐do (ḡa) ka⌐wa⌐ita.

Mr. Yamamoto

32. What do you want to drink?   Na⌐ni (ḡa) nomitai?

Mr. Tanaka

no matter what it is	na⌐ñ de⌐ mo
<u>or</u> anything at all	

33. Anything will be fine.   Na⌐ñ de mo i⌐i yo.

(h)

At a restaurant

Tanaka

34. Is this coffee?   Kore ko⌐ohi⌐i?

Yamamoto

35. Yes, that's right.   E⌐e, so⌐o.

Tanaka

isn't strange (informal)	he⌐ñ zya ⌐na⌐i

36. Doesn't it taste funny? (Lit.
Isn't it strange?) | He⌐ñ zya nai?

Yamamoto (after tasting it)

isn't delicious	o⌐isiku na⌐i

37. It isn't good, is it!   O⌐isiku na⌐i ⌐ne⌐e.

NOTES ON THE BASIC DIALOGUES

3. 'but—if I had known, I would have waited for you.'

4. Compare: <u>hoka no zassi</u> 'another magazine' or 'other magazines'; <u>zassi
no hoka</u> 'other than magazines,' 'besides magazines.'

12. Hi⌐ru⌐ means 'noon' or 'daytime.'

Compare also a⌐sago⌐hañ 'breakfast' and ba⌐ñgo⌐hañ 'dinner,' 'evening
meal.'

Note also the following, all of which are in common use: o⌐naka ḡa (or wa) sukimase⌐ñ 'I'm not hungry' (lit. 'my stomach hasn't become empty'); o⌐naka ḡa suite (i)ma⌐su 'I'm hungry' (lit. 'my stomach is in a state of having become empty'); o⌐naka ḡa (or wa) suite (i)mase⌐ñ 'I'm not hungry' (lit. 'my stomach is not in a state of having become empty').

14.   'but—will that be all right?'

15.   Both the thing which is pleasing and the person to whom it is pleasing are followed by particles ḡa or wa (depending upon emphasis). Note that su⌐ki⌐ is a na-nominal: thus, su⌐ki⌐ na mono 'pleasing things,' 'things [I] like'; o⌐suki na mono⌐ 'things pleasing to someone else,' 'things [you] like.'

16.   Wa here is the wa of comparison: 'I, for my part.'

17.   See the immediately preceding note.

18.   Si⌐ka⌐si occurs at the beginning of sentences.

      No is the nominal no 'one,' referring here to a kind of food.

22.   Ni here is the ni of goal.

25.   'but—they like most other things.'

26.   Wa here is the wa of comparison.

28.   Zutto: note also zu⌐tto ma⌐e 'a long time before or ago,' zutto usiro 'way in back,' etc.

      No⌐mi⌐mono: compare ta⌐bemo⌐no 'food,' 'edibles.'

      Kirai is the opposite of su⌐ki⌐ and enters into the same kinds of patterns (except that it does not have a polite equivalent). Ki⌐rai de⌐su is a stronger, less tactful expression than su⌐ki⌐ zya a⌐rimase⌐ñ '[I] don't like [it],' '[I] don't care for [it].'

30.   Da⌐isuki is an informal word.

31.   No⌐do ḡa ka⌐wa⌐ku occurs in the same kinds of patterns as onaka ḡa suku. See the note on Sentence 12 above.

32.   Compare: Na⌐ni o ⌐no⌐mu? 'What are you going to drink?' but Na⌐ni ḡa (or, less commonly, o) nomitai? 'What do you want to drink?' See Lesson 7, Grammatical Note 1.

28, 30, 33, and 37 contain informal non-past or past inflected words followed directly by yo or nee. Such combinations occur more commonly in men's speech.

GRAMMATICAL NOTES

1. Informal Negatives, Non-past and Past

The informal equivalent of a formal non-past negative ending in -mase˥n is an ADJECTIVAL ending in -[a] nai.

To make the informal negative adjectival from the citation form of a verbal:

>   -ru group: drop -ru and add -nai
>
>>   Example: ta⸢be⸣ru 'eat'—ta⸢be⸣nai 'doesn't eat'
>
>   -u group: drop -u and add -anai
>
>>   Example: no⸣mu 'drink'—no⸢ma⸣nai 'doesn't drink'
>
>>   but: for -u verbals ending in a vowel + -u, drop -u and add -wanai
>
>>   Example: kau 'buy'—kawanai 'doesn't buy'
>
>>   Note: The informal negative of a⸣ru 'be (inanimate),' 'have' is na⸣i.
>
>   -aru group: change -aru to -aranai [1]
>
>>   Example: ku⸢dasa⸣ru 'give me'—ku⸢dasara⸣nai 'doesn't give me'
>
>>   Note: A corresponding informal negative does not exist for go⸢za⸣ru.
>
>   Irregular group:
>
>>   suru 'do'—sinai 'doesn't do'
>>   ku⸣ru 'come'—ko⸣nai 'doesn't come'

An unaccented verbal has an unaccented informal negative equivalent; an accented verbal has an accented informal negative equivalent, with the accent occurring on the syllable immediately preceding the -nai ending.

The past informal negative ends in -nakatta; like all adjectival past informal forms, it is made by replacing the final -i of the non-past with -katta. It is accented on syllable na if derived from an unaccented non-past negative, and on the syllable immediate preceding -nakatta if derived from an accented non-past negative.

Examples:

---

[1] Or, worded differently: drop -u and add -anai.

AFFIRMATIVE	NEGATIVE	
Verbal Non-past Informal (Citation Form)	Non-past: Informal/Formal	Past: Informal/Formal
(-ru Group)		
deꜛru 'go out'	deꜛnai/deꜛmaseꜛñ	deꜛnakatta/deꜛmaseꜛñ desita
miꜛru 'see'	miꜛnai/miꜛmaseꜛñ	miꜛnakatta/miꜛmaseꜛñ desita
(-u Group)		
maꜛtu 'wait'	maꜛtaꜛnai/maꜛtimaseꜛñ	maꜛtaꜛnakatta/maꜛtimaseꜛñ desita
kaꜛeru 'return'	kaꜛeraꜛnai/kaꜛerimaseꜛñ	kaꜛeraꜛnakatta/kaꜛerimaseꜛñ desita
iu 'say'	iwanai/iꜛimaseꜛñ	iꜛwanaꜛkatta/iꜛimaseꜛñ desita
haꜛnaꜛsu 'talk'	haꜛnasaꜛnai/haꜛnasimaseꜛñ	haꜛnasaꜛnakatta/haꜛnasimaseꜛñ desita
kiku 'ask,' 'listen,' 'hear'	kikanai/kiꜛkimaseꜛñ	kiꜛkanaꜛkatta/kiꜛkimaseꜛñ desita
iꜛsoꜛg̃u 'be in a hurry'	iꜛsog̃aꜛnai/iꜛsog̃imaseꜛñ	iꜛsog̃aꜛnakatta/iꜛsog̃imaseꜛñ desita
yobu 'call'	yobanai/yoꜛbimaseꜛñ	yoꜛbanaꜛkatta/yoꜛbimaseꜛñ desita
yoꜛmu 'read'	yoꜛmaꜛnai/yoꜛmimaseꜛñ	yoꜛmaꜛnakatta/yoꜛmimaseꜛñ desita
(-aru Group)		
naꜛsaꜛru 'do'	naꜛsaraꜛnai/naꜛsaimaseꜛñ	naꜛsaraꜛnakatta/naꜛsaimaseꜛñ desita
(Irregular Group)		
kuꜛru 'come'	koꜛnai/kiꜛmaseꜛñ	koꜛnakatta/kiꜛmaseꜛñ desita
suru 'do,' 'make'	sinai/siꜛmaseꜛñ	siꜛnaꜛkatta/siꜛmaseꜛñ desita

The occurrences of non-negative adjectival forms like taꜛkaꜛi / taꜛkakatta (i.e. informal non-past and past forms) parallel the occurrences of negative adjectivals.

Examples:

Informal sentences

    Siranai. 'I don't know.'
    Ikanai yo⌐ 'I'm not going!' (men's speech)

Ma'da de⌐ki¬nai 「ne¬e. 'It hasn't been finished yet, has it.' (men's speech)

Saitoo-sañ wa 「ma'da ⌐ko¬nai? 'Hasn't Mr. Saito come yet?'

Wa⌐kara'nakatta. 'I didn't understand.'

Da⌐re mo de'nakatta yo⌐ 'Nobody answered (the telephone)!' (men's speech)

Pa'ñ ka⌐wana'katta? 'Didn't you buy any bread?'

Formal Sentences:

So⌐ñna hito' wa de⌐ki'nai desyoo. 'That kind of person probably can't do it.'

Tanaka-sañ wa i⌐rassyara'nai desyoo ka. 'Do you suppose Mr. Tanaka isn't in?'

So⌐o iwana'katta desyoo. 'He probably didn't say that.'

Wa⌐kara'nai kara, mo⌐o iti-do itte kudasa'i. 'I don't understand so please say it again.'

I⌐kana'katta kara, mi⌐mase'ñ desita. 'I didn't go so I didn't see it.'

However, note this difference: a formal equivalent of a non-negative adjectival like ta⌐ka'i/ta'kakatta is <u>ta⌐ka'i desu/ta'kakatta desu</u>. While a corresponding formal negative pattern does exist—for example, <u>na'i desu/na'katta desu</u> are frequently occurring forms—the more usual formal negative pattern is the <u>-mase'ñ/-mase'ñ desita</u> pattern derived from the corresponding formal affirmative verbal.

Note, now, the following patterns:

Non-past Negative

	Formal	Informal
Verbal Pattern	-<u>mase'ñ</u> form (or negative adjectival ending in -ʃaʃnai + desu) (wa⌐karimase'ñ or wa⌐kara'nai desu)	Negative adjectival ending in -ʃaʃnai (<u>wa⌐kara'nai</u>)
Adjectival Pattern	Adjectival ending in -<u>ku</u> + a⌐rimase'ñ or + <u>na'i desu</u> (ta'kaku a⌐rimase¬ñ or ta'kaku ⌐na¬i desu)	Adjectival ending in -<u>ku</u> + <u>na'i</u> (ta'kaku ⌐na¬i)
Nominal Pattern	Nominal + <u>zya a⌐rimase'ñ</u> or + <u>zya na'i desu</u> (ho'ñ zya a⌐rimase¬ñ or ho'ñ zya ⌐na¬i desu)	Nominal + <u>zya 「na'i</u> (ho'ñ zya ⌐na¬i)

To form the corresponding past forms of the above:
    (a) Add <u>desita</u> to -<u>mase'ñ</u> forms.
    (b) Change -<u>nai</u> to -<u>nakatta</u> and -<u>nai desu</u> to -<u>nakatta desu</u>.

An adjectival modifying a verbal o c c u r s in its -ku form (cf. Lesson 10,
Grammatical Note 4).   For negative adjectivals, occurrence before na˺ru 'become' is the most common example of this pattern:

> de˹ki˺naku ˺na˺ru 'become unable'
> wa˹kara˺naku ˺na˺ru 'reach the point of not understanding'

The a c c e n t of a -naku form is the same as that of the corresponding -nai
form.

2.   C o m p a r i s o n o f T w o I t e m s ; P a r t i c l e s yori and hodo

X to Y to, do˺tira ── asks: 'of X and Y, which is [more] ──?' [1] X and Y
are both nominals (which may be preceded by descriptive words or phrases
and/or followed by particles).   Following do˺tira is an appropriate particle—
u s u a l l y g̃a (if do˺tira is the subject) or o (if do˺tira is the object)—and an
inflected expression.

Study the following examples:

> (a) Kore to sore to, do˺tira g̃a ˹ki˺ree desu ka↲
>   'Which is prettier—this or that?'
> (b) O˹oki˺i no to ti˹isa˺i no to, do˺tira g̃a ˹i˺i desyoo ka.
>   'Which would be better—the big one or the small one?'
> (c) Tanaka-sañ no okosañ to o˹taku no˺ to, do˺tira g̃a o˹oki˺i desu ka↲
>   'Who is bigger—the Tanakas' child or yours?'
> (d) Ko˹no oka˺si to so˹no oka˺si to, do˺tti g̃a a˹ma˺i desu ka↲
>   'Which is sweeter—this cake or that cake?'
> (e) Tanaka-sañ to Yamamoto-sañ to, do˺tira o ˹yo˺ku si˹tte ima˺su
>   ka↲
>   'Which one do you know better— Mr. Tanaka or Mr. Yamamoto?'

In examples of this kind, do˺tira no ˹ho˺o 'which alternative?' is interchangeable with do˺tira 'which one?'

In the replies, the word or phrase which answers the question is followed
b y the same particle that followed the interrogative word o r phrase in the
question.   Ho˺o 'alternative' may or may not be included in the answer.

Study the following answers to the questions above:

> (a) Ko˹re g̃a ki˺ree desu.   or   Ko˹no ho˺o g̃a ˹ki˺ree desu.
>   'This is prettier.'
> (b) O˹oki˺i no g̃a ˹i˺i desu.   or   O˹oki˺i ˹ho˺o g̃a ˹i˺i desu.
>   'The big one is better.'
> (c) Ta˹naka-sañ no okøsañ g̃a ooki˺i desu.   or
>   Ta˹naka-sañ no okosañ no ho˺o g̃a o˹oki˺i desu.
>   'The Tanakas' child is bigger.'

───────────────

[1] For an alternate pattern, see Note 3 below.

(d) So⌐no oka˥si g̃a a˩ma˥i desu.   or
So⌐no oka˥si no ˥ho˥o g̃a a˩ma˥i desu.
'That cake is sweeter.'

(e) Ya⌐mamoto-sañ o yo˥ku sitte imasu.   or
Ya⌐mamoto-sañ no ho˥o o ˥yo˥ku sitte imasu.
'I know Mr. Yamamoto better.'

Yo˥ri (yori after an accented word) 'more than' follows the nominal with which another nominal is being compared. Again, the nominals may be preceded by descriptive words or phrases and/or followed by particles.

Study the following examples, noting the particles:

(a) So⌐re yo˥ri ko⌐re g̃a ki˥ree desu.   or   So⌐re yo˥ri ko⌐no ho˥o g̃a ˥ki˥ree desu.
'THIS is prettier than that.' (Lit. 'More than that, THIS [or THIS ALTERNATIVE] is pretty.')

(b) Ti⌐isa˥i no yori o⌐oki˥i no g̃a ˥i˥i desu.   or   Ti⌐isa˥i no yori o⌐oki˥i ˥ho˥o g̃a ˥i˥i desu.
'A BIG ONE is better than a small one.' (Lit. 'More than a small one, a BIG ONE [or ALTERNATIVE] is good.')

(c) Ta⌐naka-sañ yo˥ri Ya⌐mamoto-sañ o yo˥ku sitte imasu.   or
Ta⌐naka-sañ yo˥ri Ya⌐mamoto-sañ no ho˥o o ˥yo˥ku sitte imasu.
'I know MR. YAMAMOTO better than Mr. Tanaka.' (Lit. 'More than Mr. Tanaka I know MR. YAMAMOTO [or the alternative of MR. YAMAMOTO] well.')

In the above examples, the phrase ending with yori may occur after the g̃a or o phrase without any difference in meaning other than a slight change in emphasis.

Examples of the pattern X wa Y yori —— also occur; here, X is already under discussion or is being compared, and the emphasis is on what follows.

Hodo 'to the extent of' occurs in negative comparisons: X wa Y hodo /+ negative/ 'X is not as —— as Y.'

Study the following examples:

(a) Sore wa kŏre hodo ⌐ki˥ree zya a˩rimase˥ñ.
'That is not as pretty as this.' (Lit. 'That is not pretty to the extent of this.')

(b) Ti⌐isa˥i no wa o⌐oki˥i no hodo ⌐yo˥ku a˩rimase˥ñ.
'A small one is not as good as a big one.' (Lit. 'A small one is not good to the extent of a big one.')

(c) Tanaka-sañ wa Yămamoto-sañ hodo ⌐yo˥ku si˩rimase˥ñ.
'Mr. Tanaka I don't know as well as Mr. Yamamoto.' (Lit. 'Mr. Tanaka I don't know well to the extent of Mr. Yamamoto.')
      or
'Mr. Tanaka doesn't know as well as Mr. Yamamoto.' (Lit. 'Mr. Tanaka doesn't know well to the extent of Mr. Yamamoto.')

3.   Comparison of Three or More Items; i⌐ti⌐bañ

I⌐ti⌐bañ[1] 'to the greatest degree' occurs with verbals, adjectivals, nominals, and the copula:

> Ta⌐naka-sañ g̱a itibañ dekima⌐su. 'Mr. Tanaka is the most capable.'
> I⌐tibañ taka⌐i no wa so⌐re de⌐su. 'The most expensive one is that one.'
> So⌐no sara g̱a itibañ ki⌐ree desyoo ne? 'I guess that plate is the prettiest, isn't it?'
> So⌐re mo i⌐i desu g̱a, ko⌐re g̱a iti⌐bañ desu. 'That's good too, but this is the best.'

The two most common Japanese patterns for asking 'of X and Y and Z, which is most —— ?' are:

> X to Y to Z de, do⌐re + particle + i⌐ti⌐bañ ——
> Lit. 'being X and Y and Z, which to the greatest extent —— ?'

and

> X to Y to Z no uti[2] *[de]*, do⌐re + particle + i⌐ti⌐bañ ——
> Lit. '*[being]* among X and Y and Z, which to the greatest extent —— —— ?'

X, Y, and Z are nominals (which may be preceded by descriptive words or phrases and/or followed by particles); following do⌐re is an appropriate particle. These patterns are used when three or more items are specifically mentioned.   A cover phrase such as ko⌐no mi-ttu *[no uti]* *[de]* '*[being]* *[among]* these three things,' Nihoñ no yasai *[no uti]* *[de]* '*[being]* *[among]* Japanese vegetables,' etc., may be used instead of naming the specific items. Also, question words other than do⌐re may be used when they are appropriate.

Statements involving the same kind of comparison have the same general pattern as questions.

Examples:

> Gaiziñ wa, sukiyaki to teñpura to ⌐su⌐si no uti de, taitee ⌐do⌐re o i⌐ti-bañ yo⌐ku ta⌐bema⌐su ka˩ 'Which do Westerners usually eat most often— sukiyaki or tempura or sushi?'
> Ko⌐obe to Ōosaka to Yōkohama de, do⌐ko g̱a i⌐tibañ ooki⌐i desu ka˩ 'Which is the biggest place—Kobe or Osaka or Yokohama?'
> So⌐no sañ-niñ no uti de, da⌐re g̱a ni⌐hoñg̱o g̱a itibañ yo⌐ku wa⌐karima⌐su ka˩ 'Of those 3 people, who understands Japanese best?'
> Ko⌐no yo-ttu no uti de, ko⌐re g̱a itibañ suki⌐ desu kara; ko⌐re ni sima⌐-sita. 'Of these 4 I like this one best so I decided on this one.'

---

[1] I⌐ti⌐bañ is regularly accented in isolation and immediately before √da.

[2] Uti (nominal) 'among'; other meanings will be introduced later.

Eeḡo to nǐhoñḡo to hǔrañsuḡo de, i⌐tibañ hana⌐su no wa ni⌐hoñḡo de⌐su.
'Of English and Japanese and French, the one I speak most is Japanese.'

In comparing two alternatives, X to Y de ⌐do⌐tira ⸺ 'being X and Y, which
one ⸺ ?' is sometimes used as an alternant of X to Y to ⌐do tira ⸺, the
pattern introduced in Note 2 above.   Here too, a covering phrase may be used
instead of mentioning specific items: ko⌐no huta-tu⌐ de ⌐do⌐tira ⸺ 'being these
two things, which one ⸺ ?'

4.   Interrogative + de⌐ mo

An interrogative word or phrase (na⌐ñ, do⌐re, do⌐tira, i⌐tu, do⌐ko, na⌐ñ-zi,
do⌐no ⌐ho⌐ñ, etc.) + de (the gerund of da) + particle mo 'even' means '⸺ever
it is,' 'no matter ⸺ it is,' 'any ⸺ at all' (lit. 'even being ⸺). Thus: [1]

da⌐re de⌐ mo 'whoever it is,' 'no matter who it is,' 'anyone at all'

do⌐ko de⌐ mo 'wherever it is,' 'no matter what place it is,' 'any place
at all'

i⌐tu de⌐ mo 'whenever it is,' 'no matter when it is,' 'any time at all'

i⌐ku-tu de⌐ mo 'any number (of units) at all,' 'however many it is,'
'no matter how many it is'

na⌐ñ-niñ de⌐ mo 'any number of people at all,' 'however many people
it is,' 'no matter how many people it is'

The interrogative may be followed by any of the particles which normally
precede √da:

do⌐ko kara de⌐ mo 'wherever it is from,' 'no matter where it is
from'

Examples:

Da⌐re de⌐ mo de⌐ki⌐ru desyoo.   'Anyone at all can probably do it.'
I⌐tu de⌐ mo ⌐i⌐i desu yo⌟ 'Any time at all will be all right.'
So⌐no⌐ hito wa na⌐ñ de⌐ mo tabemasu. 'He eats anything at all.'
Na⌐ñ-zi kara de⌐ mo ka⌐maimase⌐ñ.   'No matter what time it starts
(lit. even being from what time), it makes no difference.'

---

[1] There is considerable variation in the accent of such combinations. The
original accent of the interrogative is sometimes retained, but is more often
lost.

5.   M a n n e r

To indicate how or in what manner something is done, the following patterns occur:

(a) a verbal gerund

Example: i⌐so⌐ide ⌐ka⌐ku 'write in a hurry'

(b) an adverbial adjectival (i.e. the -ku form)[1]

Example: o⌐mosi⌐roku ⌐ka⌐ku 'write interestingly'

(c) a nominal + particle ni of manner

Examples: i⌐ssyo ni ka⌐ku 'write together'
          ki⌐ree ni ⌐ka⌐ku 'write beautifully'

(d) a nominal alone

Examples: so⌐o ka⌐ku 'write thus'
          yu⌐kku⌐ri ⌐ka⌐ku 'write slowly'

Na-nominals are among those regularly followed by ni in patterns of manner. Otherwise, it is impossible to know which nominals are followed by ni and which may occur alone, except by observing the usage of native speakers.

6.   P a r t i c l e   to 'with'

To, the particle of accompaniment, following a nominal means 'with.' A phrase ending in to may modify an inflected word directly or it may be followed by other particles:

ni⌐honzi⌐n to kekkon-suru 'marry (with) a Japanese'
to⌐modati to hana⌐su 'talk with a friend'
to⌐modati to⌐ mo ha⌐na⌐su 'talk with a friend, too'

It may also modify certain nominals directly:

tomodati to issyo 'together with a friend'

But as a description of nominals, it is regularly followed by particle no:

a⌐merika⌐zin to no kekkon 'marriage with an American'
a⌐ni to no hanasi 'a talk with my (older) brother'

The particle to 'and' introduced in Lesson 4, Grammatical Note 1(e), joins coordinate nominals. Compare:

----

[1] This is another example of an adjectival in its -ku form modifying an inflected word—a constantly recurring pattern.

Tanaka-sañ to Yamamoto-sañ wa ha⌐nasima⌐sita.   'Mr. Tanaka and Mr. Yamamoto talked. '

and :

Tanaka-sañ wa Ya⌐mamoto-sañ to hanasima⌐sita.   'Mr. Tanaka talked with Mr. Yamamoto.'

WARNING : To never means 'with' in the sense of 'the means by which an action is performed.' Compare :

To⌐modati to hanasima⌐sita.   'I talked with a friend.'

and :

Ha⌐si de ta⌐bema⌐sita.   'I ate with chopsticks.'

For de 'by means of,' see Lesson 7, Grammatical Note 3 (d).

7.   C o u n t e r - n i ñ m a e

The counter -niñmae combines with the numerals of Series I to count portions or servings— of a single item or of everything eaten by a single person:

iti-niñmae	' 1 portion'	roku-niñmae ' 6 portions'
ni-niñmae	' 2 portions'	siti-niñmae or nana-niñmae ' 7 portions'
sañ-niñmae	' 3 portions'	hati-niñmae ' 8 portions'
yo-niñmae	' 4 portions'	kyuu-niñmae or ku-niñmae ' 9 portions'
go-niñmae	' 5 portions'	zyuu-niñmae ' 10 portions'

nañ-niñmae 'how many portions?'

DRILLS

A. Substitution Drill (based on Grammatical Note 4)

1. Anything at all will be fine.   Na⌐ñ de mo i⌐i desu yo⌡

2. Either one will be fine.   Do⌐tira de mo i⌐i desu yo⌡

3. Any one (of a group of 3 or more) at all will be fine.   Do⌐re de mo i⌐i desu yo⌡

4. Any time at all will be fine.   I⌐tu de mo i⌐i desu yo⌡

5. Anybody at all will be fine.   Da⌐re de mo i⌐i desu yo⌡

6. Any place at all will be fine.   Do⌐ko de mo i⌐i desu yo⌡

7. Any hour at all will be fine.   Na⌐ñ-zi de mo i⌐i desu yo⌡

8. Any number of people at all will be fine.   Na⌐ñ-niñ de mo i⌐i desu yo⌡

9. Any number of things (or any age) at all will be fine.   I⌐ku-tu de mo i⌐i desu yo⌡

10. Any book at all will be
fine.

Do⌐no hoñ de mo i⌉i desu yo⌐

11. No matter whose it is,
it will be fine.

Da⌐re no de mo i⌉i desu yo⌐

12. No matter what time it
starts, it will be fine.

Na⌐ñ-zi kara de mo i⌉i desu yo⌐

B. Substitution Drill

1. How much is it for one
portion?

Iti-niñmae ⌐i⌉kura desu ka⌐

2. How much is it for one
glass (ful)?

I⌉p-pai ⌐i⌉kura desu ka⌐

3. How much is it for one
bottle?[1]

I⌉p-poñ ⌐i⌉kura desu ka⌐

4. How much is it for one
(thin, flat object)?

I⌐ti⌉-mai ⌐i⌉kura desu ka⌐

5. How much is it for one
book?

Is-satu ⌐i⌉kura desu ka⌐

6. How much is it for one
hour?

I⌐ti-zi⌉kañ ⌐i⌉kura desu ka⌐

7. How much is it for one
day?

Iti-niti ⌐i⌉kura desu ka⌐

8. How much is it for one
month?

I⌐k-ka⌉g̃etu ⌐i⌉kura desu ka⌐

9. How much is it for one
person?

Hi⌐to⌉-ri ⌐i⌉kura desu ka⌐

10. How much is it for one
(thing)?

Hi⌐to⌉-tu ⌐i⌉kura desu ka⌐

C. Substitution Drill (based on Grammatical Note 5)

1. They talked slowly.

Yu⌐kku⌉ri ha⌐nasima⌐sita.

2. They talked [in] simple
[language].

Ya⌐sasiku hanasima⌉sita.

3. They talked together.

I⌐ssyo ni hanasima⌉sita.

4. They talked in a hurry.

I⌐so⌉ide ha⌐nasima⌐sita.

5. They talked that way.

So⌐o hanasima⌉sita.

6. They talked quickly.

Ha⌉yaku ha⌐nasima⌐sita.

7. They talked in the same
way.

O⌐nazi ni hanasima⌉sita.

8. They talked [in] difficult
[language].

Mu⌐zukasiku hanasima⌉sita.

---

[1] Or any long, cylindrical object.

D. Substitution Drill (based on Grammatical Note 6)

1. Last night I had dinner
    with a friend.

    Yuube to⌐modati to issyo ni syokuzi
    (o) sima¬sita.

2. Last night I went [there]
    with my mother.

    Yuube ⌐ha¬ha to issyo ni i⌐kima┤si-
    ta.

3. Last night I went out with
    my father.

    Yuube ti⌐ti¬ to issyo ni de⌐kakema┤-
    sita.

4. Last night I studied with
    my cousin.

    Yuube i⌐to¬ko to issyo ni be⌐ñkyoo-
    sima┤sita.

5. Last night I came here with
    my parents.

    Yuube ⌐ryo¬osiñ to issyo ni ki⌐ma┤-
    sita.

6. Last night I returned home
    with my children.

    Yuube ko⌐domo to issyo ni kaerima¬-
    sita.

7. Last night I saw [it] with
    my wife.

    Yuube ⌐ka¬nai to issyo ni mi⌐ma┤si-
    ta.

8. Last night I ate with my
    aunt.

    Yuube o⌐ba to issyo ni tabema¬sita.

E. Substitution Drill (based on Grammatical Note 2)

1. Which do you like better,
    this one or that one?

    Kore to are to ⌐do¬tira [no ┌ho┤o] ḡa
    o⌐suki de¬su ka⌐

2. Which is more expensive,
    this one or that one?

    Kore to are to ⌐do¬tira [no ┌ho┤o] ḡa
    ta⌐ka¬i desu ka⌐

3. Which is bigger, this one
    or that one?

    Kore to are to ⌐do¬tira [no ┌ho┤o] ḡa
    o⌐oki¬i desu ka⌐

4. Which tastes better, this
    one or that one?

    Kore to are to ⌐do¬tira [no ┌ho┤o] ḡa
    o⌐isi¬i desu ka⌐

5. Which is better, this one
    or that one?

    Kore to are to ⌐do¬tira [no ┌ho┤o] ḡa
    ⌐i¬i desu ka⌐

6. Which is easier, this one
    or that one?

    Kore to are to ⌐do¬tira [no ┌ho┤o] ḡa
    ya⌐sasi¬i desu ka⌐

7. Which is newer, this one
    or that one?

    Kore to are to ⌐do¬tira [no ┌ho┤o] ḡa
    a⌐tarasi¬i desu ka⌐

8. Which is more difficult,
    this one or that one?

    Kore to are to ⌐do¬tira [no ┌ho┤o] ḡa
    mu⌐zukasi¬i desu ka⌐

9. Which is more interesting,
    this one or that one?

    Kore to are to ⌐do¬tira [no ┌ho┤o] ḡa
    o⌐mosiro¬i desu ka⌐

F. Substitution Drill (based on Grammatical Note 3)

    (Insert na where required)

1. The one I like best is
    tempura.

    I⌐tibañ suki¬ na no wa te⌐ñpura de¬su
    yo.

2. The worst one is this pa-
    per.

    I⌐tibañ waru¬i no wa ko⌐no siñbuñ de¬-
    su yo.

3. The peppiest one is that
    child.

    I⌐tibañ ge¬ñki na no wa a⌐no kodomo
    de¬su yo.

4. The oldest one is our car.

    I⌐tibañ huru¬i no wa u⌐ti no kuruma
    de¬su yo.

5. The prettiest one is Miss Tanaka.

I⌐tibañ ki⌐ree na no wa Ta⌐naka-sañ no ozyo⌐osañ desu yo.

6. The slowest one is that bus.

I⌐tibañ oso⌐i no wa a⌐no ba⌐su desu yo.

7. The strangest one is that name.

I⌐tibañ he⌐ñ na no wa a⌐no namae de⌐su yo.

8. The busiest one is that company.

I⌐tibañ isoḡasi⌐i no wa a⌐no kaisya de⌐su yo.

9. The coldest one is the next room.

I⌐tibañ samu⌐i no wa to⌐nari no heya⌐ desu yo.

10. The most delicious (one) is the sushi at that place.

I⌐tibañ oisi⌐i no wa a⌐soko no osu⌐si desu yo.

G. Substitution Drill (based on Grammatical Note 3)

1. Which is most expensive—this one, that one, or the one over there?

Kore to sore to are de, do⌐re ḡa i⌐tibañ taka⌐i desu ka.

2. Which is most expensive—the blue one, the red one, or the black one?

A⌐o⌐i no to a⌐ka⌐i no to ku⌐ro⌐i no de, do⌐re ḡa i⌐tibañ taka⌐i desu ka.

3. Which is most expensive—this store, that store, or the store over there?

Ko⌐no mise⌐ to so⌐no mise⌐ to a⌐no mise⌐ de, do⌐re ḡa i⌐tibañ taka⌐i desu ka.

4. Which is most expensive—train, airplane, or ship?

Ki⌐sya⌐ to hi⌐ko⌐oki to ⌐hu⌐ne no uti de, do⌐re ḡa i⌐tibañ taka⌐i desu ka.

5. Which is most expensive of those three things?

A⌐no mittu⌐ no uti de, do⌐re ḡa i⌐tibañ taka⌐i desu ka.

6. Which is most expensive of these four (long, cylindrical objects)?

Ko⌐no yo⌐ñ-hoñ no uti de, do⌐re ḡa i⌐tibañ taka⌐i desu ka.

7. Which is most expensive—meat, fish, or fowl?

Ni⌐ku⌐ to sa⌐kana to to⌐ri de, do⌐re ḡa i⌐tibañ taka⌐i desu ka.

8. Which is most expensive—tea, coffee, or milk?

Otya to ko⌐ohi⌐i to ⌐mi⌐ruku no uti, do⌐re ḡa i⌐tibañ taka⌐i desu ka.

H. Grammar Drill (based on Grammatical Note 2)

Tutor: Kore wa a⌐re hodo ⌐yo⌐ku a⌐rimase⌐ñ. 'This one is not as good as that one.'

Student: Are wa ko⌐re yo⌐ri ⌐i⌐i desu. 'That one is better than this one.'

1. Ki⌐sya⌐ wa hi⌐ko⌐oki hodo ⌐ha⌐yaku a⌐rimase⌐ñ.

Hi⌐ko⌐oki wa ki⌐sya⌐ yori ha⌐ya⌐i desu.

2. Tookyoo wa Sa⌐pporo hodo ⌐sa⌐muku a⌐rimase⌐ñ.

Sapporo wa To⌐okyoo yo⌐ri sa⌐mu⌐i desu.

3. Bi⌐iru wa sa⌐ke hodo a⌐maku arimase⌐ñ.

Sake wa ⌐bi⌐iru yori a⌐ma⌐i desu.

4. Ro⌐ku-g̃atu⌐ wa ha⌐ti-g̃atu⌐   Ha⌐ti-g̃atu⌐ wa ro⌐ku-g̃atu⌐ yori a⌐tu⌐i
   hodo ⌐a⌐tuku a⌐rimase⌐n̄.   desu.

5. O⌐re⌐n̄zi[1] wa re̅mon̄[2] hodo   Remon̄ wa o⌐re⌐n̄zi yori su⌐ppa⌐i desu.
   su⌐ppa⌐ku a⌐rimase⌐n̄.

6. Ba⌐su⌐ wa ki⌐sya⌐ hodo ⌐ta⌐-   Ki⌐sya⌐ wa ⌐ba⌐su yori ta⌐ka⌐i desu.
   kaku a⌐rimase⌐n̄.

7. Nihon̄g̃o wa e̅ego hodo   Eego wa ni⌐hon̄g̃o yo⌐ri ⌐yo⌐ku wa⌐ka-
   ⌐yo⌐ku wa⌐karimase⌐n̄.   rima⌐su.

8. Ko⌐ohi⌐i wa o̅tya hodo   Otya wa ko⌐ohi⌐i yori su⌐ki⌐ desu.
   su⌐ki⌐ zya a⌐rimase⌐n̄.

I.   Grammar Drill (based on Grammatical Note 1)

        Tutor: A⌐n̄mari wakarimase⌐n̄. 'He doesn't understand very much.'
        Student: A⌐n̄mari wakara⌐nai desyoo? 'He doesn't understand very
                 much,   does he?'

1. Ma⌐da so⌐no ho⌐n̄ (o) yo-   Ma⌐da so⌐no ho⌐n̄ (o) yo⌐ma⌐nai de-
   ⌐mimase⌐n̄.   syoo?

2. Da⌐re mo kaimase⌐n̄ desi-   Da⌐re mo kawana⌐katta desyoo?
   ta.

3. Be⌐tu ni oisiku arimase⌐n̄.   Be⌐tu ni oisiku na⌐i desyoo?

4. Ni⌐hon̄g̃o de iimase⌐n̄ de-   Ni⌐hon̄g̃o de iwana⌐katta desyoo?
   sita.

5. Da⌐re mo demase⌐n̄ desi-   Da⌐re mo de⌐nakatta desyoo?
   ta.

6. Ta⌐naka-san̄ no o⌐kusan̄   Ta⌐naka-san̄ no o⌐kusan̄ (wa) ta⌐ba-
   (wa) ta⌐bako (o) suimase⌐n̄.   ko (o) suwana⌐i desyoo?

7. A⌐tarasi⌐i sakana zya a⌐ri-   A⌐tarasi⌐i sakana zya ⌐na⌐katta de-
   mase⌐n̄ desita.   syoo?

8. Bi⌐iru to sa̅ke wa no⌐mi-   Bi⌐iru to sa̅ke wa no⌐ma⌐nai desyoo?
   mase⌐n̄.

9. E⌐ego (o) ben̄kyoo-site (i)-   E⌐ego o ben̄kyoo-site (i)na⌐i desyoo?
   mase⌐n̄.

10. Ta⌐isi⌐kan̄ ni tu⌐to⌐mete   Ta⌐isi⌐kan̄ ni tu⌐to⌐mete (i)⌐rassya-
    (i)⌐rassyaimase⌐n̄.   ra⌐nai desyoo?

J.   Response Drill

        Tutor: Sore (wa) ⌐na⌐n̄ desyoo ka. /hurosiki/ 'What do you suppose
                 that is?' /furoshiki/
        Student: Yo⌐ku wa⌐karimase⌐n̄ g̃a, hu⌐rosiki zya na⌐i desyoo ka.   'I
                 can't tell for sure but isn't it a furoshiki?'

---

[1] 'Orange.'

[2] 'Lemon.'

1. Are (wa) ⌐na⌐ñ desyoo
   ka. /kusuri/

   Yo⌐ku wa⌐karimase⌐ñ ḡa, ku⌐suri
   zya na⌐i desyoo ka.

2. Koko (wa) ⌐do⌐ko desyoo
   ka. /Siñbasi[1]/

   Yo⌐ku wa⌐karimase⌐ñ ḡa, Si⌐ñbasi
   zya na⌐i desyoo ka.

3. I⌐ma ⌐na⌐ñ-zi desyoo ka.
   /sa⌐ñ-zi-ḡo⌐ro/

   Yo⌐ku wa⌐karimase⌐ñ ḡa, sa⌐ñ-zi-
   ḡo⌐ro zya ⌐na⌐i desyoo ka.

4. A⌐no⌐ hito (wa) ⌐da⌐re desyoo ka. /Ta⌐naka-sañ
   no oto⌐osañ/

   Yo⌐ku wa⌐karimase⌐ñ ḡa, Ta⌐naka-
   sañ no oto⌐osañ zya ⌐na⌐i desyoo
   ka.

5. Sore (wa) na⌐ñyo⌐obi desyoo ka. /do⌐yo⌐obi/

   Yo⌐ku wa⌐karimase⌐ñ ḡa, do⌐yo⌐obi
   zya ⌐na⌐i desyoo ka.

6. Sore (wa) ⌐i⌐kura desyoo
   ka. /sa⌐ñbyaku⌐-eñ/

   Yo⌐ku wa⌐karimase⌐ñ ḡa, sa⌐ñbya-
   ku⌐-eñ zya ⌐na⌐i desyoo ka.

7. Ta⌐naka-sañ no ho⌐ñ (wa)
   ⌐do⌐re desyoo ka. /ku⌐ro⌐i
   no/

   Yo⌐ku wa⌐karimase⌐ñ ḡa, ku⌐ro⌐i
   no zya ⌐na⌐i desyoo ka.

8. Are (wa) ⌐do⌐no da⌐iḡaku
   desyo⌐o ka. /Toodai/

   Yo⌐ku wa⌐karimase⌐ñ ḡa, To⌐odai
   zya na⌐i desyoo ka.

K. Response Drill (based on Grammatical Note 2)

> Tutor: Kore (wa) a⌐re yo⌐ri ⌐i⌐i desu ka␣ 'Is this one better than
>   that one?'
> Student: Iie, a⌐re hodo yo⌐ku a⌐rimase⌐ñ yo␣ 'Why no, it isn't as
>   good as that one.'

1. Kono miti (wa) a⌐no miti
   yo⌐ri a⌐buna⌐i desu ka␣

   Iie, a⌐no miti hodo abunaku arima-
   se⌐ñ yo␣

2. Kono kusuri (wa) a⌐no kusuri yo⌐ri ni⌐ḡa⌐i desu ka␣

   Iie, a⌐no kusuri hodo ni⌐ḡaku a⌐ri-
   mase⌐ñ yo␣

3. Ko⌐no koohi⌐i (wa) a⌐no koo-
   hi⌐i yori ⌐ko⌐i desu ka␣

   Iie, a⌐no koohi⌐i hodo ⌐ko⌐ku a⌐ri-
   mase⌐ñ yo␣

4. Ko⌐no ho⌐ñ (wa) a⌐no ho⌐ñ
   yori ya⌐su⌐i desu ka␣

   Iie, a⌐no ho⌐ñ hodo ⌐ya⌐suku a⌐ri-
   mase⌐ñ yo␣

5. Kono tokee (wa) a⌐no tokee
   yo⌐ri ya⌐su⌐i desu ka␣

   Iie, a⌐no tokee hodo ya⌐suku a⌐ri-
   mase⌐ñ yo␣

6. Kono uti (wa) a⌐no uti yo⌐ri
   ⌐ki⌐ree desu ka␣

   Iie, a⌐no uti hodo ki⌐ree zya a⌐ri-
   mase⌐ñ yo␣

7. Ko⌐no oka⌐si (wa) a⌐no oka⌐si
   yori o⌐isi⌐i desu ka␣

   Iie, a⌐no oka⌐si hodo o⌐isiku arima-
   se⌐ñ yo␣

8. Ko⌐no iro⌐ (wa) a⌐no iro⌐ yori u⌐su⌐i desu ka␣

   Iie, a⌐no iro⌐ hodo u⌐suku arimase⌐ñ
   yo␣

9. Kono o⌐su⌐si (wa) a⌐no osu⌐-
   si yori ka⌐ra⌐i desu ka␣

   Iie, a⌐no osu⌐si hodo ⌐ka⌐raku a⌐ri-
   mase⌐ñ yo␣

10. Ko⌐no⌐ ko (wa) a⌐no⌐ ko
    yori ⌐ge⌐ñki desu ka␣

    Iie, a⌐no⌐ ko hodo ⌐ge⌐ñki zya a⌐ri-
    mase⌐ñ yo␣

---

[1] Section of Tokyo.

L. Level Drill (based on Grammatical Note 1)

> Tutor: Aꜛn̄mari wakarimaseꜛn̄ kara. (Formal)
> Student: Aꜛn̄mari wakaraꜛnai kara. (Informal)
>   'Because I don't understand very much.'

1. Soꜛre wa sirimaseꜛn̄ kara. — Soꜛre wa siranaꜛi kara.
2. Oꜛoki na ꜛkoꜛe de haꜛnasimaseꜛn̄ desita kara. — Oꜛoki na ꜛkoꜛe de haꜛnasaꜛnakatta kara.
3. Koꜛn̄na iroꜛ (wa) suꜛkiꜛ zya aꜛrimaseꜛn̄ kara. — Koꜛn̄na iroꜛ (wa) suꜛkiꜛ zya ꜛnaꜛi kara.
4. Maꜛda kaꜛwakimaseꜛn̄ kara. — Maꜛda kaꜛwakaꜛnai kara.
5. Kinoo iꜛrassyaimaseꜛn̄ desita kara. — Kinoo iꜛrassyaraꜛnakatta kara.
6. Kiꜛree na uti zya aꜛrimaseꜛn̄ desita kara. — Kiꜛree na uti zya ꜛnaꜛkatta kara.
7. Koꜛn̄na hoꜛn̄ (wa) oꜛmosiꜛroku aꜛrimaseꜛn̄ kara. — Koꜛn̄na hoꜛn̄ (wa) oꜛmosiꜛroku ꜛnaꜛi kara.
8. Kinoo daꜛre mo kimaseꜛn̄ desita kara. — Kinoo daꜛre mo koꜛnakatta kara.
9. Kyoꜛo no siḡoto (wa) muꜛzukasiku arimaseꜛn̄ desita kara. — Kyoꜛo no siḡoto wa muꜛzukasiku naꜛkatta kara.
10. Goꜛhan̄ (wa) ꜛmaꜛda deꜛkimaseꜛn̄ kara. — Goꜛhan̄ wa ꜛmaꜛda deꜛkiꜛnai kara.

M. Expansion Drill

1. Is it fast? (Indirect) — Haꜛyaꜛi desyoo ka.
    Which is faster? — Doꜛtira no ꜛhoꜛo ḡa haꜛyaꜛi desyoo ka.
    Which is faster—bus or electric train? — Baꜛsu to dēn̄sya to, doꜛtira no ꜛhoꜛo ḡa haꜛyaꜛi desyoo ka.

2. It isn't ready. . . . — Deꜛkimaseꜛn̄ ḡa_
    It isn't ready yet. . . . — Maꜛda deꜛkimaseꜛn̄ ḡa_
    The toast isn't ready yet. . . . — Toꜛosuto wa ꜛmaꜛda deꜛkimaseꜛn̄ ḡa_
    The eggs are ready but the toast isn't ready yet. . . . — Taꜛmaꜛḡo wa ꜛmoꜛo deꜛkimaꜛsita ḡa, toꜛosuto wa ꜛmaꜛda deꜛkimaseꜛn̄ ḡa_

3. Please come. — Iꜛraꜛsite kudasai.
    Please come to see us (lit. to our house). — Uꜛti e iraꜛsite kudasai.
    Do please come to see us. — Doꜛozo uꜛti e iraꜛsite kudasai.
    Any time will be fine but do please come to see us. — Iꜛtu de mo ꜛiꜛi desu ḡa, doꜛozo uꜛti e iraꜛsite kudasai.

4. You know, it has grown empty. — Suꜛkimaꜛsita yo.
    You know, I'm hungry. — Oꜛnaka ḡa sukimaꜛsita yo.

You know, I'm hungry already. | Mo˺o o˹naka ḡa sukima˺sita yo.

You know, I didn't eat so I'm hungry already. | Ta˹be˺nakatta kara, mo˺o o˹naka ḡa sukima˺sita yo.

You know, I didn't eat breakfast so I'm hungry already. | A˹sago˺han̄ o ta˹be˺nakatta kara, mo˺o o˹naka ḡa sukima˺sita yo.

5. I went to the JTB.[1] | Ko˹otuuko˺osya e i˹kima˺sita.

We went to the JTB together. | Issyo ni ko˹otuuko˺osya e i˹kima˺sita.

I went to the JTB (together) with a friend. | Tomodati to issyo ni ko˹otuuko˺osya e i˹kima˺sita.

I went to the JTB (together) with a Japanese friend. | Ni˹hon̄zi˺n̄ no tomodati to issyo ni ko˹otuuko˺osya e i˹kima˺sita.

I went to the JTB (together) with a Japanese friend this morning. | Ke˺sa ni˹hon̄zi˺n̄ no tomodati to issyo ni ko˹otuuko˺osya e i˹kima˺sita.

6. I don't like them. | Su˹ki˺ zya a˹rimase˺n̄.

I don't like them as much as ships. | Hu˺ne hodo su˹ki˺ zya a˹rimase˺n̄.

I like [them] but I don't like them as much as ships. | Su˹ki˺ desu ḡa, hu˺ne hodo su˹ki˺ zya a˹rimase˺n̄.

I like [them] more than airplanes, but I don't like them as much as ships. | Hi˹ko˺oki yori su˹ki˺ desu ḡa, hu˺ne hodo su˹ki˺ zya a˹rimase˺n̄.

Trains I like more than airplanes, but I don't like them as much as ships. | Ki˹sya˺ wa hi˹ko˺oki yori su˹ki˺ desu ḡa, hu˺ne hodo su˹ki˺ zya a˹rimase˺n̄.

SHORT SUPPLEMENTARY DIALOGUES

(with questions)

1. Smith (host): O˹nomi˺mono wa ˹na˺ni o me˹siaḡarima˺su ka⌐

   Tanaka (guest): O˹sake mo bi˺iru mo i˹tadakimase˺n̄ kara, zyu˺usu[2] o oneḡai-itasimasu.

    a. Tanaka-san̄ wa ˹do˺n̄na no˹mi˺mono o ta˹nomima˺su ka⌐

    b. Do˺o site so˹re o tanomima˺su ka⌐

---

[1] 'Japan Travel Bureau.'

[2] 'Juice.'

2. Tanaka: Kyo˥o wa ki⌐no˥o hodo ⌐a˥tuku ⌐na˥i ⌐ne˥e.
   Yamamoto: Kyo˥o wa tyo⌐odo i˥i ⌐ne˥e.

   a. Kyo˥o to ki⌐no˥o to, ⌐do˥tira ga a˥tu˥i desu ka⌐
   b. Tanaka-sañ to Yamamoto-sañ wa o⌐toko˥ desyoo ka, o⌐ñna˥ desyoo
      ka⌐

3. Tanaka: Su˥misu-sañ no nihoñḡo ⌐do˥o?
   Yamamoto: A⌐no˥ hito na⌐ñ de mo waka˥ru yo⌐

   a. Su˥misu-sañ wa ni⌐hoñḡo ḡa yo˥ku wa˥karima˥su ka, a⌐ñmari waka-
      rimase˥ñ ka.
   b. Da˥re ḡa so˥o iima˥su ka⌐

4. Tanaka: Su˥misu-sañ mo ko⌐otuuko˥osya e i⌐rassyaima˥sita ka⌐
   Yamamoto: I⌐rassyara˥nakatta desyoo. Tyo˥tto ˥ma˥e ni zi⌐mu˥syo ni i˥ra-
      ssya˥tta kara.

   a. Su˥misu-sañ wa ko⌐otuuko˥osya e i⌐kima˥sita ka⌐
   b. Yamamoto-sañ wa ⌐do˥o site wa˥karima˥su ka⌐

5. Smith: De⌐ñwa-sima˥sita ka⌐
   Tanaka: E˥e, si⌐ma˥sita ḡa; da⌐re mo de˥nakatta kara, ma⌐ta a˥to de kake-
      masu.

   a. Ta⌐naka-sañ wa deñwa-sima˥sita ka⌐
   b. Do˥o site ma˥ta a˥to de ka˥kema˥su ka⌐

SUPPLEMENTARY CONVERSATION

(Mr. Saito is telephoning a restaurant to arrange for a dinner party.)

Saito: Mo˥simosi.
Restaurant Employee: Mo˥simosi. Su⌐ehiro[1] de gozaima˥su.
Saito: Kotira wa To⌐okyoo-gi˥ñkoo no Sa⌐itoo de˥su ḡa⌐
R. E.: Ma⌐ido ari˥ḡatoo gozaimasu.
Saito: Ko˥ñbañ ro⌐ku-zi-ḡo˥ro i˥ku˥ kara, o⌐neḡai-sima˥su.
R. E.: Ha˥a, ka⌐sikomarima˥sita. Ko˥ñbañ wa ⌐na˥ñ-niñ-sama[2] de go˥zaima˥-
   su ka⌐
Saito: Go-⌐ni˥ñ desu yo.
R. E.: Ha˥a. Kyo˥o wa ⌐do˥ñna mo˥no˥ ni i˥tasimasyo˥o ka.
Saito: Do˥ñna mo˥no˥ ḡa ˥i˥i desyoo ka ⌐ne˥e. Kyo˥o wa ni˥ku˥ to sǎkana to
   do˥tti ḡa ii?

---

[1] A restaurant name.

[2] Polite equivalent of na˥ñ-niñ used commonly by restaurant and hotel personnel.

R. E.: Sa⌐yoo┐ de gozaima┐su ┌ne┘e. Kyo┐o wa a⌐tarasi┘i o⌐sakana g̃a gozaima┘su kara, osasimi wa i⌐ka┐g̃a de gozaimasu ka⌐

Saito: A┐a, i┐i desyoo.

R. E.: I┐i to⌐ri mo gozaima┘su kara, tori no sukiyaki mo i⌐ka┐g̃a de gozaima-syoo ka.

Saito: A┐a, ke⌐kkoo. So⌐re go-niñmae oneg̃ai-sima┐su. Hoka ni yǎsai to ku-⌐da┐mono su⌐ko┐si oneg̃ai-simasu.

R. E.: Ha┐a, ka⌐sikomarima┐sita. O⌐nomi┐mono wa o⌐sake to obi┐iru to ⌐do┐tira g̃a yo⌐rosi┘i desyoo ka.

Saito: Tu⌐metai bi┐iru oneg̃ai-simasu.

R. E.: Ha┐a ┌ha┘a.

Saito: Iti-niñmae i⌐kura-g̃u┐rai?

R. E.: Sa⌐yoo┐ de gozaima┐su ┌ne┘e. Iti-niñmae se⌐ñ-eñ-g̃u┐rai de gozaimasu g̃a⌐ O⌐bi┐iru wa hya⌐ku rokuzyu┐u-eñ de gozaimasu.

Saito: Ke⌐kkoo. Zya┐a oneg̃ai-simasu.

R. E.: Ka⌐sikomarima┐sita. Ro⌐ku┐-zi de gozaimasu ne? A⌐ri┐g̃atoo gozaimasu.

English Equivalent

Saito: Hello.

Restaurant Employee: Hello. (This is the) Suehiro (Restaurant).

Saito: This is [Mr.] Saito at the Bank of Tokyo (but) . . .

R. E.: (Thank you for coming here often.)

Saito: Tonight I'm coming (lit. going) at about 6 so will you take care of us?

R. E.: Certainly. How many people will it be tonight?

Saito: It will be 5.

R. E.: Certainly. What kind of things would you like today?

Saito: I w o n d e r what (kind of things) would be good. . . . Which is better today—meat or fish?

R. E.: Let me see. We have fresh fish today so how about sashimi?

Saito: Oh, that would be fine.

R. E.: I have some good chicken too, so how about chicken sukiyaki (too)?

Saito: Oh, fine. I'd like 5 portions of that. In addition, I'd like a few vege-tables and some fruit.

R. E.: Certainly. For drinks, which would be better—sake or beer?

Saito: I'd like cold beer.

R. E.: All right.

Saito: About how much [will it be] per person?

R. E.: Let me see. . . . It will be about ¥1000 per person but [will that be all right?] The beer will be ¥160 [i.e. extra].

Saito: Fine. Well then, please take good care of us!

R. E.: Certainly. Six o'clock, isn't it? Thank you.

EXERCISES

1. Using appropriate magazine pictures, photographs, or line drawings, prac-tice comparisons: 'Which is more ——, X or Y?'; 'X is more —— than Y'; 'Y is not as —— as X.'

2. You have taken some Japanese friends to a restaurant for dinner as your guests. Find out what each one wants, place the orders, and make any complaints that are necessary (for example: 'I ordered beer but you brought sake,' 'I ordered rice but you haven't brought it,' etc.), and at the end, take care of the check.

3. Telephone the Suehiro Restaurant and order dinner.   Include the following information:

    a. who you are
    b. how many will be in your party
    c. when you are coming
    d. what you would like to eat and drink
    e. the price per person

4. Turn back to Drill L on page 271.   Make up questions for which the sentences of Drill L would be appropriate answers (cf. Lesson 14, Exercise 3), and then drill on the questions with their answers (informal alternants).

5. Practice the Basic Dialogues, using appropriate variations.

Lesson 16. At Home

BASIC DIALOGUES: FOR MEMORIZATION

(a)

Smith

teacher or doctor	se⌐n̄se⌐e
Teacher Wada or Dr. Wada	Wa⌐da-señse⌐e
next week	raisyuu
next Friday	ra⌐isyuu no kiñyo⌐obi

1. Dr. Wada, won't you come to our house for dinner (lit. a meal) next Friday? — Wa⌐da-señse⌐e. Ra⌐isyuu no kiñyo⌐-obi ni ūti e syo⌐kuzi ni irassyaima-se⌐ñ ka↲

Dr. Wada

take pleasure in	yo⌐roko⌐bu /-u/
gladly or with pleasure	yo⌐roko⌐ñde
visit or call on	ukaḡau ╵ /-u/

2. Next Friday? I'll be glad to come. — Raisyuu no ki⌐ñyo⌐obi desu ka↲ Yo-⌐roko⌐ñde ukaḡaimasu.

residence	su⌐mai or o⌐su⌐mai ╵

3. Where do you live? (Lit. Where is your residence?) — O⌐su⌐mai (wa) ⌐do⌐tira desyoo ka.

Smith

(a section of Tokyo)	A⌐ka⌐saka
apartment house	a⌐pa⌐ato
Harris (Apartment) House	Ha⌐risu-apa⌐ato

4. I live in (lit. it is) Harris House in Akasaka. You probably know it, don't you? — A⌐ka⌐saka no Ha⌐risu-apa⌐ato desu ḡa, go⌐zo⌐ñzi desyoo ne?

Dr. Wada

5. Yes, I do (know). — E⌐e, zo⌐ñzite orimasu.

what floor? or how many floors?	nañ-ḡai

6. What floor is your apartment? — Otaku (wa) na⌐ñ-ḡai desyo⌐o ka.

Smith

first floor or one floor	ik-kai
third floor or three floors	sañ-ḡai

7. It's number 306 on the third
   floor.

San-g̃ai no ⌐sa⌐ñbyaku ro⌐ku⌐ - bañ
desu.

Dr. Wada

8. I see.

Wa⌐karima⌐sita.

9. What time shall I come?

Na⌐ñ-zi ni u⌐kag̃aimasyo⌐o ka.

Smith

   night or night-time
10. How would about 7:30 in
   the evening be?

   yo⌐ru
Yo⌐ru no si⌐ti-zi-hañ-g̃o⌐ro i⌐ka⌐g̃a
desyoo ka.

Dr. Wada

11. That will be fine. I'll come
   at 7:30. Thank you very
   much.

Ke⌐kkoo desu. Si⌐ti-zi-ha⌐ñ ni uka-
g̃aimasu. Do⌐o mo a⌐ri⌐g̃atoo gozaimasu.

(b)

Tanaka

   gray
   blue or green
   a gray and blue car
12. Is that gray and blue car
   yours?

   haiiro
   a⌐o
   haiiro to ⌐a⌐o no kuruma
Ano haiiro to ⌐a⌐o no kuruma (wa)
o⌐taku no⌐ desu ka⌐

Smith

13. No. That's the doctor's (or
   teacher's), isn't it?

Iie. Are wa se⌐ñse⌐e no desyoo?

   brown
14. Ours is brown.

   tyairo
U⌐ti no⌐ wa tya⌐iro de⌐su yo.

(c)

Mr. Tanaka

   door
   [something] closes or
     shuts
   be closed or be shut

   to
   si⌐ma⌐ru /-u/

   si⌐ma⌐tte (i)ru or
   si⌐ma⌐tte ⌐o⌐ru+

15. Is the door closed?

To (g̃a) si⌐ma⌐tte (i)ru?

Maid

   close or shut [some-
     thing]
16. Yes. I just closed it. . . .

   si⌐me⌐ru /-ru/

E⌐e, i⌐ma si⌐mema⌐sita g̃a⌐

Mr. Tanaka

   key
   [something] locks

   ka⌐g̃i⌐
   ka⌐g̃i⌐ g̃a ka⌐ka⌐ru /-u/

be locked	ka⌐ḡi¬ ḡa ka⌐ka⌐tte (i)ru or ka⌐ḡi¬ ḡa ka⌐ka⌐tte oru⁺
17. Is it locked too?	Ka⌐ḡi¬ mo ka⌐ka⌐tte (i)ru?

Maid

lock [something]	ka⌐ḡi¬ o ka⌐ke⌐ru /-ru/
18. No. Shall I lock it?	Iie. Ka⌐kemasyo¬o ka.

Mr. Tanaka

yes	a¬a [1]
19. Yes. Lock it, will you?	A¬a, ka¬kete ne?

(d)

Mrs. Tanaka

window	ma¬do
[something] opens	aku /-u/
be open	aite (i)ru or a⌐ite o¬ru⁺
20. Are the windows open?	Ma¬do (ḡa) äite (i)ru?

Maid

have been closed or shut	si¬mete ⌐a⌐ru
21. The ones over there are open, but the ones here have been shut. . . .	Mu⌐koo no¬ wa a⌐ite orima⌐su ḡa, ko⌐tira no¬ wa ⌐si¬mete arimasu.

open [something]	akeru /-ru/
22. Shall I open them?	A⌐kemasyo¬o ka.

Mrs. Tanaka

| 23.   Yes.   It's a little hot. | E¬e. Tyo¬tto a⌐tu¬i wa⌐ |

(e)

Mr. Tanaka

heater	su⌐to¬obu

[something] becomes
  attached or turned
  on
	tu¬ku /-u/

be attached or be turned on	tu¬ite (i)ru or tu¬ite ⌐o⌐ru⁺
24. Is the heater on?	Su⌐to¬obu (ḡa) ⌐tu¬ite (i)ru?

Maid

attach or turn on [something]	tu⌐ke¬ru /-ru/

---

[1] Informal, man's word.

25. It's not on. Shall I turn it   Tu⌐ite o⌐rimase⌐n̄. Tu⌐kemasyo⌐o ka.
    on?

Mr. Tanaka

      no   i⌐ya [1]
      being that condition   so⌐no mama⌐ de
      is warm   a⌐tataka⌐i /-ku/ or
                                                                             a⌐ttaka⌐i /-ku/

26. No, it's fine as it is. (Since)   I⌐ya, so⌐no mama⌐ de ⌐i⌐i yo. Mo⌐o
    it's warm already.   a⌐ttaka⌐i kara.

(f)

Tanaka

      television   te⌐rebi
      electricity or electric   de⌐n̄ki
        light
      turn off or extinguish   kesu /-u/
        or erase [something]
27. I'm going to watch television   Te⌐rebi (o) ⌐mi⌐ru kara, de⌐n̄ki (o)
    so turn off the light.   ke⌐site.

Maid

      have been turned off   ke⌐site a⌐ru   or
                                                                             ke⌐site gozaima⌐su +
28. The ones here have all been   Ko⌐ko no⌐ (wa) mi⌐n̄na kesite gozai-
    turned off. . . .   ma⌐su ḡa—

Tanaka

      entry hall   ge⌐n̄kan̄
29. How about the one in the   Ge⌐n̄kan̄ no wa?
    entry hall?

Maid

30. Oh, that one is on, isn't it.   A⌐a, a⌐re wa tu⌐ite orimasu ⌐ne⌐e.
    I'll turn it off [right] now.   I⌐ma ke⌐sima⌐su.

(g)

Maid

      radio   ra⌐zio
      make small or turn   ti⌐isaku suru   or
        down   ti⌐isaku i⌐tasima⌐su ↓
31. Shall I turn down the radio a   Ra⌐zio(o) mo⌐o suko⌐si ⌐ti⌐isaku i⌐ta-
    little more?   simasyo⌐o ka.

---

[1] Informal, man's word.

Mr. Tanaka

being big or loud, as   o⌐oki⌐i ma┌ma┐ de
    it is
door (Western style)   do┐a
32. No, it doesn't matter if it's   I┐ya, o⌐oki┐i ma┌ma┐ de ka⌐mawa┐nai
loud but close that door,   g̱a, sono ⌐do┐a (o) ┌si┐mete ne? —
will you? —because Taro   ┌Ta┐roo (g̱a) mu┌koo de beñkyoo-
is studying in there.   site (i)ru┐ kara.

(h)

Mrs. Tanaka

is dirty   ki⌐tana┐i /-ku/
33. Hasn't this place gotten   K o k o (w a) ki⌐tana┐ku ┌na┐tta wa
dirty!   ⌐ne┐e.

clean (verb)   soozi-suru
after cleaning   so⌐ozi-site┐ kara
straighten up   ka⌐tazuke┐ru /-ru/
34. Clean it up, will you? Then   So⌐ozi-site┐ ne? Sore kara, so⌐ozi-
after you clean it, straighten   site┐ kara, ge⌐ñkañ (o) ka┌tazu┐ke-
up the entry hall.   te.

Maid

preparation   sitaku
35. What about getting dinner   Osyokuzi no sitaku wa?
ready? (Lit. As for meal
preparations?)

Mrs. Tanaka

after straightening up   ka⌐tazu┐kete kara
36. Do it after you straighten   Ka⌐tazu┐kete kara si┌te┐ ne?
up, will you?

NOTES ON THE BASIC DIALOGUES

1. Se⌐ñse┐e m e a n s 'teacher,' and 'doctor' in both the medical and non-
medical sense. It is the regular term of address for such persons, always
implying respect and deference on the part of the speaker. As a term of
address, it may be affixed to the family name or used independently.

Raisyuu 'next week': compare also rainen 'next year' and ra┐ig̱etu 'next
month.'

2. Yo⌐roko┐bu is not used in reference to the speaker except in its gerund
form, when describing the manner in which something is done (cf. Lesson
15, Grammatical Note 5). In this latter pattern, it may be used in reference to any subject. Thus: yo⌐roko┐bu desyoo '[someone other than the
speaker] will probably enjoy it or be glad'; but yo⌐roko┐ñde simasu '[some-
one] will gladly do it.'

6. A⌐pa┐ato is an apartment house. An apartment within an apartment house

is one's household—<u>uti</u> or <u>otaku</u>.

12. <u>Otaku no</u> means 'your(s),' i.e. '(the one) belonging to your household.'

14. <u>Uti no</u> means 'our(s),' i.e. '(the one) belonging to our household.'

16. 'but—is that all right?'

17-18. Note: <u>X ⌐no kaḡi⌐ ḡa ka⌐ka⌐ru</u> 'X locks';
       <u>X ⌐no kaḡi⌐ o ka⌐ke⌐ru</u> 'lock X'

21. 'but—how do you want them?'

26. Lit. 'Being that condition, it's fine.' The nominal ma⌐ma⌐ refers to an existing condition defined by the descriptive word or sequence which always precedes it.

    A⌐tataka⌐i, and contracted a⌐ttaka⌐i, mean 'warm'—i.e. 'nice and warm.' Typical days of spring, and unseasonably w a r m days of winter, are a⌐tataka⌐i.

28. 'but—is there anything else I can do?'

32. Lit. 'Even being its loud condition, it doesn't matter.'

    An informal inflected word before <u>ḡa</u> 'but' occurs in the informal speech of men.

    <u>To</u> (Sentence 15 above) is the general term for door and can refer to doors of any style. <u>Do⌐a</u>, on the other hand refers only to Western-style doors.

35. Note: <u>sitaku o suru</u> 'make preparations,' 'prepare'; <u>X no sitaku o suru</u> 'make preparations for <u>X</u>,' 'prepare for <u>X</u>.'

GRAMMATICAL NOTES

1. Verbals: Transitive and Intransitive; Gerund + $\sqrt{}$ ⌐a⌐ru

A verbal which may be preceded by a direct object + particle <u>o</u> is said to be TRANSITIVE.   A verbal which never so occurs is said to be INTRANSITIVE. Thus, <u>kau</u> 'buy' is transitive (<u>za⌐ssi o kaima⌐sita</u> 'I bought a magazine') but <u>wa⌐ka⌐ru</u> 'be comprehensible' is intransitive (<u>e⌐eḡo ḡa wakarima⌐su</u> 'I understand English').

Some other transitive verbals are: <u>ta⌐be⌐ru</u> 'eat,' <u>no⌐mu</u> 'drink,' <u>mi⌐ru</u> 'see,' <u>mi⌐se⌐ru</u> 'show,' <u>wasureru</u> 'forget'; some other intransitive verbals are: <u>iru</u> 'be needed,' <u>ka⌐ka⌐ru</u> 'be required,' <u>kikoeru</u> 'be audible,' <u>a⌐ru</u> 'be (inanimate,' 'have,' <u>iku</u> 'go.'

In Japanese, there are many pairs of verbals whose stems resemble each other phonetically, one member of which is transitive and the other intransitive. Several examples occur in this lesson:

Transitive	Intransitive

akeru 'open [something]'
  (Do˺a o a˩kema˧sita.
  'I opened the door.')

aku '[something] opens'
  (Do˺a ḡa a˩kima˧sita.
  'The door opened.')

si˹me˺ru 'close [something]'
  (Do˺a o si˩mema˧sita.
  'I closed the door.')

si˹ma˺ru '[something] closes'
  (Do˺a ḡa si˩marima˧sita.
  'The door closed.')

tu˹ke˺ru 'attach [something]'
  (De˺ṅki o tu˹kema˧sita.
  'I turned on the light.')

tu˺ku '[something] becomes attached'
  (De˺ṅki ḡa tu˩kima˧sita.
  'The light went on.')

A pair introduced previously is:

na˹o˺su 'make [something or
  someone] better'

na˹o˺ru '[something or someone]
  gets better'

Note also the following pair:

kesu 'turn [something] off'

kieru /-ru/ '[something] goes out
  or becomes extinguished'

A verbal gerund + (i)ru means that an action is now going on, or that the result of a previous action now exists (cf. Lesson 10, Grammatical Note 2). Usually the gerund of a transitive verbal + (i)ru has the former meaning, whereas the gerund of an intransitive + (i)ru has the latter meaning:

Transitive	Intransitive

Do˺a o a˩kete (i)ma˧su.
  'I'm opening the door.'

Do˺a ḡa a˩ite (i)ma˧su.
  'The door is open.'

Do˺a o ˩si˺mete (i)masu.
  'I'm closing the door.'

Do˺a ḡa si˩ma˧tte (i)masu.
  'The door is closed.'

De˺ṅki o tu˹ke˧te (i)masu.
  'I'm turning on the light.'

De˺ṅki ḡa ˩tu˧ite (i)masu.
  'The light is on.'

The subject of a gerund + √(i)ru pattern may be animate or inanimate. When the subject is inanimate, √(i)ru is replaced by √o˹ru (formal: √o˹rima˺su) in polite speech, [1] but never by √i˹rassya˺ru, an honorific which refers only to people.

A new combination appears in this lesson: the gerund of a TRANSITIVE verbal + √a˺ru 'so-and-so has been done.' [2] Like an intransitive gerund + √(i)ru, it indicates the existing result of a previous action, and the combination is itself intransitive; however, a transitive gerund + √a˺ru always implies the result of an action that HAS BEEN DONE BY SOMEONE. Thus:

---

[1] The combination is polite neutral (+), not humble (↓).

[2] This pattern includes transitive verbals in general—not only those having an intransitive partner.

Do⌐a ḡa a┌kete arima┐su. 'The door has been opened.'
Do⌐a ḡa ┌si┐mete arimasu. 'The door has been closed.'
De⌐ñki ḡa tu┌ke┐te arimasu. 'The light has been turned on.'
Ti⌐zu ḡa ┌ka┐ite arimasu. 'The map has been drawn.'
Si┌ñbuñ ḡa katte arima┐su. 'The newspaper has been bought.'

Compare these examples with one like <u>Do⌐a ḡa a┌ite ima┐su</u>, which means simply 'The door is open'; whether it was opened by someone or whether it opened by itself is not made clear by the pattern which uses the intransitive gerund.

The object of a transitive verbal becomes the subject of the corresponding gerund + √a⌐ru:

Sa┌kana o tabema┐sita. 'I ate the fish.'
Sa┌kana ḡa ta┐bete arimasu. 'The fish has been eaten.'

The subject of a gerund + √a⌐ru pattern is always inanimate.

In the informal negative, the contracted form of a transitive gerund + √iru may coincide with the transitive gerund + √a⌐ru, namely in those environments where the accent of the two forms is the same:

ta⌐bete iru '[I] am eating'
ta⌐bete inai, contracted ta⌐bete nai '[I] am not eating';
ta⌐bete ┌na┐i kara 'because [I] am not eating'

ta⌐bete ┌a┐ru '[it] has been eaten'
ta⌐bete ┌na┐i '[it] has not been eaten'
ta⌐bete ┌na┐i kara 'because [it] has not been eaten'

The coinciding forms are distinguished only by context.

2.   Verbal Gerund + <u>kara</u>

A verbal gerund (-<u>te</u>/-<u>de</u> form) + <u>kara</u> means 'after doing so-and-so' or 'since doing so-and-so.' A regularly unaccented gerund acquires an accent on its final syllable when it occurs before <u>kara</u>. Thus:

ta⌐bete kara 'after eating'
ka⌐ette kara 'after returning home'
mi⌐te┐ kara 'after seeing'
i┌tte┐ kara 'after going'   or   'after saying'

A gerund + <u>kara</u> combination regularly modifies an inflected expression without a following particle; but when it describes a nominal, it is followed by <u>no</u>.

Examples:

Ta⌐bete kara, ka┌isya e kaerima┐sita.
  'After eating, I went back to the office.'
Yo┌sida-sañ to hana┐site kara, ma┌ta koko e kite┐ kudasai.
  'After talking with Mr. Yoshida, please come back here.'
Si┌ñbuñ o yo┐ñde kara, so┌no zassi o mima┐su.
  'After I read the paper, I'm going to look at that magazine.'
Hu⌐ne ḡa ┌de┐te kara, To┌okyoo e kaerima┐sita.
  'After the ship left, I returned to Tokyo.'

Ko⌐ko e kite⌐ kara, mo⌐o ro⌐k-ka⌐g̃etu ni narimasu.
  'It is almost 6 months since I came here.'
  (Lit. 'Since coming here, it will become 6 months already.')
Sore wa zi⌐mu⌐syo o ⌐de⌐te kara no sig̃oto desu.
  'That is work [to be done] after leaving the office.'

WARNING: Be sure to distinguish between the gerund + <u>kara</u> and the informal
past + <u>kara</u>, which are easily confused by a beginner. Thus:

si⌐te⌐ kara 'after doing'   <u>but</u> si⌐ta⌐ kara 'because [I] did'
ki⌐ite⌐ kara 'after asking'   <u>but</u> ki⌐ita⌐ kara 'because [I] asked'
si⌐mete kara 'after shutting'   <u>but</u> si⌐meta kara 'because [I] shut'

3.   Color Words

<u>Akai</u>, <u>a⌐o⌐i</u>, <u>kiiroi</u>, <u>si⌐ro⌐i</u>, and <u>ku⌐ro⌐i</u> are color words which are adjectivals.
Thus:

  a. a⌐kai ho⌐n̄ 'a red book'
  b. akai 'it's red' (informal)
  c. a⌐ka⌐i desu 'it's red' (formal)
  d. a⌐ka⌐katta 'it was red' (informal)
  e. a⌐ka⌐katta desu (or a⌐ka⌐i desita) 'it was red' (formal)
  f. a⌐kaku narima⌐sita 'it's become red' (formal)
  g. a⌐kaku arimase⌐n̄ 'it isn't red' (formal)
  h. a⌐kaku na⌐i 'it isn't red' (informal)

<u>Tyairo</u> and <u>haiiro</u> are color words which are nominals. Thus:

  a. tya⌐iro no ho⌐n̄ 'a brown book'
  b. tyairo da⌐ 'it's brown' (informal)
  c. tya⌐iro de⌐su 'it's brown' (formal)
  d. tya⌐iro da⌐tta 'it was brown' (informal)
  e. tya⌐iro de⌐sita 'it was brown' (formal)
  f. tya⌐iro ni narima⌐sita 'it's become brown' (formal)
  g. tya⌐iro zya arimase⌐n̄ 'it isn't brown' (formal)
  h. tya⌐iro zya na⌐i 'it isn't brown' (informal)

Some other color words which are nominals are: <u>mu⌐ra⌐saki</u> 'purple,' <u>momo-
iro</u> 'pink,' <u>mi⌐dori</u> 'green.'

<u>A⌐ka</u>, <u>a⌐o</u>, <u>kiiro</u>, <u>si⌐ro</u>, and <u>ku⌐ro</u> are nominal alternants of the adjectival
color words listed above. While they are often used interchangeably with their
adjectival counterparts, they also have various special uses which distinguish
them from the adjectivals, including the following:

  a. Only the nominals are used to NAME the colors. Thus:

      A⌐o g̃a su⌐ki⌐ desu. 'I like blue (i.e. the color blue).'
        but:
      A⌐o⌐i no g̃a su⌐ki⌐ desu. 'I like the blue one (i.e. an object that is
        blue).'

  b. Only the nominals are u s e d when one object is described by several
      colors. Thus:

a⌐o⌐i ha⌐iza⌐ra 'a blue ashtray'
 and:
si⌐ro⌐i ha⌐iza⌐ra 'a white ashtray'
 but:
a⌐o to ⌐si⌐ro no ha⌐iza⌐ra 'a blue and white ashtray'

c. Only the nominals are themselves described by adjectivals. Thus:

a⌐o⌐i ha⌐iza⌐ra 'a blue ashtray'
 but:
u⌐sui a⌐o no ha⌐iza⌐ra 'a light blue ashtray'

akai kuruma 'a red car'
 but:
ko⌐i ⌐a⌐ka no kuruma 'a dark red car'

4. Sentence Particle <u>wa</u>

The sentence particle <u>wa</u>[1] occurs as a sentence final, or pre-final before
<u>yo</u>, <u>nee</u>, and <u>ne</u>, IN THE SPEECH OF WOMEN. It regularly follows non-past
and past inflected words in the informal style,[2] plain and polite. It is a particle which indicates friendliness and assertiveness—in a gentle way—and some
familiarity. Whereas <u>So⌐o da.</u> is abrupt and masculine, <u>So⌐o da wa⌐</u> is friend-
ly and feminine.[3]

Informal patterns consisting of an informal non-past or past directly followed by <u>yo</u>, <u>ne⌐e</u>, and <u>ne</u> are more typical of men's speech (cf. Lesson 13,
Grammatical Note 2). If sentence particle <u>wa</u> is inserted before <u>yo</u>, <u>ne⌐e</u>, and
<u>ne</u> in such sequences they become typical of women's speech. However, the
most frequently occurring women's equivalents of sentences ending in <u>da yo</u>,
<u>da ⌐ne⌐e</u>, and <u>da ne</u> simply omit the <u>da</u>.

	Men's Speech	Women's Speech
'I understand.'	Wa⌐ka⌐ru yo⌐	Wa⌐ka⌐ru wa yo⌐
'I understood.'	Wa⌐ka⌐tta yo⌐	Wa⌐ka⌐tta wa yo⌐
'Isn't it expensive!'	Ta⌐ka⌐i ⌐ne⌐e.	Ta⌐ka⌐i wa ⌐ne⌐e.
'Wasn't it expensive!'	Ta⌐kakatta ⌐ne⌐e.	Ta⌐kakatta wa ⌐ne⌐e.
'That's right, isn't it?'	So⌐o da ne?	So⌐o ne?
'It was strange, wasn't it?'	He⌐ñ datta ne?	He⌐ñ datta wa ne?

---

[1] It is best to consider this <u>wa</u> and the particle <u>wa</u> introduced previously as
different words.

[2] It also occurs with the formal style, but less frequently.

[3] In some dialects of Japanese, sentence particle <u>wa</u> occurs in men's
speech, but in standard Tokyo Japanese, it is a feminine particle.

Comparisons of some informal patterns which have already been introduced are shown in the following chart:

	Men and Women	Men	Women
'I understand.'	Wa⌐ka⌐ru.		Wa⌐ka⌐ru wa⌐
'It's expensive.'	Ta⌐ka⌐i.		Ta⌐ka⌐i wa⌐
'That's right.'	So⌐o.	So⌐o da.	So⌐o da wa⌐
'That's right!'		So⌐o da yo⌐	So⌐o yo⌐
'That's right, isn't it!'		So⌐o da ⌐ne⌐e.	So⌐o ⌐ne⌐e.
'That's right, isn't it?'		So⌐o da ne?	So⌐o ne?

5. Counter -kai 'floor'

The counter -kai combines with the numerals of Series I to count and to name the floors of a building. Numbers from one to ten are:

ik-kai	'1 floor'	or	'1st floor'
ni-kai	'2 floors'	or	'2d floor'
sañ-ḡai	'3 floors'	or	'3d floor'
yoñ-kai	'4 floors'	or	'4th floor'
go-kai	'5 floors'	or	'5th floor'
rok-kai	'6 floors'	or	'6th floor'
nana-kai	'7 floors'	or	'7th floor'
hati-kai or hak-kai	'8 floors'	or	'8th floor'
kyuu-kai	'9 floors'	or	'9th floor'
zik-kai or zyuk-kai	'10 floors'	or	'10th floor'
nañ-ḡai	'how many floors?'	or	'what floor?'

Nikai (polite, onikai[+]) occurs as the equivalent of 'upstairs' when 'upstairs' refers to the second floor of a two-story building. The equivalent of 'downstairs' is sita ('below,' 'under').

DRILLS

A. Substitution Drill

1. Shall I turn down the radio? — Ra⌐zio (o) ⌐ti⌐isaku si⌐masyo⌐o ka.
2. Shall I turn up the television? — Te⌐rebi (o) ⌐o⌐okiku si⌐masyo⌐o ka.
3. Shall I heat the tea? — Otya (o) ⌐a⌐tuku si⌐masyo⌐o ka.
4. Shall I chill the beer? — Bi⌐iru (o) tu⌐metaku simasyo⌐o ka.
5. Shall I warm this room? — Ko⌐no heya⌐ (o) a⌐ttaka⌐ku si⌐masyo⌐o ka.
6. Shall I make the coffee strong? — Ko⌐ohi⌐i (o) ⌐ko⌐ku si⌐masyo⌐o ka.
7. Shall I make the (black) tea weak? — Kootya (o) u⌐suku simasyo⌐o ka.

B. Substitution Drill (based on Grammatical Note 3)

1. It's a gray and blue car.   Haiiro to ﹁a﹂o no ku⌐ruma de⌐su.
2. It's a black and white   Ku⌐ro to ﹁si﹂ro no ha⌐iza⌐ra desu.
    ashtray.
3. It's a green and yellow   Mi⌐dori to ki⌐iro no deñsya de⌐su.
    electric train.
4. It's a gray and black   Haiiro to ﹁ku﹂ro no ⌐hu⌐ne desu.
    ship.
5. It's a red and blue   A⌐ka to ﹁a﹂o no sa⌐ra de⌐su.
    plate.
6. It's a black and red   Ku⌐ro to ﹁a﹂ka no o⌐boñ de⌐su.
    tray.
7. It's a pink and white   Momoiro to ﹁si﹂ro no o⌐ka⌐si desu.
    cake.
8. It's dark blue paper.   Ko⌐i ⌐a⌐o no ka⌐mi⌐ desu.
9. It's a light brown pen.   U﹁sui tyairo no pe⌐ñ desu.
10. It's a dark purple fu-   Ko⌐i mu⌐ra⌐saki no hu⌐rosiki de⌐su.
    roshiki.

C. Substitution Drill (based on Grammatical Note 1)

Practice this drill in two ways: (1) Omit the particles in parentheses;
(2) Include the particles in parentheses with the student supplying
them on the basis of what verbals occur.

1. Did you lock the door?   To ﹁no kaḡi﹂ (o) ka⌐kema⌐sita ka⌐
2. Is the door locked?   To ﹁no kaḡi﹂ (ḡa) ka⌐ka⌐tte (i)masu ka⌐
3. Is the window locked?   Ma⌐do no ka⌐ḡi⌐ (ḡa) ka⌐ka⌐tte (i)masu
                                   ka⌐
4. Shall I lock the window?   Ma⌐do no ka⌐ḡi⌐ (o) ka⌐kemasyo⌐o ka⌐
5. Shall I lock the car?   Ku⌐ruma no kaḡi⌐ (o) ka⌐kemasyo⌐o ka⌐
6. Please lock the car.   Ku⌐ruma no kaḡi⌐ (o) ﹁ka﹂kete kudasai.
7. Please lock the entry   Ge⌐ñkañ no ka⌐ḡi⌐ (o) ﹁ka﹂kete kudasai.
    hall.
8. Has the entry hall been   Ge⌐ñkañ no ka⌐ḡi⌐ (ḡa) ﹁ka﹂kete arima-
    locked?   su ka⌐

D. Grammar Drill

Tutor: Ki﹁tana﹂i desu yo⌐ 'It's dirty!'
Student: Ki﹁tana﹂ku na⌐rima⌐sita yo⌐ 'It's gotten dirty!'

1. Ku﹁ro﹂i desu yo⌐   Ku⌐roku na⌐rima⌐sita yo⌐
2. Ha﹁iiro de﹂su yo⌐   Ha﹁iiro ni narima⌐sita yo⌐
3. A﹁ttaka﹂i desu yo⌐   A﹁tta﹂kaku na⌐rima⌐sita yo⌐
4. Se﹁ñse﹂e desu yo⌐   Se﹁ñse﹂e ni na⌐rima⌐sita yo⌐
5. A﹁o﹂i desu yo⌐   A⌐oku na⌐rima⌐sita yo⌐
6. Ge⌐ñki desu yo⌐   Ge⌐ñki ni na⌐rima⌐sita yo⌐
7. A﹁buna﹂i desu yo⌐   A﹁bunaku narima⌐sita yo⌐
8. Mi⌐dori desu yo⌐   Mi⌐dori ni na⌐rima⌐sita yo⌐

E.   Grammar Drill (based on Grammatical Note 1)

>   Tutor: Maꜜdo o aꜛkemaꜜsita.   'I opened the window.'
>   Student: Maꜜdo ḡa aꜛkimaꜜsita. 'The window opened.'

1. Deꜜñki o tuꜛkemaꜜsita.   Deꜜñki ḡa tuꜛkimaꜜsita.
2. To ꜛo simemaꜜsita.   To ꜛḡa simarimaꜜsita.
3. Soꜛre o naosimaꜜsita.   Soꜛre ḡa naorimaꜜsita.
4. Suꜛtoꜜobu o keꜛsimaꜜsita.   Suꜛtoꜜobu ḡa kiꜛemaꜜsita.
5. To ꜛno kaḡiꜜ o kaꜛkemaꜜsi-   To ꜛno kaḡiꜜ ḡa kaꜛkarimaꜜsita.
    ta.

F.   Grammar Drill (based on Grammatical Note 1)

>   Tutor: Maꜜdo o aꜛkemaꜜsita kaↄ   'Did you open the window?'
>   Student: Maꜜdo ḡa aꜛkete arimaꜜsu kaↄ   'Has the window been
>   opened?'

1. Kuruma o naꜛosimaꜜsita   Kuruma ḡa naꜛoꜜsite aꜛrimaꜜsu kaↄ
    kaↄ
2. Tiꜜzu o kaꜛkimaꜜsita kaↄ   Tiꜜzu ḡa ꜛkaꜜite aꜛrimaꜜsu kaↄ
3. Suꜛtoꜜobu o keꜛsimaꜜsita   Suꜛtoꜜobu ḡa keꜛsite arimaꜜsu kaↄ
    kaↄ
4. Aꜛtarasiꜛi ziꜛbikiꜜ o   Aꜛtarasiꜛi ziꜛbikiꜜ ḡa gaꜛkkoo e mot-
    gaꜛkkoo e motte ikimaꜜsi-   te iꜜtte aꜛrimaꜜsu kaↄ
    ta kaↄ
5. Doꜜa o siꜛmemaꜜsita kaↄ   Doꜜa ḡa ꜛsiꜛmete aꜛrimaꜜsu kaↄ
6. Teꜜrebi o tuꜛkemaꜜsita   Teꜜrebi ḡa tuꜛkeꜜte aꜛrimaꜜsu kaↄ
    kaↄ
7. Kuꜛruma no kaḡiꜜ o kaꜛke-   Kuꜛruma no kaḡiꜜ ḡa ꜛkaꜛkete aꜛri-
    maꜜsita kaↄ   maꜜsu kaↄ
8. Paꜜñ o kaꜛimaꜜsita kaↄ   Paꜜñ ḡa kaꜛtte arimaꜜsu kaↄ

G.   Grammar Drill (based on Grammatical Note 2)

>   Tutor: Taꜛbemaꜜsita. Sore kara, kaꜛerimaꜜsita.
>   'I ate. After that, I went home.'
>   Student: Taꜜbete kara, kaꜛerimaꜜsita.
>   'After eating, I went home.'

1. To ꜛ(o) simemaꜜsita. Sore   To ꜛ(o) siꜜmete kara, maꜜdo mo miꜛñ-
    kara, maꜜdo mo miꜛñna si-   na simemaꜜsita.
    memaꜜsita.
2. Deꜜñki (o) miꜛñna kesimaꜜsi-   Deꜜñki (o) miꜛñna kesiteꜜ kara, teꜜre-
    ta. Sore kara, teꜜrebi (o),   bi (o) tuꜛkemaꜜsita.
    tuꜛkemaꜜsita.
3. Uꜛti (o) katazukemaꜜsita.   Uꜛti (o) katazuꜜkete kara, deꜛkakemaꜜ-
    Sore kara, deꜛkakemaꜜsi-   sita.
    ta.
4. Soꜛozi-simaꜜsita. Sore   Soꜛozi-siteꜜ kara, syoꜛkuzi no sitaku
    kara, syoꜛkuzi no sitaku   (o) simaꜜsita.
    (o) simaꜜsita.

5. Si⌐ṅbuṅ (o) yomima¬si-
   ta. Sore kara, ka⌐isya
   ni ikima¬sita.

   Si⌐ṅbuṅ (o) yo¬ṅde kara, ka⌐isya ni i-
   kima¬sita.

6. Ni⌐hoṅzi¬ṅ to ke⌐kkoṅ-
   sima⊣sita. Sore kara,
   A⌐merika e kaerima¬si-
   ta.

   Ni⌐hoṅzi¬ṅ to ke⌐kkoṅ-site⊣ kara,
   A⌐merika e kaerima¬sita.

7. So⌐o iima¬sita. Sore
   kara, he⌐ya¬ (o) de⌐ma⊣-
   sita.

   So⌐o itte¬ kara, he⌐ya¬ (o) de⌐ma⊣si-
   ta.

8. De⌐ṅwa (o) kirima¬sita.
   Sore kara, ma⌐ta su¬ḡu
   ka⌐kema⊣sita.

   De⌐ṅwa (o) ki¬tte kara, ma⌐ta su¬ḡu
   ka⌐kema⊣sita.

9. Byo⌐oki ni narima¬sita.
   Sore kara, o⌐sake to
   tabako (o) yamema¬si-
   ta.

   Byo⌐oki ni na¬tte kara, o⌐sake to tabako (o) yamema¬sita.

10. Zyu⌐ṅsa ni kikima¬sita.
    Sore kara, su¬ḡu mi⌐ti
    ḡa wakarima⊣sita.

    Zyu⌐ṅsa ni kiite¬ kara, su¬ḡu mi⌐ti
    ḡa wakarima⊣sita.

H. Response Drill

(Give the iie answer, same politeness and formality level, for each of
the following.)

1. A⌐kima¬su ka⌟   Iie, a⌐kimase¬ṅ.
2. A⌐ite (i)ma¬su ka⌟   Iie, a⌐ite (i)mase¬ṅ.
3. Mi¬dori?   Iie, mi⌐dori zya ⌐na⊣i.
4. Yo¬ru desu ka⌟   Iie, yo¬ru zya a⌐rimase⊣ṅ.
5. Ki⌐ete orima¬su ka⌟   Iie, ki⌐ete orimase¬ṅ.
6. Ki⌐tana¬i?   Iie, ki⌐tana¬ku ⌐na⊣i.
7. A⌐na¬ta wa se⌐ṅse¬e de   Iie, se⌐ṅse¬e de wa go⌐zaimase⊣ṅ.
   (i)⌐rassyaima⊣su ka⌟
8. A⌐tataka¬i desu ka⌟   Iie, a⌐tata¬kaku a⌐rimase⊣ṅ.
9. Na⌐o¬site (i)ru?   Iie, na⌐o¬site (i)nai.
10. Na⌐o¬site ⌐a⊣ru?   Iie, na⌐o¬site ⌐na⊣i.
11. A⌐o¬i desu ka⌟   Iie, a⌐oku a⌐rimase⊣ṅ.
12. A¬o desu ka⌟   Iie, a¬o zya a⌐rimase⊣ṅ.

I. Response Drill

Tutor: O⌐okiku si⌐masyo⊣o ka.   'Shall I make it loud?'

Student: Iie, ti⌐isa¬i ma⌐ma⊣ de
          | ⌐i⊣ desu yo⌟ |
          | yo⌐rosi⊣i desu yo⌟ | (Practice all
          | ⌐ke⊣kkoo desu yo⌟ | 4 for each
          | ka⌐maimase⊣ṅ yo⌟ | answer)
          'No, it's all right soft, as it is.'

1. Ti⌐isaku si⌐masyo⊣o ka.   Iie, o⌐oki¬i ma⌐ma⊣ de ⌐i⊣i desu yo⌟
2. A¬tuku si⌐masyo⊣o ka.   Iie, tu⌐metai mama¬ de ⌐i⊣i desu yo⌟

3. Ko˺ku si˺masyo˺o ka.   Iie, u˹sui mama˺ de ˹i˺i desu yo˺

4. Ki˺ree ni si˺masyo˺o ka.   Iie, ki˹tana˺i ma˹ma˺ de ˹i˺i desu
                                                                    yo˺

5. Ya˹sasiku simasyo˺o ka.   Iie, mu˹zukasii mama˺ de ˹i˺i desu
                                                                    yo˺

6. U˹suku simasyo˺o ka.   Iie, ko˺i ma˹ma˺ de ˹i˺i desu yo˺

7. Ka˺raku si˺masyo˺o ka.   Iie, a˹mai mama˺ de ˹i˺i desu yo˺

J.   Expansion Drill

1. Have [they] been turned   Ke˹site arima˺su ka˺
   off?

   Are [they] on, or have   Tu˺ite (i)˺ma˺su ka, ke˹site arima˺-
   they been turned off?   su ka˺

   Are the lights on, or   De˺ñki wa ˹tu˺ite (i)˺ma˺su ka, ke-
   have they been turned   ˹site arima˺su ka˺
   off?

   Are the upstairs lights   Ni˹kai no de˺ñki wa ˹tu˺ite (i)˺ma˺su
   on, or have they been   ka, ke˹site arima˺su ka ˺
   turned off?

2. It's grown cold. . . . [1]   Sa˺muku na˹rima˺sita g̃a˶

   It's grown very cold. . . .   To˹ttemo sa˺muku na˹rima˺sita g̃a˶

   It's gone out so it's   Ki˹ete (i)ru˺ kara, to˹ttemo sa˺muku
   grown very cold. . . .   na˹rima˺sita g̃a˶

   The heater is off so it's   Su˹to˺obu (g̃a) ki˹ete (i)ru˺ kara, to-
   grown very cold. . . .   ˹ttemo sa˺muku na˹rima˺sita g̃a˶

3. Hasn't it grown warm!   A˹tta˺kaku na˹rima˺sita ˹ne˺e.

   Hasn't the room grown   He˹ya˺ (g̃a) a˹tta˺kaku na˹rima˺sita
   warm!   ˹ne˺e.

   Since turning [it] on,   Tu˹ke˺te kara, he˹ya˺ (g̃a) a˹tta˺kaku
   hasn't the room grown   na˹rima˺sita ˹ne˺e.
   warm!

   Since turning on the heater,   Su˹to˺obu (o) tu˹ke˺te kara, he˹ya˺
   hasn't the room grown   (g̃a) a˹tta˺kaku na˹rima˺sita
   warm!   ˹ne˺e.

   Hasn't the room grown   Ha˺ruko-sañ (g̃a) su˹to˺obu (o) tu˹ke˺-
   warm since Haruko   te kara, he˹ya˺ (g̃a) a˹tta˺kaku na˹ri-
   turned on the heater!   ma˺sita ˹ne˺e.

4. Because I don't like it.   Su˹ki˺ zya a˺rimase˺ñ kara.

   Because I don't like it very   A˺ñmari suki˺ zya a˺rimase˺ñ kara.
   much.

---

[1]   'but—can anything be done about it?'

Because I don't like sweet
things very much.

A⌐mai mono˥ (wa) a⌐ṅmari suki˥ zya
a⌐rimase˥ṅ kara.

That's fine—because I
don't like sweet things
very much.

Ke˥kkoo desu yo—a⌐mai mono˥(wa)
a⌐ṅmari suki˥ zya a⌐rimase˥ṅ kara.

It's fine sour—as it is—
because I don't like
sweet things very much.

Su⌐ppa˥i ma⌐ma˥ de 「ke˥kkoo desu
yo — a⌐mai mono˥ (wa) a⌐ṅmari
suki˥ zya a⌐rimase˥ṅ kara.

5. It's pretty, isn't it?

Ki˥ree desyoo?

The furoshiki is pretty,
isn't it?

Hurosiki (wa) 「ki˥ree desyoo?

The purple furoshiki is
pretty, isn't it?

Mu⌐ra˥saki no hurosiki (wa) 「ki˥ree
desyoo?

The yellow and purple
furoshiki is pretty,
isn't it?

Kiiro to mu⌐ra˥saki no hurosiki (wa)
「ki˥ree desyoo?

That yellow and purple
furoshiki is pretty,
isn't it?

Ano kiiro to mu⌐ra˥saki no hurosiki
(wa) 「ki˥ree desyoo?

6. I understood.

Wa⌐karima˥sita.

After seeing [it] I understood.

Mi˥te kara, wa⌐karima˥sita.

After seeing his name
card I understood.

Me⌐esi (o) mi˥te kara, wa⌐karima˥-
sita.

I couldn't hear but after
seeing his name card
I understood.

Ki⌐koemase˥ṅ desita ḡa; me⌐esi (o)
mi˥te kara, wa⌐karima˥sita.

I couldn't hear his name
but after seeing his
name card I could tell
[what it was].

Namae (wa) ki⌐koemase˥ṅ desita ḡa;
me⌐esi (o) mi˥te kara, wa⌐karima˥-
sita.

SUPPLEMENTARY SELECTIONS

(with questions)

1. Ke˥sa to⌐temo sa˥mukatta kara, su⌐to˥obu o tu⌐kema˥sita ḡa; su˥ḡu ki⌐e-
ma˥sita.   To⌐nari no heya˥ kara ho⌐ka no˥ o mo⌐tte˥ kite tu⌐ke˥te kara,
he⌐ya˥ ḡa a⌐tata˥kaku na⌐rima˥sita.

      a. I˥tu su⌐to˥obu o tu⌐kema˥sita ka↲
      b. Na˥ze su⌐to˥obu o tu⌐kema˥sita ka↲
      c. Su⌐to˥obu o hu⌐ta-tu tukema˥sita ḡa, do˥tira mo ko⌐syoo de˥sita
         ka↲
      d. Na˥ni o si⌐te˥ kara he⌐ya˥ ḡa a⌐tta˥kaku na⌐rima˥sita ka↲

2. Kyo˥o uti ḡa 「zu˥ibuṅ ki⌐tana˥ku ⌐na˥tte ita kara, go˥ḡo no 「sa˥ṅ-zi made
so⌐ozi-sima˥sita.   So⌐ozi o site˥ kara ōtya o 「i˥p-pai ⌐no˥ṅde; sore kara,

sa⌐kanaya ni deñwa o ka⌐kete, o⌐sasimi n o sakana o tyuumoñ-sima⌐sita.
Go⌐-zi kara ro⌐ku⌐-zi made syo⌐kuzi no sitaku o sima⌐sita.   Ro⌐ku-zi-ha⌐ñ
ni ⌐syu⌐ziñ ḡa kãisya kara ⌐ka⌐ette kite;[1] sore kara, i⌐ssyo ni syokuzi o si-
ma⌐sita.

    a. Do⌐o site u⌐ti o soozi-sima⌐sita ka⌐
    b. Na⌐ñ-zi made so⌐ozi-sima⌐sita ka⌐
    c. So⌐ozi-site⌐ kara ⌐su⌐ḡu ⌐na⌐ni o si⌐ma⌐sita ka⌐
    d. Da⌐re ni de⌐ñwa o kakema⌐sita ka⌐
    e. Na⌐ni o tyu⌐umoñ-sima⌐sita ka⌐
    f. Go⌐-zi kara ro⌐ku⌐-zi made ⌐na⌐ni o si⌐ma⌐sita ka⌐
    g. Go⌐syu⌐ziñ wa ⌐na⌐ñ-zi ni kãisya kara ⌐ka⌐ette ki⌐ma⌐sita ka⌐

3. Ke⌐kkoñ-site⌐ kara ⌐mo⌐o ⌐ni⌐-neñ ni narimasu.   A⌐merika de kekkoñ-si-
   ma⌐sita ḡa, ke⌐kkoñ-site⌐ kara ⌐su⌐ḡu Ni⌐ho⌐ñ e ki⌐ma⌐sita.   Watakusi wa
   A⌐merika-taisi⌐kañ ni tu⌐to⌐mete ite, ka⌐nai wa Ni⌐ho⌐ñ no gãkkoo de e⌐eḡo
   o osiete ima⌐su.   Mo⌐o su⌐ḡu ka⌐erima⌐su ḡa; Ni⌐ho⌐ñ ḡa to⌐temo suki⌐ desu
   kara, ka⌐erita⌐ku a⌐rimase⌐ñ.

    a. I⌐ma ⌐do⌐ko ni i⌐ma⌐su ka⌐
    b. Na⌐ñ-neñ ni ke⌐kkoñ-sima⌐sita ka⌐
    c. Na⌐ñ-neñ ma⌐e ni ke⌐kkoñ-sima⌐sita ka⌐
    d. Do⌐ko de ke⌐kkoñ-sima⌐sita ka⌐
    e. Ke⌐kkoñ-site⌐ kara ⌐do⌐ko e i⌐kima⌐sita ka⌐
    f. Go⌐syu⌐ziñ wa ⌐do⌐ñna si⌐goto o site ima⌐su ka⌐
    g. O⌐kusañ wa ⌐do⌐ñna si⌐goto o site ima⌐su ka⌐
    h. I⌐tu ka⌐erima⌐su ka⌐
    i. Do⌐o site ka⌐erita⌐ku a⌐rimase⌐ñ ka⌐

SUPPLEMENTARY CONVERSATION

(In an office building)

Smith (to receptionist):   Go-⌐kai e ikita⌐i ñ desu ḡa⌐
Receptionist: Zya⌐a, asoko ni e⌐rebe⌐eta[2] ḡa gozaimasu.
Smith: Do⌐o mo.
Elevator operator: U⌐e e mairima⌐su.   Na⌐na-kai ma⌐de mairimasu.
Smith: Go-⌐kai oneḡai-sima⌐su.
Other passenger: Sañ-ḡai.
Elevator operator: Ka⌐sikomarima⌐sita. . . . Sa⌐ñ-ḡai de gozaima⌐su.
Other passenger: Do⌐o mo.
Elevator operator: Tu⌐ḡi⌐ wa go-⌐kai de gozaima⌐su. . . . O⌐matase-itasima⌐si-
    ta. Go-⌐kai de gozaima⌐su.
Smith: A⌐ri⌐ḡatoo.

---

[1] ka⌐ette ⌐ku⌐ru 'come back.'

[2] 'Elevator.'

English Equivalent

Smith: I want to go to the fifth floor. . . .
Receptionist: (In that case) there's an elevator over there.
Smith: Thanks.
Elevator operator: Going up. [This car] goes to the seventh floor.
Smith: Five, please.
Other passenger: Three.
Elevator operator: Certainly. . . . Third floor.
Other passenger: Thanks.
Elevator operator: Fifth floor next. . . . (I'm sorry to have kept you waiting.)
    Fifth floor.
Smith: Thanks.

EXERCISES

1. You ask Mr. Tanaka where he lives. He answers:

    a. In Akasaka.
    b. Near Kamakura Station.
    c. Right near the American Embassy.
    d. In an apartment in Shibuya.

2. Ask the salesgirl to show you:

    a. that green pen.
    b. that yellow ashtray.
    c. those gray teacups.
    d. those brown and white dishes.
    e. those red chopsticks.
    f. that red and blue pencil.
    g. that red and black tray.
    h. that pink paper.
    i. that light purple furoshiki.
    j. that dark blue book.

3. Tell Haruko to:

    a. open the door.
    b. shut the window.
    c. turn on the light.
    d. turn off the heater.
    e. turn the radio down.
    f. make the television louder.
    g. clean this room.
    h. straighten up the next room.
    i. get dinner ready.
    j. lock the door in the entry hall.
    k. take this upstairs.
    l. turn off the upstairs heater.

4. Indicate whether each of the following is M (more typical of men's speech),
    W (more typical of women's speech), or MW (used by men and women). If
    you are a man, give an M or MW equivalent for all sentences marked W; if
    you are a woman, give a W or MW equivalent for all sentences marked M.

> a. O⌐su¬mai ⌐do¬tira?
> b. Yameta yo↲
> c. Hoñtoo ⌐ne¬e.
> d. Ki¬ree da.
> e. Si⌐rana¬katta?
> `f. Abunai.
> g. So¬o yo.
> h. Ze¬ñbu wa⌐ka┤tta?
> i. De¬kita wa↲
> j. O⌐naka ḡa suita¬ wa yo↲
> k. He¬ñ da ⌐ne┤e.
> l. Ki⌐koena¬katta yo↲

5. Practice the Basic Dialogues with appropriate variations.

Lesson 17. At Home (cont.)

BASIC DIALOGUES: FOR MEMORIZATION

(The Smiths have just moved into a new house. Masao-sañ and
Fumiko-sañ are helping them.)

(a)

Smith (to Masao)

help or lend a hand	te⌐tuda⌐u /-u/
1. Give me a hand, will you?	Te⌐tuda⌐tte ne?
things like books and magazines	ho⌐ñ ya zãssi
study (i.e. a room)	syosai
desk	tukue
onto the desk	tukue ni
top of the desk	tu⌐kue no ue⌐
onto the top of the desk	tu⌐kue no ue⌐ ni
put or place	oku /-u/
2. Put these books and magazines and things on *[*top of*]* the desk in the study.	Kono ⌐ho⌐ñ ya zãssi (o) syo⌐sai no tukue *[*no ue⌐*]* ni oite. [1]
bookshelf	ho⌐ñdana
onto the bookshelf	ho⌐ñdana ni
put away or store	simau /-u/
3. (Because) I'll put them (away) on the bookshelves later.	A⌐to de ⌐ho⌐ñdana ni si⌐mau⌐ kara.
is small or fine or detailed	ko⌐maka⌐i /-ku/
drawer	hikidasi
into the drawer	hikidasi ni
inside	na⌐ka
inside the drawer	hi⌐kidasi no na⌐ka
into the inside of the drawer	hi⌐kidasi no na⌐ka ni
insert or put in	ireru /-ru/

---

[1] Accent of short alternant: syōsai.

295

4. Then put all those little
    things in⌊side⌋ the desk
    drawer.

Sore kara, ano ko⌐maka⌐i mo⌐no⌐(o)
⌐ze⌐ñbu tu⌐kue no hikidasi ⌊no na⌐ka⌋
ni irete. [1]

· · ·

Masao

finish putting in
following or subsequent
5. I finished putting everything
    in.   What shall I do next?

irete simau
a⌐to
Mi⌐ñna irete simaima⌐sita ḡa, a⌐to
⌐na⌐ni (o) si⌐masyo⌐o ka.

Smith

dog
hindrance or bother

become a bother   or
  get in the way
outside
to the outside
put out or send out or
  take out
6. The dog gets in the way so
    put him outside.

i⌐nu⌐
zyama /na/   or
  ozyama [+]
zya⌐ma ni na⌐ru

so⌐to
so⌐to ni
da⌐su /-u/

I⌐nu⌐ ḡa zya⌐ma ni na⌐ru kara, so⌐to
ni dasite.

(calling after Masao)

give
7. Say! Give him some water
    too, will you?

yaru /-u/
Ano ne! Mi⌐zu mo yatte⌐ ne?

(b)

Masao

8. What shall I do with these
    dishes?

Kono sara (wa) ⌐do⌐o simasyoo ka.

Smith

soap
wash
receive or get
have Fumiko wash
9. Those—have Fumiko wash
    with soap and hot water.

sekkeñ
arau /-u/
morau /-u/
Hu⌐miko-sañ ni āratte morau
Sore (wa) ⌐Hu⌐miko-sañ ni sĕkkeñ
to oyu de āratte moratte.

---

[1] Accent of short alternant: tŭkue.

cupboard (with shelves)	todana
into the cupboard	todana ni

10. (Because) I'll put them (away) in the dining-room closet later. A⌐to de syo⌐kudoo no todana ni simau⌐ kara.

. . .

Smith

on top of this	kono ue
take up _or_ take away	to⌐ru /-u/

11. Say, take away the things on top of this. Tyo⌐tto, ko⌐no ue no mono⌐ (o) ⌐to⌐t-te.

table	teeburu
kitchen	daidokoro
into the kitchen	daidokoro ni

12. (Because) I'm going to take this table into the kitchen. Kono teeburu (o) da⌐idokoro ni motte i⌐ku kara.

Masao

13. Shall I help you? O⌐te⌐tudai-simasyoo ka⌐

Smith

alone (lit. being one person)	hi⌐to⌐ri de

14. No, I can manage alone. Iie, hi⌐to⌐ri de da⌐izyo⌐obu.

(c)

Masao

throw away	suteru /-ru/

15. These old newspapers— shall I throw them away? Kono hu⌐ru⌐i siñbuñ (wa) su⌐temasyo⌐o ka.

Smith

corner (of a room)	su⌐mi
into the corner	su⌐mi ni
put for the time being	oit(e) oku

16. No, I need them so put them in that corner for the time being. Iie, i⌐ru⌐ kara, a⌐no su⌐mi ni o⌐it(e) o⌐ite.

. . .

be careful	ki⌐otuke⌐ru /-ru/
[something] spills	ko⌐bore⌐ru /-ru/
be spilt	ko⌐bo⌐rete (i)ru

17. Oh, be careful! (Because) something's spilt. A, ki⌐otuke⌐te. Na⌐ni ka ko⌐bo⌐rete (i)ru kara.

wipe	huku /-u/
have Fumiko wipe	Hu⌐miko-sañ ni hūite morau

18. Have Fumiko wipe it up!   Hu⌐miko-sañ ni hu⌐ite moratte⌐ yo.

                                Masao

19. What'll she wipe it up   Na⌐ñ de hu⌐kimasyo⌐o ka.
     with?

                                Smith

          box   hako
          into the box   hako ni
          cleaning rag   zookiñ
          dishrag or dish cloth   hu⌐ki⌐ñ
           or cloth
          things like rags and   zo⌐okiñ ya huki⌐ñ
           cloths
          go in or enter   ha⌐iru /-u/
          be in or be entered   ha⌐itte (i)ru
20. Clean rags and cloths and   Ano hako ni ⌐ki⌐ree na zo⌐okiñ ya hu-
     things are in that box   ki⌐ñ (ḡa) ⌐ha⌐itte (i)ru kara —
     (so. . .)

                        · · ·

          become tired   tu⌐kare⌐rù̃ -/-ru/
          become tired out or   tu⌐ka⌐rete simau   or
           exhausted,   tu⌐ka⌐retyau /-u/
          rest   ya⌐su⌐mu /-u/
21. You're (lit. You've become)   Tu⌐ka⌐rete si⌐matta⌐ desyoo? Tyo⌐-
     tired out, aren't you? Let's   tto ya⌐sumimasyo⌐o.
     rest for a minute.

                              (d)

               (Smith is talking to his friend Tanaka, who has
                dropped in to see how things are coming along)

                                Smith

          head   a⌐tama⌐
          is painful   i⌐ta⌐i /-ku/
22. You know, I have a terrible   To⌐temo atama⌐ (ḡa) i⌐ta⌐i ñ desu
     headache.   yo.

                                Tanaka

          give (you)   aḡeru /-ru/
23. I have medicine. Would you   Ku⌐suri ḡa arima⌐su ḡa, a⌐ḡemasyo⌐o
     like some? (Lit. Shall I   ka⌐
     give you some?)

                                Smith

          receive from Fumiko   Hu⌐miko-sañ ni morau   or
                                             Hu⌐miko-sañ kara morau
          same as this   kore to onazi
          same medicine   onazi kusuri

24. I already got this from Fu-
    miko. Is it the same medi-
    cine as this?

Hu⌐miko-san │ ni │ ⌐mo⌐o ko⌐re (o)
              │ kara │
moraima⌐sita ḡa, kore to o⌐nazi kusuri de⌐su ka⌟

                                    Tanaka

    be different from that
25. No, it's different from that.

sore to tiḡau
Iie, so⌐re to⌐ wa ti⌐ḡaima⌐su.

    is strong
26. It's a much stronger kind
    (lit. one) than that. . . .

tu⌐yo⌐i /-ku/
So⌐re yo⌐ri zu⌐tto tuyo⌐i no desu ḡa—

                                    Smith

27. Then may I have some?

Zya⌐a o⌐neḡai-sima⌐su.

                                    Tanaka

28. Aren't you hungry?

O⌐naka ḡa suita⌐ desyoo?

    order for you
29. Shall I order something for
    you by telephone?

tyuumon-site aḡeru
Denwa de ⌐na⌐ni ka tyu⌐umon-site
aḡemasyo⌐o ka.

                                    Smith

    give me
    request or order for
    me
30. Thank you but Fumiko al-
    ready ordered for me
    (so . . .)

kureru /-ru/
ta⌐no⌐nde kureru
A⌐ri⌐ḡatoo gozaimasu ḡa, Hu⌐miko-
san ḡa ⌐mo⌐o ta⌐no⌐nde ku⌐rema⌐si-
ta kara—

ADDITIONAL VOCABULARY

1. Where is the <u>stairway</u> in
   this house?

Kono uti no <u>kaidan</u> (wa) ⌐do⌐ko desyoo
ka.

       washroom or lavatory
       bathroom
       family room (Japanese
         style)

senmenzyo
hu⌐roba⌐ or ohuroba+
tyanoma

2. That I saw in the <u>bedroom</u>.

Sore (wa) si⌐nsitu de mima⌐sita.

       living room
       hall or corridor
       garden

i⌐ma⌐
rooka
niwa or oniwa+

3. Where did you buy that <u>furni-
   ture</u>?

So⌐no ka⌐ḡu (wa) ⌐do⌐ko de ka⌐ima⌐si-
ta ka⌟

       bed
       chair
       couch or sofa
       lamp

be⌐tto[1] or sindai
isu
naḡaisu
sutando

---

[1] Obsolete.

4. Put that in the refrigerator,   Sore (o) re⌐ezo⌐oko ni irete ne?
    will you?

        chest of drawers   tañsu
        closet (for clothing,   osiire
            quilts, etc.)

5. The sink is dirty!   Na⌐g̃asi⌐ (g̃a) ki⌐tana⌐i desu yo⌟

        wash basin   se⌐ñme⌐ñki
        stove (for cooking)   re⌐ñzi
        shelf   tana

6. There's a cat over there!   Asuko ni ⌐ne⌐ko (g̃a) i⌐ma⌐su yo⌟

        horse   u⌐ma⌐ or ñ⌐ma⌐
        bull or cow   usi
        goat   ya⌐ḡi
        rabbit   usaḡi
        pig   buta

7. What kind of animals are   Ni⌐ho⌐ñ ni ⌐do⌐ñna do⌐obutu g̃a ima⌐-
    there in Japan?   su ka⌟

        bird   tori or kotori
        snake   he⌐bi

8. My ear hurts!   Mi⌐mi⌐ (g̃a) i⌐ta⌐i ñ desu yo.

        tooth   ha⌐
        nose   hana
        mouth   kuti
        eye   me⌐
        neck   kubi
        arm   u⌐de⌐
        hand   te⌐
        finger   yu⌐bi⌐
        leg or foot   a⌐si⌐
        chest   mu⌐ne⌐
        back   senaka
        lower back   kosi
        body   karada

NOTES ON THE BASIC DIALOGUES

2. Particle ni here, and in Basic Sentences 3, 4, 6, 10, 12, 16, and 20, is
    the ni of goal or destination (cf. Lesson 7, Grammatical Note 3; Lesson 10,
    Note 4; and Lesson 14, Note 6).

4. Ko⌐maka⌐i means 'occurring in small pieces.' For example, in reference
    to an explanation, it indicates a detailed one.

6. Note also zyama-suru 'bother.' O⌐zyama-sima⌐sita (or -itasima⌐sita) is a
    common apology: 'I'm sorry to have bother〉d you.'

    Da⌐su is the transitive partner of intransitive de⌐ru: X g̃a ⌐de⌐ru 'X goes out'; X o ˹da˺su 'make X go out,' 'put X out.' Da˺su occurs as the opposite of both ireru 'put in' and simau 'put away.'

11. Kono ue: compare kono saki in Lesson 7, Basic Sentence 16. Other equivalents of to˺ru: 'pick up,' 'remove,' 'hand [me],' 'pass [me].' To˺ru occurs as the opposite of oku 'put,' 'place.'

13. O˹te˺tudai-suru (or -itasu) is the humble equivalent of te˹tuda˺u (cf. Lesson 13, Grammatical Note 4).

15. Note the use of particle wa. Primary interest is in what follows: 'about these old papers — shall I throw them away [or what shall I do with them]?'

17. The transitive partner of intransitive ko˹bore˺ru is ko˹bo˺su: X o ko˹bo˺su 'spill X'; X ḡa ko˹bore˺ru 'X spills.'

20. A zookiñ would be used to wipe up the floor, but a hu˹ki˺ñ to wipe a table or a dish.

Ha˺iru is the intransitive partner of transitive ireru (Sentence 4 above): X ḡa ˹ha˺iru 'X goes in,' X o ireru 'put X in.' Ha˺iru may refer to a person's entering a room or building in general; a hospital, as a patient; a school, as a student; a company, as an employee; etc.

22. N̄ is the nominal meaning something like 'matter' or 'case' (cf. Lesson 7, Grammatical Note 1).

24. The nominal onazi 'same' (onazi da 'it's the same'; o˹nazi zya na˺i 'it isn't the same'; o˹nazi ni na˺ru 'become the same') occurs directly before a nominal without particle no: onazi kusuri 'the same medicine.'

24, 25. Note the use of particle to 'with' with onazi and tiḡau: X to onazi 'same as X,' X to tiḡau 'different from X.'

25. Wa, here, is the wa of comparison: 'From that it is different.'

26. 'but—would you like to try some?'

Supplementary Vocabulary:

Hu˹roba˺ refers only to the place for bathing, in a Japanese house or inn. It is not to be confused with be˹ñzyo˺ or te˹a˺rai.

Pieces of furniture like beds, chairs, etc., though commonly found in Japan, are Western style—not native Japanese style.

GRAMMATICAL NOTES

1. Verbals of Giving and Receiving

The following four verbals all mean 'give,' with specific differences in usage:

Aḡeru means 'someone gives to an equal or a superior, or to anyone present to whom one is being polite.' It NEVER means 'give to the speaker,' i.e. 'give to me.'

Yaru means 'someone gives to an inferior or [in plain, informal speech] to an equal.'   It is regularly used for giving to animals or to things (as in 'give water to the flowers').   Like aḡeru, it NEVER means 'give to the speaker,' i.e. 'give to me.'

Ku⌐dasa⌐ru means 'someone gives to me.'[1]   It implies either that the speaker's position is inferior to that of the giver, or that the speaker is deferring to persons present for the sake of politeness.

Kureru means 'someone gives to me.'   It implies that the giver is the speaker's equal or inferior.   Sometimes it means 'he, she, or they give to you'—i.e. 'a third person gives to the person addressed,' if the giver and recipient are more or less equal. [2]

Particles (with all four verbals above): If expressed, the giver is followed by ḡa or wa, the thing given by particle o or wa, and the recipient by particle ni.

Examples:

(a) A⌐ḡemasyo⌐o ka.   'Shall I give it to you?'
(b) Se⌐ñse⌐e ni a⌐ḡema⌐sita ka┘ 'Did you give it to the teacher?'
(c) U⌐ti no Ta⌐roo wa se⌐ñse⌐e ni ⌐ho⌐ñ o a⌐ḡema⌐sita. 'Our Taro gave the teacher a book.'
(d) Musuko ni ⌐pe⌐ñ o ya⌐rima⌐sita.   'I gave my son a pen.'
(e) Ko⌐oka⌐ñsyu ni a⌐tarasi⌐i de⌐ñwatyoo o yarima⌐sita ka┘ 'Did you give the operator a new phone book?'
(f) Se⌐ñse⌐e wa ⌐ma⌐initi ko⌐domo ni ku⌐da⌐mono o yarimasu.   'The teacher gives the children some fruit every day.'
(g) Kore wa ⌐o⌐kusañ ḡa ku⌐dasaima⌐sita. 'This your wife gave me.'
(h) Ta⌐bako o kudasa⌐i. 'Please give me a cigarette.'
(i) Kore wa to⌐modati ḡa kurema⌐sita. 'This a friend gave me.'
(j) Da⌐re ḡa ⌐a⌐na⌐ta ni⌋ kureta? 'Who gave it to you?'

Situations involving giving can also be described from the point of view of receiving. The Japanese equivalent of 'receive' is morau. This verbal may refer to receiving by or from the speaker, the person addressed, or a third person. Its polite honorific equivalent is o⌐morai ni na⌐ru (↑) and its humble equivalent is itadaku (↓).

Particles: If expressed, the person who receives is followed by ḡa or wa, the thing received by particle o or wa, and the person from whom it is received by particle kara or ni.

――――――――――――

[1] Or to person(s) closely associated with me—for example, a member of my family.

[2] Be careful of this usage. To rate a third party (not present) the equal of the person addressed would, in some circumstances, be insulting.

Examples:

(k) Tomodati kara oˈkaˈsi o moˈraimaˈsita. 'I received some candy from a friend.'

(l) Kore wa ˈdaˈre ni moˈraimaˈsita ka˩ 'From whom did you get this?'

(m) Kore wa ˈdaˈre ḡa moˈraimaˈsita ka˩ 'Who received this?'

(n) Tanaka-sañ kara ˈnaˈni o oˈmorai ni narimaˈsita ka˩ 'What did you receive from Mr. Tanaka?'

(o) Oˈkusama ni ˈkiˈree na huˈrosiki o itadakimaˈsita. 'I received a beautiful furoshiki from your wife.'

A situation in which one person does something for another is indicated in Japanese by a verbal gerund followed immediately in the same phrase by the appropriate verbal of giving or receiving. For example:

kaˈite aḡeru and kaˈite yaru 'write for someone' (lit. 'give writing')
kaˈite kuˈdasaˈru 'write for me' (lit. 'give me writing')
kaˈite kureru 'write for me [or you]' (lit. 'give me [or you] writing')
kaˈite morau 'have someone write' (lit. 'receive writing')

The differences in usage of the verbals of giving and receiving described above apply equally to the combination of one of these verbals preceded by a gerund. The particles are also the same, except that the person by whom someone has something done is followed by particle ni but not kara. Also, the gerund preceding the verbal of giving or receiving may have its own direct object, goal phrase, etc. [1] Study the following examples carefully, comparing them with the corresponding examples above:

(a) Yoˈñde aˈḡemasyoˈo ka. 'Shall I read it for you?'

(b) Seˈñseˈe ni ˈkaˈite aˈḡemaˈsita ka˩ 'Did you write it for the teacher?'

(c) Uˈti no Taˈroo wa seˈñseˈe ni ˈhoˈñ o tyuˈumoñ-site aḡemaˈsita. '(Our) Taro ordered a book for the teacher.'

(d) Musuko ni ˈpeˈñ o kaˈtte yarimaˈsita. 'I bought a pen for my son.'

(e) Koˈokaˈñsyu ni aˈtarasiˈi deˈñwatyoo o tanoˈñde yaˈrimaˈsita ka˩ 'Did you ask for a new telephone book for the operator?'

(f) Seˈñseˈe wa ˈmaˈiniti kŏdomo ni kuˈdaˈmono o kiˈtteˈ yarimasu. 'The teacher cuts the fruit for the children every day.'

---

[1] Without sufficient context, some examples are ambiguous. For example, Taˈnaka-sañ ni kiite moraimaˈsita. may mean 'I had Mr. Tanaka ask [him]' or 'I had [him] ask Mr. Tanaka.' If both 'Mr. Tanaka' and 'him' are expressed, the order determines the difference:

Tanaka-sañ ni aˈnoˈ hito ni kiˈite moraimaˈsita. 'I had Mr. Tanaka ask him.'

Aˈnoˈ hito ni Taˈnaka-sañ ni kiite moraimaˈsita. 'I had him ask Mr. Tanaka.'

(g) Kore wa ⌐o⌐kusañ ḡa a⌐kete (<u>or</u> o⌐ake ni na⌐tte ꞌ) kudasaima⌐sita.
'This your wife opened for me.'

(h) Ta⌐bako o motte⌐ kite kudasai. 'Please bring the cigarettes (for
me).'

(i) Kore wa to⌐modati ḡa nao⌐site ku⌐rema⌐sita. 'This my friend fixed
for me.'

(j) Da⌐re ḡa [a⌐na⌐ta ni] site kureta? 'Who did it for you?'

(k) Tomodati ni o⌐ka⌐si o mo⌐tte⌐ kite mo⌐raima⌐sita. 'I had my
friend bring some candy.'

(l) Kore wa ⌐da⌐re ni ⌐mi⌐sete mo⌐raima⌐sita ka↲   'Who showed
you this?' (Lit. 'As for this, by whom did you receive showing?')

(m) Kore wa ⌐da⌐re ḡa si⌐te moraima⌐sita ka↲   'For whom was
this done?' (Lit. 'As for this, who received the doing?')

(n) Tanaka-sañ ni ⌐na⌐ni o ka⌐tte omorai ni narima⌐sita ka↲   'What
did Mr. Tanaka buy for you?' (Lit. 'You received the buying of
what by Mr. Tanaka?')

(o) O⌐kusama ni ⌐ki⌐ree na hu⌐rosiki o katte (<u>or</u> okai ni na⌐tteꞌ)
itadakima⌐sita. 'Your wife bought a beautiful furoshiki for me.'
(Lit. 'I received the buying of a beautiful furoshiki by your wife.')

A gerund + <u>moraitai</u> (or <u>itadakitai</u>) is an indirect request— 'I want to have
something done by someone.' Compare this with a direct request— '(you) do
something.' For example:

Mi⌐te moraitai. 'I want to have it looked at.'   But:
Mi⌐te. 'Look at it!'

A⌐ratte moraita⌐i ñ desu. 'I want to have it washed.'   But:
A⌐ratte kudasa⌐i. 'Please wash it.'

A⌐kete itadakita⌐i ñ desu. 'I'd like to have it opened.'   But:
A⌐kete kudasaimase⌐ñ ka↲ 'Would you be kind enough to open it?'

A gerund + √morau sequence occurs as a request when someone is directly
asked to have something done by someone.

Mi⌐te moratte. 'Have it looked at.'
A⌐ratte moratte kudasa⌐i. 'Please have it washed.'
A⌐kete moratte kudasaimase⌐ñ ka↲ 'Would you be kind enough to have
it opened?'

2.   Verbal Gerund + √simau

A verbal gerund + √simau means 'do so-and-so completely' or 'finish doing
so-and-so' or 'end up by doing so-and-so.' Examples:

Wa⌐surete simaima⌐sita. 'I've forgotten [it] completely.'
Kodomo ḡa o⌐ka⌐si o ⌐ta⌐bete si⌐maima⌐sita.   'The children finished
eating the candy.' <u>or</u> 'The children ate up the candy.'
I⌐kitaku na⌐katta desyoo ḡa, i⌐tte simaima⌐sita. 'He probably didn't
want to go but he ended up by going.'

In this pattern, √simau follows the verbal gerund immediately in the same phrase without pause. Compare:

> Saˈra o aratte simaimaˈsita. 'I finished washing the dishes.'
> Sara o aratte, siˈmaimaˈsita.   'I washed the dishes and put them away.'

In conversational Japanese, a gerund + √simau is very commonly contracted:

> ----te √simau **>** √----tyau
> ----de √simau **>** √----zyau

Examples:

Uncontracted	Contracted
taˈbete simau	taˈbetyau
noˈnde simatte	noˈnzyatte
wasurete simatta	wasuretyatta
aˈratte simaimaˈsu	aˈrattyaimaˈsu
iˈtte simaimaˈsita	iˈttyaimaˈsita

3.   Verbal Gerund + √oku

A verbal gerund followed immediately in the same phrase without pause by √oku [1] means 'do so-and-so and put aside,' or 'do so-and-so in advance,' or 'do so-and-so for future use or benefit,' or 'do so-and-so for the time being.' Examples:

> Tomodati ḡa ˈsuˈḡu ˈkuˈru kara, doˈa o aˈkete oˈite kudasai. 'A friend is coming very soon so please open the door (for future benefit).'
> Aˈsita iruˈ kara, kyoˈo kaˈtte okimaˈsita.   'I'll need it tomorrow so I bought it (in advance) today.'
> Sono zassi o ˈaˈto de ˈyoˈmu kara, tuˈkue no ueˈ ni oˈite oˈite kudasai. 'I'm going to read that magazine later so please put it on top of the desk for the time being.'

In conversational Japanese, the final -e of the gerund is dropped before those forms of √oku which begin oi-. Examples:

Uncontracted	Contracted
aˈkete oˈita	aˈketoˈita
oˈite oˈite	oˈitoˈite
yoˈnde oite	yoˈndoite

---

[1] The past oita and gerund oite, among other forms, acquire a first-syllable accent when they follow an unaccented gerund.

4.   Particle <u>ya</u>

The particle <u>ya</u> occurs between nominals A and B meaning 'A and B and others of the same kind,' 'A and B and so on,' 'A and B among others,' 'things like A and B.' Thus:

> oˈtoˈosañ to oˈkaˈasañ 'your father and mother'
>   but:
> oˈtoˈosañ ya oˈkaˈasañ 'your father and mother and others in your family'
>
> oˈtya to koohiˈi 'tea and coffee'
>   but:
> oˈtya ya koohiˈi 'tea and coffee and other similar drinks'

There may be more than two nominals in the series:

> hoˈñ ya zassi ya siñbuñ 'books and magazines and newspapers and the like'

A series of two or more nominals joined by <u>ya</u> occurs in the same kinds of patterns as a nominal alone.

Examples:

> Hoˈñ ya zassi wa ˈdoˈo simasyoo ka. 'What shall I do with the books and magazines and such things?'
> Peˈñ ya eˈñpitu ḡa irimaˈsu. 'I need things like pens and pencils.'
> Yaˈsai ya kudaˈmono o kaˈimaˈsita. 'I bought vegetables and fruit among other things.'

DRILLS

A. Substitution Drill

1. I finished putting in the dishes. What shall I do next?

Saˈra (o) irete simaimaˈsita ḡa, aˈto ˈnaˈni (o) siˈmasyoˈo ka.

2. I finished putting away the little things. What shall I do next?

Koˈmakaˈi moˈnoˈ (o) siˈmatte sima-imaˈsita ḡa, aˈto ˈnaˈni (o) siˈmasyoˈo ka.

3. I finished washing the glasses. What shall I do next?

Koˈppu (o) aratte simaimaˈsita ḡa, aˈto ˈnaˈni (o) siˈmasyoˈo ka.

4. I finished cleaning the kitchen. What shall I do next?

Daˈidokoro (o) soozi-site simaimaˈsita ḡa, aˈto ˈnaˈni (o) siˈmasyoˈo ka.

5. I finished straightening up the study. What shall I do next?

Syoˈsai (o) katazuˈkete siˈmaimaˈsita ḡa, aˈto ˈnaˈni (o) siˈmasyoˈo ka.

6. I finished turning on all the heaters. What shall I do next?

Suˈtoˈobu (o) miˈñna tukeˈte siˈmai-maˈsita ḡa, aˈto ˈnaˈni (o) siˈma-syoˈo ka.

7. I finished opening all the windows. What shall I do next?

Ma⌐do (o) mi⌐ñna akete simaima¬si-ta ḡa, a¬to ⌐na¬ni (o) si⌐masyo¬o ka.

8. I finished locking all the doors. What shall I do next?

To ⌐no kaḡi¬ (o) mi⌐ñna ka⌐kete si-⌐maima¬sita ḡa, a¬to ⌐na¬ni (o) si-⌐masyo¬o ka.

B. Substitution Drill

1. I'm putting away the little things.

Ko⌐maka¬i mo⌐no¬ o si⌐matte ima¬su.

2. I finished putting away the little things.

Ko⌐maka¬i mo⌐no¬ (o) si⌐matte simaima¬sita.

3. I put away the little things for the time being.

Ko⌐maka¬i mo⌐no¬ (o) si⌐matte okima¬-sita.

4. I had the little things put away.

Ko⌐maka¬i mo⌐no¬ (o) si⌐matte morai-ma¬sita.

5. Shall I put away the little things for you?

Ko⌐maka¬i mo⌐no¬ (o) si⌐matte aḡema-syo¬o ka.

6. [He] put away the little things for me.

Ko⌐maka¬i mo⌐no¬ (o) si⌐matte kurema¬-sita.

7. Please put away the little things.

Ko⌐maka¬i mo⌐no¬ (o) si⌐matte kudasa¬i.

8. Please have the little things put away.

Ko⌐maka¬i mo⌐no¬ (o) si⌐matte moratte kudasa¬i.

9. I'd like to have the little things put away. . . .

Ko⌐maka¬i mo⌐no¬ (o) si⌐matte morai-ta¬i ñ desu ḡa⌐

10. The little things have been put away.

Ko⌐maka¬i mo⌐no¬ (ḡa) si⌐matte ari-ma¬su.

C. Substitution Drill

1. [He] cut it fine.

Ko⌐maka¬ku ki⌐rima¬sita.

2. It isn't fine (i.e. in small pieces).

Ko⌐maka¬ku a⌐rimase¬ñ.

3. It isn't strong.

Tu¬yoku a⌐rimase¬ñ.

4. [He] has become strong.

Tu¬yoku na⌐rima¬sita.

5. It has become painful.

I⌐ta¬ku na⌐rima¬sita.

6. It isn't painful.

I⌐ta¬ku a⌐rimase¬ñ.

7. It isn't fast.

Ha¬yaku a⌐rimase¬ñ.

8. [He] talked fast.

Ha¬yaku ha⌐nasima¬sita.

9. [He] talked well.

Yo¬ku ha⌐nasima¬sita.

10. [He] listened carefully.

Yo¬ku ki⌐kima¬sita.

D. Substitution Drill [1]

    1. Where did you put (i.e.   Do⌐ko ni o⌐kima⌐sita ka˩
        place) it?

    2. Where did you put it (away)?   Do⌐ko ni si⌐maima⌐sita ka˩

    3. Where (i.e. into what) did   Do⌐ko ni i⌐rema⌐sita ka˩
        you put it?

    4. Where did you set it out?   Do⌐ko ni da⌐sima⌐sita ka˩

    5. Where did you take it?   Do⌐ko ni mo⌐tte ikima⌐sita ka˩

    6. What place (for example,   Do⌐ko ni ha⌐irima⌐sita ka˩
        what school) have you en-
        tered?

    7. What place did you call (on   Do⌐ko ni de⌐ñwa o kakema⌐sita ka˩
        the telephone)?

    8. Where did you go?   Do⌐ko ni i⌐kima⌐sita ka˩

E. Grammar Drill (based on Grammatical Note 3)

    Tutor: Si⌐ma⌐sita. 'I did it.'
    Student: Si⌐te okima⌐sita. 'I did it in advance, or for future reference,
        or for the time being, etc.'

    1. Kore (wa) a⌐no hako ni   Kore (wa) a⌐no hako ni irete okima-
        iremasyo⌐o ka.   syo⌐o ka.

    2. Osakana ya yasai (o) su-   Osakana ya yasai (o) su⌐ko⌐si ka⌐tte
        ⌐ko⌐si ka⌐ima⌐sita.   okima⌐sita.

    3. Syo⌐kudoo no teeburu no ue⌐   Syo⌐kudoo no teeburu no ue⌐ ni o⌐ite
        ni o⌐kima⌐sita.   okima⌐sita.

    4. Ka⌐mi⌐ ya eñpitu (o) ta⌐ku-   Ka⌐mi⌐ ya eñpitu (o) ta⌐kusañ da⌐site
        sañ dasima⌐sita.   o⌐kima⌐sita.

    5. Ni⌐kai no tañsu no na⌐ka ni   Ni⌐kai no tañsu no na⌐ka ni si⌐matte
        si⌐maima⌐sita.   okima⌐sita.

    6. Su⌐ko⌐si ya⌐sumimasyo⌐o.   Su⌐ko⌐si ya⌐su⌐ñde o⌐kimasyo⌐o.

    7. Ko⌐otuuko⌐osya de ki⌐ki-   Ko⌐otuuko⌐osya de ki⌐ite okima⌐sita.
        ma⌐sita.

    8. A⌐tarasi⌐i meesi (o) tyu⌐u-   A⌐tarasi⌐i meesi (o) tyu⌐umoñ-site
        moñ-simasyo⌐o ka.   okimasyo⌐o ka.

F. Grammar Drill (based on Grammatical Note 1)

    Tutor: Si⌐te kudasa⌐i. 'Please do it.'
    Student: Si⌐te moratte kudasa⌐i. 'Please have it done.' or 'Please
        have someone do it.'

---

  [1] In contrast with the variety of the English equivalents, the Japanese pattern here is identical throughout: a place word + particle ni of goal indicating
the place toward or into which motion occurred.

1. O⌐sara⌐ (o) aratte kudasa⌐i.   O⌐sara⌐ (o) aratte moratte kudasa⌐i.
2. Mi⌐ti⌐ (o) osiete kudasa⌐i.   Mi⌐ti⌐ (o) osiete moratte kudasa⌐i.
3. Ha⌐yaku na⌐o⌐site kudasai.   Ha⌐yaku na⌐o⌐site mo⌐ratte kudasa⌐i.
4. Se⌐ñse⌐e (o) yo⌐ñde kuda-   Se⌐ñse⌐e (o) yo⌐ñde moratte kuda-
    sa⌐i.   sa⌐i.
5. Ku⌐ruma no kaḡi⌐ (o)   Ku⌐ruma no kaḡi⌐ (o) ⌐ka⌐kete mo-
    ⌐ka⌐kete kudasai.   ⌐ratte kudasa⌐i.
6. Yo⌐kohama e⌐ no miti (o)   Yo⌐kohama e⌐ no miti (o) ki⌐ite mo-
    ki⌐ite kudasa⌐i.   ratte kudasa⌐i.
7. Ni⌐hoñḡo de itte kudasa⌐i.   Ni⌐hoñḡo de itte moratte kudasa⌐i.
8. Ki⌐ree ni ⌐ka⌐ite kudasai.   Ki⌐ree ni ⌐ka⌐ite mo⌐ratte kudasa⌐i.

G. Grammar Drill (based on Grammatical Note 1)

Tutor: Ta⌐naka-sañ ḡa site kurema⌐sita. 'Mr. Tanaka did it for me.'
Student: Ta⌐naka-sañ ni site moraima⌐sita. 'I had it done for me by
          Mr. Tanaka.' or 'I had Mr. Tanaka do it for me.'

1. To⌐modati ḡa ma⌐tte ku⌐re-   To⌐modati ni ma⌐tte mo⌐raima⌐sita.
    ma⌐sita.
2. A⌐ni ḡa si⌐ñbuñ (o) katte ku-   A⌐ni ni si⌐ñbuñ (o) katte moraima⌐si-
    rema⌐sita.   ta.
3. Hu⌐miko-sañ ḡa ha⌐ti⌐-zi   Hu⌐miko-sañ ni ha⌐ti⌐-zi made i⌐te
    made i⌐te kurema⌐sita.   moraima⌐sita.
4. Musuko ḡa si⌐ñbuñ (o) motte⌐   Musuko ni si⌐ñbuñ (o) motte⌐ kite mo-
    kite ku⌐rema⌐sita.   ⌐raima⌐sita.
5. Se⌐ñse⌐e ḡa ko⌐re (o) yo⌐ñde   Se⌐ñse⌐e ni ko⌐re (o) yo⌐ñde i⌐tada-
    ku⌐dasaima⌐sita.   kima⌐sita.
6. Ko⌐oka⌐ñsyu ḡa ba⌐ñḡo⌐o (o)   Ko⌐oka⌐ñsyu ni ba⌐ñḡo⌐o (o) i⌐tte mo-
    i⌐tte kurema⌐sita.   raima⌐sita.
7. Mu⌐sume⌐ ḡa syo⌐kuzi no   Mu⌐sume⌐ ni syo⌐kuzi no sitaku (o)
    sitaku (o) site kurema⌐sita.   site moraima⌐sita.
8. Go⌐syu⌐ziñ ḡa mi⌐ti (o) osi-   Go⌐syu⌐ziñ ni mi⌐ti (o) osiete itada-
    ete kudasaima⌐sita.   kima⌐sita.

H. Response Drill (based on Grammatical Note 1)

Tutor: Si⌐ma⌐sita ka↲ /tomodati/ 'Did you do it? /friend/ '
Student: To⌐modati ni site moraima⌐sita. 'I had it done by a friend.'
          or 'I had a friend do it.'

1. Re⌐ezo⌐oko (o) na⌐osima⌐si-   To⌐modati ni nao⌐site mo⌐raima⌐si-
    ta ka↲ /tomodati/   ta.
2. Zyu⌐ñsa ni kikima⌐sita ka↲   Ni⌐hoñzi⌐ñ ni ki⌐ite moraima⌐sita.
    /ni⌐hoñzi⌐ñ/
3. A⌐tarasi⌐i ⌐ka⌐ḡu (o) mi-   Ka⌐nai ni ⌐mi⌐te mo⌐raima⌐sita.
    ⌐ma⌐sita ka↲ /ka⌐nai/
4. Su⌐misu-sañ ni a⌐ima⌐sita   Ta⌐naka-sañ ni a⌐tte mo⌐raima⌐sita.
    ka↲ /Tanaka-sañ/
5. Kusuri (o) ka⌐ima⌐sita ka↲   Mu⌐suko ni katte moraima⌐sita.
    /musuko/

6. To (o) si⌐mema⌐sita ka‿   Hu⌐miko-tyañ ni ⌐si⌐mete mo⌐rai-
   /Hu⌐miko-tyañ/   ma⌐sita.
7. Ho⌐ñdana ni za̅ssi (o)   A⌐no⌐ hito ni si⌐matte moraima⌐si-
   si⌐maima⌐sita ka‿   ta.
   /a⌐no⌐ hito/
8. Ne⌐ko (o) ⌐so⌐to e da-   Ko⌐domo ni da⌐site mo⌐raima⌐sita.
   ⌐sima⌐sita ka‿
   /kodomo/

I.   Response Drill

         Tutor: To g̅a a⌐ite ima⌐su yo‿ 'You know, the door's open.'
         Student: Da⌐re g̅a a⌐kema⌐sita ka‿ 'Who opened it?'

1. Na⌐ni ka ko⌐bo⌐rete (i)masu   Da⌐re g̅a ko⌐bosima⌐sita ka‿
   yo‿
2. I⌐nu⌐ (g̅a) ⌐de⌐te (i)masu yo‿   Da⌐re g̅a da⌐sima⌐sita ka‿
3. Ano hako ni ⌐ki⌐ree na   Da⌐re g̅a i⌐rema⌐sita ka‿
   hu⌐ki⌐ñ ya zo⌐okiñ (g̅a)
   ha⌐itte (i)masu yo‿
4. Da⌐idokoro no de⌐ñki (g̅a)   Da⌐re g̅a tu⌐kema⌐sita ka‿
   ⌐tu⌐ite (i)masu yo‿
5. Ka⌐g̅i⌐ (g̅a) ka⌐ka⌐tte (i)ma-   Da⌐re g̅a ka⌐kema⌐sita ka‿
   su yo‿
6. Syo⌐sai no ma⌐do (g̅a) si-   Da⌐re g̅a si⌐mema⌐sita ka‿
   ⌐ma⌐tte (i)masu yo‿

J.   Level Drill[1]

1. Kyo⌐o no siñbuñ (o) su⌐te-   Kyo⌐o no siñbuñ (o) o⌐sute ni nari-
   ma⌐sita ka‿   ma⌐sita ka‿
2. A⌐tarasi⌐i ⌐ho⌐ñ (o) si⌐ma-   A⌐tarasi⌐i ⌐ho⌐ñ (o) o⌐simai ni na-
   ima⌐sita ka‿   rima⌐sita ka‿
3. Tu⌐kue no ue⌐ ni o⌐kima⌐-   Tu⌐kue no ue⌐ ni o⌐oki ni narima⌐-
   sita ka‿   sita ka‿
4. Hi⌐kidasi no na⌐ka ni i⌐re-   Hi⌐kidasi no na⌐ka ni o⌐ire ni nari-
   ma⌐sita ka‿   ma⌐sita ka‿
5. I⌐tu-g̅oro hairima⌐sita ka‿   I⌐tu-g̅oro ohairi ni narima⌐sita ka‿
6. Do⌐nata kara mo⌐raima⌐sita   Do⌐nata kara o⌐morai ni narima⌐si-
   ka‿   ta ka‿
7. Ta⌐naka-sañ ni aima⌐sita   Ta⌐naka-sañ ni oai ni narima⌐sita
   ka‿   ka‿
8. Se⌐ñse⌐e (o) yo⌐bima⌐sita   Se⌐ñse⌐e (o) o⌐yobi ni narima⌐sita
   ka‿   ka‿

---

[1] Each sentence on the right is the honorific (ꜛ) equivalent of the corresponding sentence on the left.

K. Expansion Drill

1. Is [it] in?
    What is in [it]?
    What is inside [it]?

    What is inside that big
    box?

Haᒃitte (i)masu ka⌐
Naᒃni (ḡa) ᒊhaᒃitte (i)masu ka⌐
Naᒃka ni ᒊnaᒃni (ḡa) ᒊhaᒃitte (i)ma-
  su ka⌐
Ano oᒊokiᒃi hako no ᒊnaᒃka ni ᒊnaᒃni
  (ḡa) ᒊhaᒃitte (i)masu ka⌐

2. I received help.
    I had Mr. Tanaka help me.

    I was very busy so I had
    Mr. Tanaka help me.
    Yesterday morning I was
    very busy so I had Mr.
    Tanaka help me.

Teᒊtudaᒃtte moᒊraimaᒃsita.
Tanaka-sañ ni teᒊtudaᒃtte moᒊraimaᒃsita.
Toᒊtemo isoḡaᒃsikatta kara, Tanaka-
  sañ ni teᒊtudaᒃtte moᒊraimaᒃsita.
Kiᒊnoo no aᒃsa toᒊtemo isoḡaᒃsikatta
  kara, Tanaka-sañ ni teᒊtudaᒃtte
  moᒊraimaᒃsita.

3. Have [it] fixed.
    Have this fixed.
    Have this fixed by someone
    else (lit. another person).
    [I] can't do it so have this
    fixed by someone else.
    I (comparatively speaking)
    can't do it so have this
    fixed by someone else.

Naᒊoᒃsite moratte.
Koᒊre (o) naoᒃsite moratte.
Hoᒊka no hitoᒃ ni koᒊre (o) naoᒃsite
  moratte.
Deᒊkiᒃnai kara, hoᒊka no hitoᒃ ni
  koᒊre (o) naoᒃsite moratte.
Boᒊku wa dekiᒃnai kara, hoᒊka no hi-
  toᒃ ni koᒊre (o) naoᒃsite moratte.

4. Have [them] thrown out.
    Have [them] thrown out to-
    morrow.
    [They] get in the way so
    have [them] thrown out
    tomorrow.
    [They] always get in the
    way so have [them] thrown
    out tomorrow.
    These old papers and maga-
    zines and things always
    get in the way so have
    them thrown out tomor-
    row.

Sutete moratte.
Asita sũtete moratte.

Zyaᒊma ni naᒃru kara, asita sũtete
  moratte.

Iᒃtu mo zyaᒊma ni naᒃru kara, asita
  sũtete moratte.

Kono huᒊruᒃi siñbuñ ya zassi (wa)
  ᒊiᒃtu mo zyaᒊma ni naᒃru kara,
  asita sũtete moratte.

5. Is it all right?
    I'd like to rest. Is it all
    right?
    I'd like to rest [this] after-
    noon. Is it all right?
    I'm tired so I'd like to rest
    [this] afternoon. Is it all
    right?

Kaᒊmaimaseᒃñ ka⌐
Yaᒊsumitaᒃi ñ desu ḡa, kaᒊmaimaseᒃñ
  ka⌐
Goᒊḡo yaᒊsumitaᒃi ñ desu ḡa, kaᒊmaimaseᒃñ ka⌐
Tuᒊkaᒃrete (i)ru kara, goᒊḡo yaᒊsumitaᒃi ñ desu ḡa; kaᒊmaimaseᒃñ ka⌐

I'm awfully tired so I'd
like to rest [this] afternoon. Is it all right?

Zuʹibuñ tuˡkaˉrete (i)ru kara, goˑ-
ḡo yaˡsumitaˑi ñ desu ḡa; kaˡmai-
maseˑñ ka⌐

6. It's all right.

Daˡizyoˑobu desu yo.

[She] wiped [it] up for me
so it's all right.

Huˡite kuretaˑ kara, daˡizyoˑobu
desu yo.

[She] wiped it up for me
right away so it's all
right.

Suˑḡu huˡite kuretaˑ kara, daˡizyoˑ-
obu desu yo.

Fumiko wiped it up for
me right away so it's
all right.

Huˑmiko-sañ (ḡa) ˡsuˑḡu huˡite kuretaˑ kara, daˡizyoˑobu desu yo.

I spilled [it] but Fumiko
wiped it up for me right
away so it's all right.

Koˡbosimaˑsita ḡa; Huˑmiko-sañ ḡa
ˡsuˑḡu huˡite kuretaˑ kara, daˡizyoˑobu desu yo.

I spilled sake but Fumiko
wiped it up for me right
away so it's all right.

Saˡke (o) kobosimaˑsita ḡa; Huˑmiko-sañ ḡa ˡsuˑḡu huˡite kuretaˑ
kara, daˡizyoˑobu desu yo.

I spilled sake on top of the
new table but Fumiko
wiped it up for me right
away so it's all right.

Aˡtarasiˑi teˡeburu no ueˑ ni saˡke
(o) kobosimaˑsita ḡa; Huˑmiko-sañ
ḡa ˡsuˑḡu huˡite kuretaˑ kara, daˡizyoˑobu desu yo.

SUPPLEMENTARY SELECTIONS

(with questions)

1. Aˡtarasiˑi ˡhoˑñ o taˡkusañ kattaˑ kara, aˡtarasiˑi ˡhoˑñdana mo kaˡimaˑ-
    sita. Keˡsa uˡti e motteˑ kite moˡraimaˑsita ḡa; toˡttemo isoḡaˑsikatta
    kara, hoˡñ mo ˡhoˑñdana mo syoˡsai no suˑmi ni oˡitoˑite deˡkakemaˑsi-
    ta ḡa; boku no rusu ni ˡkaˑnai ḡa hiˡtoˑri de soˡno hoˡñ o miˑñna hoˡñdana
    ni siˡmatte kuremaˑsita.

    a. Doˡo site aˡtarasiˑi ˡhoˑñdana o kaˡimaˑsita ka⌐
    b. Iˡtu uˡti e motteˑ kite moˡraimaˑsita ka⌐
    c. Sono ˡhoˑñ to ˡhoˑñdana wa ˡdoˡko ni oˡite okimaˑsita ka⌐ Doˡo
        site?
    d. Daˡre ḡa ˡhoˑñ o siˡmatte kuremaˑsita ka⌐
    e. Daˡre ni ˡhoˑñ o siˡmatte moraimaˑsita ka⌐
    f. Daˡre ḡa teˡtudaimaˑsita ka⌐

2. Kyoˡo wa ˡaˡsa kara toˡttemo isoḡaˑsikatta kara, tuˡkaˑrete siˡmaimaˑsita.
    Uˡti no Taˑroo ḡa eˡeḡo no hoˡñ o waˡsuretaˑ kara, gaˡkkoo maˑde moˡtte
    itte yarimaˑsita. Sore kara, uˡti e kaˡette; Huˑmiko to issyo ni uˡti o ka-
    tazukemaˑsita. Zyuˡuniˑ-zi ni maˑta dekakete, Giˑñza no depaˡato e iˡki-
    maˑsita. Soko no syokudoo de toˡmodati ni aˡtte, issyo ni syoˡkuzi o si-
    maˑsita. Sore kara, uˡti no syosai no sutoˡobu ḡa ˡmoˡo señsyuu kara
    dameˑ desu kara; aˡtarasiˑi no o kaˡimaˑsita. Tyoˡtto ˡoˡokikatta kara, de-
    ˡpaˑato no hiˡtoˑ ni ˡtaˡkusii made moˡtteˑ kite moratte; taˡkusii de kaˡeri-
    maˑsita. Toˡttemo tukaˡrete iˡtaˑ kara, Huˑmiko ni hiˡtoˑri de baˡñgoˑhañ

no sitaku o site moratte; i⌐ti-zikañ-ḡu⌐rai ya⌐sumima⌐sita.

    a. Na⌐ni o ga⌐kkoo ma⌐de mo⌐tte ikima⌐sita ka⌐

    b. Da⌐re ni mo⌐tte itte yarima⌐sita ka⌐

    c. Do⌐o site mo⌐tte itte yarima⌐sita ka⌐

    d. A⌐sa u⌐ti e ka⌐ette kara, na⌐ni o si⌐ma⌐sita ka⌐

    e. Hi⌐to⌐ri de si⌐ma⌐sita ka⌐

    f. Da⌐re ni te⌐tuda⌐tte mo⌐raima⌐sita ka⌐

    g. Da⌐re ḡa te⌐tuda⌐tte ku⌐rema⌐sita ka⌐

    h. Na⌐ñ-zi ni ma⌐ta dekakema⌐sita ka⌐

    i. Do⌐ko e i⌐kima⌐sita ka⌐

    j. Do⌐ko de syo⌐kuzi o sima⌐sita ka⌐

    k. Hi⌐to⌐ri de ta⌐bema⌐sita ka⌐

    l. Ta⌐bete kara ⌐na⌐ni o ka⌐ima⌐sita ka⌐ Do⌐o site?

    m. Da⌐re ḡa sore o ⌐ta⌐kusii made mo⌐tte⌐ kite ku⌐rema⌐sita ka⌐

    n. Ka⌐ette kara ⌐na⌐ni o si⌐ma⌐sita ka⌐ Do⌐o site?

    o. Hu⌐miko-sañ ni ⌐na⌐ni o si⌐te moraima⌐sita ka⌐

SHORT SUPPLEMENTARY DIALOGUES

(In each case, decide whether the speaker is best identified as M, or W, or MW. Change M utterances to W, and W utterances to M.)

1. A: Tu⌐ka⌐retyatta wa⌐
     B: Bo⌐ku mo.

2. A: Eeḡo o⌐wakari ni na⌐ru?
     B: Wa⌐suretyatta⌐ yo.

3. A: Kore ⌐do⌐ko ni o⌐kimasyo⌐o ka.
     B: A⌐suko ni oito⌐ite kudasai.

4. A: Are ⌐to⌐tte ne?
     B: Do⌐o site?
     A: Zya⌐ma ni na⌐ru kara.

5. A: Kono zibiki a̅re to tiḡau?
     B: N̄. A⌐re yo⌐ri a⌐tarasi⌐i yo⌐

6. A: Kinoo ko⌐no zassi katta⌐ wa⌐
     B: A⌐a, bo⌐ku mo o⌐nazi zassi katta⌐ yo.

EXERCISES

1. Draw a plan of your home, and describe in Japanese what each room is and the location of the doors, windows, and furniture.

2. Draw a simple house plan, including doors and windows. Using model furniture—or labeled blocks of wood or cardboard—practice giving and

following instructions on where to put each piece of furniture. (This exercise may also be done at the blackboard.   After hearing what is requested,
draw the appropriate object in the appropriate location.)

3. Speaking informally, tell someone to:

      a. put these books away.
      b. put these pens and pencils and such in the top desk drawer.
      c. throw away all these old magazines.
      d. put the beer in the refrigerator.
      e. put this on Mr. Tanaka's desk.
      f. give you a hand.
      g. put all these little things in that box.
      h. get out more paper.
      i. give this to the dog.
      j. give this to the teacher.
      k. wash this with soap.
      l. pass you the salt.
      m. put this under the kitchen table for the time being.
      n. be careful.
      o. have Fumiko buy more of this kind of medicine.

4. Practice the Basic Dialogues with appropriate variations.

Lesson 18. Visiting

BASIC DIALOGUES: FOR MEMORIZATION

(a)

Maid

guest or customer

kyaku or
okyaku⁺

put in an appearance or
show up or come

mi⌐e⌐ru /-ru/

1. Mr. Tanaka. (Lit. Master.) Your American guest has come.

Dan̄nasama⌐ A⌐merika⌐zin̄ no o-⌐kyakusa⌐ma ḡa o⌐mie ni narima⌐-sita.

Host (going to entry hall)

go up or come up or enter

aḡaru /-u/

2. Mr. Smith! It was good of you to come. Please come in.

Su⌐misu-san̄. Yo⌐ku i⌐rassyaima⌐-sita. Do⌐ozo o⌐aḡari-kudasa⌐i.

Smith

3. (Lit. I commit the rudeness [of entering your home].)

Si⌐tu⌐ree-simasu.

Host (showing Smith into the living room)

4. This way, please.

Do⌐ozo kotira e.

Smith

the other day (formal)

sen̄zitu

5. (Lit. I committed a rudeness the other day.)

Sen̄zitu wa si⌐tu⌐ree-simasita.

Host

6. (I was the one [who was rude].)

Ko⌐tira ko⌐so.

Smith

rain

a⌐me

fall (of rain, snow, etc.)

hu⌐ru /-u/

weather or good weather

te⌐n̄ki or
o⌐te⌐n̄ki⁺

7. It rained terribly [hard] yesterday but isn't it a beautiful day today!

Kinoo ⌐zu⌐ibun̄ ⌐a⌐me ḡa hu⌐rima⌐-sita ḡa, kyo⌐o wa ⌐i⌐i o⌐te⌐n̄ki de-su ⌐ne⌐e.

Host

8. [It] certainly [is].   Hoñtoo ni.

        a walk   sañpo
        for a walk   sañpo ni
        is cool   su⌐zusi⌐i /-ku/
9. I went for a walk this   Ke⌐sa sañpo ni ikima⌐sita ḡa,* su-
    morning. Hasn't it grown   ⌐zu⌐siku na⌐rima⌐sita ⌐ne⌐e.
    cool!

Smith

        fall or autumn   a⌐ki
10. Yes. Fall has come already,   E⌐e.   Mo⌐o ⌐a⌐ki ni na⌐rima⌐sita
     hasn't it. (Lit. It has be-   ⌐ne⌐e.
     come fall already, hasn't
     it.)

(Maid brings tea)

Host

11. Please [have] some tea.   O⌐tya o do⌐ozo.

Smith

12. Please don't bother. or   Do⌐ozo o⌐kamai na⌐ku.
     Please don't go to any
     trouble.

Host (serving tea)

13. It will get cold, so please   Tu⌐metaku narima⌐su kara, do⌐ozo.
     [go ahead].

Smith

14. (I'll drink it.)   I⌐tadakima⌐su.

(b)

Hostess (leading guests to dining room)

15. Please go in.   Do⌐ozo o⌐hairi-kudasaima⌐se.

Smith

16. [Excuse me for going] ahead.   Osaki ni.

        rice-straw floor mat   tatami
        room with floor mats   ta⌐tami no heya⌐
        feeling or mood   kimoti
        is pleasant or agreeable   ki⌐moti ḡa i⌐i
17. Aren't tatami rooms pleas-   Ta⌐tami no heya⌐ (wa) ki⌐moti ḡa i⌐i
     ant!   desu ⌐ne⌐e.

                        .   .   .

Hostess

        nothing   nani mo /+ negative/   or
                                                 nañni mo

18. There's nothing [worth men-   Na⌐ni⌐ mo gozaimase⌐ṅ ḡa, do⌐ozo.
    tioning] but please [eat].

                                    Smith

19. (I'll have some.)   I⌐tadakima⌐su.

                                    . . .

                                    Hostess

    second helping or   kawari   or
    additional serving   o⌐ka⌐wari⁺
20. How about some more?   O⌐ka⌐wari wa?

                                    Smith

21. No, thank you.   Mo⌐o ⌐ke⌐kkoo desu.

                                    Hostess

    reserve or restraint   eṅryo or
                                         goeṅryo ⁺
22. Please don't hold back.   or   Do⌐ozo go⌐eṅryo na⌐ku.
    Please don't stand on cere-
    mony.

                                    Smith

23. Thank you but I've already   A⌐ri⌐ḡatoo gozaimasu ḡa, mo⌐o ta-
    had a lot (so. . .)   ⌐kusaṅ itadakima⌐sita kara—

    mountain   ya⌐ma⌐
    sea or ocean   u⌐mi
    be visible or can see   mi⌐e⌐ru /-ru/
    place   to⌐ko(ro)⌐
24. How beautiful it is here, with   Ya⌐ma⌐ mo u⌐mi mo ⌐mi⌐ete, to⌐t-
    a view of the mountains and   temo ki⌐ree na to⌐koro⌐ desu ⌐ne⌐e.
    the sea! (Lit. Both the
    mountains and the sea being
    visible, it's a very pretty
    place, isn't it!)

                                    Hostess

25. Thank you.   O⌐so⌐re i⌐rima⌐su.

                                    Host

    skilled or skillful   zyo⌐ozu⌐ /na/   or
                                         ozyoozu ⁺ /na/
26. Isn't your Japanese good,   Su⌐misu-saṅ (wa) * nihoṅgo (ḡa) o-
    Mr. Smith!   ⌐zyoozu de⌐su ⌐ne⌐e.

    still or yet   ma⌐da   / + affirmative/
    learn or take lessons   na⌐ra⌐u /-u/
27. Are you still taking les-   Ma⌐da na⌐ra⌐tte (i)masu ka—
    sons?

Smith

no more	mo⌐o / + negative/
28. No, (I'm) not (taking lessons) any more.	Iie, mo⌐o na⌐ra⌐tte (i)⌐mase⌐ñ.
not skilled <u>or</u> poor at	he⌐ta⌐ /na/
these days	kono ḡoro
have time	zi⌐kañ ḡa a⌐ru
29. I'm still poor at it, but I don't have any time these days (so . . .)	Ma⌐da he⌐ta⌐ desu ḡa, kono ḡoro zi⌐kañ ḡa arimase⌐ñ kara_

(c)

Smith

by means of Japanese <u>or</u> in Japanese	nihoñḡo de
say <u>or</u> be named <u>or</u> be called	iu /-u/ <u>or</u> mo⌐osu ⌐ /-u/ <u>or</u> o⌐ssya⌐ru ⌐ /-aru/
say quote what? <u>or</u> be named quote what? <u>or</u> be called quote what?	na⌐ñ to iu <u>or</u> nañ te iu
30. What is this kind of door called in Japanese?	Koñna to (wa) nĩhoñḡo de ⌐na⌐ñ te i⌐ima⌐su ka_

Tanaka

sliding door (translucent)	syoozi
say quote shoji <u>or</u> be called quote shoji	syoozi to iu <u>or</u> syoozi tte iu
31. It's called a " shoji."	Syo⌐ozi tte iima⌐su.

Smith

32. How about that kind (of one)?	A⌐ñna⌐ no wa?

Tanaka

sliding door (opaque)	hu⌐suma⌐ [1]
say quote fusuma <u>or</u> be called quote fusuma	hu⌐suma⌐ to iu <u>or</u> hu⌐suma⌐ tte iu
33. That one is called a " fusuma."	Are wa hu⌐suma⌐ tte iimasu.

---

[1] Has commonly occurring unaccented alternant.

Smith

34. The outside ones, too?   So⌐to no mo?

Tanaka

      sliding storm door   a⌐ma⌐do
      say quote amado or   a⌐ma⌐do to iu or
      be called quote amado   a⌐ma⌐do tte iu

35. No, no. Those are called   Iie iie. Are wa a⌐ma⌐do tte iimasu.
     " amado."

(d)

Tanaka

      fine or handsome or   rippa /na/
        magnificent or im-
        posing
      Japanese-style alcove   tokonoma

36. What a handsome tokonoma!   Ri⌐ppa na tokonoma de⌐su ⌐ne⌐e.

      flower or flower ar-   ha⌐na⌐ or
        rangement   ohana⁺
      flower called quote what? na⌐ñ to iu hana or
                       na⌐ñ te iu hana

37. What kind of flowers are   Kore (wa) ⌐na⌐ñ te iu ha⌐na⌐ desyoo
     these? (Lit. These are   ka.
     flowers called quote what?)

Smith

      not know how one says [it] do⌐o iu ka siranai
        or not know how [it] is
        called

38. I don't know what they are   Ni⌐hoñḡo de do⌐o iu ka si⌐rimase⌐ñ
     called in Japanese, but there ḡa, niwa ni ta⌐kusañ arima⌐su yo_
     are a lot of them in the gar-
     den.

(e)

Maid

      during someone's absence   rusu-tyuu ni or
        from home   orusu-tyuu ⌐ ni

39. Someone (lit. a guest) came Orusu-tyuu ni o⌐kyakusa⌐ñ (ḡa) o⌐mie
     while you were out. . . .   ni narima⌐sita ḡa_

Tanaka

40. Oh? Who?   So⌐o? Da⌐re?

Maid

      be named quote Ueda or   Ueda to iu or
      be called quote Ueda or   Ueda tte iu
      say quote Ueda

41. His name was Ueda. . . .   U⌐eda to ossyaima⌐sita ḡa_

Tanaka

say quote what?   or   na⌐ꞁn to iu   or
be called quote what?   na⌐ꞁn te iu
or   be named quote
what?
42.   What did he say?   Na⌐ꞁn te itta?

Maid

say quote he'll come,   i⌐rassya⌐ꞁru to o⌐ssya⌐ꞁru   or
go, or be   i⌐rassya⌐ꞁru tte o⌐ssya⌐ꞁru
43.   He said he'd come again.   Ma⌐ta irassya⌐ꞁru tte o⌐ssyaima⌐ꞁsi-
                                               ta.

Tanaka

ask [quote] will [some-   ku⌐ꞁru ka [to] kiku
one] come
44.   Did you ask when he's com-   I⌐ꞁtu ⌐ku⌐ꞁru ka kiita?
ing?

Maid

clearly or distinctly   ha⌐kki⌐ꞁri
or precisely
say quote he doesn't   o⌐wakari ni nara⌐ꞁnai to
understand or can't   o⌐ssya⌐ꞁru   or
tell   o⌐wakari ni nara⌐ꞁnai tte o⌐s-
                                               sya⌐ꞁru
45.   Yes. I inquired but he   Ha⌐ꞁa. U⌐kaḡaima⌐ꞁsita ḡa, ha⌐kki⌐ꞁri
said he couldn't tell ex-   o⌐wakari ni nara⌐ꞁnai tte o⌐ssyaima⌐ꞁ-
actly.   sita.

NOTES ON THE BASIC DIALOGUES

1.   Remember that -sama is a more polite variant of -sañ.

2.   Aḡaru 'enter' is usually used in reference to entering a Japanese-style
building—a home, inn, restaurant, etc.—which one enters by stepping up.
Note also kaidañ o aḡaru 'go up the stairs.'

3.   Si⌐tu⌐ꞁree-simasu, lit. 'I commit a rudeness,' covers a multitude of situations in Japanese: it is an apology for entering someone's home or office
—and for leaving, for taking a seat, even for relaxing!

5.   Señzitu wa si⌐tu⌐ꞁree-simasita frequently occurs as the formal beginning of
a conversation between people who have had some recent contact with each
other. Under similar circumstances, an English speaker might say, 'It
was nice seeing you the other day.'

6.   Ko⌐ꞁso is a particle of strong emphasis. Ko⌐tira ko⌐ꞁso means 'this side,
not your side, [committed the rudeness].' Compare:

A: Go⌐ku⌐ꞁroosama desita.   'It's been a great deal of trouble for you.'
B: A⌐na⌐ꞁta koso. 'YOU're the one who has been troubled.'

This exchange might occur for example when two people have been working on a project together.

7. The gerund of hu⌐ru occurs with alternate accents: ⌐hu⌐tte and hu⌐tte⌐.

    Te⌐ṅki may be described by words meaning 'good' or 'bad,' but unmodi-
    fied it means 'good weather.'

8. Hoñtoo ni 'truly': ni is the particle of manner (cf. Lesson 15, Grammati-
    cal Note 5).

9. Ni here is the ni of goal or purpose. Note also saṅpo-suru 'take a walk.'

    Su⌐zusi⌐i means 'is cool'—i.e. 'is nice and cool.' Besides referring to
    typical days of autumn, it is used to describe pleasantly cool days of sum-
    mer.

10. Note also: hu⌐yu⌐ 'winter'; ha⌐ru 'spring,' na⌐tu⌐ 'summer.'

11. Otya o is a fragment. A possible major sentence substitute would be:
    O⌐tya o mesiaḡatte kudasa⌐i.

12. Okamai is a derivative of the verbal √ka⌐ma⌐u /-u/ 'mind,' 'care,' 'bother
    about,' from which ka⌐mawa⌐nai (formal, ka⌐maimase⌐ñ) 'I don't care,' 'it
    doesn't matter' is also derived.

14, 19. Remember that i⌐tadakima⌐su is regularly said by a guest as he begins
    to eat or drink.

16. Osaki ni, depending on context, is either an apology for doing something
    ahead of someone else, or an invitation to someone else to go ahead.
    Thus: Osaki ni si⌐tu⌐ree-simasu. 'Excuse me for taking my leave ahead
    of you.' but Do⌐ozo osaki ni. 'Please go ahead.'

17. Ki⌐moti ḡa i⌐i 'is pleasant or agreeable' and its opposite ki⌐moti ḡa waru⌐i
    'is unpleasant or disagreeable' are often used in reference to people, as
    equivalents of English 'feel well' and 'not feel well.' The person or thing
    to which these sequences refer is followed by particle wa or ḡa, depending
    upon emphasis.

22. Note also: eñryo-suru 'hold back,' 'be reserved,' 'show restraint,' 'hesi-
    tate.'

23. 'so—I don't care for any more.'

24. Toko is an informal alternant of to⌐koro⌐.

25. O⌐so⌐re i⌐rima⌐su, lit. 'I'm overwhelmed [with gratitude or shame],' is
    an extremely polite way of saying 'Thank you' or 'I'm sorry.' It is used
    more frequently by women. A commonly occurring alternate form of it is
    o⌐so⌐reirimasu.

27. Na⌐ra⌐u is used in reference to any sort of learning or instruction;
    beñkyoo-suru is usually used only for scholastic studies.

29. 'so—I've given up taking lessons.'

30. Mo⌐osu and o⌐ssya⌐ru are polite equivalents of iu. Mo⌐osu, a humble ver-
    bal, is used in reference to the speaker and persons closely connected
    with him. O⌐ssya⌐ru, an honorific, refers only to persons other than the
    speaker, in polite speech.

39.   'but— did you know he was coming?'

Rusu-tyuu: compare si͠goto-tyuu 'in the middle of work' and hanasi-tyuu 'in the middle of talking.'

41.   'but— do you know him?'

GRAMMATICAL NOTES

1.   Quotatives *[t]* te ~ to

[T] te[1] and its more formal equivalent to are QUOTATIVES.   They follow a quotation (or the gist of a quotation) consisting of any sequence whatsoever— a word, a part of a word, a sentence, a speech, an utterance in a foreign language, etc.— or nañ 'what?' substituting for a quotation.

Compare:

Ha˥yaku i˥ima˥sita.   'He said [it] quickly.'
Ha˥yaku to (or tte) i˥ima˥sita.   'He said, "Quickly."'

[T] te usually follows quotations of utterances, whereas to also follows thoughts, written words, etc.   Following utterances, *[t]* te is more common than to in rapid conversational Japanese, particularly in informal and plain speech.   Occurrences of to are usually heard in formal and honorific speech, and/or in precise speech.

Some quotations repeat the exact words of the original speaker.   Usually, however, a Japanese quotation gives— in the informal style— the gist of what was said, from the point of view of the person reporting the quotation.   The quotation does retain the tense of the original.

Thus:

Original statement: A˩͠gema˥su.   'I'll give it to you.'
Quoted: Ku˩reru tte iima˥sita.[2] 'He said he'd give it to me.'

Original statement: Ki˩noo itasima˥sita.   'I did it yesterday.' (Humble)
Quoted: Ki˩noo nasa˥tta to o˩ssyaima˥sita. 'He said he did it yesterday.'

The person who says or asks something, if expressed, is followed by particle wa or ͠ga, and the person told or asked, by particle ni.   Thus:

Tanaka-sañ wa Yamamoto-sañ ni ta˩bako o yameta tte iima˥sita.
'Mr. Tanaka said to Mr. Yamamoto that he had quit smoking.'

---

[1] Te follows ñ; tte follows vowels.

[2] Alternate accent: Ku˩reru˥ tte i˥ima˥sita., with the accent before *[t]* te ~ to the same as that before kara.

The order of the phrases is not fixed: the quotation + quotative is not always followed immediately by the inflected expression it modifies. Thus:

Tabako o yameta tte, Yaᒣmamoto-sañ ni iimaᒣsita.
'[He] said to Mr. Yamamoto that he had quit smoking.'

Sometimes only context and/or intonation distinguish parts of the quotation from modifiers of the following inflected expression. Compare :

Tanaka-sañ wa ⌐kuᒣru tte iᒣimaᒣsita.
'Mr. Tanaka said that [he]¹ would come.'
(Quotation = ku¹ru)

and :

Taᒣnaka-sañ wa ku¹ru tte iᒣimaᒣsita.
'[He]¹ said that Mr. Tanaka would come.'
(Quotation = Taᒣnaka-sañ wa ku¹ru)

Compare also:

Tanaka-sañ ni ⌐a¹tta tte iᒣimaᒣsita.
'[He]¹ said to Mr. Tanaka that [he]¹ had met him.'
(Quotation = a¹tta)

and :

Taᒣnaka-sañ ni a¹tta tte iᒣimaᒣsita.
'[He]¹ said that [he]¹ had met Mr. Tanaka.'
(Quotation = Taᒣnaka-sañ ni a¹tta)

The quotative is often omitted after a quoted question ending with ka; and before ka, the informal non-past copula da is regularly omitted. Accentuation before ka is like that before kara.

Additional examples:

Ueda-sañ wa iᒣku tte (i)tte² (i)maᒣsita ḡa_
'Mr. Ueda was saying that he would go but. . . .' (Lit. 'Mr. Ueda was saying quote he'll go but. . .')
Moᒣo ᒣmiᒣta tte iᒣimaᒣsita. 'I said that I had seen it already.'
(Lit. 'I said quote I have seen it already.')
Iᒣi to oᒣssyaimaᒣsita ka_ 'Did you say that it's all right?'
Koᒣno deñwa kosyoo da¹ tte iᒣimaᒣsita.
'He said that this phone is out of order.'
Aᒣsita kaᒣeru to kaᒣkimaᒣsita.
'He wrote that he is coming home tomorrow.'

---

¹ Or anyone else—made clear by the context.

² Following quotative /t/te, forms of √iu beginning it- (for example, itte, itta, etc.) lose their initial i- in rapid, contracted speech.

I⌐tu de mo i⌐i to, se⌐ñse⌐e ni de⌐ñwa-sima⌐sita.
  'He telephoned the teacher that any time will be all right.'
O⌐namae o ka⌐ite kudasai to i⌐ima⌐sita.
  'He said, "Please write your name."'
I⌐tu i⌐ku⌐ ka ki⌐kima⌐sita.
  'I asked when he was going.'
I⌐ssyo ni ikana⌐i ka tte Ta⌐naka-sañ ni kikimasyo⌐o.
  'Let's ask Mr. Tanaka if he won't go with us.'
So⌐no ka⌐ta ⌐do⌐nata ka ki⌐ite kudasaimase⌐ñ ka↲ [1]
  'Would you be kind enough to ask who that is?'
So⌐re wa na⌐ñ desu ka to ki⌐kima⌐sita.
  'I asked, "What is that?"'
So⌐no ho⌐ñ wa ⌐na⌐ñ te i⌐ima⌐su ka↲
  'What's the name of that book?' (Lit. 'That book is called quote
  what?')
Ma⌐tuda to moosima⌐su.
  'My name is Matsuda.' (Lit. 'I am called quote Matsuda.')

A quotation + quotative may be followed by particle wa — particularly in
negative sentences. Thus:

Ma⌐zu⌐i tte wa i⌐imase⌐ñ desita ḡa↲
  'He didn't say it tasted bad but . . .'   (Lit. 'As for quote it tastes
  bad, he didn't say but . . .')

The combination X to (or [t] te) iu Y, in which X is a name or designation
(belonging to any word class) and Y is a nominal, is the Japanese equivalent of
'a Y named X' or 'a Y called X.' Na⌐ñ to (or te) iu Y 'a Y named quote what?'
is a question equivalent.

[T] te (but not to) frequently occurs in statements and questions in sentence-
final position, or pre-final before ne⌐e, or ne, following the quotation of someone other than the speaker. Thus:

De⌐ñki ḡa ki⌐eta⌐ tte. 'He said the light went out.'
A⌐rimase⌐ñ te? 'Did you say there isn't any?'
I⌐i tte. 'He said it's all right.'
So⌐o desu tte ⌐ne⌐e. 'That's what they say, isn't it.'

This use of [t] te is informal.

----

[1] Note the omission of da before ka.

2. Indirect Questions Containing Interrogative Words

Questions containing interrogative words (na⌐ñ, da⌐re, do⌐ko, i⌐tu, etc.) and ending with particle ka occur as indirect questions before expressions of knowing, understanding, forgetting, informing, etc. They are usually in the informal style. As mentioned in the preceding note, informal non-past da is regularly lost before ka. Accentuation before ka is like accentuation before kara.

Examples:

Direct question:	Do⌐ko e i⌐kima⌐su ka⌐ 'Where are you going?'
Indirect question:	Do⌐ko e i⌐ku⌐ ka si⌐rimase⌐ñ. 'I don't know where you are going.'
Direct question:	Do⌐re ḡa i⌐tibañ taka⌐i desu ka⌐ 'Which one is most expensive?'
Indirect question:	Do⌐re ḡa i⌐tibañ taka⌐i ka wa⌐karimase⌐ñ. 'I can't tell which one is most expensive.'
Direct question:	Da⌐re desu ka⌐ 'Who is he?'
Indirect question:	Da⌐re ka wa⌐surema⌐sita. 'I forgot who he is.'

3. More Imperatives

A nominal consisting of the polite prefix o- + a verbal stem (i.e. the -ma⌐su form minus -ma⌐su)[1] compounded with ku⌐dasa⌐i or (formal) ku⌐dasaima⌐se[2] is a polite imperative. Examples:

o⌐mati-kudasa⌐i 'please wait'
o⌐yobi-kudasa⌐i 'please call'
o⌐kaki-kudasa⌐i 'please write'

If the -kudasa⌐i is dropped, the result is a more informal equivalent.

The following are all used to ask someone to wait, but they differ in their degree of formality and politeness:

	(a)	(b)	(c)
(1)	Ma⌐tte.	Ma⌐tte kudasai.	Ma⌐tte ku⌐dasaima⌐se.
(2)	Omati.	O⌐mati-kudasa⌐i.	O⌐mati-kudasaima⌐se.
(3)	O⌐mati ni na⌐tte.	O⌐mati ni na⌐tte kudasai.	O⌐mati ni na⌐tte ku⌐dasaima⌐se.

Forms in Row (2) are more polite than those in Row (1), and those in Row (3) are most polite. Forms in Column (a) are less formal than those in

---

[1] The combination o- + stem is unaccented.

[2] Forms ending in -ma⌐se are more typical of women's speech.

Column (b). Those in Column (c) are formal women's forms. (3)(a) is also typical of women's speech.

A gerund + ku⌐dasaimase⌐ñ ka (for example, ma⌐tte ku⌐dasaimase⌐ñ ka 'would you be kind enough to wait?'), though not an imperative, is a formal polite form of request. It is softer and less direct than an imperative.

WARNING: Not all verbals have imperatives of the o⌐mati-kudasa⌐i pattern. Use only those which you have heard or checked with a native speaker.

4.   ma⌐da + Affirmative; mo⌐o + Negative

Reread Lesson 14, Grammatical Note 5, carefully.

Ma⌐da + an affirmative (except for the special combination ma⌐da desu 'not yet') means 'still' or 'yet.'

Mo⌐o + a negative means '(not) any more.'

As explained in the note referred to above, mo⌐o occurs in the direct iie answer to a ma⌐da question, and ma⌐da occurs in the direct iie answer to a mo⌐o question. Thus:

> Ma⌐da e⌐eḡo o beñkyoo-site ima⌐su ka⌐ 'Are you still studying English?'
> E⌐e, ma⌐da be⌐ñkyoo-site ima⌐su. 'Yes, I'm still studying.'
> Iie, mo⌐o be⌐ñkyoo-site imase⌐ñ. 'No, I'm not studying any more.'

> Mo⌐o e⌐eḡo o beñkyoo-site imase⌐ñ ka⌐ 'Aren't you studying English any more?'
> E⌐e, mo⌐o be⌐ñkyoo-site imase⌐ñ. 'No (i.e. that's right), I'm not studying any more.'
> Iie, ma⌐da be⌐ñkyoo-site ima⌐su. 'Yes (i.e. that's wrong), I'm still studying.'

> Ma⌐da o⌐oki⌐i desu ka⌐ 'Is it still [too] big?'
> E⌐e, ma⌐da o⌐oki⌐i desu. 'Yes, it's still [too] big.'
> Iie, mo⌐o ⌐o⌐okiku a⌐rimase⌐ñ. 'No, it's not big any more.'

5.   na⌐ku in Sentence-Final Position

> O⌐kamai na⌐ku.

> Go⌐eñryo na⌐ku.

Na⌐ku is the -ku form of na⌐i (informal equivalent of a⌐rimase⌐ñ) 'there isn't [any].' The -ku form in final position in these sentences signifies a request. Thus: o⌐kamai na⌐ku 'let there be no bother'; go⌐eñryo na⌐ku 'let there be no reserve.'

Compare also: do⌐ozo yo⌐rosiku (from yorosii 'is good' or 'is favorable') 'let all be well' or 'I request your favor.'

A combination ending with na⌐ku is not limited to sentence-final position:

for example, like other -ku forms, it may occur within a sentence as the modifier of an inflected expression. Compare:

Ha⌐yaku o⌐ssya⌐tte kudasai. 'Please speak quickly.'

and:

Go⌐eñryo na⌐ku o⌐ssya⌐tte kudasai. 'Please speak freely (lit. without reserve).'

WARNING: Don't make up any —— + na⌐ku combinations. Use only those you have heard from a native speaker.

6. mi⌐e⌐ru

Mi⌐e⌐ru, an intransitive verbal, occurs in this lesson with two different meanings:

(a) mi⌐e⌐ru 'put in an appearance,' 'appear,' 'come'

The person who puts in an appearance, if expressed, is followed by wa or ḡa, depending upon emphasis. The polite o⌐mie ni na⌐ru † is used to show respect to him. This is never used in reference to the speaker.

Examples:

O⌐mie ni narima⌐su ka⌐ 'Are you going to put in an appearance?'
Ta⌐naka-sañ ḡa omie ni narima⌐sita. 'Mr. Tanaka has appeared.'
A⌐tarasi⌐i ko⌐oka⌐ñsyu ḡa mi⌐ema⌐sita. 'The new telephone operator has come.'

(b) mi⌐e⌐ru 'be visible,' 'can see'

The person who can see and the object which is visible, if expressed, are followed by wa or ḡa, depending upon emphasis. The polite o⌐mie ni na⌐ru † is used to show respect to the person who can see.

Examples:

U⌐mi ḡa mi⌐ema⌐sita. 'I could see the ocean.'
(i.e. telling what I could see)
Wa⌐takusi ḡa omie ni narima⌐su ka⌐ 'Can you see me?'
(i.e. am I visible as far as you are concerned?)
Da⌐re ḡa mi⌐emase⌐ñ ka⌐ . . . Ta⌐naka-sañ ḡa miemase⌐ñ.
'Who can't see? . . . Mr. Tanaka can't see.' or (depending upon context) 'Whom can't you see? . . . I can't see Mr. Tanaka.'
Ta⌐isi⌐kañ to ryo⌐ozi⌐kañ ḡa mi⌐ema⌐su ka⌐ . . . Ta⌐isi⌐kañ wa mi⌐ema⌐su ḡa, ryo⌐ozi⌐kañ wa mi⌐emase⌐ñ.
'Can you see the embassy and the consulate? . . . The embassy I can see, but the consulate I can't see.'

Zyo⌐ozu⌐ da 'be proficient,' su⌐ki⌐ da 'be pleasing,' wa⌐ka⌐ru 'be comprehensible,' and de⌐ki⌐ru 'be possible' are among the many other intransitive inflected words and phrases which are preceded by wa phrases and ḡa phrases but not o phrases.

DRILLS

A. Substitution Drill

1. I haven't anything. or   Na⌐ni mo na⌐i.
    There isn't anything.

2. I can't see anything.   Na⌐ni mo mie¬nai.

3. I can't hear anything.   Nani mo kikoenai.

4. I don't understand any-   Na⌐ni mo wakara¬nai.
    thing.

5. I don't know anything.   Nani mo siranai.

6. I didn't give [him] any-   Na⌐ni mo yarana¬katta.
    thing.

7. He didn't give me any-   Na⌐ni mo kurena¬katta.
    thing.

8. I couldn't do anything.   Na⌐ni mo deki¬nakatta.

9. I didn't do anything.   Na⌐ni mo sina¬katta.

10. I didn't say anything.   Na⌐ni mo iwana¬katta.

B. Substitution Drill

1. Isn't that good Japanese!   * Zyo⌐ozu¬ na ni⌐hoñgo de¬su ⌐ne¬e.

2. Isn't that poor Japanese!   * He⌐ta¬ na ni⌐hoñgo de¬su ⌐ne¬e.

3. Isn't that beautiful Japa-   * Ki¬ree na ni⌐hoñgo de¬su ⌐ne¬e.
    nese!

4. Isn't that a beautiful   * Ki¬ree na o⌐ka¬si desu ⌐ne¬e.
    cake!

5. Isn't that a wonderful   * Ke¬kkoo na o⌐ka¬si desu ⌐ne¬e.
    cake!

6. Isn't that a strange cake!   * He¬ñ na o⌐ka¬si desu ⌐ne¬e.

7. Isn't he a strange per-   * He¬ñ na hi⌐to¬ desu ⌐ne¬e.
    son!

8. Isn't he a fine person!   * Rippa na hi⌐to¬ desu ⌐ne¬e.

9. Isn't he a rude person!   * Si⌐tu¬ree na hi⌐to¬ desu ⌐ne¬e.

C. Substitution Drill

1. Fall has come (lit. it has   Mo¬o ⌐a¬ki ni na⌐rima⌐sita ⌐ne¬e.
    become fall) already, has-
    n't it!

2. Winter has come already,   Mo¬o hu⌐yu¬ ni na⌐rima⌐sita ⌐ne¬e.
    hasn't it!

3. Summer has come already,   Mo¬o na⌐tu¬ ni na⌐rima⌐sita ⌐ne¬e.
    hasn't it!

4. Spring has come already,   Mo¬o ⌐ha¬ru ni na⌐rima⌐sita ⌐ne¬e.
    hasn't it!

5. It has cleared up (lit. be-   Mo¬o o⌐te¬ñki ni na⌐rima⌐sita ⌐ne¬e.
    come good weather) al-
    ready, hasn't it!

6. You've become good at it   Mo¬o o⌐zyoozu ni narima⌐sita ⌐ne¬e.
    already, haven't you!

7. They've become the same
   already, haven't they!

Mo⌐o o⌐nazi ni narima⌐sita ⌐ne⌐e.

8. You've recovered already,
   haven't you!

Mo⌐o o⌐ge⌐ñki ni na⌐rima⌐sita ⌐ne⌐e.

D. Substitution Drill

1. What kind of flower is
   it? (Lit. It's a flower
   called what?)

Na⌐ñ te iu ha⌐na⌐ desu ka↲

2. Is it a man named Ta-
   naka?

Ta⌐naka tte iu hito⌐ desu ka↲

3. Are they cigarettes
   called " Peace" ?

Pi⌐isu tte iu ta⌐bako de⌐su ka↲

4. Is it a department store
   called " Mitsukoshi" ?

Mi⌐tuko⌐si tte iu de⌐pa⌐ato desu ka↲

5. Is it an American
   named Smith?

Su⌐misu tte iu A⌐merika⌐ziñ desu
ka↲

6. Is it the magazine
   " King" ?

Ki⌐ñgu tte iu za⌐ssi de⌐su ka↲

7. Is it the newspaper "Mainichi" ?

Ma⌐initi tte iu siñbuñ de⌐su ka↲

8. Is it an inn called "Ima-
   iso" ?

I⌐mai⌐soo tte iu ryo⌐kañ de⌐su ka↲

E. Substitution Drill

1. This kind of door is
   called a " shoji" in Japanese.

Koñna to (wa) nihoñgo de syo⌐ozi
tte iima⌐su.

2. This kind of color is
   called " aka (red)" in
   Japanese.

Ko⌐ñna iro⌐ (wa) nihoñgo de ⌐a⌐ka
tte iimasu.

3. This kind of store is
   called a " yaoya (vegetable store)" in Japa-
   nese.

Ko⌐ñna mise⌐ (wa) nihoñgo de ya⌐oya
tte iima⌐su.

4. This kind of place is
   called a " koen (park)"
   in Japanese.

Ko⌐ñna tokoro⌐ (wa) nihoñgo de ko-
⌐oeñ tte iima⌐su.

5. This kind of building is
   called a " byoin (hospital)" in Japanese.

Ko⌐ñna tate⌐mono (wa) nihoñgo de
byo⌐oiñ tte iima⌐su.

6. This kind of school is
   called a " daigaku (university)" in Japanese.

Koñna gakkoo (wa) nihoñgo de da⌐i-
ḡaku tte iima⌐su.

7. This kind of drink is
   called " kotya (black tea)"
   in Japanese.

Ko⌐ñna nomi⌐mono (wa) nihoñgo de
ko⌐otya tte iima⌐su.

8. This kind of place is
   called a " daidokoro (kitchen)" in Japanese.

Ko⌐ñna tokoro⌐ (wa) nihoñgo de da-
⌐idokoro tte iima⌐su.

9. This kind of shelf is called a " hondana (book-shelf)" in Japanese.

Koñna <u>tana</u> (wa) nĩhoñḡo de <u>ho˥ñ-dana</u> tte iimasu.

10. This kind of animal is called an " uma (horse)" in Japanese.

Koñna <u>doobutu</u> (wa) nĩhoñḡo de <u>u˥ma˥</u> tte iimasu.

F.   Substitution Drill

1. Who can't see?[1]
2. Which one can't you see?
3. Which one can't you do?
4. Who can't do it?
5. Who is good at it?
6. Who doesn't understand?
7. Which one don't you un-derstand?
8. Which one do you need?
9. Who needs it?
10. Who doesn't like it?

Da˥re ḡa mi˥emase˥ñ ka˩
<u>Do˥re</u> ḡa mi˥emase˥ñ ka˩
Do˥re ḡa <u>de˥kimase˥ñ</u> ka˩
<u>Da˥re</u> ḡa de˥kimase˥ñ ka˩
Da˥re ḡa <u>zyo˥ozu˥</u> desu ka˩
Da˥re ḡa <u>wa˥karimase˥ñ</u> ka˩
<u>Do˥re</u> ḡa wa˥karimase˥ñ ka˩
Do˥re ḡa <u>i˥rima˥su</u> ka˩
<u>Da˥re</u> ḡa i˥rima˥su ka˩
Da˥re ḡa <u>su˥ki˥ zya a˥rimase˥ñ ka˩</u>

G.   Substitution Drill

1. I don't know how they say it in Japanese.
2. I can't tell how they say it in Japanese.
3. I forgot how they say it in Japanese.
4. Please tell me how they say it in Japanese.
5. He told me how they say it in Japanese.
6. Let's ask how they say it in Japanese.
7. I had [him] ask how they say it in Japanese.
8. I inquired how they say it in Japanese.

Ni˥hoñḡo de do˥o iu ka si˥rimase˥ñ.
Ni˥hoñḡo de do˥o iu ka <u>wa˥karima-se˥ñ.</u>
Ni˥hoñḡo de do˥o iu ka <u>wa˥surema˥-sita.</u>
Ni˥hoñḡo de do˥o iu ka <u>o˥siete kuda-sa˥i.</u>
Ni˥hoñḡo de do˥o iu ka <u>o˥siete kure-ma˥sita.</u>
Ni˥hoñḡo de do˥o iu ka <u>ki˥kimasyo˥o.</u>
Ni˥hoñḡo de do˥o iu ka <u>ki˥ite morai-ma˥sita.</u>
Ni˥hoñḡo de do˥o iu ka <u>u˥kaḡaima˥-sita.</u>

---

[1] Or, depending on the context, 'Whom can't you see?' or 'Who isn't going to come?' etc.

H. Substitution Drill

1.	I don't know how they say it in Japanese.	Ni⌐hoñḡo de do⌐o iu ka si⌐rimase⌐ñ.
2.	I don't know who said that.	Da⌐re ḡa so⌐o itta⌐ ka si⌐rimase⌐ñ.
3.	I don't know what [he] got.	Na⌐ni (o) mo⌐ratta⌐ ka si⌐rimase⌐ñ.
4.	I don't know when [he] entered Tokyo University.	I⌐tu To⌐odai ni ha⌐itta ka si⌐rimase⌐ñ.
5.	I don't know what is wrong with him (lit. what place is bad). [1]	Do⌐ko ḡa wa⌐ru⌐i ka si⌐rimase⌐ñ.
6.	I don't know which one is stronger.	Do⌐tira no ⌐ho⌐o ḡa tu⌐yo⌐i ka si⌐rimase⌐ñ.
7.	I don't know which one was most difficult.	Do⌐re ḡa i⌐tibañ muzukasi⌐katta ka si⌐rimase⌐ñ.
8.	I don't know what floor it is.	Nañ-ḡai ka si⌐rimase⌐ñ.
9.	I don't know which car is his.	Do⌐no kuruma ḡa a⌐no⌐ hito no ka si⌐rimase⌐ñ.
10.	I don't know what day it was.	Na⌐ñyo⌐obi datta ka si⌐rimase⌐ñ.

I. Level Drill (based on Grammatical Note 3)

Tutor: So⌐ko de ma⌐tte kudasai. ⎫
Student: So⌐ko de omati-kudasa⌐i. ⎬ 'Please wait there.'

1.	Do⌐ozo a⌐ḡatte kudasa⌐i.	Do⌐ozo o⌐aḡari-kudasa⌐i.
2.	Ko⌐tira ni ha⌐itte kudasai.	Ko⌐tira ni ohairi-kudasa⌐i.
3.	Do⌐ozo ōsaki ni ⌐ka⌐ette kudasai.	Do⌐ozo ōsaki ni o⌐kaeri-kudasa⌐i.
4.	Koko ni o⌐namae (o) ka⌐ite kudasai.	Koko ni o⌐namae (o) okaki-kudasa⌐i.
5.	Si⌐o⌐ to ko⌐syo⌐o (o) ⌐to⌐tte kudasai.	Si⌐o⌐ to ko⌐syo⌐o (o) o⌐tori-kudasa⌐i.
6.	Kore (o) ⌐ze⌐ñbu tu⌐taete kudasa⌐i.	Kore (o) ⌐ze⌐ñbu o⌐tutae-kudasa⌐i.

---

[1] Refers to someone who is ill.

J. Grammatical Drill (based on Grammatical Note 1)

Tutor: A⌐sita kima⌐su. 'I'll come tomorrow.'
Student: A⌐no⌐ hito wa a⌐sita ku⌐ru tte (i⌐ima⌐sita). [1] 'He said he'd come tomorrow.'

1. Raineñ To⌐odai ni hai-rima⌐su.
    A⌐no⌐ hito wa raineñ To⌐odai ni ha⌐-iru tte (i⌐ima⌐sita).

2. Na⌐ñ-zi de mo kamaima-se⌐ñ.
    A⌐no⌐ hito wa na⌐ñ-zi de mo kama-wa⌐nai tte (i⌐ima⌐sita).

3. To⌐ttemo he⌐ñ desita.
    A⌐no⌐ hito wa to⌐ttemo he⌐ñ datta tte (i⌐ima⌐sita).

4. Se⌐ñse⌐e desu.
    A⌐no⌐ hito wa se⌐ñse⌐e da tte (i⌐i-ma⌐sita).

5. Te⌐tuda⌐tte aḡemasu. [2]
    A⌐no⌐ hito wa te⌐tuda⌐tte ku⌐reru⌐ tte (i⌐ima⌐sita).

6. Tomodati ni te⌐tuda⌐tte mo⌐raima⌐sita.
    A⌐no⌐ hito wa tomodati ni te⌐tuda⌐tte mo⌐ratta⌐ tte (i⌐ima⌐sita).

7. A⌐tama⌐ ḡa i⌐ta⌐i desu.
    A⌐no⌐ hito wa a⌐tama⌐ ḡa i⌐ta⌐i tte (i⌐ima⌐sita).

8. A⌐sita⌐ made i⌐ma⌐su.
    A⌐no⌐ hito wa a⌐sita⌐ made i⌐ru⌐ tte (i⌐ima⌐sita).

9. A⌐me ḡa hu⌐tte⌐ (i)ma-su.
    A⌐no⌐ hito wa ⌐a⌐me ḡa hu⌐tte⌐ (i)ru tte (i⌐ima⌐sita).

10. Kinoo de⌐kakemase⌐ñ de-sita.
    A⌐no⌐ hito wa kinoo de⌐kakena⌐katta tte (i⌐ima⌐sita).

K. Grammar Drill (based on Grammatical Note 1)

Tutor: A⌐no⌐ hito (wa) ki⌐ma⌐su ka◡ 'Is he coming?'
Student: A⌐no⌐ hito ni ⌐ku⌐ru ka [tte] ki⌐kimasyo⌐o. [3] 'Let's ask him if he is coming.'

1. A⌐no⌐ hito (wa) ⌐na⌐ni ḡa i⌐rima⌐su ka◡
    A⌐no⌐ hito ni ⌐na⌐ni ḡa i⌐ru⌐ ka [tte] ki⌐kimasyo⌐o.

2. A⌐no⌐ hito (wa) ⌐i⌐tu made i⌐soḡasi⌐i desu ka◡
    A⌐no⌐ hito ni ⌐i⌐tu made i⌐soḡasi⌐i ka [tte] ki⌐kimasyo⌐o.

3. A⌐no⌐ hito (wa) ⌐na⌐ñ-zi ni tu⌐kima⌐sita ka◡
    A⌐no⌐ hito ni ⌐na⌐ñ-zi ni ⌐tu⌐ita ka [tte] ki⌐kimasyo⌐o.

---

[1] Practice both the formal (with i⌐ima⌐sita) and informal (without i⌐ima⌐sita) alternants.

[2] Meaning 'I'll help YOU.'

[3] Practice both with and without tte.

4. Aˈnoˈ hito (wa) byoˈoki
   deˈsita ka⅃

   Aˈnoˈ hito ni byoˈoki daˈtta ka [tte]
   kiˈkimasyoˈo.

5. Aˈnoˈ hito (wa) teˈtudaˈtte kuʰremaseˈñ ka⅃

   Aˈnoˈ hito ni teˈtudaˈtte kuʰrenaˈi
   ka [tte] kiˈkimasyoˈo.

6. Aˈnoˈ hito (wa) niˈhoñḡo
   (ḡa) dekimaˈsu ka⅃

   Aˈnoˈ hito ni niˈhoñḡo (ḡa) dekiˈru
   ka [tte] kiˈkimasyoˈo.

7. Aˈnoˈ hito (wa) hiˈma
   deˈsu ka⅃

   Aˈnoˈ hito ni hima ka [tte] kiˈkimasyoˈo.

8. Aˈnoˈ hito (wa) kiˈmoti
   ḡa waruˈi desu ka⅃

   Aˈnoˈ hito ni kiˈmoti ḡa waruˈi ka
   [tte] kiˈkimasyoˈo.

9. Aˈnoˈ hito (wa) ˈdoˈo site
   kiʰmaseˈñ desita ka⅃

   Aˈnoˈ hito ni ˈdoˈo site ʰkoˈnakatta
   ka [tte] kiˈkimasyoˈo.

10. Aˈnoˈ hito (wa) ˈdoˈo site
    yaʰsumitaˈku aˈrimaseˈñ
    ka⅃

    Aˈnoˈ hito ni ˈdoˈo site yaʰsumitaˈku
    ʰnaˈi ka [tte] kiˈkimasyoˈo.

L. Response Drill (based on Grammatical Note 4)

1. Maˈda ʰaˈme ḡa huʰtteˈ
   (i)masu ka⅃ /iie/

   Iie, moˈo huˈtteˈ (i)ˈmaseˈñ.

2. Moˈo aˈno uti (o) karite
   (i)maseˈñ ka⅃ /eˈe/

   Eˈe, moˈo kaˈrite (i)maseˈñ.

3. Maˈda saˈmuˈi desu ka⅃
   /iie/

   Iie, moˈo ˈsaˈmuku aˈrimaseˈñ.

4. Maˈda eˈeḡo (o) naraˈtte
   (i)masu ka⅃ /eˈe/

   Eˈe, maˈda naʰraˈtte (i)masu.

5. Maˈda ˈheˈñ desu ka⅃
   /iie/

   Iie, moˈo ˈheˈñ zya aˈrimaseˈñ.

6. Maˈda tuˈkaˈrete (i)masu
   ka⅃ /iie/

   Iie, moˈo tuˈkaˈrete (i)ˈmaseˈñ.

7. Moˈo kōno heñ ni deˈñwa
   (wa) arimaseˈñ ka⅃
   /eˈe/

   Eˈe, moˈo aˈrimaseˈñ.

8. Moˈo ziˈkañ (wa) arimaseˈñ ka⅃ /iie/

   Iie, maˈda aˈrimaˈsu.

M. Response Drill

(Give iie answers.)

1. Moˈo oˈtomodati ḡa mie-
   maˈsita ka⅃

   Iie, maˈda miˈemaseˈñ.

2. Maˈda oˈnazi kaisya ni
   imaˈsu ka⅃

   Iie, moˈo iˈmaseˈñ.

3. Moˈo oˈnazi zya arima-
   seˈñ ka⅃

   Iie, maˈda oˈnazi deˈsu.

4. Maˈda Niˈhoˈñ ni tuˈki-
   maseˈñ ka⅃

   Iie, moˈo tuˈkimaˈsita.

5. Moˈo aˈtuˈi desu ka⅃

   Iie, maˈda ˈaˈtuku aˈrimaseˈñ.

6. Maˈda kiˈtanaˈi desu ka⅃

   Iie, moˈo kiˈtanaˈku aˈrimaseˈñ.

7. Moˈo oˈyasumi deˈsu
   ka⅃

   Iie, maˈda yaˈsumiˈ zya aˈrimaseˈñ.

8. Maꓸda iꜚssyo deꓸsu ka꜒   Iie, moꓸo iꜚssyo zya arimaseꓸñ.
9. Moꓸo kǒno kaꜚmiꓸ ya eñ-   Iie, maꓸda iꜚrimaꓸsu.
   pitu wa iꜚrimaseꓸñ ka꜒
10. Maꓸda aꜚno hoꓸñ o ꜚyoꓸñde   Iie, moꓸo ꜚyoꓸñde (i)ꜚmaseꓸñ.
    (i)masu ka꜒

N. Level Drill

    Tutor: Maꜚirimaꓸsita. 'I went (or came).' (humble)
    Student: Seꜚñseꓸe mo iꜜrassyaimaꓸsita. 'The teacher went (or came)
              too.' (honorific)

    1. Taꜚnaka to moosimaꓸsu.   Seꜚñseꓸe mo Taꜚnaka to ossyaimaꓸsu.
    2. Moꓸo oꜚtya (o) itadaki-   Seꜚñseꓸe mo ꜜmoꓸo oꜚtya (o) mesia-
       maꓸsita.   ḡarimaꓸsita.
    3. Haꜚziꓸmete Taꜚnaka-sañ   Seꜚñseꓸe mo haꜚziꓸmete Taꜚnaka-sañ
       no oꜚkusañ ni oꜜme ni   no oꜚkusañ ni oꜜai ni narimaꓸsita.
       kakarimaꓸsita.
    4. Moꓸo oꜚtutae-simaꓸsita.   Seꜚñseꓸe mo ꜜmoꓸo oꜚtutae ni nari-
                                      maꓸsita.
    5. Zyuꓸu-neñ ꜜmaꜜe ni   Seꜚñseꓸe mo ꜜzyuꓸu-neñ ꜜmaꜜe ni
       Toꜚodai de beñkyoo-itasi-   Toꜚodai de beñkyoo-nasaimaꓸsita.
       maꓸsita.
    6. Kiꓸree na huꜚrosiki (o)   Seꜚñseꓸe mo ꜚkiꓸree na huꜚrosiki
       itadakimaꓸsita.   (o) omorai ni narimaꓸsita.
    7. Aꜚmerika-taisiꜚkañ ni   Seꜚñseꓸe mo Aꜚmerika-taisiꓸkañ ni
       tuꜚtoꓸmete orimasu.   tuꜚtoꓸmete (i)ꜚrassyaimasu.
    8. Señsyuu haꜚziꓸmete koꜚti-   Seꜚñseꓸe mo señsyuu haziꓸmete
       ra e mairimaꓸsita.   koꜚtira e irassyaimaꓸsita.

O. Expansion Drill

    1. Can you see?   Miꜚemaꓸsu ka꜒
       Can you see mountains too?   Yaꜚmaꓸ mo miꜜemaꓸsu ka꜒
       Can you see ocean AND   Uꓸmi mo yaꜚmaꓸ mo miꜜemaꓸsu
         mountains?   ka꜒
       Can you see ocean AND   Otaku kara ꜚuꓸmi mo yaꜚmaꓸ mo
         mountains from your   miꜜemaꓸsu ka꜒
         house?

    2. He ended up forgetting.   Waꜚsurete simaimaꓸsita.
       He ended up forgetting   Maꜚta wasurete simaimaꓸsita.
         again.
       He said it but he ended up   Iꜚimaꓸsita ḡa, maꜚta wasurete si-
         forgetting again.   maimaꓸsita.
       He said he wouldn't forget   Waꜚsurenaꓸi tte iꜚimaꓸsita ḡa, ma-
         but he ended up forgetting ꜚta wasurete simaimaꓸsita.
         again.
       He said he wouldn't forget   Moꓸo waꜚsurenaꓸi tte iꜚimaꓸsita ḡa,
         any more but he ended up   maꜚta wasurete simaimaꓸsita.
         forgetting again.

3. I'm studying.
   I'm still studying.
   Japanese I'm still studying.
   I gave up Spanish, but
   Japanese I'm still
   studying.
   I gave up Spanish be-
   cause I have no time
   but Japanese I'm still
   studying.

Beⁿkyoo-site (i)ma⌐su.
Ma⌐da beᵣⁿkyoo-site (i)ma⌐su.
Ni⌐hoñḡo wa ma⌐da beᵣⁿkyoo-site
(i)ma⌐su.
Su⌐peiñḡo o yamema⌐sita ḡa, ni-
⌐hoñḡo wa ma⌐da beᵣⁿkyoo-site
(i)ma⌐su.
Zi⌐kañ ḡa na⌐i kara, Su⌐peiñḡo o
yamema⌐sita ḡa; ni⌐hoñḡo wa ma⌐-
da beᵣⁿkyoo-site (i)ma⌐su.

4. It's Mr. Ito.
   The one who's good at it
   is Mr. Ito.
   The one who is best at it
   is Mr. Ito.
   Mr. Yamamoto is good
   too, but the one who is
   best at it is Mr. Ito.
   Both Mr. Tanaka and Mr.
   Yamamoto are good but
   the one who is best at
   it is Mr. Ito.
   Both Mr. Tanaka and Mr.
   Yamamoto are good at
   English, but the one
   who is best at it is Mr.
   Ito.

I⌐too-sañ de⌐su.
Zyo⌐ozu⌐ na no wa I⌐too-sañ de⌐su.

I⌐tibañ zyoozu⌐ na no wa I⌐too-sañ
de⌐su.
Ya⌐mamoto-sañ mo zyoozu⌐ desu ḡa,
i⌐tibañ zyoozu⌐ na no wa I⌐too-sañ
de⌐su.
Ta⌐naka-sañ mo Yamamoto-sañ mo
zyoozu⌐ desu ḡa, i⌐tibañ zyoozu⌐
na no wa I⌐too-sañ de⌐su.

Ee⌐ḡo wa Ta⌐naka-sañ mo Yamamoto-
sañ mo zyoozu⌐ desu ḡa, i⌐tibañ
zyoozu⌐ na no wa I⌐too-sañ de⌐su.

5. [He] didn't let me know.
   [He] couldn't tell so he
   didn't let me know.
   [He] couldn't tell for sure
   so he didn't let me know.
   He couldn't tell for sure
   so he didn't let me know

   I asked but he couldn't
   tell for sure so he did-
   n't let me know.
   I asked if he would return home but he could-
   n't tell for sure so he
   didn't let me know.
   I asked by what time he
   would return home but
   he couldn't tell for
   sure so he didn't let
   me know.

O⌐siete kuremase⌐ñ desita.
Wa⌐kara⌐nakatta kara, o⌐siete ku-
remase⌐ñ desita.
Ha⌐kki⌐ri waᵣkara⌐nakatta kara,
o⌐siete kuremase⌐ñ desita.
A⌐no⌐ hito (wa) ha⌐kki⌐ri waᵣkara⌐-
nakatta kara, o⌐siete kuremase⌐ñ
desita.
Ki⌐kima⌐sita ḡa; a⌐no⌐ hito (wa) ha-
⌐kki⌐ri waᵣkara⌐nakatta kara, o⌐si-
ete kuremase⌐ñ desita.
Ka⌐eru ka [tte] ki⌐kima⌐sita ḡa; a⌐no⌐
hito (wa) ha⌐kki⌐ri waᵣkara⌐nakat-
ta kara, o⌐siete kuremase⌐ñ desita.

Na⌐ñ-zi made ni ᵣka⌐eru ka [tte]
ki⌐kima⌐sita ḡa; a⌐no⌐ hito (wa)
ha⌐kki⌐ri waᵣkara⌐nakatta kara,
o⌐siete kuremase⌐ñ desita.

I asked Mr. Tanaka by what
time he would return
home but he couldn't tell
for sure so he didn't let
me know.

Tanaka-sañ ni ⌐na⌐n̄-zi made ni
⌐ka⌐eru ka [tte] ki⌐kima⌐sita ḡa;
a⌐no⌐ hito (wa) ha⌐kki⌐ri wa⌐kara⌐-
nakatta kara, o⌐siete kuremase⌐n̄
desita.

6. What shall I do?
    [She] said it. What shall
    I do?

Do⌐o simasyoo ka.
I⌐ima⌐sita ḡa, do⌐o simasyoo ka.

    Fumiko said [it]. What
    shall I do?

Hu⌐miko-sañ ḡa i⌐ima⌐sita ḡa,
  do⌐o simasyoo ka.

    Fumiko said [he]'s wait-
    ing. What shall I do?

Ma⌐tte (i)ru tte, ⌐Hu⌐miko-sañ ḡa
  i⌐ima⌐sita ḡa; do⌐o simasyoo
  ka.

    Fumiko said [he]'s still
    waiting. What shall I
    do?

Ma⌐da ⌐ma⌐tte (i)ru tte, ⌐Hu⌐miko-
  sañ ḡa i⌐ima⌐sita ḡa; do⌐o simasyoo ka.

    Fumiko said [he]'s still
    waiting in the study.
    What shall I do?

Syosai de ⌐ma⌐da ⌐ma⌐tte (i)ru tte,
  ⌐Hu⌐miko-sañ ḡa i⌐ima⌐sita ḡa;
  do⌐o simasyoo ka.

    Fumiko said [he] came
    and is still waiting in the
    study. What shall I do?

Mi⌐ete, syosai de ⌐ma⌐da ⌐ma⌐tte
  (i)ru tte, ⌐Hu⌐miko-sañ ḡa i⌐i-
  ma⌐sita ḡa; do⌐o simasyoo ka.

    Fumiko said that a man
    named Hamada came and
    is still waiting in the
    study. What shall I do?

⌐Ha⌐mada tte iu hi⌐to⌐ ḡa ⌐mi⌐e-
  te, syosai de ⌐ma⌐da ⌐ma⌐tte (i)ru
  tte, ⌐Hu⌐miko-sañ ḡa i⌐ima⌐sita
  ḡa; do⌐o simasyoo ka.

    Fumiko said that a man
    named Hamada came
    while you were out and
    is still waiting in the
    study. What shall I
    do?

Orusu-tyuu ni ⌐Ha⌐mada tte iu hi-
  ⌐to⌐ ḡa ⌐mi⌐ete, syosai de ⌐ma⌐-
  da ⌐ma⌐tte (i)ru tte, ⌐Hu⌐miko-sañ
  ḡa i⌐ima⌐sita ḡa; do⌐o simasyoo
  ka.

GREETINGS, FAREWELLS, AND ASSORTED SMALL TALK

1. Hostess: Yo⌐ku i⌐rassyaima⌐sita. Do⌐ozo o⌐aḡari-kudasaima⌐se.
    Mrs. Tanaka: A⌐ri⌐ḡatoo gozaimasu. Si⌐tu⌐ree-itasimasu.

2. Host: Do⌐ozo o⌐aḡari-kudasa⌐i.
    Caller: A⌐ri⌐ḡatoo gozaimasu ḡa, kyo⌐o wa ⌐tyo⌐tto i⌐sogima⌐su kara_

3. Tanaka: Ma⌐tuda-señse⌐e, o⌐hayoo gozaima⌐su.
    Matsuda: O⌐hayoo gozaima⌐su.
    Tanaka: Señzitu wa si⌐tu⌐ree-simasita.
    Matsuda: Ko⌐tira ko⌐so.

4. Host: Tanaka-sañ, ⌐yo⌐ku i⌐rassyaima⌐sita. Do⌐ozo kotira e.
    Mr. Tanaka: A⌐ri⌐ḡatoo gozaimasu.
    Host: Osyokuzi wa?

Mr. Tanaka: Moꜗo siꜛmaꜗsita.
Host: Zyaꜗa, oꜛtya wa ikaꜗg̃a desu ka.
Mr. Tanaka: Doꜗozo oꜛkamai naꜗku.

5. Host: Doꜗozo goꜛeñryo naꜗku meꜛsiag̃atte kudasaꜗi. Doꜗozo ꜛdoꜗozo.
    Mr. Tanaka: Eꜗe, iꜛtadaite maꜗsu. Eꜛñryo wa simaseꜗñ kara_

6. A: Tyoꜗtto oꜛneg̃ai-sitaꜗi ñ desu g̃a_
    B: Naꜗñ desyoo ka. Doꜗozo goꜛeñryo naꜗku iꜛtte kudasaꜗi.

7. Guest: Tyoꜗtto deꜛñwa o kaketaꜗi ñ desu g̃a_
    Hostess: Doꜗozo goꜛeñryo naꜗku. Aꜛtira ni gozaimaꜗsu kara, doꜗozo.

8. Smith: Watakusi wa ꜛmaꜗda Niꜛhoꜗñ wa naꜛñni mo sirimaseꜗñ kara, oꜛu-
    kag̃ai-sitaꜗi ñ desu g̃a_
    Tanaka: Doꜗozo goꜛeñryo naꜗku.

9. A: Osaki ni.
    B: Doꜗozo.

10. A: Osaki ni. Sayonara.
    B: Sayonara.

11. A: Osaki ni siꜛtuꜗree-simasu. Sayoonara.
    B: Sayoonara. Mata asita.

12. A: Oꜛsaki ni itadakimaꜗsu.
    B: Doꜗozo ꜛdoꜗozo.

13. Hostess: Tuꜛmetaku narimaꜗsu kara, doꜗozo ꜛsuꜛg̃u meꜛsiag̃atte kudasai-
    maꜗse.
    Guest: Zyaꜗa, oꜛsaki ni itadakimaꜗsu.

14. Tanaka: Tyoꜗtto kiꜛmoti g̃a waruꜗi kara, iꜗma kaꜛeritaꜗi ñ desu g̃a_
    Smith: Doꜗo simasita ka⌐ Daꜛizyoꜗobu desu ka⌐
    Tanaka: Oꜛnaka g̃a tyoꜗtto_
    Smith: Waꜛruꜗi moꜛnoꜗ o taꜛbemaseꜗñ desita ka⌐
    Tanaka: Saꜗa.
    Smith: Odaizi ni.
    Tanaka: Doꜗo mo.

15. Host: Koꜛno isu no hoꜗo g̃a kiꜛmoti g̃a iꜗi kara, koꜛtira e doꜗozo.
    Mrs. Tanaka: Oꜛsoꜗre iꜛrimaꜗsu.

16. Hostess: Naꜛni mo gozaimaseꜗñ g̃a, doꜗozo.
    Guest: Iꜛtadakimaꜗsu.

17. Host: Naꜛni mo arimaseꜗñ g̃a, iꜛssyo ni taꜛbete kudasai.
    Mrs. Tanaka: Doꜗo mo oꜛsoꜗre iꜛrimaꜗsu.

18. Mrs. Tanaka: Go⌐tisoosama de gozaima¬sita.
     Hostess: Na¬ni mo go⌐zaimase¬ñ de‿

19. Mrs. Tanaka: O⌐so¬re i⌐rima¬su ḡa, asita mo⌐o iti-do ira¬site ku⌐dasai-
          mase⌐ñ ka‿
     Mrs. Yamamoto: Ha¬a, ka⌐sikomarima¬sita.

20. Hostess: Yo¬ku i⌐rassyaima¬sita. Do¬ozo o⌐aḡari ni na¬tte ku⌐dasaima⌐-
          se.
     Mrs. Tanaka: Ha¬a. O⌐so¬reirimasu. Si⌐tu¬ree-itasimasu.

21. Mrs. Tanaka: Nihoñḡo ḡa o⌐zyoozu de irassyaima¬su ⌐ne¬e.
     Mrs. Smith: O⌐so¬reirimasu.

22. Mrs. Tanaka: O⌐taku no ozyo¬osañ wa o⌐tya¹ o nasaima¬su ka‿
     Mrs. Yamamoto: Ha¬a, to⌐kidoki itasima¬su. I¬ma na⌐ra¬tte orimasu
          kara‿

23. Smith: Ko⌐ñna heya¬ wa nihoñḡo de syo⌐kudoo tte iima¬su ka‿
     Tanaka: Iie, so⌐o iimase¬ñ. Tya⌐noma tte iima¬su. Ta⌐tami no heya¬
          desu kara. ²

24. Mrs. Tanaka: A⌐no amerika¬ziñ wa ⌐i¬tu mo watakusi ni ăno ne! ăno ne!
          tte i⌐ima¬su ḡa‿
     Mrs. Yamamoto: Si⌐tu¬ree desu ⌐ne¬e.

25. A: Na¬ñ-zi ni i⌐kimasyo¬o ka.
     B: Matuda-sañ wa ⌐na¬ñ-zi de mo ka⌐mawa¬nai to i⌐tta¬ kara, ha¬yaku
          i⌐kimasyo¬o.

26. Mrs. Tanaka: Yosida-sañ wa ⌐ku¬-zi made ni i⌐rassya¬ru to o⌐ssyaima¬-
          sita ka‿
     Mrs. Yamamoto: Ha¬a. Syo⌐kuzi o site¬ kara ⌐su¬ḡu i⌐rassya¬ru to o⌐s-
          syaima¬sita.

27. A: Ko⌐ma¬ru tte?
     B: Iie, ka⌐mawa¬nai tte.

28. A: Su¬misu-sañ sa⌐simi tabe¬ru tte?
     B: E¬e. Da¬isuki da tte.

---

¹ Otya here refers to the tea ceremony.
² Syokudoo is usually a Western-style room.

29. A: Tanaka-sañ wa ⌜ke⌝sa de n̄sya de kima⌝sita g̃a, kuruma wa ko⌜syoo
       de⌝su ka↲
    B: Ko⌜syoo da⌝ to wa i⊦imase⁼ñ desita g̃a, ko⌜syoo desyo⌝o ⊦ne⁼e.

30. A: Kono zibiki ⌜Zi⌝roo-sañ no desu ka↲
    B: So⌝o desyoo? Tanaka ⌜Zi⌝roo to ⊦ka⁼ite ⊦a⁼ru kara—

31. Maid: Go-⌜zi-g̃o⌝ro Ueda-sañ kara o⌜de⌝n̄wa g̃a go⊦zaima⁼sita.
    Employer: A⌝a ⌜so⌝o. Na⌝ñ te?
    Maid: O⌜hima na toki⌝ ni o⌜de⌝n̄wa o ku⊦dasa⁼i to o⊦ssyaima⁼sita.
    Employer: Sore dake?
    Maid: Ha⌝a, so⌜re dake⌝ de gozaimasita.

32. Smith: Ma⌜tuda-sañ no oto⌝osañ wa ⌜na⌝ñ to o⊦ssyaima⁼su ka↲
    Matsuda: Matuda ⌜Zi⌝roo to moosimasu.

33. Mrs. Tanaka: O⌜taku no ozyo⌝osañ wa ⌜Ha⌝ruko-sañ to o⊦ssyaima⁼su
       ka↲
    Mrs. Yamamoto: Iie, Ha⌜rue to moosima⌝su.

English Equivalents

1. Hostess: I'm so glad you came. Please come in.
   Mrs. Tanaka: Thank you. (Excuse me [for coming into your home].)

2. Host: Please come in.
   Caller: Thank you but today I'm in a bit of a hurry so [I'm afraid I
       can't].

3. Tanaka: Good morning, Dr. Matsuda.
   Matsuda: Good morning.
   Tanaka: It was nice seeing you the other day. (Lit. I was rude the other
       day.)
   Matsuda: (I was the one [who was rude].)

4. Host: I'm glad you came, Mr. Tanaka. This way, please.
   Mr. Tanaka: Thank you.
   Host: What about lunch?
   Mr. Tanaka: I've had it already.
   Host: Then how about some tea?
   Mr. Tanaka: Please don't bother.

5. Host: Do please help yourself (lit. eat without reserve).
   Mr. Tanaka: Yes, I'm doing very well (lit. I'm eating). I won't hold back
       so [don't give it another thought].

6. A: I'd like to ask you a favor. . . .
   B: What is it? Please speak freely.

7.   Guest: I'd like to use the telephone. . . .
     Hostess: Please go right ahead. It's over there so please help yourself.

8.   Smith: I don't know anything about Japan yet so I'd like to ask you. . . .
     Tanaka: Please, go right ahead.

9.   A: [Excuse me for going] ahead.
     B: Go right ahead.

10. A: [Excuse me for leaving] ahead [of you].   Goodbye.
     B: Goodbye.

11. A: Excuse me for leaving ahead of you.   Goodbye.
     B: Goodbye. [See you] again tomorrow.

12. A: Excuse me for eating before you.
     B: Please go ahead.

13. Hostess: Things will get cold so please eat right away.
     Guest: Well then, I'll start (lit. eat) before you.

14. Tanaka: I don't feel well so I'd like to go home now. . . .
     Smith: What happened? Are you all right?
     Tanaka: My stomach is a bit. . .
     Smith: You didn't eat something bad?
     Tanaka: I wonder.
     Smith: Take care of yourself.
     Tanaka: Thanks.

15. Host: This chair is more pleasant so please [sit] here.
     Mrs. Tanaka: Thank you.

16. Hostess: There's nothing here [to speak of] but please [have some].
     Guest: Thank you. (Lit. I'll have some.)

17. Host: We don't have anything [special] but do eat with us.
     Mrs. Tanaka: Thank you very much.

18. Mrs. Tanaka: It was delicious.
     Hostess: There was (lit. being) nothing [to speak of]. . .

19. Mrs. Tanaka: I'm sorry but would you be kind enough to come once more
         tomorrow?
     Mrs. Yamamoto: Yes, certainly.

20. Hostess: I'm so glad you came. Please come in.
     Mrs. Tanaka: Thank you. (Excuse me for entering your home.)

21. Mrs. Tanaka: You are very good in Japanese, aren't you.
     Mrs. Smith: Thank you.

22. Mrs. Tanaka: Does your daughter do the tea ceremony?
     Mrs. Yamamoto: Yes, she does sometimes.   She's taking lessons now
       so . . .

23. Smith: Is this kind of room called a " shokudo" (dining room) in Japa-
       nese?
     Tanaka: No, we don't call it that.   It's called a "chanoma" (Japanese-
       style family room where meals are eaten)— since it's a tatami room
       [and a " shokudo" is usually a Western-style dining room].

24. Mrs. Tanaka: That American always says, "Hey, hey!" to me   but
       [what can I do?]
     Mrs. Yamamoto: Isn't it rude!

25. A: What time shall we go?
     B: Mr. Matsuda said that any time at all would be all right so let's go
       early.

26. Mrs. Tanaka: Did Mr. Yoshida say that he would come by 9 o'clock?
     Mrs. Yamamoto: Yes. He said that he would come right after he ate.

27. A: Did he say it's inconvenient?
     B: No, he said it doesn't matter.

28. A: Did Mr. Smith say he eats sashimi?
     B: Yes. He said he likes it very much.

29. A: Mr. Tanaka came by (electric) train this morning. Is his car out of
       order?
     B: He didn't say that it was out of order but it probably is (out of order),
       isn't it.

30. A: Is this dictionary Jiro's?
     B: It probably is, don't you think so? — since "Jiro Tanaka" is written
       [on it].

31. Maid: There was a call from Mr. Ueda at about 5 o'clock.
     Employer: Oh? What did he say?
     Maid: He said that you should call (lit. please call) when you are free.
     Employer: [Was] that all?
     Maid: Yes, that was all.

32. Smith: What is your father's name, Mr. Matsuda?
     Matsuda: His name is Jiro Matsuda.

33. Mrs. Tanaka: Is your daughter's name Haruko?
     Mrs. Yamamoto: No, her name is Harue.

EXERCISES

1. Using pictures, models, or actual objects, review vocabulary by taking
    turns asking and answering the question "What is this called in Japa-
    nese?"

2. As a host (or hostess):

    a. welcome Mr. Yamamoto to your home.
    b. invite him to come in.
    c. tell him to come this way.
    d. offer to let him precede you.
    e. comment on the weather.
    f. ask him if he smokes.
    g. offer him some tea.
    h. compliment him on his English.
    i. offer him a second helping.

3. As a guest:

    a. excuse yourself for going ahead.
    b. excuse yourself for your rudeness the other day. [1]
    c. refuse a cigarette.
    d. tell your host not to go to any trouble.
    e. refuse a second helping.
    f. remark on how pretty the garden is.
    g. remark on how handsome the alcove is.
    h. remark on how well you can see the mountains.
    i. remark on how pleasant this kind of room is.

_____

[1] See Basic Sentence 5 and note.

Lesson 19. Transportation

(a)

(At the station information booth)

Smith

first class	it-too
second class	ni-too
ticket	kippu

1. Where do you buy second-class tickets?

Do⌐ko de ni-┌too no kippu (o) kai-ma⌐su ka⌐

Clerk

| ticket window | ma⌐do⌐g̃uti |
| ticket window number seven | na⌐na⌐-bañ no ma⌐do⌐g̃uti |

2. It's window number seven.

Na⌐na⌐-bañ no ma⌐do⌐g̃uti desu yo⌐

(At the ticket window)

Smith

| (city near Yokohama) | Yokosuka |

3. Two second-class tickets for Yokosuka.

Yokosuka, ni-too ⌐ni⌐-mai.

Ticket seller

| round trip | oohuku |

4. Round trip?

O⌐ohuku de⌐su ka⌐

Smith

| one way | katamiti |

5. No, one way, please.

Iie, ka⌐tamiti (o) oneg̃ai-sima⌐su.

(At the information booth again)

Smith

| Yokosuka-bound | Yokosuka-iki or Yokosuka-yuki |
| track number what? | nañ-bañ-señ |

6. On what tracks are the Yokosuka trains? (Lit. The Yokosuka-bound are track number what?)

Yokosuka-iki (wa) na⌐ñ-bañ-señ de⌐-su ka⌐

Clerk

| track number seven | nana-bañ-señ |
| track number eight | hati-bañ-señ |

343

7. (They are) track number   Nana-bañ-señ to ha⌐ti-bañ-señ de⌐-
    seven and track number   su.
    eight.

Smith

    pass through or go   to⌐oru /-u/
      through or pass in
      front of
8. Do they go through Yoko-   Yo⌐kohama (o) toorima⌐su ka⌐
    hama?

Clerk

    come to a halt   tomaru /-u/
9. Yes, they stop at Yoko-   E⌐e, Yo⌐kohama⌐-eki ni to⌐marima⌐-
    hama Station.   su yo⌐

(On the platform)

Smith

    second-class car   ni⌐to⌐osya
    the second-class car   ni⌐to⌐osya ḡa tomaru
      stops
    the place where the   ni⌐to⌐osya ḡa tōmaru tokoro
      second-class car   or
      stops   ni⌐to⌐osya no tōmaru tokoro
    what part? or what   dono heñ
      section?
10. Which part [of the platform] Ni⌐to⌐osya no to⌐maru tokoro⌐ (wa)
     is the place where the sec-   do⌐no heñ de⌐su ka⌐
     ond-class cars stop?

Stranger

    frontmost or furthest   i⌐tibañ ma⌐e
      forward
11. The second-class cars are   Ni⌐to⌐osya wa i⌐tibañ ma⌐e desu
     furthest forward so it's   kara, a⌐no heñ de⌐su yo⌐
     that part [of the platform].

(b)

(At the Japan Travel Bureau)

Smith

    get on (a vehicle) or   noru /-u/
      take (a vehicle) or
      ride
    I want to get on or ride   watakusi ḡa noritai
    the one I want to get on   wa⌐takusi ḡa norita⌐i no
      or ride   or
                                    wa⌐takusi no norita⌐i no
    night   bañ
    depart or leave for a   ta⌐tu /-u/
      trip

depart late at night
express
express that departs
   late at night

bañ o⌐soku ta⌐tu
kyuukoo
bañ o⌐soku ta⌐tu kyuukoo

12. I'd like to go to Kyoto. The
train (lit. one) I want to take
is an express that leaves
late at night (but . . .)

Kyo⌐oto e i⌐kita⌐i ñ desu ḡa, wa-
⌐takusi ḡa norita⌐i no (wa) baπ o-
⌐soku ta⌐tu kyu⌐ukoo de⌐su ḡa_

Clerk

leave at 11 o'clock
special express

zyu⌐u-iti⌐-zi ni ⌐de⌐ru
to⌐kubetukyu⌐ukoo or
   tokkyuu

special express that
   leaves at 11 o'clock

zyu⌐uiti⌐-zi ni ⌐de⌐ru tŏkkyuu

13. There's a special express
that leaves at 11 o'clock
(but . . .)

Zyu⌐uiti⌐-zi ni ⌐de⌐ru to⌐kkyuu (ḡa)
arima⌐su ḡa_

Smith

transfer (from one ve-
   hicle to another)

norikae

14. That's just fine! Of course
there's no changing trains,
is there?

Tyo⌐odo i⌐i desu ⌐ne⌐e. Mo⌐ti⌐roñ
no⌐rikae wa na⌐i desyoo?

Clerk

15. No (lit. that's right), there
isn't.

E⌐e, a⌐rimase⌐ñ.

(c)

(At the station)

Smith

leaving at 11 o'clock
Kyoto-bound

zyu⌐uiti⌐-zi hatu
Kyooto-iki or
   Kyooto-yuki

16. What track [is the train]
(bound) for Kyoto leaving
at 11 o'clock?

Zyu⌐uiti⌐-zi hatu Kyŏoto-iki (wa)
nǎñ-bañ-señ?

Porter

(name of a train)

Ha⌐to

17. Do you mean the Hato?
It's track number two.

Ha⌐to desu ka↲ Ni-⌐bañ-señ de⌐-
su.

what car number?

nǎñ-ḡo⌐o-sya

18. What is your car number
and seat number? (Lit.
Your seat is what num-
ber in what number car?)

Oseki (wa) nǎñ-ḡo⌐o-sya no ⌐na⌐ñ-
bañ desu ka↲

Smith

car number three	saⁿ-ḡoⁱo-sya
19. Number 17 in car number 3.	Saⁿ-ḡoⁱo-sya no zyuⁱunanaⁱ-bañ.

(d)

Smith

(name of a train)	Tubame
(section of Tokyo)	Siⁱñbasi
20. Does the Tsubame stop at Shimbashi?	Tubame (wa) ⌐Siⁱñbasi ni toⁱmarima⌐su ka⌐

Tanaka

down-train (i.e. going away from Tokyo)	kudari
up-train (i.e. going toward Tokyo)	nobori
21. The down-train does (stop) but the up-train doesn't (stop), isn't that right?	Kuⁱdari wa tomarimaⁱsu ḡa, nobori wa tŏmaranai desyoo?

Yamamoto

opposite	hañtai
22. Isn't it the opposite?	Haⁱñtai zya arimaseⁱñ ka⌐

Tanaka

get on the train	kiⁱsyaⁱ ni nŏru
at the time [someone] gets on the train	kiⁱsyaⁱ ni noⁱru toⁱki [ni]
conductor	syasyoo
try asking or ask and see	kiⁱite miⁱru
23. Oh? Well then, when we get on the train let's ask the conductor and find out.	Soⁱo? Zyaⁱa, kiⁱsyaⁱ ni noⁱru toⁱki [ni] syaⁱsyoo ni kiite mimasyoⁱo.

(e)

(Smith and Tanaka are meeting a train)

Smith

on time	ziⁱkañ-doⁱori
24. Do you suppose it will arrive on time?	Ziⁱkañ-doⁱori [ni] ⌐tuⁱku desyoo ka.

Tanaka

information booth	aⁱñnaizyoⁱ[1]
25. I wonder. Let's ask at the information booth and find out.	Saⁱa. Aⁱñnaizyǫ de kiⁱite mimasyoⁱo.

---

[1] Has unaccented alternant.

(At the information booth)

Tanaka

leaving Kobe or coming from Kobe	Ko⌐obe hatu
arriving at one o'clock	i⌐ti⌐-zi tyaku
26. Will [the train] from Kobe due at one o'clock arrive on time?	Ko⌐obe hatu i⌐ti⌐-zi tyaku (wa) zi-⌐kañ-do⌐ori /ni/ tu⌐kima⌐su ka⌐

Clerk

fall behind or become late	okureru /-ru/
be late	okurete (i)ru
27. No, today it's about ten minutes late.	Iie, kyo⌐o wa zi⌐ppuñ-ḡu⌐rai o⌐kurete (i)ma⌐su.

ADDITIONAL VOCABULARY

1. Is there a first-class car on this train?	Ko⌐no kisya⌐ ni i⌐tto⌐osya (ḡa) a⌐rima⌐su ka⌐
third-class car[1]	sa⌐ñto⌐osya
sleeping car	si⌐ñda⌐isya
dining car	syo⌐kudo⌐osya
2. You need a berth ticket too, you know!	Si⌐ñdaikeñ mo irima⌐su yo⌐
express ticket	kyuukookeñ
special express ticket	tokkyuukeñ
passenger ticket	zyoosyakeñ

NOTES OF THE BASIC DIALOGUES

1. The former three-class system on Japanese trains has been replaced by a two-class system. First-class cars are referred to as gu⌐ri⌐iñsya or gu⌐riiñka⌐a because of their green color. The new high-speed lines are called si⌐ñka⌐ñseñ.

3. Note the use of counter -mai to count tickets.

6. -iki is derived from the verbal iku 'go,' and -yuki from yuku, an alternate form of iku which has the same meaning. Yuku is a slightly more formal form. The place which precedes -iki (or -yuki) is the final destination—the last stop.

8. The area through which (or—in some combinations—in front of which) one passes is followed by particle o. Note the following: ko⌐oeñ o to⌐oru 'pass through the park'; ko⌐oeñ no so⌐ba o ⌐to⌐oru ' pass near the park'; gi⌐ñkoo no ma⌐e o ⌐to⌐oru 'pass in front of the bank,' 'pass the bank.' The last has the shorter alternant gi⌐ñkoo o to⌐oru.

---

[1] Obsolete.

9. Tomaru 'stop'— i. e. 'come to a halt'— is the intransitive partner of the transitive tomeru 'stop'— i.e. 'bring to a halt.' Compare: Ku⌐ruma ḡa tomarima⌐sita. 'The c a r s t o p p e d .' and: Ku⌐ruma o tomema⌐sita. 'I stopped the car.' Tomaru also occurs as the equivalent of English 'stop at a place'— i.e. stay overnight or lodge.

12. 'but— is there such a train?'

Noru is the intransitive partner of transitive noseru /-ru/ 'give [someone] a ride' or 'carry' or 'take on board.'

Bañ 'night': compare ko⌐ñbañ 'tonight,' ma⌐ibañ 'every night,' ba⌐ṅgo⌐hañ 'dinner'— i.e. evening meal.

Note the following particles occurring before ta⌐tu: To⌐okyoo o ta⌐tu 'leave Tokyo'; To⌐okyoo kara ta⌐tu 'leave from Tokyo'; To⌐okyoo e (or ni) ta⌐tu 'leave for Tokyo.' The same particles occur with de⌐ru. De⌐ru is a word of more general use than ta⌐tu: if Mr. Tanaka leaves Tokyo for a trip to America, either de⌐ru or ta⌐tu may be used; if he leaves the office to go to lunch, de⌐ru is used.

13. 'but— would that be all right?'

Tokubetu occurs as an independent nominal meaning 'special.' It may be followed by particle ni of manner, meaning 'specially,' 'especially,' 'extraordinarily.'

14. Norikae is a nominal derived from the verbal no⌐rikae⌐ru /-ru/ 'change vehicles' or 'transfer.'

16. Hatu and tyaku (Basic Sentence 26) are nominals which follow time and/or place words directly without intervening particles. Note (Basic Sentence 26) that phrases ending with hatu and tyaku may also follow each other directly. Hatu and tyaku expressions are commonly used in reference to trains, ships, airplanes, etc.

22. Hañtai is a nominal: hañtai da 'it's the opposite'; ha⌐ñtai zya na⌐i 'it's not the opposite.' Note also: hañtai-suru 'oppose.'

24, 26. Ni here is the ni of manner.

27. Note: X ni okureru 'be(come) late for X.'

GRAMMATICAL NOTES

1.   S e n t e n c e   M o d i f i e r s

It has already been explained (a) that a non-past adjectival[1] is an independent sentence in the informal style (example: Ta⌐ka⌐i. 'It's expensive.') and

---

[1] With sentence intonation, of course.

(b) that non-past adjectivals directly describe following nominals (example: ta⌐ka¬i ⌐ho¬ñ 'an expensive book').

Examples in this lesson show that a sentence modifying a nominal does not necessarily consist of a non-past adjectival. Actually, any kind of informal Japanese sentence, consisting of or ending with a non-past or past form, may directly describe a following nominal— subject to the two special points noted below.

Examples:

Nominal:	modified by the sentence:	equals:
hi⌐to¬ 'man'	Ta¬bete iru. 'He's eating.'	ta¬bete iru hito 'the 'man who's eating'
hi⌐to¬ 'man'	Tanaka to iu. 'He is named Tanaka.'	Ta⌐naka to iu hito¬ 'a man who is named Tanaka'
zi⌐biki¬ 'dictionary'	Kinoo katta. 'I bought [it] yesterday.'	ki⌐noo katta zibiki¬ 'the dictionary I bought yesterday'
he⌐ya¬ 'room'	Na⌐kanaka i¬i. 'It's quite nice.'	na⌐kanaka i¬i heya 'a room that's quite nice'
ho¬ñ 'book'	Ma¬e ni wa mu˥zukasi˥katta. 'It was difficult before.'	ma¬e ni wa mu˥zukasi˥katta ⌐ho¬ñ 'a book that was difficult before'
to⌐koro¬ 'place'	Asita ikitai. 'I want to go tomorrow.'	a⌐sita ikitai tokoro˥ 'the place where I want to go tomorrow'
zassi 'magazine'	Da⌐re mo yo¬ñde inai. 'No one is reading [it].'	da⌐re mo yo¬ñde inai zassi 'a magazine no one is reading'
bi¬ru 'building'	Ta⌐isi¬kañ datta. 'It was the embassy.'	ta⌐isi¬kañ datta ⌐bi¬ru 'the building that was the embassy'

Note that there is no connecting particle between a modifying sentence and the modified nominal.

There are only two differences between an independent sentence and a sentence occurring as the modifier of a nominal, aside from the fact that the latter is almost invariably in the informal style:

(a) The informal non-past da at the end of an independent sentence has the form no or na when the same sentence modifies a nominal. The na alternant regularly occurs (1) if the following nominal is no 'one' or 'ones,' or (2) if the immediately preceding nominal belongs to the special group we designate as na words (cf. Lesson 12, Grammatical

Note (4).   Otherwise, the <u>no</u> alternant regularly occurs.

In other words, <u>no</u> and <u>na</u> are special alternants of <u>da</u> which occur only at the end of a sentence which describes a nominal.

Examples:

Nominal:	modifed by the sentence:	equals:
he⌐ya⌐ 'room'	Rippa[1] da. 'It is magnificent.'	ri⌐ppa na heya⌐ 'a room which is magnificent,' 'a magnificent room'
tomodati 'friend'	Su⌐ki⌐[1] da. 'I like [him].'	su⌐ki⌐ na tomodati 'a friend I like'
kodomo 'child'	Ge⌐ñki[1] da. 'He is healthy.'	ge⌐ñki na kodomo 'a child who is healthy,' 'a healthy child'
kodomo 'child'	Byooki da. 'He is sick.'	byooki no kodomo 'a child who is sick,' 'a sick child'
no 'one'	Byooki da. 'He is sick.'	byo⌐oki na⌐ no 'one who is sick'
musuko 'son'	Syasyoo da. 'He's a conductor.'	syasyoo no musuko 'my son who is a conductor'[2]
Ta⌐roo 'Taro'	Musuko da. 'He's my son.'	mu⌐suko no Ta⌐roo 'Taro who is my son,' 'my son Taro'
Siñtomi 'Shintomi'	Su⌐si⌐ya da. 'It's a sushi shop.'	su⌐si⌐ya no Siñtomi 'Shintomi which is a sushi shop,' 'the sushi shop "Shintomi"'

(b) The subject of a sentence occurring as a modifier of a nominal is followed by <u>g̱a</u> or <u>no</u>. <u>No</u> never follows the subject of an independent sentence.

---

[1] A <u>na</u>-nominal.

[2] This can also mean 'the conductor's son,' depending on context.

Examples:

Nominal:	modified by the sentence:	equals:
zi⌐do˥osya 'car'	Tomodati ḡa katta. 'A friend bought [it].'	to⌐modati ḡa katta zido˥o-sya or to⌐modati no katta zido˥o-sya 'the car a friend bought'
kaisya 'company'	Bo˥ku ḡa tu˥to˥mete iru. 'I am employed.'	bo˥ku ḡa tu˥to˥mete iru kaisya or bo˥ku no tu˥to˥mete iru kaisya 'the company where I am employed'
ki⌐ssa˥teñ 'tearoom'	Ko⌐ohi˥i ḡa oisii. 'The coffee is good.'	ko⌐ohi˥i ḡa o˥isii kissa˥-teñ or ko⌐ohi˥i no o˥isii kissa˥-teñ 'a tearoom where the coffee is good,' 'a tearoom with good coffee'
hi⌐to˥ 'man'	Mi⌐mi˥ ḡa i˥ta˥i. '[His] ear hurts.'	mi⌐mi˥ ḡa i˥ta˥i hito or mi⌐mi˥ no i˥ta˥i hito 'the man whose ear hurts,' 'the man with an earache'

NOTE: Four different no's have now been introduced:

(a) the nominal meaning 'one,' 'ones'

   Example: a⌐ka˥i no 'red one(s)'

(b) the copula—i.e. a special alternant of da

   Example: syasyoo no musuko 'my son who is a conductor'

(c) the particle meaning 'of,' 'pertaining to,' 'belonging to'

   Example: bo˥ku no zassi 'my magazine'

(d) the particle which follows the subject of a sentence modifier

   Example: bo˥ku no katta zassi 'the magazine I bought'

A nominal may be described by more than one modifier, any or all of which are sentence modifiers. (Modifiers of nominals which are not sentence modifiers are demonstratives—kono, sono, etc.—or phrases ending in particle no 'of,' 'pertaining to.') For example, in the following sequences, each modifier (underlined by an unbroken line) modifies the nominal at the end. In such sequences, the beginning of a new modifier is also the beginning of a new accent phrase.

tuᶜkue no ue˥ ni ᶜa˞ru kuᶜro˥i ᶜho˞ñ   'the black book which is on top
of the desk'

watakusi ḡa karita Taᶜnaka-sañ no zibiki˥   'Mr. Tanaka's dictionary
which I borrowed'

kinoo katta soᶜno ho˥ñ   'that book which I bought yesterday'

ke˥sa ᶜmi˞ta Siᶜbuya ni a˥ru oᶜoki˥i uti   'the large house which is in
Shibuya, which I saw this morning'

Or, a nominal may be described by a modifier containing or consisting of a
word which is itself modified. For example, in the following sequences, the
first modifier modifies all or part of the second modifier, which, in turn,
modifies the nominal at the end of the sequence:

taᶜisi˥kañ ni tuᶜto˞mete iru tomodati no ᶜho˞ñ

'a book belonging to a friend who works for the embassy'

ke˥sa itta giñkoo ni tuᶜto˞mete iru tomodati

'a friend who works for the bank where I went this morning'

kiᶜnoo ki˥ta tomodati no uti

'the home of the friend who came yesterday'

siᶜñbuñ o yo˥nde iru hiᶜto˞ ḡa ᶜno˞nde iru tabako

'the cigarette which the man who is reading the newspaper is smoking'

Note that while there are Japanese equivalents for English sequences like
'the man who ——,' 'the thing which ——,' 'the place where ——,' 'the time
when——,' etc., there are no Japanese equivalents for the words 'who,' 'which,'
'where,' 'when' in these sequences.

2.   toᶜki˥

Toᶜki˥ [1] 'time,' 'occasion,' 'when' is a nominal and the patterns in which it
occurs are typical nominal patterns.

---

[1] Also occurs with a first-syllable accent and with no accent.

Sentence modifier + Nominal	Literally:	Normal equivalent:
Compare:		
kinoo suteta zassi	'threw-away-yesterday magazine'	'the magazine I threw away yesterday'
with:		
ki⌐noo suteta to⌐ki	'threw-away-yesterday time'	'when I threw [it] away yesterday'
Also:		
Kyo⌐oto e iku tomodati	'go-to-Kyoto friend'	'a friend who's going to Kyoto'
with:		
Kyo⌐oto e i�ku to⌐ki	'go-to-Kyoto time'	'when I go to Kyoto'

To⌐ki⌐ is one of the time words which occur both with and without following particle ni, indicating the time when something happens: cf. Lesson 8, Grammatical Note 4(b). Followed by particles ni + wa, it refers to repeated action— 'at times when——.' Thus:

> Ko⌐obe e i╘tta toki⌐ /ni/ to⌐modati no uti ni tomarima⌐sita.
> 'When I went to Kobe, I stopped at a friend's house.'
> Ko⌐obe e i╘ku toki⌐ ni wa to⌐modati no uti ni tomarima⌐su.
> 'At times when I go to Kobe, I stop at a friend's house.'

Examples with other particles:

> Bo⌐ku ḡa i╘tta toki⌐ wa kúruma de go-⌐zikañ-ha⌐ñ ka╘karima╘sita ḡa—
> 'When I went (comparatively speaking), it took five and a half hours by car but [I don't know how long it takes now.]'
> Yamada Yūkio-sañ wa wa⌐takusi ḡa gakkoo e itte ita toki⌐ no to╘modati de╘su yo⌐
> 'You know, Yukio Yamada was a friend when (lit. is a friend of the time when) I was going to school.'
> Ko⌐domo no toki⌐ kara ⌐mi⌐ruku ḡa su╘ki⌐ desu.
> 'I've liked milk since I was a child (lit. from child time).'
> Ga⌐kkoo o de⌐ta toki kara o⌐nazi kaisya ni tuto⌐mete imasu.
> 'I've been working for the same company from the time I left school.'

3.   Verbal Gerund + √mi⌐ru

A verbal gerund followed directly in the same accent phrase by √mi⌐ru means 'do so-and-so and see,' 'do so-and-so and find out,' 'try doing so-and-so.'

Examples:

Yuube sa⌐simi⌐ o ⌐ta⌐bete mi⌐ma⌐sita.
'I tried eating sashimi last night.'
Na⌐ni ḡa ⌐ha⌐itte iru ka wa⌐kara⌐nai kara, a⌐kete mimasyo⌐o.
'I can't tell what's in it so let's open it and find out.'
Si⌐rana⌐i kara, ki⌐ite mima⌐su.
'I don't know so I'll ask and see.'

4.   Counters :   -too, -ḡoo-sya, -bañ-señ

-Too occurs with numerals of Series I to name classes as applied to train
and boat travel, theater seats, etc.

-Ḡoo-sya combines with the same series of numerals to name the passenger
cars of a train.

-Bañ-señ combines with the same series of numerals to name the tracks in
a station.

Study the following lists:

it-too 'lst class'	iti-bañ-señ	'track # 1'	i⌐ti-ḡo⌐o-sya	'car # 1'
ni-too '2d class'	ni-bañ-señ	'track # 2'	ni-⌐ḡo⌐o-sya	'car # 2'
sañ-too '3d class'	sañ-bañ-señ	'track # 3'	sa⌐ñ-ḡo⌐o-sya	'car # 3'
[higher numbers	yoñ-bañ-señ	'track # 4'	yo⌐ñ-ḡo⌐o-sya	'car # 4'
rare with this	go-bañ-señ	'track # 5'	go-⌐ḡo⌐o-sya	'car # 5'
meaning]	roku-bañ-señ	'track # 6'	ro⌐ku-ḡo⌐o-sya	'car # 6'
			si⌐ti-ḡo⌐o-sya	
	nana-bañ-señ	'track # 7'	or	
			na⌐na-ḡo⌐o-sya	'car # 7'
	hati-bañ-señ	'track # 8'	ha⌐ti-ḡo⌐o-sya	'car # 8'
	kyuu-bañ-señ	'track # 9'	kyu⌐u-ḡo⌐o-sya	'car # 9'
	zyuu-bañ-señ	'track # 10'	zyu⌐u-ḡo⌐o-sya	'car # 10'
nañ-too	nañ-bañ-señ		na⌐ñ-ḡo⌐o-sya	
'what class?'	'what track number?'		'car number what?'	

DRILLS

A.   Substitution Drill

1. What track is [the train]   Kyooto-iki (wa) na⌐ñ-bañ-señ de⌐su
    for Kyoto?   ka⌐

2. What track is [the train]   Yo⌐-zi tyaku (wa) na⌐ñ-bañ-señ de⌐-
    arriving at 4 o'clock?   su ka⌐

3. What track is [the train]   Yo⌐-zi hatu (wa) na⌐ñ-bañ-señ de⌐-
    leaving at 4 o'clock?   su ka⌐

4. What track is [the train]   Ko⌐obe hatu (wa) na⌐ñ-bañ-señ de⌐-
    from Kobe?   su ka⌐

5. What track is [the train]
   for Kobe?

   Koobe-yuki (wa) naⁿ-bañ-señ deˀsu
   ka⌐

6. What track is the 7 o'-
   clock up-train?

   Si⌐tiˀ-zi no nŏbori (wa) naⁿ-bañ-señ
   deˀsu ka⌐

7. What track is the 7
   o'clock down-train?

   Si⌐tiˀ-zi no kŭdari (wa) naⁿ-bañ-señ
   deˀsu ka⌐

B. Substitution Drill

1. The special express Hato[1]
   will arrive late tonight.

   To⌐kkyuu no Haˀto (wa) ⌐koˀñbañ
   o⌐soku tukimaˀsu.

2. My son Taro will arrive
   late tonight.

   Mu⌐suko no Taˀroo (wa) ⌐koˀñbañ
   o⌐soku tukimaˀsu.

3. My (older) brother Yukio
   will arrive late tonight.

   Aˀni no Yukio (wa) ⌐koˀñbañ o⌐soku
   tukimaˀsu.

4. My (younger) sister Haruko will arrive late tonight.

   Iˀmooto no Haˀruko (wa) ⌐koˀñbañ
   o⌐soku tukimaˀsu.

5. My daughter Akiko will
   arrive late tonight.

   Mu⌐sume no Aˀkiko (wa) ⌐koˀñbañ
   o⌐soku tukimaˀsu.

6. My friend Mr. Tanaka
   will arrive late tonight.

   Tomodati no Tanaka-sañ (wa)
   ⌐koˀñbañ o⌐soku tukimaˀsu.

7. My Japanese friend will
   arrive late tonight.

   Ni⌐hoñziˀñ no tomodati (wa) ⌐koˀñ-
   bañ o⌐soku tukimaˀsu.

8. My American teacher
   will arrive late tonight.

   Aˀmerikaˀziñ no se⌐ñseˀe (wa)
   ⌐koˀñbañ o⌐soku tukimaˀsu.

C. Substitution Drill

1. Is the train that leaves
   at 11 o'clock an ex-
   press?

   Zyu⌐uitiˀ-zi ni ˀdeˀru ki⌐syaˀ (wa)
   kyu⌐ukoo deˀsu ka⌐

2. Is the train that leaves
   late tonight an express?

   Koˀñbañ o⌐soku taˀtu ki⌐syaˀ (wa)
   kyu⌐ukoo deˀsu ka⌐

3. Is the train that stops
   at Shimbashi an ex-
   press?

   Si⌐ñbasi ni to⌐maru kisyaˀ (wa)
   kyu⌐ukoo deˀsu ka⌐

4. Is the train that you
   are going to take an
   express?

   Aˀnaˀta ḡa[2] no⌐ru kisyaˀ (wa) kyu-
   ⌐ukoo deˀsu ka⌐

5. Is the train that you
   are waiting for an ex-
   press?

   Aˀnaˀta ḡa[2] ˀmaˀtte (i)ru ki⌐syaˀ
   (wa) kyu⌐ukoo deˀsu ka⌐

---

[1] I.e. 'the Hato which is a special express.'

[2] Or no.

6. Is the train that left at 9 o'clock an express?

Ku⌐-zi ni ⌐de⌐ta ki⌐sya⌐ (wa) kyuu-koo de⌐su ka⌐

7. Is the train that is (arrived) on track #2 an express?

Ni-⌐bañ-señ ni tu⌐ite (i)ru ki⌐sya⌐ (wa) kyu⌐ukoo de⌐su ka⌐

8. Is the train that your friend is (riding) on an express?

O⌐tomodati ḡa¹ notte (i)ru kisya⌐ (wa) kyu⌐ukoo de⌐su ka⌐

9. Is the train that is (stopped) on track #4 an express?

Yo⌐ñ-bañ-señ ni tomatte (i)ru ki-sya⌐ (wa) kyu⌐ukoo de⌐su ka⌐

10. Is the train that your (older) brother just got on an express?

Ni⌐isañ ḡa¹ ⌐i⌐ma no⌐tta kisya⌐ (wa) kyu⌐ukoo de⌐su ka⌐

D. Substitution Drill

1. Is that (man) the man who wants to see Mr. Tanaka?

Ta⌐naka-sañ ni aita⌐i hito (wa) a⌐no⌐ hito desyoo ka.

2. Is that (man) the man whom Mr. Tanaka wants to see?

Ta⌐naka-sañ ḡa¹ aita⌐i hito (wa) a-⌐no⌐ hito desyoo ka.

3. Is that (man) the man whom the doctor wants to look at?

Se⌐ñse⌐e ḡa¹ mi⌐ta⌐i hito (wa) a⌐no⌐ hito desyoo ka.

4. Is that (man) the man who wants to have the doctor look at him?

Se⌐ñse⌐e ni ⌐mi⌐te moraitai hito (wa) a⌐no⌐ hito desyoo ka.

5. Is that (man) the man who wanted to go by taxi?

Ta⌐kusii de i⌐kita⌐katta hito (wa) a⌐no⌐ hito desyoo ka.

6. Is that (man) the man who doesn't want beer?

Bi⌐iru ḡa¹ i⌐ranai hito⌐ (wa) a⌐no⌐ hito desyoo ka.

7. Is that (man) the man who didn't say anything?

Na⌐ni mo iwana⌐katta hito (wa) a⌐no⌐ hito desyoo ka.

8. Is that (man) the man with the toothache?

Ha⌐ ḡa¹ i⌐ta⌐i hito (wa) a⌐no⌐ hito desyoo ka.

9. Is that (man) the man who isn't very good in Japanese?

Ni⌐hoñḡo ḡa¹ añmari zyoozu⌐ zya ⌐na⌐i hito (wa) a⌐no⌐ hito desyoo ka.

10. Is that (man) the man who doesn't have a car?

Ku⌐ruma ḡa¹ na⌐i hito (wa) a⌐no⌐ hito desyoo ka.

---

¹ Or no.

E. Substitution Drill

1. When I went to the bank this morning, I saw[1] Mr. Hamada.

    Ke⌐sa gi⌐ñkoo e itta to⌐ki, Ha⌐mada-sañ ni a⌐ima⌐sita.

2. When I opened the door, I saw Mr. Hamada.

    To ⌐(o) aketa to⌐ki, Ha⌐mada-sañ ni a⌐ima⌐sita.

3. When I bought a newspaper at the station, I saw Mr. Hamada.

    E⌐ki de si⌐nbun (o) katta to⌐ki, Ha⌐mada-sañ ni a⌐ima⌐sita.

4. When I left the house, I saw Mr. Hamada.

    U⌐ti (o) de⌐ta toki, Ha⌐mada-sañ ni a⌐ima⌐sita.

5. When I arrived at the station, I saw Mr. Hamada.

    E⌐ki ni ⌐tu⌐ita toki, Ha⌐mada-sañ ni a⌐ima⌐sita.

6. When I went into the tearoom, I saw Mr. Hamada.

    Ki⌐ssa⌐teñ ni ⌐ha⌐itta toki, Ha⌐mada-sañ ni a⌐ima⌐sita.

7. When I set out early this morning, I saw Mr. Hamada.

    Ke⌐sa ⌐ha⌐yaku de⌐kaketa to⌐ki, Ha⌐mada-sañ ni a⌐ima⌐sita.

8. When I transferred at Shimbashi, I saw Mr. Hamada.

    Si⌐ñbasi de no⌐rika⌐eta toki, Ha⌐mada-sañ ni a⌐ima⌐sita.

F. Grammar Drill (based on Grammatical Note 1)

    Tutor: Ki⌐ree na hu⌐rosiki (o) kaima⌐sita. 'I bought a pretty furoshiki.'

    Student: Ki⌐ree na no (o) ka⌐ima⌐sita. 'I bought a pretty one.'

1. Watakusi no i⌐tibañ suki⌐ na o̅sakana (wa) e⌐bi de⌐su.

    Watakusi no i⌐tibañ suki⌐ na no (wa) e⌐bi de⌐su.

2. Byooki no kodomo (wa) ⌐Ta⌐roo desu.

    Byo⌐oki na⌐ no (wa) ⌐Ta⌐roo desu.

3. Ta⌐naka-sañ no uti da⌐tta ta⌐te⌐mono (wa) ⌐i̅⌐ma ryo⌐kañ ni narima⌐sita.

    Ta⌐naka-sañ no uti da⌐tta no (wa) ⌐i̅⌐ma ryo⌐kañ ni narima⌐sita.

4. Itibañ rippa na niwa (wa) ⌐Kyo⌐oto ni ⌐a⌐ru desyoo?

    I⌐tibañ rippa na⌐ no (wa) ⌐Kyo⌐oto ni ⌐a⌐ru desyoo?

5. Nihoñg̅o g̅a i⌐tibañ zyoozu⌐ na hi⌐to⌐ (wa) ⌐Su⌐misu-sañ desyoo?

    Nihoñg̅o g̅a i⌐tibañ zyoozu⌐ na no (wa) ⌐Su⌐misu-sañ desyoo?

---

[1] I.e. 'met up with.'

G. Grammar Drill **(based on Grammatical Note 1)**

Tutor: Ke˥sa ki˹mase˥n̄ desita. '[He] didn't come this morning.'
Student: Ke˥sa ⌐ko˥nakatta hito (wa) ⌐da˥re desu ka⌐ 'Who is the person who didn't come this morning?'

1. A⌐na˥ta ḡa si˥tte (i)ma˥su.
    A⌐na˥ta no[1] si˥tte (i)ru hito˥ (wa) ⌐da˥re desu ka⌐

2. A⌐na˥ta o si˥tte (i)ma˥su.
    A⌐na˥ta o si˥tte (i)ru hito˥ (wa) ⌐da˥re desu ka⌐

3. A⌐na˥ta ni ki⌐ppu o aḡema˥sita.
    A⌐na˥ta ni ki⌐ppu o aḡeta hito˥ (wa) ⌐da˥re desu ka⌐

4. A⌐na˥ta ni ki⌐ppu o moraima˥sita.
    A⌐na˥ta ni ki⌐ppu o moratta hito˥ (wa) ⌐da˥re desu ka⌐

5. A⌐na˥ta ḡa ˥ma˥tte (i)masu.
    A⌐na˥ta no[1] ˥ma˥tte (i)ru hi˥to˥ (wa) ⌐da˥re desu ka⌐

6. A⌐na˥ta ḡa a˥ita˥i desu.
    A⌐na˥ta no[1] a˥ita˥i hi˥to˥ (wa) ⌐da˥re desu ka⌐

7. A⌐tama˥ ḡa i˥ta˥i desu.
    A⌐tama no[1] ita˥i hi˥to˥ (wa) ⌐da˥re desu ka⌐

8. Ko⌐domo ḡa arimase˥n̄.
    Ko⌐domo no[1] na˥i hi˥to˥ (wa) ⌐da˥re desu ka⌐

9. Byo⌐oki de˥su.
    Byo⌐oki no hito˥ (wa) ⌐da˥re desu ka⌐

10. O⌐sake ḡa kirai de˥su.
    O⌐sake no[1] kirai na hito˥ (wa) ⌐da˥re desu ka⌐

H. Grammar Drill **(based on Grammatical Note 1)**

Tutor: A⌐no señse˥e (wa) ni⌐hoñḡo o osiema˥su. 'That teacher teaches Japanese.'
Student: Ni⌐hoñḡo o osieru señse˥e desu. 'He's a teacher who teaches Japanese.'

1. A⌐no kisya˥ (wa) Yo⌐kohama o toorima˥su.
    Yo⌐kohama o to˥oru ki˥sya˥ desu.

2. A⌐no ba˥su (wa) Yo⌐kohama ni tomarima˥su.
    Yo⌐kohama ni tomaru ba˥su desu.

3. A⌐no yama˥ (wa) ko⌐ko kara miema˥su.
    Ko⌐ko kara mie˥ru ya˥ma˥ desu.

4. A⌐no señse˥e (wa) I⌐too to ossyaima˥su.
    I⌐too to ossya˥ru se˥ñse˥e desu.

5. Ano kodomo (wa) ⌐mi˥ruku o ko˥bosima˥sita.
    Mi˥ruku o ko˥bo˥sita ko⌐domo de˥su.

6. Ano tomodati (wa) e⌐eḡo ḡa wakarimase˥n̄.
    E⌐eḡo no[1] wakara˥nai to⌐modati de˥su.

---

[1] Or ḡa.

7. A⌐no musume⌐ (wa) byo-
   ⌐oki de⌐su.

   Byo⌐oki no musume⌐ desu.

8. Ano Tanaka-sañ (wa)
   o⌐hana ḡa zyoozu⌐ desu.

   O⌐hana no[1] zyoozu⌐ na Ta⌐naka-sañ
   de⌐su.

9. Ano kodomo (wa) mi⌐mi⌐
   ḡa i⌐ta⌐i desu.

   Mi⌐mi no[1] ita⌐i ko⌐domo de⌐su.

10. A⌐no⌐ hito (wa) a⌐tarasi⌐i
    kuruma ḡa ka⌐ita⌐i desu.

    A⌐tarasi⌐i kuruma no[1] ka⌐itai hito⌐
    desu.

I. Grammar Drill (based on Grammatical Note 3)

       Tutor: Ki⌐kimasyo⌐o. 'Let's ask.'
       Student: Ki⌐ite mimasyo⌐o. 'Let's try asking.' or 'Let's ask and
              see.' or 'Let's ask and find out.'

1. Ni⌐hoñḡo de iima⌐sita.

   Ni⌐hoñḡo de itte mima⌐sita.

2. A⌐sita no a⌐sa si⌐masyo⌐o.

   A⌐sita no a⌐sa si⌐te mimasyo⌐o.

3. Ha⌐zi⌐mete o⌐sasimi (o) ta-
   bema⌐sita.

   Ha⌐zi⌐mete o⌐sasimi (o) ⌐ta⌐bete mi-
   ⌐ma⌐sita.

4. Do⌐ñna ⌐ho⌐ñ ka wa⌐kari-
   mase⌐ñ ḡa, yo⌐mita⌐i
   desu.

   Do⌐ñna ⌐ho⌐ñ ka wa⌐karimase⌐ñ ḡa,
   yo⌐ñde mi⌐ta⌐i desu.

5. Da⌐me⌐ desu kara, mi⌐ma-
   syo⌐o.

   Da⌐me⌐ desu kara, mi⌐te mi⌐ma-
   syo⌐o.

6. Asita āno a⌐tarasi⌐i ha-
   ⌐na⌐ya e i⌐kimasyo⌐o.

   Asita āno a⌐tarasi⌐i ha⌐na⌐ya e i⌐tte
   mimasyo⌐o.

7. Amerika no tabako (o)
   i⌐ti-do nomita⌐i ñ desu
   ḡa_

   Amerika no tabako (o) i⌐ti-do no⌐ñ-
   de mi⌐ta⌐i ñ desu ḡa_

8. Na⌐ni ḡa ⌐ha⌐itte iru ka
   wa⌐kara⌐nai kara, a⌐ke-
   masyo⌐o.

   Na⌐ni ḡa ⌐ha⌐itte iru ka wa⌐kara⌐-
   nai kara, a⌐kete mimasyo⌐o.

J. Expansion Drill

1. Does it pass through?
   Does it pass in front?
   Does it pass in front of
     the embassy?
   Which bus passes in front
     of the embassy?

   To⌐orima⌐su ka↲
   Ma⌐e o to⌐orima⌐su ka↲
   Ta⌐isi⌐kañ no ⌐ma⌐e o to⌐orima⌐su
     ka↲
   Do⌐no ⌐ba⌐su ḡa ta⌐isi⌐kañ no ⌐ma⌐e
     o to⌐orima⌐su ka↲

2. It's a number.
   It's the seat number.

   Ba⌐ñḡo⌐o desu.
   Se⌐ki no ba⌐ñḡo⌐o desu.

The thing (lit. one) which is written is the seat number. | Kaⁿite ꜛaꜜru no wa ꜛseꜜki no baꜛñḡoꜜo desu.

The thing which is written here is the seat number. | Koꜛko ni kaⁿite ꜛaꜜru no wa ꜛseꜜki no baꜛñḡoꜜo desu.

3. How was it? | Doꜜo desita ka˩
How was the inn? | Ryokañ wa ꜛdoꜜo desita ka˩
How was the inn in Kyoto? | Kyoꜜoto no ryokañ wa ꜛdoꜜo desita ka˩
How was the inn in Kyoto where you stopped? | Aꜛnaꜜta ḡa tomatta ꜛKyoꜜoto no ryokañ wa ꜛdoꜜo desita ka˩

4. He's a friend. | Toꜛmodati deꜜsu.
He's a friend who is employed. | Tuꜛtoꜜmete (i)ru toꜛmodati deꜜsu.
He's a friend who is working for a bank. | Giꜛñkoo ni tutoꜜmete (i)ru toꜛmodati deꜜsu.
He's a friend who is working for the bank [I] went to this morning. | Keꜜsa itta giñkoo ni tuꜛtoꜜmete (i)ru toꜛmodati deꜜsu.

He's a friend who is working for the bank I went to this morning. | Watakusi ḡa ꜛkeꜜsa itta giñkoo ni tuꜛtoꜜmete (i)ru toꜛmodati deꜜsu.

5. It's new, isn't it? | Aꜛtarasiꜜi desyoo?
It's newer than the one [you]'re reading, isn't it? | Yoꜜñde (i)ꜛruꜜ no yori aꜛtarasiꜜi desyoo?

It's newer than the one you're reading, isn't it? | Aꜛnaꜜta ḡa ꜛyoꜜñde (i)ꜛruꜜ no yori aꜛtarasiꜜi desyoo?

The magazine on the table is newer than the one you're reading, isn't it? | Teꜛeburu ni aꜜru zassi wa aꜛnaꜜta ḡa ꜛyoꜜñde (i)ꜛruꜜ no yori aꜛtarasiꜜi desyoo?

The magazine on the dining room table is newer than the one you're reading, isn't it? | Syoꜛkudoo no teeburu ni aꜜru zassi wa aꜛnaꜜta ḡa ꜛyoꜜñde (i)ꜛruꜜ no yori aꜛtarasiꜜi desyoo?

6. I arrived. | Tuꜛkimaꜜsita.
I arrived on time. | Ziꜛkañ-doꜜori [ni] tuꜛkimaꜜsita.
[He] gave me a ride so I arrived on time. | Noꜜsete kuremaꜜsita kara, ziꜛkañ-doꜜori [ni] tuꜛkimaꜜsita.
[He] gave me a ride in his car so I arrived on time. | Ziꜛdoꜜosya ni noꜜsete kuremaꜜsita kara, ziꜛkañ-doꜜori [ni] tuꜛkimaꜜsita.

A friend gave me a ride
in his car so I arrived
on time.

I was late for the bus, but
a friend gave me a ride
in his car so I arrived
on time.

I was late for the 8
o'clock bus but a friend
gave me a ride in his
car so I arrived on
time.

Tomodati ḡa zi⌐do¬osya ni no⌐sete
kurema¬sita kara, zi⌐kañ-do¬ori
[ni] tu⌐kima¬sita.

Ba¬su ni o⌐kurema¬sita ḡa; tomodati ḡa zi⌐do¬osya ni no⌐sete ku-
rema¬sita kara, zi⌐kañ-do¬ori
[ni] tu⌐kima¬sita.

Ha⌐ti¬-zi no ⌐ba¬su ni o⌐kurema¬-
sita ḡa; tomodati ḡa zi⌐do¬osya
ni no⌐sete kurema¬sita kara, zi-
⌐kañ-do¬ori [ni] tu⌐kima¬sita.

7. It's Haruo.
   It's Haruo Yamamoto.
   [My] friend is Haruo Yamamoto.
   My friend is Haruo Ya-
   mamoto.
   There are two people,
   but my friend is Haruo
   Yamamoto.
   There are two people
   named Yamamoto, but
   my friend is Haruo Ya-
   mamoto.

   In this company there are
   two people named Yama-
   moto, but my friend is
   Haruo Yamamoto.

Ha⌐ruo-sañ de¬su.
Yamamoto Ha⌐ruo-sañ de¬su.
Tomodati wa Yamamoto Ha⌐ruo-
sañ de¬su.
Boku no tomodati wa Yamamoto
Ha⌐ruo-sañ de¬su.
Hu⌐tari ima¬su ḡa, boku no tomo-
dati wa Yamamoto Ha⌐ruo-sañ
de¬su.
Ya⌐mamoto to iu hito¬ ḡa hu⌐tari
ima¬su ḡa, boku no tomodati wa
Yamamoto Ha⌐ruo-sañ de¬su.

Ko⌐no kaisya ni¬ wa Ya⌐mamoto to
iu hito¬ ḡa hu⌐tari ima¬su ḡa, boku no tomodati wa Yamamoto
Ha⌐ruo-sañ de¬su.

8. I've forgotten.
   The name I've forgotten.
   I stopped [there] but I've
   forgotten the name.
   I stopped at an inn but
   I've forgotten the name.
   I stopped at a pleasant inn
   but I've forgotten the
   name.
   I stopped at a pretty, pleasant inn, but I've forgotten
   the name.
   When I went [there], I
   stopped at a pretty, pleasant inn, but I've forgotten
   the name.

   When I went to Kyoto, I
   stopped at a pretty, pleasant inn, but I've forgotten
   the name.

Wa⌐surema¬sita.
Na⌐mae wa wasurema¬sita.
To⌐marima¬sita ḡa, na⌐mae wa wa-
surema¬sita.
Ryo⌐kañ ni tomarima¬sita ḡa, na-
⌐mae wa wasurema¬sita.
Ki⌐moti no i¬i ryo⌐kañ ni tomari-
ma¬sita ḡa, na⌐mae wa wasure-
ma¬sita.
Ki¬ree na ki⌐moti no i¬i ryo⌐kañ ni
tomarima¬sita ḡa, na⌐mae wa wa-
surema¬sita.
I¬tta to⌐ki [ni], ki¬ree na ki⌐moti no
i¬i ryo⌐kañ ni tomarima¬sita ḡa;
na⌐mae wa wasurema¬sita.

Kyo⌐oto e i⌐tta to⌐ki [ni], ki¬ree na
ki⌐moti no i¬i ryo⌐kañ ni tomari-
ma¬sita ḡa; na⌐mae wa wasurema¬-
sita.

QUESTION SUPPLEMENT

1. A⌉sa ta⌐be⌐ru ⌐go⌐hañ wa ⌐na⌉ñ to i⌐ima⌐su ka⌐.
2. Kyuukoo no kippu wa ⌐na⌉ñ to i⌐ima⌐su ka⌐.
3. Ho⌉ñ o oku tana wa ⌐na⌉ñ to i⌐ima⌐su ka⌐.
4. To⌐okyoo no ho⌉o e i⌐ku kisya⌐ wa miñna ⌐na⌉ñ to i⌐ima⌐su ka⌐.
5. To⌐kubetu ni haya⌉i kyuukoo wa ⌐na⌉ñ to i⌐ima⌐su ka⌐.
6. Nobori no hañtai wa ⌐na⌉ñ desu ka⌐.
7. Byo⌐oki no hito⌉ ḡa ta⌐kusañ ha⌉itte iru ta⌐te⌐mono wa ⌐na⌉ñ to i⌐ima⌐su ka⌐.
8. Ta⌐tami no na⌉i ta⌐be⌐ru he⌐ya⌉ wa ⌐na⌉ñ to i⌐ima⌐su ka⌐.
9. Te⌉ ḡa ki⌐tana⌉ku ⌐na⌉tta to⌐ki⌉ ni wa ⌐na⌉ñ de a⌐raima⌐su ka⌐.
10. Zi⌐do⌉osya ḡa ko⌐syoo-sita toki⌉ ni wa ⌐do⌉o simasu ka⌐.
11. De⌐ñwaba⌉ñḡoo o si⌐ranai toki⌉ ni wa ⌐na⌉ni o mi⌐ma⌐su ka⌐.
12. Zi⌐kañ ḡa wakara⌉nai to⌐ki⌉ ni wa ⌐na⌉ni o mi⌐ma⌐su ka⌐.
13. I⌐tibañ taka⌉i kippu wa na⌐ñ-too no⌉ desu ka⌐.
14. Ue no hañtai wa ⌐na⌉ñ desu ka⌐.
15. Ho⌉ñ ḡa ka⌐itai toki⌉ ni wa ⌐do⌉ñna mi⌐se⌉ e i⌐kima⌐su ka⌐.

EXERCISES

1. Making any changes necessary, use each of the following sentences within a longer sentence, as a modifier of a nominal, and translate the completed sentence into English.

> (Example: A⌐soko ni arima⌉su. 'It's over there.'
> Answer: A⌐soko ni a⌉ru zi⌐biki⌉ wa wa⌐takusi no⌉ desu.
>   'The dictionary that's over there is mine.')

a. Mi⌉ruku o ko⌐bosima⌐sita.
b. Ni⌐hoñḡo ḡa zyoozu⌉ desu.
c. Gi⌐ñkoo ni tuto⌉mete (i)rassyaimasu.
d. Ha⌉ ḡa i⌐ta⌐i desu.
e. To⌐modati de⌉su.
f. Wa⌐karimase⌉ñ desita.
g. Wa⌐takusi ḡa kakima⌉sita.
h. Ryo⌐ozi⌉kañ desita.
i. Si⌐rimase⌉ñ.
j. Si⌐ñbuñ o yo⌉ñde (i)masu.
k. A⌐soko ni simatte arima⌉su.
l. Zu⌉ibuñ ta⌐ka⌉i desu.
m. E⌉ki no ⌐ma⌐e o to⌐orima⌐su.
n. Ko⌐ohi⌉i ḡa no⌐mita⌐i desu.
o. Si⌐ta no musume⌉ desu.
p. Kyo⌉oto e i⌐kima⌐sita.
q. I⌐ro⌉ ḡa ⌐ki⌐ree desu.

2. Express the following in Japanese.

    a. Buy the following tickets:

        (1) One second-class for Kyoto.
        (2) Two first-class for Yokohama, round trip.
        (3) One first-class for Osaka.
        (4) One second-class round trip for Nikko.

    b. Ask at the information booth:

        (1) when the next train for Yokohama leaves.
        (2) if you need an express ticket.
        (3) if the 8 o'clock train for Nagoya has already left.
        (4) if the 5 o'clock train from Nikko has arrived yet.
        (5) what track the Yokohama trains leave from.
        (6) if the Hato will be on time.

    c. Ask the conductor:

        (1) if the train stops at Shimbashi.
        (2) whether the train has a diner.
        (3) what time you arrive at Tokyo Station.
        (4) where the sleeping cars are.
        (5) where car # 3 is.
        (6) where seat # 4 is.

    d. Tell Mr. Tanaka that:

        (1) you went from Tokyo to Osaka by train and returned by plane.
        (2) you went from Tokyo to Numazu by electric train and from there to Mito by boat.
        (3) you came from New York to San Francisco by train and from San Francisco to Japan by plane.
        (4) you came from Yokohama to Shimbashi by electric car and from there to the office by taxi.

3. Using a local timetable, take turns asking and answering the following kinds of questions in Japanese:

    a. What time does the train that leaves (place) at (time) arrive at (place)?
    b. What time does the train that arrives at (place) at (time) leave (place)?
    c. Does the train for (place) that leaves (place) at (time) stop at (place)?
    d. How long does it take from (place) to (place) on the train that leaves (place) at (time)?

4. Practice the Basic Dialogues with appropriate variations.

Lesson 20. Transportation (cont.)

BASIC DIALOGUES: FOR MEMORIZATION

(a)

(At the station)

Smith

baggage or things to
   carry
is heavy
1. This baggage is terribly
   heavy, isn't it!

ni⌐motu or
o⌐ni⌐motu ⌐
omoi /-ku/
Ko⌐no ni⌐motu (wa) ⌐zu⌐ibuñ o⌐mo⌐i
desu ⌐ne⌐e.

Tanaka

porter or redcap
engage
come having engaged
  or go and engage
2. Shall I go and get a porter?

akaboo
ta⌐no⌐mu /-u/
ta⌐no⌐ñde ⌐ku⌐ru
A⌐kaboo (o) tano⌐ñde ki⌐masyo⌐o ka

Smith

3. Yes, please (go and engage).

E⌐e ta⌐no⌐ñde ki⌐te⌐ kudasai.

(b)

(At the information booth)

Smith

put into someone else's
  keeping temporarily
  or check
place where one checks
4. I'd like to check my baggage.
   Where is the checking place?

a⌐zuke⌐ru /-ru/

a⌐zuke⌐ru toko(ro)
Ni⌐motu (o) a⌐zuketa⌐i ñ desu ḡa,
a⌐zuke⌐ru to⌐ko(ro)⌐ (wa) ⌐do⌐ko
desu ka⌐

Clerk

waiting room
5. It's to the right of the waiting
   room.

ma⌐tia⌐isitu
Ma⌐tia⌐isitu no mi⌐ḡi no ho⌐o desu.

(c)

(Smith and Tanaka are on the platform after getting off a train)

Smith

subway
6. Shall we take the subway?

tikatetu
Ti⌐katetu ni norimasyo⌐o ka.

Tanaka

even though it is fast (<u>or</u> early) <u>or</u> it is fast (<u>or early</u>) but	ha⌐ya⌐i keredo
become crowded	ko⌐mu /-u/
be crowded	ko⌐ñde (i)ru

7. The subway is fast but it's always crowded so let's go by taxi.   Ti⌐katetu wa haya⌐i keredo; i⌐tu mo ⌐ko⌐ñde (i)ru kara, ta⌐kusii de i⌐kimasyo⌐o.

Smith

is near	ti⌐ka⌐i /-ku/
place for boarding vehicles	noriba

8. [Where is] the nearest stand? (Lit. As for the nearest boarding place?)   I⌐tibañ tika⌐i noriba wa?

Tanaka

exit	de⌐ḡuti
one unit of wheeled vehicles	i⌐ti⌐-dai
two or three units of vehicles	ni-sañ-dai
[something] lines up	narabu /-u/
even though they are lined up <u>or</u> they are lined up but	na⌐rañde (i)ma⌐su keredo

9. Usually two or three [taxis] are lined up at the exit (but . . .)   Taitee ⌐de⌐ḡuti ni ni-⌐sañ-dai narañde (i)ma⌐su keredo_

Smith

10. Well, let's go and see.   Zya⌐a, i⌐tte mimasyo⌐o.

(d)

(At home)

Husband

intention <u>or</u> plan	tumori
intention of going <u>or</u> a plan to go	iku tumori

11. How do you plan to go? (Lit. A plan of going by what?)   Na⌐ñ de iku tumori?

Wife

(section of Tokyo)	Sibuya
go by riding <u>or</u> ride to a place	notte (i)ku
go by transferring	no⌐rika⌐ete (i)ku

even though it is the plan
to go by transferring
or it is the plan to go
by transferring but

no⌐rika⌐ete (i)⌐ku tumori da⌐
kedo

12. I plan to ride as far as Shibuya on the bus and transfer
(lit. go by transferring) to
the subway there (but . . .)

Si⌐buya ma⌐de ⌐ba⌐su ni notte (i)t-
te, [1] asuko de ti⌐katetu ni norika⌐-
ete (i)⌐ku tumori da⌐ kedo_

Husband

go down or descend
or get off (a vehicle)

o⌐ri⌐ru /-ru/

13. Where will you get off? (Lit.
As for the place where you
get off?)

O⌐ri⌐ru toko wa?

Wife

(section of Tokyo)

Toranomoñ

14. Toranomon.

Toranomoñ yo_

Husband

15. And from there?

So⌐ko kara⌐ wa?

Wife

walk
go by walking or
walk to a place

a⌐ru⌐ku /-u/
a⌐ru⌐ite (i)ku

16. I'll walk—since it's
close.

A⌐ru⌐ite (i)ku wa_ — ti⌐ka⌐i kara.

Husband

come having gone or
go and come

i⌐tte ku⌐ru or
   i⌐tte ma⌐iru ↑ or
   i⌐tte (i)rassya⌐ru ↑

17. Well, goodbye (lit. go and
come)!

Zya⌐a, i⌐tte (i)rassya⌐i.

Wife

18. Goodbye. (Lit. I'll go and
come.)

I⌐tte mairima⌐su.

. . .

Wife (returning)

19. Hello! or I'm back!

Tadaima.

---

[1] Accent of contracted alternant: no⌐tte⌐ tte.

Husband

20. Hello!   O⌐kaeri(-nasa⌐i).

(e)

Smith

gasoline	gasoriñ
one liter	i⌐ti-ri⌐ttoru
one or two liters	i⌐ti-ni-ri⌐ttoru
be(come) left (over)	no⌐ko⌐ru /-u/
<u>or</u> be(come) left behind	
even though they're left (over) <u>or</u> they're left (over) but	no⌐ko⌐tte (i)ru keredo
airport	hikoozyoo
it will be better to have put in (for future use) <u>or</u> [I]'d better put in (for future use)	i⌐ret(e) o⌐ita hoo ḡa ⌐i⌐i

21. Even though there are still one or two liters of gasoline left, since we're going as far as the airport, it would probably be better to put [some] in now (for future use), wouldn't it.

    Gasoriñ (ḡa) ⌐ma⌐da i⌐ti-ni-ri⌐ttoru no⌐ko⌐tte (i)ru keredo; hi⌐koozyoo ma⌐de i⌐ku⌐ kara, i⌐ma i⌐ret(e) o⌐ita hoo ḡa ⌐i⌐i desyoo ⌐ne⌐e.

Tanaka

bridge	ha⌐si⌐
go over <u>or</u> go across	wataru /-u/
intersection	yotukado
gasoline station	ga⌐soriñsuta⌐ndo

22. Yes. You go over that bridge, and there's a big gas station at the next intersection.

    E⌐e. A⌐no hasi⌐ (o) watatte, tu⌐gi⌐ no yotukado ni o⌐oki⌐i ga⌐soriñsuta⌐ndo (ḡa) a⌐rima⌐su yo⌐.

• • •

(At the gas station)

Attendant

how many liters?	na⌐ñ-ri⌐ttoru

23. How many (liters)?   Na⌐ñ-ri⌐ttoru desu ka⌐

Smith

full	ippai
fill [something] (lit. make full)	ippai ni suru

24. Fill it up.   I⌐ppai ni site kudasa⌐i.

oil	o⌐iru
tire	taiya

air   ku⌐uki
be sufficient   tariru /-ru/
enough   zyu⌐ubu⌐ñ /na/

25. Look at the oil, too, and   O⌐iru mo ⌐mi⌐te; sore kara, ma⌐e
     then there's too little air   no taiya no ⌐ku⌐uki (ğa) ta⌐rina⌐i
     in the front tires so put in   kara, zyu⌐ubu⌐ñ [ni] irete.
     the right amount (lit. air
     of the front tires is insuf-
     ficient so put it in suffi-
     ciently).

(f)

Tanaka

26. I'm sorry you were kept   O⌐matidoosama de⌐sita.
     waiting.

     become punctured   pañku-suru
     become completely flat   pañku-site simau   or
                                            pañku-sityau

27. I'm late because I had a   Ta⌐iya (ğa) pañku-sityatta⌐ kara,
     flat.   o⌐soku narima⌐sita.

Smith

     awful or dreadful or   taiheñ /-na/
       terrible or a nuisance

28. Don't mention it. What a nui-   Do⌐o itasimasite. Ta⌐iheñ da⌐tta
     sance it must have been!   desyoo?
     (Lit. It was a nuisance, was-
     n't it?)

     oneself   zibuñ   or
                                             gozibuñ ⌐
     by oneself   zibuñ de
     exchange   torikaeru /-ru/

29. Did you change [it] your-   Go⌐zibuñ de torikaema⌐sita ka⌐
     self?

Tanaka

     garage   ga⌐re⌐ezi
30. No, I had [it] changed at a   Iie, su⌐ğu ⌐so⌐ba no ga⌐re⌐ezi de
     garage right nearby.   to⌐rikaete moraima⌐sita yo.

(g)

Smith

     even though there   na⌐i keredo
       isn't or there
       isn't but
     brakes   bu⌐re⌐eki
     condition   guai
     is funny   o⌐kasi⌐i /-ku/

look into <u>or</u> check
<u>or</u> investigate
it <u>will</u> be better to have
had [them] checked
<u>or</u> [I] should have
[them] checked

31. Even though we don't have
very much time, there's
something funny about the
brakes (lit. the condition
of the brakes has become
funny) so I guess I should
have them checked right
away, shouldn't I.

si⌐rabe⌐ru /-ru/

si⌐ra⌐bete mo⌐ratta ho⌐o ḡa ⌐i̊⌐i

Zi⌐kañ (ḡa) añmari na⌐i keredo;
bu⌐r̯e⌐eki no guai (ḡa) o⌐ka⌐siku
⌐na⌐tta kara, ha⌐yaku si⌐ra⌐bete
mo⌐ratta ho⌐o ḡa ⌐i̊⌐i desyoo ⌐ne⌐e.

Tanaka

important
32. Yes. You'd better do it
quickly (lit. the fast alternative is good)—be-
cause brakes are impor-
tant.

taisetu /na/
E⌐e, ha⌐ya⌐i hoo ḡa ⌐i̊⌐i desu yo⌄
—bu⌐r̯e⌐eki wa ta⌐isetu da⌐ kara.

· · ·

(At the garage)

Attendant

go around
33. Brakes? I'm sorry but
please go around toward
the back. [That's] be-
cause this (place) is just
[for] gas and oil and
things like that.

mawaru /-u/
Bu⌐r̯e⌐eki desu ka⌄ Su⌐mimase⌐ñ
ḡa, u⌐siro no ho⌐o e ma⌐watte ku-
dasa⌐i. Kotira wa ga⌐soriñ ya o⌐i-
ru da⌐ke⌐ desu kara.

NOTES ON THE BASIC DIALOGUES

1. The opposite of <u>omoi</u> is <u>karui</u> /-ku/ 'is light (i.e. not heavy).'

2. Note: <u>hi⌐to⌐ o ta⌐no⌐mu</u> 'engage a person,' 'retain a person'; <u>mo⌐no⌐ o ta-</u>
<u>⌐no⌐mu</u> 'order or request a thing'; <u>hi⌐to⌐ ni ta⌐no⌐mu</u> 'order or request
from a person.'

4. Note also: a⌐zuka⌐ru 'receive in custody,' 'take charge of,' 'keep.'

9. 'but—I don't know whether or not there are any there now.'

The opposite of <u>de⌐ḡuti</u> is <u>iriḡuti</u> 'entrance.'

<u>Narabu</u> is the intransitive partner of transitive <u>naraberu</u> /-ru/ 'line
[things or people] up'

12. 'but—do you think that's all right?'

13. Note: X o o⌐ri¬ru (or, less commonly, X kara o⌐ri¬ru) 'go down from X'
    or 'get off X.' (For particle o, see Lesson 7, Grammatical Note 3.) O⌐ri¬-
    ru is the intransitive partner of transitive o⌐ro¬su /-u/ 'lower' or 'let
    down' or 'discharge (a passenger).'

17. I⌐tte irassya¬i is the farewell regularly said by the person remaining be-
    hind, to someone leaving his own home (or, in some circumstances, his
    office, his town, city, or country, etc.).   Sayonara is not used in this
    situation.   I⌐rassya¬i (formal women's form, i⌐rassyaima¬se) is the im-
    perative of i⌐rassya¬ru.

18. I⌐tte mairima¬su, or a less polite equivalent, is the farewell regularly
    said by someone leaving his home, to the person remaining behind. It is
    the reply to Sentence 17, preceding. Men regularly use i⌐tte kima¬su or
    i⌐tte ku¬ru.

19. Tadaima, lit. 'just now'— i.e. '[I've] just now [returned],' is the greeting
    regularly said by someone returning home.

20. O⌐kaeri(-nasa¬i), an imperative of ka⌐eru 'return home,' is the greeting
    regularly said to someone who has just returned home.   It is the reply to
    Sentence 19, preceding. The formal women's form is o⌐kaeri-nasaima¬se.

21. No⌐ko¬ru is the intransitive partner of transitive no⌐ko¬su /-u/ 'leave be-
    hind,' 'leave over (for another time).'

22. For particle o, see Lesson 7, Grammatical Note 3.

    Wataru is the intransitive partner of watasu /-u/ 'hand over.'

    Yotukado is an intersection of two streets forming four corners.

24. Ippai is a nominal: ippai da '[it] is full'; i⌐ppai zya na¬i '[it] is not full';
    i⌐ppai ni na¬ru 'become full'; ippai ni suru 'fill' (lit. 'make full'). It oc-
    curs without a following particle as an expression of manner: ippai ireru
    'fill up' (lit. 'insert fully'). The opposite of ippai is ka⌐ra¬ 'empty,' also
    a nominal.

25. In expressions of manner, zyu⌐ubu¬n̄ occurs both with and without particle
    ni.

26. O⌐matidoosama (de¬sita) is used in the same kinds of situations as
    o⌐matase-itasima¬sita, but the latter is more polite.

28. Some other English equivalents of taihen da are: 'Good heavens!' 'Good
    night!' 'What a mess!' 'What a fix to be in!' Taihen also occurs without
    a following particle as an expression of manner, meaning 'awfully,'
    'very,' 'terribly.'

29. Compare: zibun̄ de 'by oneself— i.e. by one's own power or ability' and
    hi⌐to¬-ri de 'by oneself— i.e. unaccompanied.' Zibun̄ also occurs followed
    by particle no, meaning 'one's own.'

    Note: X o Y to torikaeru 'exchange X for (lit. with) Y.'

30. Ga⌐re¬ezi usually refers to a garage where cars are repaired. Garages
    attached to homes for private cars are rare in Japan.

31. Many of the Japanese words for parts of a car are, like bu⌐re¬eki and

taiya, loan-words from English. Thus: e⌐ⁿziñ 'engine,' ho⌐oñ 'horn,' ba⌐tterii 'battery,' kya⌐burettaa 'carburetor,' etc.

Note: gu⌐ai ḡa i⌐i 'be in good condition' or 'be fine' or 'be in good health'; gu⌐ai ḡa waru⌐i 'be in bad condition' or 'be out of order' or 'feel unwell' or 'be sick.'

O⌐kasi⌐i, like 'funny' in English, means either 'strange' or 'amusing.'

33. Mawaru is the intransitive partner of transitive mawasu /-u/ 'send around.'

GRAMMATICAL NOTES

1. Gerunds of Condition and Manner; Errands

(Reread Lesson 15, Grammatical Note 5.)

A verbal gerund, by itself or at the end of a sequence, may occur as the modifier of another verbal, an adjectival, or a phrase ending in √da. In one such pattern, the gerund (or sequence ending in the gerund) asks or answers the question 'how?' or 'in what condition?' For example, in ti⌐katetu ni notte kima⌐sita 'I rode here on the subway' (lit. 'I came by riding on the subway'), tikatetu ni notte describes ki⌐ma⌐sita and tells how I came.

In this pattern, the action or state represented by the gerund may precede or be simultaneous with that represented by the inflected expression it modifies.

The gerund does not always immediately precede the word or phrase it modifies.

Examples:

> A⌐ru⌐ite i⌐kima⌐sita. 'I walked (to a specific place)'— lit. 'I went by walking.'
> O⌐kurete tukima⌐sita. 'I arrived late.'
> Ki⌐otuke⌐te o⌐sara o aratte kudasa⌐i. 'Please wash the dishes carefully.'
> I⌐so⌐ide ikitai. 'I want to go in a hurry.' (informal style)
> I⌐so⌐ide u⌐ti e kaerita⌐i ñ desu ḡa_   'I'd like to go home in a hurry. . . .'
> Na⌐ñ ni notte Yo⌐kosuka e ikima⌐sita ka⌐ 'How (lit. riding on what) did you go to Yokosuka?'

This pattern also covers errand situations in Japanese— situations involving going somewhere, doing something, and coming back. In such cases, √ku⌐-ru (or a more polite equivalent) follows the appropriate gerund of doing, and the first step— the going— is usually not mentioned. (Compare English, which normally omits mentioning the last step— the coming back.) Thus, the Japanese equivalent of 'go and buy' is ka⌐tte ku⌐ru 'buy and come,' 'come having bought.'

Examples:

> Si⌐ñbuñ o katte kima⌐su. 'I'll go and buy a paper. (Lit. 'I'll come

having bought a paper.')

Kiʳite kimasyoꜗo ka.   'Shall I go and ask?'   (Lit. 'Shall I come having asked?')

Deʳñwatyoo o siraꜗbete mairimasu. 'I'll go and check the phone book.' (Lit. 'I'll come having checked the phone book.')

Actually, most uses of the gerund introduced thus far are covered by the statement at the beginning of this note. For example:

(a) aʳruꜗku + kuꜛdasaꜗi   >   aʳruꜗite kudasai 'please walk'
(b) aʳruꜗku + iru   >   aʳruꜗite iru ' [I] am walking'
(c) aʳruꜗku + kaꜗeru   >   aʳruꜗite ꜛkaꜗeru ' [I] will walk home'
(d) sañpo-suru + kaꜗeru >   sañpo-site, kaꜗeru ' [I] will take a walk, and then go home'

In patterns (a) and (b) only, the gerund is always immediately followed in the same accent phrase by the inflected word it modifies.

Patterns (c) and (d) are distinguished by intonation: in pattern (d),[1] the gerund usually ends with comma intonation and the word following the gerund starts a new accent phrase.

2.   k e r e d o 'e v e n   t h o u g h'

Keredo 'even though' or 'although' is a particle which follows verbals, adjectivals, and √da, non-past, past, and tentative. When it occurs in the middle of a sentence, it regularly ends with comma intonation. If the final inflected form in the sentence is informal, only the informal occurs before medial keredo; otherwise it may be preceded by formal or informal forms. Before keredo, an unaccented verbal or copula expression regularly acquires an accent on its final syllable and an unaccented adjectival on its pre-final syllable.

Examples:

Moꜗo waʳkaꜗtta (or waʳkarimaꜗsita) keredo, moʳo iti-do itte kudasaimaseꜗñ ka⌐   'Even though I've already understood, would you please say it again?'

Aʳtuꜗi (desu) keredo, maꜗdo wa aꜜketaku arimaseꜜñ.   'Even though it's hot, I don't want to open the window.'

Kiꜗree da keredo, aʳñmari oisiku naꜗi. 'Even though it's pretty, it's not very tasty.'

Daʳizyoꜗobu daꜜtta desyoꜜo keredo, taʳbemaseꜗñ dèsita. 'Even though it was probably safe, I didn't eat it.'

---

[1] Described in Lesson 7, Grammatical Note 5.

Like g̃a, keredo within a sentence implies contrast or is simply a clause connective (cf. Lesson 4, Note 1); but as an indication of contrast, medial keredo is a slightly stronger 'but.' Thus:

> Yo⌐mima⌉sita g̃a, mo⌉o wa⌐surema⌉sita. 'I read it but I've forgotten it already.'
> Yo⌉ñda keredo, mo⌉o wa⌐surema⌉sita. 'Even though I read it, I've forgotten it already.'

Kedo is a less formal, contracted equivalent of keredo; there is also a more formal equivalent, keredomo.

The use of keredo and kedo in sentence-final position closely resembles that of sentence-final g̃a. Thus:

> Ikitai ñ desu g̃a_
> Ikitai ñ desu keredo_ } 'I'd like to go but. . . .'
> Ikitai ñ desu kedo_

Note that whereas an informal inflected form before g̃a occurs only in men's informal speech, informal forms before keredo occur in formal and informal speech of men and women.

3. **tumori** 'intention'

Tumori (honorific, otumori⁺) 'intention' is a nominal which is always preceded by a modifier—usually a sentence modifier consisting of a non-past affirmative verbal or negative adjectival— and is followed by some form of √da (including no before another nominal). Tumori in statements usually refers to the speaker's own intentions, and in questions to those of the person addressed. Thus:

> I⌐ku tumori de⌉su. 'I intend to go,' 'I expect to go,' 'I plan to go,' etc.
> I⌐ku tumori de⌉su ka_ 'Do you intend to go?' 'Do you expect to go?' 'Do you plan to go?' etc.

A negative may precede or follow tumori. Compare:

> I⌐kanai tumori de⌉su. 'I intend not to go,' 'It is my intention not to go.'

and:

> I⌐ku tumori zya arimase⌉ñ. 'I don't intend to go,' 'It is not my intention to go.'

Additional examples:

> Ko⌉ñbañ ⌐na⌉ni o su⌐ru otumori de⌉su ka_ 'What do you intend to do this evening?'
> Ki⌐no⌉o wa de⌐kakenai tumori da⌉tta keredo, de⌐kakete simaima⌉sita. 'Yesterday I planned not to go out, but I ended up by going out.'
> Ka⌐u tumori zya na⌉katta keredo; a⌐ñmari ya⌉sukatta kara, ka⌐tte simaima⌉sita. 'Even though I didn't intend to buy it, it was so cheap that (lit. because it was so cheap) I ended up by buying it.'

Zyuᶢuniˈ-zi ni taᵇbeˈru tumori no moᵇnoˈ o zyuᶢuitiˈ-zi ni ᵇtaˈbete siᵇmaimaˈsita. 'At 11 I ate up the things I planned to eat at 12.' Doˈn̄na tumori de iᵇttaˈ ka waᶢkarimaseˈn̄ ḡa_ 'What sort of thing he had in mind when he said it I can't tell but. . .' (Lit. 'Being what kind of intention he said [it] I can't tell but. . .')

The immediately preceding sentence is an example of the pattern — tumori de suru 'do with a — intention,' 'do with — in mind'; de is the gerund of da, and suru stands for any verbal.

4.   Further Notes on Comparisons

Reread Lesson 15, Grammatical Note 2.

When comparing two courses of action, the nominal hoˈo 'alternative' is preceded by a sentence modifier consisting of— or ending with— an affirmative verbal or a negative adjectival. A non-past before hoˈo is more often used in general statements, whereas the past often refers to action on a specific occasion (lit. 'the alternative of having done will be ——').

Thus:

Koᶢn̄na hoˈn̄ no ᵇhoˈo ḡa oᵇmosiroˈi. 'This kind of book is more interesting.'

but:

Koᶢn̄na hoˈn̄ o ᵇyoˈmu hoo ḡa oᵇmosiroˈi. 'Reading this kind of book is more interesting.'

and:

Koᶢn̄na hoˈn̄ o ᵇyoˈn̄da hoo ḡa oᵇmosiroˈi. 'It will be more interesting to read (lit. to have read) this kind of book.'

The combination siᶢta hoˈo ḡa ᵇiˈi '[lit.] the alternative of having done [it] will be good' is often equivalent to English '[someone] had better do [it].' Sita may be replaced by other past verbals in this pattern.

Additional examples:

Hiᶢkoˈoki de iᵇku hoˈo ḡa haᵇyaˈi. 'It's faster to go by plane.' (Lit. 'The alternative of going by plane is fast.')
Niᶢhon̄ḡo o yoˈmu hoo ḡa muᵇzukasiˈi desyoo? 'It's more difficult to read Japanese, isn't it?'
Haˈyaku naᵇoˈsita hoo ḡa ᶢiˈi desu yo_ 'You'd better fix it quickly.' (Lit. 'The alternative of having fixed it quickly will be good.')
Koˈn̄ban̄ iᵇtta hoˈo ḡa ᶢiˈi desyoo ᵇneˈe. 'I guess I'd better go tonight!' (Lit. 'The alternative of having gone tonight will probably be good, won't it.')
Naᶢni mo iwanai hoˈo ḡa ᵇiˈi desyoo? 'It's better to say nothing, isn't it?'

A sequence consisting of— or ending with— an informal non-past affirmative verbal or negative adjectival + yori 'more than' indicates the course of action with which another is being compared. Before yori, a normally unaccented inflected word regularly acquires an accent—a verbal on its final syllable, and an adjectival on its pre-final syllable.

Examples:

> Ki⌐sya⌐ de i⌐ku⌐ yori hi⌐ko⌐oki de i⌐ku ho⌐o ḡa ha⌐ya⌐i. 'It's faster to go by plane than to go by train.' (Lit. 'More than going by train, the alternative of going by plane is fast.')
>
> Ha⌐na⌐su yori nihoñḡo o ⌐yo⌐mu hoo ḡa mu⌐zukasi⌐i desyoo? 'It's more difficult to read Japanese than to speak, isn't it?'
>
> Ra⌐isyuu ma⌐de ⌐ma⌐tu yori ⌐ha⌐yaku na⌐o⌐sita hoo ḡa ⌐i⌐i desu yo⌟ 'You'd better fix it quickly rather than wait until next week.'
>
> A⌐sita iku⌐ yori ⌐ko⌐ñbañ i⌐tta ho⌐o ḡa ⌐i⌐i desyoo ⌐ne⌐e. 'I guess I'd better go tonight rather than go tomorrow.'

5. Approximate Numbers

The combination of two consecutive numerals of Series I, from 1 to 9, plus a single counter, indicates approximation equivalent to English patterns like '1 or 2 hours,' '2 or 3 days,' '3 or 4 months,' etc.

The same pattern occurs in approximations of higher rank, like these:

ni-sañ-zeñ	'2 or 3 thousand'
si-ḡo-hyaku	'4 or 5 hundred'
ro⌐ku-siti-zyu⌐u	'60 or 70' (lit. '6 or 7 tens')

In this pattern, the consecutive numerals occurring in pairs are from 1 through 9 only. Kyu⌐uzyuu means '90'—not '9 or 10.'

Some combinations are irregular and must be memorized separately, but in general si⌐ '4' and si⌐ti⌐ '7' are the more common alternants of those numerals; and before ku⌐/kyu⌐u '9,' ha⌐ti⌐ occurs in its hak- alternant.

Examples:

iti-ni-mai	'1 or 2 thin, flat objects'
ni-⌐sañ-zi⌐kañ	'2 or 3 hours'
sañ-si-hoñ	'3 or 4 long, cylindrical objects'
si-⌐ḡo⌐-niti	'4 or 5 days'
go-⌐ro⌐p-puñ	'5 or 6 minutes'
ro⌐ku-siti-syu⌐ukañ	'6 or 7 weeks'
si⌐ti-hak-ka⌐ḡetu	'7 or 8 months'
hak-ku-neñ	'8 or 9 years'

6. Counters: -dai, -rittoru

The counter -dai combines with numerals of Series I to count units of wheeled vehicles—cars, busses, carts, carriages, etc. The numbers from one to ten are:

i⌐ti¬-dai   '1 wheeled vehicle'
ni¬-dai   '2 wheeled vehicles'
sa¬ñ-dai   '3 wheeled vehicles'
yo¬ñ-dai or yo-dai   '4 wheeled vehicles'
go-dai   '5 wheeled vehicles'
ro⌐ku¬-dai   '6 wheeled vehicles'
na⌐na¬-dai or si⌐ti¬-dai   '7 wheeled vehicles'
ha⌐ti¬-dai   '8 wheeled vehicles'
kyu¬u-dai   '9 wheeled vehicles'
zyu¬u-dai   '10 wheeled vehicles'

na¬ñ-dai   'how many wheeled vehicles?'

The counter -rittoru combines with numerals of Series I to count liters. [1]

The numbers from one to ten are:

i⌐ti-ri¬ttoru   '1 liter'
ni-⌐ri¬ttoru   '2 liters'
sa⌐ñ-ri¬ttoru   '3 liters'
yo⌐ñ-ri¬ttoru   '4 liters'
go-⌐ri¬ttoru   '5 liters'
ro⌐ku-ri¬ttoru   '6 liters'
na⌐na-ri¬ttoru or si⌐ti-ri¬ttoru '7 liters'
ha⌐ti-ri¬ttoru   '8 liters'
kyu⌐u-ri¬ttoru   '9 liters'
zyu⌐u-ri¬ttoru   '10 liters'

na⌐ñ-ri¬ttoru   'how many liters?'

-Rittoru is one of a large number of counters borrowed from English metric system terms.   Others are -meetoru 'meter,' -kiro(meetoru) 'kilometer,' -guramu 'gram,' -kiro(guramu) 'kilogram,' etc.

In the late 1950's Japan adopted the metric system as its official measurement system. Before that time, three systems were in use simultaneously: along with the metric system, there was a native Japanese system with its own terms, and the American system with another set of borrowed terms (-yaado 'yard,' -iñti 'inch,' -garoñ 'gallon,' -poñdo 'pound,' etc.). The various measures of the last two systems are being—or have already been—abandoned since the official adoption of the metric system.

---

[1] One liter = 1.06 quarts.

DRILLS

A. Substitution Drill

1.	Please get off now.	I⌐ma ⌐o⌐rite kudasai.
2.	Please let me off now.	I⌐ma o⌐ro⌐site kudasai.
3.	Please get on now.	I⌐ma no⌐tte kudasa⌐i.
4.	Please let me on now.	I⌐ma no⌐sete kudasa⌐i.
5.	Please line up now.	I⌐ma na⌐rande kudasa⌐i.
6.	Please line [them] up now.	I⌐ma na⌐rabete kudasa⌐i.
7.	Please go across now.	I⌐ma wa⌐tatte kudasa⌐i.
8.	Please hand [it] over now.	I⌐ma wa⌐tasite kudasa⌐i.
9.	Please go around now.	I⌐ma ma⌐watte kudasa⌐i.
10.	Please send [it] around now.	I⌐ma ma⌐wasite kudasa⌐i.

B. Substitution Drill

1.	There are 1 or 2 taxis left. . . .	Ta⌐kusii (ḡa) i⌐ti-ni-dai noko⌐tte (i)masu ḡa_
2.	There are 2 or 3 portions of sashimi left. . . .	Osasimi (ḡa) ni-⌐sañ-niñ-mae noko⌐tte (i)masu ḡa_
3.	There are 3 or 4 pencils left. . . .	Eñpitu (ḡa) sa⌐ñ-si-hoñ noko⌐tte (i)masu ḡa_
4.	There are 4 or 5 glasses of beer left. . . .	Bi⌐iru (ḡa) si-⌐go-hai noko⌐tte (i)-masu ḡa_
5.	There are 5 or 6 children left. . . .	Kodomo (ḡa) go-⌐roku-niñ noko⌐tte (i)masu ḡa_
6.	There are 6 or 7 liters of gasoline left. . . .	Gasoriñ (ḡa) ro⌐ku-siti-ri⌐ttoru no-⌐ko⌐tte (i)masu ḡa_
7.	There are 7 or 8 books left. . . .	Ho⌐ñ (ḡa) si⌐ti-has-satu noko⌐tte (i)masu ḡa_
8.	There are 8 or 9 sheets of paper left. . . .	Ka⌐mi⌐ (ḡa) ha⌐k-ku-mai noko⌐tte (i)masu ḡa_

C. Substitution Drill

1.	I went to the airport in a taxi.	Hikoozyoo e ⌐ta⌐kusii ni no⌐tte ikima⌐sita.
2.	I walked to the airport.	Hikoozyoo e a⌐ru⌐ite i⌐kima⌐sita.
3.	I went to the airport happily.	Hikoozyoo e yo⌐roko⌐ñde i⌐kima⌐si-ta.
4.	I went to the airport in a hurry.	Hikoozyoo e i⌐so⌐ide i⌐kima⌐sita.
5.	I went to the airport late.	Hikoozyoo e o⌐kurete ikima⌐sita.
6.	I went back to the airport.	Hikoozyoo e mo⌐do⌐tte i⌐kima⌐sita.
7.	I went to the airport, [after] transferring to a bus.	Hikoozyoo e ⌐ba⌐su ni no⌐rika⌐ete i⌐kima⌐sita.
8.	I went to the airport by way of (lit. passing through) the park.	Hikoozyoo e ko⌐oeñ (o) to⌐otte i-⌐kima⌐sita.

D. Substitution Drill

1. Shall I go and hire a por-
    ter?

    A⌐kaboo (o) tano⌐nde ki⌐masyo⌐o ka.

2. Shall I go and check the
    baggage?

    Ni⌐motu (o) a⌐zu⌐kete ki⌐masyo⌐o
    ka.

3. Shall I go and get (lit. put
    in) some gas?

    Ga⌐soriñ (o) irete kimasyo⌐o ka.

4. Shall I go and look up the
    phone number?

    De⌐ñwaba⌐ñgoo (o) si⌐ra⌐bete ki⌐ma-
    syo⌐o ka.

5. Shall I go and buy a pa-
    per?

    Si⌐ñbuñ (o) katte kimasyo⌐o ka.

6. Shall I go and ask at the
    information booth?

    A⌐ñnaizyo de kiite kimasyo⌐o ka.

7. Shall I go and call the
    doctor?

    Se⌐ñse⌐e (o) yo⌐ñde kimasyo⌐o ka.

8. Shall I go and pick up the
    baggage?

    Ni⌐motu (o) to⌐tte kimasyo⌐o ka.

E. Substitution Drill

1. Even though I didn't have
    much time, I went.

    Zi⌐kañ ḡa añmari na⌐katta keredo,
    i⌐kima⌐sita.

2. Even though I didn't feel
    well, I went.

    Gu⌐ai ḡa wa⌐rukatta keredo, i⌐kima⌐-
    sita.

3. Even though I was very
    tired, I went.

    To⌐ttemo tuka⌐rete (i)⌐ta⌐ keredo,
    i⌐kima⌐sita.

4. Even though I wanted to
    rest, I went.

    Ya⌐sumita⌐katta keredo, i⌐kima⌐sita.

5. Even though it was raining,
    I went.

    A⌐me ḡa hu⌐tte⌐ (i)ta keredo, i⌐kima⌐-
    sita.

6. Even though I didn't want to
    go, I went.

    I⌐kitaku na⌐katta keredo, i⌐kima⌐sita.

7. Even though it was winter,
    I went.

    Hu⌐yu⌐ datta keredo, i⌐kima⌐sita.

8. Even though it was awfully
    far, I went.

    Zu⌐ibuñ to⌐o⌐katta keredo, i⌐kima⌐-
    sita.

9. Even though it wasn't very
    near, I went.

    A⌐ñmari tika⌐ku ⌐na⌐katta keredo,
    i⌐kima⌐sita.

10. Even though I was very
    busy, I went.

    Ta⌐iheñ isoḡa⌐sikatta keredo, i⌐kima⌐-
    sita.

F. Substitution Drill

1. I plan to go (riding) on the
    bus (but . . .)[1]

    Ba⌐su ni no⌐tte iku tumori da⌐
    kedo_

---

[1] 'but—I'm not sure I will' or 'but—it isn't definite,' etc.

2. I plan to get off in front
   of the park (but . . .)

   Ko⌐oeñ no ma⌐e de o⌐ri⌐ru tu⌐mori
   da⌐ kedo_

3. I plan to deposit ¥ 5000 in
   the bank (but . . .)

   Giñkoo ni go⌐señ-eñ azuke⌐ru tu⌐mo-
   ri da⌐ kedo_

4. I plan to have the car
   checked (but . . .)

   Ku⌐ruma (o) sira⌐bete mo⌐rau tumori da⌐ kedo_

5. I plan to leave early in the
   morning (but . . .)

   A⌐sa ⌐ha⌐yaku ⌐ta⌐tu tu⌐mori da⌐
   kedo_

6. I plan to stop at an inn in
   Kyoto (but . . .)

   Kyo⌐oto no ryo⌐kañ ni tomaru tumori da⌐ kedo_

7. I plan to check the baggage
   at the station (but . . .)

   E⌐ki de ⌐ni⌐motu (o) a⌐zuke⌐ru tu-
   ⌐mori da⌐ kedo_

8. I plan to return to America
   next week (but . . .)

   Raisyuu A⌐merika e ka⌐eru tu⌐mo-
   ri da⌐ kedo_

9. I plan to study English next
   year (but . . .)

   Raineñ e⌐eḡo (o) beñkyoo-suru tumori da⌐ kedo_

10. I plan to transfer to the
    bus at Yokohama (but . . .)

    Yokohama de ⌐ba⌐su ni no⌐rika⌐eru
    tu⌐mori da⌐ kedo_

G. Grammar Drill (based on Grammatical Note 3)

Tutor: I⌐kimase⌐ñ. 'I'm not going to go.'
Student: I⌐kanai tumori de⌐su. 'I plan not to go.'

1. Ko⌐ñbañ de⌐kakemase⌐ñ.

   Ko⌐ñbañ de⌐kakenai tumori de⌐su.

2. Asita ki⌐mase⌐ñ.

   Asita ⌐ko⌐nai tumori desu.

3. Koñna siḡoto wa ⌐mo⌐o
   si⌐mase⌐ñ.

   Koñna siḡoto wa ⌐mo⌐o si⌐nai tumori de⌐su.

4. Ra⌐ineñ ma⌐de wa ka⌐eri-
   mase⌐ñ.

   Ra⌐ineñ ma⌐de wa ka⌐era⌐nai tumori
   desu.

5. Ze⌐ñbu wa si⌐mase⌐ñ.

   Ze⌐ñbu wa si⌐nai tumori de⌐su.

6. So⌐ñna hito⌐ ni wa na⌐ni
   mo yarimase⌐ñ.

   So⌐ñna hito⌐ ni wa na⌐ni mo yaranai
   tumori de⌐su.

H. Response Drill

Tutor: Hu⌐ru⌐i desu ka_ 'Is it old?'
Student: Hu⌐ruku a⌐rimase⌐ñ. A⌐tarasi⌐i desu yo_ 'It isn't old. It's
         new.'

1. O⌐mo⌐i desu ka_

   O⌐moku arimase⌐ñ. Ka⌐ru⌐i desu
   yo_

2. Ti⌐ka⌐i desu ka_

   Ti⌐ka⌐ku a⌐rimase⌐ñ. To⌐oi⌐ desu
   yo_

3. Zyo⌐ozu⌐ desu ka_

   Zyo⌐ozu⌐ zya a⌐rimase⌐ñ. He⌐ta⌐
   desu yo_

4. Tu⌐meta⌐i desu ka_

   Tu⌐metaku arimase⌐ñ. A⌐tu⌐i desu
   yo_

5. O⌐isi⌐i desu ka_

   O⌐isiku arimase⌐ñ. Ma⌐zu⌐i desu yo_

6. O⌐mosiro⌐i desu ka_

   O⌐mosi⌐roku a⌐rimase⌐ñ. Tu⌐mara⌐-
   nai desu yo_

7. A˹kema˺su ka⌐   A˹kemase˺ñ. Si˹mema˺su yo⌐
8. Ko˺i desu ka⌐   Ko˺ku a˺rimase˺ñ. U˹su˺i desu yo⌐
9. Ka˹ra˺ desu ka⌐   Ka˹ra˺ zya a˺rimase˺ñ. I˹ppai de˺-
                                      su yo⌐
10. Su˹ppa˺i desu ka⌐   Su˹ppa˺ku a˺rimase˺ñ. A˹ma˺i desu
                                      yo⌐

I.   Response Drill (based on Grammatical Note 4)

             Tutor: I˹kimasyo˺o ka. 'Shall I go?'
             Student: E˺e, i˹tta ho˺o ga ˹i˺i desyoo?   'Yes, you'd better go, don't
                       you think so?'

     1. Ha˺yaku si˹ra˺bete mo-   E˺e, si˹ra˺bete mo˺ratta ho˺o ga
         ˺raimasyo˺o ka.   ˹i˺i desyoo?
     2. Gasoriñ (o) i˹rete okima-   E˺e, i˹ret(e) o˺ita hoo ḡa ˹i˺i de-
         syo˺o ka.   syoo?
     3. Akaboo (o) ta˺nomimasyo˺o   E˺e, ta˹no˺ñda hoo ḡa ˹i˺i desyoo?
         ka.
     4. Ha˹si˺ (o) wa˺tarimasyo˺o   E˺e, wa˺tatta ho˺o ḡa ˹i˺i desyoo?
         ka.
     5. Kono taiya (o) to˹rikaema-   E˺e, to˹rikaeta ho˺o ḡa ˹i˺i de-
         syo˺o ka.   syoo?
     6. Oohuku no kippu (o) ka˹i-   E˺e, ka˺tta ho˺o ḡa ˹i˺i desyoo?
         masyo˺o ka.
     7. Ka˹ḡi˺ (o) ka˺kemasyo˺o   E˺e, ka˺keta hoo ḡa ˹i˺i desyoo?
         ka.
     8. A˺ma˺do (o) si˹memasyo˺o   E˺e, si˺meta hoo ḡa ˹i˺i desyoo?
         ka.
     9. To˹kkyuu ni norimasyo˺o ka.   E˺e, no˺tta ho˺o ḡa ˹i˺i desyoo?
     10. Sya˹syoo ni kiite mimasyo˺o   E˺e, ki˹ite mi˺ta hoo ḡa ˹i˺i de-
         ka.   syoo?

J.   Level Drill

             (Change all formal inflected forms except the final one to the infor-
             mal.)

     1. Zi˺p-puñ ˺ma˺e ni ta˹nomi-   Zi˺p-puñ ˺ma˺e ni ta˹no˺ñda kere-
         ma˺sita keredo, ma˺da mo-   do, ma˺da mo˺tte kimase˺ñ.
         ˺tte kimase˺ñ.
     2. I˹ti-do aima˺sita keredo,   I˹ti-do a˺tta keredo, mo˺o wa˹su-
         mo˺o wa˹surete simaima˺-   rete simaima˺sita.
         sita.
     3. I˹ti-zikañ-ḡu˺rai ˺ma˺e ni   I˹ti-zikañ-ḡu˺rai ˺ma˺e ni su˹to˺-
         su˹to˺obu (o) tu˺kema˺sita   obu (o) tu˺ke˺ta keredo, ma˺da
         keredo, ma˺da sa˹mu˺i   sa˹mu˺i desyoo?
         desyoo?
     4. To˹oi˺ desu kara, zu˺ibuñ   To˹oi˺ kara, zu˺ibuñ zi˹kañ ḡa ka-
         zi˹kañ ḡa kakarima˺su ke-   ka˺ru keredo; i˹kima˺su yo⌐
         redo; i˹kima˺su yo⌐

5. A˹no˺ hito wa wa˹karima-
   se˺ñ keredo, i˥tu mo wa˹ka˺-
   ru tte i˥tte (i)ma˺su ˹ne˺e.

   A˹no˺ hito wa wa˹kara˺nai keredo,
   i˥tu mo wa˹ka˺ru tte i˥tte (i)ma˺-
   su ˹ne˺e.

6. Mo˺o ni-˹sañ-do mima˺sita
   keredo; a˺ñmari omosiro˺i
   desu kara, ma˹ta mita˺i
   desu yo.

   Mo˺o ni-˹sañ-do mi˺ta keredo; a˹ñ-
   mari omosiro˺i kara, ma˹ta mi-
   ta˺i desu yo.

7. Se˹ñse˺e ḡa so˹o ossyaima˺-
   sita keredo, ho˹ñtoo zya
   arimase˺ñ yo_

   Se˹ñse˺e ḡa so˹o ossya˺tta keredo,
   ho˹ñtoo zya arimase˺ñ yo_

8. Ki˹koemase˺ñ desita keredo, yo˺ku mi˹ema˺sita.

   Ki˹koena˺katta keredo, yo˺ku mi˹e-
   ma˺sita.

9. I˹ku tumori de˺su keredo,
   ma˺da si˹taku wa sima-
   se˺ñ.

   I˹ku tumori da˺ keredo, ma˺da si-
   ˹taku wa simase˺ñ.

10. De˹kakenai tumori ḍe˺sita
    keredo, de˹kakete simai-
    ma˺sita.

    De˹kakenai tumori da˺tta keredo,
    de˹kakete simaima˺sita.

K. Expansion Drill

1. [He] didn't see me.
   [He] was waiting at the exit
   so he didn't see [me].
   My friend was waiting at
   the exit so he didn't see
   me.
   I was waiting in the waiting room but my friend
   was waiting at the exit so
   he didn't see me.
   I was waiting in the waiting
   room for about a half
   hour but my friend was
   waiting at the exit so he
   didn't see me.

   A˹imase˺ñ desita.
   De˺ḡuti de ˥ma˺tte (i)˥ta˺ kara, a˹i-
   mase˺ñ desita.
   To˹modati wa de˺ḡuti de ˥ma˺tte (i)-
   ˥ta˺, kara, a˹imase˺ñ desita.

   Ma˹tia˺isitu de ˥ma˺tte (i)˥ta˺ keredo; to˹modati wa de˺ḡuti de ˥ma˺tte
   (i)˥ta˺ kara, a˹imase˺ñ desita.

   Sa˹ñ-zip-puñ-ḡu˺rai ma˹tia˺isitu de
   ˥ma˺tte (i)˥ta˺ keredo; to˹modati wa
   de˺ḡuti de ˥ma˺tte (i)˥ta˺ kara, a-
   ˹imase˺ñ desita.

2. I ended up by going.
   I ended up by going (riding)
   in the car.
   There wasn't enough time
   so I ended up by going
   (riding) in the car.
   Even though I planned to
   walk (lit. go walking),
   there wasn't enough time
   so I ended up by going
   (riding) in the car.
   Even though I planned to
   walk to the station, there
   wasn't enough time so I

   I˹tte simaima˺sita.
   Ku˹ruma ni notte itte simaima˺si-
   ta.
   Zi˹kañ ḡa tarina˺katta kara, ku˹ru-
   ma ni notte itte simaima˺sita.

   A˹ru˺ite i˥ku tumori da˺tta keredo;
   zi˹kañ ḡa tarina˺katta kara, ku˹ru-
   ma ni notte itte simaima˺sita.

   E˺ki e a˹ru˺ite i˥ku tumori da˺tta
   keredo; zi˹kañ ḡa tarina˺katta
   kara, ku˹ruma ni notte itte

ended up by going (riding) in the car.	ˢimaima⌐sita.
Even though I planned to walk to the station this morning, there wasn't enough time so I ended up by going (riding) in the car.	Ke⌐sa ⌐e⌐ki e a⌐ru⌐ite i⌐ku tumori da⌐tta keredo; zi⌐kañ ḡa tarina⌐-katta kara, ku⌐ruma ni notte itte ˢimaima⌐sita.

3. I ended up by going. (M)[1]

I ended up by going (riding) on the bus.	Ba⌐su ni no⌐tte (i)ttyatta⌐[2] yo.
I arrived late so I ended up by going (riding) on the bus.	O⌐kurete tu⌐ita kara, ba⌐su ni no⌐tte (i)ttyatta⌐ yo.
I arrived at the station late, so I ended up by going (riding) on the bus.	E⌐ki ni o⌐kurete tu⌐ita kara, ba⌐su ni no⌐tte (i)ttyatta⌐ yo.
I intended to take the train but I arrived at the station late, so I ended up by going (riding) on the bus.	Ki⌐sya⌐ ni no⌐ru tumori da⌐tta kedo; e⌐ki ni o⌐kurete tu⌐ita kara, ba⌐su ni no⌐tte (i)ttyatta⌐ yo.
I intended to take a train that stops at Numazu but I arrived late, so I ended up by going (riding) on the bus.	Nu⌐mazu ni tomaru ki⌐sya⌐ ni no⌐ru tumori da⌐tta kedo, e⌐ki ni o⌐kurete tu⌐ita kara, ba⌐su ni no⌐tte (i)ttyatta⌐ yo.

4.

[He] didn't say.	I⌐imase⌐ñ desita yo⌐
[He] didn't say anything.	Na⌐ni mo iimase⌐ñ desita yo⌐
Nobody said anything.	Da⌐re mo nani mo iimase⌐n desita yo⌐
I ended up by going in but nobody said anything.	Ha⌐itte si⌐matta⌐ kedo, da⌐re mo nani mo iimase⌐ñ desita yo⌐
I ended up by going in through (lit. from) the exit but nobody said anything.	De⌐ḡuti kara ⌐ha⌐itte si⌐matta⌐ kedo, da⌐re mo nani mo iimase⌐ñ desita yo⌐
I couldn't tell so I ended up by going in through the exit, but nobody said anything.	Wa⌐kara⌐nakatta kara, de⌐ḡuti kara ⌐ha⌐itte si⌐matta⌐ kedo; da⌐re mo nani mo iimase⌐ñ desita yo⌐

---

[1] M = more typical of men's speech.

[2] Notte itte is regularly contracted to notte tte in informal speech.

I couldn't tell which was the
entrance so I ended up by
going in through the exit, but
nobody said anything.

Do⌐tira ḡa īriḡuti ka wa⌐kara⌐naka-
tta kara, de⌐ḡuti kara ⌐ha⌐itte si-
⌐matta⌐ kedo; da⌐re mo nani mo
iimase⌐ñ desita yo⌟

5. There isn't enough. (Lit.
It has become insuffi-
cient.)

Ta⌐rinaku narima⌐sita.

Again there isn't enough.

Ma⌐ta tarinaku narima⌐sita.

Even though I had [some]
put in, again there isn't
enough.

I⌐rete moratta⌐ keredo, ma⌐ta tarinaku narima⌐sita.

Even though I had enough
put in, again there is-
n't enough.

Zyu⌐ubu⌐ñ i⌐rete moratta⌐ kedo, ma-
⌐ta tarinaku narima⌐sita.

There wasn't enough (lit.
it had become insuffi-
cient) so I had the right
amount put in, but again
there isn't enough.

Ta⌐rinaku na⌐tte (i)⌐ta⌐ kara, zyu⌐u-
bu⌐ñ i⌐rete moratta⌐ kedo; ma⌐ta
tarinaku narima⌐sita.

There wasn't enough air
so I had the right amount
put in, but again there is-
n't enough.

Ku⌐uki ḡa ta⌐rinaku na⌐tte (i)⌐ta⌐
kara, zyu⌐ubu⌐ñ i⌐rete moratta⌐
kedo; ma⌐ta tarinaku narima⌐si-
ta.

There wasn't enough air in
the tires so I had the right
amount put in, but again
there isn't enough.

Ta⌐iya no ku⌐uki ḡa ta⌐rinaku na⌐tte
(i)⌐ta⌐ kara, zyu⌐ubu⌐ñ i⌐rete mo-
ratta⌐ keredo; ma⌐ta tarinaku na-
rima⌐sita.

There wasn't enough air in
the tires this morning so
I had the right amount
put in, but again there is-
n't enough.

Ke⌐sa ta⌐iya no ku⌐uki ḡa ta⌐rinaku
na⌐tte (i)⌐ta⌐ kara, zyu⌐ubu⌐ñ i⌐re-
te moratta⌐ keredo; ma⌐ta tarinaku
narima⌐sita.

6. Let's go (and come).

I⌐tte kimasyo⌐o.

Let's go to the J. T. B.

Ko⌐otuuko⌐osya e i⌐tte kimasyo⌐o.

Let's go to the J. T. B. right
nearby.

Su⌐ḡu ⌐so⌐ba no ko⌐otuuko⌐osya e
i⌐tte kimasyo⌐o.

[They] are waiting so let's
go to the J. T. B. right
nearby.

Ma⌐tte (i)ru kara, su⌐ḡu ⌐so⌐ba no
ko⌐otuuko⌐osya e i⌐tte kimasyo⌐o.

[They] are waiting in line
so let's go to the J. T. B.
right nearby.

Na⌐rañde ma⌐tte (i)ru kara, su⌐ḡu
⌐so⌐ba no ko⌐otuuko⌐osya e i⌐tte
kimasyo⌐o.

Lots of people are waiting
in line so let's go to the
J. T. B. right nearby.

Hi⌐to⌐ ḡa ta⌐kusañ narañde ma⌐tte
(i)ru kara, su⌐ḡu ⌐so⌐ba no ko⌐o-
tuuko⌐osya e i⌐tte kimasyo⌐o.

Lots of people are always
waiting in line so let's go
to the J. T. B. right nearby.

I⌐tu mo hi⌐to⌐ ḡa ta⌐kusañ narañde
ma⌐tte (i)ru kara, su⌐ḡu ⌐so⌐ba
no ko⌐otuuko⌐osya e i⌐tte kima-
syo⌐o.

Lots of people are always
waiting in line at the
ticket windows so let's
go to the J. T. B. right
nearby.

Ma⌐do⌐ḡuti ni wa ⌐i̅⌐tu mo hi⌐to⌐
ḡa ta⌐kusañ narañde ma⌐tte (i)ru
kara, su⌐ḡu ⌐so⌐ba no ko⌐otuuko⌐-
osya e i⌐tte kimasyo⌐o.

Lots of people are always
waiting in line at the
ticket windows in this
station so let's go to the
J. T. B. right nearby.

Ko⌐no e⌐ki no ma⌐do⌐ḡuti ni wa ⌐i̅⌐-
tu mo hi⌐to⌐ ḡa ta⌐kusañ narañde
ma⌐tte (i)ru kara, su⌐ḡu ⌐so⌐ba
no ko⌐otuuko⌐osya e i⌐tte kima-
syo⌐o.

QUESTION SUPPLEMENT

(The following questions are based on the Basic Dialogues of this lesson.)

(a)   1. Su⌐misu-sañ to Ta̅naka-sañ wa ⌐do⌐ko de ha⌐na⌐site imasu ka⌐
      2. Tanaka-sañ wa ⌐do⌐o site a⌐kaboo o tano⌐ñde ki⌐ma⌐su ka⌐

(b)   3. Su⌐misu-sañ wa ⌐na⌐ni o a⌐zuketa⌐i ñ desu ka⌐
      4. A⌐zuke⌐ru to⌐koro⌐ wa ⌐do⌐ko desu ka⌐
      5. Su⌐misu-sañ wa ⌐do⌐ko de o⌐siete moraima⌐sita ka⌐
      6. E⌐ki no hi⌐to o ma⌐tu he⌐ya⌐ wa ⌐na⌐ñ to i⌐ima⌐su ka⌐

(c)   7. Tanaka-sañ wa ⌐do⌐o site ti⌐katetu ni noritaku arimase⌐ñ ka⌐
      8. Tanaka-sañ wa ⌐na⌐ñ ni no⌐rita⌐i ñ desu ka⌐
      9. Ta⌐kusii no i⌐tibañ tika⌐i noriba wa ⌐do⌐ko desu ka⌐
     10. Taitee ⌐e⌐ki no ⌐de⌐ḡuti ni ⌐na⌐ni ḡa na⌐rañde ima⌐su ka⌐

(d) 11. O⌐kusañ wa ⌐na⌐ñ to ⌐na⌐ñ ni no⌐tte iku tumori de⌐su ka⌐
     12. O⌐kusañ wa ⌐do⌐ko made ⌐ba⌐su ni no⌐tte iku tumori de⌐su ka⌐
     13. O⌐kusañ wa Sï̅buya de ⌐na⌐ni o su⌐ru tumori de⌐su ka⌐
     14. O⌐kusañ wa ⌐do⌐ko de ti⌐katetu o ori⌐ru desyoo ka.
     15. O⌐kusañ wa To⌐ranomoñ de o⌐rite kara ⌐do⌐o simasu ka⌐
     16. Go⌐syu⌐ziñ mo i⌐kima⌐su ka⌐
     17. Ni⌐hoñzi⌐ñ wa zi⌐buñ no uti o de⌐ru to⌐ki⌐ ni wa ⌐na⌐ñ to i⌐ima⌐su
          ka⌐
     18. Ni⌐hoñzi⌐ñ wa zi⌐buñ no uti ni ka⌐etta to⌐ki⌐ ni wa ⌐na⌐ñ to i⌐ima⌐-
          su ka⌐
     19. U⌐ti ni iru hito⌐ wa de⌐kakeru hito⌐ ni ⌐na⌐ñ to i⌐ima⌐su ka⌐
     20. U⌐ti ni iru hito⌐ wa u⌐ti ni ka⌐ette ⌐ki⌐ta hi⌐to⌐ ni ⌐na⌐ñ to i⌐ima⌐su
          ka⌐

(e) 21. Su⌐misu-sañ no zi⌐do⌐osya ni ga̅soriñ ḡa na⌐ñ-rittoru-ḡu⌐rai no-
          ⌐ko⌐tte imasu ka⌐
     22. Do⌐o site ⌐i̅⌐ma ga̅soriñ o ⌐mo⌐tto i⌐rete o⌐ita hoo ḡa ⌐i̅⌐i desyoo
          ka.
     23. Ta⌐naka-sañ no sitte iru gasoriñsuta⌐ñdo wa ⌐do⌐ko desyoo ka.
     24. Su⌐misu-sañ wa ga⌐re⌐ezi de ⌐na⌐ni o si⌐te moraima⌐su ka⌐

(f) 25. Tanaka-sañ wa ⌐do˥o site o˩soku narima˩sita ka⌐
     26. Tanaka-sañ wa zi⌐buñ de pañku-sita taiya o torikaema˥sita ka⌐
(g) 27. Su˥misu-sañ wa ⌐do˥o site ga˩re˥ezi e i˩kima˥sita ka⌐
     28. Su˥misu-sañ wa zi⌐buñ de bure˥eki o si˩rabema˥sita ka, ga˩re˥ezi
          no hi˩to˥ ni si⌐ra˥bete mo˩rau tumori de˩su ka⌐

SUPPLEMENTARY CONVERSATION

Smith: Ga⌐soriñ o ireta˥i ñ desu g̃a, kono heñ ni ga⌐soriñsuta˥ñdo wa
            ⌐na˥i desyoo ˩ne˩e.
Tanaka: Sa˥a.   . . .   A, asuko ni zyu⌐ñsa g̃a iru˥ kara, ki⌐ite mima-
            syo˥o.
            (To policeman) Tyo˥tto u˩kag̃aima˩su g̃a, kono heñ ni ga⌐soriñ-
            suta˥ñdo wa a˩rimase˩ñ ka⌐
Policeman: Ga⌐soriñsuta˥ñdo desu ka⌐ Kono miti o mo⌐o suko˥si itte, hasi
            no temae o mi͞g̃i e mag̃atte; sore kara, ni-⌐sañ-byaku-meetoru-
            g̃u˥rai saki ni o⌐oki˥i ga⌐re˥ezi mo ga⌐soriñsuta˥ñdo mo arimasu.
Tanaka: Wa⌐karima˥sita.   Do⌐o mo a⌐ri˥g̃atoo gozaimasita.

                    . . .

Smith: A, mi⌐ema˥su yo⌐ —ha˩si˩ g̃a.
Tanaka: Mi⌐g̃i no ho˥o desu ne?
Smith: E˥e.

            (At the gas station)

Smith: O⌐neg̃ai-sima˥su.
Attendant: O⌐matase-sima˥sita.
Smith: Ga⌐soriñ oneg̃ai-sima˥su.
Attendant: I⌐ppai ni simasyo˥o ka.
Smith: E˥e.   . . .   O˥iru mo mi͞zu mo ⌐mi˩te ne?
Attendant: Ha˥a, ka⌐sikomarima˥sita.
Tanaka: Ta⌐iya wa daizyo˥obu desu ka⌐
Smith: E˥e, da⌐izyo˥obu desyoo.   Señsyuu si⌐ra˥bete mo˩ratta˩ kara.
Tanaka: Mi⌐ti g̃a waru˥i kara, taiya g̃a ⌐su˥g̃u ˩wa˩ruku narimasu ⌐ne˩e.
Smith: Ho⌐ñtoo de˥su ⌐ne˩e. Ki⌐no˥o mo ˩ma˩e no ta⌐iya g̃a pañku-sima˩-
            sita yo.
Tanaka: Kono kuruma ⌐na˥ñ-neñ no desu ka⌐
Smith: Yo-⌐neñ ma˥e no desu g̃a, e˥ñziñ no guai g̃a ⌐ma˩da to⌐temo i˥i
            desu kara⌐
Tanaka: So⌐re wa i˥i desu ˩ne˩e.
Attendant: Omatidoosama. Gasoriñ wa sa⌐ñzyuu-ri˥ttoru i˩rema˩sita. O˥iru
            mo mi͞zu mo ⌐ma˩da da⌐izyo˥obu desu kara⌐
Smith: A˥a ⌐so˥o.   Do⌐o mo go˩ku˩roosama.
Attendant: Maido a⌐ri˥g̃atoo gozaimasu.

English Equivalent

Smith: I'd like to get (lit. put in) some gas, but there probably isn't a gas
            station around here, is there.

Tanaka: I wonder.   . . .   Oh, there's a policeman over there so let's
             ask him and find out.
             (To policeman)   Excuse me but is(n't) there a gas station around
             here?
Policeman: A gas station? You go a little further along this street, turn right
             this side of the bridge, and then about two or three hundred me-
             ters ahead there's a big garage and gas station.
Tanaka: I understand. Thank you very much.

                 . . .

Smith: Oh, I see it— the bridge.
Tanaka: It's to the right, isn't it?
Smith: Yes.

             (At the gas station)

Smith: Will you wait on me?
Attendant: I'm sorry to have kept you waiting.
Smith: Let me have some gas.
Attendant: Shall I fill it up?
Smith·   Yes.   . . .   look at (both) the oil and water, will you?
Attendant: Yes, certainly.
Tanaka: Are the tires all right?
Smith: Yes, I think they're all right.   (Because) I had them checked last
             week.
Tanaka: The roads are bad so the tires go bad right away, don't they.
Smith: They certainly do.   Why, I had a flat in the front tire yesterday
             again (lit. too).
Tanaka: What year is this car? (Lit. This car is one of what year?)
Smith: It's four years old but the engine is still in very good condition
             so. . . (Lit. It's one of four years ago but the condition of the en-
             gine is still very good so. . .)
Tanaka: Isn't that fine!
Attendant: I'm sorry to have kept you waiting.   I put in 30 liters of gas.
             (Both) the oil and water are still all right (so. . .)
Smith: Oh. Thanks very much for your trouble.
Attendant: Thank you (again and again).

EXERCISES

1. Make up questions based on the immediately preceding conversation, and
    then practice the questions and answers.

2. Tell the porter:

        a. that you want to check your luggage.
        b. to take your luggage to the waiting room.
        c. to take only the heavy luggage.
        d. that you will take the light things.

3. Ask a stranger:

        a. where the waiting room is.

      b.   which way the airport is.

      c.   where you get the subway.

      d.   if the next station is Shibuya.

      e.   if there's a gas station around here.

4.   Tell the garage attendant:

      a.   that you want 20 liters of gasoline.

      b.   to fill the tank.

      c.   that there isn't enough air in the tires.

      d.   that there's something wrong with the engine.

      e.   that you have a flat.

      f.   that your brakes are out of order.

      g.   to check the oil and water.

5.   Tell Mr. Tanaka:

      a.   that you walked here.

      b.   that you came here on the subway.

      c.   that you got on at Shimbashi.

      d.   that you got off at Shibuya.

      e.   that you came here by transferring at Shibuya.

      f.   that you are going to go and buy a newspaper.

      g.   that he'd better check his luggage.

      h.   that he'd better get (lit. engage) a porter.

      i.   that it will be faster to go by taxi.

      j.   that you plan to try walking to the office tomorrow.

      k.   that you plan to walk to Mr. Tanaka's house and ride back.

      l.   that you plan to have the engine of your car checked tomorrow.

Japanese–English Glossary

Except for proper names, the following list contains all the vocabulary introduced in this text— words occurring in the Notes and as additional vocabulary as well as those appearing in the Basic Dialogues. Numbers following the entries refer to lessons: a number alone means that the entry first occurs in the Basic Dialogues of that lesson; a number followed by ‘-A’ refers to the Additional Vocabulary of that lesson; a number followed by ‘-N’ indicates that the item first occurs in the Notes of that lesson. CI and Int. refer to Classroom Instructions [1] and Introductory Lesson respectively. An asterisk (*) means that the item is included in the Index to the Grammatical Notes, with a reference to the location of the appropriate note(s).

Except in special cases, verbals and adjectivals are listed in their citation form only. Every verbal is identified as transitive /tr/ or intransitive /intr/ [2] and is assigned to the appropriate subclass; [3] its gerund is also given. For example, akeru /tr: -ru: akete/ identifies akeru as a transitive verbal belonging to the -ru subclass (i.e. the subclass to which ta⌐be⌐ru ‘eat’ and mi⌐ru ‘see’ belong), with gerund akete.

Every adjectival is identified by ‘/-ku/’ [4] after the citation form. Thus, the adjectival meaning ‘is big’ appears as: o⌐oki⌐i /-ku/.

All forms of the copula which occur in the text are listed and identified.

Nominals occur with no special designation, except that the members of the subclass of na-nominals [5] are identified by a following ‘/na/.’

Particles and quotatives are so identified. All are marked with asterisks, since all are included in the index.

Pre-nominals are identified by the designation ‘/+ nom/.’

Counters are so identified and are listed with a preceding hyphen.

‘/M/’ and ‘/W/’ follow entries typical of men’s or women’s speech respectively.

---

[1] Words designated as CI are those which occur only in the Classroom Instructions.

[2] For a description of transitive and intransitive verbals, see Lesson 16, Grammatical Note 1.

[3] For a description of verbal subclasses, see Lesson 11, Grammatical Note 1.

[4] See Lesson 2, Grammatical Note 1.

[5] See Lesson 12, Grammatical Note 4.

Except in a few special cases, words having a polite alternant that differs from the plain alternant only in the addition of the polite prefix o- or go- are listed only in the plain alternant.

For purposes of alphabetizing, hyphens and the macron of ḡ are ignored. Syllabic ñ is assigned to the position immediately following nonsyllabic n.

In most cases, combinations occurring as indented sublistings match the first occurrence in the lessons; but a simpler, more generally occurring example of the pattern is cited in cases where the combination which occurs first in the lessons seems less desirable as the model for a pattern of wide general use.

A

a oh! 4
a˺a oh! Int.
(a˺a /M/ yes 16)
abunai /-ku/ is dangerous 7
aḡaru /intr:-u:aḡatte/ go up, come up, enter 18
aḡeru /tr:-ru:aḡete/ give (to someone other than the speaker) 17
   site aḡeru do for someone 17
aida interval, space between 7
   Tookyoo to Yokohama no aida between Tokyo and Yokohama 7
akaboo porter, redcap 20
akai /-ku/ is red 4
akeru /tr:-ru:akete/ open [it] 16
a˺ki autumn, fall 18
aku /intr:-u:aite/ [it] opens 16
a˺ma˺do sliding storm door 18
amai /-ku/ is sweet or sugary or insufficiently salted 14-A
a˺me rain 18
   a˺me ḡa ˹hu˺ru it rains 18
a˺merika˺ziñ an American 10
a˹na˺ta you Int.
ane older sister 11-A
a˺ni older brother 11-A
ano* /+ nom/ that —— over there 3
   Ano ne! Say! Hey there! 13
añmari /+ negative/ not very much, not so much, not too much 3
   /+ affirmative/ so much, too much 14
añna* that kind, that kind of 5
añnaizyo, a˹ñnaizyo˺ information booth 19
a˺o blue, green 16
a˹o˺i /-ku/ is blue or green 4; is pale 14
a˹pa˺ato apartment house 16
arau /tr:-u:aratte/ wash 17
are* that thing over there 2

A˹ri˺ḡatoo (gozaimasita).+ Thank you (for what you did). Int.
A˹ri˺ḡatoo (gozaimasu).+ Thank you. Int.
a˺ru* /intr:-u:a˺tte; neg:na˺i/ be located (of inanimate objects), have 2
   si˺mete ˹a˺ru have been closed 16
a˹ru˺ku /intr:-u:a˹ru˺ite/ walk 20
a˺sa morning 9
a˹sago˺hañ breakfast 15-N
a˹si˺ leg, foot 17-A
a˹sita˺ tomorrow 1
asoko that place over there, over there 6
asuko /see asoko/ 6
a˺tama˺ head 17
   a˺tama˺ ḡa i˖ta˺i have a headache 17
a˺tarasi˺i /-ku/ is new or fresh 2
a˺t(a)taka˺i /-ku/ is warm 16
atira that one (of two); that way, thereabouts, over there 6
a˺to later, afterward 4
   a˺to de later, at a later time 4
   A˺to ˹na˺ni o simasyoo ka. What shall I do next? 17
a˺tti˺ /see atira/ 6
a˺tu˺i /-ku/ is hot 14
a˺u /intr:-u:a˺tte/ meet, see (and talk to) a person 11
   Ya˹mada-sañ ni a˺u meet or see Mr. Yamada 11
a˹zuka˺ru /tr:-u:a˹zuka˺tte/ receive in custody, take charge of, keep 20-N
a˹zuke˺ru /tr:-ru:a˹zu˺kete/ put into someone else's keeping temporarily, check, deposit 20

B

bañ night 19
-bañ /counter for naming numbers in a series/ 12
ba˹ñgo˺hañ evening meal, dinner 15-N
ba˹ñgo˺o number 12
-bañ-señ /counter for naming track numbers/ 19
ba˺su bus 8
ba˺ta butter 14-A
ba˺tterii battery 20-N
be˹ekoku˺ziñ an American 10-A

beñkyoo-suru /tr:irreg:beñkyoo-site/ study 11
be˹ñzyo˺ /M/ toilet 6-A
be˺tto bed 17-A
betu ni /+ negative/ not especially 13
bi˺iru beer 14
bi˺ru building (Western style) 6
bo˺ku, boku /M/ I, me 5
bo˺ttyañ⁺ son 11-A
bu˹re˺eki brakes 20

buta   pig   17-A
byooiñ   hospital   7

byooki   sickness, sick   11

D

da*   /copula: informal non-past/
-dai   /counter for vehicles/   20
daidokoro   kitchen   17
daiḡaku   university   13
da⌐isuki /na/   very pleasing   15
da⌐izi /na/   important, valuable   11-N
    Odaizi ni. Take care of yourself!
    11
da⌐izyo⌐obu /na/   safe, all right   7
da⌐ke⌐*   just, only   4
    so⌐re dake⌐   just that, that's all   4
    mi-⌐ttu⌐ dake   just three (units)   5
da⌐me⌐ /na/   no good, bad, broken   2
da⌐ññasa⌐ma ꜛ   master   12
da⌐re   who?   10
    dare mo /+ negative/   nobody   13
da⌐su /tr:-u:da⌐site/   put out, send out,
    take out   17
da⌐tta*   /copula: informal past/
de*   /copula: gerund/
de*   /particle/   by means of   7;
    at, in   7
de⌐ḡuti   exit   20
dekakeru /intr:-ru:dekakete/   set out,
    go out   13
de⌐ki⌐ru /intr:-ru:de⌐kite/   be possible,
    can do   9; come into being, be-
    (come) completed   15
    ni⌐hoñḡo ḡa deki⌐ru   can [speak] Japa-
    nese   9
de⌐ñki   electricity, electric light   16
de⌐ñsya, deñsya   electric train, street
    car   8
deñwa   telephone   6
    de⌐ñwa o kake⌐ru   telephone (verb)
    12
de⌐ñwaba⌐ñḡoo   telephone number   12
deñwa-suru /intr: irreg:deñwa-site/
    make a telephone call   12
deñwatyoo   telephone book   12
de⌐pa⌐ato   department store   6
de⌐ru /intr:-ru:de⌐te/   go out, leave   9

de⌐sita*   /copula: formal past/
de⌐su*   /copula: formal non-past/
de⌐syo⌐o*   /copula: formal non-past
    tentative/
-do   /counter for number of times/   1
do⌐a   door (Western style)   16
doituḡo   German language   11-A
do⌐itu⌐ziñ   a German   10-A
do⌐ko   what place? where?   6
do⌐nata ꜛ   who?   10
do⌐no*   /+ nom/   which—— ?   3
dono-ḡurai   about how long? about how
    much?   8
do⌐ñna*   what kind? what kind of?   5
do⌐o   how? what way?   2
    Do⌐o itasimasite. ꜛ Don't mention it.
        You're welcome.   Int.
    do⌐o mo   in every way   Int.
    Do⌐o mo. [Thanks] very much.   Int.
    do⌐o sita   what happened?   14
    do⌐o site   why? how?   11
    do⌐o suru   do what? act how?   13
doobutu   animal   17-A
-doori /see to⌐ori⌐/   avenue, street
    7-N
-doori   in accordance with   19
    zi⌐kañ-do⌐ori   on time   19
do⌐ozo   please   Int.
do⌐re*   which thing (of three or more)?
    2
    do⌐re de⌐ mo   whichever (of three or
        more) it is, any one at all   15
do⌐tira   which one (of two)? ; which
    way? whereabouts? where?
    6
    do⌐tira de⌐ mo   either one   15
    do⌐tira no ⌐ho⌐o   which alternative?
        15
    dotira mo   both   10
do⌐tirasama ꜛ   who?   12
do⌐tti /see do⌐tira/   6
do⌐yo⌐o(bi), doyoo   Saturday   8

E

e*   /particle/   to, into, onto   7
ebi   shrimp, prawn   14
e⌐e   yes; that's right   Int.

e⌐eḡa⌐kañ   movie theater   7
eeḡo   English language   11-A
e⌐ekoku⌐ziñ   Englishman   10-A

e⌐ki   station   6
-eñ   /counter for yen/   3
eñpitu   pencil   2
eñryo   reserve, restraint   18

ḡa*   /particle/   4
   Ha⌐iza⌐ra ḡa arimasu.   There's an
      ashtray.   4
   Ki⌐ree desu ḡa_   It's pretty but . . .
      4
gaikoku   foreign country   11-N
gaikokuḡo   foreign language   11
ga⌐ikoku⌐ziñ   foreigner   11-N
ga⌐imu⌐syoo   Foreign Office   11
-ḡaisya   /see kaisya/   company
   12-N
gaiziñ   foreigner, Westerner, Ameri-
      can   11-N
gakkoo   school   6-A
ga⌐ñneñ   the year 1, first year of an
      emperor's reign   8-N
ga⌐re⌐ezi   garage (commercial)   20
gasoriñ   gasoline   20
ga⌐soriñsuta⌐ñdo   gas station   20
ga⌐suḡa⌐isya   gas company   12-N
-ḡatu   /counter for naming the months
      of the year/   8
gekizyoo   theater   6-A
ge⌐ñkañ   entry hall   16
ge⌐ñki   /na/   health, pep, good spirits
      Int.
   (O)⌐ge⌐ñki desu ka⌐   Are you well?
      How are you?   Int.
ge⌐tuyo⌐o(bi), getuyoo   Monday   8
giñkoo   bank   6
go⌐   five   3
go⌐ḡo   afternoon, p.m.   9

ha⌐   tooth   17-A
ha⌐a+   yes; that's right   4
ha⌐ha   mother   11-A
ha⌐i   yes; that's right   Int.; here you
      are   3
-hai   /counter for glassfuls and cup-
      fuls/   14
haiiro   gray   16
ha⌐iru   /intr:-u:ha⌐itte/   enter, go in
      17
   ha⌐itte (i)ru   be inside   17

eñryo (cont.)
   Go⌐eñryo na⌐ku.   Don't hold back.
      Don't stand on ceremony.   18
e⌐ñziñ   engine   20-N

G

go⌐hañ   cooked rice, food   14-A; meal
      15
Go⌐ku⌐roosama (desita).   Thanks for your
      trouble.   1
Go⌐meñ-kudasa⌐i(ma⌐se).   Excuse me
      (for breaking away or interrupt-
      ing).   12
-ḡoo-sya   /counter for naming train
      car numbers/   19
-ḡo⌐ro*   approximate point of time,
      about   8
   ha⌐ti-ḡatu-ḡo⌐ro   about August   8
gotisoo   a feast, delicious food and/or
      drink   14-N
   Go⌐tisoosama (de⌐sita).   It was a
      feast.   Thank you for the delicious
      refreshments.   14
go⌐za⌐ru+*   /intr:-aru/   be located (of
      inanimate objects), have   Int.
go⌐zeñ   a.m.   9-N
go⌐zo⌐ñzi da†   know   13
guai   condition   20
   gu⌐ai ḡa i⌐i   be in good condition, be
      fine, be in good health   20-N
   gu⌐ai ḡa waru⌐i   be in bad condition,
      be out of order, feel unwell, feel
      sick   20
gu⌐riiñka⌐a   'green car' (i.e. first-
      class car)   19-N
gu⌐ri⌐insya   'green car' (i.e. first-
      class car)   19-N
-ḡu⌐rai*   approximate extent, about   8
   dono-ḡurai   about how much?   8
   ni-⌐syuukañ-ḡu⌐rai   about two weeks
      8
gyuunyuu   cow's milk   14-A

H

ha⌐iza⌐ra   ashtray   3
ha⌐kki⌐ri   clearly, distinctly, precisely
      18
hako   box   17
hana   nose   17-A
ha⌐na⌐   flower   6-A; flower arrange-
      ment   18
ha⌐nasi⌐   talking, a talk, a story   13
hanasi-tyuu   in the middle of talking;
      the line is busy   13
ha⌐na⌐su   /tr:-u:ha⌐na⌐site/   speak, talk   13

ha⌐na⌐ya   flower shop, florist   6-A
-hañ   half   8
    sa⌐ñ-zikañ-ha⌐ñ   three hours and a
        half   8
    go-⌐zi-ha⌐ñ   5:30   9
ha⌐ñbu⌐ñ   half, half part   14
hañtai   opposite   19
hañtai-suru /intr:irreg:hañtai-site/
    oppose   19-N
ha⌐ru   spring (season)   18-N
ha⌐si   chopsticks   14-A
ha⌐si⌐   bridge   20
ha⌐tati   20 years of age   10-N
ha⌐ti⌐   eight   3
hatu   leaving   19
    zyu⌐uiti⌐-zi hatu   leaving at 11 o'-
        clock   19
    Ko⌐obe hatu   leaving Kobe, coming
        from Kobe   19
hatu-ka   20 days; twentieth day of the
    month   8
ha⌐ya⌐i /-ku/   is fast or early   9
Ha⌐zimema⌐site.   How do you do?   11
ha⌐zi⌐mete   the first time   11
    Ha⌐zi⌐mete ome ni kakarimasu. ⊦
        How do you do?   11
he⌐bi   snake   17-A
heñ   area, section, part   6
    kono heñ   this area, around here   6
    do⌐no heñ   what part? what section?
        19
he⌐ñ /na/   strange   13
he⌐ta⌐ /na/   unskilled, poor at   18
he⌐ya⌐   room   13
hi   day   15
hidari   left   6
    hi⌐dari no ho⌐o   left side; toward the
        left   6
hikidasi   drawer   17
hi⌐ko⌐oki   airplane   8
hikoozyoo   airport   20
hima /na/   free time, leisure   12
    hi⌐ma na toki⌐   time when [someone]
        is free   12
hi⌐ru⌐   noon, daytime   15-N
hi⌐rugo⌐hañ   noon meal, lunch   15
hito, hi⌐to⌐   person   10
    o⌐ñna⌐ no hito   woman   10
    o⌐toko⌐ no hito   man   10
hi⌐to⌐-ri   one person; single (person)
    10
    hi⌐to⌐-ri de   alone, by oneself   17

hi⌐to⌐-tu   one unit   5
hodo *   approximate extent   15
    teñpura hodo su⌐ki⌐ zya ⌐na⌐i [I]
        don't like [it] as much as tempu-
        ra   15
hoka   other, another, other than   4
    hoka ni   in addition   4
    Tanaka-sañ no hoka ni   in addition
        to Mr. Tanaka, other than Mr.
        Tanaka   15-N
    hoka no hi   another day   15
ho⌐ñ   book   2
-hoñ /counter for long, cylindrical
    units/   5
ho⌐ñdana   bookshelf   17
hoñtoo   truth, true   3
ho⌐ñya   bookstore, book dealer   6-A
ho⌐o   side; direction; alternative   6
    hi⌐dari no ho⌐o   left side, toward
        the left   6
    ko⌐tira no ho⌐o   this side, this di-
        rection   6
    mi⌐gi no ho⌐o   right side, toward
        the right   6
    si⌐ta ho⌐o ğa ⌐i⌐i   it will be better
        to have done [it], [you]'d better
        do [it]   20
ho⌐oku   fork   14-A
ho⌐oñ   horn   20-N
ho⌐teru   hotel   6
hu⌐ki⌐ñ   dishrag, dish cloth, cloth   17
huku /tr:-u:huite/   wipe   17
hu⌐ne   ship, boat   8
-huñ /counter for naming and counting
    minutes/   8
hurañsuğo   French language   11-A
hu⌐rañsu⌐ziñ   Frenchman   10-A
hu⌐roba⌐   bathroom (not toilet)   17-A
hurosiki   furoshiki (cloth square for
    wrapping)   4
hu⌐ru /intr:-u:hu⌐tte, hu⌐tte⌐/   fall (of
    rain, snow, etc.)   18
    a⌐me ğa ⌐hu⌐ru   it rains   18
hu⌐ru⌐i /-ku/   is old (i.e. not new) or
    stale   2-A
hu⌐suma⌐, husuma   sliding door (opaque)
    18
hu⌐ta-tu⌐   two units   5
hu⌐yu⌐   winter   18-N
hya⌐ku⌐   one hundred   3
-hyaku /counter for hundreds/   3

I

i˹g̃irisu˺ziñ   Englishman   10-A
i˹i   /yo˺ku/   is good or fine or all
    right; never mind   2
iie   no; that's not right   Int.
i˹ka˺g̃a   how?   4
    I˹ka˺g̃a desu ka⌐   How are you?
    How are things?   How about it
    (offering something)?   4
I˹kemase˺ñ ˥ne˹e.   That's too bad.
    11
ikenai   /-ku/   it won't do, that's too bad
    11
-iki   -bound   19
    Kyooto-iki   bound for Kyoto   19
iku*   /intr:-u:itte/   go   1
i˹kura   how much?   3
i˹kutu   how many units?   5; how old (of
    people)?   10
i˹ma   now   7
i˹ma˺   living room   17-A
i˹mo˺oto   younger sister   11-A
i˹nu˺   dog   17
i˹ñdo˺ziñ   an Indian (from India)   10-A
ippai   full   20
    i˹ppai ni na˺ru   become full   20-N
    ippai ni suru   fill [something]   20
i˹rassya˺ru ✝ *   /intr:-aru:i˹rassya˺tte ∼
    i˹ra˺site/   be   6; go   7; come
    8
    I˹rassya˺i(ma˺se).   Welcome!   4
    Do˹nata de (i)rassyaimasu ka⌐ ✝
    Who is it?   Who are you?   10
ireru   /tr:-ru:irete/   put in, insert
    17
irig̃uti   entrance   20-N
i˹ro˺   color   5
    do˹ñna iro   what (kind of) color?   5
iru*   /intr:-ru:ite/   be located (of ani-
    mate beings)   6
    beñkyoo-site (i)ru   be studying   11

iru (cont.)
    hu˹tte (i)ru   be raining   18
    kekkoñ-site (i)ru   be married   10
iru   /intr:-u:itte/   be necessary, need,
    want   4
i˹sog̃asi˺i   /-ku/   is busy   13
i˹so˺g̃u   /intr:-u:i˹so˺ide/   be in a hur-
    ry   7
issyo   together   15
    Sa˹itoo-sañ to issyo   together with
    Mr. Saito   15
isu   chair   17-A
itadaku ✝   /tr:-u:itadaite/   eat, drink
    14; receive, accept   17
i˹ta˺i   /-ku/   is painful   17
i˹ta˺mu   /intr:-u:i˹ta˺ñde/   be(come)
    hurt or spoiled   14
    i˹ta˺ñda ebi   spoiled shrimp   14
itasu ✝   /tr:-u:itasite/   make, do   13
    Do˹o itasimasite. ✝   Don't mention it.
    You're welcome.   Int.
i˹ti˺   one (numeral)   3
itibañ, i˹ti˺bañ*   to the highest degree
    15
    i˹tibañ taka˺i   is most expensive   15
i˹to˺ko   cousin   11-A
I˹tte irassya˺i.   Goodbye. (Lit. Go and
    come.)   20
I˹tte kima˺su.   Goodbye. (Lit. I'll go
    and come.)   20-N
I˹tte mairima˺su. ✝   Goodbye. (Lit. I'll
    go and come.)   20
i˹tto˺osya   first-class car   19-A
i˹tu   when?   8
    i˹tu mo   always   9
i˹tu˺-tu   five units   5
iu   /tr:-u:itte/   say, be named, be
    called   1
i˹ya   /M/   no; that's not right   16

K

ka*   /sentence particle/   (question)   Int.
    O˹ge˺ñki desu ka⌐ ✝   Are you well?
    Int.
-ka ∼ -niti   /counter for naming and
    counting days/   8
ka˹do   street corner   7

ka˹eru   /intr:-u:ka˺ette/   return (home)
    9
-kag̃etu   /counter for number of months/
    8
ka˹g̃i˺   key   16
    ka˹g̃i˺ g̃a ka˥ka˹ru   [something] locks   16

kaꜛgiꜜ (cont.)
  kaꜛgiꜜ o kaꜛkeꜜru   lock [something]
    16
kaꜛg̅u   furniture   17-A
-kai   /counter for naming and counting
    floors/   16
kaidañ   stairway   17-A
kaikee   bill, accounting, check   15
kaisya   business company, company
    office   12
kaꜛkaꜜru   /intr:-u:kaꜛkaꜜtte/   be re-
    quired, take   8; be suspended
    11
  kaꜛgiꜜ g̅a kaꜛkaꜜru   [something]
    locks   16
  oꜛme ni kakaꜜru ǂ   see (a person),
    meet   11
    Haꜛziꜜmete ome ni kakarimasu. ǂ
    How do you do.   11
  ziꜛkañ g̅a kakaꜜru   take time
    8
kaꜛkeꜜru   /tr:-ru:kaꜜkete/   hang [some-
    thing]   12
  deꜛñwa o kakeꜜru   telephone (verb)
    12
  kaꜛgiꜜ o kaꜛkeꜜru   lock [something]
    16
kaꜛku   /tr:-u:kaꜜite/   write, draw   7
kaꜛmaꜜu   /intr:-u:kaꜛmaꜜtte/   mind, care
    about   18-N
  kaꜛmawaꜜnai   doesn't matter, makes
    no difference, is all right   9
kaꜛmiꜜ   paper   5
kaꜜnai   wife (one's own)   11
kaꜛñkokuꜜziñ   a South Korean   10-A
kao   face; expression   14
  aꜛoꜜi kao o suru   be pale   14
kara*   /particle/   from   8; because
    11; after   16
  sore kara   from that point, after
    that, and then, and   4
karada   body   17-A
kaꜛraꜜi   /-ku/   is spicy or salty   14
kariru   /tr:-ru:karite/   borrow, rent
    [from someone]   13
karui   /-ku/   is light (i.e. not heavy)
    20-N
Kaꜛsikomarimaꜜsita. ǂ   Certainly. I'll
    do as you have asked.   4
kaꜛtaꜜ ǂ   person   10
  oꜛñna no kataꜜ ǂ   woman   10
  oꜛtoko no kataꜜ ǂ   man   10
katamiti   one-way   19
kaꜛtazukeꜜru   /tr:-ru:kaꜛtazuꜜkete/
    straighten up   16

kau   /tr:-u:katte/   buy   4
kaꜛwaku   /intr:-u:kaꜛwaꜜite/   become
    dry   15
kawari   a change; a second helping   18
kaꜛyoꜜo(bi), kayoo   Tuesday   8
kaꜜzoku   family   11-A
kedo   /see keredo/   20
kekkoñ-suru   /intr:irreg:kekkoñ-site/
    marry   10
  kekkoñ-site (i)ru   be married   10
keꜜkkoo   /na/   fine, all right   9
  Moꜜo ꜛkeꜜkkoo desu.   I'm fine as I
    am. I've had enough already.   14
ke(re)do*   /particle/   although   20
keꜜsa   this morning   9
kesu   /tr:-u:kesite/   turn off, extin-
    guish, erase   16
kieru   /intr:-ru:kiete/   become extin-
    guished, go out   16-N
kiiroi   /-ku/   is yellow   4
kikoeru   /intr:-ru:kikoete/   be audi-
    ble, can hear   13
kiku   /tr:-u:kiite/   ask a question, lis-
    ten, hear   12
kimoti   feeling, mood   18
  kiꜛmoti g̅a iꜜiꜜ   is pleasant or agree-
    able   18
kiꜛnoꜜo, kinoo   yesterday   1
kiꜛñyoꜜo(bi), kiñyoo   Friday   8
kiꜛotukeꜜru   /intr:-ru:kiꜛotukeꜜte/   be
    careful   17
kippu   ticket   19
kirai   /na/   displeasing   15
kiꜜree   /na/   pretty, clean   3
kiꜛru   /tr:-u:kiꜜtte, kiꜜtte/   cut, cut
    off, hang up (the telephone)   13
kiꜛssaꜜteñ, kissateñ   tearoom   14-A
kiꜛsyaꜜ   (steam) train   8
kiꜛtanaꜜi   /-ku/   is dirty   16
ko   child   10
  oꜛñnaꜜ no ko   little girl   10
  oꜛtokoꜜ no ko   little boy   10
koꜛboreꜜru   /intr:-ru:koꜛboꜜrete/   [some-
    thing] spills   17
  koꜛboꜜrete (i)ru   be spilled   17
koꜛboꜜsu   /tr:-u:koꜛboꜜsite/   spill
    [something]   17-N
kodomo   child   10
koꜜe   voice   13
  oꜛokiꜜi ꜛkoꜜe de   or   oꜛoki na ꜛkoꜜe
    de   with a loud voice   13
koꜜi   /-ku/   is strong or thick (of li-
    quids); is dark (of colors)   14-A
koko   this place, here   6
koꜛkoꜜno-tu   nine units   5

ko⌐maka⌐i /-ku/ is small or fine or
　　detailed 17
ko⌐ma⌐ru /intr:-u:ko⌐ma⌐tte/ be(come)
　　distressing or troublesome or
　　annoying or inconvenient or per-
　　plexing 9
ko⌐me⌐ un⸰ooked rice 14-A
ko⌐mu /intr:-u:ko⌐ñde/ be(come) crowded 20
　　ko⌐ñde (i)ru be crowded 20
kono* /+ nom/ this — 3
kono-ḡoro these days, nowadays 18
ko⌐ñbañ this evening, tonight 13
　　Koñbañ wa. Good evening. Int.
koñḡetu this month 10
koñna* this kind, this kind of 5
Koñniti wa. Good afternoon. Int.
koobañ police box 7
kooeñ park 6-A
ko⌐ohi⌐i coffee 14
ko⌐ohiizya⌐wañ cup (with handles) 14-A
ko⌐oka⌐ñsyu telephone operator 12
koori ice 14-A
ko⌐otuuko⌐osya Japan Travel Bureau
　　12
kootya black tea 14-A
koppu glass for drinking 14-A
kore* this thing 2
ko⌐si⌐ lower part of the back 17-A
ko⌐syo⌐o pepper 14-A
kosyoo out of order 13
kosyoo-suru /intr:irreg:kosyoo-site/
　　break down 13-N
ko⌐tae⌐ru, ko⌐ta⌐eru /intr:-ru:ko⌐ta⌐ete/
　　answer CI
kotira this one (of two); this way,
　　hereabouts, here 6; this per-
　　son 11; the person speaking 12
　　ko⌐tira no ho⌐o this side, this di-
　　rection 6
kotori bird 17-A
kotosi this year 8
kotozuke message; the giving of a mes-
　　sage 13

ko⌐tti⌐ /see kotira/ 6
ku⌐ nine 3
kubi neck 17-A
ku⌐da⌐mono fruit 14-A
kudari down-train (i.e. going away
　　from Tokyo) 19
ku⌐dasa⌐i* /imperative of ku⌐dasa⌐ru/
　　give me 1
　　Ko⌐re o kudasa⌐i. Please give me
　　this one. 4
　　Ma⌐tte kudasai. Please wait. 1
　　I⌐soḡa⌐nai de kudasai. Please don't
　　hurry. 7
ku⌐dasa⌐ru ⸆ * /tr:-aru:ku⌐dasa⌐tte ～
　　ku⌐dasu⌐tte/ give me 4
　　ka⌐ite ku⌐dasaimase⌐ñ ka⌐ ⸆
　　would (lit. won't) you be kind
　　enough to write (or draw) for me?
　　7
-kuñ /M/ /suffix attached to men's
　　and boys' names; familiar/ 13
kureru /tr:-ru:kurete/ give me 17
　　ta⌐no⌐ñde kureru request (or order)
　　for me 17
ku⌐ro⌐i /-ku/ is black 4
ku⌐ru* /intr:irreg:ki⌐te⌐/ come 5
　　ta⌐no⌐ñde kuru come having engaged,
　　go and engage 20
kuruma car, cart 7
kusuri medicine 6-N
kusuriya drugstore, druggist 6-A
kuti mouth 17-A
ku⌐uki air 20
kya⌐burettaa carburetor 20-N
kyaku guest, customer 18
kyo⌐neñ last year 10-A
kyo⌐o today 1
kyo⌐odai brothers and/or sisters
　　11-A
kyu⌐u nine 3
kyuukoo express 19
kyu⌐uko⌐okeñ express ticket 19-A

M

ma⌐a oh well; I guess 4
ma⌐da* /+ affirmative/ still, yet
　　18; /+ negative/ not yet 14
　　ma⌐da da it is yet to happen; not
　　yet 14
made* /particle/ as far as; up to and
　　including 7

made (cont.)
　　To⌐okyo⌐o-eki made as far as Tokyo
　　Station 7
　　na⌐ñ-zi made until what time? 9
　　zyu⌐u-ḡatu⌐ made ni by October 9
ma⌐do window 16
ma⌐do⌐ḡuti ticket window 19

maˈe front 6; before 8
  eˈki no ˈmaˈe front of the station
    6
  ziˈp-puˈñ mae ten minutes before
    the hour 8
  ziˈp-puñ maˈe, ziˈp-puñ ˈmaˈe ten
    minutes ago 8
maḡaru /intr: -u: maḡatte/ make a turn
  7
  kaˈdo o maḡaru turn at the corner,
    turn the corner 7
maˈḡoˈ grandchild 11-A
-mai /counter for thin, flat units/ 5
maˈiasa every morning 9-N
maˈibañ every night 19-N
maido every time 4
  Maˈido ariˈḡatoo gozaimasu. +
  Thank you again and again. 4
maiḡetu every month 9-N
maineñ every year 9-N
maˈiniti every day 9
maˈiru ⸸* /intr: -u: maˈitte/ go 7;
  come 8
maisyuu every week 9-N
maitosi every year 9-N
maituki every month 9-N
maˈkitaˈbako cigarette 3-N
maˈmaˈ condition 16
  soˈno mamaˈ de being that condition
    as it is 16
-mañ /counter for ten thousands/ 3
maˈssuˈḡu straight 7
mata again 4
  Maˈta doˈozo. Please [come] again. 4
maˈtiaˈisitu waiting room 20
maˈtti match 3
maˈtu /tr: -u: maˈtte/ wait, await, wait
  for 1
mawaru /intr: -u: mawatte/ go around
  20
mawasu /tr: -u: mawasite/ send around
  20
maˈzuˈi /-ku/ is bad-tasting 14
meˈ eye 17-A
meˈe niece 11-A
meˈeḡosañ ⸸ niece 11-A
meesi name card, calling card 13
meˈezi Meiji Era (1868-1912) 8
mesiaḡaruˈ /tr: -u: mesiaḡatte/ eat;
  drink; smoke 14
miˈdori green 16-N
miˈeˈru* /intr: -ru: miˈete/ be visible,
  can see; put in an appearance,
  show up, come 18

miḡi right (i.e. not left) 6
  miˈḡi no hoˈo right side, toward the
    right 6
miˈmiˈ ear 17-A
miˈnaˈsañ ⸸ everyone 11
miˈ ñnaˈ everyone; everything 11
miˈru* /tr: -ru: miˈte/ look at, see
  12
  siˈte miˈru try doing, do and see
    19
miˈruku milk 14
miˈseˈ store, shop 6-A
miˈseˈru /tr: -ru: miˈsete show, let
  [someone] see 4
miti street, road, way 7
mi-ˈttuˈ three units 5
mizu cold water 14
mo* /particle/ also, too 4
  aˈoˈi no mo blue one(s) too 4
  deˈpaˈato ni mo in the department
    store too 6
  oˈokiˈi no mo tiˈisaˈi no mo both
    big ones and small ones 5
  doˈo mo in every way Int.
  iˈtu mo always 9
  dotira mo both 10
  dare mo /+ negative/ nobody
    13
moˈdoˈru /intr: -u: moˈdoˈtte/ go back,
  back up 7
moˈkuyoˈo(bi), mokuyoo Thursday 8
momoiro pink 16-N
moˈnoˈ thing (tangible) 14
moo* /+ quantity expression/ more,
  additional 1
  moo iti-do one time more 1
  moˈo sukoˈsi a little more, a few
    more 4
moˈo* /+ affirmative/ already, yet,
  now already, soon now 14
  /+ negative/ no more 18
  moˈo suˈḡu soon now, any minute
    now 15
moˈosu ⸸ /tr: -u: moˈosite/ say, be
  named, be called 18
morau /tr: -u: moratte/ receive, get
  17
  site morau have [someone] do [it],
    have [something] done 17
moˈsimosi hello (on the telephone);
  say there! 12
moˈtiˈroñ of course 15
motte iku take [something somewhere]
  14-N

mo⌐tte ku⌐ru bring [something] 14
mo⌐tto* more 5
mukoo beyond, over there; the far
    side 6
    bi⌐ru no mukoo beyond the building 6
    mu⌐koo no bi⌐ru the building over
        there 6

N

na* /pre-nominal alternant of da/
    12
    hi⌐ma na toki⌐ time when [someone]
        is free 12
naḡaisu couch, sofa 17-A
na⌐ḡasi⌐ sink 17-A
na⌐ihu knife 14-A
naiseñ telephone extension 12
na⌐ka inside 17
    hi⌐kidasi no na⌐ka inside the draw-
        er 17
nakanaka considerably; more than ex-
    pected 11
namae name 10
na⌐na seven 3
na⌐na⌐-tu seven units 5
na⌐ni what? 2
    na⌐ni ka something, anything 4
    nani mo /+ negative/ nothing
        18
naniiro what color? 5-N
naniziñ what nationality? 10-A
na⌐ñ what? 2
    na⌐ñ de⌐ mo no matter what it is,
        anything at all 15
nañni mo /see nani mo/ 18
na⌐o⌐ru /intr:-u:na⌐o⌐tte/ get well,
    recover 14
na⌐o⌐su /tr:-u:na⌐o⌐site/ fix, repair
    13
na⌐pukiñ napkin 14-A
naraberu /tr:-ru:narabete/ line
    [something or someone] up
    20-N
narabu /intr:-u:narañde/ [something
    or someone] lines up 20
na⌐ra⌐u /tr:-u:na⌐ra⌐tte/ learn, take
    lessons 18
na⌐ru* /intr:-u:na⌐tte/ become, get
    to be 10
    o⌐okiku ⌐na⌐ru get big 10
    ya-⌐ttu⌐ ni ⌐na⌐ru get to be eight
        years old 10

mu⌐ne⌐ chest (part of the body) 17-A
mu⌐ra⌐saki purple 16-N
musuko son 11-A
mu⌐sume⌐ daughter 11-A
mu-⌐ttu⌐ six units 5
muzukasii /-ku/ is difficult 11

na⌐ru (cont.)
    o⌐kaeri ni na⌐ru⌐ /honorific equiv-
        alent of ka⌐eru/ 9
na⌐sa⌐ru⌐ /tr:-aru:na⌐sa⌐tte ~ na⌐su⌐-
    tte/ do, make 13
na⌐tu⌐ summer 18-N
na⌐ze why? 11
ne?* /sentence particle/ isn't it
    true? do you agree? 13
ne⌐e* /sentence particle/ isn't it true!
    don't you agree! 1
    Do⌐ko desyoo ka ⌐ne⌐e. Where
        WOULD it be! I wonder where it
        is! 11
ne⌐esañ⌐ older sister 11-A
ne⌐ḡa⌐u⌐ /tr:-u:ne⌐ḡa⌐tte/ request
    Int.
    O⌐neḡai-sima⌐su.⌐ I'd like it.
        Please let me have it. Please do
        so. I have a request to make of
        you. Int.
ne⌐ko cat 17-A
-neñ /counter for naming and counting
    years/ 8
ni⌐ two 3
ni* /particle/ in, on, at 6; into,
    onto, to 7; by 17
    hoka ni in addition 4
    To⌐okyoo ni a⌐ru be in Tokyo 6
    sa⌐ñ-zi ni iku go at 3 o'clock 8
    koko ni oku put here 17
    tomodati ni iu say to a friend 18
    to⌐modati ni tuku⌐tte morau have a
        friend make [it] 17
ni⌐ḡa⌐i /-ku/ is bitter 14-A
nihoñḡo Japanese language 11
ni⌐hoñzi⌐ñ a Japanese 10
ni⌐isañ⌐ older brother 11-A
ni⌐ku⌐ meat 6-N
ni⌐ku⌐ya meat market, butcher 6-A
ni⌐motu baggage, things to carry 20
-niñ /counter for people/ 10
-niñmae /counter for portions/ 15

nippoŋ́go   Japanese language   11
niˈppoñziˈñ   a Japanese   10-A
-niti   /counter for naming and counting
      days/   10
niˈtiyoˈo(bi), nitiyoo   Sunday   8
niˈtoˈosya   second-class car   19
niwa   garden   17-A
no*   one, ones   4
      aˈkaˈi no   red one(s)   4
      kyoˈo no wa   as for today's (one)   5
no*   /particle/
      Toˈokyoo no tiˈzu   map of Tokyo   5
      kyoˈo no siñbuñ   today's newspaper
      5
      watakusi no siñbuñ   my newspaper   5
      niˈtoˈosya no tomaru tokoro   the place
         where the second-class cars stop   19
no*   /pre-nominal alternant of da/
      19-N
      byooki no kodomo   sick child   19-N
nobori   up-train (i.e. going toward To-
      kyo)   19

o*   /particle/
      Huˈrosiki o miˈsete kudasai.   Please
         show me a furoshiki.   4
      Kono miti o maˈssuˈḡu iˈtte kuda-
         saˈi.   Please go straight along
         this street.   7
oba   aunt   11-A
oˈbaˈasañ ⸗   grandmother; old lady
      11-A
obasañ ⸗   aunt; woman   11-A
oboñ +   tray   14-A
Odaizi ni. ⸗   Take care [of yourself]!
      11
Oˈhayoo (gozaimaˈsu). +   Good morning.
      Int.
oi   nephew   11-A
oˈide ni naˈru ⸗   be, come, go   9-N
oiḡosañ ⸗   nephew   11-A
oimotosañ ⸗   younger sister   11-A
oˈiru   oil (for automobiles)   20
oisii /-ku/   is delicious   14
oˈkaˈasañ ⸗   mother   11-A
Oˈkaerı-nasaˈi.   Welcome home.
      Hello.   20
okaḡesama de ⸗   thanks to you; thanks
      for asking   Int.
Oˈkamai naˈku.⸗   Don't bother.   Don't
      go to any trouble.   18
oˈkaˈsi +   cake, sweets   14-A

noˈdo   throat   15
      noˈdo ḡa kaˈwaˈku   become thirsty
      15
noˈkoˈru   /intr:-u:noˈkoˈtte/   be(come)
      left over or left behind   20
noˈkoˈsu   /tr:-u:noˈkoˈsite/   leave be-
      hind, leave over (for another
      time)   20-N
noˈmiˈmono   a drink, beverage   15
noˈmu   /tr:-u:noˈñde/   drink   14
noriba   place for boarding vehicles   20
norikae   a transfer (from one vehicle
      to another)   19
noˈrikaeˈru, noˈrikaˈeru   /intr:-ru:no-
      ˈrikaˈete/   change vehicles, trans-
      fer   19-N
noru   /intr:-u:notte/   get on (a vehicle),
      take (a vehicle), ride   19
noseru   /tr:-ru:nosete/   give [someone]
      a ride, carry, take on board   19-N
notihodo   later   12
ñ /M/   yeah   16
ñˈmaˈ   horse   17-A

O

oˈkasiˈi /-ku/   is funny (strange or
      amusing)   20
okosañ ⸗   child   10
oku* /tr:-u:oite/   put, place   17
      site oku   do in advance, do now for
      later reference   17
okureru   /intr:-ru:okurete/   fall be-
      hind, become late   19
      okurete (i)ru   be late   19
oˈkusañ ⸗   wife; madam; mistress   11
Oˈmatase-(ita)simaˈsita. ⸗   I'm sorry
      to have kept you waiting.   4
Oˈmatidoosama deˈsita.   I'm sorry you
      were kept waiting.   20
oˈme ni kakaˈru ⸗   see (a person), meet
      11
      Haˈziˈmete ome ni kakarimasu. ⸗
      How do you do?   11
omoi /-ku/   is heavy   20
oˈmosiroˈi /-ku/   is interesting, is un-
      usual, is fun   2
onaka   stomach   15
      onaka ḡa suku   become hungry   15
onazi   same   2
      onazi kusuri   same medicine   17
      kore to onazi   same as this   17
Oˈneḡai-simaˈsu. ⸗   Please (speaker
      requesting something; lit. I make
      a request).   Int.

o˩nna˩   female   10
   o˩nna˩ no hito   woman   10
   o˩nna no kata˩ †   woman   10
   o˩nna˩ no ko   little girl   10
oohuku   round trip   19
o˩oki *   /na/   big   13
   o˩oki na ˥ko˩e   loud voice   13
o˩oki˩i   /-ku/   is big   2
o˩ri˩ru   /intr:-ru:o˩rite/   go down, descend, get off (a vehicle)   20
o˩ro˩su   /tr:-u:o˩ro˩site/   lower, let
   down, discharge (from a vehicle)
   20-N
o˩ru ‡ *   /intr:-u:o˩tte/   be located (of
   animate beings)   6
   ke˩kkoñ-site o˩ru ‡   be married
      10
   be˩ñkyoo-site o˩ru ‡   be studying
      11
   hu˩tte ˥o˩ru +   be raining   18
Osaki ni. +   [Excuse me for going]
   ahead.   18
   Do˩ozo, osaki ni. +   Please [go]
   ahead.   18-N
osieru   /tr:-ru:osiete/   teach, inform
   7
osiire   closet (for clothing, quilts,
   etc.)   17-A

osoi   /-ku/   is late or slow   11
O˩so˩reirimasu.   Thank you.   I'm sorry.   18
o˩ssya˩ru †   /tr:-aru:o˩ssya˩tte/   say,
   be named, be called   13
otaku †   home, household   9
   otaku no   pertaining or belonging
   to your household
      10
o˩toko˩   male   10
   o˩toko˩ no hito   man   10
   o˩toko no kata˩ †   man   10
   o˩toko˩ no ko   little boy   10
o˩to˩osañ †   father   11
o˩tooto˩   younger brother   11-A
o˩toto˩i, ototoi   day before yesterday
   8
otya +   tea   14
oya   parent   11-A
oyaḡosañ †   parent   11-A
O˩yasumi-nasa˩i.   Good night.
   Int.
oyu +   hot water   14-A
ozi   uncle   11-A
o˩zi˩isañ †   grandfather; old man   11-A
ozisañ †   uncle; man   11-A
o˩zyo˩osañ †   daughter; young girl; little girl   11-A

P

pa˩ñ   bread   14-A
pañku-suru   /intr:irreg:pañku-
   site/   become punctured
   20

pañku-suru (cont.)
   taiya ḡa pañku-suru   have a flat
   tire   20
pe˩ñ   pen   2

R

ra˩iḡetu   next month   16-N
raineñ   next year   16-N
raisyuu   next week   16
ra˩itaa   lighter   4
ra˩zio   radio   16
re˩e   zero   12
re˩ezo˩oko   refrigerator   17-A
re˩ñzi   stove (for cooking)   17-A
re˩sutorañ   restaurant   14-A
-ri ~ -niñ   /counter for people/
   10
rippa   /na/   fine, handsome, magnifi-
   cent, imposing   18

-rittoru   /counter for liters/   20
ro˩ku˩   six   3
rooka   hall, corridor   17-A
rosiaḡo   Russian language   11-A
ro˩sia˩ziñ   a Russian   10-A
ru˩su   away from home   12
   rusu-tyuu ni   during [someone's] ab-
   sence from home   18
ryokañ   inn (Japanese style)   6-A
ryo˩ori˩ya   restaurant (Japanese style) 14-A
ryo˩osiñ   both parents   11-A
ryo˩ozi˩kañ   consulate   6

S

sa⌐a hmm... 6

sakana fish 6-N

sakanaya fish market, fish man 6-A

sake rice wine 14

saki ahead 6

  kono saki up ahead from here 7

-sama † (more polite alternant of -sañ)
    12

sa⌐mu⌐i /-ku/ is cold (of weather or
    atmosphere) 14

sañ three 3

-sañ † Mr., Mrs., Miss   Int.

sañpo a walk 18

sañpo-suru /intr:irreg:sañpo-site/
    take a walk 18-N

sa⌐ñto⌐osya third-class car 19-A

sara plate, dish 14-A

sa⌐simi⌐ sashimi (raw fish) 14-A

sa⌐to⌐o sugar 14-A

-satu /counter for books, magazines,
    etc./ 5

Sayonara. Goodbye.   Int.

sayoo that way, thus, so 12

Sayoonara.   Goodbye.   Int.

seereki Western calendar, Christian
    Era 8-N

se⌐ki, seki seat, assigned place 12

sekkeñ soap 17

senaka back (part of the body) 17-A

se⌐ñ thousand 3

-señ /counter for thousands/ 3

se⌐ñgetu last month 14

se⌐ñme⌐ñki wash basin 17-A

señmeñzyo washroom, lavatory 17-A

se⌐ñse⌐e teacher, doctor 16

señzitu the other day 18

si⌐ four 3

si⌐ba⌐raku a while (short or long) 11
    Si⌐ba⌐raku desita. It's been a long
      time [since I last saw you]. 11

siḡoto work 10
    siḡoto-tyuu in the middle of work
      12

si⌐ka⌐si however, but 15

si⌐ma⌐ru /intr:-u:si⌐ma⌐tte/ [some-
    thing] closes or shuts 16

simau* /tr:-u:simatte/ put away, store
    17

simau (cont.)
    irete simau finish putting in, put in
      for good, end up by putting in 17

si⌐me⌐ru /tr:-ru:si⌐mete/ close or
    shut [something] 16

siñbuñ newspaper 2

siñdai bed 17-A

si⌐ñda⌐ikeñ berth ticket 19-A

si⌐ñda⌐isya sleeping car 19-A

si⌐ñka⌐ñseñ new trunk-line 19-N

siñsitu bedroom 17-A

si⌐o⌐ salt 14-A

si⌐rabe⌐ru /tr:-ru:si⌐ra⌐bete/ look in-
    to, check, investigate 20

si⌐ro⌐i /-ku/ is white 4

siru /tr:-u:sitte/ come to know 10
    sitte (i)ru know 10

sita under, below, bottom, youngest
    10
    si⌐ta no ho⌐ñ bottom book 10-N
    ho⌐ñ no sita under the book 10-N

sitaku preparation 16
    sitaku o suru prepare 16

si⌐ti⌐ seven 3

si⌐tu⌐ree /na/ rudeness, rude 10
    Si⌐tu⌐ree desu ḡa_ Excuse me
      but... 10
    Si⌐tu⌐ree(-simasu). Excuse me (on
      leaving). Int.
    Si⌐tu⌐ree(-simasita). Excuse me
      (for what I did). Int.

so⌐ba vicinity 6
    e⌐ki no ⌐so⌐ba near the station 6
    so⌐ba no ⌐e⌐ki a nearby station 6
    su⌐ḡu ⌐so⌐ba immediate vicinity 6

so⌐ba noodles 14-A

so⌐ba⌐ya noodle shop 14-A

so⌐bo grandmother 11-A

so⌐hu grandfather 11-A

soko that place, there 6

sono* /+ nom/ that — 3

soñna* that kind, that kind of 5

so⌐o that way, thus, so 2
    So⌐o desu. That's right. 2
    So⌐o desu ka. Is that right? Oh?
      2
    So⌐o desu ⌐ne⌐e. That's right, isn't
      it. 2; Let me see... Hmm...
      4

soozi-suru /tr: irreg: soozi-site/ clean 16

sore* that thing 2

   sore kara after that, and then, and 4

sotira that one (of two); that way, thereabouts, there 6; that person 11; the person addressed 12

so⌐to outside 17

so⌐tti⌐ /see sotira/ 6

su⌐gi⌐ past, after 8

   ni-⌐hu⌐ñ sugi two minutes after 8

su⌐gu soon, any minute, right away 5

   su⌐gu ⌐so⌐ba immediate vicinity 6

su⌐iyo⌐o(bi), suiyoo Wednesday 8

su⌐ki⌐ /na/ pleasing; like [something] 15

sukiyaki sukiyaki (stew of vegetables with meat or chicken or fish) 14-A

su⌐ko⌐si a little, a few 4

   mo⌐o suko⌐si a little more, a few more 4

suku /intr: -u: suite/ become empty 15

   onaka ḡa suku become hungry 15

su⌐mai residence 16

su⌐mi corner (of a room) 17

Su⌐(m)imase⌐ñ. I'm sorry. Thank you for your trouble. Int.

Su⌐(m)imase⌐ñ desita. I'm sorry (for what I did). Thank you (for the trouble you took). Int.

supeiḡo Spanish language 11-A

su⌐ppa⌐i /-ku/ is acid or sour 14-A

su⌐pu⌐uñ spoon 14-A

suru* /tr: irreg: site/ do, perform, make 1

su⌐si⌐ sushi (rice with fish, seaweed, egg, etc.) 14-A

su⌐si⌐ya sushi shop 14-A

sutañdo lamp 17-A

suteru /tr: -ru: sutete/ throw away 17

su⌐to⌐obu heater 16

suu /tr: -u: sutte/ smoke (cigarettes, cigars, etc.) 14

su⌐zusi⌐i /-ku/ is cool 18

syasyoo train conductor 19

syokudoo dining room 14-A

syo⌐kudo⌐oosya dining car 19-A

syokuzi dining, a meal 15

   syokuzi o suru dine, eat a meal 15

syo⌐osyoo a little 4

syoowa Showa Era (1926–   ) 8

syooyu soy sauce 14-A

syoozi sliding door (translucent) 18

syosai study (i.e. a room) 17

-syuukañ /counter for number of weeks/ 8

syu⌐ziñ husband 11-A

T

tabako cigarette, tobacco 3

tabakoya cigar store 6-A

ta⌐bemo⌐no, ta⌐bemono⌐ food, edibles 15-N

ta⌐be⌐ru /tr: -ru: ta⌐bete/ eat 14

Tadaima. Hello, I'm back. 20

taiheñ /na/ awful, dreadful, terrible, a nuisance; very 20

taisetu /na/ important 20

ta⌐isi⌐kañ embassy 6

taisyoo Taisho Era (1912–1926) 8

taitee usual, usually 9

   ta⌐itee no Amerika⌐ziñ most Americans 15

taiya tire 20

ta⌐ka⌐i /-ku/ is expensive 3

ta⌐kusa⌐ñ, takusañ much, many 5

ta⌐kusii taxi 7

ta⌐ma⌐ḡo egg 14-A

tana shelf 17-A

ta⌐no⌐mu /tr: -u: ta⌐no⌐ñde/ make a request, place an order 14; engage, hire 20

tañsu chest of drawers 17-A

tariru /intr: -ru: tarite/ be sufficient 20

tatami rice-straw floor mat 18

   ta⌐tami no heya⌐ room with tatami 18

ta⌐temo⌐no, ta⌐te⌐mono building 6

ta⌐tu /intr: -u: ta⌐tte/ depart, leave for a trip 19

te⌐ hand 17-A

te⌐a⌐rai toilet 6-A

teeburu   table   17
temae   this side   6
  byooiñ no temae   this side of the
    hospital   6
teⁿki   weather; good weather   18
teñpura   tempura (batter-fried fish or
    vegetables)   14
teñpuraya   tempura shop   14-A
teⁿrebi   television   16
tetudaⁿu   /tr:-u:tetudaⁿtte/   help,
    lend a hand   17
tiḡau   /intr:-u:tiḡatte/   be wrong; be
    different   2
  sore to tiḡau   be different from that
    17
    Tiḡaimaˈsu.   Wrong number (on the
      telephone).   13
tiⁿisa   /na/   small   13-N
  tiⁿisa na ˈkoⁿe   a low voice   13-N
tiⁿisaⁿi   /-ku/   is small   2
tiⁿkaⁿi   /-ku/   is near   20
tikatetu   subway   20
tiⁿtiⁿ   father   11
tiⁿzu   map   5
to *   /particle/   and   4; with   15
  hoⁿñ to zassi   book and magazine
    4
  Saⁿitoo-sañ to issyo   together with
    Mr. Saito   15
to *   /quotative/   18
  naⁿñ to iu   say what?   be named <u>or</u>
    called what?   18
to   door   16
todana   cupboard (with shelves)   17
toⁿire(tto)   toilet   6-A
tokee   clock, watch   8
toⁿkiⁿ *   time, occasion   12
  noⁿru tokiⁿ /ni/   when [someone]
    rides   19
toⁿkidokiⁿ   sometimes   9
tokkyuu   special express   19
toⁿkkyuⁿukeñ special-express ticket 19-A
tokonoma   Japanese-style alcove   18
toⁿko(ro)ⁿ   place   18
tokubetu   special   19-N
toⁿkubetukyuⁿukoo   special express   19
tomaru   /intr:-u:tomatte/   come to a
    halt; stop at, lodge   19
tomeru   /tr:-ru:tomete/   bring to a
    halt   7

tomodati   friend   10
tonari   next door, adjoining   6
  eⁿki no tonari   next door to the sta-
    tion   6
Toⁿñde mo naⁿi.   Heavens no!   8
tdo   ten units   5
-too   /counter for naming classes/   19
Toodai   Tokyo University   13
tooi   /-ku/   is far   13
  deñwa ḡa tooi   have trouble hear-
    ing (on the telephone)   13
toⁿoriⁿ   avenue, wide street   7
toⁿoru   /intr:-u:toⁿotte/   pass through,
    go through, pass in front of   19
toⁿosuto   toast   14-A
tori   bird   17-A; chicken, fowl   14-A
torikaeru   /tr:-ru:torikaete/   exchange
    20
toⁿru   /tr:-u:toⁿtte/   take up, take away,
    remove, take off, pass [to someone]
    17
totemo   exceedingly, very   8
tottemo   exceedingly, very   8
toⁿziⁿru   /tr:-ru:toⁿzite/   close [some-
    thing]   CI
[t]te *   /quotative/   18
  naⁿñ te iu   say what?   be named
    or called what?   18
-[t]tu   /counter for number of units/
    5; /counter for years of people's
    age/   10
tuⁿḡiⁿ   next   7
  tuⁿḡiⁿ no ˈkaⁿdo   next corner   7
tuⁿitatiⁿ   first day of the month   8
tuⁿkareⁿru   /intr:-ru:tuⁿkaⁿrete/   be-
    come tired   17
tuⁿkeⁿru   /tr:-ru:tuⁿkeⁿte/   attach,
    turn [something] on   16
tukiatari   end of a street or corridor
    7
tuⁿku   /intr:-u:tuⁿite/   arrive   9;
    [something] becomes attached or
    turned on   16
tukue   desk   17
tuⁿmaraⁿnai   /-ku/   is dull or boring;
    is trifling   2
tumetai   /-ku/   is cold   14
tumori *   intention, plan   20
  iku tumori da   [I] intend to go, [I]
    plan to go   20
tutaeru   /tr:-ru:tutaete/   report,
    communicate, convey a message
    13

tu⌐tome⌐ru /intr: -ru: to⌐to⌐mete/ be-
    come employed 10
    tu⌐to⌐mete (i)ru be employed 10
tu⌐yo⌐i /-ku/ is strong 17
tyairo brown 16
tyaku arriving 19
    i⌐ti⌐-zi tyaku arriving at 1 o'-
    clock 19
tyanoma family room (Japanese
    style) 17-A
-tyañ ' /suffix added to children's
    given names/ 10
tyawañ cup or small bowl (Japanese
    style) 14-A
tyoodo exactly 8
-tyoome /counter for naming
    chomes/ 7

tyooseñg̃o Korean language
    11-A
tyo⌐oseñzi⌐ñ a Korean 10-A
tyo⌐tto a bit, a little 1; just
    5
    Tyo⌐tto. Say there! 4
    tyo⌐tto_ I'm afraid it won't
    do... 4
-tyuu in the middle of —, now busy
    with — 12
    sig̃oto-tyuu in the middle of work
    12
tyuug̃okug̃o Chinese language 11-A
tyu⌐ug̃oku⌐ziñ a Chinese 10-A
tyuumoñ-suru /tr: irreg: tyuumoñ-site/
    place an order 14

U

u⌐de⌐ arm 17-A
u⌐e⌐, ue over, above, top, topmost,
    oldest 10
    u⌐e no ho⌐ñ top book 10-N
    ho⌐ñ no ue top of the book
    10-N
ukag̃au ' /tr: -u: ukag̃atte/ inquire 6
    tyo⌐tto u⌐kag̃aima⌐su g̃a excuse
    me but ; I'm just going to ask
    [you something] but 6
ukag̃au ' /intr: -u: ukag̃atte/ visit 16
u⌐ma⌐ horse 17-A
u⌐mi sea, ocean 18
usag̃i rabbit 17-A
usi bull, cow 17-A

usiro back, rear 7
    ta⌐isi⌐kañ no usiro back of the em-
    bassy 7
usui /-ku/ is weak or thin (of
    liquids); is light (of colors)
    14
u⌐ti⌐, uti home, house, household
    9
    uti no our household's, our
    10
    uti among 15
    A to B to C no uti [de] [being]
    among A and B and C
    15

W

wa* /sentence particle/ /W/ 16
wa* /particle/ as for, comparative-
    ly speaking Int.
    A⌐na⌐ta wa? How about you? Int.
    Sore wa ⌐na⌐ñ desu ka_ What is
    that? (Lit. As for that, what is
    it?) 2
    Si⌐ñbuñ wa kaimase⌐ñ desita. A
    newspaper I didn't buy. 4
    Ko⌐ko ni⌐ wa a⌐rimase⌐ñ. Here
    there isn't one. 6

wa⌐ka⌐ru /intr: -u: wa⌐ka⌐tte/ be compre-
    hensible, understand, can tell 1
wañ bowl 14-A
wa⌐ru⌐i /-ku/ is bad 2-A
wasureru /tr: -ru: wasurete/ forget 4
watakusi I, me 5
    watakusi no my, mine 5
wataru /intr: -u: watatte/ go over, go
    across 20
watasu /tr: -u: watasite/ hand over
    20-N

Y

ya* /particle/ and 17
  ho⌐ñ ya zassi books and maga-
    zines and the like 17
ya⌐ḡi goat 17-A
ya⌐ma¬ mountain 18
yameru /tr:-ru:yamete/ quit, give up 14
yaoya vegetable store 6-A
yaru /tr:-u:yatte/ give (to someone
  other than the speaker) 17
yasai vegetable 14-A
yasasii /-ku/ is easy 11
ya⌐su¬i /-ku/ is cheap 3
ya⌐sumi¬ vacation, holiday, time off 8
ya⌐su¬mu /tr:-u:ya⌐su¬ñde/ rest, re-
  lax, take time off 17
ya-⌐ttu¬ eight units 5
yo* /sentence particle/ 2
  Pe⌐ñ desu yo. It's a pen (I tell
    you). 2
yobu /tr:-u:yoñde/ call, summon
  13
yo¬i /-ku/ is good 2-N
yoko side 6
  de⌐pa¬ato no yoko the side of the
    department store 6
yo¬ku /adverbial of i¬i~ yo¬i/ well,
  a good deal, often 1

yo¬mu /tr:-u:yoñde/ read 13
yo¬ñ four 3
yori* /particle/ more than 15
  ko⌐re yo¬ri ⌐i¬i is better than
    this 15
yo⌐roko¬bu /intr:-u:yo⌐roko¬ñde/ take
  pleasure in 16
yo⌐roko¬ñde /gerund of yo⌐roko¬bu/
  gladly, with pleasure 16
yorosii /-ku/ is good <u>or</u> fine <u>or</u>
  all right; never mind 5
  Do¬ozo yorosiku. (Lit. Please
    [treat me] favorably.)
    11
  Mi⌐na¬sañ ni yorosiku. Give my re-
    gards to everyone. 11
yo¬ru night, night-time 16
yo-⌐ttu¬ four units 5
yotukado intersection 20
yu⌐bi¬ finger 17-A
-yuki -bound 19
  Yokosuka-yuki Yokosuka-bound
    19
yu⌐kku¬ri slowly 13
yuku /alternant of iku/ 19-N
yu⌐ube¬ last night 11
yu⌐ubi¬ñkyoku post office 6

Z

zassi magazine 2
ze⌐ñbu all, the whole thing 1
ze¬ro zero 12
-zi /counter for naming o'clocks/
  8
zi⌐biḵi¬ dictionary 2
zibuñ oneself 20
  zibuñ de by oneself 20
  zibuñ no one's own 20
zi⌐do¬osya automobile 7
zikañ time 18
  zi⌐kañ ḡa a¬ru have time
    18
  zi⌐kañ-do¬ori on time 19
-zikañ /counter for hours/ 8
zi⌐mu¬syo office 9
zi¬syo dictionary 2
zo⌐ñzi¬nai⹁ /-ku/ don't know 13
zo¬ñzite ⌐o¬ru⹁ know 13

zookiñ cleaning rag 17
zu¬ibuñ extremely, to a considerable
  degree 3
zutto by far 15
  zu⌐tto ma¬e kara since a long time
    ago 15
zya /contraction of de¬ wa/ 2
  ⸝e⌐ñpitu zya na¬i it isn't a pencil
    2
zya¬/a/ then, well then, in that case
  2
zyama /na/ hindrance, bother 17
  zya⌐ma ni na¬ru become a bother,
    get in the way 17
zyo⌐osya¬keñ passenger ticket 19-A
zyo⌐ozu¬ /na/ skilled, skillful 18
zyu¬ñsa, zyuñsa policeman 7
zyu¬u ten 3
zyu⌐ubu¬ñ /na/ enough 20

Index to the Grammatical Notes

References are to Lesson and Grammatical Note; for example, 6.4 refers to Lesson 6. Grammatical Note 4.